# advanced JAVA™ 2

## Development for Enterprise Applications

**2ND EDITION**

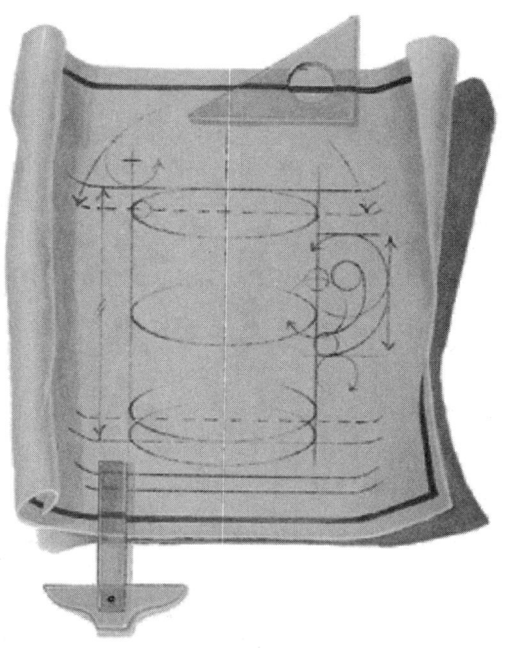

SUN MICROSYSTEMS PRESS
A PRENTICE HALL TITLE

CLIFFORD J. BERG

**Library of Congress Cataloging-in-Publication Data**

Berg, Clifford J.
Advanced Java 2 development for enterprise applications / Clifford J. Berg--2nd ed.
p. cm.-- (Sun Microsystems Press Java series)
ISBN 0-13-084875-1 (alk. paper)
1. Java (Computer program language) 2. Application software--Development.
I. Title. II. Series.
QA76.73.J38 B478 1999
005.13'3--dc21

99-051983

Cover design director: *Jerry Votta*
Cover design: *Talar Agasyan*
Composition: *Vanessa Moore*
Manufacturing manager: *Maura Goldstaub*
Acquisitions editor: *Mary Franz*
Editorial assistant: *Noreen Regina*
Marketing manager: *Lisa Konzelmann*

Sun Microsystems Press:
Marketing manager: *Michael Llwyd Alread*
Publisher: *Rachel Borden*



Prentice Hall books are widely used by corporations and government agencies for training, marketing, and resale.
The publisher offers discounts on this book when ordered in bulk quantities. For more information, contact Corporate Sales Department, Phone: 800-382-3419; FAX: 201-236-7141; E-mail: corpsales@prenhall.com
Or write: Prentice Hall PTR, Corporate Sales Dept., One Lake Street, Upper Saddle River, NJ 07458.

Printed in the United States of America
10 9 8 7 6 5 4

ISBN 0-13-084875-1

***Sun Microsystems Press***
**A Prentice Hall Title**

*To my beloved and wonderful daughter, Ariane, who inspires me every day*

# Contents

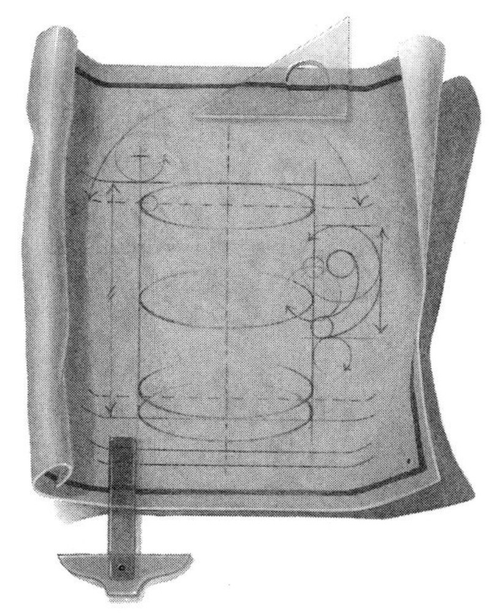

Chapter 4

## Java Security 190

# Preface

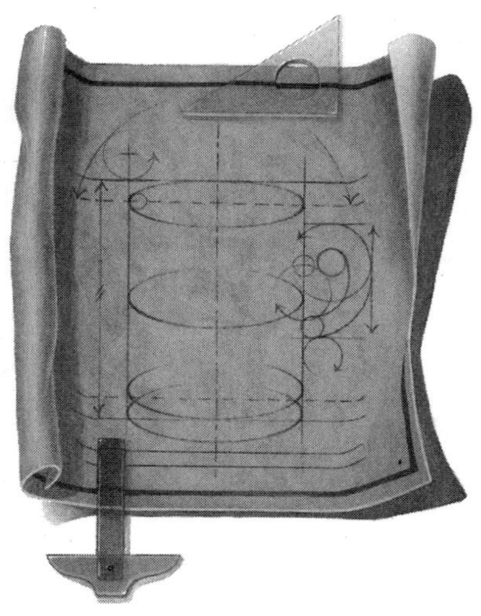

When this book first appeared in the summer of 1998, Enterprise JavaBeans™ (EJB) was a new specification, and there were only a handful of products which implemented it. There also were only a few products which implemented the Java Servlet API. Server-side Java™-based applications in general were not in widespread use, primarily because of the lack of standards-based application server products and also because of questions about reliability and performance. Java 2 was also still a beta release.

The situation today has greatly changed. The Java programming language is in widespread use as a server application technology, and there are many mature products which support its use in that role. Most of these products support Java 2 and its associated Enterprise APIs. A great many major commerce web sites now employ servlet, EJB, or other Java technologies. The combination of EJB components and Java Web servlets has emerged as a powerful and scalable tool for building electronic commerce, supply chain, and many diverse kinds of applications. It is truly amazing that this has happened in so short a time.

The questions about performance and reliability have also largely gone away, as the Java platform has proven itself on these issues. In my company we have seen Java-based application servers scale to large numbers of users and transaction rates, and the Java platform's ability to handle large volumes will certainly continue to increase. One recent benchmark we participated in demonstrated Java-based application server cluster scalability on UNIX processors at the level of more than 500 EJB transactions per second over long periods of time without any apparent instability, with relatively flat response time behavior never exceeding 600 ms.

The Enterprise JavaBeans and servlet standards have also evolved. Experience from the first version of EJB has led to improvements and clarifications, and the current generation of EJB products now incorporate these improvements and the Java 2 platform as well. EJB has become a robust and universal middle tier for transaction-based applications. The servlet standard has expanded to include provisions for security interoperability and XML messaging and the addition of JavaServer™ Pages (JSP). JSP provides a widely supported model for embedding dynamic content within web pages which leverages directly on Java technology and which is also more maintainable than earlier approaches to dynamic web content.

Perhaps the most significant development is the definition of the Enterprise Edition of the Java Platform (J2EE). This is an attempt to pull together the many Java technology specifications which are of special importance to enterprise applications, and also to specifically address issues such as interoperability, deployment, and security.

## This Book's Goals

This book explains Java-related technologies of particular importance to enterprise-wide software development. This book is not intended to be an in-depth treatment of all enterprise subjects. In fact, the topic of enterprise application development is so broad that it would require a library of books to cover each area. I therefore do not promise to even mention every topic that is relevant, much less cover each in detail. However, an advanced programmer needs to have a working knowledge of most aspects of a system in order to understand the entire system. For example, a developer working on a set of Enterprise JavaBeans does not need to understand all aspects of all security issues but does need to have a working knowledge of the security techniques used by the servers involved and the application. This book endeavors to provide a big picture, in a highly practical manner that is immediately useful to most developers, regardless of what their particular expertise is. I avoid most user-interface-related topics, because those are covered extensively in other books.

The readers of this book are expected to be advanced but with varied backgrounds. I assume that most know basic Java platform programming, but that some will know some aspects of the Java programming language and not others. I emphasize showing actual implementation details, with real products used in examples. The real-world examples give advanced developers an immediate feeling for what the code really looks like without a lot of explanatory text.

In this book I avoid Java technologies that depart from the 100% Pure Java standards. I believe that standards are extremely important for large applications and enterprise-wide development. The success of open technologies hinges on their

acceptance as standards, so it is illogical to embrace nonstandard implementations. Furthermore, standardization is in the best interest of the vast majority of the companies now building Java-based products and solutions and of the customers that depend on them.

## Companion Web Site

This edition of this book is supported by the web site:

http://www.ajdea.com

I will post new material and any errata to this web site.

## Acknowledgments

There are many people I would like to thank for their assistance or support in this effort, both for this edition and the previous edition. These include:

Susan Cheung, architect of the Java Transaction Service and Java Transaction API, for her patience in explaining nuances of the JTA and JTS specifications.

Mark Hapner for his kind and patient clarifications of issues related to EJB, JTA, JMS, and JDBC.

Li Gong, Java security architect, Sun Microsystems.

Rosanna Lee of Sun Microsystems, for JNDI.

Scott Seligman of Sun Microsystems, for JNDI.

Norbert Lindenberg of Sun Microsystems for the Input Method Framework.

Rick Cattell of Sun Microsystems for ODMG and EJB.

Luis de la Rosa, formerly of Gemstone.

Chris Noe, Cybercash.

Mike Masterton, Cybercash.

Uwe Hansmann (Secretary of the OpenCard Consortium), IBM Smart Card Alliances & Standards.

Thomas Stober, IBM Global Smart Card Solutions.

Geoff Sharon, Director of product development for Gradient Technologies.

Kenn Rugg, Vice President of Product Development, Object Design Inc.

Paul Ambrose of BEA Weblogic for his valuable insight into many things.

Sriram Srinivasan of BEA Weblogic for EJB server architecture.

Dean Jacobs of BEA Weblogic for clustering and scalability.

Mike McHugh for CD production assistance for the first edition.

Steve Oesterle, formerly of Visigenic.

Jim Stafford and Dan Weimer, for their intelligent insight into object-oriented design considerations for EJBs and CORBA integration.

Jon Siegel of the OMG.

Peter Coad of Object International.

Jeff DeLuca for his insight and feedback on many ideas.

Warwick Ford, chair of the IETF PKIX committee.

Jonathan Payne, Maurice Balick, and Dave Solin of Marimba.

Ari Luotonen, Netscape Communications, for insight on proxy security issues.

My staff, for being outstanding, especially Daniel Barclay, Paul Brigner, Doug Schnelzer, and Jeremy Smith, among many others.

My fellow company officers, for their patience, especially Steve Alexander and Dan Kohlhaas.

Mary Franz of Prentice Hall, my acquisitions editor, for her patience and foresight.

Jane Bonnell for her helpful and diligent editorial management on the second edition.

Eileen Clark for her tireless and patient editorial work on the first edition.

On a personal level, my sister, Roxanne, for her support, my daughter, Ariane, for providing the inspiration to press on through to the completion of this immense project, and my friend and love JoAnne for her support.

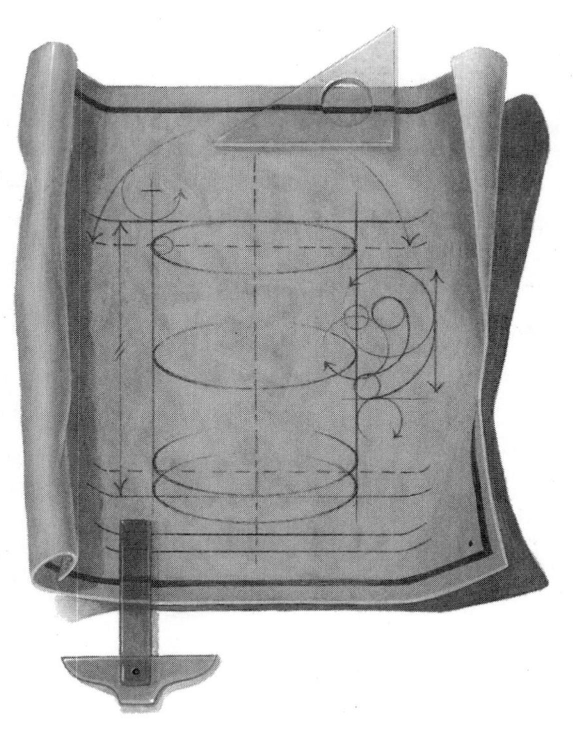

# CHAPTER 1

# *The Java Project Lifecycle*

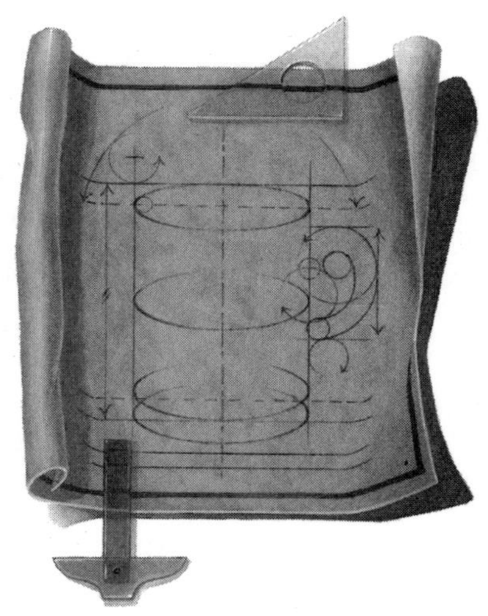

## Introduction

Spurred by the Internet, computer software technology is changing more quickly now than ever before. The days when you could wait a few years for a technology to mature and then pick a product and stay with it for ten years are gone—and will likely never return. We are now in an era when there are major technological upheavals continually, and all development nowadays carries technological risk as a result. The final twist is that new business systems must now be developed in a shorter timeframe than ever before, or risk obsolescence before they are deployed—or worse, miss valuable opportunities.

Traditional methodologies must be fine-tuned for these new paradigms, focusing on rapid delivery and incremental feature-oriented development. Ways need to be found to reduce risk while at the same time allowing for the introduction of multiple new technologies in each project. A situation in which most inhouse staff have no experience with many of the products and APIs chosen for a project is now routine. And a new system must be completed and operational within six months or less. After the system is in operation, it must be maintained in the face of constantly changing products and new releases, and it is nowadays not uncommon for technology product vendors to completely rewrite their API from one product version to the next.

Rather than provide a comprehensive treatment of software project development and lifecycle issues, which can be found elsewhere, I will focus on those aspects that are of special importance to Java technology projects.[1] I will try to answer questions such as:

- What are the issues that come up in a Java project?
- How are these issues different from other kinds of projects?
- What steps can you take to minimize risk in a Java project?
- How should you fine-tune your development methodology?
- What design guidelines should you use? coding guidelines? testing techniques? measurement techniques?

I will also try to provide software developers with an overall understanding of the issues that quality assurance and configuration management staff must deal with and what a developer must know in order to assist in and be part of these processes.

## Risk Management

Development using Internet technology—Java or otherwise—is characterized by these features:

- New technology abounds, seemingly in every area of the project.
- Rapid delivery is required—people can't wait nowadays.
- Many disparate elements are required, often from multiple vendors.

As if project development were not hairy enough, these wildcards have to be tossed in!

It seems like every six months there is an entire new *class* of products and APIs, designed to fill spaces unaddressed by those from before. Many server vendors also now make major enhancements to their core products more than once a year. This makes it hard to build a system, because there is the risk that the products are unreliable or have unanticipated behavior, or advertised features are not quite ready.

Sometimes it is wise to forego a new class of products or a new API until it has matured. The problem is, you never get to that state anymore. If something is so mature that it is no longer evolving, it is dead. The problem is not that products evolve; it is the *rate* of evolution that has sped up, as a result of the tremendous growth of the Internet and the spread of computers to mainstream and even home use.

The Java core API is a good example of an evolving technology. The hunger for enhancements is so great that people are usually willing to put up with bugs in

1. Hereafter, the term "Java" will be used to refer to the Java programming language and "Java projects" will be used to refer to projects developed with Java technology. Java is a trademark of Sun Microsystems, Inc., in the U.S. and other countries.

order to use the new features. Take the Swing API. When Swing was in beta 0.5, we already had clients using it for mission-critical applications. They could not be dissuaded. The reason was that, even though it was buggy then, it would become stable by the time it was officially released, and they wanted to base their development on a standard. Swing was also so much nicer than its predecessor, the AWT, that staying with the AWT was not even an option. One could say that this is a special case, because the AWT was flawed, but in fact it is not a special case, because in every corner of Internet technology you see this—a constant outcropping of things so new and so different that they cannot be dismissed. In the case of the aforementioned clients using Swing, it ended up being a good decision, because those applications are completed now and are very stable.

Not all of these new inventions have staying power, however. When Internet "push" technology first appeared, it was touted as the new wave that would drive our desktops from now on. As it turned out, this technology's strength is in the deployment of applications, as opposed to dynamic desktops. In only one year, the entire perception of how this technology should be used made a complete turn. It is a major challenge for a manager to sort the promising technologies from the doubtful ones, and move cautiously but at the same time without fear of using something new—because everything is new.

The viability and professionalism of the provider of a technology must also be considered when making a selection. A great many Java product companies are startups, or small organizations recently acquired by larger ones. Of course, all companies start small; in the mid-80s Oracle was a fledgling company and an underdog, battling against mainframe Codasyl and IMS databases, so smallness itself should not be a handicap. It is a red flag, however. In one project, an object-oriented "blend" product was selected to provide an object-oriented layer for a relational database. Many vendors were evaluated, and since the Java binding of the Object Data Management Group (ODMG) standard for object-oriented databases was fairly new, not all vendors had incorporated it into their products. As a result, there was quite a bit of disparity between the models used by the different vendors. The vendor that was finally selected was persuaded to agree to accelerate the schedule for certain feature enhancements of interest to the project, at the expense of others. Since they were a small vendor, and this was a large customer, convincing them was easy. They made the changes, but when the product started to be used, other unanticipated limitations were discovered. Luckily, this was during a prototype stage for the project, because the limitations necessitated reconsideration of the project's core architecture.

The constant change of technology is a major problem for staff training. It is virtually impossible to staff a project with people who have experience in all the things

you want to use. I recall seeing an ad in a newspaper in February 1996, for a programmer with "2+ years of Java development experience." Apparently the human resources person who wrote the ad was not aware that at the time there were perhaps 20 people in the world who fit that description, and they were very busy.

The cost of obtaining specialized talent can also be a factor that reduces flexibility and increases risk. One project I consulted on originally had decided that the best technology in which to implement their application was Lotus Notes. However, Java was selected because it was calculated that while Lotus Notes developers could be found, the cost of obtaining them in the required numbers would double project costs compared to using C++ programmers and training them in Java.

The incentive to tolerating these risk factors is that these new technologies promise lower-cost development, much wider deployment and end-user productivity and functionality, and greater adaptability. To get control of the risks so that these gains can be realized, a strategy is needed with new emphasis on rapid delivery in a core-capability-driven manner. To this end, I propose three rules to comprise this strategy. Surely you have heard these and other rules before, but I am putting these three at the top of the list.

### Rules for Success

The first rule is ***keep each component simple***. By keeping things simple, you can get quick turnaround in development. This is important so that you discover quickly if the project is going to have technological difficulties. Do not create unnecessary layers. Make sure each layer has a well-defined purpose that is easy to conceptualize. Otherwise, your best staff resources will be spent creating advanced local architectures, instead of understanding and applying the plethora of new technology. Also, with things changing so rapidly, you don't want to invest too much effort in in-house designs that may become obsolete or replaced by components available in the marketplace. True component-based software is finally appearing. Don't worry that staff won't be challenged: it is a tremendous challenge to understand, evaluate, assemble, and apply all these new technologies, even if custom programming is kept simple.

The second rule is ***focus on the primary mission of the application, and make that work really well***. Concentrate on what the application has to do most of the time. Tune the system for that. A system that does everything equally well is either overfunded or in fact does everything in a mediocre manner. If the primary mission is processing orders, design the system for that. If the primary mission is checking patient records, design the system for that. In large systems that are built in stages, sometimes the wrong piece is built first and then drives the rest of the design. For example, if the system must interface to an external system, a data

loading mechanism might be built early on, and the system's primary features added later. Unfortunately, when this is done, there is a risk that the system will be tuned for the data loading process, which is not the primary purpose of the system. The result is a system that may load data well, but has poor response time for calling up data—the primary mission and success criterion of the system.

The third rule is ***if using new technologies, build a prototype, and deploy it early.*** You cannot avoid using new technologies today, and things are changing all the time. The best way to deal with this unstable situation is to move quickly, to avoid obsolescence, but prudently, to manage the risk of using new features. Don't commit to an architecture without building a prototype that tests the core mission-critical functionality using the new technologies. That is the only way that technology limitations will be exposed so that a successful full-scale architecture can then be designed. Further, it takes someone with a great deal of experience with these technologies to judge where the risks might be, and what features prototype development should focus on. You should also make a point to deploy your prototype in the actual target environment, at an early phase, long before the final deployment date. Deployment is one of the most treacherous aspects of building these systems, because only then do you discover for real the interaction of security systems, application servers, and the real databases they will run with, as well as bugs and weaknesses that suddenly crop up in a great many of these products. What should take days can often take weeks, and if such delays are to occur, it is best to leave plenty of time for the inevitable workarounds.

## Deciding How to Focus Development: Features vs. Modules

Two competing views of how to approach the design of a system are:

- Decompose the system into modules and fully specify each module.
- Decompose the system into features and design the system incrementally by adding features to the design until all features are accounted for.

A project may emphasize one or the other view, but both views are needed. I believe that the predominant view should depend on the phase of the project and where the software is in its lifecycle. Regardless, both views should be maintained.

The module-oriented view can potentially result in a more well-architected system, with higher encapsulation. It is therefore most useful at the start of a project when the initial architecture is being defined. On the other hand, the feature-oriented view has advantages for incremental development, and having a process

for handling the addition of features allows detailed design work to be done in stages at the same time as releases are being generated.

Regardless which approach is used, a feature list must be maintained, since only then can a complete test plan be developed; again, regardless which approach is used, the system design should strive to abstract features into roles played by independent modules so that those modules can be developed as independently as possible. This balance is one of the challenges the system architect faces.

As the addition of new features is considered during the system's lifecycle, their impact on all modules should be examined. Again, try to recast the features as generic enhancements to modules. A feature impact analysis must be done and changes to affected modules designed. This results in changes to the specification and requirements for each affected module.

### Components Contain Components

A software system usually has many levels which can be said to contain components, starting with the smallest trackable units and ending with the outermost level comprising the entire system. The system as a whole is like a Chinese box containing one or more boxes which in turn contain other boxes, and so on.

The "package" is the outermost Java mechanism for partitioning a system. The Java language portion of a system is therefore composed of a set of packages. Much of the discussion here can apply at the total system level or at a subsystem level, and even at a module level, which in the case of Java is a single file containing a class or interface. Rather than use a term which is associated with the outermost levels, I use the term "subsystem" to refer to a component of the system, regardless of whether it is a file, a package, or a collection of packages. I use the generic term "module" to refer to a file containing a class or interface, or possibly a small number of related classes or interfaces which may be contained within a single package.

Features are hierarchical as well. The list of system requirements represents a composite feature, made up of all the individual requirements. Requirements are logical features, and a design process transforms them into physical features which are then implemented. For example, a requirement to have an alarm of some kind represents the alarm feature, and it might be implemented by a particular kind of flashing light control which is a tangible feature. The light control itself is made up of features, which might include a feature for blinking and displaying on and off modes. Collectively these comprise the system's alarm feature, which is also a logical requirement.

A feature list is a valuable document to maintain throughout a subsystem's lifecycle. It begins as the developer's first stated list of requirements, and the design

process rewrites these in terms of different but related concrete features. The design document should identify which requirements are satisfied or supported in some way by each design feature, providing continuity throughout the process. This helps to clarify the impact of removing features if the cost must be reduced.

### *Task Granularity*

Sometimes within a project it will be convenient to assign a particular class to a developer for development or enhancement. At other times, an entire package may be assigned. In general, it is preferable to make packages the level at which task responsibility assignments are made, since Java specification versions apply to a package, but sometimes the package may be too large or general-purpose for this to be practical. The decision of task granularity therefore has to be made on a case-by-case basis.

## Organizing a Project Team

The first step in beginning a project involves assigning staff and designating their roles in the project. Often there are project roles which do not directly relate to development, such as customer liaison, relationship or marketing manager, acceptance, system and network engineering, operations, and so on. I shall focus on the roles that are important for the development team. Many of these roles apply at any scale, from a project level down to a subsystem or module level, as indicated. The roles listed here are lead roles, and may be delegated. The roles may also apply at a total system level, or at a subsystem or module level.

### *Project Roles*

I shall first list the roles in summary form, and then explain them in more detail.

*Product Manager, Subsystem Manager*

- Totally responsible for the success of a unit of software, a system or a subsystem. The buck stops with this individual with regard to lifecycle and requirements issues of the product or subsystem.

*Project Manager, Task Manager*

- Responsible for ensuring that the project or task is completed successfully. Oversees other staff assigned to the project or task. A task may be the development of a component or the implementation of a new feature.
- Tracks the progress of the project or subsystem in terms of milestones, features, modules, and level of effort.

- Collaborates with the product manager to decide on priorities for releases.
- Obtains resources for completion of the project or for assigned tasks.

*Domain Expert*

- Responsible for maintaining an ongoing understanding of customer requirements.
- May play a supporting role for quality assurance testing, and therefore should not be directly involved in software implementation.

*System or Component Architect or Engineer*

- As an architect, responsible for the design of a subsystem or, at the top level, the entire system.
- The "owner" of a given system or subsystem, possibly throughout the entire lifecycle of the system or system version.
- As an engineer, responsible for the implementation of that system or subsystem.

*Feature Architect*

- Performs the design and implementation of a new feature.
- Collaborates with architects and engineers to decide how and where to implement features which involve multiple subsystems.
- This role becomes more important as the system evolves through subsequent releases.

*Quality Assurance Manager*

- Ensures that all releases meet quality assurance requirements and policies prior to delivery.
- Ensures that exceptions to policy have approval of senior management, specifically the department responsible for arbitrating marketing and production decisions.
- Develops the quality assurance test plan.
- Coordinates the execution of quality assurance testing, and provides QA test results to the Configuration Manager.
- Oversees the collection and monitoring of quality indicators, including test results during regression testing.

*Configuration Manager*

- Is associated with the system being developed, rather than the project developing it.
- Coordinates flow of change requests, change notices, and trouble reports for a module, both within a system and with other related systems.
- Owns the index of what features are and will be implemented in which builds, releases, and versions, as well as bug lists for each build and the results of regression testing; and the current and historical status of all these items.
- Responsible for the operation of the source code and documentation repository and associated directories, as well as the distribution (possibly via a web site and email or newsgroup notices) of requirements and specifications.

Let's now consider each of these roles more closely.

**Product and Subsystem Management.** Two separate views of the management of a software system are the product view and the project view. Both are needed because they serve different purposes. A product manager is someone who takes the long view and is concerned with the overall issue of the success of the product or component being constructed. Projects come and go, but products have a lifecycle that can last many years.

At a subsystem level, a subsystem manager is responsible for the lifecycle of the subsystem. Most software systems will not have a separate person for this role at a subsystem level unless the subsystem is very unique or critical, or the overall system is very large, or the subsystem is considered to be reusable.

**Project Management, Task Management, and Component Management.** The task or project view is orthogonal to the product or component view. A task manager or project manager is mainly concerned with the completion of the task at hand. This role involves obtaining resources, scheduling work, and checking progress. Most projects are highly task oriented, with tasks being assigned on a fairly granular level to individual designers and programmers. A task owner becomes a manager for that task, and is responsible for overseeing its completion.

**Domain Expert.** A domain expert is a project staff member who has or obtains expertise in the business requirements and processes. This person or team usually works closely with the ultimate user, and may spend time onsite to gain a better understanding of how the system will be used. The domain expert is usually involved in performing functional and QA testing, since that kind of testing requires knowledge of how the system will be used. A domain expert's knowledge also places them in a good position to be able to write test plans.

**System or Component Architect or Engineer.** A component architect is a technical staff member who is responsible for the design of a portion of the system, such as a package or module. A system architect is responsible for the design of the entire system. The primary tasks of an architect are to specify a well-defined set of interfaces for the system; to provide a clear definition of what the system does; to create a design for the system and verify that the design is workable; and to identify risks related to technologies used and design decisions.

**Feature Architect or Engineer.** A feature architect begins with a logical feature and casts that onto the system architecture to determine which subsystems will be affected by the feature. The feature architect recommends an implementation for the feature, which will involve changes to the design of existing systems and components. This is therefore a highly collaborative role, involving the architects of those systems. When a design is decided upon, which is determined to meet the goals of the feature and all affected systems, the feature architect is responsible for seeing the design through its implementation and for making sure that all interfaces are accounted for and modified appropriately.

**Quality Assurance on a Project.** Quality Assurance (QA) on a project is a borrowed role. Ideally, the QA staff belong permanently to a QA group and not the project. Otherwise, there is an inherent conflict of interest between the need to ensure quality and the need to ship software on schedule.

The QA staff should not be involved in development. They need to understand the application requirements, and therefore may be involved in requirements gathering. There are conceptually two components to this role: that of understanding the problem domain, and that of understanding and following the QA guidelines of the organization. A QA team therefore may be made up of two kinds of participants: those who are application experts and who participate in requirements gathering and testing, and those who belong to an independent QA group and whose primary job is to maintain and administer QA guidelines.

**Configuration Management.** Good document control and configuration management (CM) is critical for quality assurance. It is impossible to know if a system meets specifications if the current specifications cannot be found. All of the products of the analysis, specification, design, and implementation processes should be placed under configuration control, using a source-code control repository, and be made available project-wide. When the project transitions from one phase to the next (e.g., from design to development), the final versions of the documents produced in the prior phase should be published in an easily accessible form, such as an internal web site. Subsequent revisions should be published as well. Publishing this information in this way is important, because usually, extraneous items end up in the repository; a web page listing the final documents with some

explanation of what each is for can help new staff find the right information and get up to speed quickly. It also provides a place for including links to related information.

The configuration manager should be responsible for publishing any updates to these otherwise frozen documents (with the assistance of a web site administrator or librarian), and in general making sure they are current. Nevertheless, the full change history of the documents of prior phases should be maintained under configuration control at least until the system is released, in case deleted material needs to be recovered.

The configuration manager is also responsible for coordinating changes among the team, and with other teams working on related software.

### *Configuration Management and Change Control in More Detail*

Every software output needs to be viewed as a product, with a product lifecycle. A commercial product experiences high volume sales, so QA procedures are more stringent—you can't make quick fixes once products are out the door. Custom software still goes through versions, and as a result of reuse, there may at times be parallel versions. Thus, even custom software has a lifecycle, so *configuration control needs to be at a product level, not a project level.*

**CM Processes: Change Requests and Change Notices.** Change notices (CN) and change requests (CR)—which collectively may be referred to as change vehicles (CV)—are documents that provide notice about a change or a request for a change, respectively. These may be email documents, possibly composed with a web form, and are used to control and track changes to parts of a design that are deemed stable. They are normally used once a stable specification of some kind exists. They provide a means to change the product of a previous phase of development. A CN contains an announcement of a change made to some document or piece of information product, and a CR contains a request to make a specified change; both contain reference, routing, and tracking information, the originator, reason, and so forth.

During detailed design or coding, it is not useful to use CNs or CRs for most changes to that phase's product. Everything is in a state of flux, so everything would need a CV. However, a CV should be used for changes to behavior that deviate from the specification (so the specification will need to be changed as well; ideally this should be handled in the same CV). A CV should be used for a change that affects anyone else, in particular changes to implementation interfaces or protocols that may or may not be part of the specification. A CN can also be used to document a change to an item the changer is not responsible for. For example, if a change must be made to a package or class someone else is currently responsible for and they are not available to make the change, a CN should be used to document the change and provide notice of it. The configuration manager should provide a set of policies for when CVs are needed, but in general the purpose is to provide notice and create a trail of the reasons for each change that affects others.

The CV mechanism should be as automated as possible. It may make use of an email mailing list with aliases set up for the groups responsible for different packages. A private news server may also be used to provide a viewable history of changes, notices, and communication about packages and development issues.

A CR should be routed to the person or group currently in charge of the component. It should also get posted on a newsgroup for the package and any affected packages. The CR then either is approved or rejected, and, if approved, a task is assigned to make the change.

When the change has been made, a CN should be initiated. This should be routed to the original initiator of the CR and all interested or affected parties, and a news item about the change should be posted, referencing the original CR. Optionally, CRs and CNs may automatically go into a database, with a query to provide status information based on the CV number, author, package, or class.

**Version Control for Remote Teams.** If development teams are not located in the same office or geographic region, it is still possible to integrate the teams so that they operate almost as if they were co-located. In this case it is even more important to divide design and implementation responsibility into packages, so that a site knows exactly which packages it is responsible for. There is no reason a site's packages cannot be subpackages of any given higher-level package—packages are just a naming hierarchy, and subpackages may be named in any way that makes sense, even across teams or locations.

If the project is able to implement a virtual private network (VPN) with acceptable bandwidth, then all locations can use the same version control system for accessing software. Generally, however, at least a T-1 connection is required to make this practical, since most version control systems move large amounts of data when computing deltas and source versions. Some version control systems have special features to assist distributed teams. Depending on the version control system being used, this may be practical and should be tested. The disadvantage of this approach is that even with a version control system, you are dependent on some degree of human communication about who is doing what, and if a team is off site, that is inhibited. It is therefore usually more practical to treat an offsite team's work the same way you would treat a third party product: install releases at controlled times, and try to keep the shared interfaces stable. Assign release numbers to your own interface modules.

**Keeping Shared Components Stable.** Most projects have a data layer of some sort. This should be a highly stable component before coding starts. Builds of the data layer should be handled as a special case, be performed with less frequency than other project components, and be followed by testing to establish a new baseline.

The data layer will also have to be loaded with test data. Generally, at least two versions of the data layer's test data need to be maintained concurrently: a small version for development and unit testing, and a fully loaded mock-up database for full system and scalability testing. It is usually not practical to develop using a fully loaded database, due to increased load and query times, and yet a small version does not stress the system. Thus, both are needed to satisfy development and testing requirements.

**Keeping Specifications Up-to-Date.** If the coding process discovers an error in a specification, the same procedure should be used to change a specification as to change code. Ideally, design specs should be integrated by reference into the code.

The problem that arises is that coding usually results in design changes as detailed issues are resolved. It is extremely inconvenient at this stage but necessary to propagate these changes into specifications. A solution is to generate design documentation from the code, by embedding the design documentation in the code itself, e.g., in a header. This is the approach taken by the javadoc tool, which generates API documentation from the actual source code, and makes use of embedded HTML tags which the programmer can insert. This after-the-fact approach is best suited to systems which are designed incrementally or collaboratively.

Diagrams are especially problematic. One very enterprising group I worked with photographed and scanned all sketches produced in design meetings and posted them on the internal development group's web site. Eventually, these highly meaningful sketches were replaced with high-quality renderings. Code comments can refer to online diagrams, by including HTML tags that embed graphic images, or by embedding links to PDF or other document formats that have diagrammatic capability. Having entry-level staff render design sketches into online documents is a way to help get the new staff up to speed on the key aspects of the design.

Automatically generating documentation does not relieve the need to update existing specifications, however, if they are affected, nor does it relieve the need to use change control procedures, especially when interfaces or intended behavior are changed. It is extremely important that detailed actual specs be maintained in sync with the code, otherwise a "guru" system will result, with the knowledge only in the heads of key developers, and there is the possibility that management will lose control of the system and be unable to make technical judgments without relying on guru staff who have an interest in making the system more and more complex. Staff should not be blamed for this tendency: it is the natural tendency of good developers to want to tackle interesting problems; the best business solution is often the simplest, however. The real problem is making sure that the system is well documented and understood by all.

## The Phases of Development

The normal phases of a development project are requirements specification, logical design, detailed system design, implementation, final testing, deployment, and post-deployment maintenance and enhancement. Different methodologies may call these phases by different names, but they are always present. Each phase has its own products, which may be documents, code, or test results.

### *Requirements Gathering*

The effort required to collect system requirements varies enormously from one kind of system to another, and also varies depending on the prior experience of the team with the application domain. Collecting requirements is usually a multistep process, beginning with a series of discussions with the user, and progressing to more intense collaboration with users, possibly involving extended periods onsite. As part of this activity, the requirements should be documented in the form of system whitepapers initially and eventually refined into more complete documents, possibly use cases or requirements lists and concept designs for the layout of the system's primary user interface components.

When this phase is complete, requirements gathering is not done; the team members who collected the requirements may need to remain to provide an inhouse source of expertise in how the system should behave and to maintain and interpret the documents they wrote. The requirements team also has formed an important relationship with the user, and can serve as a liaison so that developers do not have to work directly with (or field calls from) the eventual users or procurers of the system.

### *Logical Design, Requirements Development, and Prototyping*

A logical design partitions the system into conceptual components and specifies their behavior. It is important that the problem domain be reflected primarily, and that minimal attention be paid to considerations having to do with performance, platform, or technology choices, unless these things are constants and known ahead of time, or are key choices that affect the functional capabilities. The reason is that this postponement allows choices of platform and technology to be deferred and left for implementation experts. The important goal of the logical design phase is to synergize the knowledge of application experts and implementation experts to produce a logical model of the system which could be implemented and would work, but perhaps not optimally.

If the system has transactional behavior, transaction partitioning should be addressed in a logical sense (what are the transactions), but not the implementation (e.g., whether DBMS locking is to be used, or implemented with an optimistic policy or other strategy). This does not mean that no thought should be given to such issues; in fact, judgment about the likely technical challenges of the alternative logical designs is crucial to coming up with a design that can be built within the project's budget. Pinning down specific implementations is probably premature, however, since at this point a prototype has not even been built, and regardless, the focus should be on making sure all the application's functionality is addressed.

In addition to the logical design per se, an important output of the logical design process is a list of system requirements. It is the natural instinct of a good engineering team to first clarify and confirm what they are to build before building it. This requirements list is just that.

You might think that if the system is now being designed, requirements should already have been compiled. This is certainly the approach taken in many traditional methodologies. However, for a development team to become efficient at designing and building a system, they must be made to express the requirements themselves. During the logical design phase, the development team reiterates the requirements in terms understood by the team, and seeks verification and signoff of these by the end user prior to beginning detailed design. This requirements list is more detailed than any before it, and becomes the final word on the system's behavior. This completes the circle in terms of understanding the system function on both sides of the table, so to speak. The requirements list developed in this phase also serves as the basis for developing the system features list. The requirements represent the logical features. Later design phases transform these into concrete features.

A prototype or proof of concept should be developed during the logical design phase if possible. If there are new technologies involved—which is almost inevitable nowadays—what are their limitations? Do they perform as advertised? What surprises do they have in store? Scale prototyping and testing should also be performed in an investigatory manner during this stage. Note that bugs such as memory leaks in key third-party components may not show up until the system is tested at scale. The prototype is not limited to proving technology: it should test critical operational assumptions and demonstrate any business process reengineering concepts that are to be implemented.

### *Detailed Design*

The detailed design phase modifies the logical design and produces a final detailed design, which includes technology choices, specifies a system architecture, meets all system goals for performance, and still has all of the application functionality and behavior specified in the logical design. If a database is a component of the system, the schema that results from the detailed design may be radically different in key places from the one developed in the logical design phase, although an effort should be made to use identical terminology and not change things that do not need to be changed. The detailed design process should document all design decisions that require schema changes, or in general any changes to the logical design, and the reasons for the change. The project manager's challenge will be to again disseminate understanding of the new design, which is replacing a logical design that had achieved credibility and consensus. This is the reason why all changes need to be well documented, so there is a clear migration, and the changes do not seem radical or arbitrary.

If a features list approach is used, it is easy to separate the project into versions, and make the detailed design and implementation phases of each version iterative. The systems's features can be analyzed for dependencies and resource requirements, and assigned to project versions based on these dependencies, critical path, and priority. The minimum set of features for a testable bootstrap system can then be determined. For each version, additional features are added, and all tests are rerun, resulting in a working system with increasing functionality and reliability. For each version, a detailed design of each feature can be performed, identifying the packages and classes affected, and with roughcut and then detailed updates to the specifications being produced, possibly in an iterative manner, and finally actual implementation in code. I have seen this technique work extremely successfully on many compiler and other projects with which I have been involved, and it is directly applicable to all kinds of systems.

Once a detailed design for a system version is agreed upon, the implementation phase should make very few changes to the system design, although some changes are inevitable. It is critical for maintainability that all changes be incorporated back into the design specifications. Otherwise, the value of the system design will be lost as soon as the system is released, and the only design documentation will be the code. A system documented only by its code is very hard for management to understand and upgrade, outsource, or disseminate.

A Java-specific reason to incorporate changes back into specifications is that Java 2 introduces the concept of package versioning. A package is viewed as a field-replaceable unit, and besides its name has two identifying pieces of information associated with it: its *specification version* and its *implementation version*. Two versions of a package that have the same specification version are implemented according to the same specifications, and should therefore be field-replaceable; the only difference between them should be that one has bug fixes which perhaps

the other does not. A user might choose one implementation version over another if the user has instituted workarounds for certain known bugs; otherwise, the latest implementation version should be the most desired one. You can see that for this methodology to work, there must exist a well-defined set of specifications for every package, and those specifications should have a version number associated with them.

### *Walkthroughs*

A walkthrough is a group session in which a design or program is reviewed and critiqued. The goal of a walkthrough is to ensure that the subject of the walkthrough (usually a particular module or subsystem) meets standards and that it agrees with the common understanding of the requirements. It is also to provide a forum for developing a collective understanding of interfaces and how the system works.

Walkthroughs are usually performed for program code, but regrettably often not for designs. For a complex system, it is extremely valuable that a walkthrough be performed for a design as well as implementation code. The walkthrough can occur as part of the design process, if it is done as a group modeling and scenario development exercise; or it can be done in a traditional sit-down walkthrough of a design spec produced by an individual. In the latter case, the designer of the subsystem should present the design first, followed by discussion. Regardless, there must be a design to review, on paper or in a computer, ideally with procedural or scenario aspects, because they are the easiest to review in a group setting and get everyone thinking.

The purpose of a walkthough is:

- To disseminate knowledge about a design in a participative way so that people absorb and understand it.
- To discover logical errors, or design flaws. An "issues list" is normally produced to identify items that need resolution.
- To discover incompatibilities between subsystems being developed by different people. A "related issues list" may be produced for distribution to potentially affected parties for future resolution.
- To verify adherence to coding or design standards.
- To boost morale and develop team spirit.

Management should participate in initial walkthroughs to establish guidelines and processes, and then leave them to senior engineering staff to manage. Development staff must feel uninhibited in a walkthrough to voice opinions. Staff should be advised ahead of time that having a defensive attitude is not permitted.

A designer's or programmer's performance should not be evaluated based on the number of problems discovered in walkthroughs, but by a trend of fewer problems over time. This encourages staff to try to create complete and correct designs without making them reluctant to discuss issues about their designs.

It is not generally necessary to perform a walkthrough for all code. For example, if several modules follow a common pattern a walkthrough can be performed for a representative module. When the representative module has been approved a quality analyst can privately review the others to ensure that they adhere to the same standards; or alternatively the other modules can be distributed ahead of time and the walkthrough of those can focus on questions or comments that others may have instead of a detailed or line by line explanation. Line by line discussion is usually only justified for critical or extremely important sections of code which need to be approved or understood by others. Non-critical code can be reviewed in a more informal manner focusing on adherence to standards and explanations of key algorithms. In short, the format and detail of the walkthrough should be appropriate for the module in question.

It is interesting and challenging that while a major purpose of a walkthrough is to create team spirit, the other purposes involve problem discovery, that is, finding fault with someone's design or implementation. Handling this is not an easy matter. It is the primary task of the person managing the walkthrough to transform this discovery process into a positive and productive exercise, which leaves the team feeling energized and that they now have a solid design and are on the right track, and that no one was reprimanded or made to feel incompetent. Humor and a pre-walkthrough pep talk are often helpful in this regard. Bringing some kind of food invariably helps because it provides an excuse for a tension-relieving break.

### *The Testing Process*

The QA process must ensure that documentation and software match, and that these match the specs. Errors discovered during QA testing and also during internal testing may show up as a list of failed tests which is routed to feature or module owners, or bug reports may be generated. Bug reports will arrive after deployment as well, when the system is in operation.

There needs to be a procedure for allocating bug reports or failed tests to engineers for investigation and bug fixing. A bug fix will not normally trigger a CV unless the change meets normal criteria for generating a CV, such as a change to a system specification, or to system interfaces, external behavior, or subsystems currently being maintained or enhanced by another group. In the last case, in which bugs are being fixed for a deployed system version in parallel with work on a new and enhanced system version (which has a new specification, according to the Java 2 versioning concepts), a CV would also be generated against the new sys-

tem, since the responsibility for fixing bugs to the deployed system version is a different responsibility than that of building the new system version. As will be discussed later, it is the responsbility of the system's configuration manager to know when a CV needs to be routed to the CM of another system or system version.

There should be a streamlined and automatic bug reporting process, accessible online to programmers and analysts. Bug reports should go into a database so that they do not accidentally collide (two different reports get assigned the same bug number), and also so that they can be tracked and analyzed. Test results, bug reports, and fixes follow statistical trends (so do CVs), and analyzing this trend (both during the project as well as making historical cross-project comparisons) is valuable to management. This is difficult for developers to understand sometimes, because developers are close to the system and do not see the components in a statistical way, just as parents do not see their children as statistics. Graphing progress in fixing bugs and posting those graphics helps to crystallize the goal for development staff during final stages of development and testing, which is to get the system as near bug-free as possible.

The bug reporting process should generate a notice to the parties responsible for the suspect module and all affected modules. A news item may also be posted in categories related to the affected features. A bug report should identify the class and, if applicable, the method or construct involved. It should identify the system build. It should possibly identify the line numbers involved, if known, and the nature of the incorrect behavior. It may recommend a fix. It should also, if practical, identify a test program that demonstrates the error; this may be attached or referenced by a network file:// URL (e.g., file://myhost/myshare/myfile.java for an NT system, or file://myhost/mydir/myfile.java for a UNIX system).

Test suites either can be based on functional requirements, such that each atomic requirement of the system is tested, or based on code coverage, such that every logical pathway and system component is exercised, or both. Functional tests generally are used for most systems; code coverage tests are used to augment testing for systems that have stringent reliability requirements.

Some systems, such as compilers, are amenable to script-driven testing. This is a highly efficient way to test a system, since a test suite can be rerun every night, and progress is easy to assess, since each night the test suite should turn up fewer bugs. Tracking progress is easy, because there is a well-defined set of tests which cover the entire scope of the system's requirements, and test passage or failure is automatically determined by the test. The process of rerunning test suites and comparing the results is known as *regression testing*. It is not uncommon for com-

piler test suites to have tens of thousands of tests, depending on the complexity of the language translated by the compiler.

Interactive systems, on the other hand, must often be tested manually. There are tools that can be used to simulate a human user, generate mouse events, and so on. These can be used for automatic testing, but in many cases it is more practical to run the system through a test procedure with a human at the helm. This will turn up previously unobserved quirks that an automatic test cannot. The larger the system, the more advantageous automated testing is.

Developing user simulation tests is also very time-consuming, and the time may be better spent in actual human-run testing. It boils down to the comparative cost of performing the test suite manually, versus the cost of developing automatic tests and then running them automatically the same number of times, which likely has negligible cost compared to running the tests manually. A strictly analytical way of looking at it is:

If

```
cost_of_developing_auto_tests <
(no_of_times_test_suite_is_run) x
   (cost_of_running_same_tests_manually)
```

then develop automatic tests.

However, even if automatic tests are developed, some manual testing still needs to be done to catch unanticipated problems. Two other considerations are that, having developed an automatic test suite, it will have to be maintained; on the other hand, it can be used and added to for every future release.

There are many Java-based automatic testing tools. SunTest (www.sun.com/suntest), a Sun Microsystems division, has a suite of high-quality testing tools, including JavaStar, for building automated test suites for UI-based applications; JavaSpec, for constructing high-coverage test suites for noninteractive code; and Java-Scope, for test coverage analysis. For test coverage, the product DeepCover from Reliable Software Technologies (www.rstcorp.com) helps you perform code coverage analysis for your test suites. Also, their AssertMate product allows you to specify correctness assertions without modifying your source code. Another coverage tool is TCAT for Java, by Software Research, Inc. (http://www.soft.com), designed for testing Java applets running in browsers.

Even if you execute user tests manually, most systems have a data layer or service layer core for which automated procedural tests can be developed. If this layer is automatically generated, based on a schema, creating a test suite for it may not be necessary. If the layer is manually coded, developing a regression suite for it is strongly recommended.

The importance of developing a test suite for a data layer component depends on the potential cost of observed and unobserved failure. Errors in a data layer may often go undetected. However, it is not difficult to develop a regression suite for the core layer, and it will have the side effect of enhancing the understanding of the system. It can be run periodically to make sure that the core system's behavior is not changing over time and deviating from specifications. Tests can be added to the regression suite throughout the system's lifetime, and the test suite's value will increase. The regression suite, in effect, becomes the proof that the system has certain characteristics. For example, if one wanted to test for year-2000 compliance, it likely would not be hard to find the tests in the regression suite that have to do with manipulating dates and times, and merely add a few tests to see if the year 2000 can be handled. The existence of a regression suite makes it easier for management to evaluate the cost of changes in future versions of the system, possibly only because of the increased precision with which the system is implemented and conforms to specifications. The suite can also be used to evaluate the impact of technology substitutions within the data layer.

Test programs and procedures should be treated as a system component and put under revision control, with changes handled by the same CR and CN procedure as the system itself. The test suite should also include scalability testing, which is often forgotten for middle-range applications and even for large ones.

Final QA testing must be treated as a separate phase of its own, and should be performed by a separate QA testing team. This team should be familiar with the problem domain, so that they can effectively exercise the system.

Developers are still busy during the QA period. They are not adding new functionality; instead, they are responding to bug reports from the QA group. The workflow is not substantially different, and all feedback mechanisms for changes and notification must still be in place. The QA group will make a "frozen" copy of the project code and test it in complete isolation, but testing of "frozen" code in this way still does not obviate feedback to the developers to subsequently fix reported problems. In fact, generating frozen releases is part of the normal build process, even though it may receive increased emphasis in the final build.

### *Acceptance Testing*

By definition, acceptance testing is performed by the receiving organization, which I will call the "customer" for purposes of discussion. It cannot be conducted by the developer. The customer is given a candidate release, and they run their tests and decide if they will accept the release.

In the course of acceptance testing, it is inevitable that deviations from expectation will be found in some areas. This can be reduced or prevented altogether by showing the customer early builds of the system and addressing those issues before final delivery. However, there may still be some problems or unresolved issues that result from the acceptance testing process.

It is critical at this time to have the requirements list that was prepared earlier during the logical design phase to which the customer agreed. This document needs to be maintained during the course of the project to reflect any changes agreed to with the customer, since it is the only document which defines in a detailed way what constitutes "success."

In the interest of promoting a good relationship with the customer and providing them with a system that meets their needs, some final changes and tweaks may be agreed to outside the scope of the contract. Nevertheless, any changes made to the software need to go through the normal process and result in a new build and modification or amendment of the requirements list if appropriate. At some point acceptance of the release occurs and future changes are worked into the next version of the system.

### *The Importance of Continuity*

Throughout all these phases, continuity is essential. A project that assigns domain analysis tasks to analysts and then reassigns those analysts during the implementation phase is operating with a severe handicap, if not doomed to failure. Domain expertise must remain within the project throughout its lifecycle. The dilemma is that once up-front analysis is complete, the analysts have less work, and their role becomes more passive. Often this cannot be justified, and these people are valuable to the business and are needed elsewhere. A solution that often works well is to keep a few domain experts assigned full time, and give them the permanent role of *facilitator.* In this capacity, they perform domain analysis, and execute all change requests to requirements specifications. They also develop user-oriented test plans, and construct system documentation. Their role therefore remains an active one, and their knowledge about the application, and contacts within the organization, can still be tapped when questions arise during development.

## More CM Issues

### *Versions, Releases, and Builds*

As a system evolves, new capabilities are usually added. The system therefore is built to increasingly rich specifications. It is important to distinguish between a system **version** and a release. Two versions of a system have different specifications—they are expected to behave differently; e.g., one version might have more capabilities than an earlier version. System versions are usually identified by major version numbers, e.g., 1.x, 2.x, and so on, or possibly by the first minor number, such as 1.1, 1.2, etc., for minor versions which add only a small number of additional features or improvements. A configuration manager should ensure that, for any version of a system, there is an identifiable feature list (under configuration control) that the version implements.

On the other hand, in this book I will use the term **release** to represent reliability improvements that do not affect the specification, except where clarifications are implemented. (A release is sometimes called an "implementation version," but I find that confusing and so I will use the term "release.") Releases usually fix bugs, but do not implement new requirements. Two releases of the same system version are expected to behave the same, except for bug fixes. System releases are designated by minor release numbers, e.g., 1.1, 1.2, or the second minor number such as 1.1.1, 1.1.2, and so on, if the first two digits represent the version. A system should have a convention for which numeric level identifies a release as opposed to a version, and the convention should be strictly adhered to.

During development of a system, builds are produced. A **build** is an instance of the system, integrated for the purpose of testing of a release. Several builds may occur before the build is deemed stable enough to be released. Build numbering or naming need not correspond in any way to release numbers, but doing so is useful, and in any case should identify the system version.

**Naming of Release Candidates.** If the project is being done under contract, a release is not official until it has been accepted by the customer. Suppose a release is delivered but the customer's acceptance testing process rejects it or requests changes. If a build has already been named to represent a release, then a subsequent build will have to be part of the next release. This is not desirable since the current release has not yet been accepted.

The solution is to first designate an unaccepted release as a "release candidate." A given release candidate is represented by a build which has passed the developer's QA process. If the customer accepts a release candidate, it becomes a release. If not, more builds are produced and eventually one of them becomes a release candidate which then is accepted. At that point the release candidate can be promoted to be a release.

**Naming of Deployment Files and Packaging.** Any deployment packaging of the system should identify the full designation of the system, including version and release. For example, if the system is packaged in a JAR file, the file should be named accordingly so that it is clear at a glance which version and release the file represents. It is very confusing to receive multiple files from a third party over time, all called something like "systemX.jar." You should always include at least the version and release in the naming of all outermost components.

It is generally undesirable to include the build number in the file name. The configuration manager merely needs to keep a record of which build was released. Still, somewhere in the system the build should be identified and easily obtained.

Using separate names for release candidates is probably confusing to the customer. If you use the same file name for each release candidate for a particular release, which is recommended, work out a process with your customer for distinguishing among them, such as including each candidate in an enclosing "release candidate package" with the candidate's name, such as "ForAcceptance-release1.4-Candidate2.zip," and have that package include the actual product. Inside the zip file the actual release candidate would reside named according to the product's normal naming and packaging design, such as "ProductX-1.4.jar," or "ProductX-1.4.exe" for a native self-extracting archive.

In the next chapter we will see that Java 2 defines a set of version control manifest attributes for the packages in a JAR file, which identify the system version (the "Specification-version" attribute) and the release and build (the "Package-version" attribute). This makes it possible to label the Java packages in each JAR file included in a product distribution. A JAR file therefore does not need to be named according to the component version or release it represents. Instead, apply release-identifying names to whatever digital envelope is used to distribute the JAR file. Do not ship "naked" JAR files as products!

**Multiple Components.** An interesting situation arises if the system is composed of multiple components which have independent version and release numbers. In that case, a manifest should be provided which identifies which version, release, and build of each component is included. Collectively these constitute a release of the overall system, which may have a separate overall number designation.

### *Module Evolution and Derived Modules*

After a system version is deployed, it goes into a maintenance phase until the version is retired or is no longer supported. During this phase, trouble or bug reports are received, which must be distributed to the group responsible for maintaining the system. It may be the case that the original developer of the module plays a role in the maintenance of the module, especially if the module represents a unique or complex technology. Alternatively, the module may be maintained by someone else, who is the new owner of the module. In either case, trouble reports need to be folded into an outstanding bug list for the system version and release.

After a system version is deployed, work may have begun on a new version. It is important that bugs fixed in a particular version result in notices to the individual

or group that owns any derived or precursor modules in other supported versions so that the impact of the bug and bug fix can be assessed for the derived or precursor modules. To accomplish this, a database needs to maintain derivational relationships for modules across any concurrently supported versions. It is the role of the configuration manager to ensure that a manual or automated system is used for routing trouble reports, bug reports, and change requests to not only the modules under development within a project, but also to other projects or module configuration managers responsible for derivational or precursor modules. The criticality of the configuration management role for a deployed and evolving system is therefore clear, and the process for handling it should be developed as soon as possible. The same system serves to document changes in system requirements, which may reflect changes in cost.

#### *Prototype Branch Threads*

If a feature requires only additions to interfaces and no semantic changes to the interface specifications, then adding the feature should have minimal impact on existing code. It can therefore be added incrementally and independently by each module owner, first adding the new capabilities and then adding code that uses the new capabilities. If, on the other hand, the feature is such that it requires changes that must be coordinated and made simultaneously in multiple modules, it is best to have one person prototype the feature by creating a parallel *branch version*, or a *branch thread*.

A branch version is a separate and parallel thread of development. To create a branch, a developer obtains the latest copy of all affected modules, for read-only access, but then makes a separate writeable local copy of the modules that need to be changed. This separate writeable copy is made without checking those modules out with respect to the main development thread. The local writeable copies are modified in their own directory or work area until they are complete. At that point, the branch is ready to be integrated with the main build thread. The developer then checks out the modules that need to be modified, and carefully incorporates the changes.

The primary difficulty with branch prototyping is the reintegration. While the prototype is being worked on, other developers are making changes to the same modules—apart from the branch. This separation is necessary to provide some stability to the branch while the prototyping is done, and at the same time it protects the main build thread from incomplete changes. In addition, when the changes are ready to be integrated, the branch developer will have to obtain delegated permission from the module owners to incorporate the changes to their modules, and will have to actually check those modules out.

Some source code control tools provide support for the reintegration process. Typically a tool will allow the programmer to view side-by-side things that have changed and make a decision about which lines to merge into the final version. This can be a difficult process, however, depending on how far the two branches have diverged. Some version control tools provide a feature in which the most recent changes are automatically merged. Such a feature is better suited to document worksharing and is risky when used for software.

### Reuse of Modules as Custom Builds

Generally only source material is put in a configuration control system. Binary code built from source is not, because it can be automatically rebuilt. The build scripts should be in the configuration database, however, because it is a form of source, and is needed to create a build. Documentation should be in a configuration control system as well. What about software obtained from third parties, or from other projects?

First of all, it must be recognized that the application of an existing component to a project (i.e., reuse) usually involves customization. For example, instantiating a JavaBeans component into a user interface typically involves placing the component and then setting its properties—i.e., customizing the instance, which results in generated code and possibly the creation of an initial state serialization file.

With non-bean components, customization may even occur through the use of compile-time variables or switches. Therefore, usage may require rebuilding binary components. The conclusion is that the mere use of a third party component usually involves some kind of configuration or customization that should be under configuration control. Since the build of the externally obtained component is likely to occur at infrequent intervals, perhaps coinciding with releases of that component, there is good reason to create a shared copy of the build, and place that under configuration control or at least some form of change control procedure, instead of merely placing its source under control or just sticking the built or configured component "out there." In fact, source may not even be available.

If a project requires a custom build of an externally produced module, a process should be created for generating that build and putting the build itself (i.e., compiled and configured code, or, for example, a configured server product) under configuration control. The project then uses the configured build, instead of accessing the original module. In this way, the build itself is controlled, so that: (1) all developers use the same build, and can be sure that the module is configured identically; and (2) a shared copy is used, instead of each programmer having to obtain and configure the module source as part of their own development process.

Most products nowadays use user interfaces for configuration. However, it is rare that there are not generated configuration files which can be placed under configuration control and used to automatically restore the system's configuration. If the system uses a database for storing its configuration, then it may be possible to copy the database and put it under configuration control so that it can be restored for each test run.

### Putting the CM Process Together

Figure 1-1 depicts a configuration management workflow. The initial entry point to the figure is at the top left in which an originator submits a change request to the configuration manager (CM) for a system. The CM is the keeper of all change requests and bug lists for the system, as well as the system's feature list, indexed by system version and release.

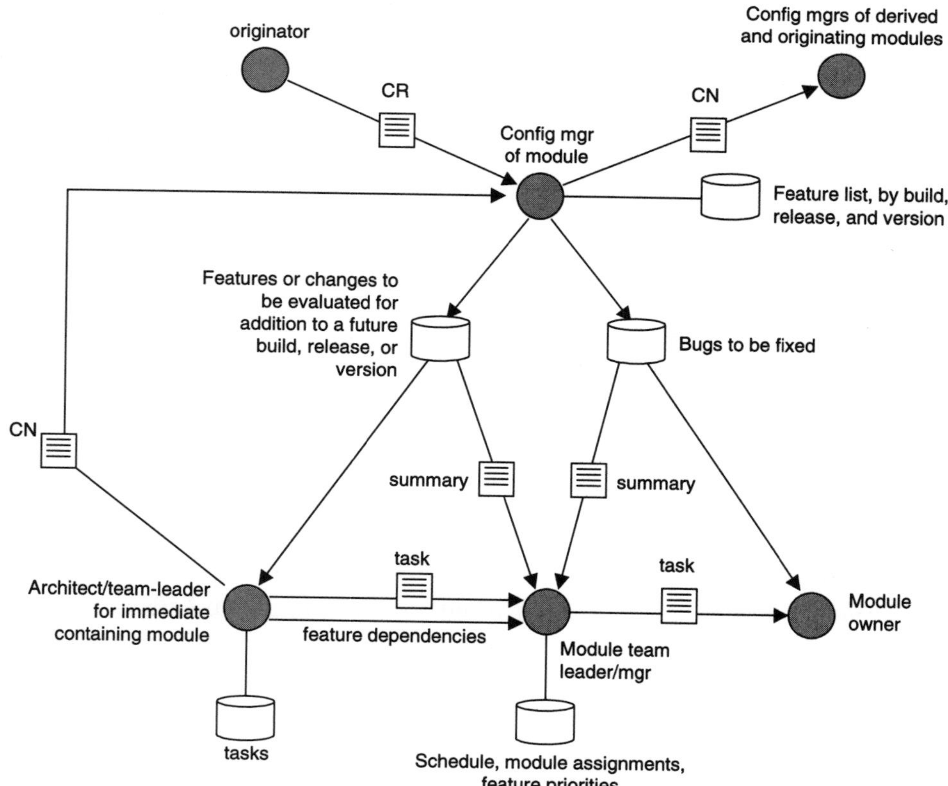


**Figure 1-1** Change propagation, which is increasingly important when software is reused.

When a change request is received, the CM evaluates the request from the point of view of determining its nature. In particular, if the requested feature is already present in the system specification but for some reason is not present or is not working in the operational system, the change request is converted to a bug report.

If a change request is determined to be legitimate, it is routed to the system architect for technical evaluation. The architect determines the viability and impact of the change on the system, and determines what additional tasks would be required to implement it. The architect also determines which tasks are interdependent and need to be implemented as a unit. This information is presented to the project manager or team leader so that it can be prioritized.

If the project manager determines that the requested changes should be implemented, the architect converts the change request into a change notice, and sends it back to the configuration manager to document that the change will be implemented. In addition, if changes are required to other systems or interfaces, appropriate change requests may be created.

An important recipient of change notices is the CM of parallel precursor or derived systems. For example, if the current system is an operational system which is being maintained with new releases, but a future version of the system is under development, then any bug fixes or changes made to the operational system need to be routed to the CM of the new system for evaluation, since each system now represents a separate and divergent set of code.

One can easily go overboard in creating a system to track all of this. It should be remembered that the goal is to maintain control of the features that are added over time and identify their impact. If manual processes accomplish this, that is satisfactory. For example, visual aids such as charts categorizing and depicting pending changes are extremely useful.

## Documenting a Design

Design is the process of producing a specification for constructing something. A "logical design" focuses on a system's behavior, which may include details of external interfaces, but overlooks many of the internal workings of the system. A logical design is different from a requirements specification in that a design begins to address *how* requirements are accomplished. It need not (should not) reiterate those requirements.

A design needs to precisely specify what the system does, however—the inputs and outputs, and the transformations or algorithms that are relevant to the application. These may appear in the system's requirements. The design makes decisions about how the requirements are to be implemented. If the requirements

contain algorithm specifications or procedures, the design addresses the form these will take in the system. The design will specify components which provide these algorithms or procedures.

A logical design is merely an abstraction of the system, with many details left out. In a logical design, many decisions about implementation are postponed to create a first-cut design that can be understood and verified by domain experts, and serve as the basis for a prototype. There is really no other qualitative or substantive difference between logical and detailed system designs, except the level of abstraction and postponement of decisions which hinge on detailed design analysis and technology choices. A logical design may therefore be viewed as a model, since it describes a hypothetical and simplified implementation.

Most projects develop a "detailed design" prior to coding. In a detailed design, features and terminology should match actual components and constructs in the real system to be built, and for this reason a detailed design is sometimes referred to as a "physical design." In contrast, only the behavior of the major components of a logical design need match the actual system. A detailed design begins with a specification of the actual top-level physical architecture of the planned system. A detailed design specification must also include decisions on issues that are postponed in a logical design; in a detailed design, no major issues are postponed. The level of detail to be included in the logical and detailed design—and even whether to separate these tasks or combine them—is a critical decision. It has been my experience that if a proof-of-concept and technology evaluation prototype is developed during the logical design phase, the knowledge gained can be used to produce a highly complete detailed design, and drastically reduce risk for the project.

### *UML—A Universal Modeling Language*

We are fortunate that there has finally been a convergence in the various object-oriented system modeling notations. Universal Modeling Language (UML), which has rapidly become the accepted standard for specifying object-oriented systems, defines a set of diagrammatic conventions for representing virtually every aspect of a system. The different kinds of diagrams specified by UML are:

> *Use case diagram*—Identifies actors and the functions (use cases) they perform in a diagrammatic manner. Useful for showing the roles users play in a system, in terms of which use cases they interact with. Appropriate for giving an overview of work processes.
>
> *Class diagram*—Identifies interfaces and classes, their attributes and operations (i.e., methods), and the cardinal, compositional, and derivational relationships between them. Most applications will have a core object model expressed with class diagrams. In a database application, certain classes will be labeled persistent.

*Sequence diagram, collaboration diagram*—Time-based diagramming techniques to show the messaging behavior of a system. A sequence diagrams is a two dimensional chart showing the flow of messages between objects versus time. A collaboration diagram does not impose a two-dimensional organization, but identifies the sequence of message flows by assigning them numbers that increase with time. A collaboration diagram has somewhat the appearance of a data flow diagram, and can be used effectively to give a high-level view of what is happening in a system. Often object instances will be represented instead of classes, to show a "typical" scenario.

*Package diagram*—Shows system partitioning. This is directly applicable to a Java application, since Java has a very analogous package construct. This is perhaps the hardest diagram to do right, although on the surface it looks like the simplest kind of UML diagram. The challenge is that in many systems—even some well-designed ones—everything uses everything, and one can end up with a package diagram that has lines between every component.

*Implementation diagram*—Similar to a class diagram, but for large-grain components. This can be used to show communication between large-grain components, such as a server object and clients. It can also be used to show how a software system is configured or deployed, in terms of which components reside in which machines.

*Activity diagram, statechart diagram*—State-based diagramming techniques for showing concurrent behavior. These are very useful for specifying aspects of a design that uses multithreading.

Let's now look at what goes into a Java design, and which of these modeling diagrammatic formats can help.

### What Should a Java Design Spec Contain?

A design specification for a software system to be developed in Java may contain some or all of the following. Depending on the complexity and requirements of the system, some aspects will be more important than others. I am assuming that use cases or requirements, or a logical features list (or all of these) have already been documented. A detailed design will address all of the following areas, except those that are not applicable to the system; a logical design will address fewer areas. By having matching sections, it is possible to map the changes from a logical design to a detailed design. A detailed design document should also explain decisions that were made that led to differences between the logical and detailed design. (Recall that differences between a logical and detailed design do not necessarily represent inconsistency; the physical model need not have the same objects as the logical model.)

In general a design should address all of these areas, at least to the extent of mentioning that each topic was considered. However, the more documentation you

generate the more lethargic you make your process, since with every change you will have to update all affected specifications. Therefore, the actual body of the sections below should be completed to a level appropriate for the project. The decision of what needs to be emphasized in the design is an important role of the architect and the project manager.

Rather than list the elements of a design and then explain each one, I will explain them within the list itself:

- *Design description:* An overview of the design, explaining how components interact and the primary logical flow. Recommended format: informal.
- *Object model:* An object model, which identifies interfaces, classes, and their cardinalities, and identifies the composite objects that will form the basis of transactions. In a logical design, it would be advisable to postpone the specification of concrete classes and leave classes abstract, focusing mainly on interfaces and roles. A clear separation of the persistent and non-persistent classes is useful. Recommended format: UML class diagrams.
- *Member specification:* An exact specification (well-commented interfaces and classes) of the methods, attributes, and associations in each of the interfaces and classes, and the purpose of each. Ultimately, you want to express the member specification in Java so that these specifications can be incorporated into the code. Consider using `javadoc` code commenting conventions, and embedding diagrams via HTML tags. An alternative, however, is to fully annotate the object model and generate these specifications automatically, using a tool such as Rational Rose or Together Java. The challenge is that the specifications are likely to be many paragraphs if not more per method, and the tool must accommodate this. For methods, these specifications should say what the methods do, and optionally how; see "Functional specification" on page 32.
- *Environment specification:* A specification of the planned deployment environment(s), and the approximate expected usage pattern, volume, and other characteristics—don't leave scalability considerations for a later phase. Format: text, UML implementation diagrams, use case diagrams, tables, and charts.
- *Design concepts:* Summary of decisions about key issues, such as transactional behavior. (See Chapter 6, "Java Database Connectivity.") Messaging between system components should be identified. A distinction between different categories of messages can be made if it is known, such as which need to be remote versus local, which need to be synchronous versus non-blocking, and

so on. An architect should be able to read this section and understand how the system works. Format: informal text and diagrams, UML collaboration or sequence diagrams, activity or statechart diagrams, and class diagrams.

- *Functional specification:* Pseudocode or scenarios describing how to implement key behavior. If the application contains visual components, their layouts and designs should be specified in this section. Applicable formats: UML collaboration or sequence diagrams, Java pseudocode, activity or statechart diagrams, and screen layouts. If the system requirements include a features list, all items in it should be referenced by the functional specifications.
- *Feature list:* An enumeration and explanation of the features of the system. In a detailed design, features are concrete things. For example, a feature of a user interface screen might be a name entry field. The features are the things which need to be implemented or provided, and each feature description should identify the requirement(s) the feature helps to satisfy. The feature list may be organized hierarchically. For example, an entire screen itself is a feature, composed of subfeatures consisting of the fields and controls on the screen. Format: text or table.
- *Package specification:* What the packages will be (the major ones); and a description of the purpose of each package, which packages are reusable, which packages are independently deployable, and the primary dependencies between the packages. Format: text, Java, and UML package diagrams.
- *External interfaces identification:* Any other schemas or components that may be required to interact with external systems. Format: text, IDL, tables, and diagrams appropriate for the external systems, class diagrams for the interfacing components in this system; collaboration, sequence, activity, or statechart diagrams; UML implementation diagram.
- *Exception specification:* Primary kinds of exceptions, and strategies for generating and handling exceptions. This should be a text document, with class diagrams, which identifies the base Java exception classes (modeled as a "signal" in UML—see below), from which all project exception classes will derive. It also specifies what information will be encoded in exception messages, and criteria for deciding at what levels of code exceptions should be handled, propagated, or converted.
- *Resource specification:* Primary categories of properties, messages, resources, and basic components and strategies for accessing and managing them. This is a textual specification; an exact specification of resource adapter classes, if any, is provided in other applicable sections as for any other system component, and may be referenced.

- *Naming specification:* Naming conventions to be followed for all named elements in the implementation. You can fold this specification into the sections above that apply to each type of named element, keep it separate, or place it in a coding style guide (see below). It is a good idea to follow and extrapolate from the naming conventions in the JavaBeans specification. (See the section "JavaBeans" on page 95, in Chapter 2.)
- *Coding style guide:* Aesthetic and quality guidelines for the implementation code and scripts.
- *Test specification:* A set of tests to be performed and test systems to be constructed. Format: text, or a test-tool-specific format.
- *Deployment specification:* A specification of the tools required, means, and manner in which the system is to be put into initial operation. This is not to be confused with the environment specification, which defines the operational environment; in contrast, this specification defines the system and procedures for installing and bringing the system into operation. Format: text, UML implementation diagram, and other charts and diagrams as appropriate.

A question that arises is, can Java be used as a modeling or domain specification language? And, if so, should analysts learn Java? My own feeling about this is mixed. Java is a low-level language, but it is object-oriented. It is not productive for domain experts to spend time learning how to code Java statements. However, it is useful for analysts on a Java project to understand the specifics of Java's object-oriented features, such as classes and interfaces. Having a concrete understanding of these helps enormously when dealing with UML abstractions. It also facilitates communication between developers and analysts.

### The Object (Class) Model

Java is an object-oriented language. As such, a Java program is itself a precise specification for an object-oriented system, which a Java compiler can translate into an actual system. The primary elements of a Java object model are:

- Packages
- Interfaces
- Classes

**Packages.** A package should serve a well-defined purpose. This purpose should be clearly documented in the package's specification. Unfortunately, Java syntax does not provide a standard way to document packages. However, most design tools provide this. It is good practice to assign a package to a single developer, and not have more than one person modify a package at a time. Subpackages can be created if necessary or convenient, to allow for delegation. Assigning a package to a single developer gives the developer a well-defined mission, as long as the package has a well-defined purpose.

A package also conceptually constitutes a field-replaceable unit, and has a version associated with it for deployment configuration control. (See "Packages Are Field-Replaceable Units" on page 139.) Viewing it this way provides some guidance about deciding how to partition a design into packages. For example, consider Figure 1-2.

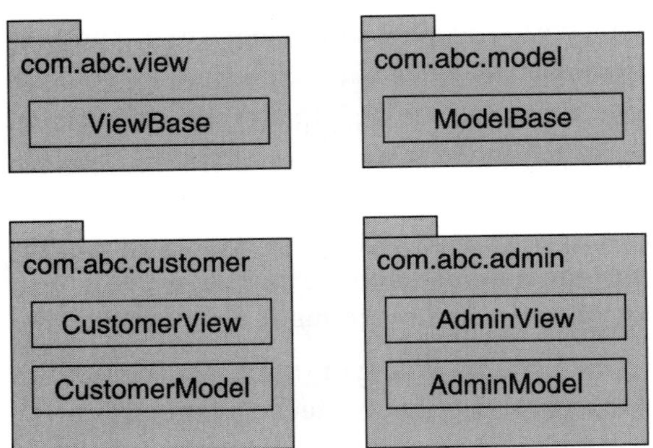


**Figure 1-2** Packages allow a system to be partitioned into generic and application-specific components.

Figure 1-2 shows an example of partitioning a small GUI-based system into packages. Note that UML identifies a package by giving it a little tab (I've bent the standard a little, by using Java syntax for the package names—UML uses "::" instead of "." to separate package name components). This diagram shows four packages: com.abc.view, com.abc.model, com.abc.customer, and com.abc.admin.

In this example, common types and behavior are abstracted out into generic layers for user interface components and data access components, and each of these is put into a separate package. There are also packages for the specific application subsystems to be developed and deployed: a customer application subsystem and an administration subsystem. The customer subsystem has two classes (or interfaces), and the administration subsystem has two classes (or interfaces) as well. The customer subsystem probably uses components from both the view package and the model package; and the administration subsystem is likely to use components from both the view and the model packages.

An alternative arrangement would have been to consolidate all of the "view"-related components into one package: a package containing ViewBase, CustomerView, and AdminView; and likewise consolidate the "model"-related components

into a package that contains ModelBase, CustomerModel, and AdminModel. The problem with doing this is that every time a new kind of subsystem is created, it impacts every package: since a subsystem will likely need both a view and a model, components will have to be added to both the view and model packages, requiring redeployment of every package. Furthermore, the role of the view and model packages is then unclear: they provide services that span the breadth of the entire application. It would be far better to isolate the discrete service components of the application, especially the reusable ones. Packages are the ideal mechanism for this.

In general it is a good idea to use separate packages for reusable components and particular uses of components. For example, if your application defines a mechanism for interfacing to an external service such as a financial trading service or credit card transaction service, this interface is a reusable component. Therefore, you should develop it as an independent package and then separately create a package in which you use the reusable component by defining an implementation of it particular to your application. This might be organized as follows:

package `com.ourcompany.someservice`:

- Interfaces for the service
- Abstract and factory classes for accessing the service
- Helper classes and implementations which can be reused

package `com.ourcompany.ourproduct.someservice`:

- Concrete class or classes which extend, aggregate, or create instances from package `com.abc.someservice`. These import `com.ourcompany.someservice`.

Other projects within your organization which later need to reuse the same services can then define their own use, by creating their own package and importing `com.ourcompany.someservice`.

**Interfaces.** Java interfaces define roles. The roles of the elements of a system are naturally the first things that get defined, because to define an object without defining its role is to create an object which has no known purpose. It makes sense to define the roles of the elements in the system first, and then define classes that can take on those roles.

Using interfaces also helps to decouple the parts of a system. If the system's behavior is defined in terms of interface types instead of concrete types, the system's designer is free to repartition the system into different concrete classes, with minimal impact.

Interfaces serve as the specification that subsystems use to communicate. In Java, a subsystem is manifest by a package. The interfaces, along with the documentation specifying the semantics of their methods, constitute the package's contract with other packages. Since all methods defined in an interface are public, defining behavior in terms of interface types guarantees that members inappropriately declared public within classes will not be accessed by other packages. If the interfaces are well-defined and do not change much during a project, programmers are largely protected from implementation changes.

UML has its own concept of an interface, which is very closely aligned with the Java concept. One difference is that UML interfaces cannot contain attributes—any attributes. Java allows interfaces to contain static final attributes.

**Classes.** Even if you use interface types extensively in your application, packages are still not completely protected from changes to other packages. Interfaces cannot have constructors, so in order to instantiate instances of classes defined elsewhere, you will have to reference at least one concrete or abstract class type.

You can isolate your code from making an explicit reference to a concrete class in another package by identifying the class via a property, and then manufacture an instance of that class by using:

```
String myClassName =
   System.getProperty("com.mycorp.myproj.myproperty");
MyInterfaceType instance =
   (MyInterfaceType)(Class.forName(myClassName).newInstance());
```

or, if the class is a bean:

```
String myBeanClassName =
   System.getProperty("com.mycorp.myproj.myproperty");
MyBeanType bean =
   (MyBeanType)(Beans.instantiate(getClass().getClassLoader(),
      myBeanClassName));
```

For this to work, the class must have a default constructor. Another solution is to use a factory:

```
String myFactoryClassName =
   System.getProperty("com.mycorp.myproj.myfactory");
MyFactoryType factory =
   (MyFactoryType)
   (Class.forName(myFactoryClassName).newInstance());

MyInterfaceType instance = factory.createInstance(...);
```

where MyFactoryType is a class you have defined that has a method createInstance()—or any method—that has the function of creating an instance based on runtime or configuration criteria such as property settings.

Finally, if two classes depend on each other in that they each need to instantiate each other, one of them always gets created first by some other means (perhaps by a main thread), and so the first class can instantiate the second one, and in the process give the second class a factory for creating new instances of the first class. This is a handy and clean way to resolve circular compilation dependencies between concrete classes. For example,

```
public interface AFactory
{
   public A create();
}
public class AImpl implements A
{
   ...
   B b = new BImpl(new AFactoryImpl(...));
   // This is ok, because AImpl knows how
   // to build a factory to create itself - and
   // it is appropriate for AImpl's own
   // factory to call new AImpl().
   ...
}

public class BImpl implements B
{
   public BImpl(AFactory af) { aFActory = af; }
   ...
   a = aFactory.create();
   ...
}
```

The reason I am making a big deal about this is because it is important to isolate packages from each other, and constructors are the leaky faucet in that house. One language I worked with years back solved this problem by requiring all classes to have an interface, and allowing you to defer the selection of an implementation class until link time, or even runtime. This way, alternative implementations could be used (e.g., a test stub package or the actual package) without affecting the code.

Abstract classes do not solve this problem, because abstract classes, while they have constructors, cannot be instantiated. They can have static factory methods, but you will still need a property or some mechanism to identify the concrete class to be instantiated.

**Relationships Between Elements of the Object Model.** The kinds of relationships between packages, classes, and interfaces that may be specified explicitly in a Java object model using Java syntax are:

*Package membership*—The package to which the class or interface belongs. We have already seen an example of how this is represented in UML.

*Implements*—A class can implement zero or more interfaces.

*Extends*—A class can extend the implementation of another class. An interface may also extend zero or more other interfaces.

In addition, for modeling our system, we would like to be able to specify:

*Instance cardinality*—Conveys cardinality semantics between instances of the connected classes or interfaces.

*Instance composition*—An object connection which indicates a "compositional" relationship, such that instances of a class are logically composed of one or more instances of another class or interface, meaning that the class is an owning or controlling class for these subordinate instances.

*Arbitrary constraints and semantics*—Enables annotated relationships, and definition of custom types of relationships.

There are, in fact, symbols in UML class diagrams for all of the above relationships. Let's look at a UML class diagram as an example (Figure 1-3).

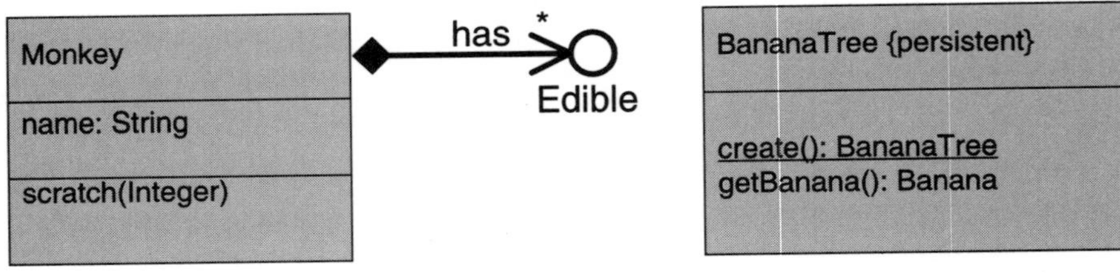


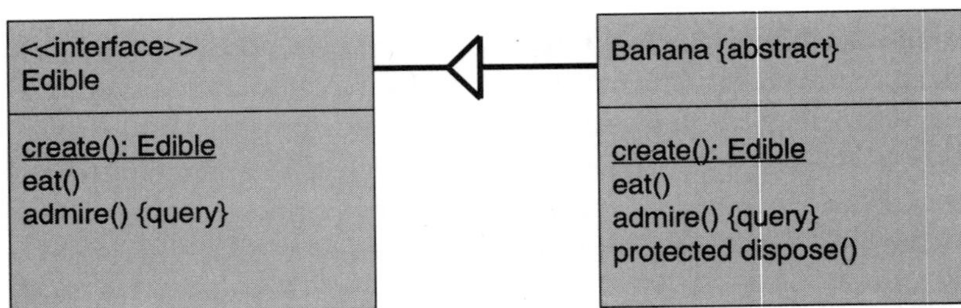


**Figure 1-3** A UML class diagram showing interface, abstract, and persistent types.

This diagram depicts one interface and three classes, one of which is labeled as abstract. Note that the kind of box used for the interface is the same as for a class, except that the interface has a UML "stereotype" symbol that says "interface" in it—a stereotype is a special role modifier that is written inside of double angle brackets (called "guillemets"). The abstract class is labeled as abstract using a different kind of label, a UML "property string." There are predefined stereotypes and property strings in UML, but you can define your own as well, unique for your application. Your design tool may have its own properties and stereotypes defined as well.

In Figure 1-3, the class Banana implements the interface Edible. This is depicted by the large triangle embedded in the line extending from Banana to Edible; the triangle points from the special to the general, or, in Java terms, from the implementor to the implementee. The same symbology is used for inheritance: if one class extends another (or several—multiple inheritance is permitted in UML, but you should avoid it for classes if your application is in Java), the triangle points from the specialized class to the class from which it extends.

Cardinal and role relationships between entities are shown by an association line connecting them, with various symbols attached. In our example, there is an association between Monkey and Edible. Edible has a stand-in, a circle with the label "Edible." This can be used any place the interface Edible is needed, so we don't have to repeat the Edible interface in its entirety on every diagram where a class implements it. The line is labeled "has" to indicate the semantic relationship between the monkey and the edible, and the arrow points in the direction required by that relationship. The "*" is an indication of cardinality between a Monkey and an Edible in this relationship: "*" is shorthand for "0..n." Other possibilities are "1," "1..2," "1..n," and so on.

The diamond on the Monkey side of the association line tells us that this is an aggregation relation: it means that an instance of Monkey has several Edibles. Well, we knew that by the "*" symbol. However, there are two forms of aggregation: simple, and composite. If the diamond is hollow, it represents simple aggregation and is merely stating that a Monkey references multiple Edibles. If the diamond is solid, as in our example, it represents composite aggregation, and means that the Monkey owns the Edibles—they are logically part of the Monkey instance to which they are attached. This is a very important distinction for defining transactions on persistent objects, as will be seen in Chapter 6, "Java Database Connectivity."

The kinds of modifiers defined in Java for classes and interfaces are:

`final`—May not be extended

`abstract`—May not be instantiated without subclassing

*Scope* (`public`, package)—Accessibility

These can be specified simply by labeling the classes or interfaces in the class diagram with UML property annotations. As we have seen, {abstract} is a property that is predefined in UML. You can define your own, however, so if, for example, security considerations mandate that a class be final, you can designate it as such using a {final} property.

It would also be nice if we could specify these characteristics:

*Persistence*—Is the type persistent, via a persistence mechanism? If so, is it indexed?

*Mutability*—Once constructed, can instances of this type be modified? Can members of this object be modified? Can they only be self-modifying, or modifiable by other instances of this type? Note that the object may be a composition of objects that are of third-party types, so we may not have control over which fields or accessors are private, and have to specify mutability policies at a composite level.

There are no built-in modifiers in UML for these characteristics, but again, we can simply label classes as such to identify them as persistent or immutable. In the example, the BananaTree class is labeled with a {persistent} property. The importance of these two characteristics is discussed in Chapter 6, "Java Database Connectivity."

The modifiers that may be specified in Java for methods and fields are:

*Scope* (`public`, `private`, `protected`, package)—Accessibility

`abstract` (methods only)—Not implemented in this class

`static`—Belongs to the class instead of an object instance

`final`—Cannot be overridden (methods) or changed once set (attributes)

`synchronized` (methods only)—Requires an object instance (for non-static methods) lock or class (for static methods) lock for entry

`native` (methods only)—Implemented by non-Java code

Of course, we don't necessarily want to specify implementation attributes in the object model—certainly not in early stages of design. On the other hand, the model should allow us to specify them when they are important for a design. We may also want to annotate the detailed design with these properties as these implementation decisions are made. UML class diagrams support method and attribute scope, using the same keywords as in Java: public, protected, and private. (There is a slight difference in semantics for "protected.") A static method or attribute is underlined in UML. UML does not have a keyword for indicating constants, but defines the {frozen} property for attributes that are unchangeable (i.e., final). Note also the {query} property shown in the example for the admire() method. This means that the method has no side effects; it does not change the state of the instance on which it is called, or of the system.

UML defines the property strings {sequential}, {guarded}, and {concurrent} for specifying the concurrent behavior of methods. {sequential} is the default and indicates an ordinary unprotected method. {guarded} is equivalent to Java's synchronized keyword, and {concurrent} means the method is fully reentrant and does not need to be synchronized.

**Exceptions.** The reliability of the system is greatly affected by the way exceptions are handled, and how consistent the system is in dealing with exceptions. Even though Java cannot (assuming a bug-free VM or JIT, and that all native code is bug-free) cause a protection fault, things can still go wrong, and it is up to the programmer to trap them in an appropriate way, and also to anticipate what kinds of exceptions might occur—especially unchecked exceptions.

Java divides exceptions into three categories (at last, something that there are not "two kinds" of!): runtime exceptions, errors, and application exceptions. Runtime exceptions are those that extend from the base type RuntimeException; these represent programming errors that should never occur in the lifetime of the system. They are the equivalent of the "bomb" symbol that displays on an Apple Macintosh when a severe error occurs, causing a program to terminate. Errors extend from the base type Error, and represent system configuration error conditions. An error does not indicate a bug in the software, but rather that something was not set up right (e.g., perhaps you have the wrong version of something). That is what errors are *supposed* to be for. The last category, application exceptions, are those that extend from Exception but do *not* extend from RuntimeException. Application exceptions are generally for user errors and anything you as the programmer want to define as an exceptional condition that should cause the program to deviate from its normal flow and back out of what it is doing.

Alas, these three categories of exceptions can be separated into two groups: checked and unchecked. Application exceptions need to be declared by your code; it will not compile unless you do. The other kinds, runtime exceptions and errors, are unchecked and do not need to be declared, and so can occur at any point. Just because you don't have to declare it, however, does not mean you do not need to be prepared for it.

In most applications, it is undesirable for the application to crash. The Java equivalent of a program crash is a stack trace, followed by program termination. To prevent this when an unchecked exception occurs you can create an exception "firewall"—an outer level throws clause that catches Throwable—the base type of *all* exception types. (More precisely, I should say it is the base type of all "throwable" types, but let's not get hung up on terminology.) You will need to do this in the outer level routine (main() or run() most likely) of every thread your program creates. It is up to you what to do when an unexpected exception occurs—perhaps you will display a window with a bomb! More likely you will want to give the user some information, such as a message to contact the system administrator. You may even give them an option to commit what they are doing, if you dare. At least they don't have a blank screen, however.

It should be noted that not all error conditions cause exceptions. For example, numeric overflows do not. In that case, you will simply get incorrect results! Thus, you should be extra careful about calculations with large numbers.

There are also some classes of exceptions that get *converted* into other kinds. For example, any exceptions that occur during static initialization of objects get caught by the system and a new ExceptionInInitializerError is thrown. In order to get the original exception which contains valuable stack trace information, you can call the getException() method on this error object. This is a good programming pattern to use for exceptions you create which are created in response to some other exception, such as a runtime exception. To summarize this: when converting an exception, preserve the original one and enclose it in the new exception.

Never consume an exception stack trace. I have seen many products which sometimes produce an error dialog indicating something has gone wrong with no indication of where! Someone needs to know where the problem is occurring if they are to fix it. A stack trace should always be printed to some console or log file, even if you also display a UI-based message.

Java does not have an assert statement, but you can achieve the same effect by creating a method that takes a boolean and, if the value is false, throws a RuntimeException. This will propagate out to your exception firewall, or to the first catch clause that catches the RuntimeException.

If your application component is not a standalone application, but is running inside of a deployment environment of some kind, such as an Enterprise JavaBeans container (see Chapter 8, "Server Frameworks and Architectures") or a servlet-enabled web server, it may be appropriate not to catch most exceptions and allow them to propagate to the containing environment. Since the containing environment probably has policies for dealing with exceptions (e.g., to unload the servlet), you should allow these policies to be employed instead of short-circuiting them. EJB in fact has very specific rules about what kinds of exceptions should propagate out to the container.

In practice, the majority of exceptions that occur in Java programs which need to be caught are related to distributed component communication failures. Any other kind of exception usually represents a programming error or deployment error and it is legitimate to allow it to propagate out and have the containing environment catch that kind of error, or if there is no containing environment, display as much information as you can and provide a graceful termination.

Exception classes should be given the UML stereotype <<signal>>.

### *Properties and Messages*

You will want to define project-wide standards for defining resources and messages. If your application is ever to be internationalized, you cannot embed text strings in the code. All strings should be defined in resource files or classes. Resources should be associated with the package in which they are used, or in a resources package if general-purpose. See Chapter 2, "Resources, Components, and Packaging," for more details on this.

In addition, all system configuration parameters should be defined as properties. The system design document should maintain a list of these properties. It is a good policy to name properties according to the class or package with which they are logically associated. Thus, for example, if your application's main class is called "com.mycompany.myproject.main.Main," and you need a property to hold the value of the startup directory for the program, you could name the property "com.mycompany.myproject.main.Main.startup," or "com.mycompany.myproject.startup." If you have a utility package, say "com.mycompany.util," and it has a class that needs a property to set a startdate value, you could call that property "com.mycompany.util.startdate." This convention helps to avoid collision of property names.

### *Design Tools*

Object-oriented software design tools allow you to define an object model in a graphical manner, and then automatically generate program code that implements the model. Nowadays, most of these tools support Java code generation; in fact, Java is gaining if not taking the lead over C++.

One such tool is Together Java by Object International (www.oi.com). This is a very elegant tool, developed by Peter Coad's company. When I first saw the Java version demonstrated before it was released, I was truly amazed at how snappy and well engineered the product was. This tool itself is an example of one of the nicer Java products available. You use the tool to construct an object model, and it generates Java code automatically, allowing you to edit method implementations. It will generate an object model even for existing code, from class files. I am told that it took only a few minutes to generate an object model for the entire Java API! It also has the capability to integrate tightly with Borland's JBuilder and Symantec's Visual Cafe.

There is also Rational Rose, from Rational Software (www.rational.com). These folks were instrumental in pushing the development of UML, which is now an OMG standard.

## Coding

The term "coding" sounds so routine and clerical. It is often said that if a detailed design is done properly, coding is merely execution. It is as though once having divided the canvas into tiny spaces and labeled them with colors, Rembrandt declared, "Now it is merely execution."

Coding is actually a highly creative exercise, and creativity, ingenuity, forethought, and experience are all necessary to fill in the gaps and convert even the most detailed design into a well-designed and well-running program. That is why coding is viewed by programmers as the "real work," because they know how critical judgment is during that phase and how much design work actually occurs as part of "coding."

For this reason it is important that the creative aspect not be managed out. Good programmers are not a commodity; in the end, it is the talent of the programmers that makes the critical difference. The experience and talent of the programmers as well as the degree to which they grasp the overall system requirements and goals both have a huge impact on what is produced.

### *Compiling and Development Environments*

Here are some tips for getting the programming effort off to a good start.

- Put someone in charge of setting up the tools and coordinating the creation of project directories, development of build scripts and all the programming infrastructure.
- Make sure everyone uses the same versions of tools, by putting them in a central location and using shared copies. In particular, you don't want people using different versions of packages or different releases of the Java SDK.
- You must decide where to put source and output. In general, keep source and class files in different directory trees, and compile from a third location. If you are using the SDK compiler, use the "-d" option to specify where to place the source. Use the "-Xdepend" option to make sure all your class files are up to date. The javac compiler options are discussed later in this chapter.
- CLASSPATH confusion: *don't set a system classpath, ever,* regardless what version of Java you are using. For development, set your project classpath in your current shell, using a command script, or simply pass it as a parameter to command line tools you run or as a project setting in an interactive tool.

The reason is that if your *system* has a classpath, you cannot reproduce the end user's system environment, which will probably not have a classpath set. If your development tool inappropriately requires a classpath to be set for your system, try invoking the tool from the command line. When you install tools, check if they have set a classpath, and unset it if they have. (Cafe is notorious for doing this—I cannot tell you how many hours I have seen projects lose due to Cafe's classpath setting. Check if it set one, and if it did, unset it. Check in all places: all startup scripts, and both your autoexec.bat file and Environment settings if you are using NT.) If you simply *must* set it automatically, set it in a user-specific script or, on NT, in the user-specific environment settings, and use a different user logon for testing.

- Use makefiles or a build configuration tool; they allow you to "clean" builds, build schemas, persistify classes, and so on, in an automated way. (*Make* and other UNIX tools are available free with optional fee-based support from Cygnus.) Cleaning is important because sometimes class or even package names may change during development, and you need a way to purge things—remember, name resolution is done by the compiler, and so if there is old stuff hanging around in directories that are still accessible, it will be visible.

  One problem you may run into with make is that Java inner classes compile into class files that contain a dollar sign ("$"), and make treats this symbol in a special way. If you refer to a class file explicitly, you can escape this symbol to prevent make from interpreting it. However, if you use wildcards in the makefile, the list of class files is generated by make, and so you cannot escape the "$" symbol. One of my engineers got around this by using an expression to first build a list of class files, and then inserting escape sequences into the list before handing it back to make.

- If using the Java launcher (i.e., "java" or "java.exe") to test your program, run without the JIT. You can do this by specifying -Djava.compiler=NONE on the java command line. The advantage is that you will never get a stack trace that says "compiled code" and is missing line numbers.

- Use a source code control system for everything that is not automatically generated.

- What about debugging? As it turns out, most people who program in Java do not use a debugger. I am included in this category. When I used to develop compilers in C and C++, I spent most of my day hopping between an editor, a shell, and a debugger. Java greatly reduces the need for a debugger, because the VM catches all error conditions. Still, debuggers can be useful, especially with problems that are hard to repeat. Furthermore, many development environments for Java come with a debugger built in. A new and very powerful debugger that deserves attention is the Metamata debugger (http://www.metamata.com).

One of the more powerful development environments is Sniff+, by TakeFive Software (http://www.takefive.com). It has features tailored to large projects, and supports integration with popular configuration control systems, makefiles, and external editors.

### *Optimization*

Do not try to optimize code during first-cut development. The first order of business should be to get the code working and meeting functional specifications. However, while programmers work they notice opportunities to make improvements later. You do not want to lose these thoughts, so encourage programmers to embed comments regarding potential optimizations, and use a project-standard way to mark such comments with searchable keywords, such as "TODO" or "REMIND."

Most of the time, the areas that need optimization can be pinpointed later on with a profiling tool. One such tool for Java applications is JProbe from KLGroup (www.klg.com). Another is OptimizeIt from Intuitive Systems (www.optimizeit.com).

I am often asked if Java's object-oriented nature makes it inefficient. It is well known that there is a performance penalty for many object-oriented features; for example, virtual method calls require runtime table lookups. Also, using object-oriented design techniques, such as accessor methods, results in a penalty: tests I have run show a fourfold time overhead in using accessors over simply referencing a variable, as a result of the VM performing an invokevirtual operation instead of a getfield operation. On the other hand, Java is a highly productive language, and using a profiler and tuning the code can result in very good performance. Well-designed Java applications are indeed very snappy. If a Java application performs poorly, it is probably not designed well. The rammification is that designing a well performing Java application requires more than logical design: it requires careful thought about the performance characteristics of the architecture, and experience with the technology. I have seen Java applications that were so heavy that they were unusable, and I have seen extremely complex and sophisticated Java applications that performed as well as native applications.

### *Developing Coding Standards*

Coding standards are the rules by which programmers on a project must live. Most programmers hate coding standards, because invariably they include rules that go against one's own aesthetic sense. Programmers take a great deal of pride in their work, and want to be able to identify a piece of work as their creation.

For this reason I don't like to go overboard in mandating a specific style. Maintainability is the goal, not uniformity except when it enhances maintainability. Rules should have significant value to be in a guideline. Compact coding standards that address tangible programming issues are interesting, and not only get read, but get discussed over lunch.

You should develop criteria for what to make JavaBeans. Decide how completely you will follow the JavaBeans guidelines, since following them to the letter and in entirety is very burdensome if applied for all work. How "bean-like" you should make something depends on what its role will be in your organization over time. (See Chapter 2, "Resources, Components, and Packaging," for more details on this issue.)

You should develop your own coding standards, but you may use the following list as a guide or starting point.

- Standard headers—Define the standard header for all your project's code. If you have legal rights to protect, state them in the header. The header can also include contact information and change history.
- Package names—Package names should be all lower case, and be prefixed with the Internet domain of your organization, but with the components of the domain name in reverse order. For example, a for-profit organization with a domain "ourcompany.com" should create packages with names like "com.ourcompany.ourproject," "com.ourcompany.anotherproject," and "com.ourcompany.ourproject.packageabc." Do not use capitals for the class A prefix (e.g., COM); this was a bad recommendation in early Java documentation and is being abandoned in favor of all lower case.
- Creating a package description—See the section "Packages Are Field-Replaceable Units" on page 139, in Chapter 2, for a description of manifest package descriptions.
- Using "import" vs. explicit scoping—Be conservative in how many packages you import with a wildcard. In general, import package classes explicitly.
- Use interfaces to shield against change, to allow overlapping of roles, and to allow for alternative implementations.
- If you must extend a class that has an interface, consider doing it like this:

```
interface A {}

class AImpl {}

interface APlus extends A {}

class APlusImpl extends AImpl implements APlus {}
```

or

```
class APlusImpl implements APlus {}
```

This makes it possible to largely hide the existence of the APlusImpl concrete type from the rest of your code. The only dependence might be when a constructor must be invoked.

- Avoid using numeric constants to implement an enumerated type. This is common practice, but is difficult to maintain, and can lead to bugs. The primary problem is that if the type is extended, then constants need to be maintained in two different interfaces or classes, and they might inadvertently be made to overlap. A better approach is to create an enumeration class, such as:

```
public class MyEnumType
{
   protected MyEnumType() {}
   public final static MyEnumType A = new MyEnumType();
   public final static MyEnumType B = new MyEnumType();
   public final static MyEnumType C = new MyEnumType();
}
```

Thus, you can now write expressions such as,

```
if (x == MyEnumType.A) ...
```

and even better, the class is extensible.

- Define all constant values in resource files or classes.
- Define properties for all configurable values, and properties to point to all resources.
- Employ a resource adapter to encapsulate accesses to resources. See the section "Encapsulating Resource Access" in Chapter 2, "Resources, Components, and Packaging."
- Avoid using nonfinal static data. Browsers use the same class loader instance for applets that have the same codebase, so one applet can clobber another's static data. (This is also a potential security weakness for signed applets.)
- Do not use public variables unless you need to for some reason, or if they are final. Also, remember that unlike methods, variables are statically bound (i.e., they are not virtual), so there is no advantage to overriding them—so declare them private, not protected.
- Declare methods public or protected. Use no modifier at all if you want other classes within the package to be able to call the method, but not classes outside the package.

- Decide where to put braces and indentation within a block, and be consistent for all kinds of constructs.

  This is by far the most "personal" issue for programmers. The location of braces affects the appearance and to some extent the organization of a program. The two most popular alternatives are:

  1. *Keep matching braces in the same column.*

     ```
     void m()
     {
     }

     class C
     {
     }

     try
     {
     }
     catch (Exception e)
     {
     }
     ```

     . . . and so on . . .

  2. *Start the first brace on the same line as any leading construct or token, and line up the ending brace with the start of that construct or token.*

     ```
     void m() {
     }

     class C {
     }

     try {
     }
     catch (Exception e) {
     }
     ```

  Most programmers indent one tab for constructs appearing inside braces. It is important also to consistently indent using either tabs or spaces, but not both. Otherwise the code may appear jumbled when viewed in an editor with different tab settings.

I will not go into all the possible nuances, variations, and minor issues related to indentation and code aesthetics, because they *are* minor and I suggest your guidelines not go into purely style details either, such as whether the "catch" token should be on the same line as the preceding brace. These kinds of rules frustrate programmers primarily because they impose restrictions with no real gain, and often the right choice depends on the complexity of the code in which a construct is used.

However, sometimes indentation is important, especially if there are many nested constructs. Consider the case of an expression that creates a new instance of an anonymous class, whose constructor takes some kind of adapter class as an argument, which must also be anonymous.

```
MyClass c = new MyClass
(
   new MyAdapter()
   {
      {
         ...initialization code goes here, since an
         anonymous class cannot have a constructor...
      }

      ...methods and variables...
   }
);
```

Using the alternative style discussed above, this would look like:

```
MyClass c = new MyClass(new MyAdapter() {
   {
      ...initialization code goes here, since an
      anonymous class
      cannot have a constructor...
   }

   ...methods and variables...
});
```

While this uses less indentation, less is not always better. It is not clear what the rules should be for a brace following another brace, and parentheses following a brace. Furthermore, with deep nesting, it is hard to match braces up unless there is a clear visual clue, such as requiring that starting and ending constructs of all kinds be placed in the same column, unless they are able to be placed on the same line.

There is also a style that is used frequently, even by Sun programmers, which surprises me greatly. I personally find it so hard to read that whenever I have to read code which uses this style, I first put it into a word processor so that I can highlight sections to remind me where they begin and end. The style uses no indentation for classes or method implementations. For example,

```
public class HardToRead {
/** Hard to read method.
 * We'll try to make this method as hard to find as
 * possible.
 */
public int hardToFindMethod() {
// This is code inside the method.
int x = 0;
if (x == 0) {
   System.out.println("Always true");
} else {
   System.out.println("Never will happen");
}
}
}
```

Without getting into aesthetics at all (I admit that its left-biased asymmetry has a stark beauty), the problem with this style is that it is extremely hard to locate features. For example, finding where a method begins is difficult because method beginnings occur in the same column as variable declarations, so columns cannot be used as a visual cue. The same holds true for braces. This kind of reminds me of Fortran-66, in which every line began in the same column. Needless to say, I do not recommend this style, and I have outlawed it within our company. Remember, just because *you* can read your code does not mean others can.

- Use parentheses in expressions. Do not rely on operator precedence or association rules, primarily because most programmers do not remember all these rules offhand, and it makes reading code difficult.
- Group overridden methods according to the superclass or interface in which they are originally declared.
- Naming: You would be advised to follow the JavaBeans naming conventions (see Chapter 2, "Resources, Components, and Packaging"), regardless of whether a class is intended as a bean or not. There are some naming issues that are not addressed in the beans spec. These include:
  - — Naming of interfaces

- — Naming of implementations
- — Naming of event signaling (generating) methods

However, for implementations there is an RMI convention in which a concrete class that implements an interface is usually named after the interface, with the suffix "Impl." Also, most beans name event signaling methods by prefixing the event name with "fire." Interfaces represent base types, so they should have names that look like types, not specific implementations. I therefore do not prefer using special prefixes or suffixes on interface names. It is also a Java convention that type names begin with a capital letter, and instance variables begin with a small letter, and both use mixed case.

- Don't consume stack traces. A stack trace is valuable information. Do not catch an exception and merely print its message. If the exception is unexpected (i.e., some kind of programming error or deployment error), always generate a stack trace on the console, even if you catch the exception and even if you display a message.
- If you create an exception, throw it from the same line. The reason is that the constructor for Throwable fills in the stack trace information, and if you throw the exception from a different line, this information will not reflect the line from which the exception was thrown.
- Distinguish between these categories of error conditions:
  - — Non-Runtime Exceptions: normal "lifecycle" exceptions that represent user errors and other conditions which can be expected to occur during the lifecycle of the system, and the cause of which can be determined in the program.
  - — RuntimeExceptions: Error conditions that should never occur, and for which the explanation cannot be deduced within the code; for these, throw a RuntimeException. Catch RuntimeExceptions at the outermost level, in a Throwable "firewall"; for RuntimeExceptions, print a stack trace and display a dialog indicating a fatal error and possibly allowing the user to attempt to save data or commit or abort transactions. A method which can throw a RuntimeException does not have to declare that exception in its throws clause.
  - — Errors: Error conditions that represent a misconfiguration of the environment, but do not represent a programming error, and for which there is no recovery. For example, a database manager might throw an error indicating that the schema is out of sync with the application; this may be unrecoverable in most cases, but not if the application is designed

to deal with this by deploying new up-to-date application code. If an application is not prepared to deal with an error, it should perform any cleanup and let the error propagate out to the Throwable firewall. Always print the stack trace of errors. Errors do not have to be declared in the throws clause.

- Inside a `finally` block, catch all possible checked exceptions that might occur within the block, to ensure that appropriate final action is actually taken.
- Never follow an if clause with a try, without braces. This avoids a bug in some versions of Java. For example,

  ```
  if (...) try {} ...
  ```

  generates incorrect code in some recent javac compilers. Instead, use:

  ```
  if (...) { try {} ... }
  ```

- For an interface method, anticipate the most general kind of Exception an implementation might throw. Consider throwing Exception in interface methods that might have unanticipated implementations. Recognize that if your interface methods do not declare a fundamental enough exception type, implementors will not be able to throw exceptions or will have to convert them to the types you have declared.
- Comments

  The most important thing about a comment is that it say more than the obvious. For example, a method called "setX()" should not be documented as "Sets the value of X." It should say what the intended purpose of the method is, for example, if it is merely an accessor or has other side effects; that is, the role the method or construct plays. Do not be overly concerned with grammatical issues. However, programmers should endeavor to *be precise and complete* when writing comments, and grammar can affect this. For example, a comment which says "Updates value of a, including a.p, a.p2, and its parent" may be highly ambiguous simply because the meaning of "its" is not clear if a, a.p, and a.p2 can all have parents.

  Comments on major features like classes and methods should give additional information. The javadoc guidelines serve as a standard for this. This standard has some drawbacks which are described below. Regardless, comment headers should include an overall description of the method, including its purpose and constraints for use, references to related items, and possibly author and version, although the latter should perhaps be used only for the entire file or class during initial development, and used at the method granularity during later maintenance phases. If you are not using javadoc, com-

ments for parameters and exceptions can be placed side by side with the associated items. This can even be done for the return value, if desired, rather than putting it in a header, far removed from the place of definition. For example, consider the following fictitious method definition:

```
/**
 * Perform any spanking that may be warranted. This is a
 * complete operation, which actually invokes the spanking
 * paddle driver to complete the execution of the spanks.
 * Spanking occurs synchronously in the calling thread;
 * i.e., this method blocks until the spanks have been
 * delivered. This method is part of this class's
 * public interface, and is intended to be called by any
 * StaffManager client.
 *
 * See also:
 * computeNumberOfSpanks()
 * SpankDriverFactory.getSpankDriver()
 * SpankDriver.spank()
 * /
public int doSpanking  // returns the number of spanks
            // actually delivered
(
   int hours,  // hours since arrival; must always be positive.
            // The input value is checked, and a
            // BadValueException
            // is thrown if it is not positive.

   boolean spank  // If true, the user should be spanked if
            // they are late logging on; i.e., if hours >
            // StaffManager.GRACE
)
throws
   BadValueException,  // Thrown if hours is not valid
   CannotSpankError  // Thrown if a device driver error
            // - we do not have to declare this, but want to
            // force calling code to handle it.
{
   ...
}
```

This is far better than having to retype (and maintain in sync) all parameters and exceptions redundantly, far from where the parameters and exceptions are declared. A well-designed document generator would easily be able to extract the comments from this method definition and associate them with

the appropriate constructs; it might even be able to generate a list of "see-also" items, based on references in the method body (which could perhaps have special comment tags next to them, directly where used). [Note: I wish someone would write an improved version of javadoc that worked this way.]

Comments should also include what the assumptions of the programmer are, what side effects occur, and the protocol of use for any construct. Can a method be called more than once? Does it rely on anything else occurring first, or is it completely self-contained? Does it modify any of its input parameters? If the return type is an object, is the object freshly constructed, or is it merely a reference to something passed in? Is the effect of the method "deep" (its effect immediately propagates and is complete) or "shallow" (the method is just an accessor, and other methods need to pick up where this one leaves off to complete the operation)? If the method is a constructor (especially a default constructor), under what circumstances can the constructor be used with `new` to create a valid instance?

If a method implements a method specification from an interface, or overrides a method from a superclass, the method's header comment should say so. Even better, you should group methods together according to which superclasses they override or interfaces they implement. For example,

```
interface A
{
   public void a();
}

interface B extends A
{
   public void b();
}

class CB implements B
{
   // From B:

   public void b() {}

   // From A:

   public void a() {}
}
```

- When returning a mutable type, never return something that was passed in unless the usage of the method specifically requires that (i.e., the method's purpose is to transform an argument). Violating this can lead to bugs that are difficult to locate because if code calls a method which returns an object, and the code thinks it is the only holder of that object and it is not, the object might change unpredictably.
- Put code that is enabled or disabled by program configuration switches in separate classes, so they do not need to be loaded if the associated switches are turned off.
- All instantiable reusable classes should override the Object methods equals(), hashcode(), and clone(). A shortcoming of the Java language is that there is no way to specify that an implementation *must always* be overridden in every subclass. Classes that override clone() as a public method should implement the Cloneable interface, and it is recommended that deep copy semantics be used for the clone() implementation.
- Make all reusable classes implement Serializable, unless there is a specific reason not to. (If a base class implements Serializable, however, derived classes retain the implementation.)
- Adhere to JavaBeans, EJB, or other applicable guidelines for what should be transient.
- Only call final methods in a constructor. You may sometimes end up creating an initialization method to initialize an object, and calling it in constructors. If you do this, you will want to make sure that this initialization method is final so that subclasses cannot override it and unwittingly change the way super() behaves.
- Don't rely on finalize().
- Watch for multiple thread access to unsynchronized objects, especially in UI adapter classes; every method that modifies a class variable (as opposed to a method variable) is suspect. Every wait() should have a corresponding notify(), and vice versa, unless proven otherwise. Always obtain object locks in the same sequence when multiple locks are needed. (See Chapter 3, "Threads in Server Applications," for details.)
- Don't kill running threads without forcing them to block in a well-defined state—or at least do so with care. Remember that when you kill a thread, it stops dead in its tracks and releases its locks, even if it was not done updating an object.

- Watch for runaway object creation. Nullify references no longer used. Java programs *can* have memory leaks, if you have lists that grow and never remove members.
- Explicitly close or dispose of resources such as server connections. When using socket connections, close any buffered stream objects, as well as the primitive socket object, since many implementations leave the socket open even after you close the buffered stream object.
- Do not rely on object serialization for long-term storage of important objects, unless you are confident that the classes involved will not change over time, or that changes will be compatible. In general, changes which add attributes and new class types are compatible, and changes which remove attributes and change structure are not.
- Build a "heartbeat" into distributed components. For some systems, it might be desirable to build in an ability to emit an "I'm alive" signal at determinable intervals. That is the only way that an application can reliably be checked to see if it is still operating. The signal should, in general, be generated before entering and at the return from any blocking action (such as file IO) which tends to have an approximate known maximum time to execute. That way, exercising the application should cause the signals to be generated, if it is still working.

## Platform-Independent Building and Deployment

Most projects use a variety of third party tools including development environments, source code control systems, and code generation tools (including EJB compilers). In many cases these tools can be counted on to be available throughout the lifecycle of the system. The productivity advantages of such tools is great, resulting from not only more rapid development but also more rapid testing.

Nevertheless, it is good practice to use a canonical process and openly available tools as a final check and for producing an actual deployable build. Java is a platform-independent language and so it does not make sense to tie its maintenance or deployment to platform-specific tools, or much of the platform independence is lost.

I will now discuss some of the ways that standard tools can be used for development. This is not to discourage the use of integrated tools, but to emphasize that the use of integrated tools does not obviate the need for a platform-independent-script-based build and deployment process using standard tools.

***The SDK Toolkit***

Java 2 Software Development Kit (SDK) is organized somewhat differently from JDK 1.1 (see Figure 1-4). For one thing, the Java Runtime Environment (JRE) is now the runtime used by the SDK when you run the java.exe program, and "java.home" is considered the JRE root directory, "`jre`". The developer tools are in their own directory above the JRE. The `jre` directory contains the `bin` and `lib` directories as in previous releases.The Java runtime classes are still in the `lib` directory, in an archive called `rt.jar`—but now you will never need to specify this, since the runtime and tools find it automatically. (When compiling, you can specify a different runtime for compile-time resolution, if you need to, using a compiler switch. This is discussed below.)

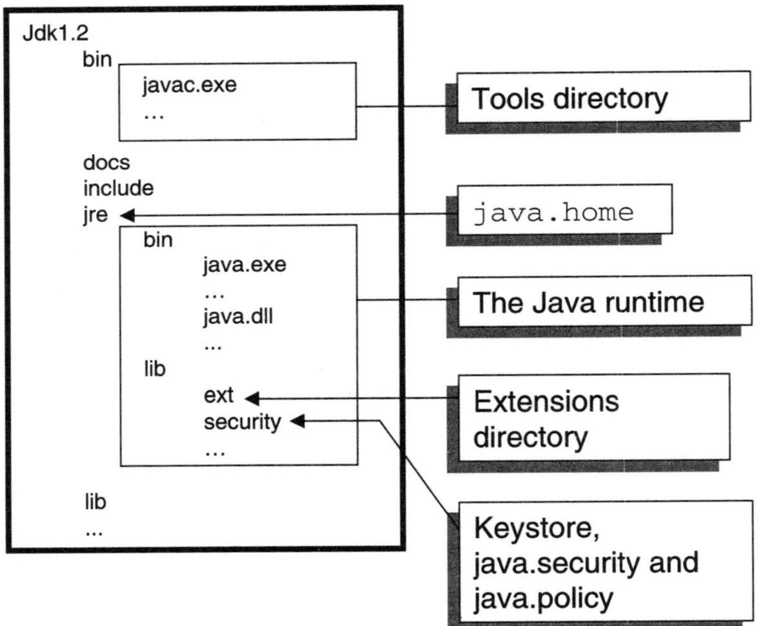


**Figure 1-4** A Java 2 SDK installation.

**What Environment Variables Must Be Set.** None. In particular, you do not—in fact you *should not*—set a classpath for your system (I have always recommended against setting a classpath). The SDK can find its own installed Java classes based on where the java (or javac) executable was run from. (For example, on Windows it looks relative to the path of the java.exe you run, and if it can't find it there, it looks in the registry to see where the JRE is installed.) You can therefore install it

(or just copy it) to a network drive on a server and share it. Simply put the tool bin directory in your path, or explicitly refer to the java or other tool with a full path (or a shell variable).

In the Windows registry, it sets values for these variables:

```
\Software\JavaSoft\Java Runtime Environment\
   CurrentVersion -
   1.2\
      JavaHome - The directory where the JRE is installed; this
         may or may not be the SDK's JRE
      MicroVersion - The portion of the release number to the
         right of the last decimal point.
      RuntimeLib - The path for the Java VM dll
         \Software\JavaSoft\Java Development Kit\
   CurrentVersion -
   1.2\
      JavaHome - The directory where the SDK is installed - not
         the jre directory that it contains.
      MicroVersion - The portion of the release number to the
         right of the last decimal point.
```

In addition to this, the "javaw.exe -jar" command is associated with .jar files for the Open operation, and the Java Plugin also makes some settings of its own.

Note that the registry setting for JavaHome may not agree with the value returned by `java.home` when you run a program, depending on which JRE you execute.

On the Windows platforms, the installation procedure will also place a second copy of java.exe and javaw.exe in your system directory (e.g., \winnt\system32). Therefore, if you need to run earlier versions of the JDK, you will need to change your path, or specify a full path for the java.exe executable. If running earlier versions of the JDK (e.g., 1.1.x), you should remember to include the JDK classes in the -classpath option of any commands you run. It is strongly recommended that you do not set a classpath for your system regardless what version of the JDK or SDK you are using.

**Compiling with the SDK.** The Java 2 SDK compiler represents a great improvement in usability over previous JDK compilers. For example, it now provides the -Xdepend option which correctly and completely handles dependencies between files, even if they are in different packages and directories. This works as long as source code is in a directory structure which matches the package structure it represents. The source code does not need to be in the same directory as the output class files, however.

For example, consider a simple example which has the following directories and files beneath your current directory:

```
.\
        src\
            com\
                ourorg\
                    productx\
                        p\
                            P.java
                            PImpl.java
                        q\
                            Q.java
                            QImpl.java
.\
        lib\
```

The contents and derivational relationships of these files are shown diagrammatically in Figure 1-5.

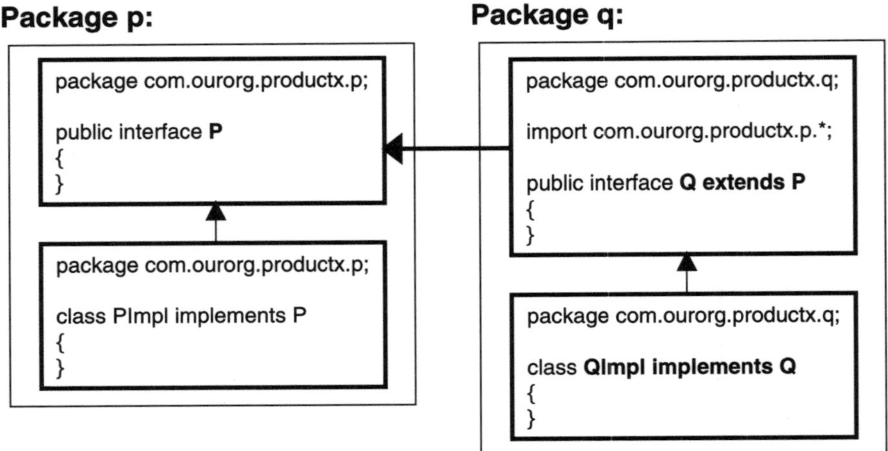


**Figure 1-5** These interdependent packages can be automatically recompiled.

The javac compiler uses the file dates of a source file and its corresponding class file to determine if one is out of date with respect to another. For this reason it is advisable to place every class definition in its own file.

Compiling with the -Xdepend option causes the compiler to check indirect dependencies. Otherwise, it only checks direct dependencies. In Figure 1-5, QImpl depends on Q, which depends on P, so compiling QImpl will cause Q and P to be compiled if they don't exist or if their source files are newer than QImpl. However, P's date will only be checked if Q ends up being recompiled or if the -Xdepend option is used, because QImpl's dependence on P is indirect. PImpl will not be recompiled, because QImpl does not depend on it directly or indirectly.

**A Basic Compile Script.** Here is an NT command script for how one could compile the above packages:

```
set SRC=.\src
set CLASSES=.\lib
set javac_classpath=.;%CLASSES%

REM Compile each package:

javac -d %CLASSES% -classpath %javac_classpath%
      -sourcepath %SRC% %SRC%\com\ourorg\productx\p\*.java

javac -d %CLASSES% -classpath %javac_classpath%
      -sourcepath %SRC% %SRC%\com\ourorg\productx\q\*.java
```

This will compile both packages. In fact, if I were to use the -Xdepend option with the javac command, I could bring both packages up to date with the single statement:

```
javac -Xdepend -d %CLASSES% -classpath %javac_classpath%
      -sourcepath %SRC% %SRC%\com\ourorg\productx\q\QImpl.java
```

If QImpl contains the "main" class, this amounts to compiling the entire system merely by specifying the main class, which directly or indirectly uses everything else at some point (as long as classes are not resolved at runtime by using the Class.forName(String) method or some other technique).

To make the automatic compilation work, I have specified several things for the compiler:

> *source file location:* The `-sourcepath` option specifies a colon-spearated (UNIX) or semicolon-separated (Windows) list of directories to search for Java files. Each directory in the list is assumed to be a root directory, with a package hierarchy under it if the Java files are in packages. Think of it as a classpath, but for Java source files. Co-dependencies across packages *are* handled.

*classpath:* The `-classpath` option specifies the classpath to use for resolution of references in your code. It consists only of your application package directories, .jar or .zip files. Do not include system or extension classes—these will be found automatically by the runtime. (If you want to compile against a different target runtime, this can be done with the `-bootclasspath` and `-extdirs` options.)

*output file location:* The `-d` option specifies the directory to write the compiled *package structure* to. This location is *not* automatically included in the compile-time classpath, so you should include it in the `-classpath` option as well.

It is a good practice to use these options instead of relying on Java files, class files, and archive files being in a particular directory relative to each other. In a large project, code often originates from multiple teams, and the build scripts must be general and flexible, without embedded assumptions about file locations.

The -Xdepend option introduces quite a bit of overhead in a compilation, and so you will probably want to use it only at intervals and definitely when doing a compile check on code that you check in to a repository, or when compiling any component that will be shared or released.

### *The Need for a Platform-Independent Build Process*

Any software product larger than a few files should have a set of automated procedures for compiling it, testing it, preparing it for deployment, and deploying it. Java is a platform-independent language, and so it stands to reason that Java programs will be deployed on multiple platforms. It may even be built on multiple different platforms over its lifecycle. The scripts should therefore be platform-independent as well, so that they do not ultimately and unnecessarily tie an otherwise platform-independent application to the platform it was originally developed on.

To accomplish this you need a command language that is portable. One of the most portable is probably the UNIX Bourne shell, "sh". If you use NT for development and have not used this and other UNIX tools before, you might feel some trepidation about going down that path. These are complex tools, with tremendous power. However, they also tend to be fairly easy to learn and become productive with, and they are easy to get information about. Open source versions are available from the Free Software Foundation (http://www.gnu.org), and these are shipped with most Linux systems. You don't have to use Linux to use them, however. If you develop on NT, go to http://www.cygnus.com and go to their download directory, and download the latest version of CygWin—a complete set of the GNU UNIX-workalike tools compiled for Windows. (Documentation of the tools can be obtained from the GNU site.) Most of the Java product

companies we have worked with use UNIX or UNIX workalike tools, even on NT, because of their power and portability.

**The File Path Syntax Problem.** The main problem you will encounter in writing platform-independent scripts is that the syntax for file paths is different between different systems, most prominently UNIX and NT. For example, a tool such as javac may require a file path as an argument. If your script is running on UNIX, this needs to be a UNIX file path. If it is running on NT, this needs to be an NT file path. If your script is a UNIX shell script running either on UNIX or in an NT port of a UNIX shell, all the paths returned by the UNIX or UNIX workalike tools are going to be UNIX-style paths. In addition, your script will probably perform operations involving concatenating directory names and file separators.

This problem can be solved partially by writing a file path conversion script or program. Unfortunately, arguments to tools can sometimes be more complex than a single file path. Take the classpath argument for example. For NT it requires a series of NT file paths separated by a semicolon. For UNIX it requires a series of UNIX file paths separated by a colon. Therefore, you need a conversion routine which is able to generate a classpath for either system, taking as input a series of file paths.

Once you have solved this problem, you can use your conversion routines to build platform-independent build and deployment scripts.

**Using Make.** In addition to a UNIX command shell, you may want to use the UNIX "make" tool. (The GNU version of make is included in the CygWin package.) The make tool allows you to define dependencies between files, so that you can write build scripts that automatically know what to do—and what not to waste time doing—whenever something in the system is modified. The fact that the javac compiler provides this capability for Java source code does not eliminate the need for this tool. Most complex software systems include non-Java components or other tools that need to be run to build the system. For example, if there is an object database layer, a tool may need to be run to postprocess certain Java class files and regenerate the interface. You don't want to run this every time you change an unrelated file, e.g., a UI file. Therefore, you need a way to specify what this interface layer depends on, so that it is rebuilt only when necessary.

It is a good idea to have a make script for the entire product being constructed as well as for each package. The package scripts should be written by the package developer and be callable from the master makefile. It should incorporate appropriate switches so that it can be conveniently used for compiling quickly versus generating a build and checking all dependencies.

If you have used make before but not used it for a Java project, you will initially assume that the natural depency rule for Java is:

```
%.class : %.java
   javac $<
```

This says that if a file ending in .java is newer than a file of the same base name but ending in .class, then the javac compiler should be called and passed the .java file.

This rule does not work, because Java files can be interdependent and so a compile can fail if a file from another package needs to be recompiled at the same time. Also, the package structure must be taken into account if the files are not all in the same directory.

JDK 1.1 necessitated using complex techniques to generate and maintain make dependencies explicitly, and we have gotten this to work. However, the Java 2 javac compiler solves this. Therefore, you should not use make to express relationships which can be handled by a Java compiler. Use make for those which cannot, including:

- Java dependencies not visible to the compiler, for example if a class is loaded by using Class.forName(classname).
- Dependencies related to generated Java or binary code.
- Dependencies related to generated schema changes.
- Any non-Java dependency which cannot be computed internally by a tool and which can be made up-to-date by running a program from the make script.

## Using a Repository

A source code or document repository is a storage system. A file system is a simple repository. Software development is usually supported by the use of a source code repository which provides the added feature of versioning, so that historical versions or snapshots can be reconstructed in case the current version is found to be flawed and needs to be rolled back to an earlier version, or in case information was deleted and needs to be retrieved.

In the software development domain, source code repositories started as file "archives" which were nothing more than large indexed files containing other files with new files appended at the end. Today there are many different kinds of "source code control" systems which provide archival and versioning as well as many other features including workflow and feature or bug tracking tools.

The UNIX tool SCCS was one of the first widely used source code control repositories. The current popular descendant of SCCS is CVS (see http://www.cyclic.com/). Some modern commercial products today include ClearCase, PVCS, and Visual SourceSafe.

For the purpose of discussion here, a repository:

- Is for storing all manually constructed content.
- Is for storing items whose configuration must be carefully controlled.
- Provides complete change history, and the ability to roll back to any earlier version of a file.

Thus, behind each item stored in the repository, there is (in a logical sense) actually the full set of earlier versions of that item, which have existed throughout its history. Further, these versions are managed hierarchically, so that one can track the history of a group of items (a "project") and roll back and forward the history of all changes that affect the group. If a problem is discovered in a project, it is then possible to roll back to an earlier version of the entire system which was known to work, even without having yet discovered which file is the culprit.

Repositories today work in one of two fundamentally different ways: there are those which operate by intercepting file system operations, and those which require actual file moves during checkin and checkout. The former is more reliable for advanced uses, for example renaming projects and moving things around. Regardless, the issues are the same for us here, and I will not distinguish between these two models.

If you include repository interaction in your build script, it is a good idea to place those operations in a separate script which gets invoked by the build script. That way the main build script is not dependent on the repository. This frees you to use a platform-specific repository while preserving a canonical and platform-independent build process.

### *Only Check In Code that Compiles*

At the beginning of a project the source code files checked into a repository will likely not compile because they are at an early stage of development. At some point an initial compile will be achieved, and after that all checkins should be required to compile. Further, they should be required to compile with a specific build script which is also checked into the repository. This helps ensures that the work of other programmers will not be disrupted by someone checking in inconsistent code.

The build script and all build scripts it references should use "canonical" tools, i.e., open tools which are universally available and which represent standards of behavior, such as the javac compiler. Programmers can still (and should) develop with higher productivity tools, but the standard tools should be used as a compatibility check before code is checked into the repository.

An interesting situation is presented by the IBM Alphaworks Jikes compiler (available from http://alphaworks.ibm.com). Most of our teams use this compiler because it is lightning fast and generates excellent error messages. (On one project it reduced our build times from two hours to 30 seconds!) It has been observed that the Jikes compiler appears to more accurately represent the Java language's subtleties than the SDK's javac compiler. Jikes is available for many platforms and therefore may be a better choice than the javac compiler as a standard tool.

### *Synchronize Before You Check In*

Most source code repositories do not maintain locks of any kind on files which have been retrieved for read-only purposes. The problem is that when one checks out a file and makes changes, those changes are usually compiled against read-only copies of additional files which are also in the repository. These other files are available for checkout by other programmers, with no notification to you.

The process of checking in one or more edited files is therefore analogous to what happens when one updates any database for which read locks have not been maintained. When checking in a file it is therefore necessary to determine in one step if anything you compiled against has changed, and if not, complete the checkin; otherwise, abort.

If your source code repository does not provide the equivalent of read locks on files you access for read-only purposes (and you wouldn't want it to), then you have no way of preventing those files from being checked out for modification. You then need to provide a mechanism for performing a checkin in such a way that it ensures consistency.

Most UI-based source code control tools support the use of command-driven operation, even if the tool is primarily UI-based. You can therefore write a script to implement a checkin process. This process needs to:

1. Briefly lock the repository when you update it, so that *all your version checks and updates occur as a unit, and are serialized with regard to other users*. To implement this, you can use a special lock file, and obtain it by checking it out for modification. All users must agree to use the same lock file.
2. Compare the modification dates of all files you currently have for read-only access, and see if any have changed since you obtained them. You can either compute this list dynamically, or maintain it.

3. If none of the files you have for read-only access have changed, check in all modified files. Otherwise, abort.
4. Release the repository lock (i.e., check the lock file back in).

If the process aborts, you should reobtain those files that have changed and recompile. This will guarantee that what you check in is consistent and will compile when someone else checks it out. This may seem picky, but it is not: inconsistency problems can lead to agonizing hours of tracking down a mysterious and inexplicable problem that is simply the result of having an old version of someone else's file: Before you checked your changes in, you retrieved the latest version of everything you use, compiled successfully, and then performed the checkin. Someone else then retrieved the latest version of everything, and your code doesn't compile! The explanation is that a person in your group checked in a new version of a file in the brief interval between when you retrieved the latest version of the file and when you actually did your checkin. In other words, your checkin operation—which performed an appropriate optimistic locking test by checking if you have the latest of everything—was nevertheless not serialized and atomic.

Some version control tools provide a means to refresh your read-only copies of files in one step. For example, CVS provides the update operation. However, there is no guarantee that someone will not check out and modify one of those files after you do the update but before you complete your checkin.

To prevent this kind of problem, every checkin script should check out a lock file while it performs its test and checkin according to the procedure above. This procedure can be encoded into a checkin script. Using a lock file adds virtually no overhead, since it is only one file, and ensures consistency.

An alternative procedure which is simpler than the one above but still correct is to check out a lock file, fetch fresh copies of all files for which you have read-only access, attempt a compile, check in your modified files if the compile succeeds, and then release the lock file. The disadvantage of this shortcut is that you will have the lock file for a longer period while your compilation is done.

A sample `bash` build script can be found at the book's web site.

## Organizing Source and Build Components

Every project should have a person designated as the process engineer for organizing and setting up the shared systems and directories needed to allow the team to integrate their work. The overall system needs to support both development and configuration management needs, but here I will focus on development and source code control.

Consider a project which is organized as shown in Figure 1-6.

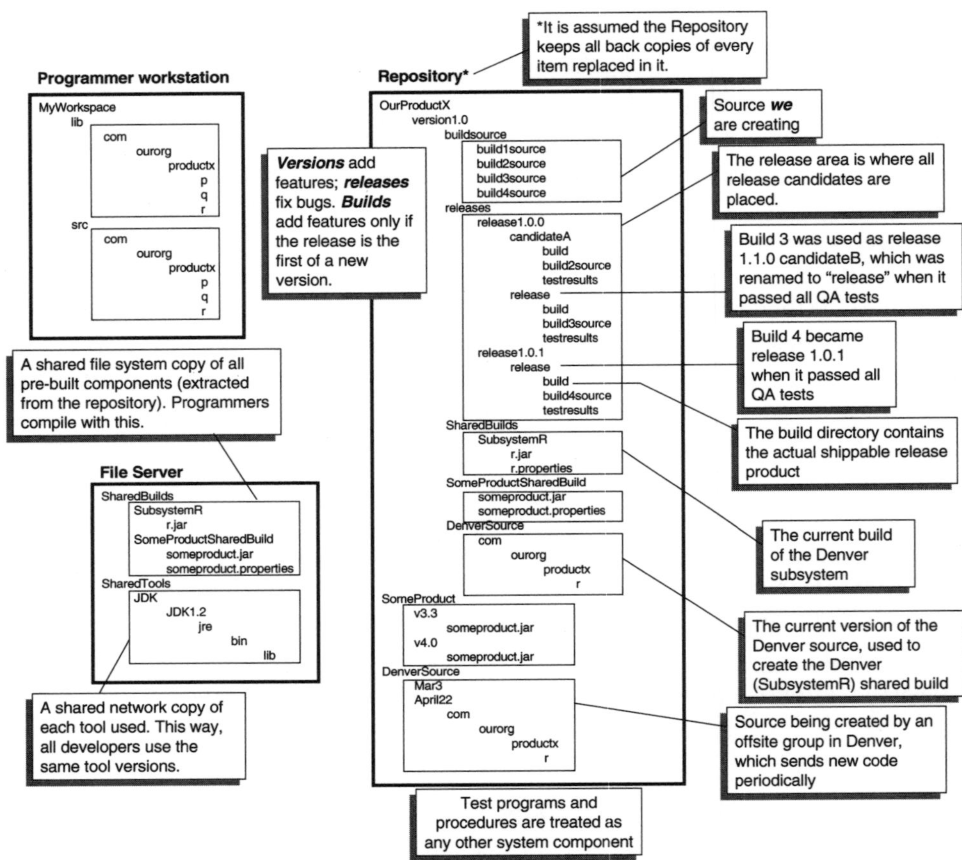


**Figure 1-6** Organizing source and build components to accommodate multiple project teams.

The figure shows three different platforms in use on a particular project: the developer's workstation, a file server, and a repository machine. The repository holds controlled versions of components, and is accessed via a repository interface, which is different from the normal file system interface. For example, it may require special checkin and checkout operations to move content in and out of it. The file server exists to provide a centralized place to post shared content, for the convenience of developers. For example, the most recent version of a configured third party package may be extracted from the repository and placed on the file server, so that it can be referenced directly in build scripts, without having to be

extracted. This would be done for stable components, which are only built at the direction of the project manager at regular and known intervals. Shared software tools can also be placed on the file server, to ensure that all staff use the same version of compilers and other tools.

### *External Teams and Shared Builds*

If an offsite team is developing some of the code on the project and shipping you updates, you need to handle that portion of the code in a special way. Ideally their code is contained in its own set of packages, but this is not necessarily the case. For example, suppose they have defined the package structure, and delegated some classes to your group. You then have a situation in which they will be sending you individual classes that you have to drop in to your development structure. Even if the offsite team's work is confined to its own package, it still needs to be integrated and synchronized with your own builds.

One solution is to tie all teams together directly via a high speed network, and put them on the same source code control system. If this is not possible, then an alternative is to place the offsite team's code in a separate place in your repository. You may even choose to create a build of that code, and place the build in the repository (for configuration control purposes), and place a shared copy on a file server for easy access. In the figure, the SharedBuilds repository archive contains a build of an offsite (Denver) group's code. It was built using whatever configuration information is required to be able to use it here. In the general case, this build will consist of components which are site-independent, and other components (perhaps generated) which are site-specific for one reason or another. The build is also placed on the file server, in a SharedBuilds directory, and this is what the staff compile and test against.

### *Third-Party Products*

A similar situation arises if components are purchased from third party sources. During the course of a project, a new version of a third-party component may be installed. In addition, the component may need site-specific configuration. The component and its configuration can be placed in the repository. If it is a large component such as an application server, the server's configuration files can be placed in the repository instead. Usually configuration files or datasets are accessible. This provides a way to easily retrieve the correct configuration if it gets destroyed somehow, which is important because the correct configuration may sometimes be difficult to determine.

### *Workstations*

A developer can use a tool provided by the repository to check out the latest copy of whatever source is needed, and obtain read-only copies of other source that is referenced. For code being developed at that site, it is best if developers obtain source and not place class files in the repository, because otherwise there is the problem of keeping the source and class files in sync. Since developers routinely inspect source code to see what it does, it is important that what they read has no chance of being out of sync with what they are running with.

It is common for Java developers to mix source code and compiled binary code during development. There is no problem with this, as long as this mixing is not relied on by build scripts. Since these same build scripts may be used to build the system for delivery, these scripts may need to accommodate code from multiple sources, stored in multiple separate directories. During development, a programmer may be using an IDE to compile and test code. When it is time to check changes in, however, the build script should be used to ensure that the code compiles with universal tools and conforms to project standards. The build script may also implement special checkin procedures for locking, as already discussed. The build script may even implement a notification mechanism, to inform other staff when certain files have been modified. All build scripts should be stored in the repository.

### *Creating a Release*

When a build appears to be sufficiently bug-free to be a candidate for becoming a release, the project manager designates it as a release candiate and the build is moved to a special manufacturing area. The manufacturing process is then run to create a shippable build. QA tests are then run. If the candidate passes all the required tests, it is wrapped in a release candidate package and provided to any third parties who need to approve the release. If it passes these final checks, the release candidate is designated as a release.

## Integration Testing and Deployment

In order to test a system which has external interfaces, it is necessary to connect to those systems. However, there are many advantages to creating a simulator of the external systems for use during development. The simulator can be hidden by an interface layer to which either the real system or the simulator can be plugged in without affecting application code.

One advantage of a simulator is that it can be written to be lightweight, non-persistent, and to have no dependencies on anything else. The team's programmers can merely link the simulator with their application code and test without having to be burdened with creating a connection to external systems or be affected by their availability or repeatability.

Another advantage to using a simulator is that the simulator's development can be delegated to someone whose job it is to specialize in and understand the interface to those external systems. By writing a simulator, the details of those external systems must be uncovered. A test suite which tests the simulator can be run against the actual external system and the results compared. The job of writing the simulator can even be delegated to the owners of the external system, since they understand their system's characteristics best. Regardless of who writes the simulator, the project team should devise the interface API at an early phase.

When integration testing is performed, all simulators need to be replaced with actual instances of the external systems they represent. Ideally this is done in a lab setting. In order to avoid affecting ongoing operations, the tests which are run should be invisible to the users of operational systems if possible. For example, if live connections are needed to operational systems such as commerce networks, test accounts should be used. Many commerce servers have a test mode so that gateways to payment systems can be exercised without actually sending a payment transaction. In the end, payment must be turned on to see if an account is properly debited and credited as expected. A test credit card account may be set up and used for this purpose. In general, it is always necessary to establish one or more test accounts with the live external systems.

Having test accounts does not obviate the need for developing a simulator. Developers need a lightweight component they can run which leaves no side effects and is the same every time they use it, without worrying about what other programmers are doing.

When the system has passed all integration tests, it is ready to be deployed in a test mode. This involves moving the system out of the lab and into the environment in which it will run. Real world tests are then run on a limited scale until there is confidence in the new systems.

Deployment is a very risky phase. During this comparatively short period, the entire relationship of trust you have cultivated with the customer over many months is at risk. A tactic which greatly reduces this risk is to deploy the system in a test mode in the real environment ahead of time. This allows you to discover unforeseen problems, and also to create a smooth deployment process.

It is common that since some data sources may preexist and be owned by the end user, an end user database administrator may be assigned to the project to make required changes to accommodate the needs of the new system. This person is usually sincerely helpful, but one has to realize that their job is to fine-tune and secure the database, and therefore they have a tendency to make last minute tweaks when you least expect it—and often do not even remember doing so. It is therefore critical that the completed system is tested with the actual data source

prior to demonstration. A data source which is not under your control is an extreme risk area, because one tiny change can break your application, which will destroy your credibility. It will usually be assumed that the application is at fault if it does not work, and not the database. Again, there is no substitute for deploying ahead of time and having a trial run prior to formal demonstration.

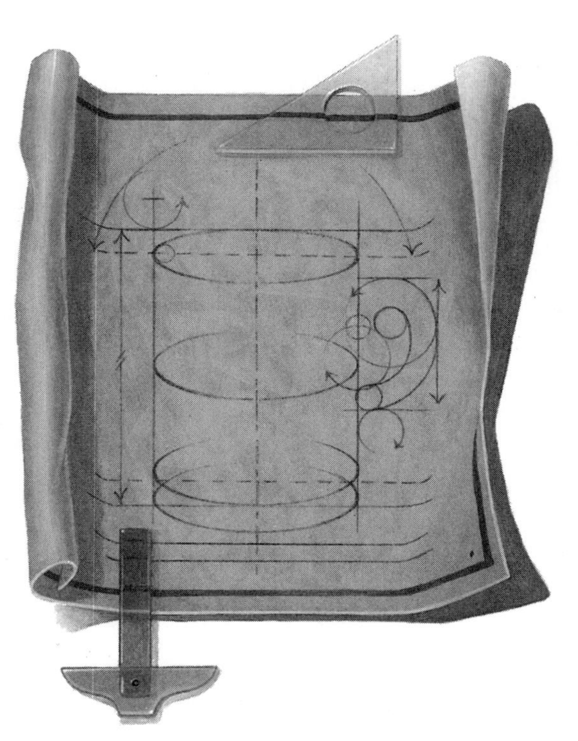

# CHAPTER 2

# Resources, Components, and Packaging

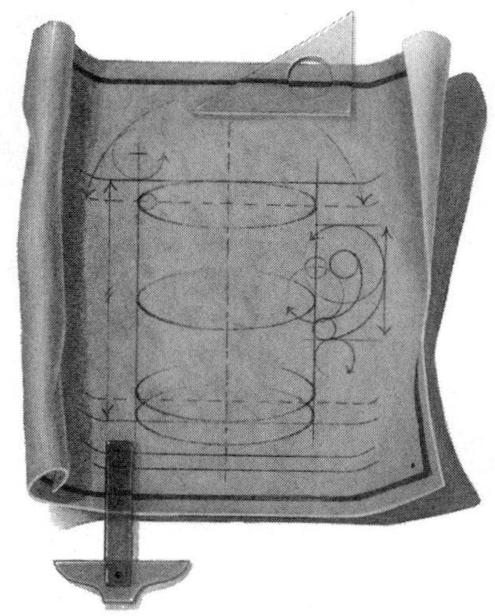

In this chapter I will summarize the important foundational component and resource models of Java. These include the JavaBeans component model, character and file resources, and how these items are packaged in JAR files with program code to produce deployable and reusable application components.

## Resource Files and Internationalization

Applications that are to support many users in a global scenario need to be internationalized to support localized currencies, time and date representations, and number formats. Such applications need to be configurable for a locale by external means without the need to change code and recompile. They also need to be easily deployable, in such a way that moving the application does not break assumptions about the locations of resources needed by the application. These are issues addressed by the Internationalization and Resource APIs.

### *Characters*

In order to understand strings, fonts, and international character sets, you first have to understand characters. A character is represented by a "code point"—a numeric value which uniquely identifies that character. Java uses the Unicode character set for all character representations. This standard defines a Universal Character Set (UCS) consisting of 16-bit characters. It is identical to the ISO 10646 UCS-2 (16-bit) character standard. The ISO standard also defines four-byte characters, UCS-4, but that is not included in Unicode.

A character is visually depicted by a "glyph," a graphic representation. This has nothing to do with Unicode, which does not address glyphs or character fonts. A "font" is a glyph set. It can cover any range of code points chosen by the font's supplier (usually a commercial font vendor). A font is a graphic and stylistic rendering of all the characters within a code point range chosen by the font supplier. A given font may also have variations—called "faces"—to represent bold, italic, and other character styles. When you obtain a font, you are obtaining someone's artistic implementation of a particular code point range.

Java 2 lets you specify fonts by the vendor-supplied font names; or you can specify a "logical" font name. The logical name specifies a generic font that is universal for all Java platforms, and therefore completely portable; each Java installation maps system fonts to these logical names via the font.properties file. You can also specify a vendor-specific font name using the Java 2 GraphicsEnvironment.getFont() method. In either case, a particular vendor font is selected, which maps some code point range to displayable glyphs. This has nothing to do with the language intended for display, except that the selected font may include Unicode ranges which represent the code points used by a particular language.

In the Unicode world, you do not get a font "for a language." The Unicode code point space is not divided by language. While some languages are represented primarily by a certain range, others share ranges. For example, the Latin-1 range, 0-255, is a set of characters shared by most Western languages. A group of related characters is called a "script," and the range of contiguous Unicode values that represent that script is called a "code block."

Unicode allows for more than one representation of certain characters. For example, composite characters such as "ü" and "ll" can be represented either by a single Unicode character or by a pair of characters, consisting of the base character followed by a "nonspacing" character to add the additional feature, such as the umlaut in "ü." Unicode defines a mechanism for transforming composite characters into base and nonspacing character pairs so that the base character can be retrieved if it is needed for operations which treat the base character and composite character the same (e.g., if "u" is to be treated the same as "ü"). Unicode has special control characters for modifying the direction of character presentation, switching from left-to-right to right-to-left midstream.

### *Converting from Other Latin-Character-Mapped Representations*

Characters in Java are represented in Unicode, but most computing platforms do not use Unicode as their normal means of storing character data in files. It is good to use the platform's normal format, because then you can exchange data with other programs more easily.

In order to support the conversion of character data native formats and Unicode, Java provides two kinds of classes:

> `Reader`—transforms an external character source to Java representation (i.e., Unicode).
>
> `Writer`—transforms Java character representation to an external form.

There are concrete implementations of these for different data sources, including FileReader, PrintWriter, and others, as well as generic InputStreamReader and OutputStreamWriter classes.

In many cases, the encoded value of a character is a value that identifies a glyph in the font sets supported by a particular platform. For example, Latin-1 font sets use the Latin-1 encoded values to identify a character within the font set for display. It is important to understand this, that encodings are usually font values, but not always—it depends on the kind of encoding, and if there are font families that support that encoding.

Most 8-bit encodings such as Latin-1 have the disadvantage that characters not representable by the encoding are lost whenever Unicode characters are written in the format. Nevertheless, it is necessary to have encoders for the 8-bit formats supported by the platform, and any platform for which you have to generate output or read input.

An 8-bit encoding that does not have this loss of information deficiency is UCS Transformation Format (UTF)-8. This format is defined in the Unicode standard as a way to represent Unicode data in a manner that is backward compatible with 7-bit ASCII.

UTF-8 represents 7-bit ASCII values (which are also identical to Latin-1 values in the 7-bit range 0–127) in their normal way. However, if the high bit is not zero, the byte is understood to begin a non-ASCII multibyte character: the number of "1" bits that occur before the first "0" bit indicate the number of bytes in the multibyte sequence. Using this scheme, the representation of a stream of ASCII-7 characters is identical to a UTF-8 stream containing the same characters. If a non-ASCII character needs to be represented, the escape sequence just described is used. UTF-8 is described in RFC 2044.

When you construct an InputStreamReader, you can choose between two forms of the constructor:

> `InputStreamReader(InputStream is, String encoding)`—Construct an input stream reader, for the specified stream encoding.
>
> `InputStreamReader(InputStream is)`—Construct an input stream reader, but use the default encoding for the platform.

The second form calls sun.io.ByteToCharConverter.getDefault() to get the platform's default encoding. This is determined by the system property "file.encoding," or the default value of "ISO8859_1" (which is Latin-1) if the property is not set.

In order to actually find the decoder, the constructor then calls

```
sun.io.ByteToCharConverter.getConverter()
```

This method uses the property "file.encoding.pkg" to construct the full package-qualified name of the byte-to-char converter class, using the template

```
<file-encoding-package>.ByteToChar<encoding>
```

For example, the name of the installed UTF-8 encoding is "UTF8," and the default value of the "file.encoding.pkg" location is "sun.io," so the converter is in sun.io.ByteToCharUTF8. Thus, to install your own decoder package, you can set the system property "file.encoding.pkg" and put all your decoder classes in there. Unfortunately, doing so causes you to lose access to the installed decoders.

### *Multinational Font Support*

As explained earlier, in a theoretical sense you do not install a font "for a language." However, in a practical sense you do, because usually a given font will contain glyphs for code point ranges that fall within the range used by a particular language. In fact, the font implementation will likely use a non-Unicode encoding for its code points, and a conversion class (a CharToByteConvertor class) will be needed when displaying the font. The conversion class is specified in the font.properties file. The font.properties file therefore contains primarily two kinds of entries: mappings from the Java "logical" fonts to actual vendor fonts (which may be designed to contain glyphs for certain languages), and the character encoding class to use for each logical font. In addition, the file can contain exclusion ranges which control which physical fonts are used for specified Unicode ranges. This way you can have several physical fonts installed from different sources, to support multiple codepoint ranges (and therefore languages) for the same logical font.

If you use logical font names, Java uses the encoder specified in the font.properties file to convert from Unicode representation to the font code representation. However, if you specify a vendor font explicitly, Java uses native system services to map between Unicode values and vendor font glyphs.

### *Locales*

A "locale" is a combination of language and geographic location. Based on a locale, it is possible to select a set of characters—hopefully contiguous—which can represent all the symbols needed by that locale.

It is up to the application or individual classes to make use of locales. However, the AWT components have a locale attribute, so that they can be localized:

```
Component comp = new Button();
comp.setLocale(java.util.Locale.US);
```

Below we will see how to make use of this.

Specifying a locale does not automatically cause different fonts to be used, and so on. The whole idea of Unicode is that you can display any character. Characters are not language-specific. Unicode defines a uniform character space. It is therefore up to the application to obtain different strings or graphics (i.e., resources) to use, depending on the locale.

There are two versions of the constructor for locale:

```
Locale(String language, String country);
Locale(String language, String country, String variant);
```

The language parameter is a string containing the (lower case) two-letter ISO-639 code for the language. (These codes are listed in Table 2-1.) The country parameter is a string containing the (upper case) two-letter ISO-3166 code for the country. (These code values are listed in Table 2-2.) If country is an empty string, the default country for the language is used. The variant parameter is provided for situations in which there may be language (or currency, etc.) variants within a region. Use Locale.getDefault() to get the system default locale.

### *Formatting and Parsing of Localized Values*

Once you have a locale defined, you can use Java's built-in locale-sensitive number, currency, and date-time formatters, from package java.text.

**Numbers.** A number formatter can be used to parse and display numeric values in different formats in a locale-sensitive manner. Different locales have different ways of representing numbers. For example, while in the United States the number "one-thousand-three-hundred-point-three-zero" would be represented as "1,300.30," in some European countries it would be represented as "1.300,30." Here is an example of getting a locale-specific number formatter, using it to parse a number value from a string, and then formatting the same value for output again:

```
NumberFormat nf = NumberFormat.getInstance(locale);
double d = nf.parse("1.2005e+3").doubleValue(); // parsing input
String s = nf.format(d);                        // formatting for output
```

**Table 2-1** **Language Codes (Languages in bold are directly supported by SDK 1.2; supported country codes are listed in parentheses.)**

| Code | Country | Code | Country |
|---|---|---|---|
| aa | Afar | gd | Scots Gaelic |
| ab | Abkhazian | gl | Galician |
| af | Afrikaans | gn | Guarani |
| am | Amharic | gu | Gujarati |
| ar | Arabic | ha | Hausa |
| as | Assamese | he | Hebrew |
| ay | Aymara | hi | Hindi |
| az | Azerbaijani | hr | Croatian |
| ba | Bashkir | hu | Hungarian |
| be | Byelorussian | hy | Armenian |
| bg | Bulgarian | ia | Interlingua |
| bh | Bihari | id | Indonesian |
| bi | Bislama | ie | Interlingue |
| bn | Bengali; Bangla | ik | Inupiak |
| bo | Tibetan | is | Icelandic |
| br | Breton | **it** | **Italian (CH, IT)** |
| ca | Catalan | iu | Inuktitut |
| co | Corsican | **ja** | **Japanese (JP)** |
| cs | Czech | jw | Javanese |
| cy | Welsh | ka | Georgian |
| **da** | **Danish (DK)** | kk | Kazakh |
| **de** | **German (AT, CH, DE)** | kl | Greenlandic |
| dz | Bhutani | km | Cambodian |
| **el** | **Greek (GR)** | kn | Kannada |
| **en** | **English (CA, GB, IE, US)** | **ko** | **Korean (KR)** |
| eo | Esperanto | ks | Kashmiri |
| **es** | **Spanish (ES)** | ku | Kurdish |
| et | Estonian | ky | Kirghiz |
| eu | Basque | la | Latin |
| fa | Persian | ln | Lingala |
| **fi** | **Finnish (FI)** | lo | Laothian |
| fj | Fiji | lt | Lithuanian |
| fo | Faroese | lv | Latvian, Lettish |
| **fr** | **French (BE, CA, CH, FR)** | mg | Malagasy |
| fy | Frisian | mi | Maori |
| ga | Irish | mk | Macedonian |

*(continued)*

**Table 2-1** Language Codes (Continued)

| Code | Country | Code | Country |
|---|---|---|---|
| ml | Malayalam | sr | Serbian |
| mn | Mongolian | ss | Siswati |
| mo | Moldavian | st | Sesotho |
| mr | Marathi | su | Sundanese |
| ms | Malay | **sv** | **Swedish (SE)** |
| mt | Maltese | sw | Swahili |
| my | Burmese | ta | Tamil |
| na | Nauru | te | Telugu |
| ne | Nepali | tg | Tajik |
| **nl** | **Dutch (BE, NL)** | th | Thai |
| **no** | **Norwegian (NO (Nynorsk), NO_B (Bokmål)** | ti | Tigrinya |
| | | tk | Turkmen |
| oc | Occitan | tl | Tagalog |
| om | (Afan) Oromo | tn | Setswana |
| or | Oriya | to | Tonga |
| pa | Punjabi | **tr** | **Turkish (TR)** |
| pl | Polish | ts | Tsonga |
| ps | Pashto, Pushto | tt | Tatar |
| **pt** | **Portuguese (PT)** | tw | Twi |
| qu | Quechua | ug | Uighur |
| rm | Rhaeto-Romance | uk | Ukrainian |
| rn | Kirundi | ur | Urdu |
| ro | Romanian | uz | Uzbek |
| ru | Russian | vi | Vietnamese |
| rw | Kinyarwanda | vo | Volapuk |
| sa | Sanskrit | wo | Wolof |
| sd | Sindhi | xh | Xhosa |
| sg | Sangho | yi | Yiddish |
| sh | Serbo-Croatian | yo | Yoruba |
| si | Sinhalese | za | Zhuang |
| sk | Slovak | **zh** | **Chinese (CN, TW)** |
| sl | Slovenian | zu | Zulu |
| sm | Samoan | | |
| sn | Shona | | |
| so | Somali | | |
| sq | Albanian | | |

**Table 2-2** **Country Codes (Countries in bold are supported for the supported languages, as listed in the Table 2-1.)**

| Country | Code | Country | Code |
|---|---|---|---|
| AFGHANISTAN | AF | BULGARIA | BG |
| ALBANIA | AL | BURKINA FASO | BF |
| ALGERIA | DZ | BURUNDI | BI |
| AMERICAN SAMOA | AS | CAMBODIA | KH |
| ANDORRA | AD | CAMEROON | CM |
| ANGOLA | AO | **CANADA** | **CA** |
| ANGUILLA | AI | CAPE VERDE | CV |
| ANTARCTICA | AQ | CAYMAN ISLANDS | KY |
| ANTIGUA AND BARBUDA | AG | CENTRAL AFRICAN REPUBLIC | CF |
| ARGENTINA | AR | CHAD | TD |
| ARMENIA | AM | CHILE | CL |
| ARUBA | AW | **CHINA** | **CN** |
| AUSTRALIA | AU | CHRISTMAS ISLAND | CX |
| **AUSTRIA** | **AT** | COCOS (KEELING) ISLANDS | CC |
| AZERBAIJAN | AZ | COLOMBIA | CO |
| BAHAMAS | BS | COMOROS | KM |
| BAHRAIN | BH | CONGO | CG |
| BANGLADESH | BD | COOK ISLANDS | CK |
| BARBADOS | BB | COSTA RICA | CR |
| BELARUS | BY | COTE D'IVOIRE | CI |
| **BELGIUM** | **BE** | CROATIA (HRVATSKA) | HR |
| BELIZE | BZ | CUBA | CU |
| BENIN | BJ | CYPRUS | CY |
| BERMUDA | BM | CZECH REPUBLIC | CZ |
| BHUTAN | BT | **DENMARK** | **DK** |
| BOLIVIA | BO | DJIBOUTI | DJ |
| BOSNIA AND HERZEGOWINA | BA | DOMINICA | DM |
| BOTSWANA | BW | DOMINICAN REPUBLIC | DO |
| BOUVET ISLAND | BV | EAST TIMOR | TP |
| BRAZIL | BR | ECUADOR | EC |
| BRITISH INDIAN OCEAN TERRITORY | IO | EGYPT | EG |
| | | EL SALVADOR | SV |
| BRUNEI DARUSSALAM | BN | EQUATORIAL GUINEA | GQ |

*(continued)*

**Table 2-2** Country Codes (Continued)

| Country | Code | Country | Code |
|---|---|---|---|
| ERITREA | ER | HUNGARY | HU |
| ESTONIA | EE | ICELAND | IS |
| ETHIOPIA | ET | INDIA | IN |
| FALKLAND ISLANDS |  | INDONESIA | ID |
| (MALVINAS) | FK | IRAN (ISLAMIC REPUBLIC OF) | IR |
| FAROE ISLANDS | FO | IRAQ | IQ |
| FIJI | FJ | **IRELAND** | **IE** |
| **FINLAND** | **FI** | ISRAEL | IL |
| FRANCE | FR | **ITALY** | **IT** |
| FRANCE, METROPOLITAN | FX | JAMAICA | JM |
| FRENCH GUIANA | GF | **JAPAN** | **JP** |
| FRENCH POLYNESIA | PF | JORDAN | JO |
| FRENCH SOUTHERN |  | KAZAKHSTAN | KZ |
| TERRITORIES | TF | KENYA | KE |
| GABON | GA | KIRIBATI | KI |
| GAMBIA | GM | KOREA, DEMOCRATIC |  |
| GEORGIA | GE | PEOPLE'S REPUBLIC OF | KP |
| **GERMANY** | **DE** | **KOREA, REPUBLIC OF** | **KR** |
| GHANA | GH | KUWAIT | KW |
| GIBRALTAR | GI | KYRGYZSTAN | KG |
| **GREECE** | **GR** | LAO PEOPLE'S DEMOCRATIC |  |
| GREENLAND | GL | REPUBLIC | LA |
| GRENADA | GD | LATVIA | LV |
| GUADELOUPE | GP | LEBANON | LB |
| GUAM | GU | LESOTHO | LS |
| GUATEMALA | GT | LIBERIA | LR |
| GUINEA | GN | LIBYAN ARAB JAMAHIRIYA | LY |
| GUINEA-BISSAU | GW | LIECHTENSTEIN | LI |
| GUYANA | GY | LITHUANIA | LT |
| HAITI | HT | LUXEMBOURG | LU |
| HEARD AND MC DONALD ISL. | HM | MACAU | MO |
| HONDURAS | HN | MACEDONIA, THE FORMER |  |
| HONG KONG | HK | YUGOSLAV REPUBLIC OF | MK |

*(continued)*

**Table 2-2** Country Codes (Continued)

| Country | Code | Country | Code |
|---|---|---|---|
| MADAGASCAR | MG | NORTHERN MARIANA ISLS. | MP |
| MALAWI | MW | **NORWAY** | **NO** |
| MALAYSIA | MY | OMAN | OM |
| MALDIVES | MV | PAKISTAN | PK |
| MALI | ML | PALAU | PW |
| MALTA | MT | PANAMA | PA |
| MARSHALL ISLANDS | MH | PAPUA NEW GUINEA | PG |
| MARTINIQUE | MQ | PARAGUAY | PY |
| MAURITANIA | MR | PERU | PE |
| MAURITIUS | MU | PHILIPPINES | PH |
| MAYOTTE | YT | PITCAIRN | PN |
| MEXICO | MX | POLAND | PL |
| MICRONESIA, FEDERATED STATES OF | FM | **PORTUGAL** | **PT** |
| MOLDOVA, REPUBLIC OF | MD | PUERTO RICO | PR |
| MONACO | MC | QATAR | QA |
| MONGOLIA | MN | REUNION | RE |
| MONTSERRAT | MS | ROMANIA | RO |
| MOROCCO | MA | RUSSIAN FEDERATION | RU |
| MOZAMBIQUE | MZ | RWANDA | RW |
| MYANMAR | MM | SAINT KITTS AND NEVIS | KN |
| NAMIBIA | NA | SAINT LUCIA | LC |
| NAURU | NR | SAINT VINCENT AND THE GRENADINES | VC |
| NEPAL | NP | SAMOA | WS |
| **NETHERLANDS** | **NL** | SAN MARINO | SM |
| NETHERLANDS ANTILLES | AN | SAO TOME AND PRINCIPE | ST |
| NEW CALEDONIA | NC | SAUDI ARABIA | SA |
| NEW ZEALAND | NZ | SENEGAL | SN |
| NICARAGUA | NI | SEYCHELLES | SC |
| NIGER | NE | SIERRA LEONE | SL |
| NIGERIA | NG | SINGAPORE | SG |
| NIUE | NU | SLOVAKIA (SLOVAK REPUBLIC) | SK |
| NORFOLK ISLAND | NF | SLOVENIA | SI |

*(continued)*

**Table 2-2 Country Codes (Continued)**

| Country | Code | Country | Code |
|---|---|---|---|
| SOLOMON ISLANDS | SB | **TURKEY** | **TR** |
| SOMALIA | SO | TURKMENISTAN | TM |
| SOUTH AFRICA | ZA | TURKS AND CAICOS ISLANDS | TC |
| SOUTH GEORGIA AND THE SOUTH SANDWICH ISLANDS | GS | TUVALU | TV |
| **SPAIN** | **ES** | UGANDA | UG |
| SRI LANKA | LK | UKRAINE | UA |
| ST. HELENA | SH | UNITED ARAB EMIRATES | AE |
| ST. PIERRE AND MIQUELON | PM | **UNITED KINGDOM** | **GB** |
| SUDAN | SD | **UNITED STATES** | **US** |
| SURINAME | SR | UNITED STATES MINOR OUTLYING ISLANDS | UM |
| SVALBARD AND JAN MAYEN ISLANDS | SJ | URUGUAY | UY |
| SWAZILAND | SZ | UZBEKISTAN | UZ |
| **SWEDEN** | **SE** | VANUATU | VU |
| **SWITZERLAND** | **CH** | VATICAN CITY STATE (HOLY SEE) | VA |
| SYRIAN ARAB REPUBLIC | SY | VENEZUELA | VE |
| **TAIWAN, PROVINCE OF CHINA** | **TW** | VIET NAM | VN |
| TAJIKISTAN | TJ | VIRGIN ISLANDS (BRITISH) | VG |
| TANZANIA, UNITED REPUBLIC OF | TZ | VIRGIN ISLANDS (U.S.) | VI |
| THAILAND | TH | WALLIS AND FUTUNA ISLS. | WF |
| TOGO | TG | WESTERN SAHARA | EH |
| TOKELAU | TK | YEMEN | YE |
| TONGA | TO | YUGOSLAVIA | YU |
| TRINIDAD AND TOBAGO | TT | ZAIRE | ZR |
| TUNISIA | TN | ZAMBIA | ZM |
| | | ZIMBABWE | ZW |

**Currencies.** Currency values are represented differently in different locales, including the unit of currency symbol, and the decimal location and style. Here is an example of getting a locale-specific number formatter, and using it to parse a currency value for that locale, and then format the value again for output for the locale:

```
NumberFormat cf = NumberFormat.getCurrencyInstance(locale);
double d = cf.parse("$1,200.50").doubleValue(); // parsing input
String s = cf.format(d);                        // formatting for output
```

**Date and Time Values.** Dates and times are represented differently in different locales. You use the Calendar class to perform most date and time operations. Here we get the current date-time, and then use a Calendar object to get the current hour value:

```
Date d = new Date();
Calendar c = Calendar().getInstance();
int h = c.get(Calendar.HOUR);
```

Use the DateFormat class to parse and format dates:

```
DateFormat df = DateFormat.getDateInstance(locale);
Date d = df.parse("12 Jan 2012");// parsing input
String s = df.format(d);// formatting for output
```

### *Resources*

A "resource" is a collection of information which can be retrieved by name, and which relocates automatically with the program. A resource can therefore be packaged with an application, and there is a well-defined mechanism for retrieving it within the program. Some examples of resources include:

- Image files
- Image icons
- Text
- Fonts (see the Swing font use categories)
- Serialized Java objects
- Audio files

The class loader knows how to find a resource based on a location relative to where it loaded its classes from. For example, the following call to getResource() looks in the class's codebase for the image resource's URL:

```
URL imageUrl = getClass().getResource("IMAGE.GIF");
```

Once you have the URL, you can use the Applet.getImage(URL) method if you are in an applet, or the Toolkit.getImage(URL) method if you are not in an applet. For resources for which a URL is inappropriate, use the getResourceAsStream() method, which returns an input stream.

A resource name is just a string, however. If you name a resource "abc.def," it does *not* interpret the "abc." as meaning package abc.

There are also other resource-retrieval mechanisms, as discussed in the section "Frameworks for JavaBeans" on page 125.

**Resources in Subdirectories.** Resources obtained via the class loader are located relative to the codebase from which the class was loaded. If the class is in a package, it will look in the subdirectory associated with that package, again relative to the codebase of the class. This is default behavior; class loaders for specific purposes (e.g., Castanet's class loader) are free to override this behavior; the only common aspect is that the application should not need to specify a hard location—it should be relative to the current class. A class loader treats JAR files just like directories, so you should put your resources into the appropriate package subdirectory before creating the JAR file.

You can refer to a resource in another package by giving a fully qualified name, using URL syntax, with a leading "/" indicating the codebase, such as

```
/package1/package2/resources/IMAGE.GIF
```

For example, the following program, which belongs to package "p," accesses an image resource in package "q," which is parallel to p in the package hierarchy:

```
package p;
import java.awt.*;
import java.net.*;
public class C extends Canvas
{
   public static void main(String[] args)
   {
      Frame f = new Frame();
      f.setSize(150, 100);
      f.show();
      Toolkit k = f.getToolkit();
      C c = new C();
      URL url = c.getClass().getResource("/q/image.gif");
      i = k.getImage(url);
      f.add("Center", c);
      f.validate();
      f.repaint();
   }

   public void paint(Graphics g)
   {
      g.drawImage(i, 10, 20, this);
   }

   static Image i;
}
```

If placed in a JAR file, the JAR file structure might be:

```
MANIFEST.MF        META-INF\
C.class            p\
image.gif          q\
```

To run this program from the command line, all you need to do is put the JAR file in your classpath and type "java p.C". The image should display, regardless of which directory you are in when you run the program. Thus, the getResource() method interprets "/q/image.gif" as meaning file resource "image.gif" in subdirectory "q" relative to the codebase of the class that getResource() is called for.

### *Resource Bundles*

A "resource bundle" is a collection of resources or resource names, representing resources associated specifically with a given locale. The class ResourceBundle has a method, getBundle(), used to obtain a resource bundle of a given name for a given locale.

There are two kinds of resource bundle; the getBundle() method looks for one kind, and then, if it does not find it, looks for the other kind. You can therefore implement your resource bundles in either of these two manners. The two kinds are:

- A subclass of ResourceBundle, according to certain naming conventions
- A resource .properties file, according to naming conventions

You can therefore provide a concrete class that has the ResourceBundle methods "hard-wired" for your application; or you can use the resource property file mechanism provided with Java. If you do the former, your bundle class name must follow the convention <bundle-name>_<locale>, where "locale" is the string representation of the locale obtained via toString(). A resource property file must be named in a similar manner, but ending in ".properties."

For example, let's suppose we have a resource properties file that is called "MyResourceNames_en_US.properties." According to the naming convention for property files, this file is for the locale whose string equivalent is "en_US"; that is, the English language as written in the United States. (We could also have used simply "US"—it would have recognized "US" as a country code, and applied the default language for that region.) To obtain the bundle called "MyResourceNames" for the US locale, we could do the following:

```
ResourceBundle bundle =
   ResourceBundle.getBundle("MyResourceNames", locale);
```

The getBundle() method will first look for a property class, named according to the conventions, and if it does not find one, will look for a .property file and use it to construct an instance of PropertyResourceBundle, which is a subclass of ResourceBundle and takes an input stream as input: the .property file. This two-step search allows you to defer the decision of which bundles to implement with ResourceBundle classes, which are potentially more efficient.

Property files contain name-value pairs. Suppose our property file contains:

```
myclass.image.filename=\\images\\MYFILE.GIF
```

This line defines the property "myclass.image.filename" to have the value "\images\MYFILE.GIF." Note that the backslash character is treated as a Java escape character (this is how you can enter Unicode values, if you do not have a Unicode text editor), so we must use two in sequence to represent one literally. (The use of a backslash in a file path looks as if it is file-system dependent, but actually it is not, because if the application is deployed in a JAR file, the JAR API will interpret it as meaning a subdirectory, regardless of what kind of system the program is executing on.)

Once you have a reference to a bundle defined in a property file, you can obtain the value of a name value pair by using the getString() method. For example, here I get the value of the "myclass.image.filename" name-value pair:

```
String imageName = bundle.getString("myclass.image.filename");
// Gets the image file resource name specified in the bundle
      property file
```

We can then get the actual resource, as already demonstrated:

```
URL imageUrl = getClass().getResource(imageName);
```

While the above resource name looks like a property and it is stored in a file that ends with a ".property" suffix, I hesitate to call it a property because we have not created any Java Property objects. This mechanism has nothing to do with Java system properties (obtained via System.getProperty()) or any Java Property object. You are free, however, if it is convenient for you, to create a Property object to contain the values obtained from the bundle, but this is not done automatically. (Note that the values of many Java system properties are defined in special property files. These files generally do not use the PropertyResourceBundle mechanism, and the mechanism for loading them is unique to the class of properties.)

**Creating a Resource Bundle Class.** If you prefer a class implementation over a .property file, you can implement your resource bundle as a class quite easily. You can either extend the ResourceBundle class and implement the handleGetObject() method, or you can extend the ListResourceBundle class, which provides a handleGetObject() method implementation. The following example creates a resource bundle base class, which is used when the specified locale cannot be found, and a German-language version of the class, which extends from it. The private Object array contains the actual resource values that are returned when a resource is asked for by name. Note that one resource is an object of a user-defined type ("StartState"), and the other is a string. In the German case, the string contains a Unicode value—the two-byte hexadecimal value for "ö," which is 0x00f6.

```
public class MyResources extends ListResourceBundle
{
   public Object[][] getContents()
   {
      return contents;
   }
   private static Object[][] contents =
   {
      { "com.ourco.ourproj.startstate", new StartState() },
      { "com.ourco.ourproj.title", "Today is a beautiful day" }
   };
}
public class MyResources_de extends MyResources
{
   public Object[][] getContents()
   {
      return contents;
   }
   private static Object[][] contents=
   {
      { "com.ourco.ourproj.startstate", new GermanStartState() },
      { "com.ourco.ourproj.title",
        "Heute ist ein sh\u00f6nes tag" }
   };
}
```

**Encapsulating Resource Access.** A useful technique for encapsulating access to the correct resources bundle and associated resources is to create a single utility class which accesses the bundle and all resources in a uniform way. Such a class is often referred to as a "resource adapter." This class implements the application's policy for determining which locale is used (e.g., by using the default locale for the platform, or by reading the locale from a property), and provides a convenient

interface for retrieving specific types of resources with specialized methods. For example, a resource adapter might have a getMessageString() method, which retrieves a particular message for the locale, according to the application's message display requirements. Other possible methods might include getImage(), getHelpURL(), and getTooltip(). In each case, the application code does not have to perform the work of determining the locale, getting the resource bundle, and extracting the required resource—this is all done by the resource adapter and its specialized methods.

### *Runtime Configurable Resources*

Resources associated with the codebase are best suited for resources which are permanent and do not need to be changed at the time of deployment. Most deployment environments, such as EJB, servlets, and Castanet, provide a separate API for obtaining deployment properties and resources, in a way convenient for that environment. Such properties are usually configurable by an administrator without programming or having to open JAR files. Usually the administrator-configured runtime settings of these configurable properties are accessible to the application via some form of "context" or "environment" object, which is passed in when a component is activated. To keep the bulk of your code as deployment neutral as possible, it is a good idea to encapsulate all resource access in a resource adapter, regardless of how the configurable resources are obtained.

### *Parameterized Resources*

You can create parameterized resource strings, and then effect parameter replacement with the MessageFormat class. For example, suppose our resource .property file contains:

```
myclass.message=Please select {0} or more recipes from {1}...
```

Once we have the bundle, we can get the resource string using:

```
String message = bundle.getString("myclass.message");
```

This string contains "Please select {0} or more recipes from {1}...". We can perform substitution on this as follows:

```
Object[] a;
String[] s1 = { "3", "the handy book" };
String[] s2 = { "4", "the big book" };
if (hunger.equals("moderate")) a = s1;
else a = s2
String substitutedMessage = MessageFormat.format(message, a);
```

In this example, the String array is used to obtain values to substitute into the message string.

The MessageFormat class has much more power than this, however. You can use it to perform type-specific formatting (e.g., to format date and time values) and to perform conditional formatting. As an illustration, suppose our message string contains:

```
"Please select {0} or more recipes from {0,choice,0#the handy
   book|2#the big book} ...";
```

The syntax "{0,choice,..." indicates the start of a choice expression, sort of like an inline switch statement; the "0#..." provides the expression to use if the {0} parameter value is 0, and the "2#..." following the " | " provides the value to use if {0} evaluates to anything greater than or equal to 2. Thus, the following code will produce "Please select 0 or more recipes from the handy book..." when "hunger" equals "moderate"; it will produce "Please select 1 or more recipes from the handy book..." when "hunger" equals "good," and "Please select 3 or more recipes from the big book..." when "hunger" is anything but "moderate" or "good":

```
Object[] a;
if (hunger.equals("moderate")) a = new Integer[] { new
   Integer(0) };
else if (hunger.equals("good")) a = new Integer[] { new
   Integer(1) };
else a = new Integer[] { new Integer(3) };
String substitutedMessage = MessageFormat.format(message, a);
System.out.println(substitutedMessage);
```

This feature is most often used to implement conditions where a choice needs to be made between using words such as "one," "both," and single versus plural forms.

### *Keyboard Entry*

Operating systems usually come in localized versions, which provide character fonts for the locale and resource files with localized messages. It is up to the application to make use of these, and many native applications come in locale-specific versions. An internationalized Java application will have resource files for the locales in which it is deployed or viewed. If the user wants to enter data, they likely have a keyboard specific to their locale, and their system's keyboard mappings will be set accordingly. As long as the application uses localized resource files using Unicode characters, the user should be able to see locale-specific messages in a font in their language.

This approach works fine for European languages, which have small alphabets. It does not work so well for many Asian languages, which have large sets of symbols. For these languages, it is necessary to provide special functions for choosing from symbol candidate lists. Entering a single symbol may require several steps using a standard keyboard.

A utility for allowing the user to enter and choose symbols in this way is called an "input method editor." Asian language versions of operating systems such as Windows come with input method editors. There are also third-party tools which use the operating system's input method API to implement additional functionality, or perhaps provide a different style of input. A popular one for Chinese is called Chinese Star. It allows the user to enter han-yu-pin-yin Latin-character representations of Chinese symbols, and maps them to the corresponding Chinese symbols. For example, if you have Chinese Star, you can use it to enter Chinese characters into an AWT text field or text area.

An input method editor provides knowledge about the language being entered. For example, it might know that a sequence of keyboard characters should be converted into the equivalent Chinese glyph, and it might even have built-in semantic knowledge about the interrelationships of characters. This knowledge should not have to be embedded in the application.

An input method editor can provide its own window, usually at the bottom of the screen (this is how Chinese Star works), for composing characters, or it can operate directly on the application's UI component, if the component supports the required interface. An input method editor which uses a separate window is called a "root window editor." The disadvantage of a root window editor is that the user has to visually switch context from one window to another when entering text. Ideally the application's UI component would be able to handle the text composition operations. An input method editor which displays input as it is composed directly on the application's UI component is said to support on-the-spot editing. This is a superior kind of UI for the user, but requires a very close coordination between the input method editor and the UI component.

It is not quite so simple, however. Asian languages often require multiple layers of conversion before a final input is arrived at. For example, a sequence of keyboard keys may be translated into an Asian character, but then it might be possible to combine that character with the Asian character preceding it to form a different character. It may or may not be possible for the input method manager to make this decision, and often the user is presented with a list of choices. The list may appear in a little side window, ideally next to the text being composed. The text being composed may also be displayed in another side window, immediately above or below the input cursor in the application's main UI component. The use of a small side composition window (not to be confused with a root window) is called over-the-spot or under-the-spot editing, depending on the location of the composition window. For brevity, I'll refer to all these variations as on-the-spot editing.

The Java Input Method Framework (JIMF) allows an application to provide on-the-spot editing. To accomplish this, it provides two interfaces, both of which must be implemented. One is the InputMethodRequests interface, and the other is the InputMethodListener interface. The InputMethodRequests interface allows the input method editor to ask the UI component for information about surrounding and selected text. It needs to know about surrounding text so it can make decisions based on context—what occurs to the left or right, or above or below, the insert point. It also needs to know where on the UI component it can graphically display small helper windows, and so the InputMethodRequests interface has methods to obtain this information as well.

The input method manager does not wait until text is fully composed to notify the application, however. The input method system works very closely with your UI component, via the two interfaces. All changes in input, whether finalized or not, are sent to the application, via the InputMethodListener interface. This interface has two methods: one for sending changes to the current composition, and the other to signal changes in cursor position in the composition. The application UI component needs this information to keep the display up-to-date, to redisplay the composition, since it is being drawn by the application!

Your application UI component must notify the JIMF what objects you have provided which implement these two interfaces. Since the underlying UI framework—the AWT— is ultimately coordinating the flow of input method messages, you are informing the AWT. To pass your InputMethodRequests implementation to the AWT, your UI component must override the getInputMethodRequests() method and return your InputMethodRequests implementation. To pass your InputMethodListener implementation to the AWT, you must call Component.addInputMethodListener() and specify your InputMethodListener implementation as the argument.

The Input Method Framework API relies on the operating system's input method manager. To use this API you will need to have an operating system version which provides an input method manager, such as an Asian version of Windows. (Windows 2000 will support this in all versions.)

The primary use of these APIs is for building UI components that can handle Asian languages. Most business applications will not use the Input Method Framework. Some advanced applications might, however. For one of our clients we built a fully customized visual business rules editor using Swing. The cus-

tomer was in Singapore, and it is not hard to envision a future version which supports Chinese character input. There are no "canned" components that could do the job, nor are there likely to be.

## JavaBeans

JavaBeans are the baseline component model of all Java application frameworks. They address important issues such as application component packaging and deployment, reuseability, and customization. New additions to the JavaBeans specifications provide frameworks for application development, to enable cross-compatibility of components created by different vendors and adaptability to different deployment environments. All of these aspects are extremely important issues for enterprise applications, which need to have a long lifecycle and be compatible with all the environments and components with which they may be combined over time. They are also important for programmer productivity, and the ability to reuse components across applications.

I will begin with some bean fundamentals, and then discuss issues related to bean event dispatching and bean contexts. I will then explain what JAR files are and how they are constructed. I will not spend much time on bean issues that pertain mainly to end-user interfaces, as is the case in most books on beans. The issues of interest here are packaging, deployment, and reuseability.

## Developing JavaBeans

### *What Are JavaBeans?*

JavaBeans are classes or sets of classes designed as a reuseable component. Components designed as beans can be assembled with minimal programming to create larger systems, typically via a drag-and-drop development tool.

A bean is the software equivalent of an electronic integrated circuit, which has self-contained and well-defined behavior, and adheres to some design framework. Anyone who has worked with electronic ICs knows that such components come in "families" which consist of components designed to work together. Components within a family share a set of protocols for communicating with each other. A protocol between electronic components consists of a set of signals with time-dependent behavior, which carry information. In an analogous fashion, beans communicate via signals in the form of EventObject objects, which may contain information within them.

In the same way that parameterized micro-electronic circuit library components are instantiated and customized for an application within an integrated circuit, beans may be customized with each use, and the customization parameters are referred to as "properties."

### *How JavaBeans Work*

Beans are extendable and customizable components. However, there is no "bean interface" that must be implemented, and no bean "base class" that must be extended. Rather, the way that bean features are identified are through a bean component's adherence to a set of design rules, or "patterns," for defining the "bean-like" features. For example, if a bean has methods of the form getXyz() and setXyz(), these are assumed to be accessors for a property called "Xyz," and that property will be identified within a bean development tool's property sheet.

To identify the properties of a bean, as well as all the other kinds of information needed to instantiate a bean, customize it, and hook it up to other components, a bean development tool uses a special bean API called the introspection API. A bean developer can provide a bean with descriptive information about the bean, in particular detailed textual descriptions of its methods and method parameters, and the introspection API is the API for accessing this information when the bean is later used. If such information has not been provided or is incomplete, the introspection API automatically resorts to a foundational API called the reflection API, which is a set of methods for discovering information about any Java class, including the names of all methods and the types of any method's parameters. Thus, there is always a way to discover at runtime what the method names and signatures are within any class, and therefore there is always a way a bean development tool can find methods that adhere to bean design patterns. It is even possible for a development tool to dynamically invoke any method at runtime—for example, an accessor method—by calling the Method.invoke() method and passing a reference to the target object.

The most important part of designing a bean is choosing the event model that the bean will use. The event model defines the signals that the bean will use to communicate with other components, whether they are beans or not. Normally when a programmer instantiates a bean, the programmer identifies which of the bean's events neighboring components will respond to, and conversely which events from other beans this bean will respond to. A response takes the form of a method invocation.

There is no built-in mechanism for dispatching bean events. That is, there is no central event system that beans must hook into. It is therefore up to the bean's developer how the bean will dispatch events to objects which are interested in those events; that is, the bean itself decides how the response methods of interested components will be invoked. Normally, invocation occurs in the same thread that generates the event: the bean simply calls the response methods of all interested components. However, the bean is free to implement an event dispatching queue. The AWT implements such a queue for dispatching its own events in a separate dispatching thread.

A bean has special packaging requirements. Beans are transported in Java Archive (JAR) files. A JAR file is a PKZIP file, which may optionally have some special files in it for describing its contents. One of these is the manifest file, which is an attributed index of the archive's contents. Any index entry which has the attribute "Java-Bean: True" is understood to be a bean. Once a bean is instantiated into a system, however, it can take any form; beans do not have to retain their identity as beans once they are used, although they may.

### *What You Should Implement*

This all sounds rather complicated, and you are probably wondering if you need to do all this just to create a bean. More fundamentally, you may even be wondering if you are a bean developer or a bean user. The answer, if you ever share your work with other programmers, is probably both: you will probably use beans made by others, and you will probably create beans for others to use.

What should you make a bean? Should all your organization's objects be made into beans? Where do you draw the line? In general, you should consider making a class into a bean if there is a good chance that the class will be reused by others, and, in particular:

- Those which encapsulate a macro service or function
- Utility classes which need customization in order to be used

Once you decide you need to develop a class as a bean, is it necessary to do all the things outlined?

You would probably document software differently if you were creating it for internal use than if you were putting it in a shrink-wrapped package for sale. The same is true for beans. Just because you are developing a bean does not mean you have to add all of the self-documenting and customization features that a bean can have. For an internal-use enterprise bean, you need some level of reuseability, and you need good documentation so that other programmers don't have to call you to ask you how your bean works. Most likely your bean will not need a customizer, or custom property editors, but it may have these if the property data types are programmer-defined (e.g., enumeration literals). If your organization is multinational, the bean may also need to be designed for localization. For a commercial bean, you would include everything already mentioned, and localization is probably more important.

Documentation, localization, and packaging can easily be delegated to a specialist in those areas. A senior designer should choose or design the event space and framework for your beans. Otherwise, you will have a proliferation of partly compatible components.

### *Bean Design*

In all likelihood you will use a tool to help you construct a bean. However, the tool cannot design the bean for you; unless your bean is a trivial UI bean, design is something that you will likely do "off-line." You are ready to sit at the tool only after the design is essentially complete. (Of course, people work differently. Some people get good results by "hacking"—designing by adding a little here and a little there, the way a chef might experiment with a new recipe. It is a very gifted person, however, who can produce good results this way for a complex design.)

**Define the Events.** The first step is to select an event model for the bean. The event model consists of the set of events that the bean will generate and respond to. This can be either an existing event model, such as the AWT component event model, or one of your own design. If your bean will be part of a larger set of reuseable components within your organization, you will want to give careful thought to this model. This step should be done by a senior designer. You are, in effect, defining the "information bus" of your and all interrelated applications and components.

Any events you use or define must extend java.util.EventObject. Event objects carry information about the event. This information is for you to define, and generally constitutes the message passed from the event source to objects that will receive and respond to the event. You should write accessor methods for setting and retrieving this information in the event object, and these methods should follow the get/set design pattern. The event class must have a constructor that takes a single Object parameter (the event source), and it must have a getSource() method—although in practice it will simply inherit the getSource() method from the EventObject class. Here is a whimsical example of an event type that signals an increase in temperature:

```
/**
 * An event for notifying interested parties that the
 * temperature has suddenly jumped!
 */
   public class ItsHotEvent extends java.util.EventObject
   {

   /**
    * The source-argument constructor; all events
    * should have this.
    */
   public ItsHotEvent(Object source) { super(source); }
```

```
    /**
     * An additional constructor for the convenience
     * of event sources.
     */
    public ItsHotEvent(Object source, float t) { this(source);
       temperature = t; }

    /**
     * Setter method; follows the setXyz() design
     * pattern.
     */
    public void setTemperature(float t)
    { temperature = t; }

    /**
     * Getter method. Follows the getXyz() design pattern.
     */
    public float getTemperature()
    { return temperature; }

    /**
     * Private property of this event type.
     */
    private float temperature;
}
```

**Define a Listener Type.** When you define an event type, you should define a type which listens for events of that type. This is an interface, containing event notification methods. The event notification methods are the methods a bean will call when it dispatches events to other components that are interested in those events. An event notification method should take a single argument of your event type, and return void. It may throw checked exceptions: those that extend java.lang.Exception, and don't extend Run-timeException. It should not knowingly throw other kinds of exceptions.

All of your event notification methods for a particular event type should be defined in an event notification interface, called a listener interface, and this interface should extend java.util.EventListener. Here is an example of a listener type for our ItsHotEvent event type:

```
/**
 * Those who are interested in rising temperature
 * should implement this interface, and
 * register themselves with all heat sources.
 */
```

```
public interface ItsHotEventListener extends
   java.util.EventListener
{
   public void temperatureRaised(ItsHotEvent e)
   throws ThermometerBrokenException;
}

/**
 * An exception needed for this bean.
 */
public class ThermometerBrokenException extends Exception {}
```

**Define Your JavaBeans Class.** A bean class should implement java.io.Serializable so that its customized state, as configured in a bean development tool, can be made persistent and packaged into a JAR file. In addition, all bean properties should be based on serializable types (all the built-in Java classes are serializable; when in doubt, see the definition for any class in question). The Serializable interface has no methods, so you don't need to do anything other than simply add the words "implements java.io.Serializable" to your class—it is just a tag, indicating that this class grants the right for others to serialize it. (Any classes it extends from should also be serializable, or their data will not be saved.) Your bean class should also have a zero-argument constructor so that a development tool can dynamically instantiate it without needing to know how to construct it. Your bean may optionally implement the Visibility interface so that environments which use the bean can determine if the bean needs a GUI environment to function, and also tell the bean whether or not it is okay to use a GUI if the bean so desires.

**Write Listener Registration Methods.** Other components that are interested in receiving events from a bean register their interest in a specific event type by calling a registration method of the form add<listener-interface-type>(<listener-interface-type>) on the bean from which it wants to receive events. This method must maintain a list of interested components ("listeners") for the bean, normally as a java.util.Vector object. The listener list should be labeled with the "transient" modifier so that when the bean is packaged into a JAR file, other attached components which are not part of the bean are not inadvertently taken with it. It is the responsibility of the instantiating component to programmatically recreate the listener hookups (by calling the addXyzListener() methods) of any embedded beans on initialization.

**Properties.** Bean properties are the parameterized values that a bean development tool will use to allow a programmer to customize your bean when using it in a project. Normally these are simply class variables, but they need not be. The distinguishing feature of a property is that if it is of an object type, it implements

java.io.Serializable (all built-in types do), and that it has accessor methods of the form getXyz() and setXyz(Xyz's-type). This naming convention is very important because it is used by bean tools to identify property accessor methods.

Note the mixed case capitalization. The actual rules for capitalization are implemented in a method called Introspector.decapitalize() which, when in doubt, you can call to obtain the "correct" capitalization for any method. Using the correct capitalization is important, because the bean introspection methods will search for features in your bean based on naming patterns. (A sequence of capitals, such as "ABC," does not become "Abc," but rather remains "ABC.")

For array properties, define methods of the form:

```
void setter(int, xxx[]) throws ArrayIndexOutOfBoundsException
XyzType getter(int) throws ArrayIndexOutOfBoundsException
void setter(XyzType[])
XyzType[] getter()
```

Property accessor methods may also throw other checked exceptions.

Here is an example of a bean class that has "temperature" and "period" (between events) properties, and which allows ItsHotEvent listeners to register for notification:

```
/**
 * A bean which generates heat, and notifies
 * interested parties when the temperature rises.
 * This is an invisible bean - it has no visual
 * appearance to the end user.
 */
public class MyHeatGeneratorBeanClass
{
/**
 * A bean should have a zero-argument constructor.
 */
public MyHeatGeneratorBeanClass()
{
   ...here you may initiate autonomous behavior for this bean
}

/**
 * Getter method for the temperature property.
 */
public synchronized float getTemperature()
{ return temperature; }
```

```
/**
 * Setter method for the event period property.
 */
public synchronized void setPeriod(long p)
{ period = p; }

/**
 * Getter method for the event period property.
 */
public synchronized long getPeriod()
{ return period; }

/**
 * Method that interested parties (listeners) call
 * to register interest in itsHot events.
 */
public void addItsHotEventListener(ItsHotEventListener listener)
{
   itsHotListeners.addElement(listener); // this is sync'd,
                                         // because Vector is
}

/**
 * Method for unregistering interest in ItsHot events.
 */
public void removeItsHotEventListener(
   ItsHotEventListener listener)
{
   itsHotListeners.removeElement(listener);
                                    // sync'd by the Vector class
}

/**
 * The ItsHot event listener list. These are the parties
 * to call back when there are "ItsHot" events. This
 * list, like all listener lists, should be transient,
 * because it is the responsibility of the listening
 * components to create event hookups on initialization -
 * hookups (i.e., listeners) should not be automatically
 * carried with the bean when it is saved.
 */
private transient Vector itsHotListeners = new Vector();

/**
 * The temperature property. Properties must be
 * serializable - this is, because all intrinsic types are.
 */
private float temperature = (float)0.0;
```

```
/**
 * The period property.
 */
private long period = 1000;          // default to once per second
}
```

**Event Generation.** The actual behavior of this bean could be such that the bean reacts to external events, and is itself an event listener; or it could generate its own events spontaneously. Here is an example implementation of the constructor which does the latter, using the "period" property to determine the time interval between events:

```
public MyHeatGeneratorBeanClass()
{
   class R implements Runnable
   {
      public void run()
      {
         for (;;)// ever
         {
            try
            {
                  Thread.current.Thread().sleep(period);
            }
            catch (InterruptedException ex) {}

            // Generate a random temperature change
            double d = Math.random();
            float f = (float)d;
            synchronized (this)
                  // temperature is accessible to
                  // other threads
            {
               float prev = temperature;
               temperature = f;
            }
            if (f > prev)
            {
               // Fire an itsHot event to each
               // listener
               Vector v = (Vector)
                  (itsHotListeners.clone());
               for (int i = 0; i < v.size(); i++)
               {
                  // Generate an itsHot event
                  ItsHotEvent e = new ItsHotEvent(
                  MyHeatGeneratorBeanClass.this, f);
```

```
                        // Note 1: We used the outer class as
                        // the event source, since that is the bean.
                        // Note 2: we used "f" instead of
                        // temperature, because f is private to this
                        // thread, and so it need not be
                        // synchronized.

                        // Fire event to listener
                       ItsHotEventListener listener =
                           (ItsHotEventListener)
                              (v.elementAt(i));
                        listener.temperatureRaised(e);
                     }
                  }
               }
            }
         }

         Runnable r = new R();
         Thread thread = new Thread(r);
         thread.start();
      }
```

In the above implementation, I defined a local class and made the local class runnable. The asynchronous behavior of the bean is encapsulated in the member class. An alternative would have been to make the bean class itself runnable. In the above implementation, however, there is the possibility of constructing the bean behavior by composition such that a runnable class is passed as a property, thereby defining the behavior at customization time.

**Examine Reentrance for Synchronization Requirements.** It is hard to anticipate how your bean will actually be used by other programmers, so it should be robust enough to handle all situations. One consideration is that the end application might be multithreaded, so there may be multiple concurrent threads running through the bean, causing it to generate events in several threads at the same time. The bean therefore needs to be designed to be thread-safe. I have made all of the accessor methods synchronized, since these methods access and modify the object's state.

One area which requires special consideration is the bean's event dispatching mechanism, which maintains a listener list and needs to access that list in a synchronized fashion. It is possible that the end application might call the addXyzListener() or removeXyzListener() methods as part of its response to event notification. You don't need to synchronize the add...() and remove...() methods, because the above implementation uses single-line addElement() and removeElement() operations on a Vector, and Vector operations are synchronized. The other section of code in this bean that accesses this list is the section that performs the event dispatching, where the event is actually generated and the list of listeners is traversed. What if someone removes a listener when we are in the midst of traversing this list?

An obvious solution is to synchronize the section of code that performs the dispatching. The difficulty is that *we don't know ahead of time what the code we are dispatching to will do.* The application code that is dispatched to may involve extended processing or may even block for a period. We don't want to hold a lock on the listener list throughout.

A solution to this potential problem is to clone the list immediately prior to delivering events, and not synchronize the event delivery mechanism. Instead, deliver events based on the cloned list, which will be under no contention since the only operation that needs to be synchronized is the brief cloning operation, which occurs prior to event delivery. This solves potential deadlock problems, but you should be aware that listeners should expect that they may sometimes be invoked even if they have just been removed from the source's list of listeners, since the cloned list might be a little bit out of date.

---

**Note**

The example presented here defines an event type that is not an AWT event. AWT events extend from java.awt.AWTEvent. (I am not talking about Java 1.0 events—I am trying to forget about those!) If your event type extends from AWTEvent, you can use a utility class in package java.awt, AWTEventMulticaster, which performs the listener list management and event dispatching functions for you, so you don't have to worry about these considerations. This is pure UI-related stuff, so I won't go into it, because this book is not about UI development; if you are interested, see the example in the AWTEventMulticaster class javadoc documentation.

---

**JavaBeans Visibility.** If your bean may be run in a variety of environments (e.g., in a servlet or an applet), you will want to implement the java.beans.Visibility interface. This allows the application to control whether the bean will attempt to make itself visible. To make your bean sensitive to visibility considerations, implement these methods:

- needsGui()—Returns true if the bean cannot be run without a GUI.
- dontUseGui()—Tells the bean not to use a GUI, assuming it is optional.

- okToUseGui()—Tells the bean it can use its GUI, if it has one.
- avoidingGui()—Returns true if the bean is not using its GUI.

### *JavaBeans Metainformation—"BeanInfo"*

All Java classes expose metainformation about their methods and variables with the reflection API, available through methods in the Class class. However, this information is incomplete, because it lacks certain details such as parameter names, and more important, it lacks descriptive information that only the programmer can provide. A developer who wishes to use a bean needs to have metainformation available about the beans methods, parameters, properties, and for what they are intended to be used. The beans "introspection" API is designed to provide this information.

Table 2-3 summarizes the introspection methods that a bean can use to publish information about itself, and conversely the methods that a bean development tool can use to obtain information about the bean. When you create a bean, you may define these classes to make this information available to users of the bean.

To get a bean's BeanInfo object, you call the static method Introspector.getBeanInfo(Class), and you pass it a Class object that describes the bean's class. (You can obtain a Class object for any object instance by calling the Object.getClass() method; or, if you don't have an instance yet, Class.forName, "<class-name>", will return a Class object.) The getBeanInfo() method returns a BeanInfo object, which completely describes the bean. The information used by getBeanInfo() to construct the returned BeanInfo object is obtained by a combination of looking for BeanInfo classes and using the reflection API, with the former taking precedence. A BeanInfo class should be named according to the following convention: "<bean-class-name>BeanInfo", and it should be placed in the same package as the associated bean class. The same rule applies to bean superclasses if the superclasses have BeanInfo objects.

Thus, if you want to provide explicit information about your bean for other developers to access, you need to create a BeanInfo class describing your bean class. To do this, you can create your own BeanInfo from scratch, according to the naming convention described above, and implement all the methods in the BeanInfo interface; or you can take the somewhat easier path of extending the SimpleBeanInfo class, which has an empty default implementation for each of the methods in the BeanInfo interface. In that case, you only need to override the methods you want to provide explicit information for, above and beyond what the Introspector will automatically derive through reflection. Once you create your BeanInfo object, you don't have to hook it to anything: just put it in the same package as your bean. Introspector.getBeanInfo(Class.forName("<bean-class-name>")) will then be able to find the BeanInfo object for your bean.

**Table 2-3** **BeanInfo and FeatureDescriptor Methods**

| **BeanInfo Methods:** |
| --- |
| **BeanDescriptor** getBeanDescriptor()<br>*BeanDescriptor methods:*<br>Class getBeanClass()<br>Class getCustomizerClass()<br><FeatureDescriptor methods - see below> |
| Image getIcon() |
| **MethodDescriptor**[] getMethodDescriptors()<br>*MethodDescriptor methods:*<br>Method getMethod()<br>ParameterDescriptor[] getParameterDescriptors()<br>*ParameterDescriptor methods:*<br><FeatureDescriptor methods - see below><br><FeatureDescriptor methods - see below> |
| **PropertyDescriptor**[] getPropertyDescriptors()<br>*PropertyDescriptor methods:*<br><FeatureDescriptor methods - see below> |
| **EventSetDescriptor**[] getEventSetDescriptors()<br>*EventSetDescriptor methods:*<br>Method getAddListenerMethod()<br>**MethodDescriptor**[] getListenerMethodDescriptors()<br>Method[] getListenerMethods()<br>Class getListenerType()<br>Method getRemoveListenerMethod()<br>boolean isInDefaultEventSet()<br>boolean isUnicast()<br>void setInDefaultEventSet(boolean inDefaultEventSet)<br>void setUnicast(boolean unicast)<br><FeatureDescriptor methods - see below> |
| int getDefaultEventIndex() |
| int getDefaultPropertyIndex() |
| **BeanInfo[]** getAdditionalBeanInfo |
| **FeatureDescriptor Methods:** |
| Enumeration attributeNames() |
| String getDisplayName(), void setDisplayName(String) |
| String getName(), void setName(String) |
| String getShortDescription() |
| void setShortDescription(String) |
| Object getValue(String), void setValue(String, Object) |
| boolean isExpert(), void setExpert(boolean) |
| boolean isHidden(), void setHidden(boolean) |

The BeanInfo.getBeanDescriptor() method returns a BeanDescriptor object, which has a method called getCustomizerClass(), which should return a Class object for the customizer if you have created one. The implementation of this method should perform a Class.forName("<your-customizer-class>"). Other BeanInfo methods include getEventSetDescriptors(), getMethodDescriptors(), getPropertyDescriptors(), getIcon(), and others which can be seen in the table.

Here is an example of a BeanInfo class for the heat generator bean:

```
/**
 * BeanInfo class, for a bean which generates heat and then
 * notifies interested parties when the
 * temperature jumps.
 */
public class MyHeatGeneratorBeanClassBeanInfo extends
   SimpleBeanInfo
{
   public EventSetDescriptor[] getEventSetDescriptors()
   {
      EventSetDescriptor[] descriptors = new
         EventSetDescriptor[1];
      try
      {
         descriptors[0] = new EventSetDescriptor
         (
            Class.forName("ItsHot"),  // source class
            "itsHot",  // eventsetname
            ItsHotEventListener.class  // listenertype
            "temperatureRaised"  // listenername
         );
      }
      catch (Exception ex) { ex.printStackTrace();
      return descriptors;
   }
}
```

**Localization of Descriptive Information.** If the developers who will be using your bean to build applications will be in different locales, you will want to localize the descriptive information that your bean info class provides. In particular, you should localize the setDisplayName() and setShortDescription() in the FeatureDescriptor class, and the getDisplayName() and getShortDescription() methods of the BeanDescriptor class. You will also want to localize the toString() method of your classes.

**Setting the Icons.** To implement the BeanInfo.getIcon(int) method, you can use the SimpleBeanInfo.loadImage() method, which obtains an image from the bean's codebase. Note that you should be prepared to deliver icons with different sizes, appropriate for different purposes and display types. Here is an example:

```
/**
 * BeanInfo class for my bean - "MyBeanClass".
 */
public class MyHeatGeneratorBeanClassBeanInfo extends
   SimpleBeanInfo
{
   ...
   public Image getIcon(int iconKind) // applications call this
                                      // if they want the bean's
                                      // icon
   {
      switch (iconKind)
      {
      case BeanInfo.ICON_COLOR_16x16:
            ResourceBundle bundle = ResourceBundle.getBundle(
               // "MyResourceNames", Locale.getDefault());
               // E.g., I have a file called
               // MyResourceNames_us.properties,
               // and "us" is my default locale.
            String imageName =
               bundle.getString("ICON16x16_IMAGE_FILE");
               // Gets the image file property specified
               // in the bundle property file
         Image image = loadImage(imageName);
               // inherited from SimpleBeanInfo
         if (image == null) throw new Error(
            "Unable to load " + imageName);
            return image;
      case BeanInfo.ICON_COLOR_32x32:
            return null;   // unsupported
      case BeanInfo.ICON_MONO_16x16:
            return null;   // unsupported
      case BeanInfo.ICON_MONO_32x32:
            return null;   // unsupported
      default: throw new RuntimeException(
            "Unrecognized icon kind");
      }
   }
   ...
}
```

### Packaging

A bean is packaged in a JAR file. JAR files are discussed in detail in the section "JAR Files" on page 130. What makes a bean's JAR file implementation unique is that JAR manifest entries which represent bean classes must be identified as such, with a "Java-Bean: True" attribute. For example, here is a manifest file containing two entries: a class file called "DirectoryLister.class," which is a bean, and an HTML file, called "a.html." Note that the bean class has a "Java-Bean" attribute following the name of the entry (actually, it need not immediately follow the Name attribute).

```
Manifest-Version: 1.0

Name: DirectoryLister.class
Java-Bean: True
Digest-Algorithms: SHA MD5
SHA-Digest: cjV76hByRA20074NyfgGdWCwrCY=
MD5-Digest: 0vpuJ65q4Y0c3JmceRp9FQ==

Name: a.html
Digest-Algorithms: SHA MD5
SHA-Digest: Dqx0MKKyU0DPoSM20jt3cJ0ICEk=
MD5-Digest: l3rHu7ylacxe+s+XkCyncA==
```

If there is no manifest file, every class and .ser file in the JAR file is assumed to be a bean. If there is a manifest file, only entries with the property "Java-Bean: True" will be recognized as beans. If the bean is packaged with its serialized state (see the discussion below about applet beans), the serialization file must have a ".ser" suffix. (If there is a .ser file, it will internally contain a reference to the bean's class name.)

The "jar" tool, used to create JAR files, automatically creates a manifest file for you and puts it in the JAR file. At present, this tool does not know how to add a bean attribute (this may change by the time you read this). However, a manifest file is just a text file, so you can edit it with a text editor to add the "Java-Bean: True" attribute. Hopefully you will have a bean development tool so you will not have to do this, but if you have to, all you need to do is extract the manifest, add the "Java-Bean" attribute, and reinsert the manifest. For example, if you used the jar tool to create your JAR file, you can extract its manifest file with a command such as:

```
jar xvf DirectoryLister.jar "META-INF\MANIFEST.MF"
```

You can then edit the manifest, and reinsert it with:

```
jar cvfm x.jar META-INF\MANIFEST.MF <your-files>
```

This will recreate the JAR file, but use the manifest created earlier with your edits included.

Another important attribute is the "Main-Class" attribute, added by Java 2. If this is set to True in the JAR file, the JAR is an "executable" JAR, and it can be executed by the java.util.jar.Exec program or directly by specifying the -jar option to java:

```
java -jar <jar-file-name>
```

This is how you can create an "executable bean." The class identified as the main class must be a valid Java application class, with a public static method called "main" and a string array argument. The Java Runtime Environment (see the section "The SDK Toolkit," on page 58, in Chapter 1) is also able to automatically invoke a main class packaged in a JAR file in this way. This makes it possible to encapsulate an executable program with all its resources. Note, however, that a main program cannot be run in a browser as an applet unless it extends the Applet class.

**HTML 2.0 Documentation in a JAR File.** A bean JAR file may contain HTML 2.0 files for documentation. These files must have names of the form "<locale>/*.html" if they are localized, or simply "*.html" otherwise, and the top-level file must have the name of the bean, for example, "us/mypackage.MyBean.html" or "mypackage.MyBean.html." The top-level HTML file may have relative links to other HTML files within the JAR file, or absolute links, for example, to a web site. Note, however, that most browsers cannot extract HTML content from JAR files, so the documentation feature is currently of most use to developers using beans to create applications (as opposed to applets deployed as JAR files); a bean development tool can extract the HTML documentation and either present it, or simply extract it and copy it to a place where the programmer's browser can access it.

### *Instantiating a Bean*

You should not instantiate a bean by calling the "new" operator. Instead, you should use one of the instantiate() methods in the java.beans.Beans class:

```
static Object instantiate(ClassLoader cl, String beanClassName
   bcn);
static Object instantiate(ClassLoader cl, String beanClassName,
   BeanContext bc);
static Object instantiate(ClassLoader cl, String, BeanContext bc,
   AppletInitializer ai);
```

The last two were introduced with Java 2, and their differences will be explained later when BeanContexts are discussed. For now, let's concentrate on the first one. The main difference between using instantiate() and using "new" is that the instantiate() method allows for the creation of a bean instance from a serialization file. This allows any property values that were set when the bean was saved to be restored to their prior values. If there is a serialized object file (a file ending in ".ser") which matches the name of the bean, it uses that and unserializes it instead of creating a new instance. If the bean name has a package prefix, it looks in that package, just as it would do for a resource name (see the section "Resources" on page 86). To get the class loader, just use the getClass().getClassLoader() sequence to get the class loader which loaded the class that wants to instantiate the bean; this will try to load the bean from the same codebase as that class, presumably a JAR file.

**If Your Bean Is an Applet.** If your bean is an applet, you need to give special consideration to how the applet will be used, and how the bean will be stored for reuse. If the bean is restored from a serialization file, when the applet is used, its init() method will not be called (nor will its constructor). Instead, it will be restored to the way it was when it was serialized, and its start() method will be called. If, on the other hand, no serialization file was stored with the bean, it will be constructed as usual and its init() and start() methods called.

Note that if the bean applet contains other embedded beans, and if a serialization file is included, any listener hookup code placed in the constructor or the init() method will not be invoked. For applets, it is generally preferable to not include a serialization file; or you can deal with the event hookups in the start() method. Note that during unserialization, the class loader will look for classes in the same place from which it got the .ser file.

### *Bound and Constrained Properties*

A bean may generate events which notify all interested parties that a property has changed. Such properties are known as "bound properties." To create a bound property, you need to provide notification of all bound property listeners or provide property-specific notification. To allow for notification of all bound property listeners, provide methods in your bean with these signatures:

```
addPropertyChangeListener(PropertyChangeListener x),
removePropertyChangeListener(PropertyChangeListener x)
```

To provide property-specific notification, provide these methods for the property:

```
addXyzListener(PropertyChangeListener x),
removeXyzListener(PropertyChangeListener x)
```

where "Xyz" denotes the property name. To provide for the property change event dispatching, use the helper class PropertyChangeSupport, as in the following example:

```
...

/**
 * Setter method for the event period property.
 *
 * In this implementation, we use the PropertyChangeSupport
 * helper class, to handle the
 * property change event propagation.
 */
public void setPeriod(long p)
{
   // Change the property value
   synchronized (this)    // needs to be synchronized, because long
   {                      // operations are not atomic
      period = p;
   }

   // Notify all interested parties that the rate has changed
   periodPCS.firePropertyChange("period", new Long(period),
      new Long(p));
}

/**
 * Getter method for the event period property - same as before.
 */
public synchronized long getPeriod() { return period; }

public void addPeriodListener(PropertyChangeListener x)
{
   periodPCS.addPropertyChangeListener(x);
}

public void removePeriodListener(PropertyChangeListener x)
{
   periodPCS.removePropertyChangeListener(x);
}

private PropertyChangeSupport periodPCS = new
   PropertyChangeSupport(this);
   // Note: the constructor parameter is the source object in
   // the events that are generated
   // by the firePropertyChange() method.

...
```

Constrained properties are bound properties that must accept vetoes; that is, a listener can prevent the change from occurring by vetoing it. To implement this, the property set methods must throw the PropertyVetoException. Again, you can notify all change listeners when there is a change:

```
addVetoableChangeListener(VetoableChangeListener x),
removeVetoableChangeListener(VetoableChangeListener x)
```

or notify them on a property-specific basis:

```
addXyzListener(VetoableChangeListener x),
removeXyzListener(VetoableChangeListener x)
```

You must notify listeners of the proposed change prior to actually making the change, and allow them to veto it. If one listener vetos it, you are required to renotify all listeners that the property is being reverted from the new value back to the old.

You can implement the required behavior yourself, or take advantage of the VetoableChangeSupport helper class, which provides this behavior just as for the PropertyChangeSupport class. Here is an example:

```
...
/**
 * Setter method for the event period property.
 *
 * Notifying that the temperature change period is changing,
 * and then, if it succeeds, notifying all interested
 * parties that it has changed: In this implementation, we use
 * the VetoableChangeSupport helper class, to handle the
 * vetoable change event propagation, and implement
 *  the specifics of the vetoable change protocol.
 */
public void setPeriod(long p) throws PropertyVetoException
{
   // Tentatively notify all interested parties that the rate
   // is about to change
   periodVCS.fireVetoableChange("period", new Long(period),
      new Long(p));
   // If any of the listeners generate a PropertyVetoException,
   // the periodVCS object catches it, then renotifies all
   // listeners that the change is being revoked,
   // and then rethrows the exception. In that case, we choose
   // to propagate the exception out of this method.
```

```
    // Change approved; implement it
    synchronized (this)  // needs to be synchronized, because
    {                    // long operations are not atomic
       period = p;
    }

    // Notify all interested parties that the rate has changed
    periodPCS.firePropertyChange("period", new Long(period), new
       Long(p));
}

/**
 * Getter method for the event period property - same as before.
 */
public synchronized long getPeriod() { return period; }

public void addPeriodListener(VetoableChangeListener x)
{
   periodVCS.addVetoableChangeListener(x);
}

public void removePeriodListener(VetoableChangeListener x)
{
   periodVCS.removeVetoableChangeListener(x);
}

public void addPeriodListener(PropertyChangeListener x)
{
   periodPCS.addPropertyChangeListener(x);
}

public void removePeriodListener(PropertyChangeListener x)
{
   periodPCS.removePropertyChangeListener(x);
}

private VetoableChangeSupport periodVCS = new
   VetoableChangeSupport(this);
      // Note: the constructor parameter is the source object in
      // the events that are generated
      // by the fireVetoableChange() method.

private PropertyChangeSupport periodPCS = new
   PropertyChangeSupport(this);
      // Note: the constructor parameter is the source object in
      // the events that are generated
      // by the firePropertyChange() method.

...
```

### *Property Editors*

A property editor is a visual component which allows a user to interactively view and modify the value of a particular bean property. A typical bean development tool will provide a property editor for entering and modifying the values of bean properties. Such a property editor will know how to parse and format values for the standard Java types (e.g., int, String, boolean); however, it would not know how to parse or format a value that was a temperature, such as a centigrade or Fahrenheit value—the property editor would not know that it had to display a ºC or ºF next to the value; or perhaps the user should even be allowed to enter an expression (e.g., 10+273 ºC).

Another consideration is that the property editor is a component that is built into the development environment, and it must accept and modify changes to values within beans the user is working on; however, the bean ought to remain in control of any changes that are made to its properties. Therefore, there is clearly a need to establish a protocol of interaction between the property editor and the bean; and also a means for the bean to take over the input and display of user-defined property data types.

A property editor provides these capabilities. It is a class that the bean developer provides, for use by property sheets. A property sheet in a development environment will find a property's property editor, if it has one, and employ it to accept and display property values. There are essentially three modes that a property editor can choose to work in: text mode; graphics mode; and it may operate as its own AWT component. Which mode is chosen is up to the property sheet, and which modes are supported by the property editor.

To register a property editor for a type, use the static method:

```
PropertyEditorManager.registerEditor(
   Class targetType, Class editorClass)
```

A property editor can be implemented in any or all of three modes: text-based, graphics-based, or component-based. A text-based property editor provides text-based entry and modification of a property value, using a text field provided by the property sheet in which it is embedded. A graphics-based property editor paints the property's value in a rectangular area provided to it by the property sheet. A component-based property editor goes even further—it provides a full-blown AWT component with which the user interacts to view and set the property value.

Here is an example of creating a property editor. It allows the bean user to enter and edit a centigrade or Fahrenheit value. It supports text, graphic, and custom (i.e., component-based) editor modes.

```
import java.awt.*;
import java.beans.*;
import java.awt.event.*;
public class TemperatureEditor
extends PropertyEditorSupport
{
   public TemperatureEditor(Object source) {super(source);}

   // -----You usually don't override these methods,
   // so I'll leave them commented out-----

   // getJavaInitializationString()

   // addPropertyChangeListener(
   //     PropertyChangeListener pcl)

   // removePropertyChangeListener(
   //     PropertyChangeListener pcl)

   // -----You may have occasion to modify these-----

   public void setValue(Object o)
   {
      super.setValue(o);
         // Sets a local copy of the value, and notifies
         // all listeners.
         // Does NOT set the actual property in the
         // bean - it is presumed that the
         // environment will listen for this event, and
         // call the property setter method
         // in the bean.
   }

   public Object getValue()
   {
      return super.getValue();
         // Returns the local copy of the value.
   }

   // -----Usually you customize some or all of this
   // part-------

   public void setAsText(String s)
   throws IllegalArgumentException
   {
      // If this property cannot be represented as
      // text, throw IllegalArgumentException.
```

```
        // Here you may want to provide localized parsing
        // of input text strings.

        // super.setAsText(s);
        // This sets the property value to the String
        // object, with no conversion.

        // I will parse a temperature value - remove
        // the "°C" or "°F" symbol, and make sure
        // that the required conversion gets performed.

        float t = parseTemperature(s);
                    // automatically converts to
                    // Centigrade. As a side effect,
                    // it sets the editor's current
                    // C or F mode.
        Float f = new Float(t);
        setValue(f);
    }

    protected static float parseTemperature(String s) throws
        NumberFormatException
    {
        try
        {
        // Extract the numeric portion
        int endOfNumber = Math.max(
            s.indexOf(' '), s.indexOf('º'));
        String ns = s.substring(0, endOfNumber);
        float t = Float.valueOf(ns).floatValue();

        // Parse the rest - if "ºF", convert to Centigrade
        // other than whitespace, throw exception
        int endOfDegree = s.indexOf('º', endOfNumber-1);
        if (endOfDegree < 0) return t;
                // assume Centigrade
        String m = s.substring(
            endOfDegree+1).trim().toUpperCase();
        if (m.equals("C")) return t;
        else if (m.equals("F"))
            return (float)((t - 32.0) * 1.8);
        else throw new NumberFormatException();
        }
        catch (Exception ex) {
            throw new NumberFormatException(); }
    }
```

```
public String getAsText()
{
    // Return null if the property cannot be converted
    // to a String representation, which can
    // be passed back into setAsText(). You may want
    // to provide localized formatting of text strings
    // for display.

    return super.getAsText();
        // This calls toString() on the property
}

public String[] getTags()
{
    return null; // The property is not an
                 // enumerated value
}

public boolean isPaintable()
{
    return true;// We know how to graphically
        // display our value. If we don't know how
        // to graph the value, return false.
}

public void paintValue(Graphics g, Rectangle r)
{
    // Graph the property value in Graphics
    // context provided,
    // within the bounds of the provided rectangle.
    // If we don't know how to graph the property,
    // simply do nothing.

    g.clipRect(r.x, r.y, r.width, r.height);
    // Draw a red bar on a white background, on a scale
    // from 0 to 120 - beyond that is off the scale.
    float t = ((Float)getValue()).floatValue();
    g.setColor(Color.white);
    g.translate(r.x, r.y);
    g.fillRect(0, 0, r.width, r.height);
    int x = ((int)t * r.width) / 120;
    g.setColor(Color.red);
    g.fillRect(0, 0, x, r.height);
}

public boolean supportsCustomEditor()
{
```

```
        return true;  // We can provide an AWT component
                      // for editing the property.
    }

    public Component getCustomEditor()
    {
        Panel p = new Panel()
        {
            // A component that lets the user select a
            // new temperature graphically.

            // Hook up the panel
            {
                // Add this component as a PropertyChangeListener
                TemperatureEditor.this.addPropertyChangeListener
                (
                    new PropertyChangeListener()
                    {
                        public void propertyChange(
                            PropertyChangeEvent evt)
                        {
                            update(getGraphics()0;
                        }
                    }
                );

                // Handle panel events

                addMouseListener
                (
                    new MouseListener()
                        // a new anonymous adapter class
                    {
                        public void mouseClicked(MouseEvent e)
                        {
                            // Convert the x-position of the click
                            // into a float temperature value
                            int x = e.getX();
                            float t =
                                ((float)x * 120.0)
                                / ((float)getSize().width);

                            // Set the new temperature and notify
                            // listeners
                            setObject(new Float(t));
                        }
                    }
                );
```

```
            . . . other MouseListener methods . . .
        }

        // Render the component
        public void update(Graphics g)
        {
            Rectangle r = new Rectangle(
                0, 0, getSize().width,
                getSize().height);
            paintValue(g, r);
        }
    };
    return p;
  }
}
```

### *Customizers*

A customizer is a property sheet developed specifically for a bean. It can take any form; it need not use a property sheet metaphor. It is an AWT component that a bean development tool can instantiate to allow the bean user to modify the bean's property values in a totally unique way for that bean.

To get the customizer, the bean development tool calls the BeanInfo.getCustomizerClass() method. A development environment can (should) choose to use the customizer instead of the environment's built-in property sheet if a customizer is provided by the bean. Following is an example of creating a customizer:

```
public class MyHeatGeneratorBeanClassBeanInfo extends
   SimpleBeanInfo
{
    private BeanDescriptor descriptor;

    public MyHeatGeneratorBeanClassBeanInfo()
    {
        descriptor = new BeanDescriptor(
            new Customizer.class());
    }

    ...

    public BeanDescriptor getBeanDescriptor()
    {
        return descriptor;
    }

    public class BeanDescriptor extends java.beans.BeanDescriptor
    {
```

```
    public BeanDescriptor(Class beanClass)
    { super(beanClass); }

    public BeanDescriptor(Class beanClass,
        Class customizerClass)
    { super(beanClass, customizerClass); }
}

public class Customizer extends java.awt.Panel
implements java.beans.Customizer,
    ActionListener, PropertyChangeListener
{
    public Customizer()
    {
        setBackground(Color.white);
        setLayout(new BorderLayout());

        // The environment will set the size, and validate

        // Create title
        Panel p = new Panel();
        add("North", p);
        p.add(new Label(
            "Set the Period and Temperature Property" +
            " Initial Values..."));

        // Create control for setting initial period
        p = new Panel();
        add("South", p);
        p.add(new Label("Period:"));
        p.add(pField = new TextField(10));
        pField.addActionListener(this);

        // Create control for setting initial
        // temperature; we elect to use our own
        // temperature editing conrol.
        add("Center", tControl =
            new TemperatureEditor(this));
        tControl.addPropertyChangeListener(this);
    }

    public Customizer(Object b)
    {
        super();
        setObject(b);
        pField.setText((new Long(period)).toString());
        tControl.setValue(new Float(temperature));
    }
```

```
public void actionPerformed(ActionEvent e)
{
    // A new property value has been entered.
    // Signal the change
    pcs.firePropertyChange(
        "period", e.getOldValue(), e.getNewValue());
}

public void propertyChange(PropertyChangeEvent e)
{
    // A new property value has been entered;
    // rebroadcast the event
    pcs.firePropertyChange(
        e.getPropertyName(), e.getOldValue(),
         e.getNewValue());
}

public void setObject(Object b)
    // gets called by environment
    // upon instantiation
{
    bean = (MyHeatGeneratorBeanClass)b;

    // Get initial property values
    period = bean.getPeriod();
    temperature = bean.getTemperature();
}

public void addPropertyChangeListener
(PropertyChangeListener x)
{
    pcs.addPropertyChangeListener(x);
        // delegate notification
}

public void removePropertyChangeListener(
    PropertyChangeListener x)
{
    pcs.removePropertyChangeListener(x);
        // undelegate notification
}

private MyHeatGeneratorBeanClass bean;
    // the bean whose properties we are setting
private long period;  // temp proxy for the real property
private float temperature;  // "
private TextField pField;   // text field for setting the
                            // period property
```

```
        private TemperatureEditor tControl;
            // component for setting for temperature property
        private PropertyChangeSupport pcs =
            new PropertyChangeSupport(this);
    }

    ...
}
```

### *Understanding JavaBeans Event Dispatching*

A client once asked me if the bean event mechanism was reliable enough for transactional applications. The challenges to relying on bean events in a transaction are:

- Nonatomicity: When a component receives an event it cannot be sure if other components have been notified, so the system is not in a well-defined state. Furthermore, listeners may have transitioned to another state by the time they get the message.
- Reliability: Event delivery is not guaranteed, so events cannot be used to deliver information reliably. For example, if an event source looks at its list of listeners and decides to message a listener, it cannot be sure that the message will get there unless it makes provisions to monitor or synchronize the delivery process, that is, synchronize the event generation with the capture of the listener list.

In other words, event delivery and handling are not *atomic*, and the *quality of service* of event delivery is *best-effort*. Event delivery has nondeterministic semantics, and event delivery is not necessarily serialized or guaranteed.

This does not disqualify beans from transactional applications by any means. However, the burden is on the application to add the required level of reliability. If bean events are used to send messages as part of a transaction, your application should treat all bean events as advisory. In other words, event delivery should not be relied on for correctness: sending a message does not mean it gets there, so your application must have another means for ensuring that all initiated transactions are completed satisfactorily. You can prove your design is reliable by reviewing it and proving to yourself that listener lists are never modified once a transaction begins and that the asynchronous closing of windows is properly handled.

One solution is to use a single event queue or a group of event queues (e.g., one per recipient) for a class of events. Simply obtain all queues and recipient lists as part of event generation and delivery, which must be synchronous. This makes guaranteed delivery possible. Event delivery (producer role) is then decoupled

from event processing (consumer role) by the queue. Thus, once an event handler begins to process an event it retrieves from a queue, it knows that the event has been delivered to the queues of all interested parties; therefore, events are serialized, and the sequence within each queue is preserved. Optionally, you may enforce that a party cannot remove its event queue from a source's interested party list unless it first scans the queue and makes sure there are no events from that party, and it must do this synchronously. This guarantees that event generation and delivery will have a well-defined effect—event sources can trust that whenever you tell them to stop sending you messages, you will have responded (and reacted) to all their prior messages.

A problem with implementing this is that present-day bean development tools implement extraneous bean adapter "glue code" according to nontransactional policies. Most of these tools are oriented toward developing UI-based application code, and these kinds of issues are not considered. In practice, design flaws that result from this usually do not show themselves unless the user clicks buttons and closes windows in quick succession.

Incidentally, the AWT uses a single queue for all GUI events; this queue is the object returned by Toolkit.getSystemEventQueue(). This works fine until a recipient needs to suspend its thread—its thread is the shared AWT queue processing thread. Suspending the current thread in an event adapter will likely cause the UI thread to be suspended and freeze the UI. For example, modal dialogs do this, and to avoid a freeze the workaround is very complex. This is, of course, not a problem if you know that your beans are well behaved (don't perform blocking operations in their event handling code).

## Frameworks for JavaBeans

### *BeanContexts*

All programs execute within some kind of environment, which provides services to the application, the most fundamental of which are application loading and unloading. Some services are implicit in the application language and standard APIs. For example, a Java application implicitly makes use of memory management services from the underlying system. A Java application may also make use of network services, for example, when it creates a socket connection. Even though a socket request is explicit, it uses the core Java API and so is considered an implicit service, since the programmer does not have to explicitly request or locate an environment-specific service.

Some kinds of Java platforms provide other standard services, which are standard for that class of platforms. An example of this is an applet context, which represents an environment interface that is unique to browsers but standard across all browser-based Java implementations. The applet context provides services to an applet that are of special use to a browser-based application (an applet), such as the showDocument() method, which allows the applet to request that remote content be retrieved and displayed in the browser.

Besides browsers, there are different ways of deploying programs. It is therefore useful to define a generic environmental context type, with a standard set of operations for interrogating what services are available and requesting services. This will allow programs to be developed somewhat independently of their deployment environment, and also to be flexible with regard to the environment they are deployed in and what services they require. This is an important feature for enterprise applications, because enterprise applications are often deployed in multiple environments, and environments change over time.

Another consideration for component-based applications is that sometimes the application needs to override the services provided by the environment. For example, suppose a component uses a print service, but a new use of the component deploys it in an environment (such as a mobile computing platform) that does not support printing, but has faxing, email, and a host-based backup service. It is not possible for the component to anticipate all these new services. The application may therefore need to *interpose* itself between the component and the default service context supplied by the environment, to in effect trap print operations and reimplement them with other methods. The context framework therefore needs to allow applications to create their own context objects, and insert them between components and the native environment's context. In a more general case, we need the ability to insert arbitrary contexts between a component and another context, thereby—in sophisticated cases—creating a context hierarchy.

Java 2 introduces a new package to package java.beans, called java.beans.beancontext, which attempts to address the need for a core application context API. It provides features for interposition and nesting of contexts, and for service interrogation and access.

**The Context Hierarchy.** The base type of all bean contexts is BeanContext. This type, which is an interface, extends java.util.Collection, which has methods add(), remove(), and other collection-oriented methods. By virtue of this extension, and a set of context-insertion and removal rules, BeanContext provides a means for creating context hierarchies. The rules for managing contexts are very complex, but there are two helper classes, BeanContextSupport and BeanContextServicesSupport, which a context may extend to provide the behavior for adding and removing contexts, notification of context events, and service registration.

**How a Bean Gets Its Context.** In order for a bean to know what its context is, the environment has to have a way to pass the context to the bean when the bean is instantiated, and there has to be a method for the bean to call to get this context. When a context's add() method is called, the object passed to it can be another context, or it can be any bean. If this object implements the BeanContextChild interface (strongly recommended), the context will automatically call the object's BeanContextChild.setBeanContext() method, and the object will implement a getBeanContext() method to retrieve this context. Otherwise, it is up to the instantiating application to know how to pass the object its context.

The parent context can then provide the resources from an application-specific source, or from the class loader, using the Class.getResource() or Class.getResourceAsStream() methods. Of course if the bean has been instantiated in an environment which does not provide a context (e.g., a standalone Java application), then the context will be null and the bean will need to obtain the requested resources directly from the current class loader instead.

```
InputStream getResourceAsStream(String name, BeanContextChild
   requestor);
URL getResource(String name, BeanContextChild requestor);
```

The context can then provide the resources from an application-specific source, or from the class loader in the standard way, using the Class.getResource() or Class.getResourceAsStream() methods.

**Defining a Context that Adds a Service.** You can define your own context class that provides a service you want to make available to beans you plan to instantiate. The context must implement the BeanContextServices interface, which extends BeanContext; if it does not, the context is not able to provide services to its subordinate objects.

For example, suppose we have developed an application framework for all the components of our application, and this framework provides a runtime context called MyContext. If we then develop a print service that we want to make available and override the built-in print service available in the native environment, we can add that new print service to our context as follows:

```
public class MyContext extends BeanContextServicesSupport
{
   public MyContext()
   {
      super();
      addService(PrintJob.class,
         new MyPrintServiceProvider());
   }
}
```

Once that context's beans have a reference to the context, they can request that context for services. A bean requests a service from its context by calling the BeanContextServices.getService() method. This method takes a service class as a parameter, in addition to some other parameters, and returns an object that represents the requested service. For example, to request a print service:

```
public class MyBean implements BeanContextChild
{
   public void setBeanContext(BeanContext bc)
   { beanContext = bc; }
   public BeanContext getBeanContext()
   { return beanContext; }

   ...
   protected PrintJob getMyPrintJob()
   {
      if (! beanContext instanceof BeanContextServices)
         return null;
      return (PrintJob)
         ((BeanContextServices)beanContext.getService(
            this, this, PrintJob.class, null, null));
   }
   ...
   private transient BeanContext beanContext;
}
```

In the example above, note that the private reference to the bean's owning context is marked transient. It is required that references to any outer context, and any services, be market-transient so that if the bean is serialized it does not take the environment with it!

If the context does not have a requested service, it may (but does not have to) propagate the request to its own containing context until either it is at the top level or the service is obtained.

**How to Create a Context and Install It Under an Existing Context.** Your application may create a context object to make a set of services available to beans that the application plans to create. The application may itself be installed under a context, or it may be the "top level," and not have a context. Regardless, to make services available to beans, it will have to create a context. For example, the following application creates an instance of MyContext and adds it to its own context:

```
public class MyApplication
{
    public MyApplication(BeanContext nativeContext)
    {
        BeanContext myContext = new MyContext();
        nativeContext.add(myContext);
    }
```

Now it can create a bean and add it to the context:

```
    protected void addMyBean()
    {
        MyBean b = (MyBean)
        (myContext.instantiateChild("MyBean"));

        b.setContext(myContext);
            // unnecessary if MyBean
            // implements BeanContextChild
        ...the bean may now request print
            services, and our context will
            attempt to serve them...
```

The overall scenario is shown in Figure 2-1.

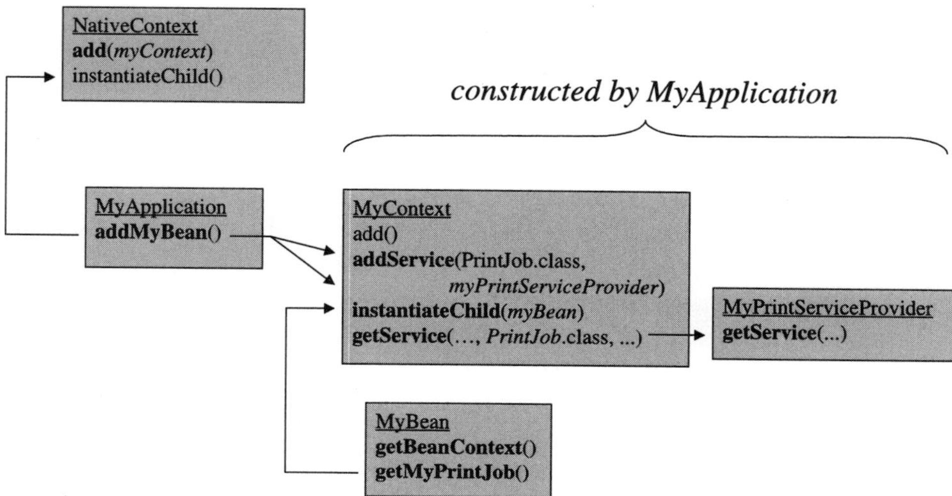


**Figure 2-1** Example of an application which creates a context to provide a print service.

**Instantiating a Bean.** A bean should always be created by calling one of the java.beans.Beans.instantiate(...) method variants. The BeanContext.instantiateChild() method is a convenience method that invokes the appropriate java.beans.Beans.instantiate() method. (Note that all beans must have a default constructor.) You could instead invoke the Beans.instantiate() method directly. These are the Beans.instantiate() methods:

```
static Object instantiate(ClassLoader cl,
    String beanClassName bcn);
static Object instantiate(ClassLoader cl,
    String beanClassName, BeanContext bc);
static Object instantiate(ClassLoader cl,
    String, BeanContext bc, AppletInitializer ai);
```

The last two variations of this method are new in Java 2, and allow you to pass in a bean context. The third version is intended for browsers to use so that a browser can instantiate an applet as a bean, using the same instantiation interface as other beans use and allowing an applet to be created with a bean context in addition to an applet context. There is no correspondence between an applet context and a bean context; the two have conceptual similarities, but the definition of applet context exists for historical reasons, and will likely remain as it is for backward compatibility.

To instantiate an applet bean using the above instantiate(..., AppletInitializer) method, the browser must construct an object that implements the AppletInitializer interface, which has methods for initializing the applet (i.e., setting its AppletStub and AppletContext)—as well as activating it (calling the applet's start() method).

**Adding a Context That Is a Component.** The bean context framework provides a set of interfaces for keeping a context hierarchy in sync with other parallel but independent hierarchies such as component container hierarchies. This is beyond the scope of this discussion, but the interested reader can study the BeanContextProxy and BeanContextChildComponentProxy interfaces.

## JAR Files

For deploying Java software, the standard container is a "JAR" file, which stands for "Java-ARchive." A JAR file is a file which contains other files. If you are familiar with ZIP files you are familiar with JAR files, because they have the same format. In addition to using the ZIP format, a JAR file contains some special files to allow a JAR to fulfill its purpose of acting as a container for Java code distribution.

The JAR format has these purposes and advantages:

- A transportable and platform-independent container for a collection of related or dependent code and resources. May constitute an executable unit as well.
- Supports hierarchical directories (again, in a platform-independent manner).
- Allows a package to be transferred more efficiently, via a single network connection.
- A package field-replaceable unit (see the section "Packages Are Field-Replaceable Units" on page 139).
- Self-describing, via a manifest file, which can contain arbitrary attributes, descriptions, and digital signatures for the archive's contents.
- Contents can be compressed (on a file-by-file basis), allowing for efficient transfer.

A JAR file may contain files of any type. Generally, it consists of Java class files and resource files (e.g., image and sound files, and property files) in either a flat structure or Java packages. It may even contain native code, although the application will have to know how to move binary code into the system's path, since that is where the loadLibrary() method looks, or the application will have to use the load() method instead of the loadLibrary() method). In addition, a JAR file contains a directory, called "META-INF," which contains a "manifest" file. The manifest file contains an attributed list of all of the files in the JAR file, and base-64-encoded MD5 and SHA-1 digital hashes of each of the JAR file's contents. (See Chapter 4, "Java Security," for a description of hashing algorithms.) The manifest file therefore contains, in effect, a fingerprint of the JAR file's contents. The manifest is in ASCII format, and so is human-readable and -editable.

Like ZIP files, JAR files can contain directories. In fact, a JAR file must have at least one directory: the directory containing the manifest file. This is "META-INF." If the JAR file is signed, this directory also contains signature instruction files and actual signature files. Signing will be discussed later.

When building a JAR file, if you are including packages from third parties, you will want to remove classes you do not use. Some IDEs have a tool to do this automatically for you. If you do not do this, you will be forcing users to download code they never execute.

**How to Create a JAR File.** To create a JAR file, you can use a ZIP tool to create the initial contents and then use the "jar" tool to add the manifest, or you can use jar to do the whole thing. The jar tool is invoked in a similar manner to the UNIX tar command. In the basic case of creating a new JAR file, this is:

```
jar cf <jar-output-file> <class-files...>
```

For example, the following command creates a JAR file from the specified list of class files:

```
jar cf MyJarFile.jar ClassA.class ClassB.class
```

To deploy a Java applet encapsulated in a JAR file, use the archive attribute in the applet tag:

```
<applet
   code="MyApplet"←or use "MyApplet.class"
   archive="archive.jar"
   width=100 height=100
   codebase="http://somewhere.com/mystuff/"←optional
>
</applet>
```

In order to find the class MyApplet, and all subsequent classes, the class loader will look in the JAR archive. You can also specify a list of JAR archive files, in which case the class loader will look in each until it finds what it wants. If it does not find a needed class or resource in any of the listed JAR files, it looks in the location from which it got the JAR file from (the codebase). The syntax for specifying a list of JAR files is as in the following example:

```
archive="archive1.jar, archive2.jar, archive3.jar"
```

Thus, the archive attribute behaves much like a classpath which contains only JAR files, and has the codebase implicitly as the last entry.

### *Signed JAR Files*

A JAR file can be signed multiple times, possibly using a different encryption algorithm each time. The reason for doing this is that you will want to sign a JAR file with a superset of the algorithms your anticipated end users will have installed on their Java platforms. For example, Netscape Navigator comes with RSA encryption installed as an available algorithm for its Java clients. This is achieved by setting a Java security property to point to the RSA provider class that implements those algorithms. (See Chapter 4, "Java Security," for an explanation of this.) Other browsers may not have the RSA provider installed, and may only have the default DSA provider. Therefore, you should sign your JAR files with DSA, and possibly with RSA as well.

A signature instructions file is essentially a list of the files to sign, and also a hash of the manifest entries of the files to be signed; and, as already explained, these entries themselves contain hashes of the actual files. It is actually the signature instructions file which gets signed. (Talk about being indirect!)

The signature instructions file is therefore derived from the manifest, which is derived from the files in the archive. This derivative relationship therefore makes signing the signature instructions file equivalent to signing the actual files themselves.

The signature instructions file is signed by encrypting a hash of it with a specified algorithm and placing the encrypted hash in the archive. This signed file has the same name as the instructions file, but with the name of the signing algorithm appended as a file extension. There can be a multiple of these files—one for each algorithm that is applied. There can also be multiple instruction files—one for each subset of files to be signed. The signing certificate is also included. See Chapter 4, "Java Security," for more information on digital signatures.

### *Signing with JDK 1.1*

(See Chapter 4, "Java Security," for a discussion of certificates and public and private keys.)

JDK 1.1 includes a tool called javakey for creating and managing certificates. Javakey produces X.509 v.1 certificates, which are not compatible with Netscape Navigator (which requires v.3). Therefore, use Netscape's own signing tool, "signtool" (discussed below), when creating certificates to be used by Navigator or Communicator.

You can use javakey for creating certificates to be used by HotJava and appletviewer; or you can obtain a certificate and key pair from a certificate authority (CA) and add those to your javakey database and use them to sign your JAR files. To do that, you must have a security provider implementation installed that matches the algorithm used by the CA. (See Chapter 4, "Java Security," for a discussion of adding a provider.)

To add a certificate and key pair to your javakey database, these are the steps:

**1.** Enter yourself into your javakey database. This creates an identity in the database which you will use to refer to the certificate and key pair associated with this identity. For example, to create an identity called "ourcompany":

```
javakey -cs ourcompany true
```

The "true" specifies that this is a trusted identity—the trust attribute is maintained in the javakey database so that applications like appletviewer can determine if certificates associated with this identity are trusted, and therefore if objects such as JAR files signed by this certificate should be trusted as well.

2. Obtain a new certificate and key pair from a source that is trusted by your target audience—either a CA or your company's certificate server.

3. Import your certificate and key pair into your javakey database; for example:

```
javakey -ic ourcompany our_certificate.cer
javakey -ikp ourcompany our_pubkey.der our_privkey.der
```

The first line imports a certificate from the file "our_certificate.cer" and associates it with the identity "ourcompany." The second line imports the public and private key pair associated with the certificate. You need both the private key and the certificate in your database to sign a JAR file.

4. Use your certificate and key pair, with javakey, to sign the JAR file:

First create a signing directives file. Here is an example, which I will store in a file called "signing.directives":

```
signer=ourcompany
cert=1
chain=0
signature.file=SIF
```

The first line specifies the identity. This must match the subject name in the certificate (see below). The second line specifies which certificate in your javakey database to use for the signing. You can list the certificates in the database with the javakey -ld command.

The third line has to do with certificate chaining (see Chapter 4, "Java Security," for an explanation of certificate chains), and is not used. The last line specifies the base name to use for the signature instructions and signature files in the JAR file; it must have no more than eight characters.

To sign the JAR file, use a command such as the following:

```
javakey -gs signing.directives OurJarFile.jar
```

All of the above assumes you have obtained a certificate from a third party. To create a certificate (instead of obtaining one), Steps 2 and 3 would be replaced with:

2. Generate a public/private key pair using javakey. For example, to generate a 512–bit DSA key pair,

```
javakey -gk ourcompany DSA 512 our_pubkey.def our_privkey.der
```

3. Generate a certificate using javakey.

   To generate a certificate from the key pair, you need to create a directives file for javakey. Suppose it is called cert.directives, and it contains this:

```
issuer.name=ourcompany
subject.name=ourcompany
subject.real.name=Our Great Company
subject.org.unit=Special Projects Division
subject.org=Our Great Company
subject.country=US
start.date=1 June 2000
end.date=1 Dec 2000
serial.number=1001
out.file=ourcompany.cer
```

   This is the information javakey uses to create an x509 v.1 digital certificate. Note that the issuer name and subject name are identical. That is because this is a self-signed certificate. If you obtain a certificate from a certificate issuer, they would be the issuer and you would be the subject. The start date and end date define when the certificate becomes valid and when it ceases to be valid. The serial number uniquely identifies the certificate, and is assigned by the certificate issuer. The certificate will be created and placed in the specified output file, "ourcompany.cer."

   To actually create the certificate, use a command such as the following:

```
javakey -gc cert.directives
```

The certificates produced by javakey are X.509 v.1 certificates, which do not distinguish between signing or authentication uses. The usage being discussed here is for signing. The normal procedure for obtaining a signing certificate from a CA is to go to the CA's web site with your browser and provide the requested information. The browser will automatically generate a key pair and blank certificate, store those in its database, and send the certificate as a certificate signing request (CSR) to the CA over the Web. The CA will sign the certificate and send it back, again over the Web or via email.

Javakey does not itself have a means of generating a CSR. You could use the browser-based procedure to get a CA-signed certificate, except that you would not be able to use the certificate for signing by javakey, since the browser will install the private key in its database, and so it will not be accessible to javakey. SDK 1.2's keytool provides a way to generate a CSR directly, without using a browser.

### *Signing with Java 2*

Java 2 replaced the javakey tool with two new tools: keytool and jarsigner. They are refreshingly easier to use than javakey (you don't have to create directive files), and much more practical for broader use, since you can generate a CSR. In addition, the javakey database is now known as a "keystore." (See Chapter 4, "Java Security," for a discussion of keystores.)

#### Entering a Signing Certificate into the Certificate Keystore—Keytool

Keytool lets you:

1. Insert a certificate from an external source into the keystore, and define it as a trusted certificate.
2. Create a new private/public key pair. The private key is stored in a specified keystore; a certificate is created, containing the public key, and put in the keystore also.
3. Create a CSR to send to a CA.
4. Import a certificate received from a CA in response to your CSR.

If you are setting up a keystore, you will need to do step 1 to define a set of trusted certificates. This is because, unlike JDK 1.1's javakey, keytool does not let you define certificates as trusted or untrusted; it assumes all certificates in it are trusted, and verifies a certificate when it is entered by checking its signature and seeing if it is signed by another certificate in its database. Self-signed certificates are a special case: they are implicitly trusted. You must therefore be certain that any self-signed certificates you import are authentic.

Here is an example of importing a trusted CA certificate:

```
keytool -import -alias verisign -file verisign.cer
```

Unless you specify the -keystore option, keytool assumes the keystore to be a file named ".keystore" in your user home directory. You will be prompted for a password to grant you access to the keystore. If the keystore does not yet exist, it will be created and the password you enter will be the one it uses from then on. You will also be prompted for a password used to encrypt and unencrypt the private key created for the alias. The term "alias" is somewhat misleading—it identifies an entity within your keystore; it is called an alias because it is not a globally defined name, such as the certificate holder's distinguished name. The alias is the

name by which you refer to all information about the key pair and certificate you are creating.

If you are testing an application, you also will need to do Step 2; for example,

```
keytool -genkey -alias ourcompany -file ourcompany.cer
```

At this time, the default implementation included with SDK 1.2 includes only the DSA signing algorithm. Thus, the key pair generated will be DSA keys, with a default key size of 1024 bits unless you specify otherwise (e.g., you could specify 512). In order to create a key pair using the RSA algorithm, you would have to install an RSA provider class implementation (this is discussed in Chapter 4, "Java Security").

You might be tempted to bypass all this and obtain a signing certificate by other means; the difficulty then is that you will not be able to use jarsigner, since jarsigner relies on your keystore: it uses the private key created by keytool and stored in your keystore to sign a JAR file. Unlike with the JDK 1.1 javakey tool, at this writing there is no way to import a private key into keytool. Therefore, if you obtain a certificate without using keytool, you will have to use another tool for signing your JAR file (e.g., Netscape's signtool, discussed later).

The certificate you create is valid for a default period of 90 days, unless you override the default with the "validity" option (e.g., "-validity 365" would make it valid for a year).

If you are deploying a final end-user application, you will need to also do steps 3 and 4 to get an actual signed certificate from a CA (or a certificate server) that uses your public key, and install that certificate in your keystore so you can use it to sign your JAR file, for example:

```
keytool -csr -alias ourcompany -file ourcompany.csr
```

The file ourcompany.csr is the output file. This is the file that needs to be sent to a CA for signing. At this time, however, you may have to make special arrangements to get the CSR processed, since most CAs are set up to do this over the Web using a browser or other automated CSR exchange software, and are not accustomed to receiving the CSR as a standalone file.

After processing the CSR, the CA will then send you a new certificate. This certificate contains your public key, and assumes you have the corresponding private key stored in your keystore (or somewhere). Suppose they send you a file called ourcompany.cer; you can import this CA-signed certificate into your keystore as follows:

```
keytool -import -alias ourcompany -file ourcompany.cer
```

It will replace the self-signed certificate that was there before.

**Note**

You do not need to send your certificate to users of the JAR file you sign; the certificate is automatically included in the JAR file by the signing process.

Keytool cannot yet handle chained certificates (certificates must be flat), but will in a future release. Make sure your CA does not send you a chained certificate. They will also want to know if you want a signing certificate or a server certificate: that depends on what you plan to use the certificate for. For signing a JAR file, you want a signing certificate. It is up to the application to decide whether it wants to be picky about this detail, which is a v.3 extension.

**Note**

Code signing is not compatible across JDK 1.1 and SDK 1.2 due to bugs in the way 1.1 tools work.

Keytool produces x.509 v.1 certificates. It can import and use v.3 certificates, however. You cannot use it to produce certificates for Netscape Navigator, SSL servers, and other server products, in general, since they require v.3 certificates; but you can use v.3 certificates obtained from your CA via the CSR process described here.

**Signing the JAR File—Jarsigner.** Once you have a certificate and key pair in your keystore, you can sign your JAR file with the certificate's associated private key (which you created in Step 2) using the jarsigner tool. You can do this as follows:

```
jarsigner OurJarFile.jar ourcompany
```

You will be prompted for the keystore's password and for the alias's (ourcompany) password. The JAR file will be signed with the private key stored in the keystore for ourcompany according to the algorithm corresponding to that key. Thus, you do not need to specify the signing algorithm here.

The signature instructions file will be automatically generated by jarsigner, and list all the contents of the JAR file. Thus, if you plan to add unsigned contents, add that after you sign it.

The type of key determines the algorithm that will be used to sign the JAR file. You must have that algorithm installed as a security provider.

### *Packages Are Field-Replaceable Units*

Java 2 adds a new dimension to Java packages and JAR files. It views a JAR file as primarily a collection of packages, and views a package as a *field-replaceable unit*—an entity which has an identifiable version number, and can be distributed and replaced as a unit for upgrades or bug fixes.

In addition to an entry for each file contained in the archive, a Java 2 JAR manifest should contain an entry for each Java package represented in the JAR archive. A package entry should have the following attributes:

> **Name**—The name of the directory within the archive that contains the package's class and resource files
>
> **Specification-Title**—The title of the API specification to which this product adheres
>
> **Specification-Version**—The version sequential number of the API specification
>
> **Specification-Vendor**—The vendor who owns the specification
>
> **Package-Title**—The Java package name
>
> **Package-Version**—The version identification of this package build; merely a string, need not be sequential in any way
>
> **Package-Vendor**—The organization that supplies this package

Here is an example:

```
Name: /com/acmeapi/ourproduct/
Specification-Title: "Our Great Product"
Specification-Version: "2.0"
Specification-Vendor: "Acme API Writers, Inc."
Package-Title: "com.acmeapi.ourproduct"
Package-Version: "2.0_bugfix3"
Package-Vendor: "Show Me The Money, Inc."
```

The concept is that a package is an implementation of a specific version of a *specification*. Packages that implement the same *specification* version should be logically interchangeable, assuming a bug-free world. A *package* version, on the other hand, is a particular release of an implementation, possibly a bug-fix release. Different package versions for the same specification version must implement the same API and functionality.

When a user upgrades by incorporating a JAR file that implements a newer specification, the user can expect to receive new and possibly different functionality.

When upgrading to a newer package version, however, no new functionality is expected, but behavior may change as a result of repairs to the implementation. The user should retain final control over whether to accept this upgrade, and perhaps return to an earlier package version if the changes have other side effects that are unexpected or not desired. For example, a newer package version might have improved performance but introduced a new bug that was not there previously. In this case, the user may want to uninstall the new package and reinstall the earlier version. To do this, the user needs to be able to ask the application what version of each package it is using, and instruct the environment to uninstall or install specific package versions. It is up to the environment or application to provide this dynamic installation capability.

Note that this model is appropriate for web-based deployment, and traditional diskette-based modes of deployment as well, but not for a code replication channel such as Castanet. A replication channel addresses version compatibility by ensuring that every client has the latest version; there is no concept of rolling back to an earlier version, and to do so would require having a separate channel for each version available at any time; one could, for example, have three channels, for the current and previous two versions. If a person wanted to go back to an earlier version, they would have to unsubscribe to the channel representing the latest version, and subscribe to a channel representing the earlier version. The channel administrator would have to stagger updates to these channels, to maintain the three versions. These versions could represent specification or package versions, depending on whether they implement the same functionality and interfaces. An alternative approach is to add logic to the channel application that allows the user to choose between different packages, which can be saved in a channel profile for the user.

So which way should you do it? The single-version Castanet approach is more appliance-like, and is more appropriate for strictly hands-off users who cannot be expected to get involved in any application maintenance or administration activities. Providing users with version information, and allowing them to choose between versions, adds flexibility, and may be appropriate for sophisticated users and applications. For example, for a very complex application some users may want to postpone upgrades for awhile, especially if they have created data using an earlier version. This can still be done with Castanet, but whether you do it with Castanet or not, it requires adding to the application the ability to choose between package versions.

### *Creating an Executable JAR File*

A JAR file can be made executable by designating one of its classes as a "main" class. The JAR file can then be selected by the `java` or `jre` program, without

having to specify the internal class name to run. To make a JAR file executable, you must modify its manifest file. To extract the manifest:

```
copy <your-archive>.jar \work
cd \work
jar xvf <your-archive>.jar
copy META-INF\MANIFEST.MF .\<your-archive>.mf
del META-INF\*.*
rmdir META-INF
```

Edit the manifest with a text editor, and give the main class a property of:

```
Main-Class: <your-main-class>
```

For example, suppose a manifest contains one entry, for a file called "C.class":

```
Manifest-Version: 1.0

Name: C.class
Digest-Algorithms: SHA MD5
SHA-Digest: FMpaHnSoID9J/w37tqwR7YFSIS0=
MD5-Digest: p0OLP5/aOPs7buzEud4L3Q==
```

You would then add the Main-Class attribute, and the resulting manifest would then contain:

```
Manifest-Version: 1.0
Main-Class: C.class

Name: C.class
Digest-Algorithms: SHA MD5
SHA-Digest: FMpaHnSoID9J/w37tqwR7YFSIS0=
MD5-Digest: p0OLP5/aOPs7buzEud4L3Q==
```

Then rebuild the JAR file with the new manifest:

```
jar cmf <your-archive>.mf <your-archive>.jar <extracted
directories or files...>
```

Now you can specify the JAR file as if it were a Java program:

```
java -jar abc.jar
```

To execute this JAR file from a program:

```
JarFile jf = new JarFile("<JAR-file-name>");
jf.exec(<args>);
```

When Java 2 is installed on NT it associates the .jar extension with the Java runtime, so double clicking on a JAR file will cause it to execute just like any program.

### *Referencing Other Included Items*

A JAR file can include other JAR files by reference. This allows you to effectively embed a classpath within the JAR file, by listing the URLs of the components to be included. For example, you could list the URL where swingall.jar can be found. The mechanics of this are discussed in Chapter 4, "Java Security," where I explain the Java Extensions Framework.

### *Sealing a JAR File*

Java 2 class loaders allow classes from a single package to be distributed across more than one JAR file. In other words, you can have some classes from package mypackage in mp1.jar, and additional classes from package mypackage in mp2.jar. You can restrict this by specifying that a JAR file or a package within a JAR file is "sealed." If a package (or JAR file) is sealed, its packages must all originate from that JAR file. For example, the JAR file attribute

```
Sealed: true
```

specifies that all the packages in the JAR file must come from this JAR file, and that some may not be loaded from another JAR file. (Of course, other packages from other JAR files can be loaded.)

You can specify sealing for individual packages. For example, consider the manifest entry for a package called "mypackage":

```
Name: mypackage/
```

If this entry has the additional attribute

```
Sealed: true
```

then the package "mypackage" is sealed. A package-specific attribute overrides the Sealed attribute for the overall JAR file.

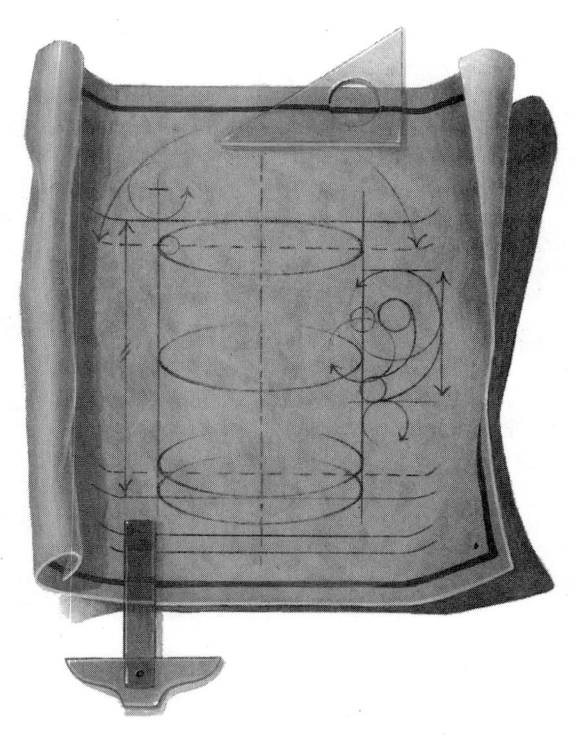

# CHAPTER 3

# Threads in Server Applications

Most operating systems today provide threads. The purpose of threads is to allow programs, executing within the context of a single process, to provide concurrent execution of separate activities. Multiple threads within a process share the same space for static and heap data, so interthread communication is achieved simply through the sharing of variables.

Threads are increasingly important for modern applications. For example, most user interface environments operate under the control of a separate thread or group of threads dedicated to delivering GUI events to application code. Web applications, such as Netscape Communicator, use multithreading to allow multiple content files to download simultaneously instead of sequentially; the net effect is that multiple images are painted at the same time instead of one at a time. Server environments such as application servers and servlet-capable web servers provide a managed multithreaded execution environment, and allocated thread resources as necessary, for application components running in the environment. The techniques and policies used by different kinds of servers are quite different, and so it is useful to be familiar with threading issues even if threads are managed by the environment.

One of the most challenging aspects of thread programming is that the specifics of thread programming APIs vary from one operating system to another. Traditionally, a programmer needs to be experienced in the thread programming models of various systems in order to avoid relying on thread primitives unique to an operating system. Java, on the other hand, defines a generic yet powerful thread programming model, with well-defined semantics, which is portable across operating systems. Sophisticated multithreaded programs can therefore be written in a portable way, which will run the same way on NT, any brand of UNIX, or any other operating system.

Nevertheless, designing a well-behaved multithreaded application, even in Java, is not a trivial task. Java provides powerful primitives for creating multithreaded applications, but Java is not a thread "design" language, in that it does not protect you in any way from creating incorrectly designed multithreaded programs. Creating a correct design is completely up to you. In this chapter, I will demonstrate how to construct correct multithreaded applications in Java.

## Java Threads[1] vs. System Threads

Most implementations of Java today use native operating system threads to implement the Java thread model. However, it is important to understand the distinction between a Java thread object and an actual system thread. A system thread is a schedulable entity within the operating system. A Java Thread object is merely a Java language wrapper or surrogate for the system-dependent thread. When you create a Java Thread object, a corresponding system thread does not yet exist, and is not created until you call the Thread's start() method. Calling start() for a Thread object causes a system thread to be created and run.

In a Java VM implemetation, a Java thread is an abstraction, and this abstraction is implemented using native system thread facilities. A Java thread has a Java VM execution stack, but a system thread has a system execution stack of its own. The Java thread's execution stack has information about the current Java methods and data visible to the Java thread; the system thread has information about the current VM functions it is executing, and VM data that identifies the associated Java thread and stack. From the Java thread's point of view, it is executing Java application code; from the system thread's point of view, it is executing VM code to service the Java thread. The start() method bridges these two worlds, creating the system thread that will be used to service a Java thread, setting up the VM data structures necessary to establish the link between the system thread and Java VM Thread object, and then launching the system thread.

## Creating and Starting a Thread

To create and start an independent thread of execution in Java, you need to create an instance of the Thread class or a subclass and call its start() method.

The start() method will invoke native code to construct a system thread for servicing this Java thread. After constructing the system thread, start() will determine if

---

1. Hereafter, the term "Java" will be used to refer to the Java programming language and "Java projects" will be used to refer to projects developed with Java technology. Java is a trademark of Sun Microsystems, Inc., in the U.S. and other countries.

a target Java object instance has been specified for it. The target object is the object containing Java code that the thread will execute. A target object can be specified when the Java Thread object is constructed as a Thread constructor parameter. The target object must implement the Runnable interface, which requires a single method with signature "void run()." If there is a target object, the new system thread uses the target object's run() method as its Java entry point.

If no target object was specified when the Thread object was constructed, its start() method will assume that it is itself the target object. Thread itself implements Runnable, so it has a run() method (empty by default, but you can override it), so in this case start() causes the new system thread to begin executing with the Thread object's run() method as the Java entry point. After initiating this sequence, start() returns to its caller.

To execute code in a separate thread, you therefore need to provide a Runnable object for a Java Thread object to execute. You can create a Runnable object by subclassing Thread, which is a Runnable, or you can create a Runnable object by using any other object which implements Runnable, and passing that object to the Thread constructor. Let us look at an example of the first approach.

```
class SleepyThread extends Thread
{
   /**
    * We override run(), which has an empty implementation in
    * the Thread class.
    */
   public void run()
   {
      for (;;)    // ever
         {
         try
         {
            sleep(1000);
         }
         catch (InterruptedException ex)
         {
            // This executes if another thread calls
            // interrupt() for this thread object.
            System.out.println("Please don't interrupt me!");
         }
         System.out.println("One more time!...");
      }
   }
}
```

Now that you have defined this Thread class, you can use it as follows:

```
public class RunMyThread extends Applet
{
   SleepyThread sleepyThread;

   public void start()
   {
      sleepyThread = new SleepyThread();    // Create a Java
                                            // SleepyThread object.
      sleepyThread.start();   // Creates a system thread, with
                           // sleepyThread.run() as its entry point.
   }

   public void stop()
   {
      sleepyThread.stop();   // Destroys sleepyThread permanently.
      sleepyThread = null;   // Allow sleepyThread instance to be
                             // garbage collected.
   }
}
```

The second way of executing code in a separate thread is to create a Runnable object by using any other object that implements Runnable, and passing that object to the Thread constructor. For example:

```
public RunMyThread extends Applet implements Runnable
{
   Thread thread;

   public void run()   // We must implement this, because Runnable
                       // requires it
   {
      for (;;)   // ever
      {
         try
         {
            sleep(1000);
         }
         catch (InterruptedException ex)
         {
            System.out.println("Please don't interrupt me!");
         }
         System.out.println("One more time!...");
      }
   }
```

```
    public void init()
    {
        thread = new Thread(this);      // Pass it the Runnable - this
                                        // object.
        thread.start();
    }

    public void destroy()
    {
        thread.stop();
        thread = null;
    }
}
```

## Reentrancy

A section of code is "reentrant" if it can be safely executed by multiple threads at the same time, without any external provisions for controlling access to data. (This property is also referred to as being "thread-safe.") There are two forms of reentrancy, which I will call "concurrent" and "guarded." (I don't like these terms much, but they are consistent with the current UML definitions of concurrent and guarded.) A section of code is concurrent reentrant if it is reentrant without using any internal provisions for synchronizing access to data. In other words, it contains no constructs that may cause it to block in order to wait for access to shared data. In contrast, a section of code is guarded reentrant if it uses synchronization mechanisms for accessing shared data, which may cause it to block on occasion.

Concurrent reentrancy can be achieved by not using global data, and not using any data that has a lifetime which extends prior or subsequent to the lifetime of the code section's execution, and if any data created by the section of code is not accessible by other sections of code or other threads. In practice, in the context of Java programming, a concurrent reentrant routine is one that does not use either static or instance variables unless they are constant. Concurrent reentrant methods are usually static. Guarded reentrancy is usually achieved using the Java synchronized modifier.

A Java method that is reentrant by either technique is completely thread-safe—it can be executed by any number of threads without concern for protecting the simultaneous access of data by multiple threads.

To illustrate, in this code the method setX() is not reentrant:

```
class C
{
    char[] x = new int[5];
    void setX(int i, char value)
    {
```

```
        x[i] = value;    // we are changing data accessible to other
                         // threads
    }
}
```

However, in this code setX() is concurrent reentrant:

```
class C
{
    void setX(char[] x, int i, char  value)
    {
        x[i] = value;   // no inherent problem here - as long as
                        // we are given parameter objects that
                        // are not shared by multiple threads;
                        // protecting against that is a matter of
                        // making the calling routine thread-safe

    }
}
```

Each thread has its own execution stack; however, class instance variables are on the shared heap. Therefore, local variables, including object references, which are created on the thread's stack exist only for the lifetime of the scope in which they are created, and so cannot be accessible to other threads. Data and object references which are part of a class's scope are accessible to any thread executing a method belonging to that class, and so are a potential source of non-reentrancy.

If a section of code cannot be concurrent reentrant because it must access a shared item of data, and it is possible that multiple program threads might access the shared item, it must be made guarded reentrant to protect against simultaneous access to the shared data. A section of code labeled "synchronized" is guarded reentrant and can be accessed by only one thread at a time for a given object instance; the virtual machine ensures this.

## Adding Synchronization

You can synchronize access to instance variables by making the code that accesses them synchronized. For example, in the following code the method setX() is declared synchronized, so only one thread at a time can execute this method *for any instance of class* C.

```
class C
{
    char[] x = new int[5];
    synchronized void setX(int i, char value)
```

```
    {
        x[i] = value;  // only one thread at a time can execute this
    }

    void m() {}

    synchronized void n() {}
}
```

The existence of the synchronized keyword on any method or section of code in the class causes a lock to be created for each instance of the class. Threads that want to enter *any* synchronized code belonging to the object instance must obtain this lock, and automatically release it when they exit the synchronized code. Using the example above, if there is an instance of C called "c," and a thread is executing c.setX(), then another thread attempting to execute c.setX() *or* c.n() will be forced to wait until the first thread is done or otherwise releases its lock on instance c. However, threads wishing to execute c.m() will not have to wait, since that method is not synchronized. An object that uses a lock to guard itself in this way is called a "monitor."

On the other hand, if there is another instance of class C, called "d," a thread wishing to execute a synchronized method in this instance will not have to wait for threads using "c" to finish, even though "c" and "d" are instances of the same class. The monitor is therefore the object, not the class. (Below we will see that a class monitor can be created as well.)

The actual VM instructions that implement synchronization are the monitorenter and monitorexit instructions. Here are their definitions.

- *monitorenter:* (assumes an objectref has been pushed on the stack)
  The interpreter attempts to obtain exclusive access via a lock mechanism to objectref. If another thread already has objectref locked, then the current thread waits until the object is unlocked. If the current thread already has the object locked, then continue execution. If the object is not locked, then obtain an exclusive lock.

- *monitorexit:* (assumes an objectref has been pushed on the stack)
  The lock on the object is released. If this is the last lock that this thread has on that object (one thread is allowed to have multiple locks on a single object), then other threads that are waiting for the object to be available are allowed to proceed.

Thus, if a thread already has a monitor's object when it tries to get it, it simply proceeds without waiting. Conversely, it does not release control of the object until it has released its last lock—exited all synchronized sections of code for that object.

The "synchronized" modifier is not considered part of a method's unique signature, and can therefore be overridden. That is, if a method is synchronized in a base class and is not in a subclass, instances of the subclass will not need to obtain a monitor to enter the method. The "synchronized" keyword is therefore a modifier that applies to a particular implementation of a method signature. You cannot even specify "synchronized" in an interface.

In general, it is necessary to synchronize access to any data that might possibly be read or updated by more than one thread at a time. A synchronized section of code can be viewed as "atomic": it executes until it completes, and it cannot be entered by another thread until then. To other threads, it is *atomic*—logically uninterruptible (even though it might be preempted by the scheduler so other threads can execute for a time—but they won't be able to execute this same code for this object instance; that is, enter this monitor).

The built-in Java operations on the Java intrinsic types and object references are defined by the Java language specification to be atomic, except for the double and long types, which will be discussed shortly. For example, arithmetic operations on a Java int value are atomic. In other words, you can be sure that when the VM begins to perform an arithmetic operation on an int, it will get all the way through once it starts. Since an int is composed of four bytes, this is important, because it would be disastrous if one thread started to read an int value when another was in the midst of incrementing it—the thread reading the value would get a corrupted result. The atomic nature of Java arithmetic operations on ints, however, makes such a corrupt value impossible. Operations on the intrinsic types double and long are not required to be atomic, and therefore accessor methods for these types need to be synchronized if access might occur from multiple threads.

Accessor methods for object attributes may or may not need to be synchronized. In particular, if a class defines an immutable object type—one which has no public methods or attributes that can modify the object—accessors to the object do not need to be synchronized, since the state of the object can never change. A good example of this is the String class. To change the value of a String object, you must create a new String, so the String's length can never change once created, and there is no reason to synchronize the length() method. On the other hand, if the object type is mutable and its internal state can change, attribute accessors—and possibly all the object's methods—should be synchronized unless the design of the application ensures that only one thread at a time will access a given object instance.

A synchronized section of code need not be an entire method. For example, in the following, the code within the synchronized block can only be executed by one

thread at a time, and that thread obtains (if it does not already have it) the monitor for the object represented by *this* when it enters the synchronized section:

```
...
synchronized (this)  // synchronize access to this object instance
{
   // synchonized code section: the thread that is executing it
   // has the object's monitor
   ...
}
// end of synchronized section: the monitor is now released by the
// thread
...
```

Like object instance data, static data must also be synchronized if it might be accessed by more than one thread at a time. Consider this problematic example:

```
class C
{
   static char[] x = new int[5];
   static void setX(int i, char value)
   {
      x[i] = value;
   }
}
```

In the above example, the static array x is accessed inside of the method setX(). If more than one thread at a time might be entering setX(), we must make sure access to x is protected so that it does not get corrupted by simultaneous accesses occurring in random order. We can do this as follows:

```
class C
{
   static char[] x = new int[5];
   synchronized static void setX(int i, char value)
   {
      x[i] = value;
   }
}
```

In this case the monitor belongs to the class, instead of an instance of the class. A class monitor is distinct from any class instance monitors. If we do not want to synchronize the entire method, we can synchronize a block in a static method by synchronizing on a static object as follows:

```
class C
{
   static char[] x = new int[5];
   static void setX(int i, char value)
   {
      synchronized (x)
      {
         x[i] = value;
      }
   }
}
```

You may be wondering what overhead synchronization imposes on an application. The overhead was significant in early versions of Java—as much as a factor of ten just to make a single synchronized method call versus a non-synchronized call in Java 1.0. However, Java 2 and newer VM's such as the HotSpot VM drastically improve this, making a synchronized method call almost as efficient as a regular method call. Regardless, it is merely good programming practice to be judicious about where you use synchronization. Rather than simply synchronizing every method that might be called by a multithreaded application, it is wise to think the design through carefully and isolate the places where multithreaded access to objects needs to occur.

## Synchronized Code Can Be Preempted

Synchronized code is often likened to a critical section. From the point of view of a typical application, the comparison is correct. There is one important difference, however: synchronized code can be preempted by the thread scheduler. The Java thread model allows low-priority threads to get some time, even if higher-priority threads are running. (The rule is that a higher-priority thread receives at least as much time as a lower-priority thread.) However, if a thread has an object's monitor, it can be guaranteed that, even if it is preempted for awhile, no other thread will be able to execute synchronized code belonging to the object (or class, if any static code is synchronized) for which the preempted thread has the monitor. Nevertheless, there might be periods of time when a thread is preempted right in the middle of a synchronized section of code. The synchronized keyword is therefore not sufficient to guarantee immediate execution, as is required for a device driver or code that must respond immediately to a request. Sun's JavaOS™ portable operating system delegates this function to C language routines for hardware interrupt handling (this is sometimes referred to as the "lower" portion of a device driver); the application-oriented part of each JavaOS driver (sometimes referred to as the "upper" portion) is always written in Java.

Another ramification of preemption is that thread priority cannot be used in place of synchronization. Just because one thread is a higher priority than another does not mean that it will execute first, so you cannot use priority to effect any kind of scheduling. (In fact, threads of different priorities may even execute concurrently on some multiprocessor systems.) Thread priority is merely a mechanism for allowing more important activities to have more CPU time. Furthermore, the Java thread priorities, which have values 1 through 10, map to different native thread priorities on different operating systems; and some Java thread priorities actually map to the same value: for example, Sun's Windows Java VM maps Java thread priorities 4, 5, and 6 to the same Windows thread priority value, so decrementing priority by one or even two will sometimes have no effect.

## Synchronized Methods in Package Java

At this point you might be wondering, if synchronization is so important, why is it not more prevalent in code in the standard Java packages? For example, how come many methods in the AWT, such as the Component paint() method, are not synchronized, since the UI event thread needs access to these routines, which can also be called by the application's main thread?

In fact, synchronization is used heavily within package java, including the AWT. It is usually encapsulated at a low level, however, out of sight. It is good practice to synchronize as small a section of code as necessary, to minimize the time other threads have to wait.

Here is an example, from MComponentPeer.java, which includes methods that get called when a component is repainted:

```
public void repaint(long tm, int x, int y, int width, int height)
{
   addRepaintArea(x, y, width, height);
   ScreenUpdater.updater.notify(this, tm);
}

private synchronized void addRepaintArea(int x, int y, int w, int h)
{
   if (updateX1 == updateX2)
   {
      updateX1 = x;
      updateY1 = y;
      updateX2 = x + w;
      updateY2 = y + h;
   }
}
```

## Threads of Execution Are Independent of Thread Object Instances

A Java Thread is merely a Java object, and it is important to recognize the distinction between a Java thread object and a thread of program execution. If you define a thread class by extending Thread, any execution thread can call any of the public methods in that class—not just the thread started by your Thread object. For example, consider this class, which extends Thread:

```
class T extends Thread
{
   public void run()
   {
      // The execution thread associated with this Thread object
      // will execute this code
      ...
   }

   public void doStuff()
   {
      // However, any execution thread may execute this code
      System.out.println(Thread.currentThread);
   }
}
```

When you create an instance of T, for example, with:

```
T myThread = new T();
```

and then start the thread, with myThread.start(), the VM will create an execution thread and give it myThread's run() method as an entry point. However, there is nothing to stop *any* execution thread from calling *any* of T's methods, e.g., doStuff(), or even run(). Figure 3-1 depicts three separate threads of execution calling myThread's doStuff() method.

## Thread Groups

A thread group is an aggregation of thread objects. Threads within a thread group can be managed as a unit. For example, you can add new threads to a thread group, set the maximum priority that any thread within the group may have, list the threads in a thread group, and interrupt all threads within the group with a single method call. A thread group can also contain other thread groups, forming a hierarchy.

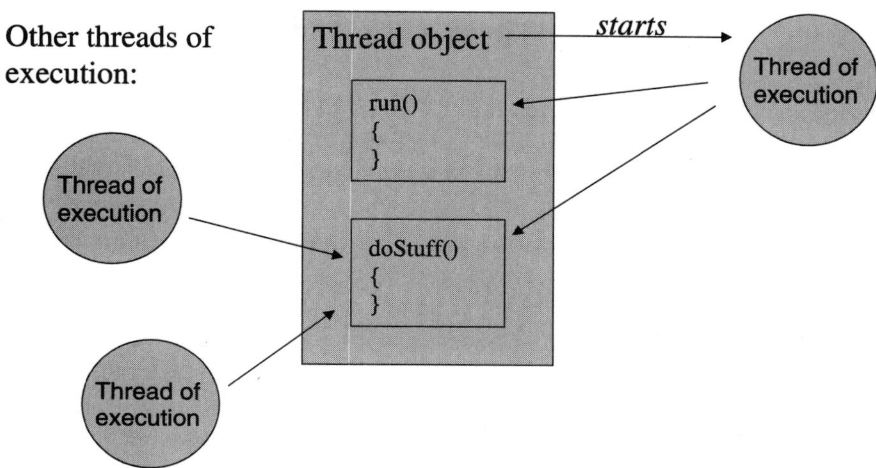


**Figure 3-1** Three threads of execution entering a Thread object.

Often, a thread group is used to collect together client threads of some kind under the management of a server or framework application. For example, the Java Commerce Client framework uses thread groups for managing commerce beans so that the independently developed commerce beans can create their own threads, but the set of threads they create can be stopped or interrupted by the Commerce Framework.

To perform operations on a thread group, you have to have permission, since all thread group operations invoke a checkAccess() operation. The default security policy allows a thread to access and modify (e.g., add new threads to) its own thread group, but not modify or access information about the thread group to which its own thread group belongs.

## The wait() and notify() Methods

The object synchronization feature of Java allows you to protect access to critical data. In addition, a means is needed for releasing a monitor in a controlled way such that it can be obtained again later. The wait() method allows a thread to release its monitor, place itself into a wait state, and then resume later at the same point when notified to do so. The notify() method allows another thread to inform the waiting thread that it should resume and reclaim the monitor. This allows the creation of producer-consumer designs, in which one thread waits for service requests, and another performs the function of generating the requests or at least notifying the service thread when a new request has arrived. The basic model is as follows:

- A synchronized object calls wait(), causing the current thread to temporarily release the object's monitor, putting the thread into a wait state (in effect, hibernation).
- A different thread later calls the object's notify() method to notify the thread waiting for the monitor that the object's monitor may be available, and that it should reenter the runnable state. If more than one thread is waiting for the object's monitor, it is undefined which will get notified.
- If there may be more than one waiting thread, use notifyAll()—all threads waiting for this monitor will attempt to reobtain the monitor.

Figure 3-2 illustrates an example.

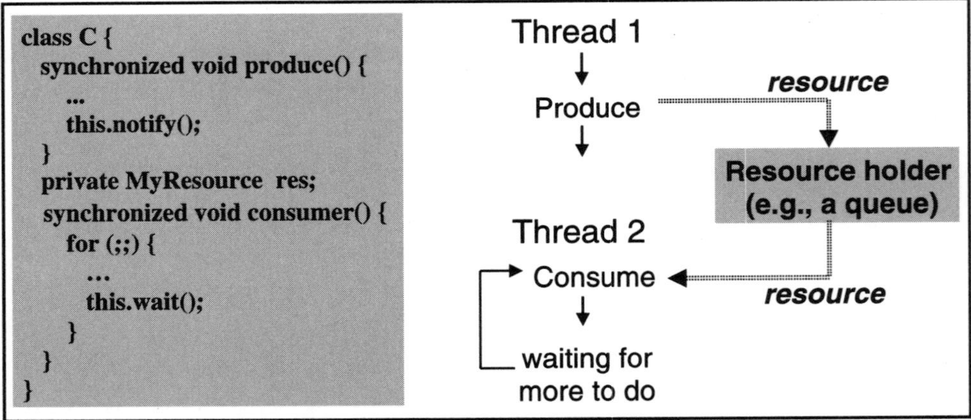


**Figure 3-2** A class that allows creation of producer-consumer thread relationships.

When a thread goes into a wait state, it is waiting for some external condition to become true; the monitor is the mechanism used to represent this condition. Subsequent notification of monitor availability is in effect notification that the waited-for condition has become true; whether it stays true for long is uncertain. The notify() method does not guarantee that the thread which gets notified will actually get the object next; if there are many threads, another thread may get it first, because threads that are notified compete on an equal basis with all other threads vying for the object, including those that were not in a wait state. When a thread returns from a wait state, it should therefore not assume anything about the condition that caused it to be notified, unless it knows it is the only thread that could have been notified.

The notify() and notifyAll() methods must be called from synchronized code, and any threads that are notified will of course wait until the notifying thread releases its lock (leaves the synchronized section). Therefore, while notify() is often called at the end of a synchronized section, it does not have to be—it could be called safely in the middle.

Notifying all threads waiting for an object with the notifyAll() method makes it possible to implement an application-specific policy about which thread should get the object after notification. In this scenario, a thread that returns from a wait() call would execute code which decides if it should go back into a wait state or not.

## Waiting for Another Thread to Terminate: The join() Method

You can use the join() method to suspend the current thread until a specified target thread object stops. The join() method will cause the calling thread to block until the target thread has stopped, and then resume; at this point, you can issue another join() on a different thread, terminate, or do anything you want.

This can be useful for gracefully coordinating the termination of threads when a program needs to exit. For example, if a user clicks the Exit button of an application while the application is performing a calculation, the button's handler should not just call System.exit()—that might corrupt data, perhaps persistent data. Instead, it should set in motion a termination sequence, perhaps as this button click adapter does:

```
public class Terminator implements java.awt.event.ActionListener,
   Runnable
{
   public Terminator(ThreadGroup g)
   {
      groupToTerminate = g;
      terminate = false;
   }

   public synchronized void
      actionPerformed(java.awt.event.ActionEvent e)
   {
      terminate = true;

      // We use a new thread, because we don't want to block the
      // UI thread
      if ((terminatorThread != null) &&
         terminatorThread.isAlive()) return;

      terminatorThread = new Thread(this);
```

```
      terminatorThread.start();
   }

   public synchronized void abortTermination()    // called from
                                                  // other threads
   {
      terminate = false;
      if (terminatorThread == null) return;
      terminatorThread.interrupt();    // interrupt this thread
                                       // object
      terminatorThread = null;
   }

   public void run()
   {
      // We are now on our way to the gallows...

      int ac = groupToTerminate.activeCount();
      Thread[] threads = new Thread[ac];
      int n = groupToTerminate.enumerate(threads);
      // Note: we should take care of the possibility that
      // more threads could join the group during this process.
      // That is omitted for simplicity.

      for (;;) try
      {
         for   // each service thread
         (int i = 0; i < threads.length; i++)
         {
            // Perform code to cause thread i to terminate
            MyThreadType t = (MyThreadType)(threads[i]);
            t.setTerminate(true);

            threads[i].join();    // blocks until this service
                                  // thread terminates
                                  // ... on to the next...
         }

         // Exit the VM - you might choose to put this call
         // elsewhere
         System.exit(0);    // "release the lever!"
      }
      catch (InterruptedException ex)
      {
         // Check if termination has been aborted
         System.out.println("Reprieve?");
```

```
            if (! terminate) return;     // reprieve from the
                                         // Governor!!!
        }
    }

    private ThreadGroup groupToTerminate;
    private Thread terminatorThread;
    private boolean terminate;
}
```

When you instantiate this adapter, you have to pass it the thread group corresponding to the set of service threads that need to be terminated when the user clicks Exit. When the button is clicked, the adapter's actionPerformed() method is called, and the adapter then constructs a thread in which to execute a termination sequence. It is important to do this in a new thread and not the current thread, because the current thread is the UI thread, and we do not want to cause the UI thread to block.

The new thread then obtains a list of all the threads in the thread group that it was passed when the adapter was constructed. This is the list of threads it will terminate before exiting the VM. It loops through the list and performs an application-specific method on each thread, which signals that thread to terminate. I have used the method name "setTerminate()" for illustration. Such a method would be a method implemented by the thread class of the threads to be terminated. In some cases, you can just call stop() for each thread, but if you do, you must be certain that it will not have undesirable consequences, since stop() will abort whatever the thread is doing midstream, release all its locks, and terminate the thread. Its use can therefore lead to inconsistencies. (For this reason, stop() has been deprecated in Java 2.)

A better approach would be to have a setTerminate() implementation which sets a flag that the thread checks periodically, and stops itself if the flag is true; or, if the thread is in a wait state, setTerminate() could call interrupt() on the thread. The interrupt() method causes the target thread to throw an InterruptedException if it is in a sleep, wait, or join state. This method did not work in Java 1.02; you had to simulate it with the stop() method as a workaround. Thankfully, though, that is history. If a thread is not in a wait (or join) state, interrupt() will merely set the isInterrupted flag in the thread, which can be tested by calling isInterrupted().

Consider this implementation of MyThreadType:

```
public class MyThreadType extends Thread
{
    public void setTerminate(boolean t)    // called from another
                                           // thread
```

```
    {
        terminate = t;
        interrupt();        // interrupt this thread object
    }

    public void run()
    {
        for (...)
        {
            try
            {
                if (terminate) return;
                wait();
            }
            catch (InterruptedException ex)
            {
                if (terminate) return;
            }
            ...do stuff...
        }
    }
    private boolean terminate;
}
```

When a thread calls setTerminate() on this thread instance, the thread instance's interrupt() method is called. This does not act on the calling thread—it acts on the *called* thread instance. After all, it would not make sense to interrupt your own thread! This is a way for another thread to interrupt this thread. If the thread object that is interrupted is in a wait state, it catches the InterruptedException and checks its terminate flag; if the flag is true, it terminates itself by returning from run().

This brings me to another issue: what if you want to abort the termination? It is easy to implement an abortTermination() method by simply calling interrupt() on this Terminator thread. This will change the terminate flag back to false, and interrupt the join() method the terminator thread is in, if any. When it resumes from the join as a result of the interrupt, it checks the flag, and, if the terminate flag is false, returns from the terminator thread's run method. Of course, by this time it may already have terminated many threads in the thread group, but at least the program has been prevented from exiting and is in a somewhat well-defined state.

Other implementations are, of course, possible, depending on the thread structure of an application; this example is intended to be illustrative.

If the number of service threads can grow during the above operations, you must iterate, checking that all threads have actually completed before you exit. Another consideration is that the above procedure will wait for child threads of the service threads as well; this should be harmless in most cases, since if a service thread terminates a child thread, the worst that can happen is that a join() will be issued on a thread that is stopped, which will have a null effect—the join will instantly return.

## Thread States

Figure 3-3 shows the thread states and transitions between states that are possible. Note that if a thread enters a wait state, it can only leave that state by an interrupt() or a notify(). In general, for each blocked state, there is a single way of entering that state and a corresponding method for exiting that state. For example, the sleep() method causes a thread to sleep for a specified period of time;[2] the sleep state can only be left by the elapse of that time or by an interrupt() call—not by any other means. Similarly, a thread that is blocked on an IO operation can only exit that blocked state by successful or unsuccessful completion of the IO operation (the latter includes interrupt calls to the thread).

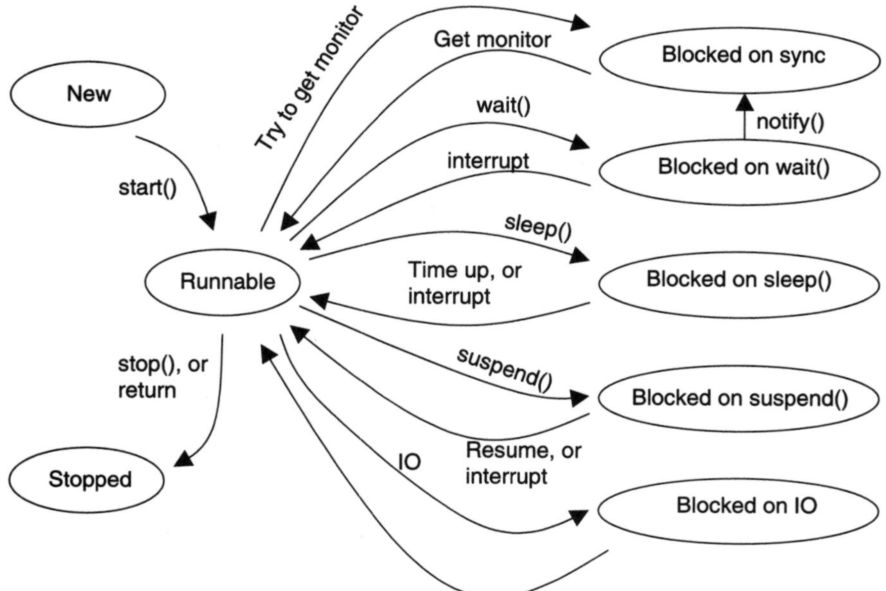


**Figure 3-3** Thread state transitions.

2. Note that the granularity of time supported by the sleep() method implementation may be different on different systems.

## Handling External System Interrupts

Java does not have a built-in way to handle external system interrupts. For example, if a server administrator types Control-C at the console to stop a server, the Java program does not normally have a way to respond to this appropriately and clean up before terminating. However, you can provide a native signal handler to do this, which calls a Java method in your code. Here is an example, taken from a newsgroup posting by Mark Gritter of Stanford University, showing how to write a native signal handler for UNIX, installable from Java:

```
/**
 *  CatchSignal.java
 */
public class CatchSignal implements Runnable
{
   static { System.loadLibrary("CatchSignal"); }
   public native static void setControlCHandler();
   public static void callback()
   {
      System.err.println("Control-C hit!");
   }
   public void run()
   {
      setControlCHandler();      // never returns
   }
   public static void main(String[] args)
   {
      Thread t = new Thread(new CatchSignal());
      t.setDaemon(true);    // Allow program to end even through
         // signal-handling thread doesn't ensure signals are
         // handled
      t.setPriority(Thread.MAX_PRIORITY);
      t.start();
      // Go about normal business...
      ...
   }
}
/*
 * CatchSignal.c -- Compile as shared library libCatchSignal.so
 */
int pipefd;
void ctrl_c_handler()
{
   int foo = SIGINT;
   write(pipefd, &foo, sizeof(int));
   signal(SIGINT, ctrl_c_handler);
}
```

```
JNIEXPORT void JNICALL
Java_CatchSignal_setControlCHandler (JNIEnv * env, jclass cls)
{
   int filedes[2], sigfd, s;
   jmethodID mid = (*env)->GetStaticMethodID(env, cls,
      "callback", "()V");
   pipe(filedes);
   pipefd = filedes[0];
   sigfd = filedes[1];
   signal(SIGINT, ctrl_c_handler);
   while(1)
   {
      read(sigfd, &s, sizeof(int));
      (*env)->CallStaticVoidMethod(env, cls, mid);
   }
}
```

## Avoiding Thread Deadlock

Thread deadlock is an undesirable situation in which two different threads are waiting for each other, in such a way that they will wait forever. For example, if thread A has a lock for an object and is waiting for a lock held by thread B, but B is waiting for the lock on the object held by thread A, then a deadlock results. This can occur in the real world, say, if you play in a band and are waiting for permission to marry Mary; but Mary's parents are waiting for you to quit the band before they will give permission (this is the old days), but you can't quit until you marry Mary and the two of you can move to Colorado where you can find a new job. This is deadlock—semingly unresolvable!

To avoid deadlock, always obtain locks in the same sequence. In the case of Mary, you joined the band before you asked Mary to get married; but her parents, who apparently have a lock on Mary, have had that lock since Mary was born. You should try to obtain this lock in the same sequence as her parents: get Mary's lock before you get the "band lock." In other words, ask Mary to get married before you join the band. In the case of a Java application, design the application such that in case thread A ever needs access to two synchronized objects, make sure that every other thread accesses those objects in the same order A does. This strategy works if one assumes that each method has a means of completing and will not *explicitly* block for some resource.

Two Thread methods which are deadlock-prone are suspend() and resume(). The suspend() method causes a thread to explicitly go into a blocked state until some other thread calls the resume() method on the blocked thread. In the meantime, the blocked thread holds all of its locks. These methods have been deprecated in Java 2, so you should not use them.

The elimination of these methods does not prevent us from using the wait() method to write code that explicitly blocks and cannot be resumed. *The wait() method only releases the lock for the object instance on which it is called.* If the thread holds locks for other objects, it will not release them while it is waiting. This has nothing to do with calling order; it has to do with going to sleep while someone is waiting, and they can't call to wake you up because your phone is off the hook! Let's look at a Java example:

```
class Outer
{
   Inner inner = new Inner();
   Outer()
   {
      synchronized (this)
      {
         inner.selfishBlock();    // We are now blocked; the
                                  // current thread now holds
                                  // this object's lock, but has
                                  //  released inner's lock
      }
   }
   synchronized void wakeInnerUp()
   {
      // no thread can ever get this lock, because the waiting
      // thread holds it
      inner.notify();
   }
}
class Inner
{
   synchronized void selfishBlock()
   {
      wait();     // current thread releases inner's lock, but still
                  // holds all other locks - yet it is blocked
   }
}
```

A waiting thread only releases the lock of the object for which the wait was called. If the wait () call occurs inside synchronized code that holds a lock to another object, the notify () method had better not be called from that other object. In the above example, the class Inner is in a wait state; but it also holds Outer's lock, and Outer is the "telephone"—it has the only method that can be called to release the lock. Thus, no one can call, and Inner sleeps (waits) forever. This situation of an object explicitly waiting for a call to an object it has locked is called a "nested monitor."

A way around this is not to rely on Inner's phone; use the front door. Have an unsynchronized method in Outer that calls a synchronized method in Inner, to wake Inner up, to call notify(). The tip-off of a potential problem in the code above is the fact that wait() is called in an Inner method, and the corresponding notify() call occurs in an Outer method; they are in different classes. Here is a version that does not deadlock:

```
class Outer
{
   Inner inner = new Inner();
   Outer()
   {
      synchronized (this)
      {
         inner.selfishBlock();     // We are now blocked; the
                                   // current thread now holds
                                   // this object's lock, but has
                                   // released inner's lock
      }
   }
   void wakeInnerUp()
   {
      inner.wakeupBuddy();
   }
}
class Inner
{
   synchronized void selfishBlock()
   {
      wait();    // current thread releases inner's lock, but still
                 // holds all other locks - yet it is blocked
   }
   synchronized void wakeupBuddy()
   {
      notify();
   }
}
```

Any thread can call the wakeupBuddy() method, because it is not synchronized. This method can then successfully call the wakeupBuddy() method, which is synchronized, because the lock it needs is released.

## A Simple Multithreaded Server Application

Threads allow for lightweight servicing of concurrent client requests. The basic approach is to assign a separate thread to service each incoming request. Since

threads have access to the same virtual machine, care must be taken in the design of the service applications, and consideration should be given even to writing a security manager specific to the needs of the server application. (This is demonstrated in Chapter 4.)

The following program demonstrates a simple server application using threads. It is a "chat" server, which performs a simple function: it receives incoming text from each of multiple clients, and broadcasts all text received to *all* clients. If you like, you can embellish this program to provide logon identity and other features that are commonly found in real chat programs. The program consists of two classes: the server's main class and a thread class. Let us first look at the main class:

```
import java.util.*;
import java.net.*;
import java.io.*;
public class ChatServer
{
   public static void main(String[] args)
   {
      int port = 0;
      try { port = Integer.parseInt(args[0]); }
      catch (Exception ex) { System.out.println
         ("Must enter port no."); return;}
      ServerSocket ss = null;
      try
      {
         ss = new ServerSocket(port);
      }
      catch (Exception ex)
      {
         ex.printStackTrace();
         return;
      }
      ChatServer cs = new ChatServer();

      for (;;)   // ever
      {
         Socket s = null;
         try
         {
            s = ss.accept();  // blocks until next connection
                              // request
            SocketServiceThread t = new
               SocketServiceThread(s,cs);
            t.start();
         }
         catch (Exception ex)
```

```
            {
                ex.printStackTrace();
            }
        }
    }

    Vector instreams = new java.util.Vector();
    Vector outstreams = new java.util.Vector();
}
```

The first thing the server program does is attempt to create a server socket on a user-specified port for listening for incoming connection requests. Assuming this succeeds, it then creates an instance of its own class. The only reason it does this is to create a single object on which it will synchronize access to two data structures: a list of input streams and a list of output streams; the need for this will be clear shortly. It then enters an endless loop, in which it repeatedly blocks on an accept() call. The accept() returns when a new connection request has arrived, and the server then immediately allocates resources to service that request: it creates a new Java thread specifically for the request, and starts it. If requests were known to arrive at a high rate, a more sophisticated implementation could first enqueue the request and then reenter the accept(); the enqueued request could then be serviced by a separate queue manager thread. However, connection requests are a small part of the service demands for this application.

The threads that are created to service requests are defined as follows:

```
class SocketServiceThread extends Thread
{
    public SocketServiceThread(Socket s, ChatServer chatServer)
    {
        setDaemon(true);

        this.chatServer = chatServer;

        dis = new DataInputStream(s.getInputStream());
        ps = new PrintStream(s.getOutputStream(), true);

        synchronized (chatServer)
        {
            chatServer.instreams.addElement(dis);
            chatServer.outstreams.addElement(ps);
        }
    }

    public void run()
    {
```

```
         for (;;)   // ever
         {
            String data = "";
            try
            {
               data = dis.readLine();
            }
            catch (Exception ex) { data = null; }

            if (data == null)
            {
               synchronized(chatServer)
               {
                  int index =
                     chatServer.instreams.indexOf(dis);
                  PrintStream ps =
                  (PrintStream)(chatServer.outstreams.
                     elementAt(index));
                  ps.println();
                  ps.flush();
                  ps.close();
                  try { dis.close(); } catch
                     (IOException ex2) {}
                  chatServer.instreams.removeElementAt(index);
                  chatServer.outstreams.
                     removeElementAt(index);
               }
               stop();
            }
            // Write to all clients

            synchronized(chatServer)
            {
               for (int i = 0; i < chatServer.outstreams.size();
                  i++)   // all clients
               {
                  PrintStream ps =
                  (PrintStream)(chatServer.outstreams.
                     elementAt(i));
                  ps.println(data);
               }
            }
         }
      }

   private DataInputStream dis;
   private PrintStream ps;
}
```

When this thread is constructed, it first sets the daemon flag to true, to indicate that it is a daemon thread. This is desirable because if the main program thread terminates, we want all service threads to terminate as well. It then constructs streams to use for input and output on the socket that it is servicing. At this point, it adds these newly constructed streams to two lists. These lists are needed later when the thread needs to broadcast data to all other clients, and also when it needs to disconnect itself from a client. Since these lists are shared objects, used by all service threads, access to them must be synchronized. Furthermore, while it is true that the methods that operate on the Vector class, which is what we are using for our lists, are synchronized themselves, this is not sufficient, because we want operations that we perform on *both lists at the same time* to be atomic; we do not want the two lists to get out of sync, even for an instant. That is why we wrap accesses to both lists in synchronized blocks of code, and synchronize *on the object which owns (contains) the lists:* the instance of ChatServer.

This last point is an important point: you should either synchronize on the object you are trying to protect access to, or you should synchronize on an object that is a single identifiable owner of that object. Many other objects may have references to a protected object, and synchronizing them does not accomplish your goal of protecting access to the object. For example, consider a class D which references a class C:

```
class C
{
   Vector v = new Vector();
   public static void main(String[] args)
   {
      C c = new C();
      D d1 = new D(c);
      Thread t1 = new Thread(d1);
      D d2 = new D(c);
      Thread t2 = new Thread(d2);
      t1.start();
      t2.start();
   }
}

class D implements Runnable
{
   public D(C c)
   {
      this.c = c;
   }
   public void run()
   {
```

```
      // synchronized (this)  // Wrong - we are synchronizing on
                              // the wrong thing
      synchronized(c)         // Right - synchronize on the actual
                              // object being changed,
                              // or its logical composite parent.
      {
         c.value++;
      }
   }
   private C c;    // This object does not own this instance of C -
                   // it merely references it.
}
```

Each instance of D merely references a common instance of C. Synchronization therefore should be on the shared instance, since that is what must be protected, or on an object that is the single logical parent of the common instance. In the ChatServer example, the latter approach is used: access to the instreams and outstreams lists is serialized by synchronizing on the single object that owns both lists: the ChatServer object.

Returning to the ChatServer, the thread's run() method merely loops forever, blocking on a read of the socket's input stream. Whenever the read returns data, the thread scans the list of output streams and broadcasts the data to each. This operation must be synchronized, since one of the server sockets could close during this process, and the thread servicing it would then remove it from the list of output streams; this could change the position of elements in the list, at the same time as another thread is broadcasting. There is a flaw in this design, however—can you spot it? In many cases, where service time is short or the number of clients small, this approach is workable. In a high-throughput application with a large number of clients, however, it would be unacceptable to lock the client list while data is broadcast to all clients, which might take a long time compared to the normal time between the arrival of new data. A more scalable approach would be to first make a copy of the client list, in a synchronized fashion, and then release the list and use the copy, and make provisions for the fact that the copy might become out-of-date while we are using it. Thus, we might rewrite the last section of the class as:

```
class SocketServiceThread extends Thread
{
   ...

   public void run()
   {
      for (;;)    // ever
      {
```

```
            ...
            // Write to all clients

            java.util.Vector outstreams = null;
            //synchronized(chatServer)
            //{
               outstreams = chatServer.outstreams.clone();
            //}
            for (int i = 0; i < outstreams.size(); i++
                                          // all clients
            {
               try
               {
                  PrintStream ps =
                     (PrintStream)(outstreams.elementAt(i));
               }
               catch (ArrayIndexOutOfBoundsException ex)
               {
                  continue;
               }
               try
               {
                  ps.println(data);
               }
               catch (IOException ex)
               {
                  continue;
               }
            }
         }
      }

      ...
   }
```

Thus, we clone the chatServer.outstreams list of client output streams, and then use that list for determining to whom to broadcast. I have even commented out the synchronization specification, since the Vector.clone() method is synchronized and we only need to clone the outstreams list in this operation, not both lists.

The only difficulty lies in taking care of the possibility that the real list of outstreams may change while we are using the cloned list, so some of the outstreams may become invalid and some new ones be added that we will not know about. The price is a small one, since in this application failing to deliver a line of text to a newly arrived client is a very minor and acceptable failure, so we are not worried about not knowing of a new connection occurring during a broadcast. The other situation—that a connection may be terminated after we clone the list and before we complete the broadcast—will potentially result in the list ordering changing, and also a possible attempted broadcast to someone who is already disconnected. The list ordering is not important, since we are broadcasting the same thing to all clients (we might encounter an array index out of bounds exception, which we can catch), and a broadcast to a disconnected client will at most result in an IO exception, which we can also catch.

## Implementing a Thread Pool

These improvements work fine, but for large numbers of clients the system will start to run out of resources. A thousand clients would require a thousand connections and a thousand threads. This would not occur in a chat application (at least not in a single chat room—it would be a noisy chat room indeed!). However, it can occur in many transactional applications. Applications that require access to data, often intermittently, from large numbers of clients are designed as transaction-oriented instead of session-oriented to improve scalability. The application only needs to retain state about a client for the duration of a single transaction. With this simplification resources can be reused, including system threads.

Transaction-oriented applications may maintain a persistent connection to a server; but the server does not allocate processing resources until the client makes a request, and the resources are freed when the request has been serviced. For example, a DBMS requires the client to maintain a connection to the DBMS, but each transaction is serviced by a thread allocated for the duration of that transaction; or, if the transaction spans multiple queries, it may not even be the same thread. Another example is a CORBA ORB, which may maintain connections to a large number of clients, but may maintain a thread pool for servicing incoming remote call requests. It is then up to the application to retain any required client-specific state between requests.

### *A Producer-Consumer Thread Pool Model*

One way of implementing a thread pool is to view it as a set of consumer threads which service requests manufactured by a producer. The basic approach is:

- Create a producer: this is the main server object.
- Create *N* consumer thread objects; start each, and put each into a wait state.
- Loop: whenever a request comes in, create a new service object (includes the socket), add the object to a queue, and call notify().
- When a consumer thread object resumes, it attempts to get a single service object from the queue. If it fails, it goes back into a wait state. If it succeeds, it processes that object and then tries to get another object, or goes back into a wait state.

I will now explain an example implementation using this technique. For simplicity, I will assume a pool of a fixed (ungrowable) size. I will also assume that the calling routine manages client connections, and only invokes the pool manager when a new request arrives; that is, there is a new connection, or there is data on a connection. The client manager may be a single-threaded routine, looping until data is available on the socket's SocketImplementation. (There is unfortunately not an equivalent to the UNIX select() call, which blocks until there is either new data, or a new connection request.)

The PoolManager class (makes me think of summer days gone by) provides a server program with the required consumer functionality, to service manufactured (incoming) service requests. The entry point a server program would use is the PoolManager's service() method, which takes a Runnable object as a parameter. When this method is called, the PoolManager takes care of making sure that the object's run method is called in its own thread.

```
class PoolManager
{
   private ServiceThread[] threads;          // the thread pool
   private Vector serviceRequests = new Vector();
   public PoolManager(int noOfThreads)
   {
      threads = new ServiceThread[noOfThreads];
      // Create the thread pool
      for (int i = 0; i < threads.length; i++)
      {
         ServiceThread thread = new ServiceThread(this);
         threads[i] = thread;
         thread.start(); // this will start a separate thread,
                  // which will then call getObject() and block
      }
      // We can now be sure that all threads are created and are
      // in a blocked
      // state, waiting for us to call notify(). That is what
      // service() does.
   }

   /**
    * This method is the entry point for the server's main
    * routine, whenever it wants to pass us a Runnable object
    * to service in a thread.
    */

   public synchronized void service(Runnable object)
   {
      serviceRequests.addElement(object);
```

```
        notify();
    }

    /**
     * This is the method that our service threads call in order to
     * get new Runnable
     * objects to service; these threads block in this call until
     * the above service()
     * method results in a notify to one of them.
     */

    public synchronized Object getObject()
    throws InterruptedException
    {
        while (true)
        {
            try
            {
                Object o = serviceRequests.firstElement();
                serviceRequests.removeElementAt(0);
                return o;
            } catch (Exception ex) { wait(); }
        }
    }
    /**
     * Gracefully stop the threads in the thread pool.
     */

    public void finalize()
    {
        // Stop all the threads that are not blocked...
        for (int i = 0; i < threads.length; i++)
        {
            if (threads[i].isAlive()) threads[i].stop();
        }
    }
}
```

The getObject() method is called by service threads waiting in the pool when they want another object to service. This method blocks those threads until a notify() wakes one of them up, at which point the awaken thread can check if an object is available to be serviced; if not, it goes back into a wait state. If an object is available, it returns, and the thread's run() method proceeds and calls the object's run() method. When the object's run() method returns, the thread's run() method loops back to the getObject() call.

The finalize() method above takes care of graceful termination of service threads. A more complete implementation would not call stop(), but would signal the service threads to terminate, and join() on those threads, as illustrated earlier in this chapter.

The ServiceThread class is the thread class for the threads used to service requests. Its run() method contains a loop, as just described. This loop executes forever, repeatedly blocking on a getObject() call, and then calling the returned object's run() method.

```
class ServiceThread extends Thread
{
   private Runnable object;
   private PoolManager poolManager;
   public ServiceThread(PoolManager pm)
   {
      poolManager = pm;
   }
   public synchronized void run()
   {
      for (;;)
         // ever
      {
         //
         // Wait to be notified; blocks until an object is
         // returned
         //
         try
         {
            object = (Runnable)(poolManager.getObject());
         }
         catch (InterruptedException ex)
         {
         }
         //
         // Do the callback, at the specified priority
         //
         try
         {
            if (object != null) object.run();
         }
         catch (ThreadDeath td)    // We simply want the thread to
                                   // go back to the pool
         {
         }
         catch (Throwable t)   // Exception "firewall"
         {
```

```
                t.printStackTrace();
            }
            finally
            {
                object = null;     // Allow runnable object to be
                                   // collected and finalized
            }
        }
    }
}
```

### *A Thread Assignment Model*

A problem with the previous implementation is that you don't know if the service request is being handled right away. In particular, if there are not enough threads in the thread pool, there is no way to find out—the notify() method will fall on deaf ears. In that case, the request will not be serviced until another thread is done. You also cannot control or manage priority changes if you want to, since thread allocation is handled completely automatically by the Java VM.

You can take direct control of thread assignment to service requests by implementing your own thread allocation mechanism. Here is an implementation that does not rely on notify() to select a thread. The changes from the previous pool implementation are indicated in bold.

```
class PoolManager
{
    private ServiceThread[] threads;    // the thread pool
    private boolean[] allocated; // allocation flag for each thread
    public PoolManager(int noOfThreads)
    {
        threads = new ServiceThread[noOfThreads];
        allocated = new boolean[noOfThreads];
```

Above I have added a set of flags to indicate if a given thread in the pool is assigned or not. The next section of code gets a little more complicated, because we have to take care of the situation in which our threads no longer call getObject(). Instead, we need to cause the threads to start, and then block on a wait() from which we can extricate any particular one of them. We must be careful to know the state of all threads before we allow any of them to be allocated to a service request. To accomplish this, the following code must block after each thread's start() method is called, until the thread signals that it has started and is waiting.

```
        // Create the thread pool
        for (int i = 0; i < threads.length; i++)
        {
           allocated[i] = false;
           ServiceThread thread = new ServiceThread(this);
           threads[i] = thread;
           synchronized (thread)
           {
              thread.start();    // this will start a separate
                 // thread, which will then call wait() and
                 // block (which releases its monitor so
                 // we can get past the next line)
              try
              {
                 thread.wait();    // this blocks until the thread
                 // calls notify() and then blocks (which
                 // releases its monitor,
                 // allowing this statement to return)
              }
              catch (InterruptedException ex)
              {
              }
           }
        }
        // We can now be sure that all threads are created and are
        // in a blocked
        // state, waiting for us to call notify(). That is what
        // allocate() does.
     }
```

The following method replaces the service() method in the previous implementation. Its purpose is to allocate a thread from the pool, and cause that thread to execute the passed object's run() method. This routine immediately returns with a reference to the thread used to service the object. This thread reference could be used in a more advanced implementation to perform thread management functions, such as changing the thread's priority or unscheduling the thread. (These features will be seen in the next example.) Note also that this routine can throw an exception type I have defined, InsufficientThreadsException, indicating that there are not enough threads to service the request. A more complete implementation, which is left to the reader to implement, would dynamically grow the thread pool.

```
public synchronized ServiceThread allocate(Runnable object)
throws
   InsufficientThreadsException
{
   // Pick a thread from the thread pool
   ServiceThread thread = allocateAThread();
   if (thread == null) throw new
      InsufficientThreadsException();
   // Allocate that thread
   thread.allocate(object);
   // Return a unique identifier for the thread
   return thread;
}

/**
* Allocate a thread from the thread pool.
 */

protected ServiceThread allocateAThread()
{
   for (int i = 0; i < threads.length; i++)
   {
      if (allocated[i]) continue;
      allocated[i] = true;
      return threads[i];
   }

   return null;
}
```

The following method returns a thread to the thread pool. The service threads automatically call this after they have completed servicing a request.

```
/**
 * Return a thread to the thread pool.
 * This method must be synchronized in case multiple threads in
 * an application
 * call this method for this Scheduler object, and also because
 * threads call
 * this to return themselves to the thread pool.
 */

public synchronized void deallocateThread(ServiceThread thread)
{
   for (int i = 0; i < threads.length; i++)
   {
      if (threads[i] == thread)
```

```
            {
               allocated[i] = false;
               return;
            }
         }
      }
      /**
       * Gracefully stop the threads in the thread pool.
       */

      public void finalize()
      {
         // Stop all the threads that are not blocked...
         for (int i = 0; i < threads.length; i++)
         {
            if (threads[i].isAlive()) threads[i].stop();
         }
      }
   }
   class ServiceThread extends Thread
   {
      private Runnable object;
      private PoolManager pm;

      public ServiceThread(PoolManager pm)
      {
         poolManager = pm;
      }
```

The following method is the method called by the PoolManager to allocate this thread to a service object. It has the effect of bringing the thread out of the wait state into which it puts itself below in the run() method.

```
      public synchronized void allocate(Runnable object)
      {
         this.object = object;
         // Now, resume this thread
         notify();
      }
      public synchronized void run()
      {
         notify(); // this merely notifies the pool manager, which is
                   // waiting to be notified, that it should
                   // unfreeze itself in the thread's
                   // monitor queue. This helps to ensure that all
                   // threads have been started before the
                   // PoolManager starts allocating them.
```

```
        for (;;)
           // ever
        {
           //
           // Wait to be called upon; blocks until a call to
           // allocate() results in a notify()
           //

           try
           {
              wait();
           }
           catch (InterruptedException ex)
           {
           }

           //
           // Do the callback, at the specified priority
           //
           try
           {
              object.run();
           }
           catch (ThreadDeath td)    // We simply want the thread to
                                     // go back to the pool
           {
           }
           catch (Throwable t)    // Exception "firewall"
           {
              t.printStackTrace();
           }
           finally
           {
              object = null;    // Allow runnable object to be
                                // collected and finalized
           }

           //
           // Thread's work is done; return it to the pool
           //

           poolManager.deallocateThread(this);
        }
     }
  }
```

```
/**
 * If there are insufficient threads in the thread pool.
 */
class InsufficientThreadsException extends Exception {}
```

## Implementing a Thread-Based Service Scheduler

A service scheduler is a server application which allows clients to schedule processing to occur at a future time. An example of such a requirement is the UNIX cron utility. Ideally, a scheduler allows you to not only schedule processing, but unschedule it as well if circumstances change. (The algorithm employed for this kind of application is very similar to a discrete event simulator, which schedules and unschedules future events in a synchronous way.)

We can extend the thread pool manager developed in the previous section to provide thread scheduling. We have the basic framework; a thread pool manager is just a special case of a scheduler in which threads are scheduled to service requests immediately instead of at a future time. What we must add to create a true scheduler is delayed servicing, and also the ability to unschedule a service that has already been scheduled. We can also add some additional features to make the scheduler more functional, such as variable service thread priority, an application-specific service argument, and a feature for scheduling services that recur at regular intervals.

To implement this, we only have to make a few additions to the previous implementation. Most of the program is very similar to the previous one, so I will only present the changes. First of all, I will rename the class "Scheduler," since that is more descriptive of its new purpose.

Next, instead of requiring service objects to implement the Runnable interface, I will define a new interface, more appropriate for a schedulable object:

```
/**
 * Callback object interface.
 */

interface Schedulable
{
   public void onEvent(Object arg);
   public void onAbort();
}
```

The onEvent() method will be called by the scheduler when a future scheduled event arrives, and the onAbort() method will be called when an exception of any type occurs while the event is being serviced.

Next I will rename the allocate() method to schedule(), and give it this implementation:

```
/**
 * Schedule thread to run at a future time.
 * The Schedulable.onEvent() method will be called for object
 * after a real-time delay of "delay" milliseconds.
 * The thread's handle is returned, which
 * we can later use to reschedule the thread.
 * If "recurring" is true, then a new event will be scheduled
 * automatically each time onEvent() is called.
 * This method must be synchronized in case multiple threads in
 * an application call this method for this Scheduler object.
 */

public synchronized EventThread schedule(long delay,
   Schedulable object, Object arg, int priority, boolean
   recurring)
throws
   InsufficientThreadsException
{
   // Pick a thread from the thread pool
   EventThread thread = allocateAThread();
   if (thread == null) throw new
      InsufficientThreadsException();

   // Schedule an event for that thread
   thread.schedule(delay, object, arg, priority, recurring);

   // Return a unique identifier for the event
   return thread;
}
```

As you can see, there are parameters for a time delay and an execution priority. I will also define a reschedule() method as follows:

```
/**
 * Unschedule the future event for a thread, and reschedule it.
 */
public void reschedule(EventThread thread, long delay,
   Schedulable object, Object arg, int priority, boolean
   recurring)
throws
   InsufficientThreadsException
{
   thread.reschedule(delay, object, arg, priority, recurring);
}
```

The above method can be used to reschedule future events that have already been scheduled. This is important, since it is often the case that scheduled processing must be unscheduled or moved to a new time. The rest of this class is the same as before.

I will now modify the EventThread class by adding these class variables to it:

```
private long delay;          // wait for this time
private Object arg;          // a parameter for onEvent()
private int priority;        // execute onEvent() at
                             // this priority
private boolean recurring;   // reschedule the event every
                             // time
```

and redefining its allocate() method—which I will also rename "schedule"—as follows:

```
public synchronized void schedule(long delay, Schedulable
   object, Object arg, int priority, boolean recurring)
{
   this.object = object;
   this.delay = delay;
   this.arg = arg;
   this.priority = priority;
   this.recurring = recurring;

   // Now, resume this thread to tell it how long to wait for
   notify();
}
```

I will also give this class an unschedule() method.

```
/**
 * Reschedule this Thread object. Note that this will be called
 * from a different thread.
 */
public synchronized void reschedule(long delay, Schedulable
   object, Object arg, int priority, boolean recurring)
throws
   InsufficientThreadsException
{
   // stop(new InterruptedException());   // This was the only
                                          // way in JDK 1.0
   interrupt();                           // This is the
                                          // right way
   try
```

```
      {
         wait();// wait until the stopped thread blocks
      }
      catch (InterruptedException ex)
      {
      }
      schedule(delay, object, arg, priority, recurring);

}
```

I will re-implement the run() method as follows:

```
   public synchronized void run()
   {
      notify();    // this merely notifies the scheduler, which is
                   // waiting to be notified,
                   // that it should unfreeze itself
                   // in the thread's monitor queue.

      for (;;)
         // ever
      {
         //
         // Wait to be called upon; blocks until a call to
         // schedule() results in a notify()
         //

         try
         {
         if (! recurring) wait();
         }
         catch (InterruptedException ex)
         {
         }

         //
         // Sleep until the specified time has elapsed
         //

         try
         {
            // This is the real wait, requested by the
            // scheduler
            wait(delay);
         }
         catch (InterruptedException ex)
         {
            // We are being rescheduled: abort the current
            // sleep
```

```
                recurring = false;
                notify();
                continue;
            }

            //
            // Do the callback, at the specified priority
            //
            int savep = getPriority();
            setPriority(priority);
            try
            {
                object.onEvent(arg);
            }
            catch (ThreadDeath td)
            {
                try
                {
                    object.onAbort();
                }
                catch (Throwable ta    // Exception firewall
                {
                    ta.printStackTrace();
                }
            }
            catch (Throwable t         // Exception firewall
            {
                t.printStackTrace();
            }
            finally
            {
                object = null;
            }
            setPriority(savep);
            //
            // Thread's work is done; return it to the pool
            //

            if (! recurring) scheduler.deallocateThread(this);
        }
    }
}
```

The main change to the run() method is the division of processing into two steps: a delay step, which effects the time delay, and a service step, which actually invokes the service object's onEvent() method. The delay step must accommodate the possiblity that the event gets rescheduled, by catching InterruptedException and performing a `continue` to go back to the start of the loop and back into a wait state. I have also added a "recurring" feature for events that need to occur at regular intervals: the schedule method has a boolean argument which is set to true for recurring events, and in that case the event occurs again and again after the passage of the specified time period.

## Thread-Local Variables

Java 2 has a new feature, called "thread-local" variables, which provides a convenient mechanism for implementing multithreaded programs that must service an arbitrary number of clients and be stateful. It allows you to defer the replication of your object data until the moment at which a new thread actually enters your code. For example,

```
public class MyClass
{
   private static ThreadLocal myData = new ThreadLocal()
   {
      protected Object initialize()
         // called when a new thread accesses this thread local
      {
         return new SomethingOrOther(...);
      }
   };

   public synchronized void doStuff()    // some method that many
                                         // threads may call
   {
      ...
      SomethingOrOther soo = (SomethingOrOther) (myData.get());
      ...
   }
}
```

If we then create an instance of MyClass and call its doStuff() method, then the instance's initialize() method gets called. If we subsequently call doStuff() again from the same thread, initialize() is *not* called. However, if we call doStuff() on the object from a different thread, initialize() will be called, and each thread will have its own instance data—its own copy of SomethingOrOther. Thus, each thread will be operating on a different SomethingOrOther when it calls doStuff, even though both threads access a single instance of MyClass.

The advantage of this approach is that we did not have to anticipate in the design of our thread class that we would want to have a copy of SomethingOrOther for each thread instance—we added that later to the reentrant doStuff() method, just by declaring a ThreadLocal variable.

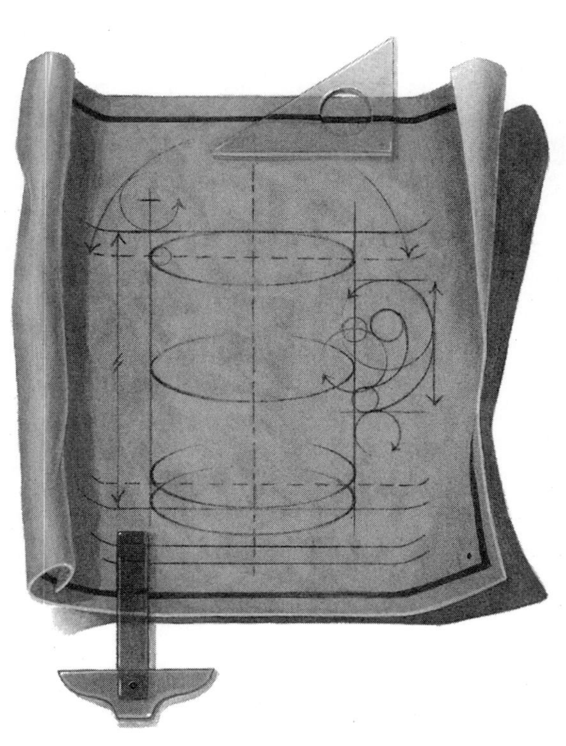

# CHAPTER 4

# Java Security

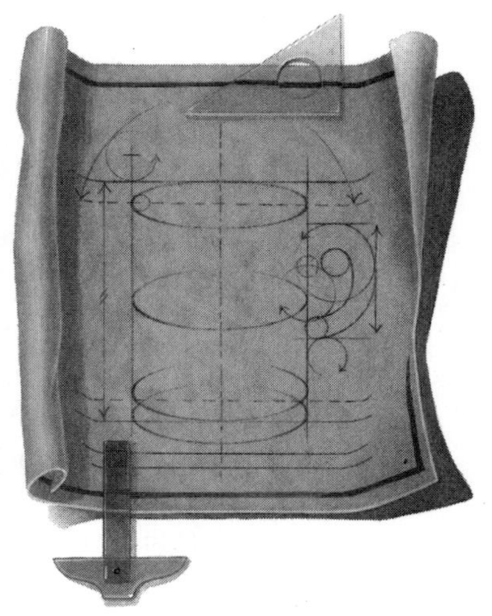

**S**ecurity is the first concern of any serious large-scale application. Business applications invariably convey sensitive information, to which access must be authorized. Mission-critical systems must further be protected against the destruction or theft of information. Single-user systems must also be protected, because in the aggregate they constitute a large part of the business computing environment.

Security concerns for business applications generally fall into these domains:

- *Security of content*—The protection of *information at its point of origin,* prior to transmission or retrieval
- *Security of communications*—The protection of *transmitted information* against theft or modification while in transit or being retrieved
- *Security of the corporate computing infrastructure*—The protection of *the local environment* from the actions of newly installed content after transmission and acceptance into the local environment

Within *each* of these three domains, there is a need to:

- *Establish proof of identity*: The source and destination of the information are who they say they are.
- *Establish proof of information integrity:* The information has not been altered since the originator created it.
- *Ensure privacy:* The information cannot be read by an unauthorized party.

The specific needs and emphasis on each of the above depend on the application and the environment. Java provides an extremely secure base infrastructure from which applications that have all of the above requirements can be met. This security derives from the fundamental design of the Java Virtual Machine, and from the extensive security features of the standard and extended APIs.

The subject of security is very complex; however, it should not be necessary for a developer to read several books on encryption and security before being able to grasp what is important, and how the APIs fit together. The goal of this chapter is therefore to make sense of these different Java APIs and aspects of Java security to the extent necessary to evaluate and apply them. To accomplish that, it is necessary to provide a background on many security fundamentals—some very new, and some long-established.

Before proceeding, I should stress that the term "secure" means different things to different people. To the average person—who thinks nothing of signing a credit card imprint in a restaurant and leaving it behind in the hands of restaurant staff—the definition of "secure" is far different than what the National Security Agency means when it uses the term "secure." In this book, which focuses on Java applications that use security, the term "secure" is relative to the levels of security that are commonly expected and tolerated in business and commercial applications.

## Data Encryption, Keys, and Certificates

Encryption is the process of converting data from a readable form to an unreadable form, such that only the intended recipient knows how to reconvert it back into a readable form. This is usually accomplished by inputting the readable information into an algorithm for encryption. The information is then transported to the recipient, by any means, and the recipient then inputs the received encrypted information into an algorithm that reverses—*decrypts*—the encrypted information, thereby retrieving the original text.

Encryption is the primary means used to transmit data securely over the Internet. The reason is that since the Internet is a public network, it is not possible to rely on exclusive use of network equipment or lines to separate one's data from the outside world; one has little control over which routers a message will pass through before reaching its destination, and who might be capturing or analyzing messages which pass through that equipment. Therefore, it is necessary to make sensitive data unintelligible to all but the sender and the receiver, and this is the role encryption plays.

In addition to encrypting the data, it is necessary to make sure that the data is being received from or sent to the right party, not an impostor; it may also be nec-

essary in some circumstances to prove after the fact that a particular party *did* take part in a communication or transaction. It is therefore often important, for a variety of reasons, to authenticate one or both parties when communicating. The primary mechanisms used for authentication are passwords, digital certificates, and physical identification tokens.

A digital certificate is an electronic document, conforming to a well-defined standard, which contains verifiably correct information. I will discuss the kinds of certificates that are important for Java applications, including what is inside of certificates and what they are used for.

Encryption algorithms fall into two main categories: symmetric and asymmetric key encryption, and I will start by discussing these. I will explain the techniques used for exchanging cryptographic keys, and the practical legal restrictions that exist for using cryptographic keys and cryptography. I will then explain some of the implementations that use these techniques, including SSL, CORBA, and various Java deployment platforms.

### Symmetric Key Encryption

Symmetric key encryption algorithms are used to achieve efficient high-throughput encryption of information. For example, a symmetric key algorithm would be used to implement encryption for a secure socket stream connection to transmit arbitrarily large amounts of data securely. A symmetric key algorithm uses a single key for both encryption and decryption, and therefore both parties—the sender and the recipient—must have privately exchanged this key ahead of time, by some other means. This kind of key is usually referred to as a "secret key." Figure 4-1 depicts encryption and decryption using a secret key.

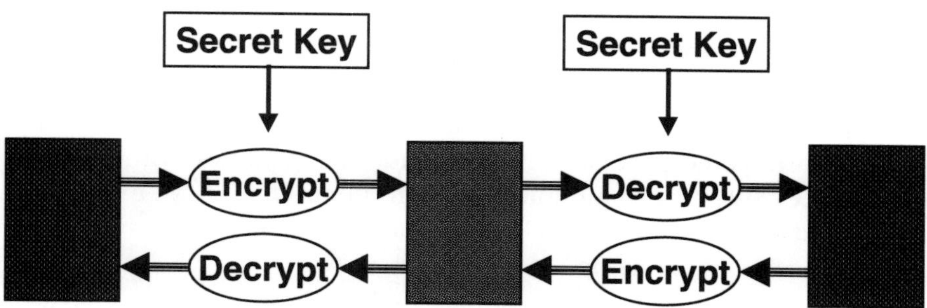


**Figure 4-1** Encrypted communication with a symmetric key.

**Symmetric Key Algorithms.** Symmetric encryption algorithms generally fall into the categories of block ciphers and stream ciphers. A block cipher takes as input a block of information at a time, whereas a stream cipher operates on a stream of input data a byte at a time. Here is a list of some of the more prevalent symmetric encryption algorithms.

**DES** Data Encryption Standard; U.S. government standard. It is a block cipher, normally used with a 56-bit key. Recently it has been broken through brute force methods in less than 24 hours using ordinary networked computers, and so it is no longer considered secure for very sensitive data. **Triple-DES (3DES)**, which is currently the algorithm of choice in banking and secure Internet Mail (S/MIME), applies the algorithm three times, resulting in an encryption that is approximately twice as hard to break. DES is defined by the NIST in FIPS 46-1 and 46-2. Recently 3DES has also been shown to be no stronger than DES under certain conditions.

**RC2** A block cipher that was a trade secret of RSA Data Security until very recently (they published it in 1997; however, the algorithm had been anonymously published prior to that).

**RC4** A stream cipher. This was a trade secret of RSA Data Security; however, it was also anonymously published. RSA still considers it proprietary.

**RC5** A block cipher, published and patented by RSA.

**IDEA** The International Data Encryption Algorithm (IDEA) from ASCOM Systec, Switzerland; used by the Pretty Good Privacy (PGP) system; patented.

In addition, the U.S. government (through NIST) is leading an effort to develop a new algorithm, to be an open and nonproprietary standard, called the Advanced Encryption Standard (AES), to replace DES. At the time of this writing, the candidate algorithms are being evaluated.

### *Public Key Encryption*

A public key encryption algorithm requires two different keys. One key is typically designated the "private key," the other the "public key." The public key can be revealed to parties other than one of the communicating parties, without compromising the security of the communication. Algorithms which have two keys are often referred to as "asymmetric" algorithms, and the public and private key pair are referred to as "asymmetric keys."

The important characteristic of public key encryption algorithms is that if data is encrypted using one of these two keys, it can only be decrypted with the other. Thus, for example, if you have a pair of asymmetric encryption keys, you can give one of them to other people to encrypt messages to be sent to you, and then only you will be able to decrypt them by using the other key, which you have not given out.

The advantage of asymmetric encryption is therefore that you can send the encryption key using unsecure means, knowing that the party who receives it will be able to send secret messages to you that only you can decipher. This does not prevent someone else, however, from receiving the key and forging messages, pretending to be the other party. If you exchange keys via an unsecure means, it is therefore necessary to *authenticate* the messages subsequently sent to you (i.e., prove that they are all from the intended party).

Asymmetric keys are usually used in such a way that each party has a separate public and private key pair and they exchange their public keys using any (unsecure) means. In practice, however, this technique is used only to transmit small amounts of data, since it is computationally inefficient compared to symmetric algorithms. For example, the Secure Socket Layer (SSL) protocol first allows both parties to exchange a secret (symmetric) key by transmitting it securely using asymmetric encryption or a secret key exchange algorithm. Once the parties both know what the symmetric secret key is, they use it for all subsequent communication during that session; the symmetric secret key is referred to as a "session key." (Note: the details are more complex; SSL actually uses multiple keys, but that is not important for this discussion.) Figure 4-2 illustrates encryption and decryption using a public key algorithm.

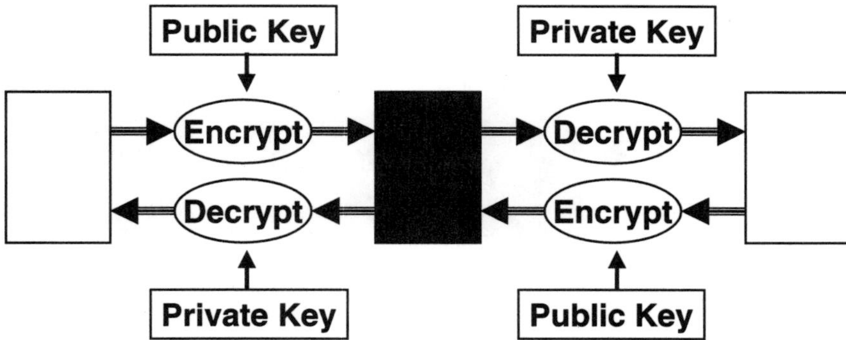


**Figure 4-2** Encrypted communication with public and private keys.

In addition to asymmetric encryption algorithms, there are other kinds of asymmetric key algorithms, including signature algorithms and key exchange algorithms.

A signature algorithm is a one-way encryption algorithm which allows you to create and verify a digital signature. One key (the private key) is used for signing, and the other (the public key) is used for verifying. A key exchange algorithm is an algorithm which allows two parties to cooperatively compute a common symmetric key, without directly exchanging that key. Examples of these techniques will be discussed under "Asymmetric Key Algorithms" on page 198.

### *Asymmetric Keys for Authentication*

In addition to encrypted transport of symmetric keys and other small amounts of information, asymmetric encryption can be used for authentication. The concept is as follows: if one of your asymmetric keys is known only to you (i.e., is private), only you will be able to generate messages that can be decrypted with the other key. The other key can be made public, and given to others for the purpose of authenticating your messages.

All you need to do is send a short message encrypted with your private key, and the mere fact that others can decrypt it proves that the message originated from you. (This assumes that no one has stolen your private key!) In this situation, the authentication message is something that you want others to be able to decrypt—it is not private—so you use your private key to encrypt it so that others can use your public key to decrypt it. If you wanted to send encrypted information, you would instead use the recipient's public key to encrypt it so that only they could decrypt it. The authentication process is shown in Figure 4-3.

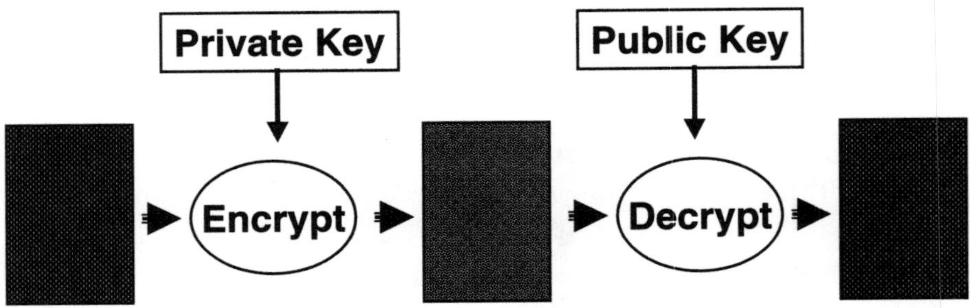


**Figure 4-3** Authentication (proof of identity): they use your public key to decrypt a signature.

There is still the risk that someone could intercept your authentication message and then use it later to pretend to be you. Recipients would receive a message purporting to be from you, encrypted with your private key—the very same message you sent some time before. They may believe it, or instead this "replay" attack can be protected against by challenging you, issuing you the command: "If you are who you say you are, then encrypt this for me," followed by a random[1]

1. Ordinarily you would add some data of your own to their random message, in effect saying "this is a test," otherwise, they could dupe you by asking you to sign something that they can then pass off as authenticated by you.

message for you to encrypt. If you can encrypt a message randomly constructed by the other party on demand, and they can decrypt it using your public key, then indeed you must be the holder of the private key.

In the scenario just described, we used authentication to prove the identity of a party in a communication. Suppose instead you want to prove that an item of data is authentic, regardless of who is sending it? A piece of data which has the ability to authenticate itself could be sent around within a network, and even posted for general use. Users of the data could use the data without fear that it had been altered. Data can be authenticated by attaching to it a verifiable encrypted signature of the data. A signature is an encrypted hash value that is a function of the data itself, and if it is encrypted using the private key of the data's creator, users who have the public key can decrypt it and compare the signature with a recomputed hash of the data. Thus, users need to know the public key and the hash algorithm.

### *Message Digests*

The hash functions used in signatures are often called "message digests," or simply "digests" for short. They are algorithms which take a message of arbitrary length as input, and produce a (usually fixed-length) numeric value. Properties of good hash algorithms include irreversibility: the practical impossibility of finding one or more input messages that produces a given hash value; apparent randomness, such that the input acts like a random number seed, and even the tiniest change in the input results in an output with no similarity to the previous value; and the near impossibility of finding *collisions*, or two messages that have the same hash value. These properties are important for applications where a hash value is used to represent or identify a piece of data, but should not reveal anything about the data, and to be able to prove message validity.

Some of the more important message digest algorithms include:

**Secure Hash Algorithm-1 (SHA-1)**—Developed by the U.S. government, it takes as input a message of arbitrary length and produces as output a 160-bit "hash" of the input. SHA-1 is fully described in FIPS 180-1. IETF has selected SHA-1 as the preferred one-way hash function for the Internet Public Key Infrastructure (PKI).

**Message Digest 2 (MD2)**—This is used by privacy enhanced mail (PEM) for certificates [RFC 1422] [RFC 1423] [RFC 1319]; now considered obsolete for new uses.

**Message Digest 5 (MD5)**—Used in many existing applications (including Marimba's Castanet), it was developed by Ron Rivest in 1991. It takes an input message of arbitrary length and produces a 128-bit hash result, specified in RFC 1321. At this time, the algorithm appears to have potential weaknesses, so new uses are not recommended.

### *Asymmetric Key Algorithms*

The most widely used asymmetric key algorithms in use today are the DSA, RSA, and Diffie-Hellman algorithms. These are used for two primary purposes: implementing symmetric key exchange or negotiation, and as a digital signature.

**Digital Signature Standard (DSS) and Digital Signature Algorithm (DSA).** The terms DSS and DSA are often used interchangeably. The DSA algorithm is defined in Digital Signature Standard, NIST FIPS 186, and was developed by the U.S. government. It is a digital signature algorithm that uses the RawDSA asymmetric transformation (also described in FIPS 186) along with the SHA-1 message digest algorithm.

When signing, the DSA algorithm generates two values. These values are commonly referred to as "r" and "s." X.509 v3 certificates represent these as a sequence of two integers, and together they represent the signature. The s value is a function of the private key used, which is a random number, and of a 160-bit SHA digest of the message being signed; and the r value is a function of a random number and prime modulus and divisor. The signature can later be proved to be valid by checking that it satisfies certain equations involving the public key, which is itself a function of the private key. The verification algorithm also needs to know the values of three public parameters, known as "p," "q," and "g," used when signing.

One aspect of this algorithm is that it is designed specifically for signing. Unlike the RSA algorithm, you cannot use DSA for encrypting data, only for verifying it. Nor can you use a private key as a public key, and vice versa—a DSA private key can only be used as a private key, and a DSA public key can only play the role of a public key. For this reason, DSA is often described as a "one-way" or "irreversible" algorithm.

The U.S. government holds patent 5,231,668 on the Digital Signature Algorithm (DSA), which has been incorporated into Federal Information Processing Standard (FIPS) 186. The patent was issued on July 27, 1993. However, NIST has stated publicly that DSA is available "royalty-free to users worldwide."

**RSA (Rivest, Shamir, and Adleman).** The RSA asymmetric key encryption algorithm is the predominant public key algorithm used worldwide. Unlike DSA, the RSA algorithm can be used for either signing or encryption. Furthermore, it is bidirectional, in that a public key can decrypt messages encrypted with the private key, and vice versa. A key is composed of a set of two numbers, known as the "modulus" and the "exponent." Thus, a private key consists of a modulus and a "private" exponent, and a public key consists of the same modulus and a "public" exponent. No other parameters need be known to decrypt messages or perform verification.

The RSA algorithm, which is described in RSA Laboratory (http://www.rsa.com) Technical Note PKCS#1, is typically used in combination with either the MD2, MD5, or SHA-1 message digest algorithms for computing digital signatures.

The patent for the RSA algorithm is actually owned by the Massachusetts Institute of Technology, which has granted RSA Data Security, Inc., exclusive sublicensing rights. The patent (U.S. patent no. 4,405,829) expires on September 20, 2000. This patent is not recognized in Europe, which has led to widespread use of the algorithm there.

The Internet Engineering Task Force (IETF) has specified RSA as an algorithm for digital signatures in its PKIX standard. Therefore, those who implement products using the PKIX standard may be required to obtain a license from RSA. RSA has stated a policy of granting nonexclusive licenses to users of the patent, with royalties currently computed at 2% of the selling price of a product that makes use of the patent (of course, subject to change). Normally, of course, you would obtain a cryptographic package that includes an RSA license. RSA itself markets such a package for Java applications, called Crypto-J.

An interesting development has occurred at the time of this writing. Quite amazingly Security Dynamics, the parent company of RSA Data Security, has asked the cryptography community to stop using the term "RSA" to refer to the RSA algorithm, so that they can apply for trademark status of the term. The creators of the RSA algorithm were researchers. Imagine if other researchers did this: Euler's Number would not be Euler's Number; a Laplace Transform would not be a Laplace Transform; and Moore's Law would not be Moore's Law—because he and others had all trademarked their names!

The result of this ridiculous situation is that alternative names are now being proposed. You can expect there to be some confusion about the term "RSA" until this is sorted out, and it appears possible that the term itself may be replaced. At this time, the Java Software division of Sun has no plans to rename any of its RSA-related security algorithm names.

**Diffie-Hellman (DH) Key Agreement.** The Diffie-Hellman key agreement protocol is different from RSA and DSA in that it is not intended for encryption or verification; its purpose is to allow two parties to exchange a symmetric key without actually transmitting the value of the key.

The algorithm works as follows. Consider a function $f(g, x)$ known to two parties, A and B, wishing to exchange a secret, and assume that the value of $g$ is a nonsecret algorithm parameter known to both parties. Suppose also that A has a secret key, $a$, known only to A, and that similarly B has a secret key, $b$, known only to B.

Both parties now apply the known (and public) formula *f(g, x)*, supplying their secret key for *x*, and they exchange their results.

```
A computes ka = f(g,a), and sends this to B.
B computes kb = f(g,b), and sends this to A.
```

Both parties now apply the formula again, but this time substituting the value they were sent for the parameter g:

```
A now computes Ka = f(kb, a) = f(f(g,b), a)
B now computes Kb = f(ka, b) = f(f(g,a), b)
```

If $f(g,x)$ has the property that $f(f(g,a), b) = f(f(g,b), a)$ for any *a* and *b*, then both recipients have in fact computed the same value (i.e., Ka = *K*b)—this is their *shared* secret key—but no one else can know the value, because no one else knows either secret key (*a* or *b*), and the information publicly exchanged cannot be used to reverse-compute *a* or *b*.

A function that has the property specified above is exponentiation: ((*g* exp *a*) exp *b*) has the same result as ((*g* exp *b*) exp *a*) for any *a* and *b*; these are equivalent to (g exp (*a* * *b*)). Exponentiation is therefore used as the function; in order to bound the value to a certain size, the computation is done modulus a large number, which is chosen as a prime.

The algorithmic parameters that need to be specified are therefore the modulus and *g*, which for various mathematical reasons is required to be a primitive root of the modulus. The values for *a* and *b* can be chosen at random. This is an important fact, because it means that they can be unique for each session, and do not need to be stored. In other words, the Diffie-Hellman key agreement algorithm does not require that a private key of any kind be maintained, so there is no risk that a private key might be discovered over time. This is one reason that it is increasingly becoming an algorithm of choice in new Internet standards.

A variation of the technique, called "ephemeral Diffie-Hellman," is used when the public parameters (the modulus and the value of *g*) are not known ahead of time. In this case, one party can specify the values to be used for the parameters, and sign the specification. As long as the other party can authenticate the signed parameter specification, these parameters can then be trusted as originating from the communicating party, and used to perform the key agreement algorithm. Any signing algorithm, such as DSA or RSA, can be used to sign the parameter specification. (The reason for being so careful about making sure the parameters originate from a trusted party is that you do not want to take a chance that someone might give you a unique set of parameters which have a mathematical property that can be exploited to more easily guess your session key.)

The Diffie-Hellman key agreement algorithm is covered by patent no. 4,200,770, which expired on August 19, 1997.

**Elliptic Curves.** Elliptic curve algorithms are a class of algorithms that are just starting to come into use. At present, few products use elliptic curve algorithms, but this may change. Some standards under development related to elliptic curves are ANSI X9.62 and ANSI X9.63, and IEEE P1363.

### *Import and Export Laws*

Applications and software that are deployed via the Internet can reach any location in the world. It is therefore important to have a basic understanding of the restrictions that exist regarding the transport of encryption software, since encryption is a major component of most software that provides security features.

**The United States.** The export of cryptographic software from the United States is regulated by the U. S. Department of Commerce, Bureau of Export Administration (BXA). Posting or distributing cryptographic software on the Internet is considered to be exporting, unless you have a means of preventing foreigners from accessing it (e.g., by verifying that their host is located within the United States). This includes any software that bundles cryptographic packages.

The policy for exporting authentication-related algorithms is more lenient than for exporting encryption, and the BXA is willing to review applications on a case-by-case basis. The current guidelines limit asymmetric keys to 1024 bits. The restriction for symmetric keys is 56 bits.

Financial institutions, foreign subsidiaries of U.S. companies, health and medical organizations, and on-line merchants can apply for an exception for any key length. It should be pointed out that regardless of whether a product fits any of these criteria, an encryption exporter must still apply for a license, unless the encryption product is already licensed for export. Refer to the BXA (http://www.bxa.doc.gov/Encryption/) and the Federal Register (U.S. Government Printing Office Databases, http://www.access.gpo.gov/su_docs/) for the current rules.

Any restrictions are quite ineffective. Encryption algorithms and products are widely available worldwide; a foreign entity does not need to obtain them from the United States. Many people think that the export control restrictions are being used, in reality, to slow the use of encryption in domestic applications, because the government knows that U.S. companies need to operate multinationally nowadays, and so will use a level of encryption that can be deployed uniformly for all their locations. What the government is really worried about is that if everything starts to be encrypted, they will not know where to invest their decryption efforts.

Only a lawyer can truly evaluate the legal obligations you have with regard to these issues, so the information presented here is for general informational purposes only; you should consult an attorney before importing or exporting any technologies that you think might be restricted, especially since the situation changes almost monthly.

**International.** Import and export rules for encryption technology vary from country to country. The "Wassenaar Arrangement on Export Controls for Conventional Arms and Dual-Use Goods and Technologies," usually referred to as the Wassenaar Arrangement, was formed in 1996, and modified in December 1998. The 1996 agreement basically allows licensed export except to certain countries, but does not appear to address the export of encryption software via the Internet. The 1998 modifications specify certain restrictions including a 56-bit key length. The agreement is not itself enforceable; it is up to participating countries to enact laws that implement it. As of this writing, most participating countries have not yet enacted laws supporting the 1998 modifications.

Here is a survey of the current rules that exist in some countries. Remember, again, that only a lawyer can truly evaluate the legal obligations you have with regard to these issues, so this list is for general informational purposes only, and to give you a feel for the kinds of restrictions that exist; you should consult an attorney before importing or exporting any technologies that you think might be restricted. These rules, and their interpretation, also change frequently.

Canada—Unrestricted export between the United States and Canada, but if originally exported from the United States, re-exportation from Canada is subject to U.S. rules. For export to countries other than the United States, Canada adheres to 1996 Wassenaar Arrangement.

United Kingdom—Export over the Internet is unrestricted except to embargoed countries.

Sweden—Adheres to 1996 Wassenaar Arrangement, and restricts export via Internet.

Spain—Adheres to 1996 Wassenaar Arrangement.

Singapore—Must apply to import or send encrypted data over telecom lines.

Japan—Adheres to 1996 Wassenaar Arrangement.

Germany—Export outside the European Union (EU) is restricted by license.

France—Export of authentication is permitted, but you must file; export of encryption requires a license. Some restrictions on import. Earlier restriction on the domestic use of encryption are being rescinded at this writing.

### *Java Security Providers*

The Java security architecture allows security algorithms to be plugged in using the Provider interface. A security provider is a package that implements a set of security algorithms, which may include algorithms for message digests, key generation, encryption, signing, and random number generation. A provider package must also have a class which extends java.security.Provider; it is the job of the constructor of this Provider class to actually install the different algorithms. It does this by setting certain properties in itself (the Provider class extends java.utl.Properties, which extends Hashtable), which identify the algorithms it supports. These properties basically take the form

```
<engine_type>.<the algorithm_name, cert type, or keystore type>
```

where <engine_type> is one of

- AlgorithmParameterGenerator
- AlgorithmParameters
- KeyFactory
- KeyPairGenerator
- MessageDigest
- Signature
- SecureRandom
- CertificateFactory
- KeyStore

For each of these there is an abstract class in package java.security with the name <engine_type>Spi, and also a class <engine_type>, which extends <engine_type>Spi. A provider must extend the engine classes to provide security algorithms. For example, if a provider wishes to implement a Signature algorithm, it must extend java.security.Signature and implement the abstract methods defined in SignatureSpi.

In order to make the engine class (and therefore the algorithm) available, the provider class adds it to its list of properties.

Unless you are developing security algorithms, you will not need to worry too much about this. If you are using the algorithms implemented by a security provider, you will merely need to install and possibly specify the provider. Once a provider is installed, the Security class knows how to examine the properties of each installed provider and find the ones that implement specified algorithm names.

**Adding a Security Provider.** To statically add a provider to your Java installation, you must make an entry for the provider in the java.security file in the lib/security directory of your Java runtime, of the form

```
security.provider.n=<provider-master-class-name>
```

where *n* is a sequential number consistent with the other providers defined in the file (i.e., no gaps), beginning with 1. The provider master class name will be specified in the documentation that comes with the provider implementation. It is the class that extends the Provider base class. The class must be locatable by the runtime (e.g., included in the runtime, or in the classpath or the extensions directory).

To add a provider programmatically, you can use the Security.addProvider() method. The Security class has additional methods for managing providers. The changes you make in this way are not permanent, however, since they are not reflected in your java.security file.

The SDK runtime's default provider is named "SUN." There is also an additional provider, "SunJCE," which comes as part of the Java Cryptography Extensions (JCE) packages. These are in a separate package, because they implement encryption algorithms that may not exportable to some locations and so cannot be as freely distributed as the rest of the SDK. The SUN provider contains freely exportable algorithms, including hashcode algorithms and digital signature algorithms.

### *Encryption Algorithms Included with the Java APIs*

The Java Cryptography Extensions (JCE) consists of a set of packages that implement cryptographic algorithms. JCE includes implementations for DES and Triple DES encryption among others. These features are distributed separately from the SDK because of the restrictions on the export of encryption technology imposed by the U. S. Department of Commerce Export Administration Regulations.

Application developers will not typically use the cryptographic APIs directly for an application, because more convenient packages are available from third parties that provide higher level functionality, such as SSL.

There is the temptation for simple applications that need to communicate over the Internet to use JCE to create an encrypted stream without authentication. However, this is not wise, because authentication is a large part of the problem, and an encryption solution must address it. Providing stream encryption for Internet tunneling, without authentication, is like sending a securely locked package to someone and not having it signed for at the receiving end.

There are situations, however, in which simple encryption is appropriate. For example, a colleague of mine markets a program called BackOnline, which provides web-based backup for data. This product encrypts the data when it is transferred to the server, but never decrypts it until it returns to the client. Authentication is therefore less of an issue, because no one reads the data except the originator. On the web site that accompanies this book, I provide an example of password-based encryption using the JCE.

The following list specifies the algorithms recognized by the Java API. Included algorithms are marked with an asterisk, or two asterisks if they are part of the JCE. These are the "standard" names by which the Java API knows these algorithms.

**Standard names defined by JDK 1.1 and SDK 1.2:**

*Included with SUN provider for JDK 1.1 and SDK 1.2

**Included with SunJCE Provider for JCE 1.2

**Digest algorithms:**

- **SHA***(aliases **SHA** and **SHA1**)
- **MD5***
- **MD2**

**Key pair generation:**

- **DSA** (aliases **OID.1.3.14.3.2.12** and **OID.1.2.840.10040.4.1**)
- **RSA**

**Digital signature algorithms:**

- **SHA1withDSA*** (aliases **DSA, DSS, SHA/DSA, SHA-1/DSA, SHA1/DSA, OID.1.3.14.3.2.13, OID.1.3.14.3.2.27,** and **OID.1.2.840.10040.4.3;** known in JDK 1.1 as simply "**DSA**")—Signature created by applying RawDSA to an SHA-1 digest
- **SHA1withRSA** (known in JDK 1.1 as **SHA-1/RSA**)—Signature created by encrypting an SHA-1 digest with an RSA cipher
- **MD5withRSA** (known in JDK 1.1 as **MD5/RSA**)—Signature created by encrypting an MD5 digest with an RSA cipher
- **MD2withRSA** (known in JDK 1.1 as **MD2/RSA**)—Signature created by encrypting an MD2 digest with an RSA cipher

**Standard names added by SDK 1.2:**

**Random number generation:**

- **SHA1PRNG**—Pseudo random number generator using SHA1 and implementing an algorithm described in IEEE P1363 Appendix G.7

**Certificate types:**

- **X.509**

**Keystore types:**

- **JKS**—The Java Keystore implementation
- **PKCS12**—A PKCS#12 keystore which defines a transportable keystore file format for importing and exporting private keys and certificates

**Standard names defined by JDK 1.1 but not defined in SDK 1.2:**

- **DES****
- **IDEA**
- **RC2**
- **RC4**

**Standard names defined by JCE 2.1** (all these are included in the SunJCE provider):

**Symmetric cipher algorithms:**

- **DES**
- **DESede**—DES-EDE (3DES)
- **PBEWithMD5AndDES**—Password-based encryption using MD5 digest and DES encryption. Refer to PKCS#5
- **Blowfish**—Drop in replacement algorithm for DES and IDEA. See http://www.counterpane.com/blowfish.html

**Cipher block modes:**

- **ECB**—Electronic Codebook Mode, as defined in the National Institute of Standards and Technology (NIST) Federal Information Processing Standard (FIPS) 81
- **CBC**—Cipher-Chaining Mode, as defined in NIST FIPS 81
- **CFB**—Cipher-Feedback Mode, as defined in NIST FIPS 81
- **OFB**—Output-Feedback Mode, as defined in NIST FIPS 81
- **PCBC**—Plaintext Cipher Block Chaining, as defined by Kerberos

**Cipher padding:**

- NoPadding—No padding is used (padding forces encryption blocks to be a multiple of a certain size)
- PKCS5Padding—The padding schemes defined in PKCSS#5
- SSL3Padding—Padding as defined by SSL version 3

**Key agreement:**

- **DiffieHellman—**Diffie-Hellman key agreement

**Key generation:**

- DES
- DESede
- Blowfish
- HmacMD5—An HMAC-MD5 key as defined in RFC 2104
- HmacSHA1—An HMAC-SHA1 key as defined in RFC 2104

**Key pair generation:**

- DiffieHellman

**Secret key factory:**

- **DES**
- **DESede**
- **PBEWithMD5AndDES—**Password-based encryption, as per PKCS#5

**Key factory:**

- DiffieHellman

**Algorithm param gen:**

- DiffieHellman

**Algorithm param:**

- DiffieHellman
- DES
- DESede
- PBE—for password-based encryption (PKCS#5)
- Blowfish

**MAC (message authentication code):**

- HmacMD5
- HmacSHA1

**Keystore type:**

- JCEKS—The JCE keystore. Keys are encrypted using PBE with 3DES.

### *Overview of X.509 Certificates*

A digital certificate is a digitally signed document which serves the purpose of providing a specific set of authenticated information. The information is authenticated because the signature is verifiable proof that the document has not been altered, and because the signature can be proved to have been created by a trusted party. Generally, the signed content includes the identity of the originator of the certificate and their public key. A certificate is therefore a reliable way to distribute one's public key.

Let us consider an example. Suppose you have a public key and want to send it to someone. You could create a certificate that includes your name and your public key, and then have a trusted third party sign the certificate. Anyone who receives the certificate can verify the contents of the certificate simply by verifying the signature. Basically, they prove that the name and public key were used to create the signature, and therefore have not been modified since the signature was created.

The signature is created using the private signing key of the trusted third party. To perform the verification, you need the trusted third party's public key. It seems that to get this, you need their certificate—and so we have kind of a catch-22, since to verify a certificate we need another certificate, and so on. Where does it end? The assumption is that at some point you obtain the certificate of a trusted party through some physical means that you trust, such as by obtaining it from someone on a diskette, or perhaps the certificate was included with a product such as a browser. Such "trusted certificates" are usually issued by entities called "certificate authorities" (CA), whose main business is to issue these certificates. A CA provides a strong guarantee that their certificate keys are kept in a safe place, just as a bank guarantees that your money is kept in a safe place.

Practically the only kind of certificate you are likely to encounter nowadays on the Internet is an X.509 certificate. The X.509 certificate standard was first published in 1988 as part of X.500, revised as version 2 in 1993, and again as version 3 in 1996.

Version 3 has a loophole: using the "extensions" provision, it is possible to create X.509 v.3 certificates of different kinds particular to an application. Thus, just because your certificate is X.509 v.3-compliant does not give you any indication whether it will work in your application, because your application may need certain extension fields to be filled in. This means that the providers of certificates are in a position of being the providers of unique certificates for potentially each user, and for potentially every application that user uses. What a nice position to be in!

This is what is contained in an X.509 certificate, in exactly this sequence:

```
version (i.e., version 1, 2, or 3)
serial no.
signature algorithm id
issuer distinguished name
validity period
subject distinguished name
subject public key info (algorithm, key)

Version 2 extensions (IETF recommends against using these):
   issuer unique id
   subject unique id

Version 3 extensions:
   triplets, {extension name, criticality, extension value}

digital signature
```

Here is an example. This is a human-readable dump of the CA certificate for RSA Data Security, included with Netscape Communicator 4.0. It is a self-signed certificate—hence the subject and issuer are the same. As you can see, it is a version 1 certificate. The actual certificate is encoded in a format called "DER-encoding."

```
Version: 1 (0x0)
   Serial Number:
       02:41:00:00:16
   Signature Algorithm: md2WithRSAEncryption
   Issuer: C=US, O=RSA Data Security, Inc., OU=Commercial
      Certification Authority
   Validity:
      Not Before: Nov  4 18:58:34 1994 GMT
      Not After : Nov  3 18:58:34 1999 GMT
   Subject: C=US, O=RSA Data Security, Inc., OU=Commercial
      Certification Authority
   Subject Public Key Info:
      Public Key Algorithm: rsaEncryption
      Public Key (RSA): (1000 bit)
         Modulus (1000 bit):
            00:a4:fb:81:62:7b:ce:10:27:dd:e8:f7:be:6c:6e:
            c6:70:99:db:b8:d5:05:03:69:28:82:9c:72:7f:96:
```

```
                3f:8e:ec:ac:29:92:3f:8a:14:f8:42:76:be:bd:5d:
                03:b9:90:d4:d0:bc:06:b2:51:33:5f:c4:c2:bf:b6:
                8b:8f:99:b6:62:22:60:dd:db:df:20:82:b4:ca:a2:
                2f:2d:50:ed:94:32:de:e0:55:8d:d4:68:e2:e0:4c:
                d2:cd:05:16:2e:95:66:5c:61:52:38:1e:51:a8:82:
                a1:c4:ef:25:e9:0a:e6:8b:2b:8e:31:66:d9:f8:d9:
                fd:bd:3b:69:d9:eb
            Exponent: 65537 (0x10001)
    Signature:
        76:b5:b6:10:fe:23:f7:f7:59:62:4b:b0:5f:9c:c1:68:bc:49:
        bb:b3:49:6f:21:47:5d:2b:9d:54:c4:00:28:3f:98:b9:f2:8a:
        83:9b:60:7f:eb:50:c7:ab:05:10:2d:3d:ed:38:02:c1:a5:48:
        d2:fe:65:a0:c0:bc:ea:a6:23:16:66:6c:1b:24:a9:f3:ec:79:
        35:18:4f:26:c8:e3:af:50:4a:c7:a7:31:6b:d0:7c:18:9d:50:
        bf:a9:26:fa:26:2b:46:9c:14:a9:bb:5b:30:98:42:28:b5:4b:
        53:bb:43:09:92:40:ba:a8:aa:5a:a4:c6:b6:8b:57:4d:c5
```

Note that the signature algorithm may be different from the subject public key algorithm. The signature algorithm is what the CA uses to sign the certificate; the subject public key algorithm specifies the type of key the subject has generated. Very frequently these are the same algorithm, but there is no strict reason why they have to be. (Some protocols may require that they be the same.) As a practical matter, if the algorithms are different, the probability is higher that software using the certificate will not have one of the algorithms.

Different kinds of keys have different value components, as explained earlier when asymmetric algorithms were discussed. Also, a Diffie-Hellman certificate will have DH parameters. Still, a DH certificate will be signed with some signature algorithm, such as DSA or RSA.

**Version 3 Extensions.** The X.509 version 3 extensions are:

Authority key identifier—Identifies a particular issuer public key in cases when the issuer has more than one signing key

Subject key identifier—Identifies the subject's public key; may be a hash-code of the key

Private key usage period—Specified if the private key has a different validity period than the certificate

Policy information—Identifies CA policies that apply to the certificate; may specify a notice to be displayed for users, and identify a Certification Practice Statement

Policy mappings—Only used in CA certificates; correlates end-usage policies with CA policies

Subject alternative names—Provide additional identities for the subject in addition to the distinguished name, such as email address, DNS name, IP address, and a URI

Issuer alternative names—Provides additional identities for the issuer

Subject directory attributes—Not usually used

Basic constraints—Indicates whether the subject of the certificate is a CA and how deep a certification chain may be through that CA

Name constraints—Identifies a name space in a certification chain which must contain all subjects in subsequent certificates

Policy constraints—Specifies that each certificate in a chain contains a policy identifier, or excludes policy mapping

CRL distribution points—Identifies how CRL information is obtained (CRLs are discussed below)

Key usage—Defines the CA's intended purpose of the key contained in the certificate (e.g., encryption, signing)

Extended key usage—Identifies additional purposes for usage, typically specific to the enduser's (as opposed to the CA's) domain

IETF extension—The only IETF extension: identifies an online validation service supporting the CA

**Key Usage and Extended Key Usage.** As shown above, X.509 version 3 defines a "key usage" extension and an "extended key usage" extension. The key usage extension specifies the intended purpose of the public key contained in the certificate. The usages (which may be combined in certain ways) defined for the key are:

digitalSignature—Authentication

nonRepudiation—Nonrepudiation service which protects against the signing entity falsely denying some action

keyEncipherment—For enciphering keys for transport

dataEncipherment—For enciphering user data

keyAgreement—Key agreement, for example, when a Diffie-Hellman key is to be used for key management

keyCertSign—Verifying a signature on certificates (for CA certificates only)

cRLSign—Verifying a signature on CRLs

encipherOnly—Enciphering data while performing key agreement

decipherOnly—Deciphering data while performing key agreement

The extended key usages proposed by the IETF at the time of this writing are:

serverAuth—Web server authentication

clientAuth—Web client authentication

codeSigning—Signing of downloadable executable code

emailProtection—Email protection

ipsecEndSystem—IP security end system (host or router)

ipsecTunnel—IP security tunnel termination

ipsecUser—IP security user

timeStamping—Binding the hash of an object to a time from an agreed-upon time

These must be consistent with the key usage indicators, according to a set of consistency rules. These extended uses are not at present used by the Java security implementations, however.

The most common kinds of certificates a user or system administrator will encounter are client certificates, server certificates, signing certificates, and CA certificates. Client certificates are used by end users to authenticate themselves to a server. A client certificate would have its clientAuth flag set, as well as its digitalSignature flag and perhaps its nonRepudiation flag. A server certificate is used to authenticate a server to clients, and provide a key for encrypting session keys that are exchanged, which may then be used for encryption. A server certificate would have its serverAuth flag set, its digitalSignature and nonRepudiation flags set, and perhaps others. A signing certificate is for signing data (e.g., applets or other content distributable to clients), and would have its codeSigning flag set. A CA certificate is usually self-signed, and serves the purpose of a top-level trusted item used to verify other certificates. Assuming a CA certificate has been obtained by a satisfactorily secure means (e.g., bundled with a product in a physically sealed software product package), or is posted somewhere against which it can be compared, the CA certificate's public key can be used by clients to verify a server's certificate.

You will not normally have to know what key usage modes are in effect for a certificate unless your certificate is not working, and you cannot get support from your certificate vendor or certificate server vendor, and you need to diagnose what is wrong yourself. This could occur if you have your own certificate server, and the certificates you are creating do not seem to work.

**What SET Uses.** SET is the Secure Electronic Transaction standard, developed by Visa, Mastercard, and others. It is a standard that will be used for consumer credit card purchases over the Internet. While SET is a closed system, and SET certificates can only be used for SET applications, the world is watching SET to see how certificates measure up in volume use. Lessons learned from SET will surely be applied elsewhere.

---

**Different Kinds of Certificates (sigh...): My Soapbox**

Sometimes things go so far awry that one just has to stand up and say something about it.

A certificate should contain one assertion: I AM <a-specified-entity>; and it should provide the capability to sign things, and/or seal (encrypt) things. It should be that simple. A certificate should *not* be used to transfer information (messages) other than what is required to accomplish its main purpose: authentication of identity. Messages should be defined in protocols, and encrypted or signed if necessary for authentication and privacy. Certificates should *not* contain things like "Vendor no. XXX," "Point-of-origin," "Address," "Host name," and so on. Would you want your current address in your birth certificate? Of course not, because if you move, you would need to update your birth certificate and have it reprinted—kind of silly, right? And imagine if each time you had to make such a change, it cost you $400!

A certificate is merely a digitally signed document. However, it should be a special kind of document. As long as an entity's identity can be verified, using a certificate signed by a trusted party, that entity can use their certificate to sign, and therefore verify, any other information that needs to be exchanged by an application or protocol. There is no need to go back to a certificate authority to sign protocol-specific information. That signing can be delegated.

The obstacle to this is that server vendors are using the X.509 v.3 extensions feature to add application-specific information to the certificates required by their servers, and then requiring you—the user—to go to the CA to obtain a certificate just for their server. The result is that you need to get separate server certificates for your Netscape server, your Microsoft server, your Castanet server, and so on. In fact, you need to get a separate certificate for *each machine* on which these servers run; if you move a server from one host to another, you usually have to go back to the CA and pay another fee (around $400 at the time of this writing)! (Embedding the hostname protects the administrator against stolen keys, but there are better ways to do this.) It does not have to be this way. (Complain to your server vendor!)

---

SET uses X.509 v.3 certificates with these standard extensions:

- Authority key identifier
- Key usage
- Private key usage period
- Certificate policies (several extensions related to this)
- Subject alternative names
- Basic constraints
- Issuer alternative names

SET has also added these "private extensions," which are unique to SET:

- HashedRootKey
- CertificateType (SET defines these types: Cardholder, Merchant, PaymentGateway, GeoPoliticalCertificateAuthority, BrandCertificateAuthority, RootCertificateAuthority, CardholderCertificateAuthority, MerchantCertificateAuthority, PaymentCertificateAuthority, and various combinations of some of these)
- MerchantData
- CardCertRequired
- Tunneling
- SETExtensions

**What Java Uses.** As you can see, all of the different kinds of certificates we have looked at claim to be X.509 v.3 compatible. However, they all have extensions of various kinds—extensions not recognized by each other. Again, this is because these certificates are being used as customized signed documents, to carry information. In some cases, as with SET, there is good reason to define a closed system, since these uses are new, and the participants want to maintain control to ensure success. Hopefully the tendency to create closed systems will not continue, however.

The Java security APIs can handle any X.509 certificate that uses algorithms for which there is a provider installed. The tools which generate certificates, however, generate a X.509 v.1 certificate.

### *Obtaining a Server Certificate*

Obtaining a server certificate (e.g., for a secure web server or a secure CORBA ORB) is normally done through a user interface included with the server product itself. The server knows what X.509 v.3 extension attributes to write into the certificate request, usually including the hostname or IP address of the machine the server is running on (which must be the same machine on which you create the request).

The server will guide you through the process of key pair generation, storing the private key in the server (encrypted with a user-supplied password), generation of a blank certificate with the new public key to send to the CA, wrapping it in a Certificate Signing Request (CSR; usually as defined in RSA PKCS#10 or the newer RFC 2511), and sending it out for signing; at this point, you may have to prove your identity to the CA.This is usually a particular CA with whom the server vendor has a relationship.

The CA will then add information to the certificate such as expiration date and CA information. The CA encrypts a hash of the information in your certificate using their private key (i.e., signs it) and stores the result in your certificate. They then send the certificate back to you.

You then go back to the server's certificate request user interface, and tell it the file name where the returned certificate resides. (The CA may have sent it to you via email.) Some server products require you to enter the certificate via pasting its text value into a UI form instead of by specifying a file. Regardless of how it is entered, the server then will install the certificate into its certificate database, replacing the self-signed certificate it created earlier with the one signed by the CA.

### *Key Management*

An application that wants to provide user authentication must have a way to manage client and CA certificates and keys. For this purpose, the application needs to have, or have access to, a key and certificate database. For example, Netscape Communicator has one for each user, located in files called key3.db and cert7.db.

Currently, the key databases in these products are not accessible to you programmatically. This may change when these and similar products incorporate Java 2, since Java 2 includes a key database facility called a KeyStore. The key store is by default stored in a file named .keystore in the user's home directory, as determined by the "user.home" system property.

**Creating a Key Manager.** A key management tool allows users to manage their keys and certificates—both the certificates that pertain to them, and the certificates they receive from others. Such a tool would allow users to:

- List certificates
- Import/remove certificates
- View certificates (before and after installation)
- Verify certificates

To implement this, you can use an existing key store implementation, or write your own. In either case, we are still dealing with a key store, so the rest of the code is the same. We will use Sun's default KeyStore, sun.security.tools.JavaKeyStore.

First we must instantiate the keystore manager. We do this as follows:

```
KeyStore ks = KeyStore.getInstance("JKS");
```

This will create an instance of a "JKS" keystore. The first provider listed in the java.security properties file which can make a keystore of this type is used. "JKS" is the type of keystore provided by the built-in SUN provider.

All this does is create an empty keystore. To load a keystore database:

```
// Specify where the key database is - this can be anywhere
String fname = System.getProperty("user.home") +
   System.getProperty("file.separator") + ".keystore";
// Load the key database; skip this if keystore is new
FileInputStream is = new FileInputStream(fname);
String pswd = "myCertDBPassword";
char[] buf = new char[pswd.length()];
pswd.getChars(0,  buf.length, buf, 0);
ks.load(is, buf);
is.close();
```

Our application, however, could allow the user to select a keystore manager class, and a keystore database as well.

Next, we can list the certificates in the key store:

```
TextArea list = new TextArea(5, 30);
add(list);
Enumeration entries = ks.aliases();
for (; entries.hasMoreElements();)
{
   String alias = entries.nextElement();
   if (ks.isKeyEntry(alias)) list.append("Key: ");
   else if (ks.isCertificateEntry(alias)) list.append("Cert: ");
   list.append(alias + "\n");
}
```

To select and instantiate a client certificate,

```
Certificate[] certChain = ks.getCertificateChain(alias);
```

(Make sure you import java.security.cert.Certificate, and not java.security.Certificate, which is deprecated.) The first certificate in the array is the certificate associated with the alias; the rest are the certificates of CAs which signed the first certificate, and then each other, ending with the root CA's certificate.

(If you store server certificates in your database, you will need to use the getCertificateAlias(Certificate cert) method to match them.)

This would be done to view a certificate. It would also be done by SSL code that wanted to use a certificate from this database, either to verify a trusted server certificate, or to provide a client certificate for user authentication.

The user will want to view a selected certificate. These methods can be used for x.509 certificates:

```
checkValidity()—Check if the current date and time are within the
  certificate's validity period, and thrown an exception if not.
checkValidity(Date)—Check if the specified date/time value is
  within the certificate's validity period, and throw an exception
  if not.
equals(Object)—Return true if the encoded form of this certificate
  is the same as that of the argument.
getBasicConstraints()—Applies to CA certificates only. Return the
  Basic Constrains value, which specifies the maximum number of CA
  certificates that may follow this certificate in a certification
  chain. Zero indicates that only an end-user certificate may
  follow.
getEncoded()—Return the encoded form of the certificate. An X.509
  certificate would return the certificate's DER encoded byte
  representation.
getPublicKey()—Return the public key of the certificate.
getType()—Returns a string representing the type of the
  certificate, e.g., X.509.
getIssuerDN()—Return the issuer distinguished name value from the
  certificate.
getIssuerUniqueID()—Return the issuerUniqueID value from the
  certificate.
getKeyUsage()—Return the BitSet for the KeyUsage extension, (OID =
  2.5.29.15).
getNotAfter()—Return the notAfter date from the validity period of
  the certificate.
getNotBefore()—Return the notBefore date from the validity period
  of the certificate.
getSerialNumber()—Return the serialNumber value from the
  certificate.
getSigAlgName()—Return the signature algorithm name for the
  certificate signature algorithm.
getSigAlgOID()—Return the signature algorithm OID string from the
  certificate.
getSigAlgParams()—Return the DER-encoded signature algorithm
  parameters from this certificate's signature algorithm.
getSignature()—Return the signature value (the raw signature bits)
  from the certificate.
getSubjectDN()—Return the subject (subject distinguished name)
  value from the certificate.
```

getSubjectUniqueID()—Return the subjectUniqueID value from the certificate.
getTBSCertificate()—Return the DER-encoded certificate information, the tbsCertificate from this certificate.
getVersion()—Return the version number value of the certificate.
hashCode()—Compute a hashcode value from the certificate's encoded form.
toString()—Return a readable string representation of the certificate.
verify(PublicKey)—Verify the certificate's signature using the specified public key which is known to be associated with the certificate's signer.
verify(PublicKey, String provider)—Same as above, but use the specified security provider implementation.

For example, we might want to display the certificate owner's distinguished name, the issuer's distinguished name, the key usage (what the certificate can be used for), the validity period, the serial number, the signing algorithm, the version number, and the actual public key of each certificate in the chain:

```
Panel p = new Panel();
p.setLayout(new GridLayout(7, 1));
for (int i = 0; i < certChain.length; i++)
{
   Certificate cert = (X509Certificate)(certChain[i]);
   p.add(new Label("Owner: " + cert.getSubjectDN().getName()));
   p.add(new Label("Issuer: " + cert.getIssuerDN().getName()));
   boolean usage = cert.getKeyUsage();
   if (usage != null) p.add(new Label("Key Usage: "
      + "Authentication: " + (usage.set(0) ? "yes" : "no") + "    "
      + "Encryption: " + (usage.set(3) ? "yes" : "no") ));
   p.add(new Label(
      "Valid from " + cert.getNotBefore().toString()
      + " to " + cert.getNotAfter().toString()));
   p.add(new Label("Serial No.: "
      + cert.getSerialNumber().toString()));
   p.add(new Label("Sig. Alg.: " + cert.getSigAlgName()));
   p.add(new Label("Version: " + cert.getVersion()));
}
add(p);
validate();
```

Key usage bits are:

| Bit | Usage |
|---|---|
| 0 | digitalSignature |
| 1 | nonRepudiation |
| 2 | keyEncipherment |
| 3 | dataEncipherment |
| 4 | keyAgreement |
| 5 | keyCertSign (CAs) |
| 6 | cRLSign |
| 7 | encipherOnly |
| 8 | decipherOnly |

Surprise, this is just what is defined in the evolving IETF standard!

To read in a certificate from a source other than a Java keystore, you must construct a Certificate object from the bytes that compose the certificate. A CertificateFactory allows you to construct certificates:

```
InputStream fis = new FileInputStream("MyCertFile");
CertificateFactory cf = CertificateFactory.getInstance("X.509");
X509Certificate cert =
   (X509Certificate)(cf.generateCertificate(fis));
fis.close();
```

Whenever you obtain a certificate, you should verify it. Certificate verification involves decrypting the signature stored in the certificate, using the signer's (usually a CA) public key. Applying the signer's public key to the certificate's encrypted signature should yield a decrypted message that contains a reproducible hash of the identity of the signer. If this is successful, it proves that the signer's private key was used to produce the encrypted signature. To verify a certificate, you can use the verify() method:

```
try
{
   cert.verify(cert.getPublicKey()); // public key should also
                                     // be compared with its
                                     // known value
}
catch (java.security.GeneralSecurityException)
{
   System.out.println("Whoooaaaa—certificate does not verify!");
}
```

A certificate alone is sufficient for validating messages sent to you by the certificate owner, and for sending encrypted messages back to the certificate owner. If you want to sign messages or read messages sent to you, or authenticate yourself in an SSL session, you need the certificate's private key as well. Normally this is generated on the workstation where it is used, and it is put into that workstation's keystore at that time. If you have obtained it from an external source, however, you need to read it in and insert it into the keystore.

To read a key from a file, you have to first read in the bytes, and then use a key factory to construct a key from those bytes. To do this, you need to know two things: the algorithm which generated the key, e.g., DSA or RSA, and the encoding format which was used to write the key to serialized form. The encoding formats supported by Java 2 are X.509 and PKCS#8.

Depending on the encoding, you use one of two key containers to decode the key file. Java 2 provides the X509EncodedKeySpec and PKCS8EncodedKeySpec classes for this purpose. You then pass the key spec container to a key factory for the key algorithm, and use the generatePrivate() method to reconstruct the key:

```
File f = new File("MyKeyFile");
fis = new FileInputStream(f);
byte[] bbuf = new byte[(int)(f.length())];
int n = fis.read(bbuf);
KeyFactory kf = KeyFactory.getInstance("DSA");
KeySpec keyspec = new PKCS8EncodedKeySpec(bbuf);
key = kf.generatePrivate(keyspec);
```

A private key and its accompanying certificate can be added to a keystore using the setKeyEntry() method:

```
String pswd = "MyNewPassword";
char[] pswdbuf = new char[pswd.length()];
pswd.getChars(0,  pswdbuf.length, pswdbuf, 0);
ks.setKeyEntry
(
   alias,        // identifier to use in keystore for this entry.
   key,          // key we obtained above.
   pswdbuf,      // password, as a char array.
   new Certificate[] { cert }  // cert chain, containing
                               // our cert from above.
);
FileOutputStream os = new FileOutputStream(fname);
ks.store(os, "myCertDBPassword");
os.close();
```

### Smartcards and Embedded Keys

A smartcard is a credit-card-sized device which has an embedded microprocessor and nonvolatile memory. Metal contacts on the surface of the card allow it to connect to a communication bus when inserted into a smartcard reader. A smartcard can serve many functions, ranging from holding medical information to storing electronic cash ("E-cash"), or it may simply provide a tamper-proof token for authenticating a user.

Since a physical token can be made tamper-proof, it can itself serve as a kind of certificate. This is what currency is: tamper-proof documentation of a debt. However, just as with currency, techniques evolve over time to defeat tamper-proofness or to duplicate tokens. Relying on physical tamper-proofness, alone is not sufficient if there is a lot at stake. That is why many smartcards also require a password (i.e., a PIN number), which the user must enter each time the card is used, just as with a bank card. The user must therefore be in possession of the card and also must know the password.

Since smartcards contain computers, their function is only limited by the ingenuity of smartcard designers. Some smartcard APIs have built-in support for encryption and even certificate management. The smartcard can therefore be used to store certificates and encrypted private keys. This obviates the need to keep private keys on a user's machine, making it possible for users to roam from computer to computer, and carry their certificate and key database with them.

Sun has developed a version of the Java VM for smartcards. The JavaCard API, in version 2.1 at this writing, is now supported by a range of smartcard manufacturers. The standard cryptographic API includes support for random number generation, message digests, and public key operations. The security extensions package includes support for ciphers.

Interestingly, the JavaCard Java VM fits in 40K of read-only memory. Yes—that is "K," not "M." (This takes me back 20 years!) This was achieved by eliminating most of the APIs that it was felt were not relevant for smartcard applications, which do not have user interfaces and don't need to connect with any device except for a smartcard reader. JavaCard programs also do not have automatic garbage collection, so if your program creates an object, the object never goes away. Since JavaCard programs run for the life of the card, the strategy is to create all the objects you need at initialization and reuse them.

Smartcards—Java or otherwise—require support on the computer in which they are used.

Unfortunately, a standard security provider class for smartcards is not planned at this time. Therefore, it is a little difficult to integrate smartcard use into Java security applications in a streamlined way.

**OpenCard Framework (OCF).** The OpenCard Framework (OCF) is a standard Java smartcard API developed by a consortium of companies including Sun, IBM, Visa, Gemplus, Siemens, Dallas Semiconductor, Schlumberger, and many others. OCF is a high level API, and provides application level services so that applications do not generally have to be programmed down to the message level when they need services from smartcards. Many smartcard readers support the OCF standard. A list of currently supported devices can be found on the OpenCard web site, at http://www.opencard.org/index-devices.html.

Another important smartcard API standard is the PC/SC standard, developed by Microsoft and others for the Wintel platform. This API is much lower level than OCF, and does not therefore compete with it. Also, it is a native API. In fact, the OCF reference implementation includes a PC/SC based implementation, so that card readers which have PC/SC drivers can plug right into OCF.

There are three primary aspects to using a smartcard in an application. One is initialization of the card terminal and service interfaces. In OCF, this is accomplished by registering a set of factories, which are used to query a card when it is inserted and determine which factory can handle the card. OCF defines two kinds of factories: card terminal factories and card service factories. The classes which implement the factories must be listed in Java properties, so that the runtime can find them. These factories are shown in the Figure 4-4.

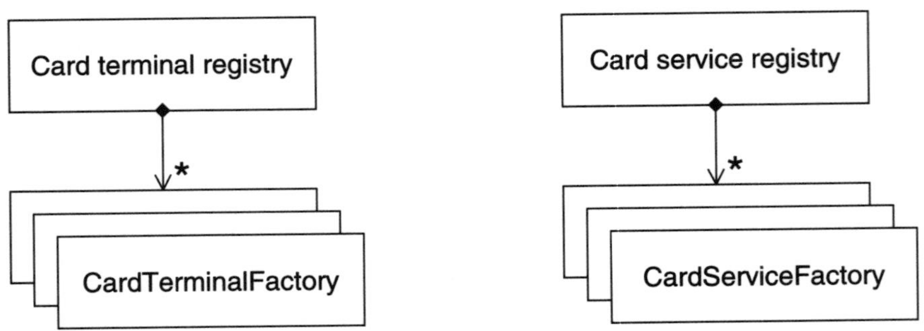


Properties:

OpenCard.loaderClassName=<class name of property loader>
(must implement opencard.core.util.OpenCardConfigurationProvider; this property must be defined before the runtime starts, e.g., by a -D switch)

OpenCard.terminals=<terminal factory class list...>

OpenCard.services=<service factory class list...>

**Figure 4-4** Configuration of the terminal interface.

A second aspect of using a smartcard is authentication. There are three kinds of authentication:

**Card holder verification (CHV)**—The user is authenticated, possibly by prompting the user for a PIN number or through biometric authentication.

**External authentication**—The card authenticates the application, e.g., by providing the application with a random number and asking the application to encrypt it, and then verifying the encryption.

**Internal authentication**—The application verifies the card, e.g., by providing the card with a random number and asking the card to encrypt it, and then verifying the encryption.

For security applications, all three kinds of authentication may be used. Often, external authentication is not necessary, because the application is not tamper-proof and so it cannot be effectively authenticated anyway. On the other hand, a security application such as SSL, which needs to authenticate a user holding a smartcard, will make use of CHV and internal authentication, to verify the user's PIN number (when "logging in" to the card) and to verify the card itself.

Internal authentication may require that the card have some cryptographic capability, especially if the application is a PKI application, such as SSL is. In this case, the card must have the ability to store a private key in a secure way, to store and verify a PIN number, and to sign or encrypt messages presented to it. The card therefore must be able to play the roles of a keystore and a cryptographic provider.

The third aspect of card usage is actually using the authenticated card—invoking services required by the application such as signing or encrypting application messages, storing and retrieving information, etc. For example, an application may require that documents be signed using the card's private key. The card can do this, if the document or a digest of it is provided to the card. In most cards, these capabilities are disabled until the user is authenticated by a CHV procedure, typically involving presenting to the card a PIN number. If the PIN number is correct, the card enables its cryptographic and other services. OCF performs card holder verification automatically when a service is requested which requires it. The CHV process effectively logs in the user (assuming CHV succeeds), and the enabled services then remain accessible until the card is removed from its terminal. OCF provides a default CHV password dialog, but application programmers can substitute their own.

Smartcards have many uses. In a numerical sense, the most widespread usage is in phone cards. In many countries, especially in Europe, smartcards are also used for storing medical and other information. In the U.S., perhaps the most important use of smartcards presently is for security applications. This is the application that is important to most readers of this book, since application builders need a secure PKI mechanism for authenticating users, and a smartcard can provide a portable and user-specific keystore and security provider.

Unfortunately, some work needs to be done to streamline this. One problem is that believe it or not, there is no Java 2 security provider implementation based on OCF. Since a smartcard can be both a keystore and a security provider, and OCF is a high level card-independent interface to smartcard terminals, you would think that it would be relatively straightforward to create a Java 2 keystore and security provider implementation on top of OCF. That has not been done to date. In addition, while OCF is largely card-independent, there are certain features which are important to security applications which don't yet have direct support in OCF, most notably authentication.

The problem may be geographic in origin. Smartcards are more widely used in Europe and are used for data-carrying applications as opposed to mere authentication tokens. The major smartcard providers are therefore European companies, and their entire focus is on smartcard applications, which the United States is not ready for. The United States needs smartcards for authentication applications, and smartcard penetration into the U.S. market will not occur unless that need is addressed first and independently. Smartcard efforts here for banking and commerce have largely failed. On the other hand, if users become accustomed to logging onto their computers at work with smartcards, it will not be long before they will get the idea and want to extend those cards to do everything else.

Authentication is the foundational feature of smartcards, and work is underway as of this writing to add an authentication service to OCF. In the meantime, to encode authentication using OCF, one has to write ISO 7816 messages directly and pass them through to the card using OCF's command message interface. That is doable but requires an intimate understanding of smartcards and smartcard message protocols. The upcoming authentication service will abstract this out and make it simple. An interesting scenario is that the smartcard must not provide the security implementation used to authenticate the card!

Part of the problem is the tremendous variety of smartcards. OCF is trying to accommodate all the different kinds of cards that are out there. As smartcards become more standardized in terms of their capabilities, it will be feasible for application vendors to add them ubuiquitously to all applications, and for PC manufacturers to make card readers a standard or optional hardware feature.

At present, the Java Wallet uses a Java extension API called javax.smartcard. This package serves the purpose of providing a standard Java API for interfacing to card reader drivers. It is likely that at some point when OCF has matured, the Java Wallet will be enhanced to use OCF instead, and javax.smartcard will go away.

OCF is viewed as an important standards effort, complementary to other Java APIs, and will be well-supported by the industry. The various Java smartcard APIs and their interactions are shown in Figure 4-5.

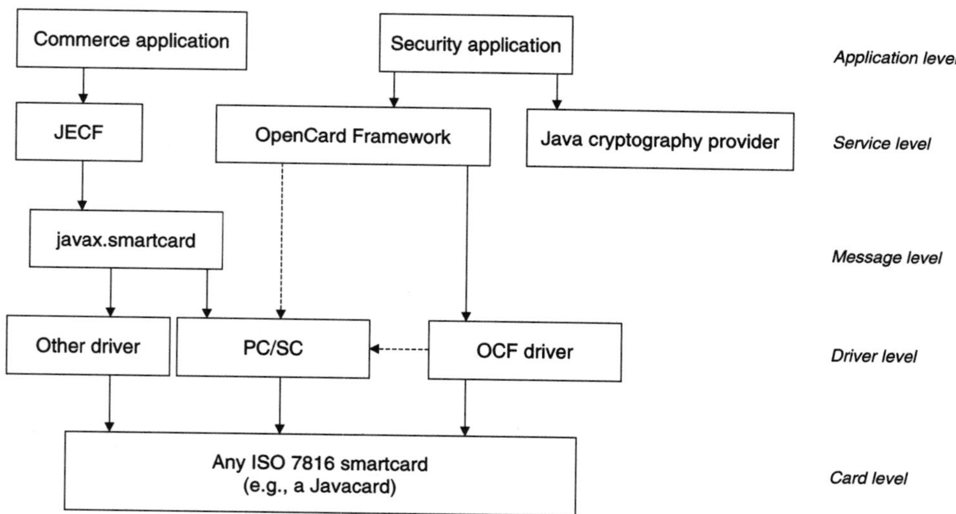


**Figure 4-5** Java smartcard APIs and their interactions.

Note that if your application is deployed in a container environment (a browser, Castanet, EJB, etc.) which provides smartcard-enabled services, your application automatically inherits smartcard support. For example, a client SSL session running in a browser can be authenticated using a smartcard if the client uses the browser's HTTPS connection factory. All smartcard interaction is then separated from the application. This is discussed later under "Secure Communication Protocols" on page 234.

Smartcards contain hierarchically organized EEPROM data structures called "files." Logically these are similar to files on a disk drive. These files can contain application-specific data, PIN numbers, and keys. The syntax used for a file name is a two-byte hex number, with colons (":") used as path separators.

Let's take a look at a simple smartcard application. I would like to present an authentication application, but since this part of the API is not available yet, I will show instead a digital signature application.

I'll explicitly list all the imported classes, so that you can easily see which classes are mine and which come from the OCF packages.

```
import opencard.core.terminal.CardTerminalRegistry;
import opencard.core.terminal.Slot;
import opencard.core.terminal.CardNotPresentException;
import opencard.core.service.SmartCard;
import opencard.core.event.CTListener;
import opencard.core.event.CardTerminalEvent;
import opencard.opt.security.SecureService;
import opencard.opt.security.PrivateKeyFile;
import opencard.opt.iso.fs.CardFilePath;
...
static final String cardFilePath = ":0001";
CardTerminalRegistry ctRegistry;
SmartCard smartCard;
Slot slot;
CTListener handler;
SignatureCardService sigService;
SmartCard.start();
```

In the code above, the variable "cardFilePath" is the name of the file containing the internal authentication key of the card. When the card was created, a different key could have been created and stored in a different file, but I am assuming that this is the location of the key we want to use here.

Next I create a card terminal listener. The listener handles card insertion and removal events. The listener is effectively an application-level driver, and should execute quickly, without blocking on IO or other long-duration application functions. The listener must have two methods: cardInserted(...) and cardRemoved(...), for handling card insertion and removal events, respectively. When an insertion event occurs, I then will obtain the service I want, as an instance of SignatureCard-Service. The "slot" variable merely records which card slot is used by the card, in case there is more than one.

```
handler = new CTListener()
{
   public void cardInserted(CardTerminalEvent event)
   {
      if (smartCard == null)
      {
         synchronized (this)
         {
            try
            {
                  smartCard = SmartCard.getSmartCard(event);
                  slot = event.getSlot();
                  sigService  =
                        (SignatureCardService)
```

```
                        smartCard.getCardService(
                        SignatureCardService.class, true);

                  // A password dialog will open when the
                  // card's signing service is accessed.
                  // However, we can provide our own
                  // branded dialog instance here if
                  // we choose:
                  // signatureService.setCHVDialog(
                  // new MyCHVDialog());
            }
            catch (Exception ex)
            {
                  ex.printStackTrace();
                  smartCard = null;
                  smartSlot = null;
            }
         }
      }
   }

   public void cardRemoved(CardTerminalEvent event)
   {
      if (event.getSlot() == slot)
      {
         synchronized (this)
         {
            smartCard = null;
            slot = null;
         }
      }
   }
};
```

Now I must add the listener to the card terminal registry, so that it will receive card terminal events. I must then call a special method to generate a simulated card insertion event, to cover the case in which the card was already inserted.

```
ctRegistry = CardTerminalRegistry.getRegistry();
ctRegistry.addCTListener(handler);

// Generate card insertion event for cards already
// inserted and send them to our handler.
try
{
   ctRegistry.createEventsForPresentCards(handler);
}
```

```
catch (Exception ex)
{
   ex.printStackTrace();
}
```

Now I define a method for signing a message digest. I could sign an entire data file, but that would be inefficient. As discussed earlier in this chapter, signing involves a two-step process of first computing a digest and then encrypting the digest. Since only the second step uses the private key, the first step can be done outside the card, using the faster processor of the user's machine. My signing method therefore takes a digest as input instead of a data stream, and it is up to the calling application to first compute the digest. In this implementation, the digest is assumed to be an SHA-1 digest.

```
public byte[] signDigest(byte[] digestBytes)
throws OpenCardException
{
   if (!signatureCardPresent())
      throw new CardNotPresentException();

   // Obtain the key to be used for signing.
   PrivateKeyFile pkf =
      new PrivateKeyFile(new CardFilePath(cardFilePath), 0);

   // Generate and return the signature.
   return sigService.signHash(pkf, "DSA", digestBytes);
}
```

Finally, when it is time for the program to exit, I unregister the card terminal listener, and shut down smartcard services.

```
ctRegistry.removeCTListener(handler);
SmartCard.shutdown();
```

To use this code to sign a message, you first would use the normal Java cryptography APIs to compute an SHA-1 digest of the message, and then pass it to the above signDigest(...) method. For example:

```
byte[] data = ...your data to be signed...
MessageDigest md = MessageDigest.getInstance("SHA");
byte[] digestBytes = md.digest(data);
byte[] signature = signDigest(digestBytes);
```

The long-term potential for smartcards goes way beyond security applications. For example, looking down the road to when smartcards have more memory, imagine if you could store your email on a smartcard, or your computer desktop preference settings. Java smartcards also have the ability to be updatable in the field, due to their inherently secure design. Eventually smartcards will be able to store applications from multiple sources—your banks, telephone company, airlines, your office, and so on—so you can carry your entire e-commerce and security world with you on a single card. This will require many details to be worked out before it can happen, such as the ability of applications on cards from different sources to trust each other, but it is definitely coming.

### *Obtaining a Certificate*

A common way of obtaining a certificate is from a web site. Certificates obtained in this way usually are intended for use in the respective client, e.g., Communicator or IE. The application/x-x509-ca-cert and application/x-x509-user-cert MIME types are used by both Communicator and Internet Explorer for transferring client certificates from a certificate server to the browser. (The MIME type application/pkcs7-mime could also be used, but at this writing Communicator does not recognize that type.) A certificate transferred in this way will be automatically installed into the browser's certificate database (or in the case of Internet Explorer, in the registry). This is fine if the browser is your application, or if your application will be using browser-based security facilities, e.g., its secure socket implementation. Once it is in the browser you can export it to a file, but this creates an encrypted PKCS#12 message containing your certificate and its private key in encrypted form. To store that in a different keystore, you need software that can parse a PKCS#12 message.

A better approach is to enable your application to request a certificate from a certificate server. This is not as difficult as it sounds. Unfortunately, the negotiation that occurs between a client application and a certificate server is not yet completely standardized. This means you have to select the brand of certificate server you plan to use, and build the proprietary negotiation protocol into your application. Yet, there are aspects that are standardized. For example, the certificate request is usually a CSR (PKCS#10) message (but not always—e.g., Communicator sends a signed public key along with HTML form variables specified by the certificate server), which I have already discussed. When the certificate is sent back to the client, it is usually sent in a PKCS#7 message (but not always—a plain DER-encoded certificate is sent by some certificate servers). The MIME type is also *partially* standardized, as explained above. What is not standardized is the parts in between. Let's look at an example, using Phaos Technology's Centuris certificate server.

```
import com.phaos.cert.X500Name;
import com.phaos.cert.CertificateRequest;
import com.phaos.cert.BASE64Encoder;
import com.phaos.https.HttpsURLStreamHandlerFactory;
            // provides SSL functionality
...
URL.setURLStreamHandlerFactory(new
   HttpsURLStreamHandlerFactory());
X500Name n = new X500Name("cn=John Smith, o=My Org, c=US");

// Generate key pair.
java.security.KeyPairGenerator kpg =
   java.security.KeyPairGenerator.getInstance("DSA", "Phaos");
kpg.initialize(1024);
KeyPair kp = kpg.genKeyPair();

// Save the private key to a file.
FileOutputStream fos = new FileOutputStream("MyPrivateKey.der");
(kp.getPrivate()).output(fos);
fos.close();

// Generate a PKCS#10 certificate signing request.
CertificateRequest cr = new CertificateRequest(n, kp);

// Open a secure connection to the cert server.
URL theServer = new URL("https://MyOrgsCertServer");
HttpURLConnection theConnection =
(HttpURLConnection)theServer.openConnection();
theConnection.setRequestMethod("POST");
theConnection.setDoOutput(true);
OutputStream os = theConnection.getOutputStream();

// Get the DER encoded representation of the cert
// request, and Base64 encode that.
String requestBytes =
(new BASE64Encoder()).encodeBuffer(cr.getEncoded());

// Now URL encode it, and construct an HTTP POST message,
// with the variables "csr" and "response_format". Different
// certificate servers may use different POST variables.
String content = "csr=" + URLEncoder.encode(requestBytes) +
"&response_format=pkcs7";

// Send the request.
os.write(content.getBytes());
os.write("\r\n".getBytes());
```

At this point, most certificate servers would not automatically send a certificate in their response. To do so would represent a weak security policy, since there is no physical verification that the person requesting the certificate is who they say they are—and to give them a certificate would be like giving someone a new driver's license without seeing proof of identity. Therefore, most certificate servers use a two-step process, in which they add the newly created certificate to a repository, and instead send out a retrieval code to a secure address, e.g., an administrator's address. (Type 1 certificates are granted on the Internet and the pickup code is emailed to the person's email address—not very secure!) The certificate owner then obtains the pickup code from the administrator and makes another web request, providing the pickup code. The certificate server then responds with the actual certificate, and the client can obtain it as follows:

```
// Read the response and check for the MIME type.
if(! theConnection.getContentType().equals(
    "application/x-x509-user-cert"))
{
    throw new Exception(
    "MIME type \"application/x-x509-user-cert\" expected.");
}

// We requested a PKCS#7 response, so attempt to
// construct that from the response stream.
InputStream is = theConnection.getInputStream();
CertificateFactory cf = CertificateFactory.getInstance("X.509");
Certificate[] certs = cf.generateCertificates(is).toArray();

// Store the private key and certificate in our keystore.
KeyStore ks = ...as in earlier examples...
ks.setKeyEntry
(
    "jsmith",     // keystore alias (userid)
    kp.getPrivate(),    // private key
    new char[] { 'm', 'y', 'p', 's', 'w', 'd' },  // password
    certs  // certificate chain
);
```

Note the connection to the certificate server is an HTTPS connection. This is standard practice, and ensures that the connection to the server is private. The standard Java packages do not provide HTTPS, so you have to obtain an implementation elsewhere. In this example I am using the implementation provided by Phaos with their `HttpsURLStreamHandlerFactory`. The Java security packages also do not provide a means to generate a certificate request, and here

I am using the Phaos `CertificateRequest` class for that purpose, which encapsulates PKCS#10 certificate request functionality.

Many certificate servers can store the certificates they generate in an LDAP directory. You can then obtain the certificate using the LDAP userCertificate attribute. For example,

```
Properties env = new Hashtable();
env.put(Context.INITIAL_CONTEXT_FACTORY,
"com.sun.jndi.ldap.LdapCtxFactory");
env.put(Context.PROVIDER_URL, "ldap://ldaphost");
if (userDN == null)
   env.put(Context.SECURITY_AUTHENTICATION, "none");
else
{
   env.put(Context.SECURITY_AUTHENTICATION, "simple");
   env.put(Context.SECURITY_PRINCIPAL,
      "cn=John Smith, o=My Org, c=US");
   env.put(Context.SECURITY_CREDENTIALS, "MyPassword");
}

DirContext ctx = new InitialDirContext(env);
Vector certs = LDAPUtils.getUserCerts(subjectDN, ctx);
if ((certs == null) || (certs.size() == 0))
{
   System.err.println("No user certificates found");
   return;
}
X509 cert = (X509)certs.elementAt(0);
```

At the present time there are some new standards pending, being developed by the IETF as part of their Public Key Infrastructure (PKIX) effort. These standards will supplant many of the tried and true PKCS standards, and so PKCS#7, for example, will have a newer counterpart, as will CertificateRequest. The negotiation between a client and a certificate server may also become standardized.

**Certificate Revocation.** A certificate is only as good as its associated private key. If the key is compromised, the certificate is worthless. Public certificate authorities have safeguards to keep their private keys in a safe place, because their entire business depends on it. Nevertheless, there is always the possibility that a key may be discovered, either through theft, accidental disclosure, or cryptographic analysis, and therefore a mechanism for revoking certificates is needed. The problem is more immediate with certificates issued by organization level certificate servers, since the safeguards applied vary with the organization.

An electronic message which specifies that one or more certificates are no longer valid is called a certificate revocation list, or CRL. Traditionally a CRL is embedded in a digital envelope, as specified by the PKCS#7 standard. The ongoing IETF PKIX effort has developed a newer standard which now supplants this, specified in RFC 2459. It is the latter which is implemented in the Java X509CRL and X509CRLEntry classes.

These classes provide a means to read in a compliant CRL from an external source (such as a file or a network connection) and construct an instance representing the CRL:

```
InputStream fis = new FileInputStream("MyCRL.crl.der");
CertificateFactory cf = CertificateFactory.getInstance("X.509");
X509CRL crl = (X509CRL)(cf.generateCRL(fis));
fis.close();
```

To test if a certificate is revoked, call the isRevoked() method and pass the certificate in question as a parameter:

```
if (crl.isRevoked(cert))
{
   System.out.println("Hey - this certificate has been revoked!");
}
```

A certificate revocation list is normally stored on a server which manages certificates. For example, a web server which provides SSL capability may have a CRL capability. CRLs can be served from a web server using the application/pkcs7-crl MIME type. A certificate server can obtain the latest CRL posting and update its own internal CRL. A CRL normally specifies a date and time when the next revision to the CRL is anticipated. You can obtain this using the X509CRL's getNextUpdate() method. In this way, a server's internal CRL can be kept up-to-date.

**Real-Time Certificate Status.** The problem with the above method of obtaining CRLs is that it may not be timely when it most needs to be—when a certificate has been compromised. Posting a CRL on a web site is a passive notification method. Servers need to be notified actively and immediately when a certificate is revoked; or alternatively, the server needs to contact a timely source of CRL information whenever it needs to check the status of a certificate. The PKIX protocol designed for that purpose is the Online Certificate Status Protocol (OCSP).

The primary difference between obtaining a CRL and making an OCSP request is that a CRL is a listing of all known revoked certificates for a specified CA, whereas an OCSP request is for a particular certificate. OCSP is designed for high-volume real-time validation of certificates, for applications which have a critical need to know the current status of any certificates being used in a transaction. An OCSP application may even query an OCSP server more than once during a session.

## Secure Communication Protocols

### *The Secure Socket Layer (SSL) Protocol*

The Secure Socket Layer (SSL) protocol is a protocol for creating secure connections between a client and a server across a network. Netscape developed the SSL protocol to create a way for their browser to be used with their server products to conduct electronic commerce, securely, and with the confidence that consumer financial data—in particular, credit card data—transmitted over the Internet could not be compromised. Ironically, the mere fact that they developed this mechanism may have heightened fears about Internet commerce rather than quelled them (just as the fact that Java has built-in security protections has raised consciousness about Java security issues). A consumer's actual financial liability with any credit card purchase is usually quite limited in practice, so Internet credit card fraud may have received more attention than it deserves—at least from the consumer's point of view. Nevertheless, the need for secure transmission of information via the Internet is a real one for many applications, financial and otherwise. The SSL protocol was a breakthrough in making this possible.

SSL attempts to solve the full end-to-end secure transmission problem: it provides for identity authentication of both the client and server (although client authentication is optional in many server products that use SSL), and it encrypts the data that is transmitted. The protocol is flexible, and allows for dynamic specification of cipher algorithms. It is also largely automatic from the user's point of view. The only complication is that one or both ends of the communication link must have a digital certificate or private/public key pair, which must be installed in some way by the administrator or user.

It should be noted that SSL is a secure connection protocol and does not address the issue of logging. If an application needs to record who did what, and when, the application needs to provide for this. While SSL can authenticate users, it does not automatically record sessions, much less what takes place in them. If you need to provide logging of any kind, your application generally must add this.

The protocol can be used in many ways. However, the basic operation of the SSL protocol commonly uses this sequence:

1. Exchange digital certificates (usually server certificate, sometimes client certificate as well).
2. Verify the certificate(s) and authenticate identity.

3. Securely (via asymmetric key encryption or negotiation) exchange symmetric encryption keys to use for subsequent data transmission.
4. Begin data transmission.

This exchange is depicted in Figure 4-6.

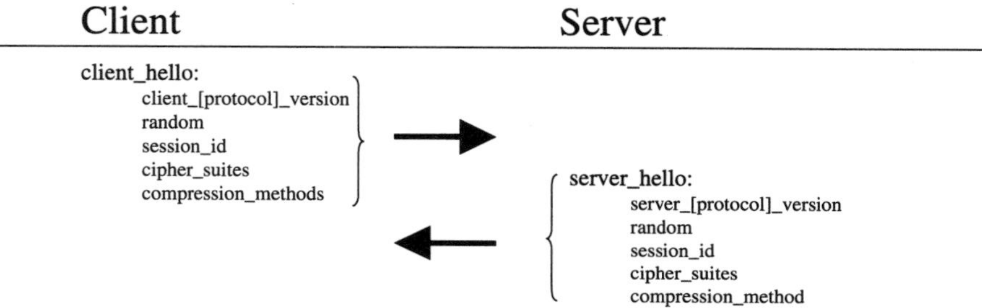


*We now have established protocol version, session ID, cipher suite, and compression method*

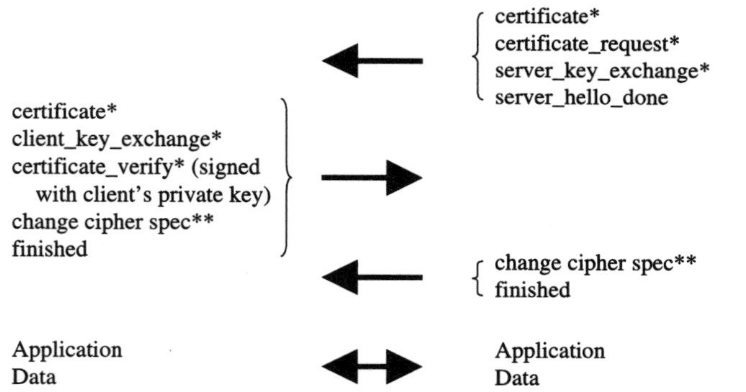


* Optional or situation-dependent messages that are not always sent.
** Belongs to SSL Record Protocol.

**Figure 4-6** SSL handshake protocol messages.

The actual protocol has many additional features. For example, either communicating party can request at any time that the cipher be changed. (It is a common technique in secure communication systems to change keys at frequent intervals during a session.) Authentication of the client (the originator of the connection) is optional in most uses, and some SSL APIs do not mandate authentication of either party.

The protocol actually is layered into multiple protocols. The two primary layers are the SSL Handshake Protocol and the SSL Record Protocol. The Handshake Protocol defines the session establishment messages that travel between the client and server at the start of a session. The Record Protocol defines a lower-level messaging band in which the Handshake Protocol and all application data is wrapped. Error conditions that generate alerts travel in this band.

The Record Protocol message types are:

- change_cipher_spec
- alert
- handshake
- application_data

The SSL Handshake protocol message types are:

- hello_request
- client_hello
- server_hello
- certificate
- server_key_exchange
- certificate_request
- server_hello_done
- certificate_verify
- client_key_exchange
- finished

Session key exchange can be by any of the following techniques:

- Diffie-Hellman
- RSA encryption
- Fortezza Key Exchange Algorithm (similar to Diffie-Hellman; uses a hardware token)

One difficulty with a session-oriented protocol like SSL is that web traffic is often not session-oriented. HTTP sessions are usually created on demand, and may be closed and reopened for each request. To handle this, SSL has the ability to resume an SSL session if the connection is closed. If a client wishes to resume a previous SSL session instead of opening a new one, the client sends a client_hello message using the session_id of the session to be resumed. If the server is willing to re-establish the connection, it will send a server_hello with the same session_id value. At this point, both client and server must send change cipher spec messages. All of this happens automatically as part of the SSL protocol, and is transparent to the client and server applications.

Netscape has a patent on SSL, but allows royalty-free implementation, providing that those implementations do not claim their own patent rights that infringe on Netscape's patent.

### *Transport Layer Security (TLS)*

Transport Layer Security is an IETF specification aimed at standardizing the SSL protocol. It is anticipated that most future implementations of SSL will move to TLS, and support SSL only for the sake of backward compatibility. This is not hard to do, however, since TLS is extremely similar to SSL 3.0. TLS is defined in RFC 2246. TLS supports using RSA for authentication and key exchange, or Diffie-Hellman for key exchange with authentication using DSS or RSA signatures.

Unless a particular usage requires otherwise, the following cipher suite is always included in a TLS implementation. See the next section for an interpretation of this name.

```
TLS_DHE_DSS_WITH_3DES_EDE_CBC_SHA
```

### *Interpreting Cipher Suite Names*

The SSL and TLS Hello handshake involve the negotiation of a cipher suite to be used between the client and server, among other things. A cipher suite is a set of algorithms, including the key exchange protocol, the symmetric cipher algorithm to be used, and the hashing algorithm to be used. The identification of the cipher suite is numerically encoded, but the specifications define a set of names for recognized cipher suites.

Consider the cipher suite name:

```
TLS_RSA_WITH_RC4_128_MD5
```

The basic sequence for deciphering these (no pun intended) is:

```
<protocol>_<key-exchange-algorithm>_<cipher-algorithm>_<hash-
algorithm>
```

Therefore, "TLS_RSA_WITH_RC4_128_MD5" uses RSA encryption for exchanging secret keys; those keys are 128-bit RC4 keys, and the hashing algorithm for computing digests is MD5.

Now let's consider:

```
TLS_DHE_DSS_WITH_3DES_EDE_CBC_SHA
```

This suite specifies DHE_DSS for key exchange. The "DHE" part stands for ephemeral Diffie-Hellman, and DSS specifies that the DSS algorithm should be used for signing the Diffie-Hellman parameters so they can be authenticated by the other side. Moving down to the cipher algorithm, "3DES_EDE_CBC" specifies triple-DES with Cipher Block Chaining, a technique applicable to block ciphers such as DES. "SHA," of course, specifies SHA as the hashing algorithm to use.

What about this:

```
TLS_DH_DSS_EXPORT_WITH_DES40_CBC_SHA
```

This suite specifies Diffie-Hellman key exchange, using DSS for authentication. The session encryption algorithm will be DES, with a 40-bit key (i.e., exportable, for mass-market software), and so on.

#### *Use of HTTPS (HTTP/SSL or HTTP/TLS) URLs*

Java platforms such as browsers and the Castanet tuner provide their own URL stream handler factory to allow URLs for recognized protocols to be handled. For example, Communicator does something like the following when it initializes a virtual machine:

```
java.net.URL.setURLStreamHandlerFactory(new
   netscape.net.URLStreamHandlerFactory());
```

In a Communicator applet or a Castanet application, you can therefore use an SSL URL to access a location that uses SSL, and cause the browser's or tuner's built-in SSL stream handler to be used. For example, you could do something like the following:

```
URL url = new
   URL("https://securehost.mycompany.com/privatestuff.cgi");
URLConnection uc = url.openConnection();
uc.connect();
OutputStream os = uc.getOutputStream();
...write posted output (securely)...
InputStream is = uc.getInputStream();
...get response (securely)...
```

In the above example, a port is not specified in the URL, so in all likelihood the stream handler will use port 443, which is the default port for HTTPS connections (for either SSL or TLS).

Of course, you can only use the connection in a manner supported by that type of connection, as defined by the stream handler created for you by the stream handler factory. In particular, an HTTP or HTTPS connection will probably have restrictions on when and how you can read and write from the stream, and it will also depend on the object (URL) to which you are connecting (i.e., whether or not it is a program or a static object). See Chapter 5 for more information.

## The Java Security Model: Protecting the Local System

So far I have discussed security as it relates mainly to the transmission of information. I will now shift to discussing the local environment, and what Java provides to protect it from invasion or attack by malicious software downloaded into the user's environment. This issue has become famous, in the context of "malicious applets," but it applies to any kind of software obtained from an untrusted source, whether the software is installed as an applet, a local application, a remotely installed Java servlet, or any other form. Luckily, Java has a security architecture to protect against such risks.

### *What Could a Malicious Applet Do Without Security Management in Place?*

First of all, we should question if the risk is real: what can a malicious piece of software do, once installed in our system? Here are some hypothetical examples:

- It can peruse your internal network, and thereby discover your internal IP address structure.
- It can upload your Windows registry, or look for particular installed programs or data.
- It can steal your (or your company's) information.
- It can pretend to be you (placing orders, sending emails).
- It can mislead you, by masquerading as other applications.
- It can install other daemon programs, viruses, and backdoor patches which remain after you have removed the malicious program.
- It can overwrite your java.security file, so that the next time you start a VM, you are using a security provider with a Trojan horse.
- It can replace classes in package java.

Because of the speed and automatic nature of computerized activities, it is conceivable that a suitably designed scheme could cheat a large number of people in a very short time, with the perpetrators long gone before it is discovered. Money is not the only concern: large amounts of private information could be transferred in a very short interval of time—e.g., an office's entire customer database (imagine an applet that searched for *.ACT, uploaded it when it found it, and then erased all trace of this activity, and three days later the URL is "Not Found," and the perpetrators have by then stolen hundreds or thousands of customer databases and are now selling them overseas for cash!). It is not hard to think of other even scarier examples. Ideally, you would want the applet to have to ask permission to access a directory such as your ACT directory—which would surely tip you off!

### *The Sandbox Model*

The Java sandbox is a metaphor for the concept that a piece of Java code obtained from an external source is untrusted, and therefore executes within a restricted environment. Within this environment, it is not permitted to access resources in the local system that are deemed sensitive from the point of view of security. The sandbox policy is implemented by a component called the SecurityManager, and all system code which provides access to sensitive capabilities requests permission from the security manager prior to each and every access.

Java 1.1 relaxes this model somewhat, and allows digitally signed applets to access the local system as if they were outside of the sandbox. In effect, if an applet is signed, the restrictions are disabled. Netscape and Internet Explorer modified this by adding their own supplementary models, much like the domain model to be discussed below. The Marimba Castanet client framework allows locally installed channels that are signed to run as local code.

Signing downloaded code is not sufficient, however. I recall a Dilbert cartoon in which Dilbert installs a new program, and at the end the program prompts innocently, something to the effect, "Do you want to contact the program's manufacturer to register?" Dilbert pondered for a moment and then clicked "Yes," after which events proceeded beyond his control. At one point the program announces that it is removing files from his hard disk to make room for new software it is automatically ordering for him, using a credit card number that it has found on his machine.

The point is, if you obtain a program about which you do not have much information, you need to give it permission to do things in a step-by-step manner—not wholesale. Permission to access files should be limited to a user-specified directory or set of directories. Permission to access other hosts should be on a host-

name-specific basis, and so on. It should not be all or nothing. Fine granularity of access permission is the direction in which Java is moving.

**Logging—Does It Protect You?** Both Communicator and IE now provide logging for applets. However, if an applet is able to access any part of your hard disk, it can easily find the log and erase it after it has done its dirty work. It is therefore my opinion that a Java security manager should not allow an applet—even a signed one—to erase or modify the security log, replace any classes in package java, or change the security provider. Java 2 makes it possible to distinguish between local applications and system classes, thereby allowing even local classes to be somewhat restricted.

**Protection Domains.** A *protection domain* is a logical entity which has associated with it a level of trust (permissions). Based on this trust, and a set of policies, an entity which regulates access to protected resources—an *access controller*—can decide if a domain should be allowed access to any specific resource.

Java 2 implements a protection domain model, in which it identifies a collection of Java classes that came from the same source as belonging to a protection domain. Code from that domain may attempt to access protected resources, such as a hard disk. System code responsible for monitoring those resources has the responsibility to ask the system if the domain has permission to use the resource.

A *codesource* object identifies a codebase (where the code came from) and the set of public keys (if any) that signed the code. This represents the level of granularity in the current protection domain model. A smaller granularity may be implemented in the future, perhaps at the runtime (signed) object level.

In Java 2, a *policy* object implements the policy (including granularity) for assigning *permissions*. A set of permissions is associated with each protection domain (i.e., each codesource). There is only one policy object in effect at any one time. This policy object is consulted by an AccessController for making actual access right determinations whenever final system code that provides resource-level services requests it to by calling AccessController.checkAccess(). (Policies are set using a policy configuration file. This is discussed in "The Policy File" on page 252.

To determine if a domain should be allowed to access a resource, the checkAccess() method must determine which domains are actually making the request. In other words, it must trace the thread of codesources that are currently active, and determine which domains are involved: it must walk back along the current thread's stack, checking permissions along the way.

There is a complication, though. Sometimes system code needs to access protected resources in a very specific way for a specific purpose, without giving the user application more general access to the same resource. For example, system code might need to access a property file; but this does not mean that the application which is calling the system routine should necessarily be given read access to the file system. The access to the property file occurs under the supervision of the system routine, and requires a temporary suspension of checking the permissions of the application's domain. This is accomplished by a mechanism that allows a system routine (or any routine for that matter) to say, in effect: "The buck stops here; I am going to do something, and assuming you let me do it, don't bother to check if my caller can do it, because I know what I'm doing." Such a section of code is called a *privileged section*, even though it is really a responsible section, rather than privileged, because even *a privileged section is not exempt from its domain requiring permission to access a resource.*

A section of code specifies that it is *privileged* (not really privileged, responsible) as follows:

```
public void somePublicService(...) // some service which
// requires no permission to use
{
   Whatever w = null;
   try
   {
      w = (Whatever)
      (AccessController.doPrivileged(new MyAction(...)));
   }
   catch (SomeException se)
   {
      ...
   }
   catch (Exception ex)
   {
   }

   class MyAction implements PrivilegedExceptionAction
   {
      public MyAction(...) {}
      public Object run() throws SomeException
      {
         // privileged code:
            ...the code requiring privilege goes here...
         return whatever;    // can be null
      }
   }
}
```

The doPrivileged() method executes the run() method of the PrivilegedExceptionAction (or PrivilegedAction, for run() methods that don't need to throw an exception) instance passed to it. The execution scope of the run() method is treated as a privileged section.

The privileged code should be code that is algorithmically safe. That is, a non-privileged caller should not be able to misuse it. A privileged section assumes total responsibility for its actions, and so it must ensure that everything it does cannot result in harm. Therefore, you should not write a general purpose privileged utility which, for example, deletes an arbitrary specified file; instead, the privileged code should perform whatever steps are necessary to ensure that deleting a file is appropriate or what the user intends. In addition, it is extremely important that *any resources that privileged code obtains, e.g., network connections, remote service connections, or local system resources, not be shared or handed or returned to unprivileged code! Privileged code should use its resources, and then release them.* If you must return a system resource, return a secure proxy for the resource.

Lower-level system code that guards access to resources calls the security manager when resources are accessed, which in turn calls the AccessController.checkPermission() method. The checkPermission() method is normally used by final system code like this:

```
FilePermission p = new FilePermission("somedir/somefile",
   "write");
SecurityManager sm = System.getSecurityManager();
sm.checkPermission(p);
```

The security manager in turn delegates this decision to the AccessController, by calling the AccessController's checkPermission(p) method:

```
AccessController.checkPermission(p);
// throws exception if we don't have permission
// If no exception occurred we are ok, and we can proceed
```

If no exception results, the original sm.checkPermission() call returns normally and the calling routine proceeds to access the resource.

The permission and action combinations that are defined in Java 2 are shown in Figure 4-7.

| Permission | Action |
|---|---|
| java.awt.AWTPermission | "accessClipboard" |
| java.awt.AWTPermission | "accessEventQueue" |
| java.awt.AWTPermission | "listenToAllAWTEvents" |
| java.awt.AWTPermission | "readDisplayPixels" |
| java.awt.AWTPermission | "showWindowWithoutWarningBanner" |
| | |
| java.io.FilePermission | "{path}", "read" |
| java.io.FilePermission | "{path}", "write" |
| java.io.FilePermission | "{path}", "execute" |
| java.io.FilePermission | "{path}", "delete" |

(The path can be a file or directory, and can end in a * or - wildcard, where * means all files immediately contained, and - indicates recursive containment.)

| | |
|---|---|
| java.net.NetPermission | "setDefaultAuthenticator" |
| java.net.NetPermission | "requestPasswordAuthentication" |
| java.net.NetPermission | "specifyStreamHandler" |
| | |
| java.util.PropertyPermission | "{key}", "read" |
| java.util.PropertyPermission | "{key}", "write" |

(The key can be a * wildcard, or a . can be followed by a * wildcard)

| | |
|---|---|
| java.lang.reflect.ReflectPermission | "suppressAccessChecks" |
| | |
| java.lang.RuntimePermission | "createClassLoader" |
| java.lang.RuntimePermission | "getClassLoader" |
| java.lang.RuntimePermission | "setContextClassLoader" |
| java.lang.RuntimePermission | "setSecurityManager" |
| java.lang.RuntimePermission | "createSecurityManager" |
| java.lang.RuntimePermission | "exitVM" |
| java.lang.RuntimePermission | "setFactory" |
| java.lang.RuntimePermission | "setIO" |
| java.lang.RuntimePermission | "modifyThread" |
| java.lang.RuntimePermission | "stopThread" |
| java.lang.RuntimePermission | "modifyThreadGroup" |
| java.lang.RuntimePermission | "getProtectionDomain" |
| java.lang.RuntimePermission | "readFileDescriptor" |
| java.lang.RuntimePermission | "writeFileDescriptor" |
| java.lang.RuntimePermission | "loadLibrary.{library name}" |
| java.lang.RuntimePermission | "accessClassInPackage.{packagename}" |

| Permission | Action |
|---|---|
| java.lang.RuntimePermission | "defineClassInPackage.{packagename}" |
| java.lang.RuntimePermission | "accessDeclaredMembers" |
| java.lang.RuntimePermission | "queuePrintJob" |
| (The target can be a * wildcard, or a . can be followed by a * wildcard) | |
| | |
| java.security.SecurityPermission | "getPolicy" |
| java.security.SecurityPermission | "setPolicy" |
| java.security.SecurityPermission | "getProperty.{key}" |
| java.security.SecurityPermission | "setProperty.{key}" |
| java.security.SecurityPermission | "insertProvider.{provider name}" |
| java.security.SecurityPermission | "removeProvider.{provider name}" |
| java.security.SecurityPermission | "setSystemScope" |
| java.security.SecurityPermission | "setIdentityPublicKey" |
| java.security.SecurityPermission | "SetIdentityInfo" |
| java.security.SecurityPermission | "addIdentityCertificate" |
| java.security.SecurityPermission | "removeIdentityCertificate" |
| java.security.SecurityPermission | "printIdentity" |
| java.security.SecurityPermission | "clearProviderProperties.{provider name}" |
| java.security.SecurityPermission | "putProviderProperty.{provider name}" |
| java.security.SecurityPermission | "removeProviderProperty.{providername}" |
| java.security.SecurityPermission | "getSignerPrivateKey" |
| java.security.SecurityPermission | "setSignerKeyPair" |
| | |
| java.io.SerializablePermission | "enableSubclassImplementation" |
| java.io.SerializablePermission | "enableSubstitution" |
| | |
| java.net.SocketPermission | "{host}", "resolve" |
| java.net.SocketPermission | "{host}:{port}", "connect" |
| java.net.SocketPermission | "localhost:{port}", "listen" |
| java.net.SocketPermission | "{host}:{port}", "accept" |

**Figure 4-7** Java 2 permissions.

You can see then that the AccessController class, which is a final class consisting of primarily native methods, is the ultimate gatekeeper, and implements the runtime's core immutable security policies. These policies include association of privileges with codesource, thread association of security context (which includes the codesources traversed by the current thread), and demarcation of responsibility based on privileged sections.

The algorithm used by checkPermission() is as follows:

```
beginning with the current domain n, winding back through n
   domains on the stack,
domain = n;
while (domain > 0)
{
   if (domain does not have the specified permission)
      throw AccessControlException("request denied");
   else if (domain is privileged)
      return;   // i.e., ok
   domain--;
}
return;
```

This is summarized in Figure 4-8.

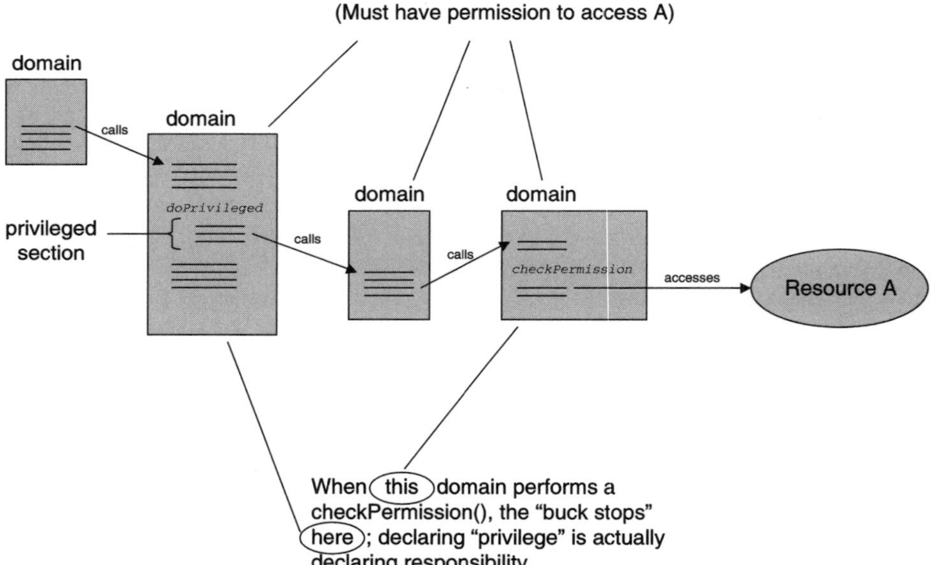


**Figure 4-8** How a thread, which calls many domains, determines if it can access a resource.

In addition, the runtime needs to check permissions for any threads which we used to create the current thread. This is because when one thread creates another, the new thread inherits the complete security context of the original thread as it exists at that moment. Thus, whatever the current thread is trying to do, the creat-

ing thread must have permission as well, or it must have performed the creation while in a privileged section. Further, this must hold for the creating thread's creating thread, and so on, back to the original creating thread. The checkPermission algorithm above is therefore performed not only for the current thread, but for all threads along the chain of creation of the current thread, until a privileged section is detected, or until all domains in the current thread and all creating threads, have been checked.

### *Locally Installed Application Code*

Java 1.0 and 1.1 divided Java code into two categories: code loaded from the local machine via the classpath (as specified by the property java.class.path or an environment variable), and code obtained via a class loader. Code resident on the local system is always completely trusted in Java 1.0 and 1.1. This simplification does not lend itself to Java platforms that allow for self-installing downloadable software, such as Castanet or Netscape's UpdateNow. It is necessary to be able to distinguish between local system code and locally installed applications.

For this reason, Java 2 redefines the Java classpath. In Java 2, the property java.class.path, set by the CLASSPATH environment variable or by a command line switch, no longer includes the Java system classes, which are assumed to reside in the installation's <java.home>/lib/rt.jar file and <java.home>/lib/i18n.jar JAR files, unless the command-line flag -Xbootclasspath: specifies a different path. The location of <java.home> is the jre directory containing bin/java.exe. Classes in the classpath, which no longer include system classes, are now loaded with a special class loader. This allows the controlled installation of system extensions, and classes on the classpath must conform to policies specified in the policy file, even if they come from the local disk.

### *The Extensions Framework*

The Java 2 Extensions Framework defines two separate mechanisms, with two different purposes:

- Allows the permanent installation of a trusted application
- Allows a remotely loaded application to reference other components, using a remote classpath mechanism

**Installing a Trusted Application.** The default security.policy file distributed with the Java 2 platform includes this line at the top:

```
grant codeBase "file:${java.home}/lib/ext/-" {
   permission java.security.AllPermission;
};
```

The security.policy file syntax is discussed in "The Policy File" on page 252. However, the effect of the statement above is to grant all permissions to all code placed within the indicated directory. For example, if your Java runtime is installed in a directory called jre, then all code placed within the jre/lib/ext directory will be granted all permissions and effectively treated as if it were part of the installed runtime, as far as security is concerned. Therefore, if an application installation program installs an application in this directory, the application will operate as an extension of the system and be equally trusted.

The directory i386 within the extensions directory is appended to the path searched for native libraries such as DLLs or shared libraries on Intel UNIX systems. On SPARC systems, the directory called sparc within the extensions directory is appended to the search path for shared libraries. In general, a port to a given architecture will use a directory named after that architecture within the extensions directory for shared libraries.

**Bundled Extensions.** A bundled extension is nothing more than a JAR file or directory referenced by another JAR file. Very often an application is deployed on a web site in the form of a JAR file, but the application requires additional components which are in their own JAR file, e.g., the Swing library, or the additional components may be deployed in a subdirectory on the web server. The application's main JAR file can include these additional components by reference. It does this with a manifest attribute called Class-Path, in which it lists all the additional JAR files or directories it requires by relative URL. For example, the classpath attribute:

```
Class-Path: swingall.jar FromDenver/otherstuff.jar FromDenver/
```

appends the two JAR files swingall.jar and otherstuff.jar to the classpath, as well as all files within the FromDenver subdirectory, which must be relative to the codebase of the JAR file containing the Class-Path attribute (this restriction will be relaxed in the future). The / after the FromDenver directory name is required to indicate that it is a directory and not a JAR file.

A bundled extension is not a true extension in that it has no predefined security permissions, and is not installed in any way. It is merely a means of referencing additional components in a convenient way. To give permissions to a bundled extension, you must grant permission to its codesource in your system's java.policy file.

### *Class Loaders*

Class loaders are the mechanism Java uses to retrieve and dynamically link Java classes at runtime. A class loader loads classes from one or more domains—that is, one or more codesources, and more typically a single codesource. To invoke a class loader, a Java VM runtime invokes a class loader's loadClass(...) method from native code whenever it needs to resolve a class reference. The loadClass(...) method of a class loader is required to be declared `synchronized`.

Java runtime system classes—the classes in package java—are loaded by the "primordial" class loader. This is the class loader which is built into the runtime, and is used to load all classes until another class loader is itself loaded and used. The primordial class loader is often referred to as the "null" class loader, because it is not represented by any Java class implementation, and if one invokes the getClassLoader() method on a class which has been loaded with the primordial class loader, it returns null.

Class loaders are themselves instances of classes (except for the primordial class loader). These class loader classes must be loaded as well, using the same class loading mechanism as for any other class.

Each class loader instance defines a disjoint class namespace. Therefore, if you declare a static variable in a class, and two different class loaders load the same class, they will be unable to share the value of the static variable. This is useful for container environments which need to keep multiple deployed applications logically separate. For example, a web browser permits multiple applets deployed on the same web page to share static data by sharing classes, but applets on other pages are unaffected. This is true because matching codebases on the same web page share a class loader instance, but all other codebases and pages use different class loader instances.

Java 2 allows class loaders to be chained together, forming a hierarchy. The primordial class loader is always at the top of the hierarchy. This is a classname resolution hierarchy. Class loaders are expected to first delegate class loading to their parent class loader, and use other methods only if that fails. The hierarchy therefore also represents an order of preference for how to obtain classes, with installed system classes of highest preference. The parent-child relationship between a class loader and its parent is established when a class loader instance is created, usually through a constructor parameter. An example of a class loader hierarchy is shown in Figure 4-9.

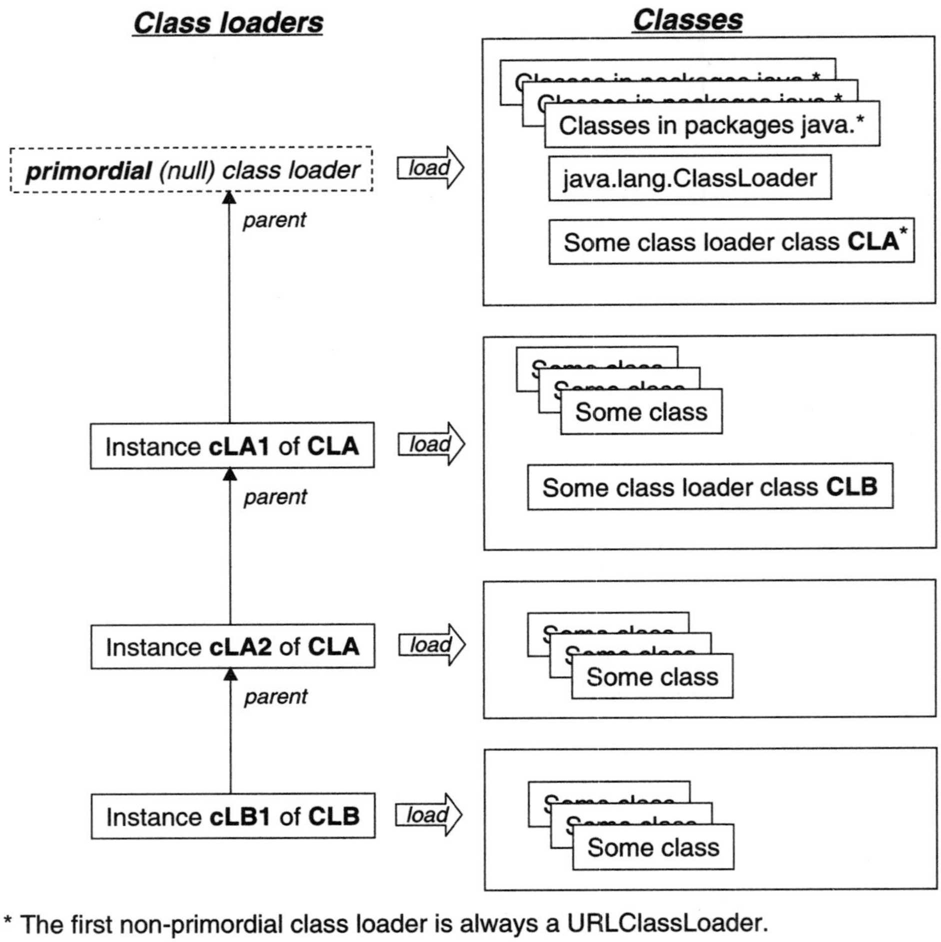

***Class loaders*** | ***Classes***

***primordial*** *(null) class loader* → *load* → Classes in packages java.* / java.lang.ClassLoader / Some class loader class **CLA***

*parent*

Instance **cLA1** of **CLA** → *load* → Some class / Some class loader class **CLB**

*parent*

Instance **cLA2** of **CLA** → *load* → Some class

*parent*

Instance **cLB1** of **CLB** → *load* → Some class

* The first non-primordial class loader is always a URLClassLoader.

**Figure 4-9** How class loader classes are loaded.

Let's look at how a class loader actually works. The main part of the base class java.lang.ClassLoader.loadClass(String name, boolean resolve) method is reproduced here:

```
// First, check if the class has already been loaded
Class c = findLoadedClass(name);
if (c == null) {
   try {
      if (parent != null) {
         c = parent.loadClass(name, false);
```

```
        } else {
           c = findBootstrapClass(name);
        }
     } catch (ClassNotFoundException e) {
        // If still not found, then call findClass in order
        // to find the class.
        c = findClass(name);
     }
  }
  if (resolve) {
     resolveClass(c);
  }
```

As you can see, the base class loader first checks to see if the class is already loaded. If not, it then delegates the load operation to its parent, or to the primordial "bootstrap" class loader if parent is null. If this fails, it then calls the findClass(String) method, which always throws a ClassNotFoundException in the java.lang.ClassLoader implementation. Therefore, subclasses of ClassLoader must override findClass(String).

The findClass(String) method is the method which actually obtains the bytes representing the class, and then constructs a class object from it by calling defineClass(...). The resolveClass(...) method performs name resolution on the symbolic references within the class. A customer class loader normally only has to override the findClass() method. However, if a custom class loader must manage its class cache differently, it may need to do more than override findClass(String).

Normally a class is loaded in response to an attempt by the VM to resolve a class name. In Sun's VM, the runtime calls the C method FindClassFromClass() which in turn calls ClassLoaderFindClass(), which natively invokes the Java loadClass(...) method on the current thread's class loader. However, a class loader can also be invoked explicitly from your Java application, by calling its loadClass(...) method from Java; it can also be invoked by calling Class.forName(<classname>).

In the case in which a class loader's loadClass(...) method is invoked explicitly, there is no ambiguity about which class loader to use, since it is being explicitly specified. In the latter case of calling Class.forName(String classname), the class loader of the calling class is used. (Note that there is an error in the Java documentation about this.) You can also specify a class loader by using the overloaded version Class.forName(String classname, boolean initialize, ClassLoader loader).

In most Java runtime implementations, the first non-primordial class loader created by the runtime is an instance of URLClassLoader (in browsers or other container environments it may be different). This class loader is used to load application classes. Applications can then install their own class loaders under the URLClassLoader if they desire. URLClassLoader extends from SecureClass-Loader, which associates the newly created class with a protection domain. This inheritance relationship is shown in Figure 4-10.

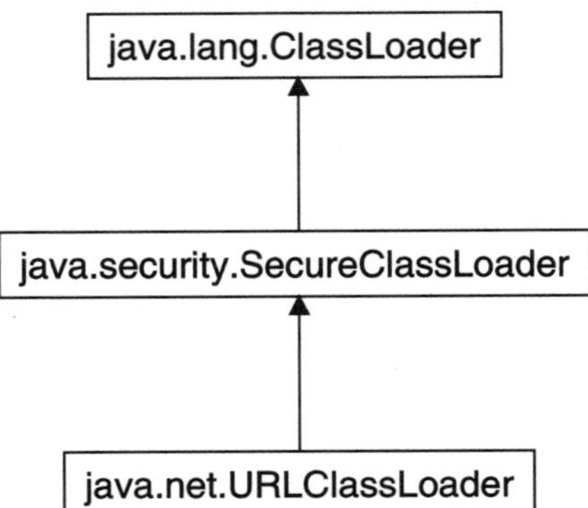


**Figure 4-10** Inheritance relationships of the built-in class loaders.

### *The Policy File*

The purpose of a policy file or a policy database is to prevent users from "clicking away security." What good does it do the user if the browser asks the user if an applet can open a socket to a remote host, if the user does not understand the ramifications of that? Or if the user is so tired of being asked such things that he or she automatically clicks "yes" to each request?

A policy file or database allows the administrator of a system to configure the system's security policy to allow certain operations, so that the user does not have to be asked dynamically. In fact, a browser such as Netscape Communicator, which supports its own capabilities API, has its own policy database, which gets updated automatically whenever the user clicks "yes" or "no" on such a permission dialog. An organization that needs to deploy Java software in a secure way needs a way to preconfigure policies, based on a list of trusted hosts. Applications which are trusted can even be given the right to update this database, for example through a trusted host's list control panel.

There can be more than one policy file. The default policy implementation (implemented by java.security.PolicyFile) uses the property values policy.url.* to find policy files. These property values are specified in your java.security file. The default values are:

```
policy.url.1=file:${java.home}/lib/security/java.policy
policy.url.2=file:${user.home}/.java.policy
```

where the values in ${} get expanded to their Java system property values. For example, the property user.home, on an NT computer that belongs to a network domain, will normally expand to C:\WINNT\Profiles\<your-domain-logon-id>. The URL is relative to the policy file location, or may be an absolute URL.

The determination of <java.home> is dependent on which Java runtime is executing. For example, if you have a copy of the JRE installed in the NT Program Files directory (which is very common, especially if you have installed the Java Plugin), and you ran that copy of the java.exe launcher to start your application, then that JRE directory will be treated as <java.home>, and the java.policy file in that JRE's lib/security directory will be used (in addition to your <user.home> one). If, however, you ran a different java.exe launcher, e.g., the one included with the Java 2 installation, then that version's java.policy file will be used.

The intended approach therefore is to have a single system-wide policy file, and a policy file in the user's home directory. Since policy files are loaded in the order specified by the policy.url.* trailing number, the default is to have the system policy file load first, followed by the user's policy file. If no policy file is specified, the built-in sandbox policy is used. In assigning policy URL property names, do not skip a number, because if you do, those following the skipped number will not be seen.

You can also specify an application-specific java.policy file to use, by setting the runtime property -Djava.security.policy property=<your policy file> when you run your application. This will cause the specified policy file to be logically concatenated onto the system and user policy files. If you want the file you specify to be the only one used, use a double-equals instead: -Djava.security.policy==<your policy file>. You can specify your policy file as a file path or as a URL.

### *Policy File Syntax*

The policy file has entries that grant privileges. Each entry consists of a "grant" statement, which contains a set of permission declarations. The grant may be unconditional, or may be conditional based on a codebase and/or a signing alias. For example:

```
grant signedBy "marketing", codebase "http://sales.theircompany.com"
{
   permission java.io.FilePermission "C:\\orderlogs\\*", "read,
      write";
   permission java.net.SocketPermission
      "orders.ourcompany.com:6000", "connect";
};
```

grants file read and write permission to the C:\orderlogs\ directory on a Windows system. The "*" indicates that the permission is to be applied recursively, to all subdirectories; if it were not present, the permission would only apply to the specified file or directory. The signedby clause is optional, as is the codebase clause. If neither appears, the permission is granted unconditionally. If one or both appear, the permission is granted based on whether the code is signed and comes from the specified codebase, respectively.

Note that URLs always use forward slashes, even on a Windows system, whereas a file specification should use the syntax appropriate for the host on which the policy file resides. You can use the syntax ${/} instead of a slash or backslash pair if you want a file specification to be platform independent.

The syntax ${<property>} can be used to expand Java system properties. You could therefore have a permission in your policy file as follows:

```
permission java.io.FilePermission "${user.home}\\*", "read,
   write";
```

This would grant read and write permission to all files under the user's home directory.

### *Implementing a Customized Policy*

The policy file mechanism is provided with the Java 2 runtime as a default implementation. A Java platform could instead implement a policy database. This would allow centralized and real-time configuration and administration of Java policies within a network. Another application of this would be, for example, if you are writing a server that you want to be extensible, such that users can add their own plugins to the runtime without threatening the stability of the server. Basically, for each plugin you would assign a URL, and keep a database of URL (codesource) vs. permissions. When a plugin is installed, you would update the permission database. You would need to extend java.security.Policy, and implement the evaluate() method.

```
public class PluginPolicy extends java.security.Policy
{
   public PluginPolicy() {}

   public void init()
   {
      // Load default policy configuration, in case database
      // cannot be opened
      super.init();
       ...open your policy database...
   }
```

```
    public PublicKey[] getPublicKeys(Object signers[])
    {
        return super.getPublicKeys(signers);
    }

    public Permissions evaluate(CodeSource codesource)
    {
         ...check the database...
    }

    public void addPermission(String permissionClassName, String
        targetResource, String action,
            String codebase, String signerAlias)
    throws GeneralSecurityException
    {
        ...add the permission to your database...
    }

    public void revokePermission(String permissionClassName,
        String targetResource, String action,
            String codebase, String signerAlias)
    {
        ...remove the permission from your database...
    }
}
```

To enable this new policy class, just edit the policy.provider entry in your java.security file:

```
policy.provider=PluginPolicy
```

### *Using Thread Groups to Segregate Rights Within a VM*

Sometimes you need to restrict access to resources based on criteria other than where the code originates from. For example, you might have a server program which creates threads to satisfy user requests. Depending on the user, you might want to associate a different policy for each thread for the thread's lifetime.

You can accomplish this by writing your own security manager for the server application. The server manager can create different thread groups for different classes of user requests, and associate policies on a thread-group basis. Since it is possible to restrict a thread's ability to access or modify its thread group, there is no way the thread can "escape" from the thread group sandbox. This is shown in Figure 4-11.

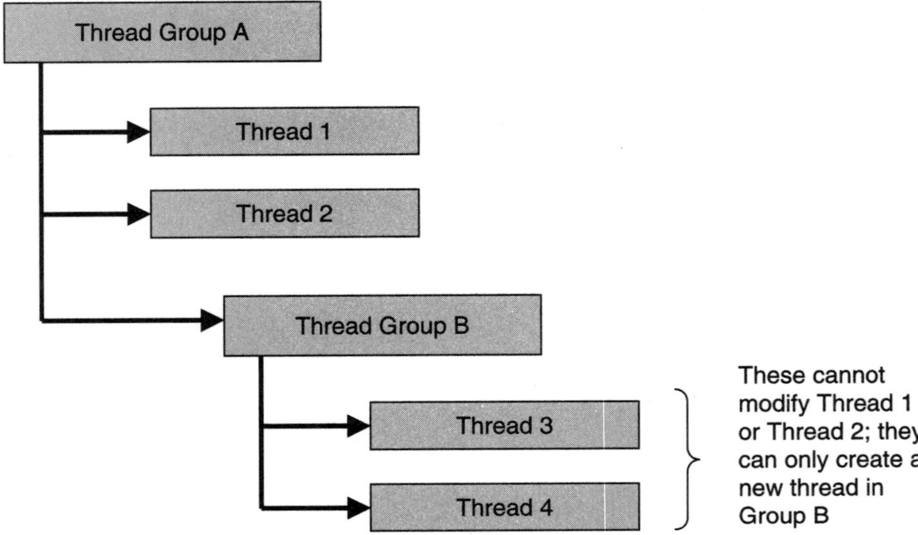


**Figure 4-11** Our thread group access policy.

Let's consider an example in which we want to restrict our service threads such that they can only write files in a specified directory; furthermore, if a file name has the suffix ".private," the service thread cannot modify it. I will assume that the service threads are implemented by a class called "Gremlin," which implements Runnable. Here is an outline of the security manager class:

```
class GremlinWatcher extends SecurityManager
{
   private ThreadGroup seniorThreadGroup;
   private String gremlinDirectory;
   public GremlinWatcher(ThreadGroup seniorThreadGroup,
      String gremlinDirectory)
   {
```

Note that in the constructor we specify the thread group that will own the gremlin thread group. We also specify the directory in which gremlin threads can write:

```
      super();
      this.seniorThreadGroup = seniorThreadGroup;
      this.gremlinDirectory = gremlinDirectory;
   }
```

We need to protect against gremlins trying to modify their thread group, to defeat our thread-group-based security restrictions:

```
public void checkAccess(Thread t)
{
   super.checkAccess(t);
   if (! threadGroupAccessAllowed(t.getThreadGroup()))
   {
      checkPermission(new RuntimePermission("modifyThread"));
   }
}
public void checkAccess(ThreadGroup g)
{
   super.checkAccess(g);
   ThreadGroup tg = Thread.currentThread().getThreadGroup();
   if (! threadGroupAccessAllowed(g))
   {
      checkPermission(
         new RuntimePermission("modifyThreadGroup"));
   }
}
/**
 * Implements our thread access policy. This is our
 * own method.
 */
protected boolean threadGroupAccessAllowed(ThreadGroup g)
{
   ThreadGroup tg = Thread.currentThread().getThreadGroup();
   return (tg.parentOf(g));
}
```

The checkPermission() call in both checkAccess() methods is to allow Java system code to bypass our policy. This is really unnecessary in this case, since a Java system thread will not belong to our gremlin thread group, but I have coded it this way just in case.

Next we need to implement our file write restriction policy: a gremlin can write files within its gremlin directory, but not if the file name ends in ".private":

```
public void checkWrite(String file)
   {
      ThreadGroup tg = Thread.currentThread().getThreadGroup();
      if (tg != seniorThreadGroup)
      {
         // Perform checks; if checks fail, throw exception

         java.io.File f = new java.io.File(file);
```

```
            String path = f.getAbsolutePath();
            if (! path.regionMatches(
               true, 0, gremlinDirectory, 0,
                gremlinDirectory.length()))
            {
               // Cannot write file outside of Gremlin Directory
               super.checkWrite(file);
            }

            if (f.getName().regionMatches(true, f.getName().length()
               - 8, ".private", 0, 8))
            {
               // Cannot write private file
               super.checkWrite(file);
            }
         }

         // return ok
         System.out.println("File " + file + " may be written");
      }
```

Here is a program which instantiates the gremlin security manager:

```
public final class GremlinWorrier
{
   private static ThreadGroup gremlins;

   private GremlinWorrier() {}
// private - we don't want any gremlins instantiating it

   public static void main(String[] args)
   {
      // Create the gremlin security manager, and a
      // thread group for any gremlins to run it.

      SecurityManager sm = new GremlinWatcher(
         Thread.currentThread().getThreadGroup(), args[0]);
      System.setSecurityManager(sm);
      gremlins = new ThreadGroup("Gremlins");
      try
      {
```

Now let's create a gremlin, and run it in the gremlin thread group:

```
            Runnable gremlin    = (Runnable)(new Gremlin());

            // Create a new thread for gremlin, in the gremlin's
            // thread group.
            // Within that thread group, they can do whatever they
               want!
        Thread t = new Thread(gremlins, gremlin);
        t.start();
        }
        catch (Exception e)
        {
            e.printStackTrace();
        }
    }
}
```

## Authorization and Access Control

An access control list (ACL) is a list which enumerates a set of access rights for an entity such as an individual. Rights can be negative, such that an access control entry may specify that the entity is to be denied a right, or they may be positive and allow a right. Access control lists are commonly used by many systems, including application servers, file systems, and security systems to store access permission information about users.

I have already discussed the access control mechanism applied by the Java runtime's AccessController. This mechanism relies on privileges being associated with a codesource. What if your application needs to apply its own access control policies? We have seen an example of thread-group based access control, in which a user is associated with a specific thread group, and access rights are granted on a thread group basis. Other, more general, kinds of access control requirements may exist, however. For example, if we need to store arbitrary access control permissions on a per-user basis, we need a general mechanism for aggregating and storing that kind of information. The java.security.acl package is a utility package for that purpose.

The interface java.security.acl.Acl defines a container for ACL entries. Each entry is associated with a Principal. A Principal identifies an individual or any entity which may have privileges. An entry may be either positive or negative. Positive entries enumerate permissions to be granted, whereas negative entries enumerate permissions to be denied. Further, within an ACL, a Principal may have only one positive entry and one negative entry. We therefore have a structure which is logically like the one shown in Figure 4-12.

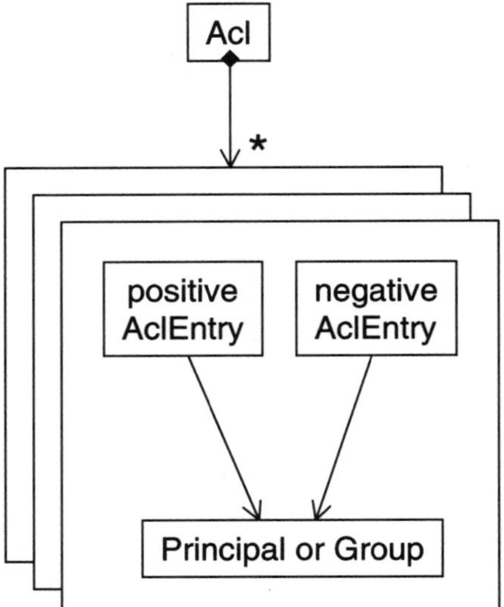


**Figure 4-12** An access control list.

Notice that an entry can be associated with a Group as well as a Principal. In fact, Group extends from Principal.

Using an ACL, you can check if a given principal has a given permission by calling the Acl.checkPermission(Principal, Permission) method. How you implement your ACL is up to you. It could, for example, be a serializable object which is stored in a directory server or database.

In addition, it is up to your application to implement Principal in the way that is convenient. Therefore, you can return whatever you want for the Principal.getName() method. However, note that there are some implementations of Principal built into the Java packages, including sun.security.x509.X500Name, which is returned by the method X509Certificate.getSubjectDN(). The X500Name.getName() method returns an X500 distinguished name string. ACLs which are used for checking permissions for users who are authenticated using PKI techniques will therefore find it convenient to use distinguished name strings.

### *The Java Authentication and Authorization Service (JAAS)*

As already explained, the Java sandbox security model addresses access control based on the codesource of an executing class, and a set of privileges granted to that codesource. There is no consideration of the *user* in determining access control or capabilities. I have already shown a thread-group-based user access control model, but that example was not a framework and required coding the specific

access control rules to be applied to each thread group. In the previous section, I showed how access control lists can be used to build data structures, which can then be used to determine access control rules. Applying those rules is still up to the application, however. What we need is a framework, which extends the basic Java security model to account for users.

The Java Authentication and Authorization Framework (JAAS) extends the access control model of the Java runtime to include users. User association is implicit, in that a thread of execution is associated with a user, and access control is then applied to the thread as it traverses through code. The JAAS framework therefore adds two primary features to Java security: user and thread association, and privilege assignment based on users.

It is necessary to enhance the AccessController to accomplish this, which is a core part of the Java runtime, and so JAAS is not available in the current release of Java 2 (SDK 1.2). However, it is anticipated in the next major release.

# CHAPTER 5

# Java Network Programming and Internet Server Protocols

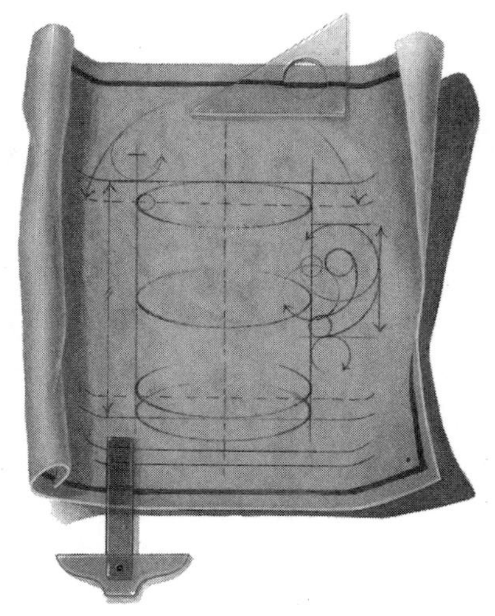

One of the great assets of the Java language is its built-in support for TCP networking. This is what makes the language Internet-ready, and an easy platform on which to build networked and distributed applications. The network model provided by Java is simple, and conveniently abstracts socket operations which otherwise might be host-specific or OS-specific. This is certainly not the only OS-independent socket API there is, but the spread of Java is sure to make it one of the most widely used.

In addition to basic networking, Java provides higher level functionality for application protocols such as HTTP and FTP. With a few statements, a programmer can establish an HTTP connnection to talk to a web server. It is unnecessary to find and include network or protocol libraries or encode protocol headers. Support for proxies such as SOCKS and HTTP proxies is built in. Many other protocols such as IIOP or SSL are easily added by including implementations of these, which ride on top of the basic Java networking API.

In this chapter I will attempt to explain the basic facilities at a detailed level in preparation for discussion of techniques which include writing your own socket implementations and adding or configuring security features. This preparation is intended to help the reader understand later discussions of other protocols and how they can be used in real network environments which include firewalls and security systems.

### *Writing Your Own Protocol*

Since Java has built-in networking support, it is easy to write one's own application level protocol. I have done this myself many times. The first one I ever wrote in Java implemented a protocol for a shared whiteboard applet, which allowed multiple users to share a common drawing and painting surface across the Internet. Written in 1995, this was possibly one of the first Java applications of that kind. I designed a (somewhat inefficient) protocol of my own for that application because no suitable protocol existed in Java. If I were to write that application today I would use RMI.

Generally it is advisable to use standard protocols instead of inventing your own. The reason is that you can then take advantage of features which you would otherwise have to implement, such as proxy tunneling, or scalability features, such as the ability to manage connections.

Sometimes it is necessary to do it yourself, however, especially if you have specific requirements that are not met by an existing protocol implementation. A custom protocol has the opportunity to be faster and more efficient than a general purpose remote invocation or messaging protocol, such as CORBA's IIOP or RMI's JRMP. With a custom protocol, you can avoid general purpose overhead, and send just what is needed, and know exactly what to do with each message received. You can reduce the number of layers of software, and establish a direct connection between a client object and server object, avoiding application-level method call routing between the two. The disadvantage is that the protocol will be specific to that application, and you will have the burden of maintaining it. In choosing to build a custom protocol, you must also consider if the quality of service of the underlying network is sufficient to provide the desired performance, even if the application protocol is extremely efficient. For example, a real-time multi-player game implemented over today's Internet will suffer from unpredictable and sporadic transmission and routing delays, especially if players are far apart.

It seems as if every major corporation I have worked with has at one point developed its own remote object protocol, analogous to CORBA, if not developing their own CORBA ORB. Now that standardized technologies like CORBA have matured, many of these home-grown solutions are being shelved. However, the fact that these organizations went to the trouble to create re-usable solutions for the remote invocation problem shows that there are significant advantages of a general purpose protocol that outweigh use of a custom one.

Even if you use a general purpose solution like CORBA or RMI, it is useful to understand the underlying Java network model and how these technologies work.

# Understanding Java Networking[1]

## Sockets and Server Sockets

There are many types of network transport protocols in use today. A transport protocol provides application-to-application delivery of data, usually in sequence and with a fairly high degree of reliability. A transport protocol API (in combination with its underlying network protocol) provides an abstraction for applications to use, to send data from one application to another, without worrying about physical device characteristics such as device addresses and the path to the destination machine. I am tempted to say that issues like flow control and retransmission are taken care of also, but in a practical sense they are only taken care of up through the network transport level—application programmers must still allocate buffers (unless a buffered API is used for reading data), and worry about end-to-end acknowledgment. (See also the discussion about the TCP reset problem on page 268.) Still, at least you don't have to find out the Ethernet address of the network card on the machine with which you are trying to communicate! What a transport service does provide is routing to the final destination and application, and automatic retransmission of pieces that don't make it on the first try, with all data arriving in the correct sequence.

With most protocols, however, it is still up to you to define things such as message record boundaries (how does the receiver know when it has read the entire message? It cannot check for EOF, since the connection is still open, and more data may arrive as part of the next message).

Java provides a built-in binding for TCP/IP, which is the protocol used by the Internet. Other protocols may be used from Java, but if you want to use another protocol, you will have to import a package that implements it, and it will likely require loading some native code to access the native communication services. An alternative is to use a TCP/IP gateway.

Implementations of TCP normally use two kinds of logical connection: a client socket, for transmitting and receiving data, and a server socket, sometimes referred to as a "passive socket," for receiving connection requests. A server socket is actually just a socket that has bound itself to a port so it can receive connection requests. Most TCP APIs, however, encapsulate the socket creation and bind into one operation. Java goes further and uses a separate object class for server sockets.

A server socket is opened by a server application, and responds to connection requests from prospective clients by creating client sockets. The server program waits on a server socket read (in UNIX implementations this is often a "select()"

---

1. Hereafter, the term "Java networking" will be used to refer to Java-based networking or networking in the Java programming environment. Java is a trademark of Sun Microsystems, Inc., in the U.S. and other countries.

function), and when a request comes in, creates a new client socket to service the client and then returns to its blocking read. Usually, the server will also allocate a thread or process to service the new socket, although an alternative approach is to service it right away (or at least read and enqueue the data), and combine the server socket read and all client socket reads into one read operation in a loop. This is not usually the approach of Java programs, because the Java socket API does not lend itself to this design, since sockets and server sockets are implemented by separate objects.

The Java socket API specifies a Socket object type for servicing client socket connections, and a ServerSocket object type for handling connection requests. I will first discuss the Socket class, and then the ServerSocket class.

### *The Socket Class*

The Socket class encapsulates creation of a socket. There are two instances in which a Socket is created—by a server socket for the purpose of servicing a client connection, and by a client application wishing to communicate with a server program.

Once you create a Java socket, it is already open and ready for use—the act of creating it establishes the connection. With a Socket instance, you can perform reads and writes using the input stream and output stream associated with the socket. Thus, one socket services communication in both directions, unlike some TCP APIs in other languages, which associate a separate socket object or structure for each direction.

When you write a socket program in a language such as C, you have to worry about an important issue called "network byte ordering." Different computer architectures order bytes differently, the two schemes being "Big-Endian" and "Little-Endian." The Big-Endian scheme, which is used by the Java VM, gives the high order bytes of a multi-byte numeric value a lower address in memory than the low order bytes. This ordering is also referred to as "network byte order," and is the standard ordering used by Internet protocols for transferring numeric values such as protocol port numbers between different machines. (Actually, values usually are transferred as they are, and re-ordered if necessary when they reach their destination.) Intel machines use Little-Endian byte ordering. The Java socket layer takes care of byte order conversion for you and re-orders received bytes when needed, so your application does not have to worry about it—a big relief in comparison with socket programming with most UNIX socket libraries.

Here is an example of creating a client socket from a client program to communicate with a server:

```
Socket socket = new Socket("myhost.com", 1000);
```

This attempts to open a bidirectional socket to host "myhost.com" on port 1000. The port is not a physical port with wires coming out of it—it is a logical port, as defined by TCP/IP. The port routes the connection to the server application on the specified host; this number is specified by the server application when it starts accepting connections, as will be seen below when I discuss server sockets.

If you were writing this in C, you would also have to worry about name resolution—obtaining the IP address for the destination host, based on the domain name myhost.com. In BSD UNIX, a client application calls the gethostbyname() function to do this. The Java socket layer takes care of this for you too—it automatically calls the hosts's name resolution API, which will either use a local name directory, or go out on the network to a name server to look up the specified host. It is all transparent to your application. You can also specify an IP address, thereby avoiding name resolution, e.g., by creating a socket with:

```
Socket socket = new Socket("127.0.0.1", 1000);
```

To read from the socket you have created, you can do something like the following:

```
BufferedReader br = new BufferedReader(new
   InputStreamReader(socket.getInputStream()));
String s = br.readLine();
```

One advantage of using BufferedReader is that it is buffered: its readLine() method will read all the data that is available at any moment and block until it finds a line terminator sequence (CR-NL, CR, or NL—whichever it finds), which it treats as a record boundary. This is very useful for many Internet application protocols, such as HTTP, which use CR-NL as a logical record boundary.

To write to the socket, you can call getOutputStream(), and construct a more convenient output writer object, exemplified by the following:

```
PrintWriter pw = new PrintWriter(socket.getOutputStream());
pw.println("hi there");
```

### *The ServerSocket Class*

A Java server socket exists to create client sockets. That is its role. By itself it does not participate in client communication, but merely acts to respond to connection requests from remote clients, and to create local client sockets to actually service those requests. Here is an example:

```
ServerSocket ss = new ServerSocket(1000);
for (;;)
{
   Socket s = ss.accept();
   SocketServiceThread t = new SocketServiceThread(s);
   t.start();
}
```

In this example, I have assumed that the programmer has defined a class called SocketServiceThread, which extends Thread and implements the functionality required by the application to actually communicate with the client and service client requests. The basic flow of control is this: the main server program sits in an endless loop, blocked on a ServerSocket.accept(), waiting for a connection request. When a connection request comes in, the ServerSocket manufactures a client Socket, which can be used to communicate in logical duplex mode with the new client. In my example, I then create a separate service object specifically for that new connection, and I implement this service object with a new thread so that it will run concurrently with other service objects. I then return to the accept() call, and wait for the next connection request.

It is possible to extend the Socket and ServerSocket class to provide your own implementation, for example, to add encryption to a socket stream. In Chapter 4, I provided an example of doing so.

### *The TCP Reset Problem*

Consider a situation in which a client sends a request to a server, and instead of waiting for a response, proceeds to send more requests, assuming that the server will handle the first request successfully. If the server fails on the first request and closes its connection, unread data will be left in the TCP buffers, and the TCP connection may be reset by the server ("connection reset by peer"), causing all the data on the server side to be discarded, including any response sent by the server. The problem is that the client does not know if the first request succeeded or if the connection was closed for other reasons. In this case, the client has no choice but to retry the original request, and this process happens all over again. The client and server can end up in an endless loop of trying and not succeeding.

While it is true that TCP provides a reliable transport mechanism that delivers all data while two entities are connected, anomalies like this can occur when connections are broken unexpectedly. To prevent this problem, one should avoid using the data transport mechanism as an application queue, and send only the data required for the current operation. You can relax this restriction if you are sure that you handle all possible error conditions.

If you have written the server program, you can also control the reset behavior by setting the "linger" interval, by calling setSoLinger(true, <delay>) on the socket. This is the time (in milliseconds) that the socket will remain open after a close if there is still data that has not been processed. When the linger interval is expired or all data has been processed (whichever comes first), the socket is reset. Not all platforms support this feature, so use it with care.

### *How TCP Applications Assign Ports*

It is important to understand sockets and ports, and the distinction between a remote port and a local port.

The fundamental communication system to application routing abstraction in TCP is the socket. The address of the socket is its port number. Both the client and the server have a port. Application programmers usually do not specify a client port number for a socket connection, but it has one.

TCP does not distinguish between client and server sockets. Once a connection is established, it is symmetric. The only asymmetry exists in the establishment of the connection. Java encapsulates the connection process in an object type called ServerSocket. The job of a ServerSocket is to accept connection requests and manufacture Sockets to service those new connections.

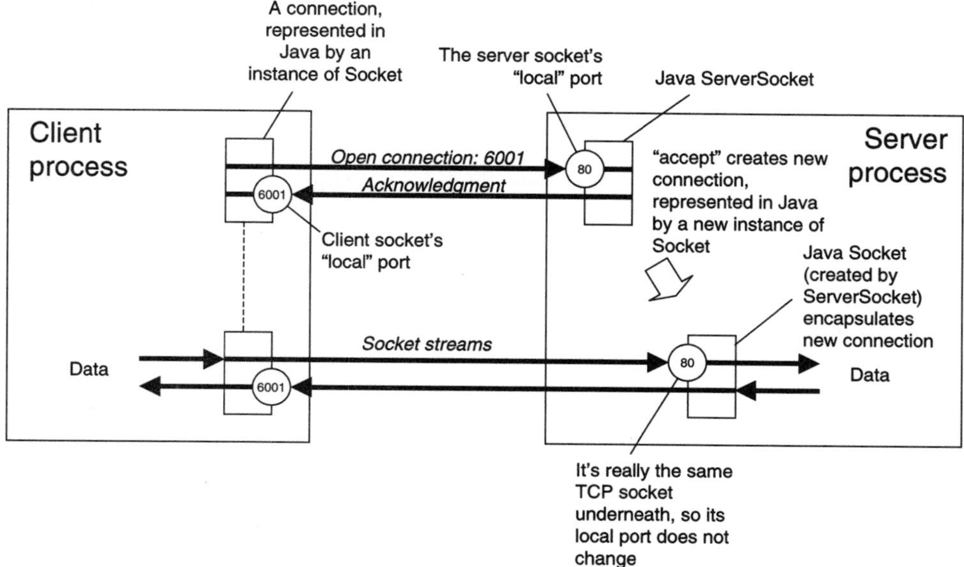


**Figure 5-1** Example of a client Socket obtaining a server Socket connection.

### Socket vs. Connection

In TCP parlance, it is not really a new "socket," but a new "connection." A "socket" is a combination of {host, port}, and a "connection" is a combination of one socket talking to another. Thus, the new Java Socket object created by the ServerSocket.accept() operation is really just a new connection on the same server TCP socket.

As shown in Figure 5-1, this is the sequence of events, from a Java programmer's perspective:

1. The server *binds* a server port—its "local port"—and begins to *accept* connections from clients. In the example in the figure, the server chooses port 80. The Java API does not provide a way at this time to specify allowed client hosts and ports—so any incoming request is allowed.
2. A client *binds* a local port, and *opens* a connection to a server port. In Java, the client does this by creating an instance of Socket. Typically, the client specifies 0 for the local port, which means that it doesn't care, and the OS will choose the number. In the example in the figure, the OS (or the client application) chooses port 6001.
3. When the ServerSocket *accepts* a connection, it creates a new internal connection record identifying the new connection to the client host and client port. A Java Socket object encapsulates operations specific to this new connection. However, from the TCP perspective, this new connection belongs to the same TCP socket as the ServerSocket instance.
4. The new connection is established, and the client and server begin to communicate.

These Socket methods give you information about the ports associated with the socket's connection:

> **getPort()**—Returns the remote server port to which this socket is created. This is the port you specify when you create the Socket object. From the server's perspective, this is the server's "local port" of the ServerSocket that is listening for connection requests. This is the port number usually associated with the application—the one that clients "connect to."
>
> **getLocalPort()**—Returns the local OS TCP port to which this Socket is bound. This is the port on the client machine that is receiving data from the server.

This ServerSocket method provides the server socket's port number:

**getLocalPort()**—This is the port number of the socket that is listening for client connection requests, and it is also the port number used for all Java Socket objects created by a given ServerSocket.

## Firewall Issues

The term "firewall" is a very general term and encompasses many different kinds of hardware and software. At the most basic level, a firewall can consist of a router which connects an internal network to an external network. Routers can provide packet level filtering to ensure that packets coming from the outside do not have forged IP addresses indicating they are from the inside. Many routers can also provide session level filtering in which they remember which session a packet belongs to and use relaxed rules for packets belonging to sessions that originated from the inside. Routers traditionally extend an address space, bridging one network to another with a common address space.

Many routers have advanced features which allow them to be configured to permit traffic along certain routes between hosts and to remap addresses so that an internal address space can be hidden. Firewall routers go a step further and provide filtering based on transport level information and even information which is embedded in certain application protocols such as SSL client identifiers. Software firewalls provide the maximum protection by parsing the application protocol itself and by providing filtering for specific application level protocols. The tradeoff is that software firewalls do not have the same performance as a hardware firewall, which can operate at near network speed. Usually software firewalls are used in general purpose networks for allowing a campus to access the Internet, and hardware firewalls are used in special purpose networks that need to provide a controlled set of services to the public. On the other hand, software firewalls can achieve the same throughput as hardware firewalls by replicating them.

Figure 5-2 summarizes the features typically provided by firewall products. It is important to realize that there is a tremendous variety of products and overlap among their features. For example, some routers can provide authentication.

This is not a book on network design, and so I will not go further into the tradeoffs of different kinds of firewalls. I have presented them only to explain what they do so that you will be able to understand the discussions on application configuration and firewall traversal which follow in this chapter. Since software proxy firewalls are so prevalent nowadays for better or worse and are considered the most secure, I will assume as a default that the firewalls discussed from here on are of that type unless otherwise noted.

| Security-enhancing: | Router | Proxy |
|---|---|---|
| IP filtering (source, target, session) | X | X |
| IP translation/hiding | X | X |
| host name translation/lookup/hiding | | X |
| port filtering | X | X |
| application protocol parsing and filtering | | X |
| content filtering | | X |
| authentication | | X |
| Flexibility features (security relaxing): | | |
| pass-through port mappings | X | X |
| pass-through service mappings (SOCKS) | | X |

**Figure 5-2** Firewall services provided typically by routers or proxies.

***Overview of Software Firewalls***

There are many different kinds of software firewalls. A software firewall, usually referred to as a "proxy firewall," is a program which monitors and filters TCP port connections on one or more network adapters on a machine. The program acts as an intermediary and forwards allowed traffic across two domains, usually manifested by two different adapters. Once a connection is established on a network adapter using an allowed logical (TCP) port, all traffic on that connection is forwarded to another host and port, usually on a different adapter and network. This is referred to as a "multi-homed" configuration, referring to the existence of multiple network adapters on a single machine. A less robust alternative is to use a single adapter and rely on the router to restrict incoming traffic to the firewall host.

Software proxy firewalls can provide many advanced services which can easily be configured as hosts are moved around and applications are changed. There are generally two categories of software proxy firewall: (1) connection-oriented proxies, and (2) application-level proxies. Connection-oriented proxies are represented by the singularly predominant example of the SOCKS protocol, which allows an

application to request an opaque session to a remote host on a specified port. The proxy does not care or check what kind of traffic travels on this connection. In contrast, an application-level proxy pretends to be the remote service that the client is trying to contact, and as such must parse and understand the protocol. For example, an HTTP proxy must parse HTTP requests to extract the URL being requested, fetch the content, and return it to the client. Application level proxies therefore have the ability to filter content.

I will now discuss the major kinds of proxies and how Java can be used to communicate with them and build applications which use them effectively.

### SOCKS

SOCKS is a protocol which can be used to build a proxy for allowing and disallowing connections to hosts and ports on a network. A SOCKS proxy is generally deployed as a firewall or a part of a firewall, for controlling inbound and outbound connections.

SOCKS operates at the socket level in that it does not care what data is being transmitted over the connection. All SOCKS cares about is the origin and destination of the socket connection. This is different from application level firewall proxies which operate at the application level and can therefore provide filtering and other application-related proxy services.

Most firewall products today implement SOCKS in addition to providing application proxy and gateway services for select protocols. SOCKS therefore provides a common denominator mechanism for allowing any application to pass, subject to host and port restrictions.

For an application to pass through a SOCKS proxy, the application must connect to the network's SOCKS server and make an explicit request for a proxy connection. This request takes the form of the CONNECT message, with a parameter specifying the desired endpoint destination. If a connection is granted, the application is informed of the port on the SOCKS server to connect to. The application then connects to this port, and all traffic is relayed to the ultimate destination. SOCKS also allows an application to establish a connection to be used for callbacks to the application from outside the firewall, although this feature is not directly supported by the default Java socket implementation.

For an application to use SOCKS, it must implement the SOCKS protocol. This can be done by coding the protocol into the application itself, or it can be done by using a socket library which transparently supports the protocol. It can even be implemented in the host's native TCP socket library, in which case it is completely transparent to the application. An application or system which implements SOCKS is often referred to as being "socksified."

The latest version of SOCKS is version 5. Version 4 is widely supported, and most implementations which support version 5 support version 4 clients as well.

Support for SOCKS (version 4) is implemented in the default Sun socket implementation (PlainSocketImpl). This makes sense because SOCKS is a connection level protocol. It is therefore automatically available to all protocols which use the default socket implementation. SOCKS is often the protocol used for passing many basic Internet protocols such as SMTP and POP. To use SOCKS, all a Java application has to do is define the SOCKS related properties listed below.

If a Java client is behind a SOCKS firewall and needs to communicate with an application outside the firewall, and the user's workstation is not socksified (i.e., SOCKS is not implemented natively), you will need to set these properties in the client application to instruct its Java VM to use SOCKS:

> **`socksProxyHost`**—The host address of the SOCKS proxy, as addressed from the client network.
>
> **`socksProxyPort`**—The port SOCKS is running on in the client network (defaults to 1080).
>
> **`user.name`**—The "ident service" username which is permitted to use the specified port. The SOCKS server may or may not require this setting.

The most common use of SOCKS is to allow outbound connections to designated destinations. It is also possible to allow inbound connections. If a Java server is behind a SOCKS firewall, the server port must be known (not dynamic) and the SOCKS firewall must be configured to permit inbound connections to the server. In addition, external clients accessing the server must be socksified, and must be configured to access the SOCKS firewall. (Most likely, the firewall also supports mapped ports, and that is an alternative. Mapped ports do not require external clients to engage in any special protocol.) If those clients are behind their own SOCKS firewall as well, then the clients need to be configured instead to access their own SOCKS firewall, and that firewall needs to be configured to permit connections to the server's SOCKS firewall. This is in essence a virtual private network, and indeed SOCKS version 5 supports VPNs by providing for encrypted connections between two SOCKS firewalls.

### *Application Proxies*

An application-level proxy operates by pretending to be the endpoint destination. To do so it must do two things:

1. Receive the socket level connection from the application.
2. Parse the traffic so that it can intercept things like URLs, which it uses to contact the actual destination, receive data, and relay it back to the requestor.

To accomplish 1, firewalls use one of two approaches. Either they can require applications to know about the proxy location, in which case the application creates a socket connection to the proxy instead of the endpoint host whenever a connection is required; or the proxy can operate as a stateful router and provide its service transparently. (A third approach is for client machines to install special proxy libraries which route communication traffic to the proxy.) Since the second approach is transparent to clients, I will focus on proxies which use the first approach and require clients to make explicit connections to them.

Most application-level proxy firewalls support common web application protocols, including HTTP, FTP, and POP and SMTP (for email), and possibly others. The Java default implementations for HTTP and FTP URL connections have built-in support for HTTP and FTP proxies. To redirect HTTP requests to a proxy, you will need to set these properties as follows:

> **`http.proxyHost`**—Sets the hostname or IP address of the HTTP proxy host. All HTTP requests are routed to this host. If a value is not set, no proxy is used. Alternatively you can set the property **`proxyHost`**, which sets the proxy host for all supported protocols (i.e., HTTP, FTP, Gopher).
>
> **`http.proxyPort`**—The port to route HTTP proxy requests to.
>
> **`http.nonProxyHosts`**—A string containing a list of hosts separated by a "|" character. Hosts in this list are assumed to be directly routable (i.e., on the local network inside the firewall) and are contacted directly.

For FTP, these properties need to be set:

> `ftp.proxyHost` (or `ftpProxyHost`)—The host running the FTP proxy.
>
> **`ftp.useProxy`**—If the above are both null, and this is true, the **`proxyHost`** property is used.

In addition, Java 1.1 used this property for FTP:

> **`proxySet`**—"true" or "false"

There is also a property called "trustProxy." If the trustProxy property is set to true, the privilege manager allows the use of invalid (unresolvable) hostnames when making connections—the program trusts the proxy to police which hosts can be connected to.

### *Proxy Configurations and Where to Put Your Application*

The issue of the relative position of firewall components, web servers, application servers and database servers is important to consider in designing the overall architecture of an application. It affects throughput and can affect design, since a decision might be made to implement more or less behavior in servlets as opposed to backend components, or to change the way application server creden-

tials are stored and accessed. Let's look at some of the typical configurations. I will discuss these in generic terms, and defer detailed discussion until later when I discuss specific protocols.

Note that the selection of the type of firewall is also a critical decision, but that is not the topic of this book. I will assume a software firewall, and I will assume that all routers only have stateful filtering capability that allows them to track host-to-host connections on an application-unaware basis.

**Typical Partner-Access and Low Throughput Public Access Configuration.** The simplest moderately secure configuration is to place everything behind a single proxy firewall. You can then have relative confidence that if the firewall is properly configured, only intended protocol traffic will travel through it. No configuration files of any kind should be outside the firewall. This configuration also hides your network's internal IP address space since the proxy firewall remaps permitted connections to an internal address.

The main vulnerability is then any active server side content you might have, such as CGI programs or servlets. If you have confidence in these, you can have reasonable confidence in the overall system's security against simple attacks. The proxy firewall can be configured to allow public unauthenticated traffic to specific hosts for specific protocols and ports, or it can be configured to require a password for access by partners or offsite staff. The configuration is shown in Figure 5-3.

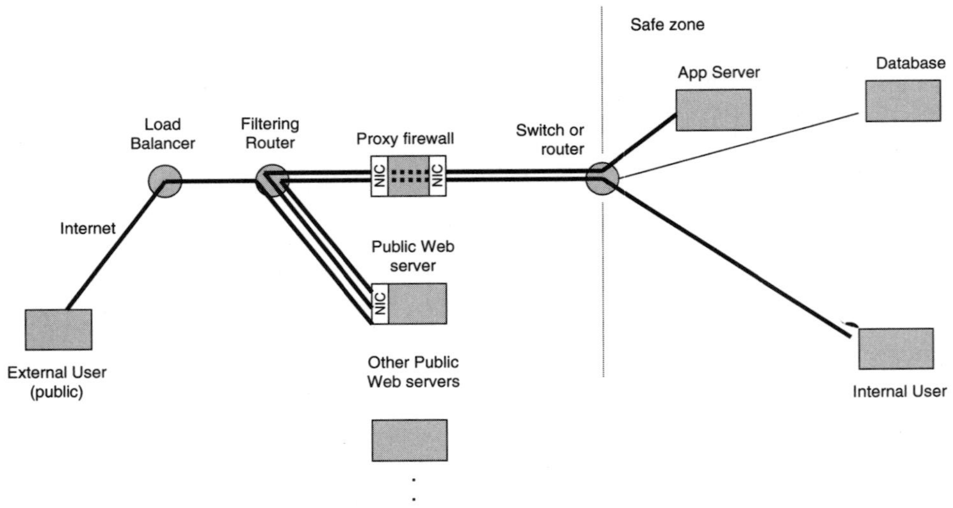


**Figure 5-3** Allowed routes for partner-access web server behind firewall.

One problem with this configuration is that it is not very scalable. Proxies are computers, and the operating system and hardware of a standard computer are not designed for routing messages. If the web site is a high traffic site, the proxy will become a bottleneck. Another problem is that the configuration is not very secure. Let's first see how the scaling deficiencies can be addressed.

**High Throughput Public Access Configuration.** A solution to the scaling problem is to move the public web servers outside the proxy firewall and use load balancing technology such as a load balancing router. Web servers and servlets behind the load balancer can be replicated for arbitrary scalability. A router can be configured to allow the web servers to create connections through the proxy, but external clients are not allowed to.

Any servlets running on the web servers must be configured to pass through the proxy. This is sometimes difficult if the servlets use many services, including name services and remote protocols such as IIOP and RMI. In that case, the application must communicate through the proxy. Many database drivers support firewall traversal, and some firewalls support the traversal of database protocols, such as SQL*Net.

A replicated web server configuration is shown in Figure 5-4.

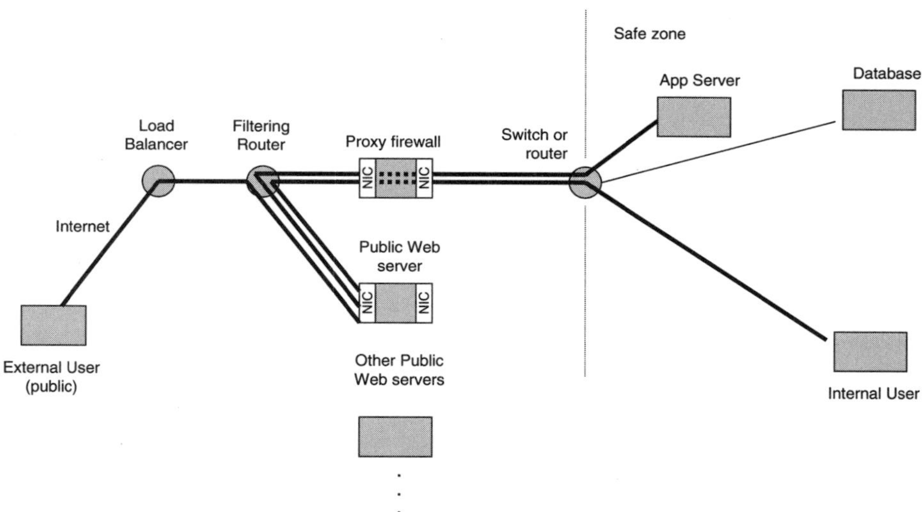


**Figure 5-4** Allowed routes for public web server outside firewall.

**More Secure Public Access Configuration.** The problem with the previous configuration is that the web servers are only protected by a router, which is much more difficult to configure and maintain than a proxy firewall, and does not provide the same protection. The web servers may contain configuration data and possibly credential information to allow them to access backend services. It would be desirable to have as much protection for these machines as possible.

A more secure and flexible arrangement is to connect the load balancer to a bank of one or more firewall machines, and place the web servers behind those. That decouples the router configuration from the web server configuration, and also allows for easier management of which ports and protocols are permitted. It also provides the best protection for the web and application servers. The overall configuration is shown in Figure 5-5.

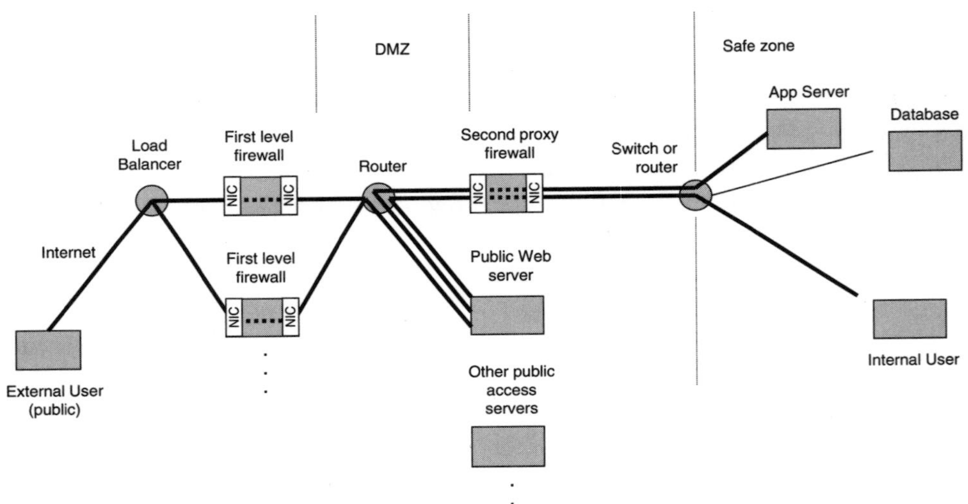


**Figure 5-5** Allowed routes for public web servers in DMZ.

No arrangement is completely secure. If at some point you allow traffic through a firewall to access data, your system is only as secure as the protocol and application which performs that access. For this reason, it is advisable to avoid writing home-grown gateways and use standard and well-supported services such as HTTP servers for traversing the first firewall. An extremely secure alternative is to replicate all data to databases that sit outside your internal network, but this is not always practical.

In later sections I will revisit these issues in the context of specific protocols and services.

**Load Balancing Problems When Clients Are Themselves Behind Firewalls.** Normally a load balancer can identify a client session based on the socket connection. This is possible even if the client itself is behind a proxy firewall because each client connection with the proxy will have a corresponding unique proxy connection to the destination server. However, many server protocols or services employ stateful sessions of some kind which may live beyond the lifetime of the actual socket connection. For example, HTTP sessions can span the actual socket connection to the web server. HTTP clients can use "cookies" or other techniques to store a session identifier on the client so that when a client returns, the client can be associated with an application session. When a server recognizes a session id in a new connection as belonging to a prior session, it needs to associate that client with the prior session. The load balancing technology being used must be able to recognize session identifiers in order to route connections to the correct server. To do this, it must be able to at least partially parse the application protocol since that is where the session identifier resides.

An alternative is to place the burden on the servers and require the servers to move session information to the physical server that needs it at any moment. For example, a servlet server can provide a distributed implementation of servlet state, so that a client returning to a servlet on a given servlet session can access the correct session state regardless of which server it actually runs on that time around.

Generally it is difficult for load balancers to load balance servers which use stateful protocols. However, there are exceptions. For example, some load balancers can properly handle SSL traffic on a preconfigured TCP port by reading the session id in the SSL Hello message (the SSL protocol is discussed in detail in Chapter 4), allowing the load balancer to reassociate new connections with prior SSL sessions.

### *The Mechanics of Passing Through a Firewall*

One of the greatest technical challenges today for implementing Internet and extranet applications is firewalls. Most firewalls only permit certain protocols to pass, including HTTP access via port 80 and FTP access via port 21 (with special provisions for the FTP data connection), so endusers behind such firewalls — which includes users in most corporations—cannot access many important protocols from hosts external to the firewall.

**Port Mapping.** A firewall is normally configured to prevent connections to all ports on the firewall machine, except for a specific set. On those, it runs proxy services which either emulate the actual service sought by the client or directly forwards the data to an allowed second destination. A firewall port on which such direct forwarding is allowed is called a "mapped port." Port mapping works as long as the protocol does not embed host addresses in its stream, since with port mapping, the proxy is merely forwarding packets.

**Gateways and Application Protocol Tunneling.** Port mapping is one way to "open" a firewall. Another way is to simply allow connections on a certain port, and run a gateway program or separate proxy on that port. This places the port out of the purview of the firewall, and therefore should only be done if the separate proxy is trusted and there is a strong need to provide that service. You might do this, for example, if you need to run a separate proxy for an important protocol not supported by your firewall, and for which the mapped port technique will not work. An example is an IIOP proxy.

Another technique for passing through a firewall is "HTTP tunneling." Many middleware vendors have such tunneling components, which allow their protocol to be wrapped inside of an HTTP connection, to allow the protocol data to hide inside an HTTP stream. For this to work, the protocol must be able to survive HTTP's request/response mode of operation, and the closing and reopening of connections.

At the receiving end of a tunneled connection, the destination can either receive the HTTP stream and unwrap the tunneled data itself, or it can make use of a gateway program running in a web server. The latter is necessary if the destination is behind a firewall which only allows web traffic.

**Proxy Tunneling.** A superior technique to HTTP tunneling is to create a persistent passthrough connection through a firewall to a well-known port number on the other side of the firewall. This can either be done with authentication of the destination server, or without authentication. A simple extension to the HTTP protocol, known as "proxy tunneling," provides the capability to create such a passthrough connection.

Proxy tunneling began as a means to pass SSL-encrypted sessions through a firewall proxy, and was called "SSL tunneling." Since the session is encrypted and opaque, the proxy cannot perform any protocol and content filtering functions, and therefore SSL traffic cannot be filtered by a proxy except on the basis of destination host and port number. If the endpoint is trusted, however, or if at least the destination is a well-known port, there is a corresponding level of assurance that the traffic is trustworthy, and can be allowed. This is an administrative decision.

To support the passthrough of opaque sessions through a proxy, the HTTP CONNECT method was devised. Unlike with the HTTP GET or POST method, which create a transient connection to send a request or data and get a response, the CONNECT method establishes a persistent bidirectional passthrough, creating a socket connection to the destination host and port and forwarding the SSL or other protcol as is.

Proxy tunneling is alot like SOCKS. Both establish circuit connections across a firewall. The difference is that SOCKS is usually implemented in the socket libraries whereas proxy tunneling is specific to the HTTP protocol.

To use proxy tunneling, the client application as well as the proxy must support the proxy tunneling extension to HTTP. In the case of a Java client, there are normally two ways to approach this. If the Java client is running in a browser, it can use the browser's built-in SSL and tunneling capability to establish the tunneling session. This is achieved by using an HTTPS URL as previously discussed. (Netscape Communicator's SSL implementation is tunnel-aware via the "Proxies/Security" setting.) If, however, the client is not running in a browser, then this is not an option, and the SSL package or connection factory (or whatever application protocol you are using, e.g., HTTPS) must support tunneling. These two scenarios are shown in Figure 5-6.

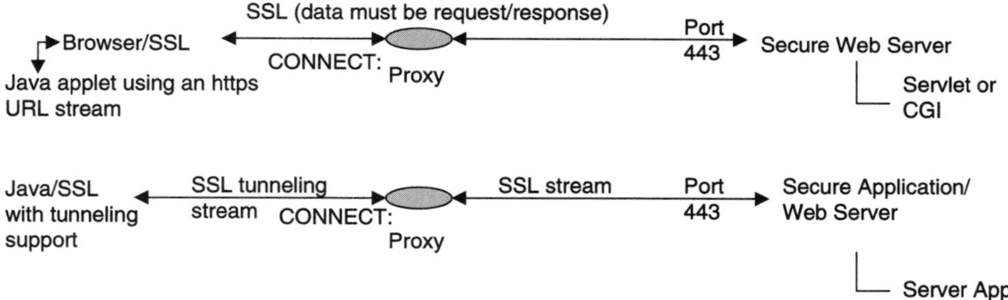


**Figure 5-6** Two forms of SSL firewall tunneling.

Now let's discuss the server side of things. If the server is a web server, and the server application is implemented by a servlet or CGI program, data will have to be request/response, as is required by web-based content transfer. If, however, the server is an application server that supports SSL, it will have to pretend to be an HTTP server and listen on an allowed port (such as the HTTPS 443 port), but in fact it is free to set up full-duplex connections between clients and server applications.

In the first case above, a Java applet uses the browser's HTTPS protocol to access the browser's built-in SSL capability. In this case, the destination server will need to use a protocol supported by the browser—i.e., HTTPS. The Java client merely accesses the HTTP stream for sending and receiving data, as discussed earlier.

In the second case, a Java client—probably one written using an application server's client development toolkit—establishes a proxy tunneling connection through the firewall to the destination application server. The application server routes the data to the requested application.

If two proxies are involved, which would be the case if the server itself is behind a firewall, the client proxy would establish a tunneling connection to the second proxy. In such a situation, however, communication is between two parties who trust each other (at least partially), and so those organizations may consider setting up a limited virtual private network (VPN) to link two of their subnets together.

**Using a VPN.** A VPN uses encryption and authentication to create a secure link across an open network, in such a way that parties participating in the VPN can share data as if it were within their own private network. There are two primary ways to establish a VPN. One is by using routers which implement the required encryption and authentication (e.g., IPSEC) transparently to applications. This is the most robust solution, but it is difficult at present since the required standards are still evolving, and you and your partners would have to use compatible equipment on both ends.

A more flexible and simpler approach is to use software proxies to set up a VPN. In this scenario, the VPN software supplies the secure connection as its authentication method. For example, SOCKS 5 compliant VPNs allow the use of alternative authentication methods, and SSL is a popular one used by VPNs. A VPN connecting two networks using SSL authentication and encryption is depicted in Figure 5-7.

In a VPN scenario, the Java client and the server are not involved at all in the establishment or management of the secure connection—in fact, they are not even aware of it. Source and destination authentication is handled completely by the VPN. Most VPN software allows for single sign-on authentication at the user (client) end, so the user does not have to supply a password or smartcard each time a new connection is established, because the VPN operates at the network level and so this information is remembered between applications. Note that at the server side, however, most secure servers do not interoperate with VPN software for SSL authentication, although this may change in future releases of SSL.

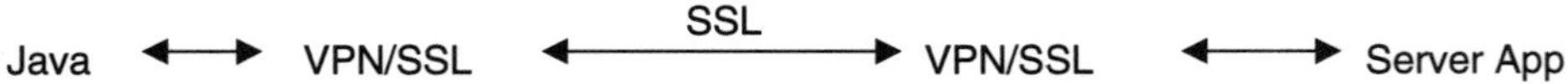


**Figure 5-7** SSL supplied by a proxy-based Virtual Private Network.

## Internet Server Protocols

Internet server protocols include those Internet protocols that provide application-level services requiring a server. These protocols are generally specified in Internet "RFCs" which constitute official specifications and are maintained by the Internet Engineering Task Force (IETF). There are literally thousands of RFC specifications, but out of all of these there are a few which are of major importance and which are important to understand when developing distributed Java applications. These include Hypertext Transfer Protocol (HTTP) and Lightweight Directory Access Protocol (LDAP), and possibly others including File Transfer Protocol (FTP) and the email protocols (POP, IMAP4, and SMTP).

These protocols are important generic utility layers that can be used to move data between applications and between users. They provide a common set of client-server building blocks available ubiquitously within the Internet, and are the means by which most work is done on the Internet today.

Sun Microsystems has added support for many important Internet server protocols to the Java core API, but in such a way as to allow third parties to provide their own implementations. Thus, most of these protocol APIs are specified with interfaces, abstract classes, and factory methods, rather than concrete implementations. In nearly every case, however, Sun has provided a built-in implementation that you can use at no cost, or you can use an implementation that provides features important to your application, for example, SSL encryption, or particular implementations of generic services such as email.

Internet services use URLs to identify resources. The prefix of a URL specifies the protocol to be used to obtain the resource. For example, in the URL http://www.somewhere.com/abc.txt, the protocol "http" is specified, indicating that the server providing the resource is an HTTP server (i.e., a web server). The java.net package contains a base class URLConnection which contains behavior common to all connections to URL-based services.

### *HTTP*

Hypertext Transfer Protocol (HTTP) is probably the most important Internet server protocol. It is the protocol that sparked the tremendous growth and popularization of the Web, and it serves as a backbone protocol on which many diverse kinds of services depend. The Java core API provides built-in support for HTTP, in the form of classes that can open connections to HTTP servers and parse HTTP messages. Let's take a look at some of these classes.

The HttpURLConnection class is an HTTP-specific class that extends URLConnection, and provides functionality specific to HTTP-based resources. This is an abstract class, but the factory method URL.openConnection() returns a concrete implementation. Different Java platforms will return different implementations of a URLConnection. The standard Java release returns an instance of sun.net.www.protocol.http.HttpURLConnection if you give it an http:// URL. This class is an implementation of HttpURLConnection. The constructor of the concrete class has the signature:

```
public sun.net.www.protocol.http.HttpURLConnection
(
   URL url, // the URL
   String proxy, // if there is a proxy
   int proxyPort// the proxy port
);
```

Let's consider an example:

```
import java.net.*;
import java.io.*;

public class C
{
   public static void main(String[] args) throws Exception
   {
      HttpURLConnection c;

      //
      // Writing to a URL
      //
      // Construct an HttpURLConnection object - no connection
      // exists yet
      c = new sun.net.www.protocol.http.HttpURLConnection(
            new URL(args[0]), null, 0);
      c.setRequestMethod("PUT");
      c.setDoOutput(true);
      c.connect();
      OutputStream os = c.getOutputStream();
      if (os == null) throw new Exception("os is null");
      PrintStream ps = new PrintStream(os);
      ps.println("hi");
      InputStream is = c.getInputStream();
      if (is == null) throw new Exception("is is null");
      DataInputStream dis = new DataInputStream(is);
      String s = dis.readLine();
      System.out.println("response body=" + s);
      c.disconnect();
```

For the Apache 1.1.1 server, if the specified URL is a CGI program, the response body displayed on the terminal window will simply be the contents of the specified URL, minus any HTTP header fields. This is somewhat puzzling, since that release of the server does not support HTTP 1.1 or the PUT method. It probably should return a message saying "Not Supported." This is what happens if the URL is a static file.

Now let's see how we would read from a URL. Note that:

```
//
// Reading from a URL
//
// Now let's construct a new connection object, for reading
// what we wrote:
c = new sun.net.www.protocol.http.HttpURLConnection(new
    URL(args[0]), null, 0);
c.setRequestMethod("GET");
c.connect();
is = c.getInputStream();
if (is == null) throw new Exception("is is null");
dis = new DataInputStream(is);
s = dis.readLine();
System.out.println("response body=" + s);
c.disconnect();
```

The output of this is the contents of the specified URL.

Now let's try a POST. Note that the URL must specify a CGI program, or we will get a "Not-Supported" message from the server.

```
//
// Writing to and reading from the same URL, via a POST
//
c = new sun.net.www.protocol.http.HttpURLConnection(new
   URL(args[0]), null, 0);
c.setRequestMethod("POST");
c.setDoOutput(true);
c.connect();

os = c.getOutputStream();
if (os == null) throw new Exception("os is null");
ps = new PrintStream(os);
ps.println("Here is some data to write");
ps.flush();
```

```
        is = c.getInputStream();
        if (is == null) throw new Exception("is is null");
        dis = new DataInputStream(is);
        s = dis.readLine() + s.readLine();// just read two lines
        System.out.println("response body=" + s);

        // Get header data for the fun of it...
        for (int i = 1;;i++)
        {
           String k = c.getHeaderFieldKey(i);
           if (k == null) break;
           String f = c.getHeaderField(i);
           System.out.println(k + ": " + f);
        }
        c.disconnect();
    }
}
```

If the specified URL is a CGI program, the response body display is the output of that program. If that program is an echo program, it will echo the output written to the output stream ("Here is some data to write"). If the URL is not a CGI program, the server will generate a "Not Supported" message.

The request methods supported are:

GET
POST
HEAD
OPTIONS
PUT
DELETE
TRACE

You can, of course, simulate the function of the HttpURLConnection by creating your own socket connection and implementing the HTTP protocol yourself, by sending request headers and data and parsing the responses headers.

### *java.net.Authenticator*

Sun's sun.net.www.protocol.http.HttpURLConnection class, which is their implementation for java.net.HttpURLConnection, automatically negotiates HTTP proxy and web server authentication. Basically, if a proxy or web server replies with a "Proxy-authenticate" or "WWW-Authenticate" header, respectively, the

HttpURLConnection knows it must provide authentication credentials for the user.

Sun's HttpURLConnection class supports "basic" authentication (base-64 encoded userID and password) for HTTP proxies, and "basic" authentication and "digest" authentication (hash encoding of a challenge and userID and password) for web servers. Both basic and digest authentication require a userID and password. To obtain the userID and password, it calls the static method Authenticator.requestPasswordAuthentication(...), which in turn obtains the instance of java.net.Authenticator which has been registered with the runtime by a prior call to java.net.Authenticator.setDefault(Authenticator). A typical implementation of an Authenticator would display a dialog requesting a userID and password. If no Authenticator has been registered, then the connection will fail.

It is up to the application to set a default Authenticator if proxy or HTTP authentication is required, as none is set by default. It is up to the Authenticator implementation whether and for how long to cache a userID and password entered by the user.

In general, applications should consider following the browser model, which maintains multiple authentications even if they are from different realms (different web servers, even for content on the same page), but allow the authentications to expire.

### *LDAP*

The Lightweight Directory Access Protocol (LDAP) version 3, defined in RFC 2251, defines a simplified protocol for accessing X.500-style directory services. Organizations use LDAP servers to store and consolidate information about employees, applications, and other aspects of their operations. Many other kinds of server products today are capable of using an external LDAP server as their repository for user information, thereby allowing an organization to centralize this type of information in an application independent way. Some of the types of products that use LDAP include application servers, certificate servers, email servers and clients, PBXs, IPSEC-capable routers, VPN software, and in general any product or application which requires information about users, application services, or access control. LDAP allows an administrator to have a single hierarchical view of all the things in the enterprise that need to be managed, and store information about them in a way accessible to applications and other servers.

To accomplish this, most server products that support the use of LDAP provide a means of configuring, or mapping, the data they need to an external LDAP server's schema. For example, if a server needs to access the digital certificate associated with any user that accesses the server, the server must be configured to obtain this data from the LDAP attribute "userCertificate." (LDAP attributes are explained below.) In this case, the attribute "userCertificate" is a standard LDAP attribute, and so the application server will likely know to access that attribute without configuration. User name, group, and password information is also commonly stored in LDAP servers for access by application servers and other products. For example, the Castanet Transmitter product can be configured so that it accesses an LDAP server for user and user group information. It interprets the LDAP attribute "org" to be the user's group, "uid" to userID, and "userPassword" to be the user's password. Optionally, it can instead map "groupOfNames" to the group and "member" to the userID, following the convention used by Netscape server products.

For other less common types of information for which there are no standard attributes, configuration is necessary.

An LDAP server itself must be configured as well. This amounts to defining its schema. An LDAP server is a form of object database. The schema consists of three primary kinds of definitions: syntax definitions, attribute definitions, and class definitions. Syntax definitions define the primordial types and the way they are represented at the bit level. Examples of standard LDAP syntax types are Binary, Bit String, Boolean, and Certificate (these are their informal descriptive names; their actual identifying names are numeric, as explained below). Attribute definitions define user-level scalar types, and in some cases their internal representation so they can be parsed by client applications. Class definitions define the kinds of entries that can be made in the database. A class definition consists of a set of attributes. An entry in an LDAP database can in fact implement more than one class, in which case the entry has the sum of attributes defined for each class it implements. The standard LDAP v.3 syntax definitions are listed in RFC 2252, and the standard attributes are listed in RFC 2256. An organization is free to augment the standard definitions in it own schema.

Let's look at an example. As mentioned above, a unique number is used to represent each type defined in a schema, much the way an IP address is used to uniquely identify an IP network node. These schema identifiers are called Object IDs (OID). If an organization wants to define its own schema types, it can contact the Internet Assigned Numbers Authority (IANA)—eventually to be replaced in this function by the new Internet Corporation for Assigned Names and Numbers (ICANN)—and request an "Enterprise Number," which is a unique numeric prefix. The organization then creates new OIDs by appending to the prefix. For example, IANA has assigned the prefix 1.3.6.1.4.1.9 to Cisco Systems. If Cisco wants to define new OIDs, they can do so simply by defining 1.3.6.1.4.1.9.1, 1.3.6.1.4.1.9.2, and so on, and even add more levels to the hierarchy.

Now consider the standard LDAP attribute definition with OID `2.5.4.36:`

```
( 2.5.4.36 NAME 'userCertificate'
   SYNTAX 1.3.6.1.4.1.1466.115.121.1.8 )
```

*This defines the attribute type 2.5.4.36, specifies it has the equivalent name "userCertificate," and says that it is to be represented as a "1.3.6.1.4.1.1466.115.121.1.8"*

This defines "2.5.4.36" as an attribute with name "userCertificate." (The attribute name is not necessarily unique, but the OID is.) It specifies that a userCertificate is to be encoded as a "1.3.6.1.4.1.1466.115.121.1.8," which is the OID that defines the encoding for a certificate as stored in LDAP:

```
( 1.3.6.1.4.1.1466.115.121.1.8 DESC 'Certificate' )
```

*This defines the object type "1.3.6.1.4.1.1466.115.121.1.8." For this type, a rule is specified that objects of this type must be transferred as binary values.*

Now suppose an organization with assigned OID prefix 1.3.6.1.4.1.9999 wants to store information on all staff, including name, department, phone number, and their personal digital certificate. The standard attribute names for common name, surname, department, country of operation, and certificate are CN, O, OU, C, and userCertificate, respectively. They could define an object class as follows:

```
( 1.3.6.1.4.1.9999.123
   NAME 'staff'
   DESC 'General staff member'
   SUP top
   STRUCTURAL
   MUST (CN, SN, O, OU, C, userCertificate)
)
```

They could then add entries to the database by specifying the class "staff" and all the required attributes. The "STRUCTURAL" keyword specifies that database entries which implement this class type do not need to implement any other class types; every entry must implement a class which is STRUCTURAL, and zero or more AUXILIARY class types.

When you add an entry to an LDAP directory, you must specify several things. These include:

- The name of the entry. Note that a name can have multiple parts. This is not to be confused with the fact that the name itself is part of a hierarchy.
- The place in the hierarchy to insert the entry—the context.

- The class(es) which the entry implements—this defines which attributes it may or must have. Exactly one of these classes must be defined as a "structural" class. Thus, structural classes act as primary node types in the hierarchy and define the structural elements of the directory. You specify these classes by specifying one or more values for the "objectclass" attribute.
- The object's attribute values (in addition to the "objectclass" attribute).

An organization can configure other LDAP-enabled servers to access LDAP attributes for required data. The organization can even write its own applications which access organization-specific attributes as well as standard attributes.

An important class of attributes often defined by applications and servers is access control lists. These are usually application specific. For example, Netscape's Certificate Server defines an LDAP attribute called "userPKCS12," which contains a PKCS#12 message containing an encrypted private key and certificate. This attribute comes predefined in Netscape's own LDAP ("Directory") server product, as you might imagine. Therefore, no special configuration is necessary to make their certificate server work with their own LDAP server. If you were to use someone else's certificate server, you would have to either configure it to use that attribute for storing generated user certificates and keys, or you would have to define an analogous attribute in the LDAP schema to store what your certificate server produces.

To find information in an LDAP database, an LDAP client contacts the LDAP server and presents a search query. The query consists of a set of attribute values and a set of matching criteria. The LDAP server searches through its data and returns all matches. The matching entries can then be accessed one by one to obtain additional attributes. For example, if entries had been made using the above "staff" class, an employee could be found by name, and then the userCertificate attribute could be obtained.

**Storing Java Objects.** Sun Microsystems has proposed an IETF standard schema for representing Java objects in LDAP. There is not a number assigned to this pending RFC yet, but its title will likely end up being "Schema for Representing Java™ Objects in an LDAP Directory," so you can obtain it from the IETF or from Sun. As of this writing, the proposed attribute definitions are shown in Figure 5-8 and consist of:

- **javaClassName**—The fully qualified Java class name of the object being stored.
- **javaCodebase**—The URL from which to obtain the object's classes.
- **javaSerializedData—**The serialized Java object.

```
javaClassName
(UTF-8 Directory String)

javaCodebase
(IA5 String)

javaSerializedData
(binary)
(single valued)

javaClassNames
(UTF-8 Directory String)

javaFactory
(UTF-8 Directory String)
(single valued)

javaReferenceAddress
(UTF-8 Directory String)

javaDoc
(IA5 String)
```

**Figure 5-8** LDAP attributes for storing Java objects.

- **javaClassNames**—The fully qualified names of the inherited classes and interfaces of this object.
- **javaReferenceAddress**—Defines a syntax for storing a parsable or serialized JNDI Reference (see Chapter 7).
- **javaFactory**—The fully qualified class name of a JNDI ObjectFactory (discussed in Chapter 7).
- **javaDoc**—A URL reference for the object class's Javadoc documentation.

The proposed object class definitions are shown in Figure 5-9 and consist of:

- **javaContainer**—A container type. All the Java object types defined below must be stored with a javaContainer, or with another LDAP class which is STRUCTURAL. The only required attribute is CN.
- **javaObject**—An abstract class which must have a javaClassName attribute, and may have a javaCodebase attribute. The following three classes extend this type.
- **javaSerializedObject**—Adds to javaObject the required binary attribute javaSerializedData.
- **javaMarshalledObject**—Adds to javaObject the required binary attribute javaSerializedData.
- **javaNamingReference**—Adds to javaObject the optional attributes javaReferenceAddress and javaFactory. See the discussion of JNDI in Chapter 7 for an explanation of JNDI references and how JNDI objects are stored.

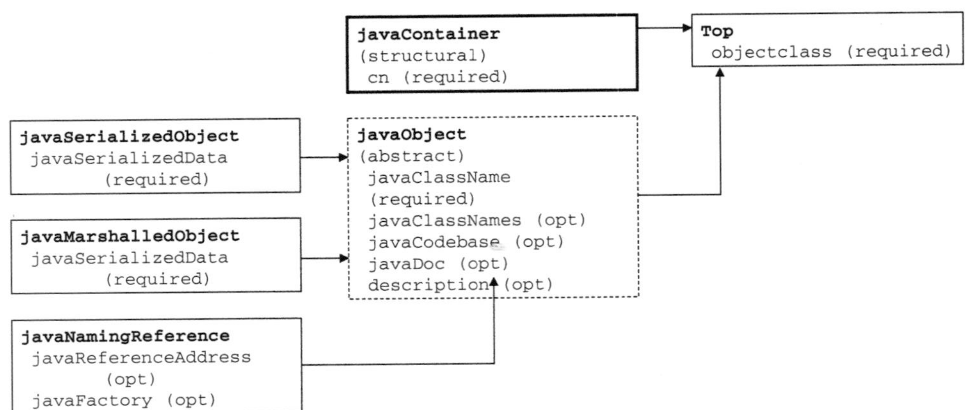


**Figure 5-9** LDAP object classes for storing Java objects.

These definitions define how to store these types of Java objects natively in an LDAP database. Without a standard, implementations of JNDI would have to independently come up with their own way of mapping these kinds of objects to an LDAP schema. Having these standards allows for interoperability across implementations. These mappings will be especially important for JNDI LDAP provider implementations, which are discussed in Chapter 7.

Since this standard is new, it is not implemented in most LDAP products at the time of this writing. Therefore, to store Java objects in this way (these schema types are used by the JNDI LDAP provider), you must add these definitions to your LDAP schema. Sun Microsystems provides a utility program to make these definitions, called UpdateJavaObjects. However, making schema changes over the wire is not very portable, and you need to check the resulting definitions and make sure they are correct. The schema is still undergoing revision at this writing, so you should obtain the latest from the IETF or from the JNDI distribution you are using. Note that if your LDAP server does not support the matching rules specified in the schema, you can most likely get away with editing the schema and substituting different (more lenient) matching rules.

**LDAP Names.** LDAP uses X.500 distinguished names to identify entities according to the conventions for representing those as strings, as specified in RFC 2253; for example:

```
"CN=Frank N. Stein, O=MyCompany, OU=Body Parts, C=RO"
```

where the keywords preceding the "=" are standardized X.500 keywords, including Common Name (CN), Organization (O), Organizational Unit (OU), and Country (C). (The country code "RO" is the ISO code for Romania. A complete listing of these codes is given in Chapter 2.)

It is peculiar and unfortunate that in many existing server security products which use distinguished names to identify certificate owners, the spaces and sequence of elements within the string must be identical for equality comparison operations, such as comparing the name embedded in a certificate with the user's distinguished name stored in an LDAP server. LDAP server search operations, however, are attribute-oriented and are not affected by the form of the original string representation.

**LDAP Programming.** Let's look at a basic example of an LDAP client application. The program below uses Netscape's LDAP API to open a connection to an LDAP server, and searches for all occurrences of the name "Frank N. Stein" within the country "RO" (Romania) and the organization "My Company." The program was tested using Netscape's LDAP Directory Server:

```
import java.util.*;
import netscape.ldap.*;

public class DemoLDAP
{
   public static void main(String[] args) throws LDAPException
   {
      LDAPConnection connection = new LDAPConnection();
      connection.connect("myhost", 389 /*port*/);

      // Authenticate to the directory, as nobody
      connection.authenticate("", "");

      // Search for all entries with the specified surname
      LDAPSearchConstraints constraints =
       connection.getSearchConstraints();
      constraints.setBatchSize(1);
      // Note: specifies the number of results to retrieve with
      // each request;
      // a value of 0 specifies to retrieve all results in one
      // request.

      LDAPSearchResults r = connection.search
      (
         "o=My Company,c=RO",    // search base
         LDAPConnection.SCOPE_ONE,
         "cn=Frank N. Stein",    // filter
```

```
                null,
                false,
                constraints
            );

            // Retrieve and display results
            while (r.hasMoreElements())
            {
                // Next directory entry:
                LDAPEntry e = (LDAPEntry)r.nextElement();
                System.out.println("name=" + e.getDN);

                // Get entry attributes
                LDAPAttributeSet as = e.getAttributeSet();
                Enumeration ea = as.getAttributes();

                // for each attribute...
                while (ea.hasMoreElements())
                {
                    LDAPAttribute a = (LDAPAttribute)ea.nextElement();
                    System.out.println("\t" + a.getName());
                    Enumeration ev = a.getStringValues();
                    while (ev.hasMoreElements())
                    {
                    System.out.println("\t\t" + ev.nextElement());
                    }
                }
            }

            connection.disconnect();
        }
    }
```

I have specified a search scope of SCOPE_ONE. This means that I only want to search the children of the immediate context. Two other possible values for the search scope are:

- SCOPE_SUB—Search the entry at the immediate context and all entries at all subordinate levels.
- SCOPE_BASE—Search only the single entry at the immediate context. This is used to retrieve a single entry.

An important use of directory servers today is to centrally store an organization's user names with corresponding distinguished names, and possibly digital certificates as well (although the latter is not usually done unless required by security or VPN software). That way there is a central repository for retrieving user distin-

guished names for comparison with authenticated names. Just because a user presents a valid signed certificate saying they are John Smith does not mean they are the John Smith you think they are—there could be two John Smiths in an organization. The distinguished name stored in a certificate serves to uniquely identify an entity, and if it is possible to look that entity up in an LDAP or other database, then it can be verified and compared, possibly using other information in the database. Common aliases and computer userIDs can be stored as well to serve as a cross-reference.

If you are writing a business application, you will probably not use the LDAP API. Instead, you will access an LDAP server using JNDI and a JNDI LDAP service provider implementation. Even if you don't program to LDAP directly, it is valuable to understand it, because it is a cornerstone of distributed application development, and is increasingly important for access control and authentication.

**Referrals and Chaining.** LDAP version 3 specifies a mechanism for a server to respond to a request with a new address, effectively redirecting a client to a new location. This technique is called a *referral*. The referral is fully exposed to the client, so the client has the choice of following the referral or ignoring it and abandoning the request.

In addition, some X.500 servers also provide a mechanism for chaining servers together transparent to client applications, to create a federation of servers that acts as one from the perspective of clients. The use of the referral and chaining techniques allows an organization to distribute management of its directories to the groups most familiar with the entities represented in each directory, without losing the advantage of having a single virtual and global hierarchical namespace for all client applications. For this to work reliably, it is generally advantageous for the organization to create an organization-wide standard schema to ensure that a distributed request does not fail because an intermediate server does not recognize an attribute type or object class.

The details of these techniques are related to administration and are beyond the scope of this discussion. It is useful for programmers to know that they exist, however. In addition, the JNDI discussion in Chapter 7 will explain how referrals are handled in the JNDI API.

### *FTP*

The interhost File Transfer Protocol (FTP) is defined in Internet RFC 959. It is a protocol for the transfer of files between hosts, under the control of a client program. An FTP client can initiate the transfer of data between itself and an FTP server, or between two FTP servers (peer-to-peer transfer).

Transfer between the client and server is the mode implemented in most personal FTP client programs that people use to obtain data from FTP sites. Remote peer-

to-peer transfer is important, however, for back-end services that need to effect file transfer without user intervention; for example, a program which must periodically make fresh data available from an external system to another application, such as a Castanet Publish tool, or to a data mining application.

Most systems that support FTP have an FTP client program which can be invoked from a script. Using a script, however, has the disadvantage that FTP command scripts vary from one system to another, and therefore scripts tend to be somewhat nonportable. A program is also more flexible, and can be integrated with other functions, and even implemented in a transactional manner; this is difficult to do with scripts in a portable way.

I will not go into the details of the FTP protocol here. However, this book's web site has an implementation of an FTP client program that has peer-to-peer transfer capability. An example of its use is also provided there. It can be used to remotely effect the transfer of files between any two machines that each have an FTP server running.

### *SNMP and the Java Management API (JMAPI)*

Simple Network Management Protocol (SNMP) is a messaging protocol for building interoperable systems management applications. Such applications are normally in the computing system domain, but the protocol is general purpose and can be used to build any type of application which sends and receives status messages. SNMP is currently in version 3, and is described in RFCs 2271-2275.

The Java Management API (JMAPI) is an application interface for building such applications, and as such has direct support for SNMP. Many of JMAPI's components are redundant (although nicely done) with regard to other Java packages, but some of the unique features include:

- Managed Container Interfaces
- Managed Notification Interfaces
- Managed Data Interfaces
- Managed Protocol Interfaces
- SNMP Interfaces
- Applet Integration Interfaces

JMAPI is intended for system and server vendors who need to provide operational management features for their products, and want to do so using a browser-based application. However, the API is accessible enough that it can be used by application developers as well to build application management functionality into their applications.

### SMTP, IMAP, and POP

Email plays a large role today in business and the activities of any large organization. More information is exchanged by email than by any other means. In many cases, the recipient of an email is not even human; it might, for example, be a list server, to which a person sends an email in order to subscribe to a mailing list. Emails can also be generated by non-human agents, such as mailing list servers, the most well-known being a product called Majordomo. Besides these mainstream mechanisms, email can also be used to implement a conduit of information in an automated business process. For example, changes to a database object could trigger an email to all "interested parties." In this situation, the email establishes an important link in a system, for change notification. In such a system, email features need to be integral to the application, in particular because a human is not generating (or perhaps even receiving) the messages, so an ordinary email client program cannot be used; the application has to directly interact with an email infrastructure.

Building basic email capability into an application is not difficult. I will focus on Internet email protocols, since those are open protocols that are rapidly growing and will likely subsume other email protocols. These protocols have evolved from very simple mechanisms into a rich set of standards for sending data of many different kinds. The protocols are also extensible, so one can create new kinds of data to send, and even submit the new type as a proposed standard if desired.

The type of data in an email message is called its "MIME" type—for Multipurpose Internet Mail Extension. When a message is constructed by an email program, it is given a header which describes information such as the recipient's email address, the MIME type, and other information. A receiving email program examines the MIME type in the header, and uses that to determine how to view the message content. If the program cannot handle the MIME type, it will usually save the message data to a file and tell the user where the file is. Most email programs also allow you to identify a program to be used to view a specific MIME type. Such programs are called "content handlers," "viewers," or "plugins."

There are three primary protocols for the transport and receipt of email messages within the Internet: Simple Mail Transfer Protocol (SMTP), Post Office Protocol (POP), and Internet Message Access Protocol (IMAP). There are many supporting protocols as well, such as RFC 822, which defines the Internet mail message header structure. I will discuss these protocols very briefly, spending the most time with IMAP, and then introduce Java's email client package, JavaMail. JavaMail is a large and complex package, so I will only discuss its main features. It is an extensible framework that can be used to easily build mail functionality into an application, or to construct an entire email client application.

**SMTP.** The SMTP mail transport standard is defined in Internet RFC 821, and a series of service extension RFCs that follow it. The primary purpose of SMTP is to define how mail messages are entered into or provided to an email server, and how email servers cooperate to deliver a message to the host on which the recipient resides. In practice, SMTP servers are very complex programs, because they must interface between different incompatible mail systems in a way that is transparent to the user. I recently experienced a real-world nonelectronic analog to this: I had to send a letter to Thailand, and I discovered that if I addressed it in English, it would not get to its destination; so I had to find out how to write the address in Thai. To my amazement, the letter got there; and it made me reflect on how we take for granted issues such as the compatibility of mail systems that we deal with. Sometimes the translation is not straightforward.

To send an email to a local SMTP network service, there are two techniques. One way is to make API calls directly to an SMTP library. This library will interface to the SMTP program running on your system. The other way is to send a message directly to the SMTP port on which the SMTP daemon is listening. If your SMTP server is not on your host, you will have to use the second technique. You basically need to send these command lines:

```
HELO
MAIL FROM: <your email address>
RCPT TO: <email address of sender>
<data> (this should be prefixed with a mail header)
.      (single period on a line by itself)
```

Here is a snippet that does this:

```
// Open connection to SMTP server
String smtpHostName = ...
int smtpPort = 25;// the SMTP standard port
socket = new Socket(smtpHostName, smtpPort);

// Send an email message to an SMTP server
rina = socket.getInetAddress();
lina = rina.getLocalHost();
ps = new PrintStream(socket.getOutputStream());
dis = new DataInputStream(socket.getInputStream());

// Send message
sendline("HELO " + lina.toString());
sendline("MAIL FROM:" + senderEmailAddress);
sendline("RCPT TO:" + recipientEmailAddress);
```

```
sendline("DATA");
sendline(...message data...);
sendline(".");

// Close connection
socket.close();
```

This snippet uses a sendline() method, for sending a line and receiving a response in one step, defined as follows:

```
String sendline(String data) throws IOException
{
   ps.println(data);
   ps.flush();
   return dis.readLine(); // we should check these responses
}
```

Conceptually it is quite simple, and you can implement very basic mail-sending functionality in this way. Note that no password is required; however, most ISP routers will only grant you access to their SMTP server if your IP address is part of their subnetwork, to prevent every Tom, Dick, and Harry from using their mail server.

**POP3.** The POP protocol, now at revision 3, is defined in Internet RFCs 1957 and 1939. I will not go into all the details of the protocol, but instead will show a basic usage example before proceeding to discuss IMAP, which is a more advanced protocol.

The purpose of the POP protocol is to provide a means for users to access their mail remotely. Originally, Internet email was oriented toward user account names, because most users had time-sharing "shell" accounts on UNIX systems, and each account had an email directory associated with it. SMTP routed email to the host that contained the account for the user appearing in the email address, and delivered it to that user's email directory. Using the UNIX mail program, a user could then read his or her mail. POP makes it possible to access your mail even if you are not logged into your account, by providing a remote service for perusal and transfer of your own mail messages between the system containing your account and any email client program that supports POP (Netscape, Eudora, etc.). Nowadays, most email users do not have real shell accounts; they have email accounts instead, so while the user cannot log on and get a shell, their POP client can connect to the system's POP server and transfer their email.

For example, here are the commands that your email client would send to a POP server to query how many messages you have:

```
USER <user-id>
PASS <password>
STAT
```

The first two lines log you into the POP server. The last line asks for status information (how many messages). There are other commands to list, transfer, and delete messages.

One problem with POP is that it allows for two levels of operation: one in which some servers can give messages permanent identifiers, which never change over time and are never (or not for a long time anyway) reassigned, and another in which messages are identified by their sequence in the user's mailbox or mail directory. The problem is that if messages are identified by sequence number, it is easy for a remote client to get out of sync with the mailbox. For example, suppose the client tells the mailbox to delete message 3, and there are 10 messages total. When 3 is deleted, 4 becomes 3, 5 becomes 4, and so on. The client has to know to reorder its own list of messages as well. This works fine until you start the practice (as I do often) of connecting to your POP server with more than one email client. When a client connects, it has to get a list of the messages on the server, determine which it has, and transfer those it does not have. If message identifications can move around, this is very difficult. I have not disassembled their code, but I strongly suspect, based on observed behavior, that programs like Eudora and Netscape actually transfer all messages and compute a checksum to determine which they don't have yet—and then wastefully discard the rest. On the other hand, if the POP server supports the capability to identify messages by permanent ID, the email client does not have to struggle with this ambiguity.

Here is a snippet to ask a POP server how many messages we have; note that I am using my sendline() method again:

```
String popHostName = ...
int popPort = 110;
String userid = ...
String password = ...
Socket socket = new Socket(popHostName, popPort);
ps = new PrintStream(socket.getOutputStream());
dis = new DataInputStream(socket.getInputStream());

// Check for messages
sendline("USER " + userid);
String response = sendline("PASS " + password);
if (response.charAt(0) != '+') throw new Exception("Incorrect
password");
response = sendline("STAT");
```

```
// Parse result
int r = Integer.parseInt(response.substring(4, response.indexOf("
messages")));
System.out.println("User " + userid + " has " + r + " messages on
host " + popHostName);
```

**IMAP4.** The IMAP protocol, now at version 4, revision 1, is a more advanced protocol than POP. It provides authentication, and a richer command set than POP. The JavaMail model is based largely on IMAP, so I will go over the standard in more detail than for POP.

An IMAP server listens for connection requests on port 143. The standard does not define mail transport; that is handled by SMTP. In the IMAP protocol, client and server streams are asynchronous; that is, when you send a command, you do not, except for some commands, block on a response. For this reason each command sent by the client is tagged, so the server can reference a particular client command in response messages. For example, in the following, the client sends a SELECT command, tagged with the identifier "A391" and some time later the server sends a response to that command, identifying the original command by its tag:

***Client:*** `A391 SELECT INBOX`

...

***Server:*** `A391 OK [READ-WRITE] SELECT completed`

The IMAP protocol defines six standard "flags" that a message can have set. These are:

- **\Seen**—The message has been read.
- **\Answered**—The message has been replied to.
- **\Flagged**—The message is "flagged" for urgent or special attention.
- **\Deleted**—The message is marked for deletion by later EXPUNGE.
- **\Draft**—The message is incomplete, i.e., is marked as a draft.
- **\Recent**—The message has recently arrived; set until notification has been made.

These flags are used by commands such as SEARCH to filter messages based on the flag value. A server tells the client which flags it supports by sending the FLAGS message (in response to a SELECT or EXAMINE command; commands are discussed below), such as

*Server:* `* FLAGS (\Answered \Flagged \Deleted \Seen \Draft)`

When a client first connects to an IMAP server, it can connect as a pre-authenticated client if the server supports client authentication by other means, or a client can connect and enter a nonauthenticated state from which it will be required to log on. Once authenticated, the client can perform a SELECT or EXAMINE command to select a mailbox, and enter the "selected" state. The states for a client are shown in Figure 5-10.

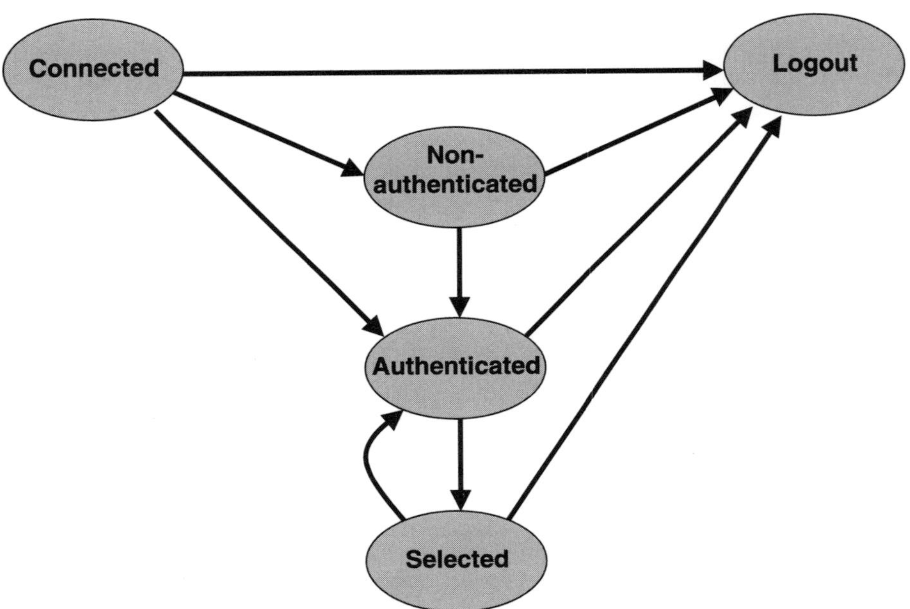


**Figure 5-10** IMAP4 client states.

The client commands supported by IMAP4, and the states from which they can be invoked, are as follows:

- *Universal*

  **CAPABILITY**—Request a listing of supported features ("capabilities"). The server must indicate if it has IMAP capability, and the types of authentication mechanisms and specification extensions supported.

  **LOGOUT**—Disconnect from the server.

  **NOOP**—Merely cause the server to respond, but take no specific action.

- *Nonauthenticated*

  (all Universal commands)

  **LOGIN**—Connect to the server.

  **AUTHENTICATE**—Initiate a specified client authentication protocol. Certain commands can only be performed if the client is authenticated.

- *Authenticated*

  (all Universal commands)

  **SELECT**—Select a specified server mailbox.

  **EXAMINE**—Select a specified server mailbox, but for read-only access.

  **APPEND**—Add a new mail message to the specified mailbox.

  **CREATE**—Create a mailbox.

  **DELETE**—Delete a mailbox.

  **LIST**—List the contents of a mailbox.

  **LSUB**—Return the list of subscribed mailboxes for this user.

  **RENAME**—Rename a mailbox.

  **STATUS**—Request status information for a mailbox, including number of messages, number of messages with the \Recent flag set, number of unread messages, and others.

  **SUBSCRIBE**—Add a specified mailbox to the user's list of subscribed mailboxes, as returned by the LSUB command. The client can use this list to decide which mailboxes to display automatically in its UI.

  **UNSUBSCRIBE**—Unsubscribe a specified mailbox.

- *Selected state*

  (all Universal and Authenticated commands)

  **CHECK**—Request a checkpoint of the current mailbox; implementation-dependent.

  **CLOSE**—Permanently remove all messages marked for deletion from the current selected mailbox, and unselect the mailbox.

  **EXPUNGE**—Permanently remove all messages marked for deletion from the current selected mailbox.

  **COPY**—Copy a specified message from one mailbox to another.

  **FETCH**—Retrieve portions of or an entire specified message.

  **STORE**—Modify the flags for a specified message.

  **UID**—Perform a COPY, FETCH, STORE, or SEARCH command, but using unique message IDs instead of message sequence numbers.

  **SEARCH**—Search for messages matching a specified search criteria.

**JavaMail.** The JavaMail API, represented by packages javax.mail and the subpackages therein, provide a very powerful and flexible framework for adding email capabilities to applications. The framework abstracts email functionality, and separates protocols like POP, IMAP, and SMTP from the application by wrapping them in a service provider layer. Protocols are selected dynamically, depending on the type of email address and selections made by the client. New protocols can be added simply by updating configuration files.

Unfortunately, JavaMail suffers from the deficiencies that exist in the POP and IMAP protocols, in particular that messages are allowed to be identified by message sequence number, and the sequence of a message can change over time. This is not the fault of JavaMail, but rather of the email protocols. The impact is that client design is complicated by the situations that can arise when multiple clients access the same mailbox, or if the client is multithreaded.

JavaMail defines the concept of a "store"—a user mailbox. To connect to a store, you must first establish a session object, as follows:

```
// Create a session
Properties p = new java.util.Properties();
p.put("mail.store.protocol",
p.put("mail.transport.protocol",
p.put("mail.host", <my-email-host>);
p.put("mail.user", <my-user-name>);
p.put("mail.from", <my-email-address>);
Session session = Session.getInstance(p, null);
```

Having created the session, you connect to a store by specifying which kinds of mail protocols you want to use. For example, you might want to access IMAP mailboxes and use SMTP as your mail transport mechanism. To specify this, you get a Provider object that describes each protocol and pass it to the session, as follows:

```
// Query which implementations are available
Provider[] providers = session.getProviders();

// Decide which protocols to use
...you might use a UI, or options panel, for the user to select
   protocols...
Provider[] userChosenProviders = ...

// Pass the list of protocols to the session
for (int i = 0; i < userChosenProviders.length; i++)
session.setProvider(userChosenProviders[i]);
```

Now you can obtain a store object, which you can use to access mail services using the chosen protocols. The store is a proxy for dealing with the mail servers on the specified host (as set by your session). To obtain a store, call the session's getStore() method, and then connect to the store:

```
// Get a store implementation of each protocol. The
// implementations are defined
// in mail.store.protocol
try
{
   Store store = session.getStore();
   store.addConnectionListener(...adapter for responding to
      ConnectionEvent's...);
   store.addFolderListener(...adapter for responding to
      FolderEvent's...);
   store.addStoreListener(...adapter for responding to
      StoreEvent's...);

   store.connect();// the Store implementation will probably
      // display a password dialog
} catch (MessagingException mex) {}
...
```

As you can see, once a store is created, it generates events, which you must handle. The event types defined by JavaMail are:

**ConnectionEvent**—Generated by a store or folder when the store or folder is opened or closed, respectively.

**FolderEvent**—Generated by a folder when it is created, deleted, or renamed. A folder listener can register with the store, or with a particular folder; in either case, it will receive all events for the folder.

**MessageCountEvent**—Generated by a folder when the number of messages in the folder changes as a result of an addition or a removal.

**MessageChangedEvent**—Generated by a folder when a message has been modified.

**StoreEvent**—Generated by a store to signal alerts and notices to be displayed to the user.

**TransportEvent**—Generated by a session's transport implementation (i.e., its mail sender); supports status returned by SMTP or another mail sender interface, indicating if a message was successfully sent.

Figure 5–11 shows which JavaMail components generate these events.

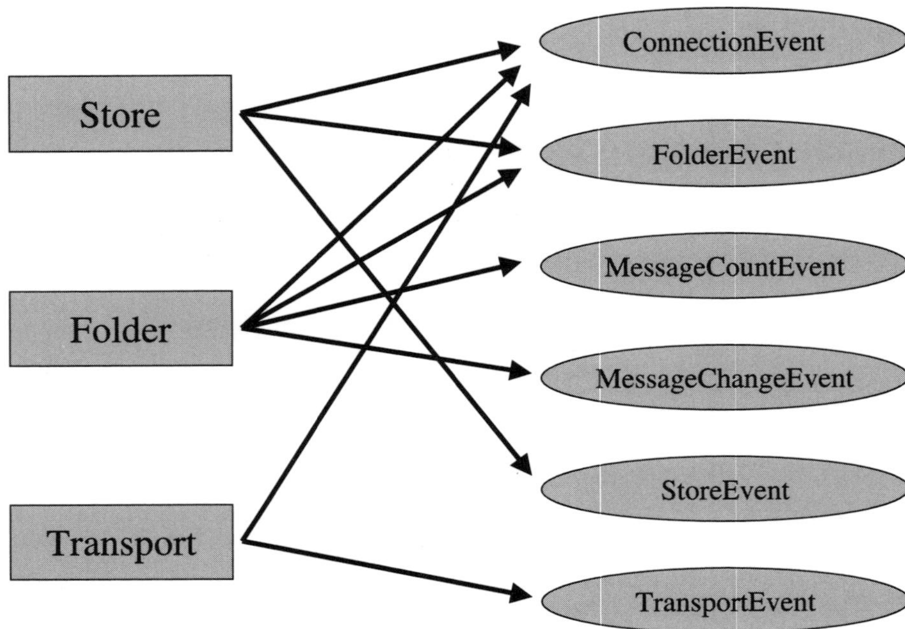


**Figure 5-11** Events generated by JavaMail components.

As we saw in the IMAP4 protocol, you must connect to a particular mailbox folder to perform certain operations. To connect to a folder in a JavaMail store, first get the root folder for the store using getDefaultFolder(), and then use that object to list folders and connect to specific folders. Connecting to a folder involves creating a proxy object for the folder, from which you can receive events and to which you can issue commands.

```
Folder rootFolder = store.getDefaultFolder();
Folder[] folders = rootFolder.list();
...display list of folders...

inFolder = rootFolder.getFolder("INBOX");
if (! inFolder().exists()) throw new Exception("You don't have
   an INBOX!");
myCurrentFolder = inFolder;

myCurrentFolder.addConnectionListener
(
   new ConnectionListener()
```

```
   {
      public void opened(ConnectionEvent e)
      {
         if (e.getSource() == myCurrentFolder)
            refreshFolderDisplay();// (see below)
      }

      public void closed(ConnectionEvent e)
      { ...folder closed; clear display; attempt to recover by
         reconnecting... }

      public void disconnected(ConnectionEvent e) { ...folder
         disconnected... }
   }
);

myFolder.addFolderListener( ...my FolderEvent adapter... );

myFolder.addMessageCountListener( ...my MessageCountEvent
   adapter... );

myFolder.addMessageChangedListener( ...my MessageChangedEvent
   adapter... );

myFolder.open(Folder.READ_WRITE);
```

The above-referenced refreshFolderDisplay() method could be implemented as follows:

```
protected void refreshFolderDisplay()
{
   Message[] messages = myCurrentFolder.getMessages();
   // This does not actually transfer messages, just as an IMAP
   // LIST command does not transfer messages

   // Now get the header information for each message, so we can
   // display in on the client
   FetchProfile fp = new FetchProfile();
   fp.add(FetchProfile.Item.ENVELOPE);
   fp.add(FetchProfile.Item.CONTENT_INFO);
   fp.add(FetchProfile.Item.FLAGS);
   myCurrentFolder.fetch(messages, fp); // Get the information
                                        // for each message

   // Display information for each message - this may either
   // fetch the information
   // dynamically, or use information retrieved in the previous
```

```
    // fetch() operation
    for (int i = 0; i < myCurrentFolder.getMessageCount(); i++)
    {
       Message m = messages[i];

       Address[] from = m.getFrom();
       String subject = m.getSubject();
       Flags[] flags = m.getFlags();
       Date receivedDate = m.getReceivedDate();
       Address[] recipients = m.getAllRecipients();
       Address replyTo = m.getReplyTo();
       Date sentDate = m.getSentDate();

       ...display this information on a line in the client's
          display...
    }
}
```

In the above, I first get an array of message objects from the folder; these are lightweight proxies for the actual messages; no message content is transferred in this operation. I then define a message information retrieval profile object, and perform a fetch using this profile—an implementation will normally use this profile to retrieve the kinds of information specified in the profile object for each message, and store that information in the message objects. In this way, the information can be retrieved in one step, instead of going back to the server for each message one by one. Some implementations may implement this more efficiently than others. After this, I then iterate through each message in the folder and display the message information, presumably in a scrollable list of messages. Most likely the user would be able to select a message from this list and retrieve the message content, or the content for all messages could be retrieved automatically.

Note that in the above example, I retrieve each message's flags: the JavaMail predefined flag values are ANSWERED, DELETED, DRAFT, FLAGGED, RECENT, and SEEN; these are exactly the flags defined in the IMAP protocol. User-defined flags are also supported by the API, although not all stores may support this feature.

To actually get the contents of a mail message, you can use the getContent() method. This returns an object of a type that depends on the MIME type of the content. Some of the possible object types returned are:

- Multipart, MimeMultipart—These are nested objects which contain message parts; when you get this, you must handle each nested content type recursively.

- Message, MimeMessage—Use the getContent() method again.
- String
- InputStream
- Image

or potentially any other kind of object for which a MIME type exists. Alternatively, if there is a viewer included with the mail application for the message's MIME type, you can use the data handler for that MIME type:

```
DataHandler dh = message.getDataHandler();
CommandInfo ci = dh.getCommand("view");
Component c = dh.getBean(ci);
...add and show the viewer component...
```

To send a newly composed message, use the static Transport.send() method:

```
Transport.send(message);
```

The default transport implementation is used to send the message to all the recipients in the message's recipient list. The javamail.providers property file identifies the transport and store provider implementations that are available; and the javamail.address.map property file maps transport address types to transport protocols. For example, the providers property file might contain the line:

```
protocol=smtp; type=transport;
 class=com.sun.mail.smtp.SMTPTransport;
```

and the map property file might contain:

```
rfc822=smtp
```

This maps an RFC822-style address to the SMTP mail transport protocol. This makes it possible for the Transport class to determine that an RFC822 message requires an SMTP transport, and that the available implementation exists in com.sun.smtp.SMTPTransport, which of course must be in the classpath.

The JavaMail API encapsulates a broad set of email functionality so that applications which need email features do not have to wrestle with protocol details or protocol dependencies. Furthermore, the use of the Java Activation Framework for the incorporation of content viewers makes it possible to support new kinds of content without modifying the application.

# CHAPTER 6

# Java Database Connectivity

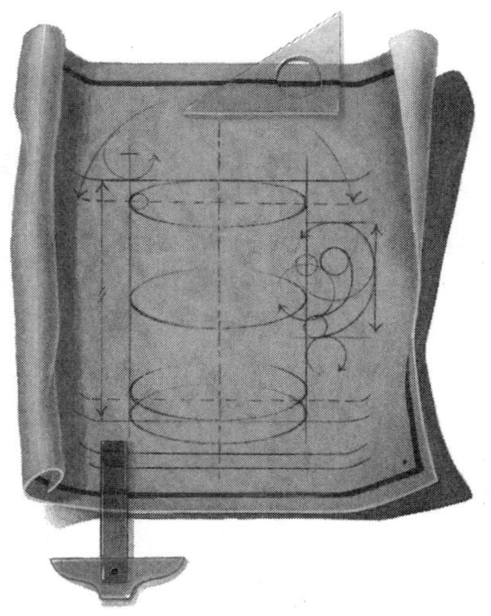

Most multiuser computing applications center around access to data. At the core of any large application there is a database of some kind, which stores the state of the system. Business applications usually use relational databases today, which provide multiuser concurrency and transaction control, high throughput, and advanced features for data recovery in the event of system failure. These are necessary features for a mission-critical system.

Standards such as SQL have provided programmers with tools to define data in powerful and universal ways so that the data model can be developed independent of the decision of which database to use. The relational model, which was controversial in the mid-'80s, is now a universally accepted standard. The Java JDBC (Java Data Base Connectivity) API defines a standard way of accessing a relational database from a Java application, regardless of where the application is running and where the database is (i.e., it supports remote clients in a transparent way).

This location independence is a powerful feature. It means that database programs can be written which can easily be deployed as an application or as a web applet. Web-deployed applets can be inserted into web pages, providing instant access to realtime data as easily as if the database were running on the user's machine. While it is possible to provide access to databases using CGI programs, Java programs are orders of magnitude more maintainable, more robust, easier to develop, and more secure than equivalent CGI-based solutions. Furthermore, the decision of how to deploy the program—as an applet, a stand-alone application, or a "push" channel, and as either a thin-client design or a heavy client—can be deferred, and a change in decision does not require a significant new investment in staff or training.

Having a universal and portable implementation language—Java—also makes it possible to develop platform-independent object models directly in the implementation language: the resulting object models are then portable. This has opened up the field of object-oriented databases, which were niche products prior to Java but are now rapidly gaining acceptance. These products, which are quickly maturing, are beginning to provide the same fail-safe features and scalability, and nearly the performance of relational systems. In addition, they come in many varieties, from small-footprint systems to high-performance distributed database engines. The developer has a great deal of choice in selecting a database system suited to the application. Object-oriented databases, by their very nature, provide many benefits that relational systems do not, which I will discuss. In terms of acceptance, object-oriented databases are now where relational databases were in the mid-'80s: at the threshold of their time. The challenge to the providers of these products is to prove that they are scalable and reliable.

In this chapter I will first provide a foundation for the JDBC API. I will then explain object-oriented databases, and discuss their unique characteristics. With these established, I will then give an overview of transaction and concurrency concepts, and provide a framework of transaction models that are applicable to persistent objects and databases. Throughout this, I will use as many examples as possible, to make the discussion concrete and show actual implementations. I will wind up by addressing synchronization issues that pertain to database client deployment.

## Using JDBC

The JDBC API is a "thin" API, which wraps SQL and query responses in an object layer. The API is contained in package java.sql. In this section I will examine the features of JDBC, and how to use it.

Most JDBC programs do these things:

- Load a JDBC driver.
- Establish a connection to a database by specifying the database's URL.
- Optionally interrogate the database for what capability subset it has.
- Optionally retrieve schema metainformation.
- Construct an SQL or callable statement object, and send queries.

- Process query results; the transaction completes when the results have all been retrieved.
- Close the connection.

JDBC is based on ODBC, so there is a great deal of conformance between the two. In fact, Sun supplies a bridge between them so that you can access any data source that has an ODBC driver (this is a large set of applications) using the JDBC API.

An important component of a JDBC implementation is the JDBC driver. The driver establishes the connection to the database, and implements any protocol required to move queries and data between the client and the server. From an API perspective, the driver does this by manufacturing an object that implements the java.sql.Connection interface for the client to apply JDBC calls against. From a protocol perspective, the Connection object created by the driver must either convert query transport requests into DBMS native API calls (for a type 1 or 2 driver), or marshall the requests into a stream and send them to a remote middleware component (which may have its own driver, for connecting to the database on the server side; this middleware driver has nothing to do with JDBC).

In addition, the driver must therefore perform data type mapping between JDBC and database types, and interpret SQL escape sequences. The JDBC specification permits data type extensions, so the driver can map vendor-specific database types to a vendor-specific package of Java types.

### *Two-Tier vs. Three-Tier*

Products like Oracle's SQL*Net/Net8 allow database clients to access a database remotely, so distributed clients are nothing new. SQL*Net is a multiprotocol proxy which forwards database requests from the current host to the host that has the data, in a way which is largely transparent to the application, even to the extent of allowing transactions to overlap between hosts. This proxy component can be thought of as a middle tier, sitting between the application and the databases the application uses. The component is a generic utility that is largely transparent to the application, so it is sometimes viewed as merely a communication layer rather than a tier in its own right—it depends on your perspective.

Protocols like SQL*Net are proprietary, however. You cannot use SQL*Net, for example, to access a Sybase database. JDBC does not define a standard wire protocol for database access—not even a default one—but it does define a standard programmatic way of accessing databases, independent of where they are located and what brand they are. It is up to the JDBC driver manager to locate the driver for that database, and it is up to the driver to make the connection and transport the data.

Building two-tier and three-tier applications with JDBC is therefore easy, because the developer can focus mostly on the application rather than where the database is or what kind it is. The developer further has the choice of programming their own middle tier, using a generic technology like CORBA, or obtaining a multitier driver product like Symantec's dbANYWHERE or a full-fledged application server such as BEA WebLogic. Regardless, the client-side application which actually makes the queries is the same, and it need not know if the database is installed locally or remotely. Since Java clients are web-deployable, this means that the client can be used from anywhere in a local or wide area network, and can access multiple databases anywhere—potentially around the world.

### What Is a "Thin Client"?

A heavy client architecture is one in which a program resident on each client machine interacts with a server. This is called "heavy" because the client application is usually large, and makes substantial use of client-side services for its operation. A great deal of application logic usually resides on the client in such a system.

By contrast, a thin client architecture is one in which the client is a general-purpose component, such as a web browser (or other deployment component), and most application logic resides on a server. Unfortunately, the term "thin client" has come to be somewhat muddled, and now can also mean a heavy client written in a transportable language like Java, and which uses a "thin" server driver. For example, a large Java client program which uses an all-Java JDBC driver is often referred to as a thin client design, when in fact the client is anything but thin. In this book I will use the term "thin client" to mean either server-generated HTML, or a lightweight program, with a small footprint, which makes limited use of client-side services; and I will use the term "thin driver" to refer to a lightweight server protocol component, which has a small footprint and makes limited use of services for the system in which it executes (the client).

### JDBC Driver Types

Selecting the right driver is an extremely critical decision for a project. Do not assume "all drivers are alike," and do not treat a driver as a commodity item. Drivers add significant value to a system, and their features vary tremendously. Furthermore, there is significant risk that you may take certain features for granted, only to find the driver you have selected does not support those features. You should create a checklist of the features you need and desire, and verify that the driver you select has those features. This chapter will help you to prepare such a list.

Ultimately, the database drivers have the burden of providing the flexibility and features allowed by JDBC. Java has defined these numbered driver categories:

Type 1: JDBC/ODBC
Type 2: Native-API
Type 3: Open Protocol-Net
Type 4: Proprietary Protocol-Net

I will now discuss each one.

**Type 1: JDBC/ODBC.** Type 1 drivers do not have any host redirection capability, and require that an ODBC driver for the database be installed. A type 1 driver merely translates queries obtained by the driver into equivalent ODBC queries and forwards them, typically via native API calls, directly to the ODBC driver. Since native API calls are involved to access an ODBC driver, a type 1 JDBC driver usually needs to load a native library component and access it with native methods. The JDBC/ODBC bridge driver (sun.jdbc.odbc.JdbcOdbcDriver) provided by Sun with the Java SDK is an example of a type 1 driver.

It is noted that a type 1 driver does not itself provide any host redirection capability. However, if the ODBC driver is itself a network driver, it does not preclude it.

The basic usage configuration for a type 1 driver is shown in Figure 6-1.

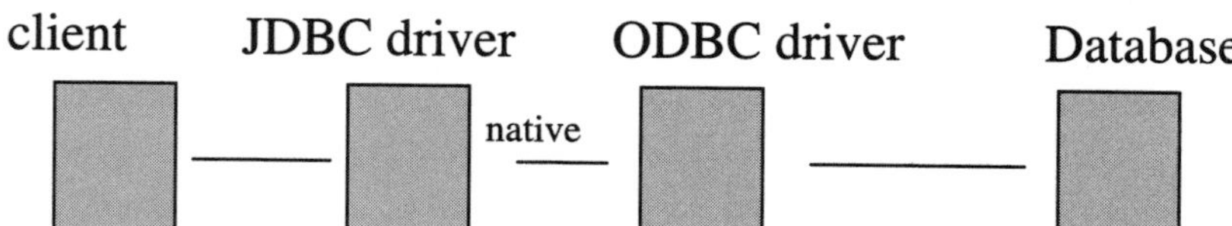


**Figure 6-1** Type 1 JDBC driver.

**Type 2: Native-API.** Like a type 1 driver, a type 2 driver provides no host redirection for database queries; however, it does not use ODBC, but instead directly interfaces to a vendor-specific driver or database API, such as Oracle's OCI (Oracle Call Interface).

The basic usage configuration for a type 2 driver is shown in Figure 6-2.

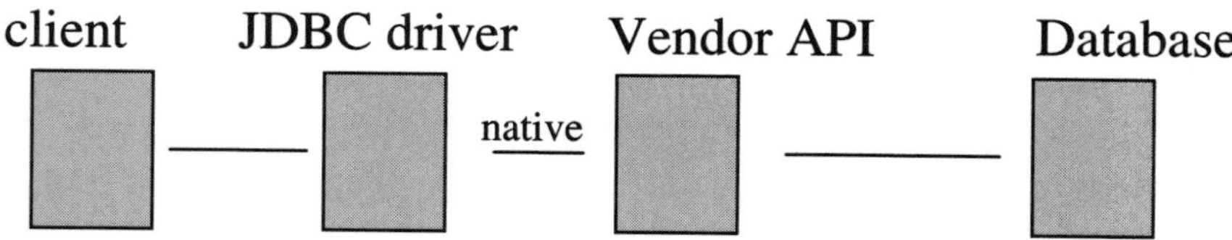


**Figure 6-2** Type 2 JDBC driver.

**Type 3: Open Protocol-Net.** A type 3 driver is one that has the capability to forward database requests to a remote data source. Furthermore, type 3 drivers can interface to multiple database types, and are not vendor-specific. This is, of course, a matter of degree, as such drivers usually have a set of database types to which they can connect.

In this configuration, all native code is relegated to a net server gateway component, which may run on a remote machine. The net server component may or may not use ODBC to actually access the database; this is transparent to the client. To make matters confusing, this net server component often requires a driver of its own. From the point of view of the JDBC client, however, the client driver, which is written completely in Java, communicates with the net server using a database-independent protocol, and the net server translates this protocol into database commands for whatever type of database it is connected to.

The basic usage configuration for a type 3 driver is shown in Figure 6-3.

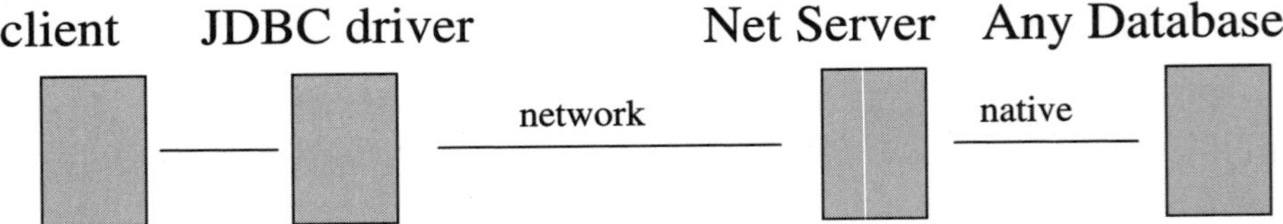


**Figure 6-3** Type 3 JDBC driver.

An interesting type 3 driver in the public domain is the RmiJdbc driver, developed by the INRIA/France Mediation Project (http://dyade.inrialpes.fr/mediation/download/). It is based on RMI as a wire protocol, and one can even obtain the remote interface definition to make RMI calls to it directly.

**Type 4: Proprietary Protocol-Net.** A type 4 driver has the same configuration as a type 3 driver; however, it uses a wire protocol specific to a particular vendor, and is intended for accessing only that vendor's brand of database. Client-side code is unaffected, and it should be possible to substitute a type 4 driver for a type 3 (or a different type 4) if database brands change.

JDBC does not define a standard wire protocol for database access, which is a good thing, because it opens the door for type 4 drivers that provide optimized access to specific databases without any change to the client code.

The basic usage configuration for a type 4 driver is shown in Figure 6-4.

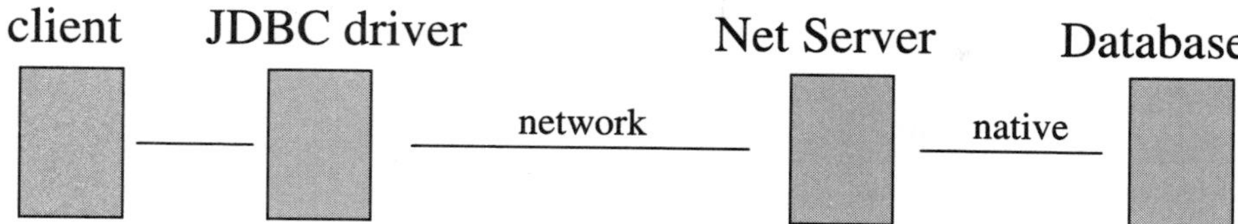


**Figure 6-4** Type 4 JDBC driver.

While type 4 drivers have the greatest opportunity to have good performance compared with the more generic type 3 drivers, they tend to be the most problematic in terms of implementing the JDBC functionality, because they are usually implemented on top of the DBMS's native stream protocol, which was most likely developed before JDBC existed. For example, one widely used type 4 driver we tested, from a major vendor, did not allow us to retrieve column names, presumably because this information is not available via the native protocol used by the driver.

Often type 3 and 4 drivers do not implement concurrency models supported by their type 1 and 2 counterparts. This may be because middleware implementations associate a transaction with a thread, so the stream protocol must know how to reconnect to the same thread to retain transaction context across JDBC calls. (ORB products such as Inprise's VisiBroker allow a single-thread-per-connection model as an optional connection mode, which is compatible with the JDBC model of one transaction per connection.) Given these considerations, there seems to be an inclination for driver vendors to take a shortcut and not support certain isolation modes. Often it is the drivers from the database vendors themselves that have such limitations, while drivers from "driver companies" are more fully developed.

### *Driver Comparisons*

Internally we have done extensive testing of drivers provided by different manufacturers, and have been amazed at the variety of performance characteristics. Drivers change continually, so I will not attempt to compare them by vendor here, and the list below leaves the providers anonymous. This list is a sampling of results for the driver products of a few vendors. The list shows the divergence—in some cases not as one would expect—in driver performance from different providers.

*Time to Retrieve 5000 Bytes**
(*Result set retrieval and data transport to close transaction)

*Type 1*
JDBC/ODBC bridge: **0.65**

*Type 2*
Vendor A: **0.96**

*Type 3*
Vendor A: **2.3**
Vendor B: **0.97**

*Type 4*
Vendor C: **1.28**

This indicates that it is worthwhile to compare drivers and select the best one, since it can change the performance of your application by a factor of two or even more. Note also that comparing type 1 or 2 drivers with type 3 or 4 is like comparing apples and oranges. When selecting a driver brand, one should only compare a type 1 or 2 with another type 1 or 2; or a type 3 or 4 with another type 3 or 4. Drivers of type 1 or 2 can only be compared with drivers of type 3 or 4 for the purpose of evaluating an overall system design. Also, there is more to drivers than raw performance; driver features are discussed in the next section.

### High Performance Driver Features

Drivers vary enormously in their features. Some features may be important to you, and others may not. I will now discuss the major categories of features.

**Thread/Connection Model.** JDBC requires that a driver support multiple connections per client. This implies that the client application can open several connections and perform a separate transaction on each of these concurrently in a separate thread.

How the driver implements this is not specified. The driver may open a separate socket connection for each connection, or it may multiplex JDBC connections on a single socket. This has performance implications with regard to scalability for large numbers of clients. It is impossible to anticipate beforehand which approach will yield better performance for the application, since it depends on the details of how connections are demultiplexed in both the server-side driver component and the network software as well, and the latter may be operating-system-dependent. The only way to know is to run tests simulating the loading factor the application is expected to encounter, and compare drivers by running tests under load.

It should be noted that the JDBC/ODBC bridge driver is intended to provide JDBC access for arbitrary ODBC applications such as desktop databases and is not designed as a highly scalable component. For example, the bridge is not

multithreaded and therefore serializes all client accesses. High-volume applications should use higher performance drivers.

**Firewall Traversal and Security.** Some drivers have the ability to tunnel through a proxy firewall, by embedding their protocol inside of the HTTP protocol. The driver may require the application to configure it by setting a property (a proxy address). (The Driver.getPropertyInfo() method can be used to obtain the properties a driver requires to be set.) This issue is discussed in more depth later in this section.

Some drivers use IIOP as their wire protocol. In this case, if the firewall is designed to allow IIOP to pass (usually by mapping all IIOP requests to a single port, and filtering out non-IIOP traffic on that port), the driver will be able to operate without tunneling. This is a very open approach, and is being used by more and more driver vendors. Similarly, if the driver uses RMI, the driver vendor may provide the capability to pass the RMI traffic using a mapped port. This capability must be included with the driver and is not an automatic capability of RMI.

Some drivers also provide secure connections using SSL. If your connection will be traversing the Internet and you are concerned about privacy, you should investigate using a driver that provides SSL connections.

An example of a driver that has all of these capabilities is WebLogic's Tengah JDBC driver. This product provides HTTP tunneling, and can use IIOP as its wire protocol. It uses SSL to provide a secure connection between the client and the component WebLogic server. Another example is Sybase's JConnect, which provides both HTTP tunneling for penetrating a firewall, and SSL for secure connections between the client and the Sybase database server.

**Caching.** Drivers can perform caching of various kinds to speed up queries. Some of these are:

- *Row prefetching*: When you retrieve a result set, the rows are not actually transferred until you request them one by one. Some drivers perform row prefetching in anticipation that you will ask for the next row before you actually do.
- *Row caching* ("array fetch"): This is related to row prefetching; the driver retrieves a block of rows at a time.
- *Connection caching:* A driver may maintain a set of reusable database connections for a given user; clients that connect as this user transparently reuse this persistent connection, thereby avoiding database connection time and reducing the overall server-side footprint per client.

- *Schema caching:* Drivers have the job of translating SQL from generic SQL into a vendor's specific SQL. To do this, they often need to consult the database schema. A driver may perform schema caching to speed this up.

**Early Binding of Stored Procedures.** A driver may instruct the database to locate and load stored procedures (in JDBC, "callable statements") while the SQL is being processed by the driver so that the procedures are ready to execute as soon as the database engine needs them.

**Support for Hints.** Hints are constructs that appear in an SQL construct to tell the database engine what strategy to use for implementing a query. A driver will ordinarily pass hints on through to the database. A general-purpose thin type 3 driver might strip hints out, since hints are DBMS specific—this is something to evaluate when choosing a driver.

**Support for DDL.** Some drivers allow you to perform DDL operations, and some do not. If your application needs to do things like "DROP TABLE," you should check whether your driver allows this operation. Note that SQL92 assumes that any DDL operations constitute a new transaction.

**Database Feature Support.** Your database may have specific features that you want to use, and you should test your driver to make sure it supports these. For example, outer joins may be supported by the database but not the driver. There are methods defined in the java.sql.DatabaseMetaData class which you can call to determine if a particular feature is supported by the database or driver servicing that connection.

**JTA Support.** JDBC 2 adds support for distributed transaction management allowing pure Java JDBC drivers to participate in global transactions coordinated by a transaction manager. This enables the application to access multiple databases of different kinds and perform the separate operations within the context of a single global transaction which can be committed or rolled back as a unit.

Before JDBC 2, many application server vendors provided multi-database support, but often had the restriction that the databases had to be of the same kind. This is because the driver relied on the database's built-in support for distributed transactions across multiple instances of the database product. Support for distributed transactions for databases of different brands was generally lacking, however, and those which did support heterogeneous distributed transactions did so by using horrendous workarounds to enable them to link with existing native XA database drivers. This support required IIOP or custom RMI protocols as well.

JDBC 2 adds support for distributed transactions in a standard way. This topic is discussed extensively in the section on JDBC 2 and in Chapter 7. JTA support gen-

erally goes hand-in-hand with an application server environment and is not usually used in a standalone manner (although it can be). If your application may be communicating with multiple databases of different kinds, make sure that the application server and database drivers include JTA support.

### *JDBC Compliance*

The method java.sql.Driver.jdbcCompliant() can be used to determine if a driver has passed Sun's JDBC compliance test. If this method returns false, it does not necessarily mean the driver is not JDBC-compliant; however, if it returns true, it *is* compliant. Compliant drivers support the full JDBC API and have full support for SQL 92 Entry Level. A compliant driver will return true when tested for these features:

- **nullPlusNonNullIsNull** (concatenation between a null and nonnull value is null)
- **ANSI92EntryLevelSQL** (supported)
- **CorrelatedSubqueries** (supported)
- **LikeEscapeClause** ("{escape 'escape-char'}" is supported)
- **MinimumSQLGrammar** (the ODBC Minimum SQL grammar is supported)
- **MixedCaseQuotedIdentifiers** (mixed-case quoted identifiers are case sensitive)
- **NoNullableColumns** (columns can be defined as nonnullable)
- **SubqueriesInComparisons** (subqueries in comparison expressions are supported)
- **SubqueriesInExists** (subqueries in "exists" expressions are supported)
- **SubqueriesInIns** (subqueries in "in" statements are supported)
- **SubqueriesInQuantifieds** (subqueries in quantified expressions are supported)
- **TableCorrelationNames** (table correlation names are supported)

and false for:

- **MixedCaseIdentifiers** (mixed-case unquoted identifiers are case sensitive)

### *Loading a Driver*

The driver manager (java.sql.DriverManager) uses the Java property "sql.drivers" to identify the classes that contain JDBC drivers. The driver manager will register the drivers in this list. Any application can set this property, but in practice, drivers are usually registered automatically by causing their class to be loaded: a driver is required to automatically register itself by executing code in a static block in the driver's class. Thus, all you have to do is either instantiate the driver, for example,

```
MyVendorsDriver driver = new MyVendorsDriver();
```

or explicitly load its class, for example,

```
Class.forName("MyVendorsDriver");
```

When a driver is subsequently needed to complete a database connection, specified by a URL, the driver manager will try each registered driver until a driver reports that it can handle the URL's protocol (returns true to the acceptsURL() method).

### *JDBC from an Application*

A Java application which uses JDBC can identify the driver to use by listing the driver's class in the sql.drivers property, or by explicitly loading the driver class. In either case, the driver class must be in the virtual machine's java.class.path property (i.e., the classpath).

Once the driver is loaded, a type 1 or 2 driver should be able to connect to a database identified by a local URL (i.e., on the same machine), or any database reachable by any native driver that the JDBC driver supports. For example, if you are using Java's ODBC bridge driver, you would be able to connect to any database on that machine which has an ODBC driver installed. This is shown in Figure 6-5.

As another example, if your driver is Oracle's OCI driver, which is a native driver that uses Oracle native call interface, you would be able to connect to any Oracle instance on that machine, or any Oracle database reachable from your machine, via SQL*Net.

Using a type 3 or 4 driver, an application should be able to connect to a database identified by a local or remote URL. In the latter case, a middleware daemon running on the database machine would process streamed requests and convert them into native driver calls. An example of a type 3 remote driver is Symantec's dBANYWHERE product.

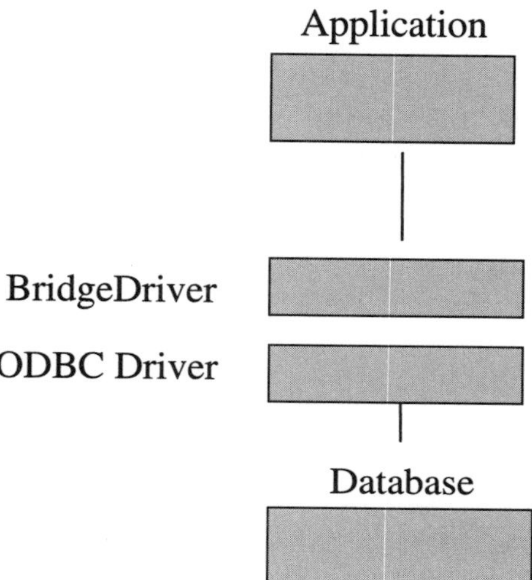


**Figure 6-5** Type 1 JDBC on the same machine as the database.

### *JDBC from an Applet*

Connecting from an applet presents some special problems that do not exist for an application. These include:

- Driver in the codebase
- Middleware
- Firewall issues
- Security of transmitted data
- Authentication

The last three items are related to security, and they are discussed them later in this chapter and also in Chapter 4. For this discussion, let me address the first two, which are architectural issues.

For the driver manager to locate the driver, it must be able to find the class, as specified either in the java.sql property or if you explicitly load the class. In either case, a class loader must physically locate the class, from either the user's local disk or the codebase from which the applet was obtained. When deploying a JDBC applet, therefore, you will need to make sure that the driver's classes are in the codebase for the applet. Assuming the driver is packaged in a JAR file, this can be achieved by adding that JAR file to the HTML ARCHIVE tag for the applet.

The next consideration is the configuration of the server middleware component that intermediates between the communication connections to its drivers and the database. Consider the following scenario.

The driver in Figure 6-6 is an applet-deployed JDBC driver. This kind of driver is often referred to as a "thin" driver, because it is written purely in Java and does not make use of any native or client-based services other than those provided by Java. It is merely a communication manager for connecting to the server-side middleware.

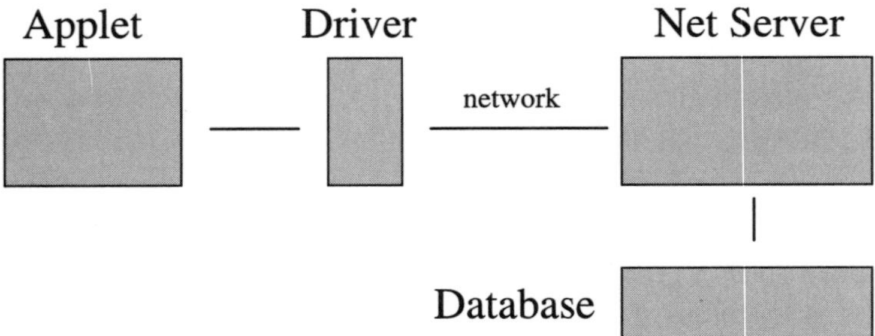


**Figure 6-6** Applet-deployed JDBC driver and server-side proxy middleware.

The middleware has the task of managing multiple sessions with all of the JDBC applets connecting to the database, and proxying requests and results between the client-side driver and the database.

Database connection establishment overhead can be mitigated by using a middle tier that maintains a connection pool. However, you still have the delay of connecting to the middle tier.

### *Connecting to a Database*

To open a connection to a database, you call the driver manager's static getConnection() method and provide it with a URL to locate the database:

```
Connection con = DriverManager.getConnection(
   "jdbc:my_vendors_driver://host:port/datasourcename", userid,
      password);
```

If the database is not actually on the same machine as the middleware, but is being accessed from there by the middleware using a proprietary network database protocol such as SQL*Net, the middleware will need to know the ultimate

location of the database so it can provide this to the network software. Thus, the URL can be somewhat more complex, and actually requires two hostnames in it. The exact format is specified by the driver manufacturer.

If the client is an applet running in a browser outside of your firewall, and the client's network has its own firewall, the driver may have to wind its way through two proxies. In addition, if your organization's policy does not permit running applications (such as middleware) other than a web server on the applet host, you will need to redirect the driver's connection yet again to the ultimate middleware host. Often this web server redirection program is implemented as a Java servlet so that it can be run on a web server. If you put all of this together, you obtain a picture something like the one in Figure 6-7.

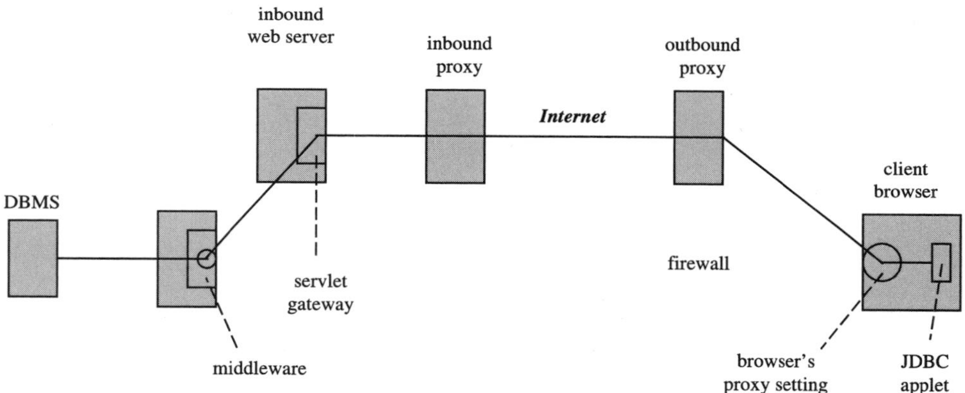


***Proxy settings for a client JDBC driver:***

- **The client network HTTP proxy (because the driver may not recognize the browser's proxy setting)**
- **The servlet gateway**

**Figure 6-7** Using a servlet to redirect DBMS requests.

As you can see, there are many opportunities for a bottleneck to occur in a scenario such as this. In particular, several routing components are effectively application-level routers (proxies or middleware), rather than packet routers optimized for the task. If there are a large number of clients, some percentage of them will have open database connections, each of which increases the resources required by the driver as well as network resources. In some cases it may be desirable to locate an authenticated application server outside of the organization's inner firewall as a front end to requests from extranet clients.

The driver may also require your applet to set a Java property to specify the parameters required by a Java servlet redirection gateway. The applet may even have to obtain the location of the user's own network proxy from the user and set this as a property so that the driver can communicate out through the user's firewall. This depends on how the driver is written, and whether it uses the browser's socket facility or a pure Java one.

The bottom line is, design and test your planned configuration early. I have seen many projects progress to an advanced point, only to find that the driver did not support a critical capability.

### Displaying Database MetaData

The JDBC DatabaseMetaData class allows your application to obtain information about the database and DBMS, including its catalog (if any), tables, and features. Here is an example of getting a database's metadata object, and then requesting a list of all of the tables in the database.

```
DatabaseMetaData dmd = con.getMetaData();
ResultSet tables = dmd.getTables(null, null, null, null);
```

The parameters on the getTables() statement are selection criteria, including name matching. Null values cause "any" to match. The return type is a result set, which can be scrolled through to obtain information about the selected tables, such as the column names and data types.

### Result Sets: Making a Simple Query

To perform a query, you need to first construct a Statement object. You can reuse this object for multiple queries. Using the statement object, you can call the executeQuery() method to transport SQL to the database:

```
Statement statement = con.createStatement();
ResultSet   rs = statement.executeQuery("SELECT *
      from PRODUCTS");
```

The object returned is a ResultSet. A ResultSet is a table of rows. The rows are accessed in sequence; you can't go back and reread a row once you have read it, though JDBC2 will relax this. (Thus, repeatable reads are not an issue within a result set; this is discussed later.) To access the first and each successive row, you must call the ResultSet's next() method.

The row you are currently on represents a logical cursor into a result table returned from the query. To retrieve column values by name or position from the current row, you can specify a column by either name or ordinal position. For example, both of these retrieve int values from the current row:

```
rs.getInt("COL1");     // gets int value from column COL1 of
                       //current row
rs.getInt(2);    // gets int-value from the second column of the
                 //current row
```

To retrieve a column value as an object, use the Object-type accessor.

```
rs.getObject("COL1");     // returns a java object, depending
                          // on type of COL1
rs.getObject(2);    // returns a java object, depending on
                    // type of column 2
```

ResultSet is an interface, so you can implement your own ResultSet object from any base class. Thus, there is no reason why, for example, you could not in theory create a serializable ResultSet or other exotic types of ResultSet.

### *Cursors*

A result set has an implied cursor. You can get the cursor name using the getCursorName() method. If the database supports operations using cursors, you can use this cursor name in subsequent statements. Use the supportsPositionedUpdate() and supportsPositionedDelete() methods to determine if the database (and driver) support these operations. Even if the database supports them, the driver may not, especially for some type 3 and 4 drivers.

### *Joins and Outer Joins*

There are many different ways to specify an outer join, and there is a way preferred by JDBC. First, however, we must understand what a join and an outer join are.

A "join" is a query made against two or more tables, in which columns from each table are selected based on a criterion that "joins" the tables (e.g., that a value in one table must equal a value in another table).

Consider Tables 6-1 and 6-2.

**Table 6-1** Employee

| EMPNO | ENAME | DEPTNO |
|---|---|---|
| 7521 | WARD | 30 |
| 7782 | CLARK | 10 |
| 7839 | KING | 10 |
| 7844 | TURNER | 30 |
| 7900 | JAMES | 30 |
| 7934 | MILLER | 10 |

**Table 6-2** Department

| DEPTNO | DNAME | LOC |
|---|---|---|
| 10 | ACCOUNTING | NEW YORK |
| 30 | SALES | CHICAGO |
| 40 | OPERATIONS | BOSTON |

Here is a join, and its results are shown in Table 6-3:

```
rs = stmt.executeQuery("SELECT D.DNAME, E.ENAME FROM DEPT D, EMP E
   WHERE D.DEPTNO = E.DEPTNO");
```

**Table 6-3** Join

| DNAME | ENAME |
|---|---|
| SALES | WARD |
| ACCOUNTING | CLARK |
| ACCOUNTING | KING |
| SALES | TURNER |
| SALES | JAMES |
| ACCOUNTING | MILLER |

An ambiguity occurs if some of the values in one table do not appear at all in another table being joined. In the above example, department 40 is not represented at all in the EMP table (Table 6-1). Perhaps it is a new department. We still might want it included in the join, however, so we do not forget about it. In other words, if we are trying merely to create a cross-reference of department name to employee, do we want departments without employees to be left out of the list? If the answer is no, we need to tell the query engine to do an "outer join." Here is an outer join, shown in Table 6-4, using Oracle's syntax.

```
rs = stmt.executeQuery("SELECT D.DNAME, E.ENAME FROM DEPT D, EMP E
WHERE D.DEPTNO = E.DEPTNO (+)");
```

**Table 6-4** **Outer Join**

| DNAME | ENAME |
|---|---|
| ACCOUNTING | CLARK |
| ACCOUNTING | KING |
| ACCOUNTING | MILLER |
| SALES | JAMES |
| SALES | TURNER |
| SALES | WARD |
| **OPERATIONS** | **null** |

Here is an outer join, using JDBC standard escape syntax.

```
rs = stmt.executeQuery("{oj DEPT D LEFT OUTER JOIN EMP E ON
   D.DEPTNO = E.DEPTNO}");
```

Not all drivers support this syntax. For example, on Oracle 7.3 with Oracle's thin JDBC driver, this results in the error "Nonsupported SQL92 token: oj."

With these DatabaseMetaData methods, you can find out if outer joins are supported:

```
supportsOuterJoins()
supportsFullOuterJoins()
supportsLimitedOuterJoins()
```

### *Statements that Don't Return a ResultSet*

SQL INSERT, UPDATE, and DELETE operations do not return a result set. For these kinds of statements, use the Statement's executeUpdate() method instead of the executeQuery() method. For example,

```
stmt.executeUpdate("INSERT...");   // for INSERT, UPDATE, and
                                   // DELETE operations
```

Some JDBC drivers allow you to execute DDL statements, and some do not. In general, use the metadata interface to determine the capabilities of the database; for example, the rather long-winded method:

```
supportsDataDefinitionAndDataManipulationTransactions()
```

returns true if DDL operations are allowed.

### *Prepared Statements*

A prepared statement is one which is precompiled and potentially preoptimized, with placeholders for parameter substitutions. In theory, the DBMS can create a query plan ahead of time for a prepared statement, and have it ready to run each time the query is invoked. Prepared statements are useful in loops, which execute the same SQL repeatedly with minor variations. While it is true that most databases keep query caches so that they do not need to create query plans all over again if an SQL statement is repeated, in theory a prepared statement could save a lot of overhead, or the DBMS having to determine if the query is similar to one executed previously.

Here is an example of a JDBC prepared statement:

```
java.sql.PreparedStatemet ps = con.prepareStatement(
   "SELECT * FROM TAB1 WHERE COLA=?");
```

This creates a prepared statement that is ready to be executed. To execute the statement, you must supply values for the positional parameters placemarked by "?" symbols. You use the set<type>() method to do this, where the <type> depends on the data type of the column. For example:

```
ps.setInt(1, 1000);    // sets the first "?"
                       // parameter to "1000"
```

sets the value of the first positional parameter (the first position is indicated by the "1") to the value 1000. Having supplied values for all positional parameters for the statement object, you can then execute a query with:

```
ResultSet rs = ps.executeQuery();
```

For some databases, prepared statements execute as ordinary statements, because the database caches them regardless, and handles them in that manner.

### *For Large (BLOB and CLOB) Parameters*

Binary Large Objects (BLOBs) are often used to store media data and documents in a database. To pass a BLOB value in JDBC, construct a prepared statement, create an input stream to read the BLOB data, and pass the input stream to the prepared statement as follows:

```
PreparedStatement ps = con.prepareStatement(
   "INSERT INTO TAB1 VALUES (?, ?)");
ps.setString(1, "Anatoli Knapsackovitch");
java.io.File f = new java.io.File("mug.jpeg");
ps.setBinaryStream(2, new java.io.FileInputStream (f),
   f.length());
```

The PreparedStatement.setBytes() method can be used to pass a Java byte array to a BINARY, VARBINARY, or LONGVARBINARY column value instead of passing the bytes via a stream.

For reading binary values as a stream from a result set column, you can use the getBinaryStream(), getAsciiStream(), and getUnicodeStream() methods; or you can use the getBytes() method to obtain the value as a byte array.

You can request a conversion of a binary stream to character format by using the getAsciiStream() and getUnicodeStream() methods. The PreparedStatement setAsciiStream() and setUnicodeStream() methods will send an ASCII and Unicode stream data (CLOBs) to the database, respectively, performing any conversion required by the database to store the data in the database's internal format.

Similarly, Character Large Objects (CLOBs) can be passed as streams using the setUnicodeStream() and setAsciiStream() methods. You can retrieve CLOBs from a result set as a stream, using the getAsciiStream() and getUnicodeStream() methods, or as a string using the getString() method.

When retrieving a BLOB or CLOB as a stream, you must read the stream before performing any more getXXX() operations on the result set, because the stream is automatically closed on the next getXXX() call.

### *Dates and Times*

To represent dates and times, use the JDBC "escape" syntax, which consists of curly braces with a command/parameter pair inside. For a date value, the command is "d." For example, to represent a date, use:

```
{d 'yyyy-mm-dd'}
```

To represent a time, use:

```
{t 'hh:mm:ss'}
```

To represent a timestamp, use:

```
{ts 'yyyy-mm-dd hh:mm:ss.f . . .'}
```

Note that some systems have restrictions on timestamps. For example, some databases (such as MS SQL Server) do not allow more than one timestamp column per table.

### *Data Type Mappings*

To write a portable application, you should avoid using database data types that are specific to a brand of database. This is often easier said than done, because some databases do not provide needed types or combine the use of types. For example, Oracle uses DATE for time and timestamp values. In contrast, SQLServer has DATE, TIME, DATE&TIME, and TIMESTAMP.

JDBC defines the type mappings from SQL types to corresponding Java types; and also from the Java types to SQL types. The mapping of SQL types to and from Java types is listed in Table 6-5.

**Table 6-5** Type Mappings Between SQL and Java

| | | | | | |
|---|---|---|---|---|---|
| CHAR | ➡ | String | | ➡ | VARCHAR or LONGVARCHAR |
| VARCHAR | ➡ | String | | | |
| LONGVARCHAR | ➡ | String | | | |
| | | | *converts to* | ⇨ | (any) |
| NUMERIC | ➡ | java.math.BigDecimal | | ➡ | NUMERIC |
| DECIMAL | ➡ | java.math.BigDecimal | | | |
| | | | *converts to* | ⇨ | TINYINT, SMALLINT, INTEGER, BIGINT, REAL, FLOAT, DOUBLE, DECIMAL, (NUMERIC), BIT, CHAR, VARCHAR, LONGVARCHAR |

**Table 6-5** Type Mappings Between SQL and Java (Continued)

| BIT | ➡ | Boolean | | ➡ | BIT |
|---|---|---|---|---|---|
| | | | *converts to* | ⇨ | (same as BigDecimal) |
| TINYINT | ➡ | Integer | | ➡ | INTEGER |
| SMALLINT | ➡ | Integer | | | |
| INTEGER | ➡ | Integer | | | |
| | | | *converts to* | ⇨ | (same as BigDecimal) |
| BIGINT | ➡ | Long | | ➡ | BIGINT |
| | | | *converts to* | ⇨ | (same as BigDecimal) |
| REAL | ➡ | Float | | ➡ | REAL |
| | | | *converts to* | ⇨ | (same as BigDecimal) |
| FLOAT | ➡ | Double | | ➡ | DOUBLE |
| DOUBLE | ➡ | Double | | | |
| | | | *converts to* | ⇨ | (same as BigDecimal) |
| BINARY | ➡ | Byte [] | | ➡ | VARBINARY or LONGVARBINARY |
| VARBINARY | ➡ | Byte [] | | | |
| LONGVARBINARY | ➡ | Byte [] | | | |
| | | | *converts to* | ⇨ | BINARY |
| DATE | ➡ | java.sql.Date | | ➡ | DATE |
| | | | *converts to* | ⇨ | CHAR, VARCHAR, LONGVARCHAR, TIMESTAMP |
| TIME | ➡ | java.sql.Time | | ➡ | TIME |
| | | | *converts to* | ⇨ | CHAR, VARCHAR, LONGVARCHAR |
| TIMESTAMP | ➡ | java.sql.Timestamp | | ➡ | TIMESTAMP |
| | | | *converts to* | ⇨ | CHAR, VARCHAR, LONGVARCHAR, DATE, TIME |

While many drivers will automatically convert Java values into the type of the corresponding table column, even if the column is a proprietary type, it is a good idea—if possible—to define the schema in terms of the standard types common to most systems, and for which a Java-to-SQL mapping is defined.

### *Functions*

Most databases provide a set of scalar functions for constructing expressions. JDBC does not require that a particular set of functions be supported, but rather defines a list of functions which can be supported, and, if they are, should have the specified profile (or be convertible to that profile by the driver).

To call a function, use the escape syntax with the "fn" keyword, as shown in this example:

```
ResultSet rs = statement.executeQuery("{fn ABS(" + alpha + ")}");
```

It is the responsibility of the driver to map these functions to functions actually provided by the database where possible. These DatabaseMetaData methods can be used to obtain a comma-separated String list of which of the functions are supported:

getNumericFunctions()
getStringFunctions()
getTimeDateFunctions()
getSystemFunctions()

The numeric functions defined are:

ABS(number)
ACOS(float)
ASIN(float)
ATAN(float)
ATAN2(float1, float2)
CEILING(number)
COS(float)
COT(float)
DEGREES(number)
EXP(float)
FLOOR(number)
LOG(float)
LOG10(float)
MOD(integer1, integer2)
PI()
POWER(number, power)
RADIANS(number)
RAND(integer)
ROUND(number, places)
SIGN(number)
SIN(float)
SQRT(float)
TAN(float)
TRUNCATE(number, places)

The string functions are:

- ASCII(string)
- CHAR(code)
- CONCAT(string1, string2)
- DIFFERENCE(string1, string2)
- INSERT(string1, start, length, string2)
- LCASE(string)
- LEFT(string,count)
- LENGTH(string)
- LOCATE(string1, string2, start)
- LTRIM(string)
- REPEAT(string,count)
- REPLACE(string1, string2, string3)
- RIGHT(string, count)
- RTRIM(string)
- SOUNDEX(string)
- SPACE(count)
- SUBSTRING(string, start, length)
- UCASE(string)

The time and date functions are:

- CURDATE()
- CURTIME()
- DAYNAME(date)
- DAYOFMONTH(date)
- DAYOFWEEK(date)
- DAYOFYEAR(date)
- HOUR(time)
- MINUTE(time)
- MONTH(time)
- MONTHNAME(date)
- NOW()
- QUARTER(date)
- SECOND(time)
- TIMESTAMPADD (interval, count, timestamp)
- TIMESTAMPDIFF(interval, timestamp1,timestamp2)
- WEEK(date), and YEAR(date)

The system functions are:

- DATABASE()
- IFNULL(expression, value)
- USER()

A data type conversion function is also specified:

CONVERT(value, SQLtype)

where SQL type may be BIGINT, BINARY, BIT, CHAR, DATE, DECIMAL, DOUBLE, FLOAT, INTEGER, LONGVARBINARY, LONGVARCHAR, REAL, SMALLINT, TIME, TIMESTAMP, TINYINT, VARBINARY, or VARCHAR.

### *Callable Statements*

Most DBMS provide stored procedures, also referred to as *persistent stored modules* (PSM). These are program routines, stored in a database, which are invoked by SQL. JDBC supports this model with the CallableStatement object. To call a stored procedure, you first construct a CallableStatement, using positional parameter notation as for a prepared statement. For example:

```
CallableStatement cs = con.prepareCall("{ call DAILY (?, ?) }");
```

creates a callable statement, with two parameters.

You must register each parameter that can return a value (i.e., each OUT or INOUT parameter). You do this with one of the registerOutParameter() methods. For example:

```
cs.registerOutParameter(2, java.sql.VARCHAR);
```

You must set the values of input parameters the same way you set positional parameters in a prepared statement. In fact, CallableStatement extends from PreparedStatement. Once you set parameter values, you can execute a callable statement the same way you execute a prepared statement.

To retrieve the values of returned parameters, you can use the get<type>() methods. For example:

```
cs.getInt(2);
```

retrieves the value of the second parameter, which must be an OUT parameter. Before retrieving any OUT parameter values, however, you must retrieve all statement result sets. Many stored procedures return one or more result sets; you must scroll through all of these before OUT parameters are accessible. For example:

```
if (cs.execute())
{ // there is a result set...
    ResultSet rs = cs.getResultSet();
    // get rows
    for (; rs.next(); ) { …get any row values… }
}
String s = cs.getString(2);    // get the OUT parameter value
```

If there is the possibility that the statement might return more than one result set, you can use the getMoreResults() method to check if there is another result set.

Stored procedures can also return values. If a stored procedure returns a value, define the callable statement as such:

```
CallableStatement cs = con.prepareCall("{ ? = call SUMMARY(?) }");
```

Note that the result is identified as an OUT parameter by the first "?" symbol. A return value is treated as the first OUT parameter, and it must be registered as any OUT parameter.

```
cs.registerOutParameter(1, java.sql.INTEGER);
cs.registerOutParameter(2, java.sql.REAL);
```

### *Transactions*

A database transaction is a discrete set of database operations with a well-defined begin point and a well-defined end point, such that the entire set of operations can be treated as a unit for controlling change to the database. The end point of a transaction is when the transaction is committed and made permanent, or aborted ("rolled back") and the changes discarded. JDBC specifies these policies related to transactions:

- One transaction exists at a time per connection: the concept of multiple nested transactions is not supported. However, implementations can allow clients to create multiple connections.
- Drivers are required to allow concurrent requests from different threads on the same connection; if the driver cannot multiplex them, they are performed in series.
- You can cancel a statement asynchronously by calling the statement's cancel() method from another thread.
- Each statement is a transaction by default (autocommit mode). In auto-commit mode, commit() is called automatically when the statement completes (all ResultSet rows have been retrieved). Use setAutoCommit(false) to turn auto-commit off.
- Deadlock (a situation in which two transactions are waiting for each other, with no means of resolving the wait) detection behavior is not specified. Most implementations throw an exception, but it could be an SQLException or a RuntimeException, or even an Error.

If autocommit is disabled and you perform a transaction that obtains locks (such as when using SELECT ... FOR UPDATE with Oracle), your locks will remain in effect until either you explicitly call commit() or abort(), you close the connection, or the statement is otherwise closed. (A statement is closed automatically when the statement object is garbage collected, but you can also call close() explicitly.)

### *Isolation Levels Defined by JDBC*

An important issue with transactions is to what degree other transactions can observe or participate in the effects of changes your transaction has made, prior to when those changes are committed: this is known as the "isolation" policy. JDBC does not impose transaction isolation requirements on an implementation. It does, however, define these isolation modes in the java.sql.Connection class. (See "Database Locking and Isolation" on page 416 for more explanation of isolation and locking modes and the terms used below.)

*TRANSACTION_NONE*: Transactions are not supported. (This would be applicable, for example, if one were using JDBC to access a nontransactional data source, such as a file or spreadsheet.)

*TRANSACTION_READ_UNCOMMITTED*: Dirty reads, nonrepeatable reads, and phantom reads can occur. (SQL Isolation Level 0)

*TRANSACTION_READ_COMMITTED*: Dirty reads are prevented; nonrepeatable reads and phantom reads can occur. (SQL Isolation Level 1)

*TRANSACTION_REPEATABLE_READ*: Dirty reads and nonrepeatable reads are prevented; phantom reads can occur. (SQL Isolation Level 2)

*TRANSACTION_SERIALIZABLE*: Dirty reads, nonrepeatable reads, and phantom reads are prevented. (SQL Isolation Level 3)

You can call the DatabaseMetaData.supportsTransactionIsolationLevel() method to see if the driver and database support a given isolation level, and if so attempt to set it with the Connection.setTransactionIsolation() method.

### *Deadlock Detection and Response*

Given the same application, it is possible that deadlocks can occur on some systems and not others, because it is affected by locking granularity (table vs. row or page) and policies (e.g., lock escalation) of the DBMS. For example, Oracle never escalates locks within the same granularity, but it does escalate lock modes within a level of granularity, whereas Sybase escalates locks from the page to the table level. Also, the application can unwittingly cause lock escalation by requesting objects for update, or simply by making additional read requests. Again, different databases have different policies.

In general, your application must be prepared to catch deadlock errors. Sun claims that the correct behavior for a JDBC driver when deadlock is detected is to generate an SQLException. This makes sense because deadlock is logically an application condition. However, the programmer should be aware that the probability of deadlock varies from one kind of database to another.

### *Asynchronous Execution*

JDBC does not support multiple transactions per connection. However, a client application may create multiple connections, and perform a separate concurrent transaction on each connection, by executing them in separate threads. A JDBC driver is supposed to allow this mode of operation. As will be discussed later, some object database products do not allow this. Surprisingly, there are mainstream relational database products that do not even allow multiple connections per client process using the DBMS's own drivers. Multithread concurrency is an important capability, and you should not take for granted that a given JDBC driver in combination with a given DBMS provides it.

Operations on java.sql objects is multithread-safe. Thus, multiple client threads can access result sets and other JDBC objects without fear of corrupting those objects.

Multithreading is important in applications that support the workstation paradigm, as opposed to the transaction terminal paradigm: a user can have several things going on at once, in different windows. An example from our own work is a bank loan system's "minimize" feature, which allows the user (a loan officer) to handle impromptu telephone inquiries from customers without interrupting other loan applications being worked on at that moment.

A JDBC program can participate in multiple transactions concurrently, and have result sets open from multiple databases. However, a single java.sql.Statement can only provide one result set at a time. If the application requires multiple result sets to be open concurrently, they must be created by different Statement instances. Any Statement operation which creates a result set will automatically close any open result sets owned by that Statement.

### *Handling Connection Loss*

It is a common occurrence that a client application may lose its connection to the database unexpectedly. This may be a result of loss of a communication link, an administrative shutdown, or an unrecoverable protocol error detected by the driver. Since connection loss is asynchronous, an error will be thrown during the next or current attempt to access the connection. This kind of error should not be treated as an unrecoverable error, but handled gracefully.

Such an error will result in an SQLException which is a checked exception, and therefore must be caught. If all database accesses are encapsulated in access routines, the throws clause can be in the access routine to avoid cluttering code. Some database drivers will attempt to reconnect transparently when a connection is lost, and, if a connection is reestablished, determine if the original transaction's thread can still be connected to; and if not, throw an exception. Regardless, if the connection is ultimately lost and an exception thrown, it is up to the application to either try to reestablish the connection and replay the transaction (if possible), or inform the user of any changes that were lost.

### *Dealing with the Time Delay of Connecting to a Database*

Connecting from a client to a remote database (or any remote server) can require from tens of milliseconds to several seconds. More typical is a delay of a hundred milliseconds or more. When combined with network traffic, application load, and the overhead of middle-tier software, the actual delay to create a connection can be protracted. While the connection is being established, the user is free to click about on the user interface and try to use the connection before it actually exists. The client application design must take this possibility into account.

Three states which are important are the states of "have not attempted connection yet," "in process of connecting," and "have completed a connection." Rather than setting a synchronized flag to indicate these states, it is usually sufficient to rely on the fact that java.sql method implementations are required to be thread safe. However, your application should also be prepared for users who are impatient and click on "connect," then "cancel" twice in a row, then "connect," "cancel," "connect" and then "get data." If you have a progress window indicating that a connection is in progress, it needs to be resilient to any order of delivery of events, as well as any java.sql.SQLException.

Premature clicking will not happen if the connection was initiated by user action and the GUI system employs a single thread to handle user events, such as the AWT does, but this behavior should not be relied on. Alternatively, connection establishment and long-running transactions may be implemented in separate threads. Performing connection establishment or time consuming queries in the GUI's event thread (which handles button clicks) is not generally a good idea, because the time delay of a database operation is indeterminate, and menus and other GUI elements will be inaccessible in the meantime. Doing so will also prevent the user from being able to click on "Cancel" if you provide such a feature (which you should). (Note: A Cancel function should not kill a connection establishment or query thread; it should signal it instead with an InterruptedException.)

Here is a very basic sample template for how this can be addressed.

```
public interface Connector
{
    public void addConnectorListener(
        ConnectorListener listener);
    public void removeConnectorListener(
        ConnectorListener listener);
```

```
    public Connection getConnection();
    public void cancel();
}

public interface ConnectorListener
{
    public void gotConnection(Connection c);
}

public class ConnectorImpl
extends Thread implements Connector
{
    private Connection connection;
    private Vector listeners = new Vector();

    public void addConnectorListener(
        ConnectorListener listener)
    {
        listeners.addElement(listener);
    }

    public void removeConnectorListener(
        ConnectorListener listener)
    {
        listeners.removeElement(listener);
    }

    public Connection getConnection() { return connection; }

    public void run()
    {
        Connection c = null;
        ConnectionProgress cp = null;
        try
        {
            cp = new ConnectionProgress(this);
            //c = DriverManager.getConnection(...);
            // Simulate the above with a sleep for one minute:
            Thread.currentThread().sleep(1000*10);

            // Success.
            Vector v = (Vector)(listeners.clone());
            for (Enumeration e = v.elements(); e.hasMoreElements();)
            {
                ConnectorListener listener =
                    (ConnectorListener)(e.nextElement());
                listener.gotConnection(c);
            }
```

```
        }
        catch (InterruptedException ex)
        {
            // Someone clicked on cancel?
            System.out.println("Connection aborted");
            return;
        }
        cp.dispose();
        cp = null;
    }

    public void cancel()
    {
        // Called from other threads (e.g., the UI thread) in
        // response to a Cancel button click.
        try
        {
            interrupt();// Tell this Thread object to interrupt
                // the thread it is associated with.
        }
        catch (Throwable t)
        {
            // This is here in case the thread has already
            // been cancelled (interrupted), to catch any
            // IllegalThreadStateExceptions.
            // Will rarely occur, and is probably OK.
            t.printStackTrace();// Print trace just in case...
        }
    }
}

public class MyClientClass
{
    public static void main(String[] args)
    {
        ConnectorImpl connector = new ConnectorImpl();
        connector.addConnectorListener
        (
            new ConnectorListener()
            {
                public void gotConnection(Connection c)
                {
                    // We are still in the Connector's thread.
                    System.out.println("hurray!");
                }
            }
        );
```

```
        connector.start();
    }
}

class ConnectionProgress extends Frame implements ActionListener
{
    private Connector connector;
    private Button cancelButton;

    public ConnectionProgress(Connector c)
    {
        super("Connector");
        setSize(300, 100);
        connector = c;
        cancelButton = new Button("Cancel");
        add(cancelButton);
        cancelButton.addActionListener(this);
        show();
    }

    public void actionPerformed(ActionEvent e)
    {
        dispose();
        connector.cancel();
    }
}
```

### *The Problems with "Active" Controls*

Many database component libraries provide control components such as scrollable lists and tables that maintain an active connection to the database and are self-updating. This approach works best for small databases used by a few people or a single user. If the system is a multiuser system, the isolation level impacts the manner in which the component is updated, and in some situations the user may think they are seeing current data when in fact they are seeing a snapshot. JDBC also does not require that a result set be backward scrollable (although JDBC 2 will add this feature), so JDBC does not provide a standard way for JDBC component vendors to implement this, although most do. Reverse scrolling may be implemented by the driver or the control. If this feature is used, the precise semantics of the mechanism should be examined to determine if it is desirable for the application.

### Unicode Support

Most databases have no problem storing multibyte character strings. For example, if you store the Java string value "W\u00e4hrung" ("Währung," which means "currency" in German) in Oracle with the following statement:

```
stmt.executeUpdate("INSERT INTO DEPT VALUES (60, 'W\u00e4hrung',
    'Berlin')");
```

and then retrieve it with a query, you will get back the same identical string value. In general, if you plan to internationalize your application, you should make sure that the database and driver can handle Unicode strings.

### Sorting and Comparing Unicode Using the Collator and CollationKey Classes

Java has two classes for performing locale-sensitive comparisons and sorting of Internationalized string values. These are the Collator and CollationKey classes. For comparing individual strings, use the Collator class. For performing multiple comparisons using a single string, use the CollationKey class. Here is an example of using the Collator class:

```
Collator c = Collator.getInstance(Locale.US);
c.setStrength(Collator.IDENTICAL);
c.setDecomposition(Collator.FULL_DECOMPOSITION);
int r = c.compare(string1, string 2);
if (r < 0)
   System.out.println("string1 < string2");
else if (r == 0)
   System.out.println("strings are equals");
else
   System.out.println("string1 > string2");
```

In the above, the "IDENTICAL" strength setting specifies that the strings must be identical to match, and that, for example, the comparison is case sensitive. The possible strengths are:

**IDENTICAL**—This is the strongest (most "picky") form of comparison. Only lexically equivalent strings are considered identical. Unicode has multiple ways of representing many characters, including a single-character representation, and a compound "base" and "nonspacing" representation; and also, sometimes a pair of characters are considered equivalent to a different single character, such as "ll" and "l" followed by "l." The comparison result depends on the locale.

**TERTIARY**—Very small differences result in the characters being considered distinct, including case.

**SECONDARY**—A middle ground, usually representing case insensitivity.

**PRIMARY**—The least strong (least picky) form. If the two characters cannot be considered equivalent in any way for the specified locale, they have a primary difference. For example, "a" and "b" have a primary difference because they are completely different characters, whereas "a" and "ã" would probably be considered the same in most locales; case insensitive as well.

The decomposition level specifies the Unicode compatibility mode for multicharacter forms and variations that are considered lexically equivalent. There are three possible settings for this:

**NO_DECOMPOSITION**—Accents will not be taken into account, leading to incorrect sorting order for languages that have accents.

**CANONICAL_DECOMPOSITION**—Accents are taken into account.

**FULL_DECOMPOSITION**—Multicharacter forms are sorted correctly. This is important for some Asian languages.

Use the CollationKey class to repetitively compare a string value with other strings. For example:

```
CollationKey ck1 = c.getCollationKey(string1);
for (int i = 0; i < strings2.length; i++)
{
   CollationKey ck2 = c.getCollationKey(strings2[i]);
   if (ck1.equals(ck2)) { return; }
}
// not found
throw new Exception();
```

### *Searching with LIKE*

Some drivers we have tested support the LIKE clause, and some do not. LIKE expressions are used to match strings based on wildcard expression rules, rather than exact character-by-character matching. This can be used to implement very powerful searching for person and place names, and other strings for which a record must be identified but the complete spelling is not known.

In a LIKE expression, "%" matches zero or more characters, and "_" matches exactly one character. You can override this and cause these characters to be treated literally by escaping them with an escape character. The escape character may be different on different systems, however. JDBC lets you use the "{escape 'escape-character'}" syntax to specify an escape character in LIKE expressions. For example, in this example we are saying "treat any character immediately following '$' literally, rather than as a wildcard":

```
stmt.executeQuery(
"SELECT FNAME FROM DOCFILES WHERE FNAME LIKE '%$_%' {escape'$'}");
```

Unicode may also not be directly supported by the DBMS, so characters may get converted internally to ASCII for searching and queries. If you are storing Unicode, in particular character sets for languages other than English, make sure that queries perform as you expect when searching based on a Unicode string. Again, most databases can handle this. For example, Oracle in combination with its "thin" all-Java driver has no trouble finding "Währung." However, you should run a test to make sure.

---

**The Name Ordering Problem**

A problem with international applications is that different cultures order name components differently. While most Western cultures list the family name last, most Eastern cultures list the family name first. For example, the English name John W. Smith identifies John W. as belonging to the Smith family; while the Chinese name Tan Sai Cheong identifies Sai Cheong as belonging to the Tan family. Some cultures do not even recognize the concept of a family name. It used to be a practice in Scotland to use the father's first name as the last name for a child (e.g., William, of Jonathan); if William then has a son, he might name him Stephen, of William. This practice is rare nowadays, however.

A solution for name searching is to be agnostic with regard to the ordering of name components, and search every possible combination. Also, international applications should not force a cultural bias on users. A field for family name should be labeled as such, not as "last name."

---

### *Representing Decimal and Monetary Data Types*

Representing monetary types is problematic for two reasons: precision and locale-specific representation. In choosing a representation, one must be sure that it can handle the range of values which will be represented, and that precision, rounding, and arithmetic and conversion rules specific to the application are adhered to. For example, for monetary types, a given legal jurisdiction or accounting practice may require rounding up according to a certain formula or alternating up/down technique. In parsing and displaying values, locale-specific rules require displaying the correct currency symbols in the right positions, and radix and point separators following the correct number of digits. What would seem to be a simple problem turns out to be extremely complex.

**Using Long.** The advantage of using long to represent monetary values is that it is a built-in type, and thus efficient. The disadvantages are that the range may not be enough for some applications.

A long is a 64-bit signed quantity. This yields a numeric range of $2^{63}$, or $8\times10^{18}$; so, to represent a monetary value to 3 decimal places (i.e., thousandths of a currency unit), we have a range of $8\times10^{15}$ currency units, or 8 million billion. If your application might be computing account totals larger than this, using long may require special provisions for your largest accounts.

You may also want control over rounding behavior. This is only an issue with percentage, fractional multiplication, and division calculations, and for those you can write special routines that implement the rounding rules you prefer; but you would probably need to do this regardless of the representation used.

**Using BigDecimal.** The BigDecimal type is a Java class, defined in package java.math. This means that all of its operations are defined as methods, and simple operations such as addition will need to be expressed as a method call. Java, unlike C++, does not support operator overloading, so there is no way to get around this.

In practice, using the BigDecimal type is not as inconvenient as you might think. Arithmetic routines are usually encapsulated into other higher-level routines that perform specific calculations for an application; it would be extremely poor design not to encapsulate such code into a well-defined "business rules" package that performs these calculations. Therefore, the actual impact on your code, from an aesthetic and programming convenience point of view, should be minimal. The main drawback is speed. Calculations using the BigDecimal type will be thousands of times slower than calculations using the long type. Depending on how often these calculations are done, this may or may not be a problem.

It may be possible to use a hybrid approach in some applications. Account balances, for example, could be represented by long values and converted to BigDecimal values whenever division and multiplication are required. Again, this conversion should be encapsulated within the calculation routines and hidden from the rest of the code.

Here are some examples of using BigDecimal:

```
BigDecimal oneThousandPointOhSevenFive = new
BigDecimal("1000.075");
    the scale is 3
    the intValue() is 1000
```

To round a value and specify that rounding should use the "half-even" method, in which the calculation rounds up if the digit to the right of the discarded fraction is >= .5 and the digit to the left is odd, and otherwise round down:

```
BigDecimal dollarsAndCents =
   oneThousandPointOhSevenFive.setScale(2,
      BigDecimal.ROUND_HALF_EVEN);
        the scale is 2
         the intValue() is 1000
         the full value is 1000.08 - we have rounded, and lost
            precision
```

To perform arithmetic operations, use the add(), subtract, multiply(), and divide() methods, such as in:

```
BigDecimal difference =
dollarsAndCents.subtract(oneThousandPointOhSevenFive);
   the scale is
   MAX(dollarsAndCents.scale(),
      oneThousandPointOhSevenFive.scale()) = 3
   the intValue() is 0
   the full value is 0.005
```

To convert BigDecimal values to other types, there are conversion methods—one for each Java intrinsic numeric type. Of course, depending on the value being converted, a loss of data may result.

### Creating Incremental Queries

A search query can potentially return result sets of highly variable or unpredictable size. For example, if one is searching for all objects for which a name attribute matches "Huckstable," there will probably only be a few. If one searches for "Smith" in the United States or England, however, or for "Tan" in Singapore, there are likely to be a great many values in the result. This is problematic for an interactive application, since one does not want to have a huge result set, and suffer the delay associated, or have to scroll through them once they finally arrive.

The solution for cases in which this might occur is to design an incremental query capability. In order to allow the transaction to be completed with each iteration, so as not to keep the database locked, the application can construct an index that allows it to figure out where it left off each time. For example, if the query returns the first 100 matches for "Smith," and they consist of Alan Smith through Barney Smith, the value "Barney Smith" could be passed the next time, to obtain matches from that point on. Of course, there is a uniqueness problem to deal with (there might be two Barney Smiths), and so you probably need to pass additional infor-

mation, such as a number specifying the number of names which have been sent already which match the last name sent—i.e., how many Barney Smiths have been sent so far (usually the value of this will be one). The JDBC Connection method setMaxRows(int) is useful for limiting the size of a returned result set.

### *Is Java Year 2000-Compliant?*

The Date type is internally represented as a long, with the value zero set to January 1, 1970. This does not mean dates prior to 1970 cannot be represented; they are simply negative numbers (internally). Nor does it mean you have to subtract 1970 from all your years: this is taken care of for you by the Date and Calendar class methods. In fact, when you retrieve the year value using the Calendar class, the number you get is simply the year (e.g., for the year 2000, you get 2000).

Year values are also continuous across the year 2000 threshold. Thus, if you add one (1) day to December 31, 1999, you end up with January 1, 2000.

One way in which the year 2000 is kind of unique is that it is divisible by 400, and also by 100. The rule for leap years is that a leap year occurs if a year is divisible by 4 but *not* divisible by 100—unless it is divisible by 400, in which case it is still a leap year. The year 2000 is therefore a leap year, because it is divisible by 400. The JDK correctly reports that the year 2000 is a leap year, and that there are 29 days in February 2000. Here is the output of a test:

```
calendar with year set to 1999: Thu Dec 30 22:23:30 EST 1999
one day later...Fri Dec 31 22:23:30 EST 1999
another day later...Sat Jan 01 22:23:30 EST 2000
Add 58 days:Mon Feb 28 22:23:30 EST 2000
another day later...Tue Feb 29 22:23:30 EST 2000
```

The Date type can represent a time range of $2^{63}$ milliseconds, which corresponds approximately to 250,000,000 years. This clearly encompasses the year 2000, as well as any conceivable long-term mortgages!

What about java.sql.Timestamp? That is a date/time class as well. The Timestamp object is a composite of a Date and a separate nanosecond value. It therefore can handle any range that Date can handle.

There have been some bugs reported for some versions of Java prior to JDK 1.1.6, and also in the Java 2 SDK 1.2.1. These have been related to the parsing of shorthand date representations containing abbreviated year strings, such as 1/1/02, and also to the year 2000 February 29 date. These have been fixed in the current Java 2 release (SDK 1.2.2) and in JDK 1.1.6. Sun also runs an extensive Y2K compliance suite against each release. Sun Microsystems claims to have accounted even for leap seconds.

Note also that some DBMS implementations of SQL dates run out in the year 2036! This is a while from now, so you might think we don't have to worry about this just yet; but what about a banking loan application? A 40-year mortgage created in 1998 would mature in the year 2038. Make sure that the data range handled by the database—not just Java—supports the range you need and beyond!

---

### My Soapbox: When to (and Not to) Store Serialized Data

The term "impedance mismatch" is often used to identify the inefficiencies that result from using a relational database with an object-oriented language. The fact that a term from electrical engineering has been appropriated to describe a computer science problem is indicative of the fact that these inefficiencies are hard to summarize. In fact, relational databases can be used quite effectively with object-oriented languages. The JDBC API is an object-oriented API for accessing relational systems. JDBC queries return objects—ResultSet objects—which are objects just like any other in Java. Using JDBC, a relational system can be accessed with no less inherent efficiency than if it were accessed by a query from any other language.

The real impedance mismatch comes into play when systems are not used correctly. For example, a relational database should not be used to store objects. This is a different situation from products which implement an object model using a relational database engine. Those products take account of caching and data integrity requirements, and allow an object model to be efficiently implemented directly on legacy relational systems. A different, and sad, scenario is when objects are stuffed into a relational database, and the resulting system is described as object oriented.

This may sound so absurd that no one would do this, but in fact I have seen it done many times. The justification is usually that the data is being stored in the form of the objects that will later be needed, so there will be a single query to obtain the object. This is rarely the case once the system starts to be used, however. As more queries are added, a situation soon results where in order to obtain a small piece of data, one has to retrieve and reconstitute an entire large-grain object, only to throw most of it away. What usually happens is that the application starts to evolve bizarre caching strategies to implement an incremental query capability, which should be performed by the DBMS.

It is almost never advisable to store serialized objects in a database, unless it can be guaranteed that those objects have nothing to do with the database's application domain. Such a situation is exemplified by a user interface, in which it is desirable to restore the client's GUI appearance, based on the user's identity, from any client machine. In this case, storing the GUI state as a serialized object for later retrieval makes a roaming client possible. Of course, the system must know what to do if the same user is logged on in more than one location.

---

A final caution about storing serialized objects in a database is that doing so embeds in the database assumptions about the structure of the serialized objects. If a later release of the software changes the implementation of the serialized object classes, all of the serialized objects in the database may become unreadable. If the changes satisfy compatibility rules, this can be solved by implementing a readObject() method[a] in the new version of the class, unloading all of these objects, and reloading them. Otherwise, an unload, convert, and reload program will have to be written; or, if the objects are not critical data (e.g., they might simply be the visual GUI state), they may be simply be deleted.

*[a]If a class has a readObject() method with the signature void readObject(ObjectInputStream), this method is used instead of the default method for reconstituting the object. See the explanation in the javadocs for the Serializable interface.*

## JDBC 2

A large set of new features are added to JDBC in JDBC version 2. These new features are optional for an implementation, and therefore the task of selecting a database driver is now even more complex than before, as driver providers are free to implement features as appropriate for the intended use of their product.

The enhancements are divided into two groups: core feature enhancements and extended feature enhancements. The core enhancements take the form of new methods and capabilities added to the existing java.sql classes, and new classes added to package java.sql. The extended enhancements are provided by a new package: javax.sql. I will first explain the enhancements to the core java.sql package, and then discuss the extended enhancements.

### *Result Sets*

So far the ResultSet type we have discussed in this chapter is an object type that has the ability to scroll forward through a query result. Depending on the implementation, rows in the result set may be obtained dynamically as it is scrolled, or the result set may be built statically all at once when the query statement is executed. Regardless, there is no mechanism defined for a result set to scroll backwards, and in this way, the issue of repeatability of data read by a result set is avoided. Many vendors have nevertheless provided their own backward scrolling capability, with semantics particular to their implementation.

To address this, JDBC 2 defines three types of result sets:

*forward-only*—Same as before: the JDBC ResultSet type. Exact behavior depends on the implementation: may be computed at creation, or as it is scrolled.

*scroll-insensitive*—Filled when created. Static. Does not even reflect changes made in the current transaction.

*scroll-sensitive*—Dynamic. Reflects current state of the transaction's data. Exact behavior depends on the isolation policy of the database and transaction.

A scroll-insensitive result set is logically a fully constructed object, which represents the state of the database at the moment the query is performed. The result set is a snapshot of the database, and so depending on the way the result set is implemented, scrolling need not involve any database interaction.

A scroll-sensitive result set is dynamic, and may—*may*—reflect changes made to the database during the course of the user's transaction. Whether it does or not depends on the isolation mode in effect for the transaction. I will not get into the details of this now, as these issues are discussed later in this chapter. Suffice it to say that a scroll-sensitive result set has the ability to reflect database changes, whereas a scroll-insensitive result set does not.

In addition, a result set may now be declared to be of one of these types:

*read-only*—The contents have, at most, read locks.

*updatable*—The contents have write locks or an automatic optimistic mechanism, and the result set may be modified by the transaction. (Provides a platform-independent way of saying "SELECT ... FOR UPDATE.")

These modes determine whether a transaction can use a set of new updateXXX() methods on the result set to change the values of its rows. A read-only result set may not be so modified, whereas an updatable result set can. In addition, an implementation will likely map these settings to multi-transaction concurrency control policies, which affect the ability of others to obtain access to the data represented by the result set at the same time that our transaction is in progress. A read-only result set allows all other transactions read access to the data, whereas an updatable result set may place write locks on the affected data, thereby preventing others from accessing the data until the transaction is complete. Again, exactly what the system will do depends on the concurrency control policies and techniques used by the database and the driver. Database concurrency control and locking is discussed later in this chapter.

Here is an example of creating a statement that is both scroll-sensitive (dynamic) and updatable:

```
Statement s = connection.createStatement(
   ResultSet.TYPE_SCROLL_SENSITIVE,
   ResultSet.CONCUR_UPDATABLE);
ResultSet resultSet = s.executeQuery("SELECT N FROM TALLIES");
```

Since the statement is updatable, we can use the ResultSet updateXXX() methods on it:

```
resultSet.next();
resultSet.getInt("N");
resultSet.updateInt("N", 45);
```

Since the result set is scroll-sensitive, we should see the change we made if we re-read the current row:

```
int newN = resultSet.getInt("N");    // should return 45
```

In addition, we can be confident that the database will prevent others from reading or modifying this data until our transaction commits, since the result set data is locked for update. The semantic details of this and how it is implemented depends on the concurrency control and locking mechanisms of the database, and the driver implementation.

The possible values for the result set type parameter of a statement are:

TYPE_FORWARD_ONLY

TYPE_SCROLL_INSENSITIVE, and

TYPE_SCROLL_SENSITIVE.

The possible values for the concurrency parameter are:

CONCUR_READ_ONLY and

CONCUR_UPDATABLE.

You can test how the database and driver handle updates with the following new DatabaseMetaData methods:

```
supportsResultSetType(int type)
supportsResultSetConcurrency(int type, int concurrency)
ownUpdatesAreVisible(int type)
ownDeletesAreVisible(int type)
ownInsertsAreVisible(int type)
othersUpdatesAreVisible(int type)
othersDeletesAreVisible(int type)
othersInsertsAreVisible(int type)
updatesAreDetected(int type)
```

```
deletesAreDetected(int type)
insertsAreDetected(int type)
```

If the result set is declared to be updatable but the driver discovers for some reason at runtime that it cannot support this capability, for example, if the result set is computed such as the result of a join, then the driver chooses an alternative supportable result set type and adds an SQLWarning to the Statement that produced the ResultSet. The warning can be retrieved by calling the statement's getWarnings() method, and the actual result set type and concurrency mode by calling the get ResultSet's getType() and getConcurrency() methods, respectively.

You can also add a row to a result set. To do this, you must temporarily move to the virtual "insert row," using the moveToInsertRow() method, perform updateXXX() calls to add column values to the new row, and then finally call the insertRow() method. For example, to insert a *new* row in the result set that has one int-valued column,

```
resultSet.moveToInsertRow();
resultSet.updateInt(1, 60);
resultSet.insertRow();
```

In addition to the standard ResultSet next() method, scroll-insensitive and scroll-sensitive result sets can use these new ResultSet methods for effecting positional control:

`first()`—Set the position to the first row in the result set.

`last()`—Set the position to the last row.

`previous()`—Set the position to the previous row.

`afterLast()`—Prepare to decrement backward from the end, using the previous() method.

`beforeFirst()`—Prepare to increment forward from the first row using the next() method.

`relative()`—Increment or decrement the current row position. (There must be a current row—can't be before the first or after the last.)

`absolute()`—Set the position to a specified row.

`isAfterLast()`—Return true if the position is after the last row (false if there are no rows).

`isBeforeFirst()`—Return true if before the first row (false if there are no rows).

New methods are also added to provide hints to the driver to allow it to optimize its operations when fetching and scrolling. These are the setFetchSize() and setFetchDirection() methods. For example:

```
resultSet.setFetchDirection(ResultSet.FETCH_FORWARD);
```

tells the driver that we will be scrolling primarily forward, and that it can optimize its operations for that. The possible values for the setFetchDirection parameter are FETCH_FORWARD, FETCH_REVERSE, and FETCH_UNKNOWN. To help the driver perform array-fetching optimizations (discussed earlier), the setFetchSize() method can be used to recommend to the driver how many rows it should fetch at once. For example:

```
resultSet.setFetchSize(20);
```

tells the driver it should retrieve twenty rows at a time, in anticipation of all of those rows being read by the current transaction. You can also set fetch direction and size hints for the statement object.

The new ResultSet methods are summarized in Table 6-6.

**Table 6-6** **New ResultSet Methods**

| |
|---|
| Object getObject(String columnName) |
| int findColumn(String columnName) |
| java.io.Reader getCharacterStream(int columnIndex) |
| java.io.Reader getCharacterStream(String columnName) |
| BigDecimal getBigDecimal(int columnIndex) |
| BigDecimal getBigDecimal(String columnName) |
| boolean isBeforeFirst() |
| boolean isAfterLast() |
| boolean isFirst() |
| boolean isLast() |
| void beforeFirst() |
| void afterLast() |
| boolean first() |
| boolean last() |
| int getRow() |
| boolean absolute(int row) |
| boolean relative(int rows) |

**Table 6-6** New ResultSet Methods (Continued)

| |
|---|
| boolean previous() |
| void setFetchDirection(int direction) |
| int getFetchDirection() |
| void setFetchSize(int rows) |
| int getFetchSize() |
| int getType() |
| int getConcurrency() |
| boolean rowUpdated() |
| boolean rowInserted() |
| boolean rowDeleted() |
| void updateNull(int columnIndex) |
| void updateBoolean(int columnIndex, boolean x) |
| void updateByte(int columnIndex, byte x) |
| void updateShort(int columnIndex, short x) |
| void updateInt(int columnIndex, int x) |
| void updateLong(int columnIndex, long x) |
| void updateFloat(int columnIndex, float x) |
| void updateDouble(int columnIndex, double x) |
| void updateBigDecimal(int columnIndex, BigDecimal x) |
| void updateString(int columnIndex, String x) |
| void updateBytes(int columnIndex, byte x[]) |
| void updateDate(int columnIndex, Date x) |
| void updateTime(int columnIndex, Time x) |
| void updateTimestamp(int columnIndex, Timestamp x) |
| void updateAsciiStream(int columnIndex, java.io.InputStream x, int length) |
| void updateBinaryStream(int columnIndex, java.io.InputStream x, int length) |
| void updateCharacterStream(int columnIndex, java.io.Reader reader, int length) |
| void updateObject(int columnIndex, Object x, int scale) |
| void updateObject(int columnIndex, Object x) |
| void updateNull(String columnName) |
| void updateBoolean(String columnName, boolean x) |
| void updateByte(String columnName, byte x) |
| void updateShort(String columnName, short x) |
| void updateInt(String columnName, int x) |
| void updateLong(String columnName, long x) |

**Table 6-6** New ResultSet Methods (Continued)

| |
|---|
| void updateFloat(String columnName, float x) |
| void updateDouble(String columnName, double x) |
| void updateBigDecimal(String columnName, BigDecimal x) |
| void updateString(String columnName, String x) |
| void updateBytes(String columnName, byte x[]) |
| void updateDate(String columnName, Date x) |
| void updateTime(String columnName, Time x) |
| void updateTimestamp(String columnName, Timestamp x) |
| void updateAsciiStream(String columnName, java.io.InputStream x, int length) |
| void updateBinaryStream(String columnName, java.io.InputStream x, int length) |
| void updateCharacterStream(String columnName, java.io.Reader reader, int length) |
| void updateObject(String columnName, Object x, int scale) |
| void updateObject(String columnName, Object x) |
| void insertRow() |
| void updateRow() |
| void deleteRow() |
| void refreshRow() |
| void moveToInsertRow() |
| void moveToCurrentRow() |
| Statement getStatement() |
| Object getObject(int i, java.util.Map map) |
| Ref getRef(int i) |
| Blob getBlob(int i) |
| Clob getClob(int i) |
| Array getArray(int i) |
| Object getObject(String colName, java.util.Map map) |
| Ref getRef(String colName) |
| Blob getBlob(String colName) |
| Clob getClob(String colName) |
| Array getArray(String colName) |
| Date getDate(int columnIndex, Calendar cal) |
| Date getDate(String columnName, Calendar cal) |
| Time getTime(int columnIndex, Calendar cal) |
| Time getTime(String columnName, Calendar cal) |
| Timestamp getTimestamp(int columnIndex, Calendar cal) |
| Timestamp getTimestamp(String columnName, Calendar cal) |

### Batch Updates

A "batch update" mechanism has been added to support a more efficient execution of updates, allowing several updates to be processed by a DBMS with a single DBMS call. For example, the following creates a statement and adds two batched INSERT operations to it, to be performed in series. It then executes the batched statement and commits the results. Note that an exception can occur as a result of any portion of a batched update, so we should disable auto-commit so that we can treat the entire batched operation atomically as a single transaction:

```
connection.setAutoCommit(false);
try
{
   Statement s = connection.createStatement();
   s.addBatch("INSERT ...");
   s.addBatch("INSERT ...");
   s.executeBatch();
   connection.commit();
}
catch (SQLException ex)
{
   try { connection.rollback(); } catch (Exception ex2) {}
}
```

Prepared and callable statements can participate in batch updates as well. The following example creates a prepared statement, and batches two executions of the statement, each using different parameters:

```
connection.setAutoCommit(false);
try
{
   PreparedStatement ps = connection.prepareStatement(
      "INSERT INTO TABA VALUES (?, ?)");
   ps.setString("ID", "A-210-003");
   ps.setString("Name", "Ima Lemmon");
   ps.addBatch();

   ps.setString("ID", "C-101-001");
   ps.setString("Name", "Rob R. Barron");
   ps.addBatch();

   ps.executeBatch();
   connection.commit();
}
catch (SQLException ex)
{
   try { connection.rollback(); } catch (Exception ex2) {}
}
```

A batched callable statement works the same way. However, a batch update callable statement may not have OUT or INOUT parameters.

You can test if the database and driver support batch updates with the new DatabaseMetaData supportsBatchUpdates() method.

### *New Types*

To accommodate SQL3, and in addition the storage of persistified Java objects in a standard RDBMS-supported way, JDBC 2 adds new column types to the java.sql.Types class. The additions are:

JAVA_OBJECT—A persistified Java object. Objects of this type can be retrieved directly using the ResultSet's getObject() method, and stored using the updateObject() method.

DISTINCT—Analogous to an IDL typedef. Effectively aliases for type specifications. For example, "CREATE TYPE NAME VARCHAR(10)." The standard Java-to-SQL type mappings apply, based on the underlying actual type of the data.

STRUCT—Analogous to an IDL struct. Manifest by the new java.sql type Struct. The contents of a Struct are retrieved when the Struct is retrieved, and have normal Java object lifetime semantics. The Struct method getAttributes() can be used to retrieve the Struct's contents. Use the ResultSet getObject() methods to retrieve a Struct. Use the PreparedStatement setObject() method to store a Struct.

ARRAY—An array of values of a specified type. Manifest by the new java.sql type Array. Only valid for the duration of the transaction that created it.

BLOB—Binary large object. Manifest by the new java.sql type Blob. The contents of the object is not transferred to the client unless explicitly requested, via the Blob's getBytes() or getBinaryStream() methods. A Blob object is only valid for the duration of the transaction that created it.

CLOB—Character large object. Manifest by the new java.sql type Clob. Similar to BLOB, value is not actually transferred unless explicitly requested via the getCharacterStream() or getAsciiStream() methods. Only valid for the duration of the transaction that created it.

REF—For retrieving and passing (e.g., to an UPDATE) references to database data without actually retrieving the data. Manifest by the new java.sql type Ref. Valid for the duration of the connection. Useful for handling large data objects without having to transfer them to the client environment over a network.

The DatabaseMetaData class has the following new method to get information on the data types supported by the database:

```
ResultSet getUDTs(String catalog, String schemaPattern, String
   typeNamePattern, int[] types)
```

Each returned row contains:

TYPE_CAT—String or null; the type catalog in which the type is defined, if any.

TYPE_SCHEM—String or null; the type's schema, if any.

TYPE_NAME—String; the type name.

JAVA_CLASS—String; the fully-qualified name of the Java class that is constructed for values of this type.

DATA_TYPE—short; the type code for this type (the value defined in java.sql.Types).

REMARKS—Comment.

The JAVA_CLASS column identifies the Java class that maps to the database type, as discussed above. Actual instances used to update column values must be of this type or a subclass. The DATA_TYPE column specifies the typecode for uniquely identifying the JDBC database type.

### *Type Maps*

Normally objects retrieved from columns of type DISTINCT or STRUCT result in a Java object of the mapped Java object type or a Java Struct object. However, a facility called "type maps" is provided to automatically encapsulate the conversion of database types to arbitrary client application types. All you have to do is implement the SQLData interface in your type, and register the type map with the database connection by calling its setTypeMap() method. For example, the following class encapsulates the construction of a user-defined type, Name, from a DISTINCT type which would otherwise map to a Java String:

```
public class Name implements SQLData
{
   public void readSQL(SQLInput is, String type)
   throws SQLException
   {
      sqlType = type;
      name = is.readString();
   }

   public void writeSQL(SQLOutput os)
   throws SQLException
   {
      os.writeString(name);
   }
```

```
    private String name;
    private String sqlType;
}
```

This code registers the type:

```
java.util.Map map = connection.getTypeMap();
map.put("NAME", Name.class);
```

Whenever a distinct type of type NAME is read from the database, an instance of Name will automatically be constructed, using the Name.readSQL() method. Similarly, Name objects inserted into the database will be converted to NAME column values using the Name class's writeSQL() method.

### Java Objects

JDBC 2 supports database columns of type JAVA_OBJECT. Columns of this type represent persistified Java objects—perhaps objects which have been serialized, or stored as persistent objects in a database-supported manner. These can be objects such as Java documents or potentially large application objects of arbitrary types. The problem with doing this is that such objects are not accessed the way an RDBMS is designed to access its data. A serialized large object (SLOB) is not accessible to the database's normal mechanisms, and so it cannot be as efficient in a product designed for high performance relational access. All the code in the RDBMS designed to optimize table access is not applicable. The issue of code deployment, versioning, and object obsolescence must also be addressed; these are not addressed by the current version of the JDBC 2 specification, and it will be interesting to see what support vendors provide for these requirements.

If one must store many Java objects, one might as well use an object database. However, admittedly there are cases in which objects need to be stored essentially for transfer or archival, and not accessed internally by the database. If used in this way, the object is just a BLOB. Providing special support for it in a relational database is of questionable value. These products are getting too big anyway.

In order to support Java object storage, the ResultSet getObject() method is extended to handle this new type. There is also an updateObject() method for updating rows containing Java objects.

### Use of JNDI

JDBC 2 provides in package javax.sql a new type called DataSource, which allows JDBC databases to be located and connected to by using Java Naming and Directory Interface (JNDI). This provides an alternative to specifying a database URL, thereby freeing application code from having to know in advance the hostname on which a database is deployed, and even the name of the dataset. Once the data source is obtained, a client can log onto the database by using the data source's getConnection() method. For example:

```
Context context = new InitialContext();
DataSource ds = context.lookup("jdbc/MyDataset");
Connection connection = ds.getConnection("scott", "tiger");
```

establishes a database connection to a database dataset identified as MyDataset, regardless where the database resides, as long as it is registered with a directory service accessible by the JNDI interface. The DataSource is therefore viewed as a "resource factory," which manufactures a connection to a data resource, i.e., a database.

### *Other Additions*

JDBC 2 adds a new ResultSet type, called "RowSet." RowSet is an extension feature (in package javax.sql) that extends the ResultSet interface but provides JavaBeans style design time support features. This is a feature of most interest for user interface design and is outside the scope of this book.

JDBC 2 also adds support for distributed transactions using Java Transaction API (JTA), and connection pooling for allowing implementations to implement database connection pools in an API-supported manner.

### *Connection Pools and Distributed Transactions*

JDBC 2 defines a set of extension features which define an interoperable API for vendors to build connection pooling and transaction management into database drivers. Prior to this API, these features could only be proprietary, leading to an inseparable dependence between an application server and the drivers provided by the application server vendor. JDBC 2 separates these functions into well-defined layers so that it is possible to mix and match compliant drivers (resource managers) from different vendors within an application server. The driver-related interfaces defined by the JDBC 2 extended API are shown in Figure 6-8.

The objective of a client when using these interfaces is of course to merely obtain a JDBC Connection. The client does this by calling a connection factory, which is defined by the DataSource interface. A client obtains an instance of DataSource by looking one up using JNDI. The set of connections available to clients on a particular application server instance are most likely preconfigured by the server's system administrator, with appropriate credentials specified administratively so that applications do not have to specify them.

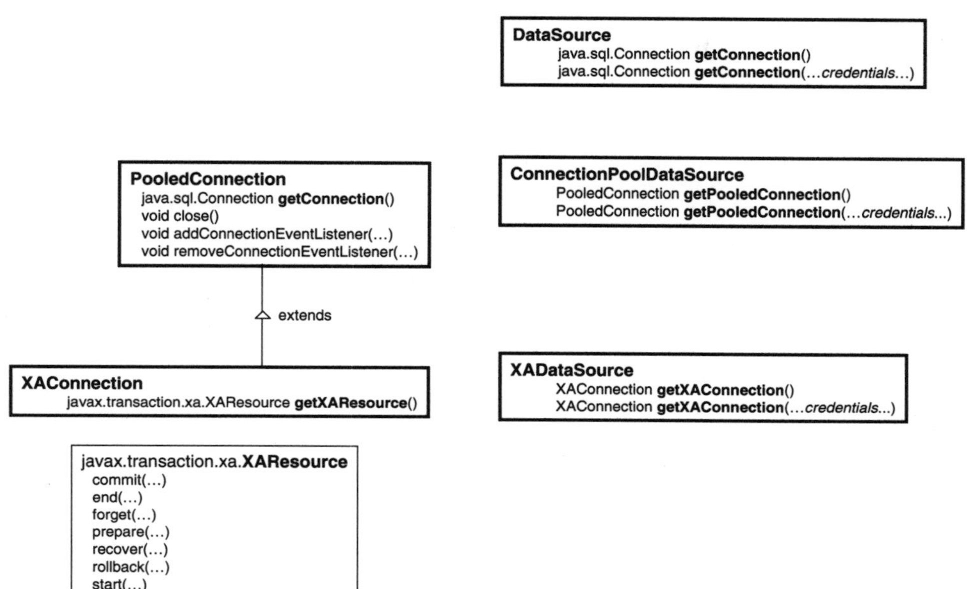


**Figure 6-8** The JDBC 2 extended API for connection pools and resource factories.

The DataSource's getConnection() method returns a Connection to the client. As far as the client can tell this is a regular JDBC Connection. (Note that if the Connection supports global transactions then one cannot start and end transactions on it the way one would with a local JDBC Connection; this is discussed below. Global transactions are discussed in detail in Chapter 7.)

Behind the scenes the DataSource accesses its PooledConnectionDataSource to obtain a Connection from an internal connection pool. If there is no available connection in the pool and the pool size limit has not been reached, the PooledConnectionDataSource will create a new connection on the fly and return it; otherwise it will merely return a connection from the pool which is not currently in use. The Connection object the DataSource returns is actually a PooledConnection which provides a Connection facade interface. This facade intercepts attempts to close the connection and instead returns unused connections to the pool instead of actually closing them. The use of a pooled connection is shown in Figure 6-9.

The connection interface for connections which can participate in global transactions is the XAConnection interface. Notice that an XAConnection is a PooledConnection. This does not mean that connection pooling must be implemented

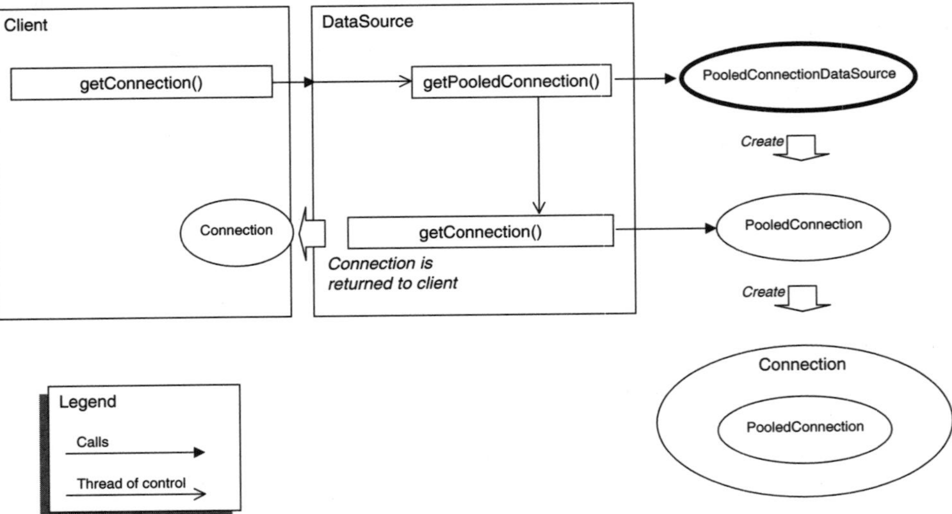


**Figure 6-9** How a DataSource provides connections from a connection pool.

for all connections which support global transactions; it only means that the driver must provide a PooledConnection interface—perhaps with a pool of size zero.

Many application servers which provide DataSource implementations for JDBC connection pooling also provide support for global transactions. Global transactions are transactions which are managed by a transaction manager and which can encompass multiple data resouces within a single transaction, possibly on different servers. If the connections returned by a DataSource can support global transactions, the connections delegate their calls to an XAConnection implementation which is responsible for coordinating the activities of each global transaction that the connection participates in. This scenario is shown in Figure 6-10.

You can see that drivers which expose an XADataSource or ConnectionPoolDataSource interface (there is no need to provide both) can be plugged into an application server and accessed by the application server's DataSource implementations in a standard way. It is therefore up to the driver vendor to build drivers with either a ConnectionPoolDataSource or XADataSource interface so that the driver can be used with any JDBC 2 compliant application server; and it is up to the application server vendor to use the ConnectionPoolDataSource and XADataSource interfaces so that other drivers can be used instead of just the application server's drivers.

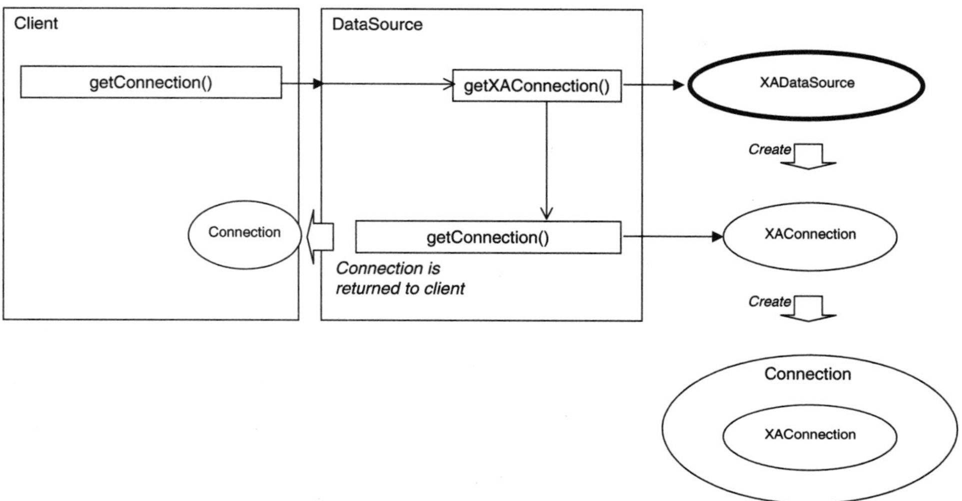


**Figure 6-10** How a DataSource provides global-transaction-capable connections from a connection pool.

Connection pooling is an extremely important strategy for building distributed applications. It allows a system to scale by providing a framework for sharing connection-oriented resources. This model can be extended to IIOP connections, connections to external transaction processors such as Tuxedo, and so on. In concert with this, the ability to coordinate operations on these shared remote resources through a global transaction manager allows applications to be designed which are free to be deployed at will across an enterprise.

## SQLJ (aka J/SQL)

In a joint effort, IBM, Oracle, Sybase, Tandem, Microsoft, Informix, and XDB have defined a standard for embedding SQL in Java programs. Analogous to embedded SQL for other languages such as C and C++, SQLJ leverages the host language and adds SQL features. SQLJ can be implemented either with a preprocessor that translates source into pure Java, or as a compiler which integrates SQLJ and Java source analysis into a single step.

There are three aspects to the effort, each identified by an associated subsection of the standard. These are:

- Part 0: A definition of Java language grammar extensions and rules for embedding SQL statements in Java programs.

- Part 1: A definition of how database stored procedures are to be written in Java.
- Part 2: SQL extensions to accommodate the storage and parameter passing of Java-specific objects and data types.

At this writing, Part 0 has been completed and Part 1 has been demonstrated. Part 2 is still being worked on.

A principal advantage of using SQLJ is that errors which would otherwise be detected at runtime can often be caught as type mismatch errors at compile time. For example, if the SQLJ compiler has access to the schema for the database the program is targeted for, it can check if query variables are matched to compatible Java types. By comparison, in a JDBC program such an error would only be detected when the actual query is run.

### Basic Syntax

SQLJ is defined as a set of extensions to the Java language. Each SQLJ statement is preceded with a "#"; however, such a statement may continue onto any number of lines. As illustrative examples, the basic syntax of a select and insert is shown below, using SQLJ. Source and target Java variables are preceded by colons:

```
int age = 20;
#sql { SELECT NAME INTO :name FROM GREATVIOLINISTS
WHERE AGE < :age };
String attraction = "Tyrannosaur";
#sql { INSERT INTO THEMEPARK VALUES ( :attraction ) };
```

At present, only Java variables may appear following a colon. It is likely that an upcoming release of the SQLJ specification will permit Java expressions as well, such as:

```
String[] team = { "Sculley", "Mulder" };
#sql { INSERT INTO XFILE VALUES ( :team[0], :team[1] ) };
```

### Creating a Connection

To create a connection to a database at runtime, your SQLJ program must first declare a *context*. A context compiles into a class that contains information about a database connection. The generated class has four constructors which may be used to establish a live context instance. Parameters to these constructors include the URL of the database. There is also a static method generated which can be used to set a default context instance for the generated context class so that the context does not need to be specified in subsequent statements which would require a context.

An example follows. In this example, it is assumed that when the programmer invokes the SQLJ compiler, he or she specifies that class CarTable is the default context class; the default context instance of this class will then be used whenever a default context is determined:

```
#sql context CarTable;  // this generates a context class (but not
                        // an instance)
public class MyClass
{
   public static void main (String argv[]) throws SQLException
   {
      // Now we create a context instance, and make it the default
      // for the CarTable context class
      CarTable.setDefaultContext(new CarTable(argv[0]));
      double average;
      #sql { SELECT AVG(PRICE) INTO :average FROM CARDATA };
      // The above uses CarTable as the default context class,
      // because the programmer
      // specified that when compiling, and obtains the default
      // context instance by
      // calling CarTable's generated static method
      // getDefaultContext()
   }
}
```

Note that in this example, the main method's argument, which presumably contains a database connect string, is passed to the constructor of the generated context class, CarTable. The CarTable context instance created as a result of the new operation is passed to CarTable's static setDefaultContext() method. The #sql statement that then follows executes in the default context of the CarTable class.

### *Improved Support for Cursors—Iterators*

SQLJ expands on the Java result set and SQL cursors by defining *iterators*. An iterator automates the mapping of SQL query result columns to Java objects, thereby reducing potential runtime errors when trying to convert column values.

Iterators may be bound *by-position* or *by-name*. Positional iterators require you to use a FETCH ... INTO ... clause when retrieving a row to associate columns with Java variables that will hold the results. In contrast, by-name iterators generate Java-typed accessor methods uniquely for the result columns.

Here is an example of a positional iterator:

```
// Define an iterator - this generates an iterator class
#sql iterator Secrets (String, String, String);
```

```
Secrets i;   // this is a reference to an iterator of the type we
             //defined
String org;
String secret;
String mole;
// Now perform a query that returns a result set with an
// iterator
#sql i = { SELECT ORG, TRADESECRETS, MOLE FROM COMPETITORS };
while (true)
{
   #sql { FETCH :i INTO :org, :secret, :mole };
   if (i.endFetch()) break;
   System.out.println(
   "Pssst - " + mole + " discovered " + org +
   " has this: " + secret);
}
```

Here is the same example, rewritten using a by-name iterator:

```
// Define an iterator - this generates an iterator class
#sql iterator Secrets (String org, String secret, String mole);

Secrets i;   // this is a reference to an iterator of the
             //type we defined
// Now perform a query that returns a result set with an
// iterator
#sql i = { SELECT ORG, TRADESECRETS, MOLE FROM COMPETITORS };
while (i.next())
{
   System.out.println(
   "Pssst - " + i.mole() + " discovered " + i.org() +
   " has this: " + i.secret());
}
```

### *Stored Procedures*

The goal of SQLJ Part 1 is to define a capability for database stored procedures to be written in SQLJ. This would make it possible to write database programs in the same language which is used for database client applications. It also makes available to database programs the same powerful features which are available to Java applications, including standard APIs for messaging and remote invocation.

SQLJ stored procedures are implemented using Java static methods. A Java class is written containing one or more static methods, the class is wrapped in a JAR file (discussed below), and then installed on the target database. An SQLJ stored procedure is callable from Java, such as remote JDBC clients, non-Java clients including

other Java or non-Java stored procedures, and tools such as a command-line interface. In other words, it is accessible just as any other stored procedure.

For now parameter and result types must map to SQL types. Eventually it will be possible to use any Java type. The current specification actually does not preclude the passing of arbitrary Java types—it is simply a limitation of current implementation goals.

Let's look at an example of an SQLJ stored procedure. Here is an SQLJ class which contains a stored procedure called getPrice(...):

```
public class MyStoredProcedures
{
    public static int getPrice(String carType)
    throws SQLException
    {
        Connection connection = DriverManager.getConnection(
            "jdbc:default:connection");
        Statement statement = connection.createStatement();
        ResultSet rs = statement.executeQuery(
            "select price from cardata where cartype = '"
            + carType + "'");
        return rs.getInt("PRICE");
    }

    ...other static methods...
}
```

Note in the above example that the driver creates a connection to the current database which is executing the stored procedure, using the special URL jdbc:default:connection.

### *Installing SQLJ Stored Procedures*

The tools provided by your SQLJ implementation will compile this code and build a JAR file for you to install in your database. A standard way of installing a JAR file containing Java stored procedures has been defined. The SQL procedure SQLJ.INSTALL_JAR does this. Here is an example:

```
sqlj.install_jar(
    'file:/MyJavaPSMs/MyStoredProcedures.jar',
    'my_stored_procs_jar');
```

This loads the JAR file at file:/MyJavaPSMs/MyStoredProcedures.jar into the database's PSM repository and specifies that this loaded JAR file should be identified by the name "my_stored_procs_jar." At this point the contained Java classes and their methods must be bound to SQL procedure names in order to be accessible to an SQL runtime. This can be done using the CREATE PROCEDURE and CREATE FUNCTION SQL statements. Here is an example:

```
create function get_price(carType string)
    external name
        'my_stored_procedures_jar:MyStoredProcedures.getPrice'
    language Java
    parameter style Java;
```

Note that the SQL name defined for this Java method is different from the actual name of the Java method. I could have made them the same, but I made them different to illustrate that they are different. The SQL name is the name used by the database for identifying the stored procedure. This is the name the administrator will see when all installed stored procedures are listed on the console. It is also the name you should use when referring to the stored procedure from a JDBC CallableStatement.

### *OUT Parameters*

In the Java method, if a parameter needs to be an OUT parameter and it is of type X, declare it to be of type X[]. In the Java method, assign a value to x[0]. When you call create procedure or create function and declare the parameter to be an OUT parameter, the system will assume the Java parameter is an array type and will automatically bind the variable to the zero-th element of the parameter. Here is an example:

```
public static void getPrice(String carType, int[] price)
throws SQLException
{
    Connection connection = DriverManager.getConnection(
        "jdbc:default:connection");
    Statement statement = connection.createStatement();
    ResultSet rs = statement.executeQuery(
        "select price from cardata where cartype = '"
        + carType + "'");
    price[0] = rs.getInt("PRICE");
}
```

Then declare this in SQL as follows:

```
create procedure get_price(carType string, out price integer)
    external name
        'my_stored_procedures_jar:MyStoredProcedures.getPrice'
    language Java
    parameter style Java;
```

### *Deployment*

SQLJ programs have neutrality of execution context, in that they are required to run the same whether they are run as a client program or a stored procedure. This is a powerful advantage because it means that Java SQLJ modules can be written in a reusable way and deployed in various environments without changing the source code or even recompiling. Environmental differences are encapsulated in the resource bindings encoded in a set of serialized Java objects which are stored in the JAR file containing the generated and compiled code. These special resources, called "profiles," follow a standard naming pattern so that deployment tools can locate them.

The profiles are the means by which compiled SQLJ modules can be redeployed at will without changing the code, because they contain all the required bindings to the target environment. Each SQLJ Context declared within an SQLJ file results in the compile-time generation of a profile, and each use of that context within the application results in a profile "entry" which describes the usage of the context. Deployment tools for a database customize the stored procedures for the environment by modifying the profiles of the procedures. The relationship between a SQLJ module, its contained contexts, and the resulting JAR file and contained profiles is shown in Figure 6-11.

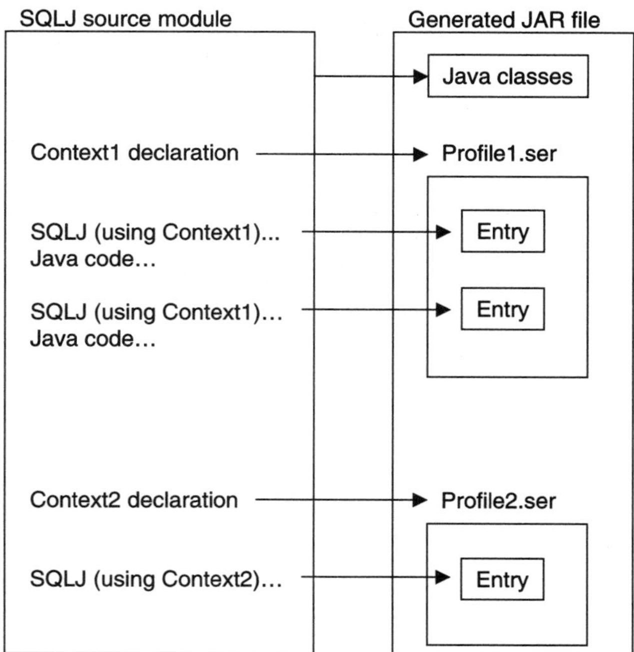


**Figure 6-11** An SQLJ module JAR file.

In addition, the JAR file may contain a deployment descriptor file, which is a text file that lists SQL statements that the DBMS should execute when it installs the JAR file. Here is an example:

```
SQLActions[] =
{
   "begin install
      create function get_price(carType string)
      external name
      'my_stored_procedures_jar:MyStoredProcedures.getPrice'
      language Java
      parameter style Java;
   end install",
   "begin install
      create prodedure ...etc.
}
```

The SQLJ standard is still evolving. Therefore, do not be surprised if some API changes occur.

## Persistent Object Databases

A persistent object database provides a permanent storage mechanism for program objects. A Java persistent object database allows the programmer to define Java objects and save them in a database for later retrieval, possibly by a different virtual machine.

### *Why Use a Persistent Object Database?*

JDBC defines an API for accessing a relational database (and many other data sources as well) using an SQL statement model. This approach suffers from some disadvantages, namely:

- The programmer must work with two very different languages: Java and SQL.
- SQL is primarily a runtime bound language, which makes testing difficult (this disadvantage can be addressed by using SQLJ, as discussed in this chapter).
- SQL is a very complex language, and understanding it thoroughly is a major career decision—it may be hard to find developers who understand both the implementation language and SQL sufficiently to develop effective and reliable applications.

An alternative approach is to use one language, and Java is a good choice for this. A persistent Java object database extends the Java semantic model to allow for

persistent objects, using the reliable and easy-to-understand Java object model (or Object Design Language, ODL, model, which can be converted into Java), which retain their state between and across virtual machine instances. A significant performance advantage of this approach is that relationships between objects are maintained explicitly, rather than computed at runtime as is the case with a relational query. (Actually, relational performance is not so bad in this regard if foreign keys are used to define relationships between tables.)

Another benefit is that some object databases make implementing optimistic locking easier, by allowing you to use object references outside of a transaction; then when you begin a new transaction, an exception is thrown if a reference is dirty. This will be discussed later in this chapter.

The Object Data Management Group (ODMG) is a consortium of companies formed to standardize the interface to object database systems. By having a standard it should be possible to write object-oriented applications and store objects in a persistent manner without becoming dependent on a particular object database product. The ODMG standard includes a Java language binding.

More recently Sun Microsystems has initiated an open process for defining a new standard tailored toward Java. This new standard, called the Java Data Objects Specification (JDO), will essentially replace the ODMG standard for Java applications. However, it is likely that it will not be too different from the ODMG standard because many of the same companies which participated in the latter are involved in the JDO effort, and the project has stated "This Specification will incorporate parts of the Object Data Management Group 3.0 persistent storage interface." You can find out more about the status of this effort at http://java.sun.com/aboutJava/communityprocess/jsr/jsr_012_dataobj.html. For now I will concentrate on the ODMG standard for all OODB examples since it is a completed standard.

ODMG does not define a mechanism for how Java object persistence is implemented. Implementing a persistent object layer can be accomplished in a variety of ways. Some techniques used by current products are:

- Post-process Java class files (e.g., ODI's ObjectStore and PSE products; this is sometimes referred to as a "static" implementation.
- Post-process Java source code (some object/relational mapping products, such as O2's Java Relational Binding, worked this way when first introduced, but since then have been upgraded to use the above technique); this is also a "static" implementation.
- Provide a modified (persistent) virtual machine implementation (e.g., GemStone); this is sometimes referred to as an "active" implementation.

With static implementations, the basic idea is to replace normal Java object dereferencing operations in the code (bytecode or sourcecode, depending on the implementation) with calls to methods that operate on the database. Since this is done by a postprocessor, the persistence mechanism is transparent to the application, and the application only has to worry about concurrency issues, associated with multiuser access to the data. An active implementation is even more transparent, since the code is not modified at all; rather, the VM itself implements the persistence.

In addition, there are object-to-relational mapping products, often called "blend" products, which provide an object-oriented layer on top of a relational database. These will be discussed in a separate section.

### *How ODBMSs Work*

Regardless of which implementation technique is used, a Java object database allows the programmer to deal strictly with Java objects of programmer-defined types. Predefined "database" types such as ResultSet are not used. This has the tremendous advantage that the business's object model can be defined explicitly in terms of a universal and well-defined language, making it portable and easy to understand across products, technologies, and methodologies.

To make a class persistent in a static implementation, all you do is run it through the persistent database product's persistence post-processor. Most implementations impose restrictions on what classes can be made persistent, however. For example, it is a common limitation that classes which are not user-defined cannot be made persistent. For example, java.awt.Applet or from somethirdparty. SomeClass could probably not be made persistent, because the persistence post-processor will not want to modify standard or prepackaged classes from external sources. Some persistence products also require that your own classes not extend from a base class which cannot be made persistent.

In practice this may not be as big a limitation as it sounds. Usually the classes you want to make persistent are of your own design, and are data containers of some sort—they constitute your database. Sometimes, however, you may want to make an AWT GUI component's state persistent, and to be able to do this, you will have to make sure the persistent database product has the capability to make classes that extend from package java (or other sources) persistent. Rather than making a user's GUI state persistent, a solution could be to serialize the GUI object's visual state using Java object serialization, and store that in the database or on the client machine. Of course, with this solution any database object references maintained by the GUI (as well as references to the GUI from database objects) would have to be transient, and rebuilt programmatically when the component is reinstantiated.

**States of a Reference.** Most ODBMSs use these concepts for references to persistent objects:

Hollow / shadow—A reference to an object exists, but the object itself has not yet been loaded.

Active—A valid reference, for an object that has been loaded.

Stale—The object has not been reloaded since the last transaction (references do not necessarily remain valid between transactions—it depends on the ODBMS).

When you commit a transaction, some ODBMSs allow you to specify an option to keep references from becoming stale so that you can reaccess them in the next transaction. Otherwise, you would have to look up the root objects and traverse to the objects you need all over again.

Note that you can put a transaction "on hold" by calling leave(), and later calling join() to resume. (This is discussed below.) The object references will still be valid in the joined transaction. However, the transaction will hold all of its locks for the entire time period, which may not be desirable.

**States of an Object.** An object referenced in an ODBMS application may be in either a transient state or a persistent state. To be in a persistent state, the object must be persistent-capable as defined by the persistence mechanism of the ODBMS. The definitions for persistent and transient are:

Persistent—Stored in the database.

Transient—Not persistent at this instant (but may become persistent if later referenced by a persistent object). This is not to be confused with the Java `transient` keyword. An object referenced by an object attribute that has a Java `transient` modifier may still be a nontransient (i.e., persistent) database object, if it is referenced by any other persistent object in the database.

### *The ODMG Object Model*

The ODMG model attempts to unify the object database world by defining a standard model for object database products. The model has object-definition, query, and manipulation subsets. The object definition language (ODL) is based on the OMG IDL standard. The query subset (OQL) is based on SQL, but is greatly simplified. Object manipulation is normally accomplished with an API, and there is now a Java language binding.

The ODMG Java binding defines the following object classes:

- Database
- Transaction

- These collection classes:
  - SetOfObject—implements DSet, described below
  - BagOfObject—implements DBag, described below
  - ListOfObject—implements DList, described below

Unlike the Java binding for OMG (CORBA), which defines a set of org.omg packages, the ODMG Java binding does not define any predefined packages of its own; rather, vendors are free to put the ODMG classes into a package of their choosing.

**The Database Class.** The ODMG Java API standard does not define a method for creating a database, and leaves that up to the implementation (e.g., some implementations have a static create() method). Once created, however, the Database class has these methods for opening and operating on a database:

```
public static Database open(String name, int accessMode)
   throws ODMGException;
public void close() throws ODMGException;
public void bind(Object object, String name);
public Object lookup(String name) throws
ObjectNameNotFoundException;
public void unbind(String name) throws
   ObjectNameNotFoundException;
```

**Defining Root Objects.** Before you can work with an existing database that you have opened with the open() method, you have to first get references to at least one object in the database. Once you have a reference to a persistent object, you can traverse through the object network using Java object references, just as you would in any Java program; however, you need a starting point.

Usually a starting point is some object that is a collection type. For example, you might want to find a particular employee, so you need to get a reference to an employee list. For this purpose, the employee list will need to have a name so that applications can find it. You can use the Database class's bind() method to give an object a name; for example:

```
myDatabase.bind(myEmployeeCollection, "EMPLOYEES");
```

From then on, you can always find this list—even from other processes and even after your program terminates—by calling lookup ("EMPLOYEES") after opening the database. Notice that you would not use the bind() method to give each

employee a lookup name: it is not intended for that purpose. It is intended for identifying "root" entry points.

Some ODBMS products provide the ability to construct "extents." An extent is a collection of object instances which represent the total set of all objects in the database of a specific type. For example, you might construct an extent for class Employee, and thereby obtain a set of all employees. The ODMG specification does not specify support for extents at this time.

**Collection Types.** These collection interface types are defined by the ODMG Java binding:

- DCollection—Extends java.util.Collection.
- DSet—Extends DCollection, java.util.Set. An unordered DCollection, with no duplicates allowed.
- DBag—Extends DCollection. An unordered DCollection, with duplicates allowed.
- DList—Extends DCollection, java.util.List. An ordered DCollection, duplicates allowed.
- DArray—Extends DCollection, java.util.List. A resizable array.

Notice that DCollection, and therefore all of the ODMG collection types, implement the java.util.Collection interface defined in Java 2. In addition, the DList and DArray types extend the Java 2 java.util.List type. Some of the methods in these types return the type java.util.Iterator, which is also a Java 2 type. The Iterator type is similar to the Java 1.0 Enumeration, but allows elements to be removed from it. Since an Iterator is not intended to be a persistent type, there is no corresponding DIterator interface defined by ODMG.

An implementation must provide concrete types that implement these, consisting of at least SetOfObject, ListOfObject, and BagOfObject. The only constraint on membership is that all members be Java Objects (i.e., there is effectively no type constraint). Other ODMG language bindings provide for other concrete collection types, of the general form SetOf<type>, and so on, but the Java binding only specifies those listed here. Thus, these collection types permit membership of mixed object types.

Collections are considered nonprimary containers: cloning a DCollection instance only clones the container, not the members; in other words, copies are shallow. The Java binding does not define the copy operation, however. It is up to the implementation or application to define such a shallow copy operation. These types are also mutable.

Notice that there is no hashtable object. Most implementations provide a persistent hashtable or dictionary class. You can also use the DCollection query() and selectElement() methods to find objects in any collection; these methods take a query predicate (i.e., the part of a WHERE clause that follows the "WHERE") as a parameter. However, beware that some "ODMG-compliant" products do not yet support this feature.

Of course, regular Java arrays are supported also.

Table 6-7 lists the methods defined in java.util.Collection, java.util.List, java.util.Iterator, and the ODMG collection interfaces.

**Persistence by Reachability.** A class must be persistent-capable to be made persistent. It is not defined how classes are made persistent-capable. In practice, products use one of the techniques discussed earlier to make objects persistent-capable (i.e., using a postprocessor to insert database calls into class files, or providing a persistent VM).

**Table 6-7** **Collection Types**

**java.util.Collection:**

```
public int size();
public boolean isEmpty();
public boolean add(Object obj);
public boolean remove(Object obj);
public boolean contains(Object obj);
public java.util.Iterator iterator();
public boolean containsAll(Collection c);
public boolean addAll(Collection c);
public boolean removeAll(Collection c);
public boolean retainAll(Collection c);
public int size();
public boolean isEmpty();
public boolean add(Object obj);
public boolean remove(Object obj);
public boolean contains(Object obj);
public java.util.Iterator iterator();
public boolean containsAll(Collection c);
public boolean addAll(Collection c);
public boolean removeAll(Collection c);
public boolean retainAll(Collection c);
```

**Table 6-7 Collection Types (Continued)**

**java.util.List (extends java.util.Collection):**

pubic void add(int index, Object obj) throws ArrayIndexOutOfBoundsException;
public void set(int index, Object obj) throws ArrayIndexOutOfBoundsException;
public Object remove(int index) throws ArrayIndexOutOfBoundsException;
public Object get(int index) throws ArrayIndexOutOfBoundsException;

**java.util.Iterator (An iterator over a Collection):**

public boolean hasNext()
public Object next()
public void remove()

**DCollection (extends java.util.Collection):**

public Object selectElement(String predicate) throws QueryInvalidException;
public java.util.Iterator select(String predicate) throws QueryInvalidException;
public DCollection query(String predicate) throws QueryInvalidException;
public boolean existsElement(String predicate) throws QueryInvalidException;

**DSet (extends DCollection, java.util.Set):**

public DSet union(DSet otherSet);
public DSet intersection(DSet otherSet);
public DSet difference(DSet otherSet);
public boolean subsetOf(DSet otherSet);
public boolean properSubsetOf(DSet otherSet);
public boolean supersetOf(DSet otherSet);
public boolean properSupersetOf(DSet otherSet);

**DBag (extends DCollection):**

public DBag union(DBag otherBag);
public DBag intersection(DBag otherBag);
public DBag difference(DBag otherBag);
public int occurrences(Object obj);

**DList (extends DCollection, java.util.List):**

public DList concat(DList other);

**DArray (extends DCollection, java.util.List):**

public void resize(int newSize);

Assuming an object is persistent-capable, the database will convert it from transient to persistent as needed. The ODMG specification says that when a persistent-capable object references other persistent-capable objects, those objects become persistent when the referencing object is saved. Thus, if you look up an object using the Database.lookup() method, and you attach other persistent-capable objects to that object by setting object references, all of those objects (and all persistent-capable objects they point to) will be saved when the transaction is committed, because they are all reachable from the root persistent object.

**Object Locking.** The ODMG object locking model is a simple one, which uses the concept of an "intention-write" lock (see "Database Locking and Isolation" on page 416). These three lock modes are defined:

READ—Allows shared read access

WRITE—Exclusive access; does not permit concurrent reads by other transactions

UPGRADE—An intention-write lock

Read locks are obtained automatically (implicitly) as objects are accessed. Write locks are obtained automatically (implicitly) as objects are modified. Use Transaction.lock(object, mode) to explicitly request or upgrade a lock.

The lock() method is used to explicitly request a lock on an object. Normally you will only call this method when you need to request an UPGRADE (intention-write) lock, since read and write locks are obtained implicitly as needed when you perform access and modify an object.

Request an UPGRADE lock for any object for which you intend to eventually implicitly or explicitly ask for a WRITE lock within the current transaction. Other concurrent transactions cannot get WRITE or UPGRADE locks for an object if there is an UPGRADE lock for that object. This allows other transactions to read the object until the moment you decide you are ready to request the WRITE lock, providing greater concurrency than if you requested the WRITE lock from the outset.

A transaction is terminated when you perform a commit() or abort(). At that time all locks are released, and object references become stale.

**Transactions.** ODMG supports Isolation Level 3 (serializability). (See "Database Locking and Isolation" on page 416.) This provides a complete guarantee of correctness of operation with regard to concurrent transactions.

The Transaction class has one constructor and these methods:

```
Transaction();     // intended to be "public" - implementations
                   // make it public
public void begin();
public void join();
public void leave();
public static Transaction current();
public boolean isOpen();
public void commit();
public void abort();
public void checkpoint();
public void lock(Object obj, int mode);
```

It is important to distinguish between an instance of the Transaction class and a database transaction. Your program may perform several transactions over time using the same Transaction instance.

The join() operation connects the current thread to a Transaction instance. A thread cannot perform any database operations unless the thread is joined to some Transaction instance. This even includes connecting to a database. Thus, before you can open a database, you must create a Transaction instance first and join to it.

Instantiating a Transaction object implicitly joins the current thread to that instance, so you do not have to call join() unless you want to join the thread to a different Transaction instance. You might do the latter if you put that transaction on hold for a moment by calling leave(); the join() method lets you return to it.

To begin a database transaction, you call begin() on the thread's Transaction instance. To terminate a transaction, call either commit() or abort() to save changes or abandon them, respectively. In both cases, all locks held by the transaction are released. The checkpoint() method saves changes, but does not release the transaction's locks. The abort() method does not restore the prior program state of nonpersistent (i.e., transient) objects.

Thus, a Transaction object manages database transactions, and at any one instant may or may not have an actual transaction in progress. Your thread must be attached to a Transaction object to create objects in the context of that transaction. You cannot call begin(), commit(), abort(), checkpoint(), or leave() for a transaction to which you are not attached. Also, more than one thread can be joined to a transaction. In that case, the threads operate within the context of that transaction, and are responsible for synchronizing access to objects they share—even persistent objects. However, two threads that are *not* joined to a transaction should not share objects. In other words, do not allow one of your threads to read a persistent object reference obtained from a transaction to which your thread is not joined.

When you commit, references become stale. You can refresh them by refetching, starting from a root object. Some ODBMSs allow you to keep them from becoming stale, but then in your next transaction you may have to catch an exception for the object being dirty, since your commit released your lock on the object. Keeping references between transactions is a valuable feature, but is not specified in the ODMG standard, so use it with care, recognizing that it may make your program nonportable.

**OQL (Object Query Language).** The OQLQuery class provides an SQL-like query capability for object databases, for retrieving objects and object collections based on a selection expression. To perform a query, you either can use one of the DCollection query methods, or create a OQLQuery object and execute its create() and execute() methods. The former is appropriate when you merely want to select some objects from an existing collection. For example:

```
DList mySalespersonList = (DList)(d.lookup("Salespeople"));
...
// Get the salespeople named 'Flint'
java.util.Iterator i = mySalespersonList.select("this.name
   like 'Flint'");
for (;;)
{
   try
   {
      Salesperson s = (Salesperson)(i.next());
      System.out.println(s.name);
   }
   catch (NoSuchElementException ex) { break; }
}
```

To perform a query, create an OQLQuery object, and initialize it with an OQL SELECT expression. Then call its execute() method. For example:

```
OQLQuery q = new OQLQuery(
   "select list.region from Salespeople where list.region.name
      like 'North America'");
DCollection regions = (DCollection)(q.execute());
```

**Exceptions.** The ODMG standard defines a list of Java exceptions, including the base type ODMGException. Again, these classes do not go into any particular package; that is up to the vendor. Nor is their inheritance defined; they may extend from a vendor's own exceptions.

One significant difference between an object database and a relational database is that with a relational database, an exception only can occur during a database operation. With an object database, since every object dereference is potentially a database operation, virtually any operation can result in a database exception. You must therefore treat database exceptions as a general kind of event that may occur in any statement. Note that an implementation may generate Runtime-Exceptions or Errors as well for some database events (like deadlock), so do not simply catch ODMGException—this will probably not get them all.

As already mentioned, some ODBMS products allow a persistent object reference to span transactions. What if a subsequent transaction attempts to use a reference from an earlier transaction, and the referenced object is modified (i.e., has been modified by someone else)? If the database automatically reloads the object, it will probably invalidate other references; what if you try to use one of these? In general, if an object database allows references to span transactions, there must be a class of exceptions for dealing with dirty and stale references, and you will have to catch these in your code. Most likely, when you detect an object has changed, you will reload the object by going back to the object used to get to it, or even by reperforming a lookup() in the database and starting from scratch. You may then need to refresh all objects obtained from the invalid object.

An important class of exceptions that are generated by some products, but are not defined in the ODMG standard, are lifecycle exceptions, which indicate mismatches in database schema between the client and the server. This capability is very valuable for implementing replicated code architectures, as described in detail at the end of this chapter. If the database schema has been modified, applications should have a way to know, other than the system administrator taking the system down and sending everyone an email. Look for exceptions with names like "DatabaseUpgradeException" or "SchemaEvolutionException."

**Portability.** ODMG compliance does not include binary compatibility. It is up to the DBMS vendor to decide what packages the ODMG classes go into, or what exception type ODMGException extends from. Therefore, even source code is not portable until you insert the appropriate import statements at the start of each source file, and then recompile. In addition, if your code creates databases, it must do so in a vendor-specific manner, since the ODMG standard does not define a Java API for creating a database. Finally, the form of the constructors for the SetOfObject, ListOfObject, and BagOfObject classes is not specified in the standard and thus is vendor-specific.

Since the ODMG exception types may derive from a vendor-specific type, it is not usually possible to combine two different implementations in the same program.

If you do this, you cannot, for example, check if a returned exception was of a particular type, unless you fully qualify the package name.

Many ODMG-compliant DBMSs also have significant features that are not defined in the ODMG standard. For example, the ODMG standard does not require that object references remain valid from one transaction to the next, even if the transactions occur in the same thread. Thus, if your application does multiple commits, it has to refetch all data at the start of every transaction. The checkpoint() method, which allows you to combine what would have been two transactions into one, is not a solution when the first commit and the final commit are separated by a significant amount of time, during which all locks would have to be held. ObjectStore, however, allows you to keep your references from becoming stale after a commit; if you use their proprietary Transaction type and the following method:

```
myTransaction.commit
   (COM.odi.ObjectStoreConstants.RETAIN_READONLY);
```

A feature like this is very valuable; but, as with all extensions, you must evaluate the cost. In particular, does the requirement to use a proprietary type propagate, and preclude you from using other ODMG-compliant types? For example, if you use a proprietary transaction type, must you then use a proprietary database type, and so on, and so on? What starts out as an ODMG-compliant project may turn out to be completely noncompliant, merely as a result of a decision to use a single extension. Also, if the database is created using the vendor's proprietary API, can it later be accessed with the vendor's ODMG API, or do they create incompatible databases?

### *An Example: Creating a Persistent Database Application*

I will now show an ODMG-compliant example, of a simple case of a program which updates a single field of a persistent object. The persistent class is Task, which contains merely a single field, called "name," which represents the name of a task. This persistent class has two accessor methods: getTask() and setTask(String). The class must be processed in some way, by a persistence tool supplied by the vendor of the persistent database, to make it persistent-capable. Here is the Task class:

```
/**
 * Process this class with ODBMS's postprocessor to make it
 * persistent.
 */
public class Task extends Anything
```

```
   // some products require Anything to be a class you define,
   // and not
   // a third party or Java class; or, if they do, there are
   // restrictions
{
   public void setName(String n)
   {
      // Assume we are in a transaction
      name = n;
   }
   public String getName()
   {
      // Assume we are in a transaction
      return name;
   }

   private String name;
}
```

Below I define a program which attempts to open a database, find a persistent task list, find a particular task within the list, and then modify the name of that task.

```
/**
 * Transaction to rename a task. This class does not need to be
 * persistent, since it is not stored
 * in the database.
 */
public class RenameTask
{
   public static void main(String[] args)
   {
      String oldname = args[0];   // the old name
      String newname = args[1];   // the new name

      // Create a transaction object; this must be done before
      // you can open the database
      Transaction t = new Transaction();

      // Open the database
      Database d = null;
      try
      {
         d = Database.open("MyDatabase",
            Database.openReadWrite);
      }
      catch (Exception ex)
```

```
        {
            System.out.println("Unable to open database");
            System.exit(1);
        }
        // Start a transaction
        try
        {
            t.join();    // Attach transaction t to the current
            // thread
            // The above is not necessary, since t's constructor
            // joins us automatically.
            // All database operations will now take place using
            // the transaction
            // of the current thread

            t.begin();    // Start a transaction
        }
        catch (Exception ex)
        {
            System.out.println("Unable to start transaction...");
            ex.printStackTrace();
            System.exit(1);
        }
```

Below I use the Database lookup() method to find a persistent named object which I previously created. This object is a persistent collection type, in this case a DList. Note that the LockNotGrantedException can be thrown, indicating a sharing violation (i.e., the object is in use). Normally we might want to try again if that happens, but in this simple example, we just terminate.

```
// Find the list of all tasks
DList tasklist = null;
try
{
    tasklist = (DList)(d.lookup("OurTaskList"));
}
catch (LockNotGrantedException exa)
{
    System.out.println("Unable to get task list; perhaps
        someone is modifying it");
    t.abort();
    System.exit(0);
}
catch (Exception exb)
{
    System.out.println("Unable to locate task list!");
```

```
    exb.printStackTrace();
    t.abort();
    System.exit(1);
}
```

Once we have the persistent task DList object, we can use the collection selectElement() method to evaluate a query selection on that list. Here I tell it to select the element for which the "name" field is equal to the value of oldname.

```
// Find the task we are interested in Task task = null;
try
{
    Object o = tasklist.selectElement("this.name=\"" +
        oldname + "\"");
    task = (Task)o;
    t.lock(task, Transaction.UPGRADE);
        // state our intention to modify it
}
catch (LockNotGrantedException exa)
{
    System.out.println("Unable to get task; perhaps
        someone is modifying it");
    t.abort();
    System.exit(0);
}
catch (Exception exb)
{
    System.out.println("Could not find task '" +
        oldname + "'");
    t.abort();
    System.exit(0);
}
```

Above, after we obtain the desired task, we attempt to promote the read lock we implicitly have on it to an UPGRADE lock. This tells the database that we *intend* to modify this object, and that it should prevent other transactions from obtaining an UPGRADE or UPDATE lock on it (i.e., prevent other transactions from modifying it).

```
// Attempt to set the task name, and commit the change
    try
    {
        task.setName(newname);    // promotion to WRITE lock is
                                  // automatic
        t.commit();
        // At this point, any object references you have are
        // now stale
```

```
      // ObjectStore allows the following to keep your
      // references from becoming
      // stale; if you do this, you can still use the
      // reference to task in the next
      // transaction without re-fetching it:

      // t.commit(COM.odi.ObjectStoreConstants.
      // RETAIN_READONLY);

      // However, you would have to use ODI's
      // COM.odi.Transaction type, instead
      // of their ODMG-compliant COM.odi.odmg.Transaction
      // type. With any
      // ODMG-compliant product it is important to evaluate
      // if deviations like this
      // propagate, and cause you to have to use other
      // types that are also not
      // compliant.
   }
   catch (LockNotGrantedException exa)
   {
      System.out.println(
         "Unable to get task for update; perhaps someone"
         + "is reading it");
      t.abort();
      System.exit(0);
   }
   catch (Exception exb)
   {
      t.abort();
      exb.printStackTrace();
      System.exit(1);
   }
   System.out.println("Name updated");

   // Get the task name, to see if our previous transaction worked
   String s = null;
   try
   {
      // Start new transaction
      t.begin();

      // We have to refetch task
      ... do everything we did before to find task, but now
          we have to look for it by its new name...
```

```
        // With an ODBMS that allows us to retain active
        // references between
        // transactions, we can just do this instead:
        // s = task.getName();

        t.commit();
        d.close();
     }
     catch (LockNotGrantedException exa)
     {
        System.out.println("Unable to get task; perhaps
           someone is modifying it.");
        System.out.println("Your change is being aborted");
        t.abort();
        System.exit(0);
     }
     catch (Exception exb)
     {
        t.abort();
        exb.printStackTrace();
        System.exit(1);
     }
        System.out.println("confirmed that task's new name=" + s);
     }
}
```

### *Serializing or Externalizing Database References; Interdatabase References*

Maintaining references to objects between transactions is an important requirement, and your application will probably need a strategy for doing that. The references can be either "lightweight," such that they actually only constitute an index of some kind for quickly looking up the object, or "heavyweight," representing actual ODBMS references.

One valuable type of reference is an externalized object reference. Many products support reference externalization. An externalized reference is one the ODBMS can use to automatically locate the corresponding object and reconstruct a true persistent reference. Externalized references can be maintained outside of the transaction, and even outside of the process or application; they can even be written to disk.

As an example, ObjectStore allows you to do the following:

```
ExternalReference er = null;
try
{
   new ExternalReference(myPersistentObject);
```

```
}
catch (Exception ex)
{
   ...
}
transaction.commit();
...

...start new transaction...
try
{
   myPersistentObject = er.getObject();
}
catch (ObjectNotFoundException exa)
{
   ...(object is gone)
}
catch (Exception exb)
{
   ...
}
```

In this example, an external reference is created in one transaction, and later another transaction uses that value to recreate a true persistent object reference without having to look up the object all over again.

### *Building an Object Database Application Server*

There are lots of reasons why you might choose to build an application server instead of implementing a heavy client and using a network driver for your object database application. One is that you might want to implement a custom security policy or facility for accesssing the database (e.g., with user identities stored and accessed via an LDAP server), and wrap all database accesses in a server-side object layer. Another is that your available network database drivers have limitations, such as restricted support for full transaction isolation.

Some problems you will need to consider in implementing an object database tier include object serializability, transaction context loss across remote calls, and remote class deployment.

With some products, persistent objects cannot be made serializable, so the objects you send as remote query results cannot be persistent objects. Instead, you may need to define an equivalent serializable "message" version of the object, for transport to clients and back.

Regardless, before you serialize a persistent object or its message equivalent, you may need to perform a deep fetch operation on the object, to convert all of its references into active references, and their references, and so on, for all objects reachable from the object via nontransient references. You cannot rely on the seri-

alization mechanism to do this, because it uses Java reflection, which will bypass the persistence mechanism entirely. In short, you should build your own serializable object by reading persistent objects first, and then use writeObject() to serialize it.

When performing remote transactions, you may want to invoke a remote method which initiates a transaction, does some work, and returns some partial results without committing the transaction yet. For example, the method may be for an incremental query. The difficulty is that, if you use RMI, you cannot know which thread will be used to perform the remote method call on the server. From the point of view of the ODBMS your transaction is on the server; if you disconnect from the transaction and the thread goes into a wait state (and most likely back into a thread pool), you will need to have a way of identifying the Transaction object on the next call, so you can call join() to reattach to it. Thus, your server application will need to maintain a look-up table that correlates clients with transactions. You will probably want to make this as transparent as possible, and pass a transaction handle of some sort (a lightweight index into your table) as a parameter on incremental query calls.

Another alternative is to use middleware that associates a thread or server object uniquely with a client session. For example, some CORBA products allow this as an option. Using this technique, all you need to do is have your server return incremental results. Then, on each successive call, the thread merely uses the same transaction object. In other words, each session keeps a transaction object to reuse. The disadvantage of this approach is that it is not scalable to large numbers of client connections.

Thus, there are three approaches to dealing with over-the-wire transactions:

**(a)** Retain transaction context, by coding server methods so that they leave() a transaction when they complete, and join() it when they start. This requires a look-up mechanism in the server implementation to identify the transaction. (Transaction is not serializable, so you cannot send it back and forth.)

**(b)** Use middleware which maintains an association between client connection and server transaction.

**(c)** Complete each remote call in a single transaction. In that case, each remote method implementation will have to start a transaction, look up whatever objects it needs, perform its work, and commit.

If you serialize true persistent objects and send them over the wire, you may have to provide for what happens when persistence facilities get called by those objects. Some products require you to deploy a "stub package" in your client classpath (or your archive tag if the client is deployed in a browser) to provide access to stub versions of classes that normally implement persistence facilities on the host and are referenced by persistent classes that you serialize. These stubs may either implement a remote protocol for interacting with the DBMS (i.e., as a network client), or they may merely be no-ops, specifically for serialized objects.

I will now present an example of an application that implements a middle-tier server to access a persistent object database using RMI. The example implements a remote object server, connected to clients via RMI, and illustrates some of the issues that you may encounter in building a distributed application that uses persistent object technology.

For simplicity, this example is coded as if it were a single-user application, and does not check for concurrency exceptions the way the earlier Task example does. In a multiuser application, you would have to do these checks, as in the Task example. Also, I use strategy (c) from above: implementing each remote call as a separate and self-contained transaction.

First I define interfaces: a remote interface for the task server, and a base-type interface for the task objects that will be sent back and forth as messages, and persistified:

```
/**
  * These are the remote methods exported by the task server, which
  * the client may call. Each of these methods represents a remote
  * transaction.
  */
  interface TaskServer extends java.rmi.Remote
  {
    /**
    * Return a list of RemoteTask objects. We return RemoteTask
    * objects instead of SerializableTask objects, so that we can
    * reference the server's tasks when we manipulate the server's
    * task list (e.g., with the delTask() method).
    */
    public java.util.Vector getTasks() throws
       java.rmi.RemoteException;

    /**
     * Add a new task definition to the server's task list.
     */
    public RemoteTask addTask(SerializableTask task) throws
       java.rmi.RemoteException;

    /**
     * Remove the specified task from the server's task list.
     * Return false if the task was not found.
     */
    public boolean delTask(RemoteTask task) throws
       java.rmi.RemoteException;
}
```

```
/**
 * A Task is the object that the user defines and the system
 * tracks. This is the base type that defines what a Task does. In
 * this example, it is trivial: it merely sets and gets its name.
 */
interface Task
{
   /*
    * Accessor: set the name of this task.
    */
   public void setName(String name);
   /*
    * Accessor: get the name of this task.
    */
   public String getName();
}
```

Now I will define a remote task interface, to define the remote operations possible on a task. These operations occur on a remote proxy for a persistent task, which in turn operates on an actual persistent task. Note that this interface does not extend the Task interface. The reason is that a remote implementation may have to throw exceptions—in particular RemoteException—that are not appropriate for a local task implementation, and I do not want to be forced to add inappropriate throws clauses to Task, so I define a completely separate RemoteTask interface:

```
/**
 * Remote version of a Task.
 * Redefine the Task interface with the required remote
 * exceptions.
 * RemoteTask objects are remote proxies for PersistentTask
 * objects.
 * Each of these methods represents a remote transaction.
 * We would like to extend this from Task; however note that
 * if we extended this from Task, each method of Task would have
 * to throw Exception, or an exception type that RemoteException
 * derives from.
 */
interface RemoteTask extends java.rmi.Remote
{
   public void setName(String name) throws
      java.rmi.RemoteException;
   public String getName() throws java.rmi.RemoteException;
}
```

Now let's look at the class implementations. (I will use Object Design's slightly variant version of their API, which allows me to use their RETAIN_UPDATE flag, for maintaining object references across transactions.) The task-server object has to implement the TaskServer remote interface, and extend the RMI Unicast-RemoteObject class, to obtain the desired remote behavior:

```
class TaskServerImpl extends java.rmi.server.UnicastRemoteObject
   implements TaskServer
{
   public TaskServerImpl() throws java.rmi.RemoteException
   {
      this.initThread = Thread.currentThread();

      // Open the database; create it if necessary

      COM.odi.ObjectStore.initialize(null, null);

      try
      {
         database = COM.odi.Database.open(
            "taskmaster.odb", COM.odi.Database.openUpdate);
         COM.odi.ObjectStore.initialize(getInitThread());
         COM.odi.Transaction tr =
            COM.odi.Transaction.begin
            (COM.odi.Transaction.update);
         persistentTasks =
            (COM.odi.util.OSVector)(database.getRoot
            ("PersistentTasks"));
```

I have now retrieved a collection object, called "PersistentTasks," which I stored at some previous time. I retain my reference to this object, even after I commit this transaction, by committing with the RETAIN_UPDATE flag. That way, I do not have to perform the potentially expensive look up on the "PersistentTasks" collection every time I make a query transaction that requires this collection.

Below I perform another optimization, which may be very inappropriate in some circumstances. For each persistent task, I construct a remote task proxy object, which can support remote calls of its own. I do this mainly for illustration, to show that we can create all kinds of server objects, standing in for persistent objects that have to remain on the database machine. If the list of tasks is long, you probably would not want to create all these remote objects ahead of time, and would only create them as needed.

```
      System.out.println("There are " +
         persistentTasks.size()
            + " tasks in the database");
      // Create remote proxies
      for (int i = 0; i < persistentTasks.size(); i++)
      {
         RemoteTask rt = new RemoteTaskImpl(
            this, (PersistentTask)
            (persistentTasks.elementAt(i)));
         remoteTasks.addElement(rt);
      }
      tr.commit(COM.odi.Transaction.RETAIN_UPDATE);
      System.out.println("Database opened without error");
   }
   catch (COM.odi.DatabaseNotFoundException e)
   {
      System.out.println("Database not found; creating...");
      database = COM.odi.Database.create(
         "taskmaster.odb", COM.odi.Database.ownerWrite);
      COM.odi.ObjectStore.initialize(getInitThread());
      COM.odi.Transaction tr =
         COM.odi.Transaction.begin (COM.odi.Transaction.update);
      persistentTasks = new COM.odi.util.OSVector();
      database.createRoot("PersistentTasks",persistentTasks);
      tr.commit(COM.odi.Transaction.RETAIN_UPDATE);
      System.out.println("Database created without error");
   }
}
```

Having opened the database for this stateful object and initialized the Persistent-Tasks reference, our remote methods can be called to operate on the Persistent-Tasks collection. Here is the implementation of those remote server methods:

```
public java.util.Vector getTasks() throws
   java.rmi.RemoteException
{
   System.out.println("Returning task list (" +
      remoteTasks.size() + " tasks)");
   return remoteTasks;
}
public RemoteTask addTask(SerializableTask task) throws
   java.rmi.RemoteException
{
   System.out.println("Attempting to add task...");
   COM.odi.ObjectStore.initialize(getInitThread());
   COM.odi.Transaction tr =
```

```
      COM.odi.Transaction.begin
      (COM.odi.Transaction.update);

   PersistentTask pt = new PersistentTaskImpl(task);
   persistentTasks.addElement(pt);
```

Above I have constructed a new persistent task, using a serializable task message object sent by a client, as the sole constructor parameter. This message object contains enough information about the task to be created to create a persistent version of it. Then I have added the newly created persistent task object to the persistent list of tasks; to keep things in sync, I also create a new remote task proxy object for the newly-created persistent task, and add it to the remote task list:

```
   RemoteTask rt = new RemoteTaskImpl(this, pt);
   remoteTasks.addElement(rt);

   tr.commit(COM.odi.Transaction.RETAIN_UPDATE);
   System.out.println("...Task added.");
   return rt;
}
```

Deleting a task is complicated by the fact that I am keeping separate but synchronized lists of persistent tasks and their corresponding remote task objects. Therefore, when I delete one, I must delete the other. Aside from this, it is straightforward:

```
   public boolean delTask(RemoteTask task) throws
      java.rmi.RemoteException
   {
      COM.odi.ObjectStore.initialize(getInitThread());
      COM.odi.Transaction tr =
         COM.odi.Transaction.begin
         (COM.odi.Transaction.update);

      // Remove the task from the remote task list,
      // if it is in there; if not, return false
      for (int i = 0; i < remoteTasks.size(); i++)
      {
         RemoteTaskImpl rt = (RemoteTaskImpl)
            (remoteTasks.elementAt(i));
         if (rt.equals(task))
         {
            try {remoteTasks.removeElementAt(i);}
            catch (ArrayIndexOutOfBoundsException ex)
            { throw new RuntimeException("Should not happen!"); }
```

```
            // the remote handle is now stale
            // Remove the task from the persistent task list
            persistentTasks.removeElement
               (rt.getPersistentTask());
            tr.commit(COM.odi.Transaction.RETAIN_UPDATE);
            return true;    // success
         }
      }
      // did not find it - it must have already been deleted
      tr.commit(COM.odi.Transaction.RETAIN_UPDATE);
      return false;
   }

   /**
    * Accessor: return the thread that initialized the database.
    */
   public Thread getInitThread() { return initThread; }
   /**
    * The task server is a program, and needs a static entry
    * point.
    */
   public static void main(String[] args) throws
      java.rmi.RemoteException
   {
      // Create and install a security manager

      System.setSecurityManager(new
         java.rmi.RMISecurityManager());
      // Publish the server
      TaskServer obj = null;
      try
      {
         obj = new TaskServerImpl();
         java.rmi.Naming.rebind(args[0], obj);
         System.out.println(
         "TaskServerImpl created and bound in the registry to
            the name " + args[0]);
      }
      catch (Exception e)
      {
         e.printStackTrace();
      }
   }
   private java.util.Vector remoteTasks = new java.util.Vector();
   private Thread initThread;
   private COM.odi.Database database;
   private COM.odi.util.OSVector persistentTasks;
}
```

The next class is the persistent task class. This class will be processed by the ODI post processor (or whatever persistence tools you might choose to use) to make it persistent. I would like to make this class serializable, so that it could be sent to clients by value, but some ODBMSs and blend products will not let me do this, because the postprocessor will add a base class that is not serializable. Check if the product you choose allows persistent objects to be serializable, and what the restrictions are, e.g., if your class extends from a serializable class in package Java. (ObjectStore does not have this restriction, but it is done this way here to show the general case.)

Ideally, I would also like to make this class double as the remote version of a task, but I cannot because remote objects should extend UnicastRemoteObject, and I am assuming here that persistent objects must be postprocessed to extend an implementation-defined persistent base class (although as already explained, some products do not have that restriction), so I create a separate remote object type to serve as a remote proxy for the persistent object. I could elect to not extend UnicastRemoteObject, but then I would be losing out on the encapsulation of remote behavior provided by this type.

```
/**
 * A persistent representation of a task.
 */
class PersistentTaskImpl implements Task
{
   public PersistentTaskImpl(SerializableTask serializableTask)
   {
      name = serializableTask.getName();
   }
   public void setName(String name) { this.name = name; }
   public String getName() { return name; }
   private String name;
}
```

Next I define the lightweight message object that describes a task. I define this separately because I am assuming that persistent tasks are not serializable. This is used to send new task definitions between the client and server.

```
class SerializableTaskImpl implements Task, java.io.Serializable
{
   public void setName(String name) { this.name = name; }
   public String getName() { return name; }
   private String name;
}
```

Here is the implementation of a remote task. This serves as a remote proxy for a persistent task. Every operation performed by a client on a remote task propagates to the corresponding persistent task. Note that each of its remote methods encapsulates a complete transaction.

```
class RemoteTaskImpl extends java.rmi.server.UnicastRemoteObject
   implements RemoteTask
{
   public RemoteTaskImpl(TaskServerImpl taskServer, PersistentTask
      persistentTask)
   throws java.rmi.RemoteException
   {
      this.taskServer = taskServer;
      this.persistentTask = persistentTask;
   }
   public void setName(String name) throws
      java.rmi.RemoteException
   {
      COM.odi.ObjectStore.initialize
         (taskServer.getInitThread());
      COM.odi.Transaction tr =
         COM.odi.Transaction.begin
         (COM.odi.Transaction.update);
      persistentTask.setName(name);
      tr.commit(COM.odi.Transaction.RETAIN_UPDATE);
   }

   public String getName() throws java.rmi.RemoteException
   {
      COM.odi.ObjectStore.initialize
         (taskServer.getInitThread());
      COM.odi.Transaction tr =
         COM.odi.Transaction.begin
         (COM.odi.Transaction.update);
      String s = persistentTask.getName();
      tr.commit(COM.odi.Transaction.RETAIN_UPDATE);
      return s;
   }

   /**
    * This method is not part of the remote interface.
    */
   public PersistentTask getPersistentTask()
      { return persistentTask; }

   private TaskServerImpl taskServer;
   private PersistentTask persistentTask;
}
```

An alternative architecture is one in which the middle tier is supplied by the object database product. In that case, the issue of serializing the persistent objects for transport goes away, because it is handled automatically by the persistent object layer. It is possible to design a heavy client, which accesses an object database on a remote server, while coding the application completely as if the database were local to the client. Most object database products provide remote access in this way.

The previous example does not address the issue of database object locking, for the sake of simplicity.

### *Evolution and Enterprise Integration*

Once you have built an object database, you will have the problem of maintaining it, which may include any or all of the following:

- Changes to the schema
- Moving the database—to different architecture machines, and maybe to different brands of database
- Interconnecting the applications to other kinds of database

When schema changes occur, there is the possibility that you will have to unload and reload the database. Before choosing a database, you should ask:

- What kinds of schema changes require a reload?
- Is a partial reload possible, or do I always have to reload the entire database?
- What tools are provided for building the reload process?

If you should have to migrate the database to a new platform, you will need to consider if the new platform supports the ODBMS product; and even if it does, is the database format compatible across platforms? If you need to perform a cross-ODBMS load, the ODMG standard includes the specification of a standard format for unloading and storing object database data. This format can be used for unloading data from one database and loading it into another. You should make sure that your ODBMS has a tool for writing a database snapshot in this format, which is called Object Interchange Format (OIF). Also, what if the database becomes corrupted: do you have to reload the database from a snapshot, or is it possible to make spot repairs?

Even if your application is to be written in Java, what if you need to provide access to the database from other applications that are not written in Java? If this is a possibility, the ODBMS should support bindings for other languages. The primary issue is then compatibility between the database when accessed via multiple languages—e.g., can a database written from Java be read from a C++ application?

Application integration frequently involves event notification. If the ODBMS provides an event service, is it compatible with existing standards, such as the OMG Event Service?

### *Network Implementations*

If your client application is to be deployed across a network, the application can either be designed as a two-tier or a three-tier configuration. A two-tier design will require that the ODBMS support a network implementation, in the same manner that a type 3 or 4 JDBC driver supports transparent remote access by clients.

Some ODBMS products use common protocols to implement the connection with the central database. For example, Poet uses IIOP as its wire protocol. Using a common protocol can help in establishing a pathway through a firewall. Also, you will want to check if the network client requires a native component, or if it is pure Java ("thin"). Is the network implementation secure, and can it tunnel through a firewall?

### *Concurrency and Performance*

The ODMG specification does not specify anything about database physical lock granularity. From an API point of view, objects are locked. However, the ODBMS is free to implement this with segment or page locking. While it is often claimed that very granular locking reduces performance, this is only true in a system that is primarily read-oriented. If the application involved updates during prime time, the highly granular locking can help improve concurrency. Some database systems claim to use very granular locking, but it turns out that when you implement serializable operations, the locking granularity has to become much larger; so evaluate this carefully in terms of what type of locking is actually used in different situations.

If the ODBMS provides an administrator with the ability to organize data, e.g., grouping objects by type (extent) or by relationships, this can help to tune the application.

Some ODBMSs now provide multiversion concurrency control (MVCC), which is discussed later in this chapter. MVCC is a very sophisticated capability which gives good benchmark results, and therefore makes the database vendor look good, but it is very hard to build reliable applications using this model unless it is limited to read-only applications; use in applications which update should be with care.

The quality of the database's OQL implementation will affect the speed with which OQL queries are processed. Also, the ODMG specification does not say anything about how queries are processed, such as whether they are atomic. The implication is that they are, since that would be consistent with the rest of the specification, but it is not explicitly stated. You should make sure that your implementation provides atomic query semantics. The specification also does not say if data retrieved in the process of performing a query is locked as a side effect.

### *Replication and Scalability*

A system often performs well for a small number of users, but performs poorly when lots of users are added. A high performance ODBMS will probably have a multithreaded design, with full isolation between threads. Various limitations can still come into play, however, as the number of database connections is increased. For example, as locks increase, can the system still maintain a high level of concurrency? Does lock management overhead scale linearly? And what is the resource footprint of a single connection? What is the overhead of an application that has a lot of persistent objects loaded? Or of maintaining object references across transactions?

What if the system fails? Does the ODBMS product provide any mirroring features? Does it allow you to switch over to a mirror system without loss of service? Another important feature for scalability is object clustering: the ability to organize the way the data is actually stored using knowledge of how it is accessed most of the time. Some object database products also provide the ability to interlink multiple database instances, achieving a federated network of databases which can grow to any size.

Finally, some products act primarily as object repositories and do not have a server-resident capability to execute methods on the object or to perform queries, relying on clients to do that. The problem is that the client cache may not be large enough for some queries, and it is also inefficient for some queries to transfer all the objects needed.

### *Multiple Client Connections*

Some object database products do not allow a single client process to open more than one database connection at a time. Further, some products I am aware of have this kind of limitation on some platforms, but not on others. (This problem also exists with some very popular relational databases.) The ability to open multiple database connections is often very valuable for work-process applications, in which users must juggle several tasks at the same time, so you should consider carefully if this is an important requirement, and check that the ODBMS can support it on your target platform.

### *Finding Objects*

There are primarily two approaches to finding an object in an object database: obtaining an extent, and performing a query or search on the extent; or maintaining a collection object for aggregating objects to search on, and performing the query or search on that. While extents are not supported by the ODMG standard at this time, many products provide an extent capability. Usually people who have mostly worked with relational databases in their career prefer the extent approach, and people who have done object-oriented programming prefer the collection object approach.

Both approaches suffer from potentially variable or large return collection sizes. This can be addressed by building an incremental query capability, as has already been discussed in the context of JDBC.

**OQL vs. Programmatic Traversal of Persistent Collections.** To perform the search—again regardless of whether you use extents or collection objects—you can use OQL, or implement your own search using a hashtable object, for example. The ODMG standard does not specify any indexed persistent object types such as hashtable, but many products provide them. As already discussed, however, all ODMG DCollection types have a query() method, which can be used to perform a search. This may not help you find multinational names, however. (See "Sorting and Comparing Unicode Using the Collator and CollationKey Classes" on page 344.)

### Storing Persistent Object References Inside of Controls

Often the contents of user interface controls are obtained from a database. For example, your application might allow the user to select a brand of car by picking from a drop-down list. The list of car brands available might be stored in the database, and if it is, a query will have to be performed to build the list. If the database has an object representing each car brand, you might want to store a persistent reference to that object in the list itself, so that when the user clicks on a selection, the associated object can be immediately identified.

This is not usually workable for a number of reasons. First, it means that your application will have to keep a transaction open for the duration of whatever the user is doing. An open transaction ties up resources. And what if you need to commit the transaction? When that happens, all of the references stored in the controls will immediately become stale, unless your ODBMS allows references to remain valid between transactions—and that has its own set of problems anyway.

There are other problems as well. For example, many controls which allow you to store general objects use the equals() method to determine which item was selected by the user. That means that you will have to implement the equals() method for your persistent objects.

In general, it is far better to store lightweight objects such as strings in controls, and have a mechanism for refreshing them when you receive an indication that they may be out of date.

### *Initial Instantiation of Control Objects*

One disadvantage of the object/relational blending products is that they usually generate a substantial amount of code for mapping the object model to a relational model. While it is usually the case that mapping classes only need to be loaded as they are used, and so one does not have to load all this code at one time, this may be unacceptable if user interface elements need to display choice lists and other tabular kinds of displays of database data. For example, suppose the application needs to give users a choice of geographic regions. To do this, the application will have to obtain the available regions from the database. This data, and the associated object/relational mapping classes, could be loaded as needed but this would result in an unacceptable delay the first time the drop-down list is selected. Depending on the nature of the user interface, and what data will be needed up front with each visual interface component, a strategy may need to be devised for anticipating when classes will be needed and loading them "just in time"—before the user actually requests them.

The alternative is to load all persistence classes at application startup. This may take a long time, especially if the classes are located on a server, and the connection between workstations and the server is not a fast one. It may be acceptable if the application is usually left running, or if it is locally deployed, e.g., with Castanet, or installed as an application.

Even if the class loading problem is solved, there is still the delay of going to the database to fill the contents of a dropdown list. An alternative is to embed this kind of data into Java classes. Since the class loading delay has been solved, according to our assumption, it will be fast or done before actually needed. An example from my own work was the embedding of a medical terminology index into Java classes, which were then deployed via Castanet. Lookups to the dictionary were then avoided, and the data was kept current via the Castanet update protocol.

A different solution is to presume that the user will pause a little while to think before clicking on something on a user interface, and use this time to populate the controls in a separate thread. Care must be taken to ensure that the controls are thread safe.

All of this may not be implemented in the initial stages of the project, and a solution still must be found to allow the application to start quickly, so that programmers can test effectively. It will therefore be necessary to create a small test database, with a restricted subset of control data, so that dropdown lists that would ordinarily come up with a choice of 40 geographic regions instead come up with a choice of two—sufficient to demonstrate functionality and test against.

### *Object/Relational ("Blend") Persistence Mapping Products*

Most organizations have relational databases. When a new object-oriented application is built, an important issue that comes up is whether or not to use that database or build a new one that is object based. If the relational database contains company data that is needed by the new application, then a link of some kind is needed to get data from the relational database to the object application. If, on the other hand, data generated by the object application will be used by other applications based on other technologies, then it may be necessary to provide a bridge from the object application to the others; often a relational database is used as such a bridge, although this is not a very effective way to implement such a bridge.

So-called "blend" products are products which bridge the object-relational gap, either by mapping an object model to a relational database, or by generating an object model from a relational schema, or both. Some examples of such products include the Object People's TopLink and Sun's JavaBlend™.

It generally makes sense to map a relational system to an object model, to allow relational data to be incorporated into object-oriented software without embedding SQL. From a purely technical point of view, however, it rarely makes sense to map an object model to a relational database. Organizations which do this usually do it for nontechnical reasons, such as the desire to limit the number of kinds of database servers that must be administered. An organization which has a lot of expertise in maintaining an existing relational server may have confidence in its robustness or security features, and be justifiably reluctant to bring in another product when the existing one could be used instead. In such a situation, using an object-to-relational mapping may be a way to develop software using an object model, with the intention of eventually transitioning it to an object database. The mapping can be used as an interim solution to allow the relational server to be used. The object layer does not mitigate programming problems, however, in dealing with transactional issues and data consistency.

Some of these products do not allow you to access more than one kind of database, or multiple databases at the same time; so if you need to do this, you should check that the product supports it.

Object-to-relational mapping products generally work adequately for simple applications. They tend to have difficulty when the application deals with relationships between objects, due to the fact that the way object oriented applications deal with relationships is so different from the way relational databases do. Some implementations need a separate database cursor for every object instance accessed by a client, which is not very scalable.

## Logical Object Transaction Models

Dealing with Java objects does not relieve the programmer from the need to consider transaction semantics. One must still define the boundaries of a transaction, when to commit, and potentially when to rollback. A model which omitted these features would fail to address the important requirement of defining isolation modes, and controlled commit of changes, which is extremely important in multiuser data applications. Persistent Java object databases therefore provide methods for defining transactions and their states. While most object databases define the granularity of a transaction as an object, the programmer must still consider the issue of what constitutes a logical transaction—which sets of object operations should be implemented as an atomic unit; and related to this, which sets of objects constitute pieces of a larger whole, and therefore should be changed together and kept consistent. It is therefore necessary to develop some concepts for defining the boundaries of a transaction that changes objects, rather than tables. For now, I will focus on transaction boundaries, and leave discussion of locking and isolation modes for a later section.

### *Transaction Boundaries*

To successfully build a persistent object multiuser application, one must consider factors similar to building a comparable relational application; specifically, transaction boundaries, granularity, and correctness, and object locking and concurrent access policies. The considerations are the same—the implementation and specific techniques are different.

The basic rule of thumb in designing a transaction application for a relational database is: when a transaction completes, it leaves the database in a well-defined, self-describing state, so that any subsequent transactions by any other user can proceed based only on the content of the database. Sometimes a distinction is made between "logical" and "physical" transactions, in that the former represent a self-defining unit of work, and the latter represent actual and potentially incomplete physical updates to the data. When a physical transaction represents only a portion of a logical transaction, a mechanism must be designed into the application to ensure that other users do not use the results of the physical transaction until the entire logical transaction completes, which may consist of a series of physical transactions over time.

The reason that logical transactions may be divided into distinct physical transactions is because a logical transaction may require a long duration, and locking the relevant data for that period may have performance consequences for other database users. This distinction adds complexity to a design, but it is a valuable concept for large-scale applications.

An object-oriented database has the same considerations. Rather than designing tables, however, one designs an object model of the system under consideration. The object model is the same model that programmers write code against. The only difference between code that accesses the object model and the rest of the application code is that code that accesses persistent objects must occur within a transaction. Thus, one is still faced with the task of defining the logical transactions for the system.

### *Defining Objects by Composition*

Transactions in an object-oriented database result in the creation or modification of objects and object trees—modification when history is not required, and creation when it is. Before explaining these distinctions, we must first understand an important concept: object composition. Consider the following:

```
class Book
{
   String title;
   int nPages;
   Date whenPublished;
}
```

Class Book contains references to two Java objects: one String and one Date. It also contains an embedded value: an int, containing the number of pages of the book. In Java, objects may only be contained within other objects by reference, and so an instance of Book does not physically contain the corresponding title string or the whenPublished date—it merely references them, as distinct objects. In the Book class, however, it is easy to see that the objects referenced by an instance of Book are logically part of that instance—they are unique to it, and inextricably linked. In such a case, one can imagine that if one were to make a copy of (clone) a Book, one would want to make a complete copy of all of its embedded objects as well, because we would then have two complete and distinct instances of book, rather than two Books which really point to the same internal data. In other words, if we make a copy of a Book, we want to be sure that we can modify that instance of book without affecting the original book. We can do this only if we clone all of its internal data when we copy it. (We will ignore the issue of immutable objects for the moment.)

Now consider the following modification to Book:

```
class AuthoredBook
{
   String title;
   int nPages;
```

```
   Date whenPublished;
   Author author;
}

class Author
{
   String name;
   String address;
   List otherBooks;
}
```

In this example, we have added an author reference. The question is: if we clone an AuthoredBook, do we want to clone the author as well? Probably not, because the author is distinct in its own right, and we really only want to maintain a reference to an independent Author object. In that way, if the author changes address, the new address will be reflected in all objects that references the author. In AuthoredBook, the piece of information that is *part of* (composes) the book is not the author, but the *reference* to an author. Defining which instance objects (i.e., class variables that are objects) logically belong to the containing class, and which are merely references to independent objects, is called *defining the composition* of a class. Note that an instance object can belong to only one containing class; a composition therefore represents a hierarchy. Some nomenclatures refer to composition paths as "primary links."

In designing a persistent object system, it is very important to define the logical composition of objects. A transaction usually begins at the root level of some composition, and requires locks on contained objects down to some level along some path in the hierarchy for that composition. Depending on whether history is required for that composition, the transaction may result in an entirely new object subtree; or, if history is not required, some links or values may simply be modified.

A transaction is therefore viewed as the construction or modification of a complete composite object hierarchy. Object databases typically provide transaction isolation mechanisms to ensure the integrity of object modifications, but isolation is at the granularity of a Java class. An object database has no knowledge of object compositions. This is analogous to the distinction between logical and physical transactions in a relational database. The DBMS will ensure the integrity of a physical transaction, but it is up to the application to provide guarantees for logical transaction completeness and correctness (consistency). In other words, by explicitly defining transaction boundaries, the application design must not permit partial logical transactions to occur; and in the context of an object database, the application must make sure, through the design of its update processes, that the object composition model intended by the schema designers is adhered to. Using the example of the Book class above to illustrate, note that the whenPublished class variable is a Date object. It would be possible to go into the database and modify the Date object of any book, without locking the corresponding Book instance. Doing so, however, risks that at the same time, someone else is modifying the book, and setting the whenPublished reference to point to a different date object—and so, while we think we have reset the date, we have not succeeded, because someone else made the book point to a different date! The solution is to recognize that a Book object owns its whenPublished Date object, and we cannot allow any transaction to obtain the whenPublished Date without first obtaining (and locking) the book, i.e., we must obtain the composite subtree, from the root book down to the whenPublished object.

**clone(), equals(), and Deep vs. Shallow Copy.** The terms "deep" and "shallow" copy are used frequently to mean copying an object and all the things it points to (contains); and copying just the object's nonreference data, respectively. In Java, this distinction is not syntactically explicit because Java objects contain *all* their instance objects by reference. Further, as we have seen, it is important to distinguish between compositional and noncompositional links, and so a deep copy, if applied blindly, may copy too much.

C++ has the concept of a copy constructor, which serves the purpose of making a copy (clone) of an object. C++ confuses the issue, however, by allowing objects to physically contain other objects. It is often the case, in C++ and in Java, that an object logically contains another object, *regardless of whether it physically contains it* (e.g., several objects may share a single immutable copy of the contained object, by reference; this is often the case with string classes). The programmer is led to believe that if an object is included by reference, then a copy operation should not include the referenced object. This is not the case, however, and *the semantics of a copy operation require that contained or referenced objects are copied if they are logically owned by the containing object.* In C++ you would achieve this by writing the copy constructor with an initializer list that uses the members of the class to initialize the copy; if you don't do this, a shallow copy is effectively performed, since default constructors are then used for members. In Java, the equivalent decision comes into play in how you code the clone() method.

The Java Object class has a clone() method, which serves the purpose of a copy constructor. This method must be overridden, and implemented with compositional copy semantics, for any class which needs to provide a copy operation. If your class needs a copy operation, you should redefine the clone() method as public, and provide a correct compositional implementation for it. A cloneable class should implement Cloneable, call super.clone() as its first statement, call clone() on each of its primary mutable object members, and ensure that all its object members are cloneable. An object is "mutable" if it can be modified, and a class member is considered to be "primary" if the class can be said to own the member, with the restriction that an object can only be owned by at most one other object at any time. These concepts will be discussed further below, but for now consider this example of implementing the clone() method:

```
public class A implements Cloneable
{
    int x;
    public Object clone() { return super.clone(); }
}
public class B implements Cloneable
{
    int y;
    String s;
    A a;
    public Object clone()
    {
        Object o = super.clone();
        o.a = a.clone();
        return o;
    }
    ...
}
```

This clone() method will successfully make a deep copy of any instance of B. Remember that you only explicitly clone *primary* mutable object members. Also, note that the clone() methods of most built-in Java collection types implement shallow copy semantics; so if you need deep copy semantics, you must manually clone each collection member.

The Object class also defines a method called equals(), which can be used to compare the values of two objects. Comparing an object with its clone should return true. The default implementation of the equals() method is to simply compare the reference values of the target and parameter, which is not correct, because Java already has a built-in operator for comparing object references—the "==" operator. If your class needs to provide an equals() method, you must implement correct semantics for this method, and compare the class members one by one. If your class extends Object directly, do not include super.equals() as a required condition in your implementation.

**Predefined Collection Types.** A composite may consist of or contain a collection object of some kind. Most collection types do not implement clone() as a deep copy operation. However, many have a deep copy operation, and in fact must to be useful for defining object compositions. You may want to extend the type and implement clone() and equals() for the collection type, to make sure it has the semantics that are consistent with your application. In general, you will need collections that are "owning" collections, and collections that are "referencing" collections—i.e., not owning.

Thus, if you have a third-party collection type called Collection, and it has deepCopy() and shallowCopy() methods, and you are satisfied that its equals() method implements the behavior you want, you might extend it as follows:

```
public class NonPrimaryCollection extends Collection
{
   public Object clone() { return shallowCopy(); }
}

public class PrimaryCollection extends Collection
{
   public Object clone() { return deepCopy(); }
}
```

**Defining Mutability.** Cloning entire composite objects is potentially very expensive. In practice, it is actually not very expensive, if care is taken to define object mutability. A *mutable* object is one which can be modified after it is constructed. Conversely, an *immutable* object cannot be modified once constructed.

The Java String class is an example of an immutable object. Once created, a String cannot be changed. Thus, in the previous Book class example on page 407, if one constructs an instance of Book, and sets the value of the title in the process, the String object pointed to by the title reference can never be changed. To change the book title, one must create a new String object, and set the title reference to point to it.

Immutable objects have an advantage in that they can be shared. If a single immutable object is shared by multiple other objects, those objects can rest assured that their shared copy will not be changed—because it is immutable. Thus, they have the perception that they have their own virtual private copy of the object, since its value will never change unless they change it—and in that case, they simply create a new immutable object (which might end up being shared).

Composite objects can use the immutable object concept to economize on object duplication during cloning. If a root object logically is composed of a tree of objects, then when the root object and its subtree is constructed, the subtree objects can be marked as immutable. A clone operation on the root would then know to copy immutable objects by reference, rather than by physical copy. Thus, when cloning an object tree, the only new storage required is for copying any objects that are not immutable.

A composite class may be treated as immutable, and then all child objects of the class should be treated as immutable—they should never be changed once constructed. Creating a new composite object would typically consist of cloning an existing object as a starting point (or creating an empty object), and then setting its references to point to new instances of child objects, resulting in a new composite. The new composite might share immutable members with the cloned composite, but it has the appearance of having its own copy of everything.

You can enforce immutability by simply using discipline within your code (i.e., by defining policies for object modification); or, you can take advantage of the ability to define it explicitly using features of the programming language or API. Java allows you to define data values and object references which are final, but can be initialized explicitly. In other words, you can assign to them, but only once. If such a final reference is to an immutable object, you have effectively defined an object constant: Once given a value, the value cannot be changed. For example:

```
public class MyImmutableComposite
{
   public final String name;    // this is a "blank final" - it
                                // becomes final once it is set
   public final int value;      //    "        "      "      "       "

   public MyImmutableComposite(String n, int v)
   {
      name = n;     // once set here, can never be changed
      value = v;    //              "       "       "    "
   }
}
```

The above class defines an immutable type, because once an instance is created, its members can never be changed. This may be too restrictive an implementation, however, especially if the process of construction cannot be nicely encapsulated into a single routine, but rather is a long process involving user interaction. In that case, an immutable flag may be used. For example:

```
public class MyImmutablyFlaggedComposite
{
   private boolean mutable = true;
```

```
    private String name;

    public MyImmutablyFlaggedComposite()
    {
        // This is initial incomplete construction only
    }

    public String getName() { return name; }
    public void setName(String n)
    {
        if (! mutable) throw new RuntimeException(
            "Attempt to alter immutable object");
        name = n;
    }

    public boolean getMutable() { return mutable; }
    /**
     * Routine for setting this object's mutability. This is
     * package protected, so that only other
     * classes within this package can call this method. In
     * effect, we only want "friends" to call this.
     */
    void setMutable(boolean m) { mutable = m; }
}
```

If a class that must be treated as immutable is from an external source and you therefore cannot modify its behavior, then immutability will have to be handled as a policy implemented by the clients of the class, or you could extend the class and add (im)mutability constraints.

**The `transient` Keyword.** The keyword "transient" should not be interpreted to mean "nonprimary." Primary links are nontransient; but nontransient links may or may not be primary. If a link is marked as transient, it will not be made persistent—we want even nonprimary links to be persistent.

Unfortunately, serializing an object will collect all nontransient links (i.e., nonprimary links as well). Thus, to serialize a persistent object, you may need a method to construct a self-contained object for transport; but you would likely need this anyway, since it does not make sense to serialize persistent objects—you would likely construct a serializable "message" or "command" object.

### *Saving Change History*

An important issue in most business applications is whether to save change history (which I will refer to as simply "history" for short) or not. Some transactions require history, and some do not. For example, a hospital application which records changes to a patient chart will likely require history, to show the complete picture of the patient's progress and treatment. On the other hand, a system which schedules the movement of materials in a manufacturing plant probably does not care where a certain item was last week—it only cares where it is right now—and so history is not needed.

Classes that do not need history should not be immutable. When we need to modify the object, we do it "in place"—simply modify it, without cloning. On the other hand, those classes that need history should be immutable. This especially applies to the root composite class of a transaction. When we need to change an immutable class instance, we are forced to clone the existing one and make a new copy. This ensures that the old copy is not modified (although, of course, we need to implement a change history retrieval mechanism to be able to find it).

To illustrate: If, for example, your application consisted of updates to flight reservations for passengers, the root object in a transaction would perhaps be an instance of an itinerary for a particular passenger. Since we would not care what changes had been made to the itinerary over time, prior to travel, and are only interested in the final flight bookings, we do not need change history. When making a change, we simply modify the reservation's references to existing flights. History is lost. If, on the other hand, we did care about history for some reason, then to make a change we would clone the existing complete itinerary for the passenger, and then make modifications as required.

It is important to realize that the clone operation does not necessarily physically copy all flight information. The only references that are traversed deeply by a clone operation are those that are not immutable, and those which are also owned by the current composite object (i.e., primary links). Thus, a clone operation may in fact be very economical, if the design allows for the designation of which links are primary, and which objects are immutable.

In summary, if we need to keep history, we must make the root transaction object immutable, so that when it must be changed, an entire new one must be created, preserving the old (which is presumably added to a history list of some sort).

For cloning, immutability means that copy-by-reference is feasible. It is purely an implementation consideration. Immutable or not, objects that are strict members of a composite object should not be changed, unless the root composite is obtained exclusively first. Since a clone operation assumes that an immutable object has immutable members, that means that no primary member of a subtree of an immutable object may be treated as mutable by any operation within the entire system. This guarantees that the clone operation can copy by reference, and be assured that members of the composite are correctly included in the copy. Further, mutability is a property that, once set to *immutable*, cannot be changed back, unless it can be guaranteed that all composite references to the object will be converted into new clones.

### *Views*

Conceptually, views are noncomposite objects, which represent an alternative way of looking at a composite object, or some kind of cross section. A view does not own the objects that it is a view of. It may be a composite object in its own right, with attribute members, but it is not a view of those—it is the root composite. For example, a view may contain its own timestamp information, indicating an event, and indicating by reference which composite objects participated in that event. With regard to the timestamp information, the view object is a composite; but with regard to the references to other composites, the view object is merely a view.

As an example, a summary of all passengers on a specified flight would be a view. The view references the itinerary objects of various passengers, and associates them with a flight. The view does not own the itineraries—it merely references them—and cloning the view should at most result in copying references to itinerary components, and never actually copying the itinerary components, since the latter may change if the itinerary is updated. An exception is if a "snapshot" is taken, in that case, the view owns the snapshot—the snapshot is part of the view's composition—and the copy is therefore merely part of the process of constructing the view. From that point on, the snapshot is not related to the original itinerary—it is merely a snapshot of a historical itinerary.

Another type of view would be a proposed change to an object hierarchy. If the change is approved, the view can replace the actual object—the proposed view becomes the current approved version of the object.

### *Garbage Collection of Resources Assigned to Voided Objects*

Just like Java, object databases have automatic garbage collection mechanisms that reclaim objects that are no longer referenced. As with Java, however, such mechanisms are not totally hands off: the programmer must still make sure that references to unused objects are set to null so that the mechanism will recognize an object as being unused. Dangling references to retired objects will prevent those objects from being reclaimed, and constitutes a memory leak.

An example of when this can occur is with nonprimary links. If an object is logically owned by another object, then the owning object has a primary link to the owned object. If the owning object is retired, then links to it will be programmatically set to null, freeing it to be collected—or so one would hope. Suppose, however, that the owned object still is pointed to by some other object that references it for some purpose. In that case, the object will never be reclaimed, because something points to it. Further, if the owned object has a pointer as well back to its parent, the parent will never be reclaimed, as a result of its child never being reclaimed. This cascading effect can tie up a lot of storage.

A concrete example may help. Consider the case of a banking application, in which a customer has obtained a loan, secured by securities. When the loan matures, it may be archived and deleted from the database. However, the securities used to secure the loan may still exist. The loan will surely reference the securing instruments, and those instruments will probably have pointers to all the loans they are currently being used to secure. If these "used-to-secure" pointers are not set to null when the loan is removed from the database, the loan objects may never get reclaimed, because the securities still point to them. This is a garbage collection issue, especially if the loan application cannot be sure who is making references to its objects. The solution is to have a database schema that is well documented and controlled by a database administrator; to have well-defined object composite hierarchies; and for each object type, to define the removal process for that object.

## Database Locking and Isolation

### *Understanding Transaction Isolation*

A database's transaction isolation level defines how it handles various situations involving simultaneous access to data by more than one transaction. Three important situations to consider are the cases of dirty reads, repeatable reads, and phantom reads.

**Dirty Read.** A dirty read is when a transaction reads uncommitted changes made by another transaction. There is the risk that these changes may not be committed, and so the reading transaction will have read invalid data and not know it. From a transaction processing point of view, dirty reads are always undesirable. A collaborative groupware system, however, may permit dirty reads, although more likely it would use a versioning capability.

**Repeatable Read.** Repeatable reads are guaranteed if the data read by a transaction is locked against changes from other transactions, until the current transaction is done. Thus, the transaction can presume that if it reads the same data twice, it will get the same result.

Some databases claim to have repeatable reads by implementing a technique in which they present the user with a snapshot that remains static for the duration of the transaction—even though the data represented by the snapshot may be changed by another transaction. In effect, your snapshot represents an old version of the database. The usefulness of this way of achieving "virtual" repeatable reads depends on whether an application needs to have up-to-date data at all times.

**Phantom Read.** Phantoms are undetected items of data added to the database by another transaction while a transaction is in progress. The data that is added is undetected, because the current transaction is using the results of a query made when it started. In a system that is serializable, the entire set of data would be locked against updates, and so the phantom could not be created until the first transaction is done.

These isolation levels are recognized by the SQL2 standard:

*0 ("Read Uncommitted"):* Dirty reads, nonrepeatable reads and phantom reads can occur.

*1 ("Read Committed"):* Dirty reads are prevented; nonrepeatable reads and phantom reads can occur.

*2 ("Repeatable Read"):* Dirty reads and nonrepeatable reads are prevented; phantom reads can occur.

*3 ("Serializable"):* Dirty reads, nonrepeatable reads and phantom reads are prevented.

**Locking.** To address these phenomena, we have to distinguish between read locking and write locking, and various exclusivity modes of access. Read locking ensures that other transactions cannot obtain the data for update while one or more transactions that hold read locks on the same data are in progress.

Write locking, which can only be granted for an element of data if no other transaction holds a write lock on that data, obtains the data for update. Write locking can be exclusive (prevent other transactions from making dirty uncommitted reads of this transaction's changes) or not. If not exclusive, the isolation level determines the semantics of simultaneous reads while the update transaction is in progress.

The granularity for read locking may be a single row (ensures cursor stability), the portion of a result set read so far (repeatable reads), a full result set (ensures serializability), an object (for an object database), an arbitrary-sized block or page of records, or an entire table.

The terminology used to describe database locks may be slightly different from one product to another. In addition, the concepts of isolation and locking are often mixed, since they so strongly affect one another and isolation may be implemented using locks. For the purpose of the discussion here, I will define the following kinds of locks. This terminology is compatible with most products across both the relational and object database domains.

- **read lock**—Concurrent reads by other read-locking transactions are allowed, but writes by this or any other transaction are prevented. Prevents other transactions from obtaining an exclusive write lock. Note that some databases may permit reading without obtaining a read lock—reading and read locks are separate concepts.

- **write lock**—Concurrent writes by other transactions are not allowed. Prevents other transactions from obtaining a read or write lock. Other transactions may read the data (as long as they do not need to obtain a read lock to do so), but may not see your modifications until you commit them, depending on the isolation level. If you must escalate this lock to an exclusive write lock (see below) before actually making writes, then the write lock is known as an ***intention* write lock**. An intention write lock prevents other transactions from obtaining a lock (of any kind), and effectively reserves an exclusive lock while allowing reading (as long as reading does not require a read lock). This allows others to read the data until you are ready to obtain the exclusive lock and actually do the update.
- **exclusive write lock**—Concurrent *write or read* locks by other transactions are not allowed. Prevents other transactions from obtaining a read lock or any type of write lock.

A no-wait policy for lock conflicts is very useful. With such a policy, if a transaction tries to obtain a lock and cannot, due to a conflict, it would immediately throw an exception. This allows the application to possibly report to the user that the requested data is in use, or perhaps try the transaction again a few times. A system which automatically retries or waits will be dependent on the locking granularity of the particular DBMS for its design correctness.

**Achieving Consistency.** A database is "consistent" if its transactions do not make conflicting changes to the data.

Two approaches to providing true consistency across changes that must be made in two or more steps are:

- **Pessimistic Policy**: Lock all data you use (write *or read*) and perform all the work within a single physical transaction.
- **Optimistic Policy**: Before you commit your transaction, verify that nothing you have used (written *or read*) has been changed by another transaction—if so, raise an error condition and do not make any changes.

A pessimistic approach can be implemented if all transactions obtain at least read locks on data they read, and write locks on data they write, and hold those locks until they commit. This approach is not the default update mode of many products, however. For example, Oracle has two kinds of isolation modes, which they call "Read Committed" and "Serializable." Neither mode guarantees correct and serializable transactions, unless queries occurring in update transactions use the "FOR UPDATE" construct, which enforces a write lock policy.

Unfortunately, different database products have different levels of locking granularity. Some databases lock at the record level, some at the page level (which corresponds to no boundary visible to the application!), and some at the table level. Locking an entire table for every read is not practical if the system is update-intensive. However, it may be the only way to guarantee correct and consistent results. It may be necessary to batch updates to optimize the use of tables once the required exclusive table locks are obtained. If the application is update-intensive, it is critical to choose a database which provides the right level of locking granularity.

### *The Importance of Locking Data You Have Read*

Many relational and object database products provide built-in support for a kind of optimistic locking, in which they can detect if changes have been made by another transaction to data you have modified. That is, you do not need to hold a read lock, because the system does a check before committing your change and tells you if someone else has changed something you are trying to change. If using such a feature, you must recognize that it is also important to either lock or check data which is merely read as part of a transaction.

Suppose, for example, that your application computes and stores a total based on values it reads in separate queries. If in the process another user's transaction modifies one of those values, your computed result will be out of sync with regard to the values it has read; that is, the stored total will not equal the actual total of the other values. For this reason, if an update transaction must always reflect an accurate relationship of some kind with respect to other data, all that data—including all data read, not just data which is updated—must be either locked during the full duration of the transaction, or all the data must be checked for changes before the update transaction is committed.

In some cases it is possible to encode such integrity relationships in the database, using triggers and other mechanisms. This is not possible, however, if the relationship cannot be explicitly encoded, such as if it is a result of a judgment involving a human. As an illustration, a doctor might make a diagnosis based on the latest information on a patient. In that case the diagnosis, which may include the prescription of treatment and drugs, is based on the doctor's professional analysis of the current data. If new data arrives while the doctor is preparing the diagnosis, the diagnosis may be based on obsolete data when it is actually committed.

Such long duration interactions should always include an automated verification step at the end to see if any data which was read during the operation has changed. Even if long duration update locks are used, the results cannot be trusted unless all data which is read is also locked, or unless data which was read is also verified at commit time. Alternatively, a separate process could be used to notify the user when any data which was read has been updated. The use of advisory events to help provide consistency is discussed later in this chapter.

Often the consequences of inconsistency are tolerable and are outweighed by the performance gain of always allowing read access to data. The cost of ensuring complete consistency must be weighed against the cost of those inconsistencies and any manual handling they may require. Applications which are retrieval oriented and do not need to be absolutely current can safely use relaxed concurrency control strategies such as not using read locks or by using database snapshots, which is discussed next.

**Multi-Version Concurrency Control.** Multi-Version Concurrency Control (MVCC) is a technique for achieving a form of virtual serializability, without paying the price of obtaining exclusive locks for data being read, or in many cases, even written. Each transaction is given a unique view of the database, representing a "snapshot" of the state of the data at the moment at which the transaction begins. This snapshot is computed, based on record modification timestamps. Many current database products provide this model as an option, indluding Oracle and ObjectStore. The ObjectStore version of MVCC, however, is a read-only model.

Since the transaction has a snapshot computed at an instant in time, it is fully consistent within itself. For example, one can be sure that any relationship constraints between the data will hold, such as an account balance field being equal to the sum of account entries. MVCC is a way of putting blinders on, and saying, "I don't care what the rest of the world is doing—I'm operating on yesterday's assumptions, and results based on those assumptions are what you will get." This is often sufficient with read-only applications but an application which updates usually needs the current value of the data.

MVCC can be claimed to be serializable in the sense that it provides data update consistency, and so your transaction yields the same result whether someone else's transaction begins just after yours and proceeds in parallel, or waits until yours is almost done before it starts—your transaction behaves as an atomic unit. However, in many situations this is not good enough, as we saw above. It sometimes is vital to have the latest data, and to know if someone has changed assumptions you have made. Sometimes MVCC is good enough, though. In applications that mainly provide data, and which do not need to be completely up-to-date, this tends to be adequate. MVCC systems are also vulnerable to the "Snapshot too old" message, indicating that the transaction has lasted too long and a snapshot can no longer be computed.

MVCC protects consistency within the isolated world of your snapshot, but does not guarantee correct operation in the context of the database as a whole unless read locks are also used. Global data integrity is therefore guaranteed relative to transaction start time, rather than transaction commit time.

In general, data consistency must be measured at commit time, not transaction start time, as is the case with some MVCC implementations. If measured in this way, MVCC without read or write locking of all data read, and write locking of all data modified, is not truly serializable.

### *Implementing Pessimistic Locking*

Let's look at an example of using pessimistic locking. In the following program, I obtain data using Oracle's FOR UPDATE clause, which has the effect of obtaining an exclusive lock on the data. This ensures that locks are acquired on the data being read as well as written. Other transactions that read any of the same data *should also use* FOR UPDATE; otherwise, they may read obsolete data—this policy can be relaxed only if it is proven on a case-by-case basis that the results will still be correct.

```
Class.forName(drivername);
Connection con = DriverManager.getConnection(urlString, userid,
   password);
con.setAutoCommit(false);

// Perform a query, and lock all rows that are involved
Statement s = con.createStatement();
ResultSet emps = null;
try
{
   emps = s.executeQuery
      ("SELECT * FROM EMP WHERE DEPTNO=30 FOR UPDATE");
   // The above is pessimistic, because we lock the required
   // records and don't release them
   // until we are completely done - see below.
}
catch (Exception ex)    // We catch Exception instead of
                        // SQLException, because we don't know if
                        // the driver will throw a
                        // RuntimeException if it detects deadlock
{
   // May be contention for this data, or even deadlock...
   // notify user of potential contention
   con.rollback();
   return;
}

// Here we perform another query; locks are still in effect
Statement t = con.createStatement();
```

```
ResultSet nrs = null;
int n;
try
{
   nrs = t.executeQuery
      ("SELECT COUNT(*) FROM EMP WHERE DEPTNO=10"); nrs.next();
   n = nrs.getInt(1);
   System.out.println("There were " + n
      + " employees in Dept. 10");
}
catch (Exception ex)
{
   // May be contention for this data, or even deadlock
   // ...notify user of potential contention
   con.rollback();
   return;
}
// Assign top-producing employees to dept 10, based on salary
try
{
   for (; emps.next();) // each employee
   {
      int eno = emps.getInt("EMPNO");
      int sal = emps.getInt("SAL");
      int deptno = emps.getInt("DEPTNO");
      if ((sal > 2000) && (deptno != 10)) s.executeUpdate(
         "UPDATE EMP SET DEPTNO=10 WHERE EMPNO=" + eno);
   }
}
catch (Exception ex)
{
   // May be contention for this data, or even deadlock...
   // notify user of potential contention
   con.rollback();
   return;
}

try
{
   // Re-do the count; notice that we can see the effect of our
   // own update - others cannot
   // (Some databases have modes in which you cannot see your own
   // updates, until you commit)
   nrs = t.executeQuery
      ("SELECT COUNT(*) FROM EMP WHERE DEPTNO=10");
   nrs.next();
   n = nrs.getInt(1);
   System.out.println("There are now " + n +
      " employees in Dept. 10");
```

```
    // Now we commit, and free all rows that were locked.
    // According to a pessimistic policy,
    // we held all locks until our commit.
    con.commit();
}
catch (Exception ex)
{
    // May be contention for this data, or even deadlock...
    // notify user of potential contention
    con.rollback();
    return;
}
```

It is interesting that often the modes supported by a driver, especially a remote client driver, can be limited and in some cases may not even include the modes supported by the database itself. For example, one driver we tested threw the following exception if you attempted to set the isolation mode to SERIALIZABLE:

```
java.sql.SQLException: setTransactionIsolation: Only supports
TRANSACTION_READ_UNCOMMITTED
```

Yet in this case the database itself only supported the READ_COMMITTED and SERIALIZABLE modes (i.e., the driver claims it only supports an isolation mode that the server itself does not support)! Shop around for a driver from a third party that specializes in JDBC drivers.

Other drivers have other problems. One driver we tested, for example, does not allow you to call setAutoCommit() with a value of true—i.e., auto-commit is always off. As you can see, while the JDBC API is a generic API, the behavior of an actual application written with JDBC will vary from one database to another.

Using pessimistic locking for long durations—in "user time"—is generally a bad idea, for these reasons:

- A transaction will hold ALL its locks until it is committed, and some may have been converted to table locks (e.g., Oracle uses table locks when SELECT FOR UPDATE is used).
- Sequence numbers (such as Sybase's timestamp value) wrap eventually.
- The chance that the system will go down during the transaction is greatly increased.
- If the system uses MVCC, the chance that a "snapshot-too-old" or "rollback-segment-too-small" message being generated is greatly increased—the system can no longer construct query results for a transaction that began a long time ago.

It may seen improbable that a user would take so long that some of these things could occur frequently. However, computers today are multiwindow, and if the work is process-oriented rather than transaction-oriented, it is very conceivable that users will often leave windows minimized or applications open for long periods—even weeks.

User-time locks are often used acceptably in situations when the data that is locked is limited to data specific to a user "session" and is of interest primarily by a single user. Contention for the data is then not an issue because only that user needs to access the data. If sessions are still relatively short compared to the time between server restarts, and the risk of losing session data in the event of a system loss is not a concern, then user-time locks for session-specific data are a viable model. This is in essence a special case, however, and the database design should be checked to make sure that the data that needs to be locked does not result in a lock promotion causing other data to be locked which is not part of the session. Session data is typically better handled using an application server which can maintain session state without relying on a database. This is discussed in Chapter 8.

If user-time locks are needed, reexamine the design to see if they can be eliminated, and if not, consider a checkout model, as described later in "Checkout-based Locking (Application-based Write Locking)" on page 433.

### Implementing Optimistic Locking

You can use a database's built-in optimistic mode to implement an optimistic policy, if it has one, or you can use granular and short-lived pessimistic locks and implement an overall optimistic policy yourself. The latter is necessary if the database does not have a truly serializable optimistic mechanism—one which prevents concurrent modification to data you have read—data which you have used to compute your own update.

Oracle maintains a "System Control Number" (SCN) to represent each database snapshot it uses. This is used by Oracle's SERIALIZABLE mode to implement an optimistic policy: When an Oracle "serializable" transaction commits, the SCN of the transaction is compared with the SCN of records it is trying to modify, and if their SCN is higher, the commit fails. Thus, the check is done at commit time, and so it is optimistic. However, this particular implementation does not prevent other transactions from updating data we have *read*, and therefore getting inconsistent data, as we have seen.

A true optimistic policy must check not only that data it wants to modify has not been changed by someone else, but in fact it must check that all data it has accessed in any way—has read, or wants to modify—has not been changed by

someone else. With Oracle, to prevent that, a transaction modifying *anything* should, in general, use the FOR UPDATE clause for read queries, to lock the data that it reads, regardless of whether it updates that particular data or not. This, however, converts the policy from optimistic to pessimistic.

If this is done, the SERIALIZABLE mode is largely redundant, since it protects against data you are modifying from changing, but using FOR UPDATE will lock the data you read and thereby prevent it from changing—and usually you read data before you modify it. The downside of this is that it can severely affect performance. Therefore, use FOR UPDATE only when updates represent computed values that must be absolutely consistent with other data items. If an update is merely the addition of information and does not produce a computed result, it may be possible to avoid using FOR UPDATE.

To implement your own optimistic locking, you can either compare the actual values of data read and written to see if they have changed, or you can compare instead something else that tracks with the value of the data. An example of the latter is a hashcode of the data. Another example is a timestamp of when the data was written. Some systems automatically timestamp or sequence records, and if that is the case and the sequence number or timestamp value is accessible, you can use it, or you can write your own timestamp.

**Optimistic Locking Using Explicit Timestamps.** Here is a simple example of using a manually written timestamp to verify that input data has not changed in the course of a transaction, and thereby implement an optimistic policy. (The TableArea class is not shown, but is assumed to be a TextArea which generates an ActionEvent when a row is clicked on, with the event's action command set to a string containing the row number that was clicked on by the user.)

```
import java.awt.*;
import java.awt.event.*;
import java.sql.*;
import java.util.*;

public class DBDemo3 extends Panel
{
   static String drivername = "oracle.jdbc.driver.OracleDriver";
   static String urlString = "jdbc:oracle:thin:@a1:1521:ORCL";
   static String userid = "scott";
   static String password = "tiger";

   public static void main(String[] args)
   {
      Frame f = new Frame();
      f.setSize(600, 300);
```

```
      try
      {
         BDemo3 d = new DBDemo3();
         f.add("Center", d);
      }
      catch (Exception ex)
      {
         System.out.println("Could not complete query - try
            later");
         System.exit(0);
      }
      f.show();
   }

   Connection con;
   // Now display employees in a list, and allow user to select
   // one...
   Vector vn = new Vector();
   Vector vi = new Vector();
   Vector vt = new Vector();
   TableArea textArea = new TableArea(5, 60);
   TextField salField = new TextField(10);

   public DBDemo3() throws Exception
   {
      Class.forName(drivername);
      con = DriverManager.getConnection(urlString, userid,
         password);
      Statement s = con.createStatement();
      ResultSet emp = s.executeQuery(
         "SELECT * FROM EMP WHERE ENAME = 'JONES'");
      // We did not specify "FOR UPDATE", so locks will be
      // released as soon as
      // we are done reading the result set

      for (int r = 0;emp.next(); r++)
      {
         String name = emp.getString("ENAME");
         int id = emp.getInt("EMPNO");
         Timestamp ts = emp.getTimestamp("TS");
         vn.addElement(name);
         vi.addElement(new Integer(id));
         vt.addElement(ts);
      }
      textArea.set(vn);
      con.commit();    // this guarantees we are freeing locks,
                       // regardless of the autocommit state
```

```
    textArea.addActionListener
    (
       new ActionListener()
       {
          public void actionPerformed(ActionEvent e)
          {
             // Figure out which row was selected
             int row = Integer.parseInt
                (e.getActionCommand());
             // (we assume that the GUI component
             // triggering this
             // event has the ability to determine which
             // row the user selected)

             // Now correlate the row with the vector of
             // customers
             String name = (String)(vn.elementAt(row));
             int eid = ((Integer)(vi.elementAt(row))).
                intValue();
             int newsal = Integer.parseInt
                (salField.getText());
             Timestamp ts = (Timestamp)
                (vt.elementAt(row));
             try { updateSalary(eid, newsal, ts); }
                catch (Exception ex)
             {
                System.out.println(
                "Unable to update salary...stack " +
                   "trace follows");
                ex.printStackTrace();
             }
             System.out.println("Update completed");
          }
       }
    );
    add(textArea);
    add(salField);
}
/**
 * This action handler is called much later - in user time.
 */
public void updateSalary(int eid, int newsal, Timestamp ts)
    throws Exception
{
    // Look up the selected employee - lock records for the
    // time it takes to do this update only
    Statement s = con.createStatement();
```

```
        ResultSet rs = s.executeQuery(
            "SELECT ENAME, SAL, TS FROM EMP WHERE EMPNO = "
            + eid + " FOR UPDATE");

        // It is unlikely, although possible, that the person's
        // info has changed
        // since the earlier transaction - if it has changed, we
        // cannot be sure that we are using the right values
        rs.next();
        Timestamp newts = rs.getTimestamp("TS");
        if ((ts == null) || ts.equals(newts))
        {
            // ok - apply update
            String q = "UPDATE EMP SET TS=SYSDATE, SAL=" + newsal +
                " WHERE EMPNO=" + eid;
            System.out.println("Applying update: " + q);
            s.executeUpdate(q);
            con.commit();
            System.out.println("Salary modified: " + newsal);
        }
        else
        {
            // stuff has changed - all bets are off
            System.out.println("Salary not modified");
            con.rollback();
            throw new Exception("Must retry transaction - data is
                stale");
        }

        // Locks are now released
    }
}
```

**Optimistic Locking Using Object Comparison.** Comparing timestamps has the disadvantage that a timestamp value has to be written to every record. Some databases (such as Sybase) write a timestamp automatically (actually, Sybase automatically writes a sequence number, called a timestamp, if a timestamp column is defined in a table), and in that case the trouble of writing a timestamp is not an issue. However, for other DBMSs, writing a timestamp to every record may be an impractical approach. In that case, an actual data comparison may be necessary.

A disadvantage of comparing data values directly, however, is that if new columns are added to a table, your code will have to be examined in many places to make sure that the new columns also are compared, if required by the application. Also, the entire set of data needed by the update transaction needs to be sent as well by the query transaction—i.e., it is sent twice.

If you are implementing your own multitier design, using an object streaming or application-specific protocol, you can put the above consistency-checking logic into the middle tier. For example, the middle tier could perform a query, compute a digest of the query results and send it to the client, along with any data the client needs from the query, and then later during the update transaction it can redo the query and recompute the digest—an exception could be thrown if the digest value is different from last time. Consider the following example which uses an RMI-based middle tier database server object. Remember that, unless you are sure you can get away with not doing so, you must compare data you read as well as data you intend to update.

```
public class Digest implements java.io.Serializable
{
   public void equals(Object d)
   {
      if (! (d instanceof Digest)) throw new Error();
   }

   public String getValue() { return md5Value; }

   public Digest(byte[] data)
   {
      ...compute the MD5 digest value for the byte array...
   }

   private String md5Value;
}

public class CustomerData implements java.io.Serializable
{
   public CustomerData(int id, String name, String address,
      String ssn, int age, String comments)
   {
      this.id = id; this.name = name;
      this.address = address;
      this.ssn = ssn; this.age = age;
      this.comments = comments;
      digest = computeDigest();
   }
   public int id;
   public String name;
   public String address;
   public String ssn;
   public int age;
   public String comments;

   protected Digest computeDigest()
   {
```

```
      // Concatenate all fields into a byte array, b
      ...

      // Construct a digest object
      return new Digest(b);
   }

   public Digest digest;
}

interface DBServer extends java.rmi.Remote
{
   public CustomerData getCustomerData(int id)
      throws java.rmi.RemoteException, Exception;
   public void updateCustomerData(CustomerData)
      throws java.rmi.RemoteException, Exception;
}

public class DBServerImpl extends
   java.rmi.server.UnicastRemoteServer
implements DBServer
{
   public DBServerImpl(URL url)
   {
      // Create connection pool
      ...
      connection[i] = java.sql.DriverManager.getConnection(url);
      ...
   }

   public CustomerData getCustomerData(int id)
      throws java.rmi.RemoteException, Exception
   {
      // Get a connection
      java.sql.Connection con = ...get connection from pool

      CustomerData cd = null;
      try
      {
         CustomerData cd = getCustData(con, id);
         con.commit();
      }
      catch (Throwable t)
      {
         con.rollback();
         throw t;
      }
      finally
      {
```

```
        // Return the connection to the pool
        ...
    }

    // Return the customer data to the remote caller
    return cd;
}

protected CustomerData getCustData(java.sql.Connection con,
    int id) throws Exception
{
    java.sql.Statement s = con.createStatement();
    java.sql.ResultSet rs = s.executeQuery(
        "SELECT * FROM CUSTOMERS WHERE ID = " + id +
        " FOR UPDATE");
    // there should be only one row in the result set
    rs.next();
    String name = rs.getString("NAME");
    String address = rs.getString("ADDRESS");
    String ssn = rs.getString("SSN");
    int age = rs.getInt("AGE");
    String comments = rs.getString("COMMENTS");

    CustomerData cd = new CustomerData(id, name, address,
        ssn, age, comments);
    return cd;
}

public void updateCustomerData(CustomerData cd)
    throws java.rmi.RemoteException, Exception
{
    // Get a connection
    java.sql.Connection con = ...get connection from pool

    try
    {
        CustomerData cdPrime =
            getCustData(java.sql.Connection con, cd.id);
    }
    catch (Throwable t)
    {
        con.rollback();
        ...return the connection to the pool
        throw t;
    }

    try
    {
        if (cdPrime.digest.equals(cd.digest))
```

```
            {
               // ok - no change since last time; apply update
               Statement s = con.createStatement();
               s.executeUpdate(
                  "INSERT INTO CUSTOMERS VALUES (" +
                  cd.name + "," + cd.address + "," +
                  cd.ssn + "," + cd.age + ", " +
                  cd.comments + ")" + " WHERE ID = " +
                  id);
               con.commit();
            }
            else
            {
               // oops! - the checksum is not the same as
               // last time  - someone did an update!
               con.rollback();
               throw new Exception(
               "Data is stale!!! - retry transaction please");
            }
         }
         catch (Throwable t)
         {
            con.rollback();
            ...return connection to pool
            throw t;
         }
      }

      public static void main(String[] args)
      {
         try
         {
            // First try to establish database connection
            String driver = args[0];
            Class c = Class.forName(driver);   // likely a type 1
                                               // or 2 driver
            String url = args[1];

            // Now publish this server object
            DBServerImpl s = new DBServerImpl(url);
            java.rmi.registry.Registry r =
               java.rmi.registry.LocateRegistry.getRegistry();
            r.rebind("DBServer", s);
         }
         catch (Exception ex) ex.printStackTrace();
      }

      private java.sql.Connection[] connection;
   }
```

The primary advantage of this scenario is that the application data does not have to traverse the network again just so the client can verify it has not changed—we have one round trip for the data, instead of a round trip and a one-way verification trip. However, note that this implementation has an update granularity equal to the size of the data retrieved, whereas the earlier examples allow the client to send back to the server only the changes desired. The choice of which strategy to use is actually part of the overall decision of which distributed architecture and protocols to use, and cannot therefore be made in isolation. There are also other variations on this technique, including implementing a customized object marshalling protocol, and calculating a digest as a side effect of transmission.

### *Checkout-based Locking (Application-based Write Locking)*

The pessimistic and optimistic locking models owe their origin to transaction-based database applications, in which user operations are relatively short in duration—certainly less than the typical time between system restarts. As we have seen, the pessimistic model deals well with very discrete updates that are completed quickly—instantaneously to the user. The optimistic model allows for prolonged user access in the process of an update, but still assumes that such interaction is short compared to the expected time between accesses by other users, and also is shorter than the average time interval between system restarts. What about situations that do not fit either of these assumptions, for example when the user requires prolonged access, for days or more? Applications that fit this model include process-oriented applications that range from commercial loan preparation to engineering design. The salient feature is that work must be allowed to proceed in an uninterrupted and protected manner, for a long time, until the user is ready to submit it.

A checkout-based model assumes that:

- The system can be expected to restart during the course of a user operation, making pessimistic locking impractical.
- Other users can be expected to try to access the data during the course of the user operation, making optimistic locking impractical. This may result either from usage patterns, or from the underlying DBMS failing to support the required lock granularity needed by the application.

It is further assumed that it would be unacceptable for other users to modify the data that the current user is working on. Still, they may either be granted read access to the work in progress, or to the last saved state of the data, depending on the requirements.

Checkout is generally designed into an application, although there are Java products that support it as a built-in feature. One such product is offered by Kinexis (http://www.kinexis.com), called Proposal Based Architecture. In this approach, a composite object is viewed as a "proposal," which is checked out for development. The object is a collection of information, together comprising a logical whole—a composite. While the object is being worked on, it is in the possession of a single party—perhaps even in a physical sense, e.g., in a mobile computer, separated completely from the primary database or server. When the proposal is completed, it is checked back in. Inherent in this approach is multiversioning, optimistic locking, and viewing a transaction as the construction of a composite object. The Proposal Based Architecture provides an infrastructure for implementing this functionality in a reusable way.

Implementing a checkout-based design requires careful designation of which objects represent composites. The target of a checkout operation is always the root of a composite. Often the object checked out is created as a side effect of the checkout operation; in this case the user process which checked out the object is viewed as performing a long-term construction of a new composite object—it is filling it in—and when it is done, it will check it in for the first time. Subsequent changes are either prohibited (if the object is immutable), or must be performed via a checkout.

Here I show a simple example of how one can implement checkout in a reusable class that can be incorporated into other classes that want to implement checkout. The basic idea is simple: you are merely giving each composition root object an owner attribute, and applications should attempt to become the owner before using the composition.

```
public interface Checkable
{
   public final void checkout(User u) throws InUseException;
   public final void checkin(User u) throws
      TokenNotOwnedException;
}

public class CheckableDefault   make this persistent
{
   public final void checkout(User u) throws InUseException
   {
      if (u == null) throw new RuntimeException("Null user");

      // Check validity of User object
      User.checkUser(u);

      // Perform a test-and-set on this object's token
      Transaction tr = new Transaction();
```

```
    tr.join();
    tr.begin();
    try
    {
        tr.lock(this, Transaction.WRITE);
        if (user != null)
        {
            if (user.equals(u))
            {
                tr.abort();    // we already have it
                return;
            }
            else
            {
                throw new InUseException();
            }
        }
        user = u;
        tr.commit();
    }
    catch (Exception ex)
    {
        // Object is locked by anther transaction; or it
        // is dirty
        tr.abort();
    }
}
public final void checkin(User u) throws TokenNotOwnedException
{
    if (u == null) throw new RuntimeException("Null user");

    // Check validity of User object
    User.checkUser(u);

    Transaction tr = new Transaction();
    tr.join();
    tr.begin();
    try
    {
        tr.lock(this, Transaction.WRITE);
        if (user == null) throw new TokenNotOwnedException();
        if (! user.equals(u)) throw new
            TokenNotOwnedException();
        token = null;
        tr.commit();
    }
    catch (Exception ex)
```

```
        {
            // Object is locked by another transaction; or it
            // is dirty
            tr.abort();
        }
    }
    private User user;
}
```

The User class can be declared final, with a private constructor, and a static dispenser method for dispensing instances of User under a security policy. Thus, one cannot create an instance of User without legitimately obtaining it, and further, the system can check if a given User instance is still valid.

Here is an example of use:

```
public final class Task implements Checkable   a persistent class
{
    private Task() {}
    public Task(String n) { name = n; }

    //
    // Checkable methods
    //

    public final void checkout(User u) throws InUseException
    {
        checkableDelegate.checkout(u);
    }
    public final void checkin(User u) throws TokenNotOwnedException
    {
        checkableDelegate.checkin(u);
    }
    final String name;                // primary
    private Checkable checkableDelegate
        = new CheckableDefault();     // primary
}
```

This example assumes that the ODBMS allows the object reference to remain valid outside the context of a transaction; otherwise, the transaction initiation and completion must be taken out of the checkout method and implemented by the caller. Alternatively, the checkout() and checkin() methods could be declared static and take an object external reference or an object key as a parameter, and fetch the object based on that.

### *Defining the Transaction Layer*

In designing a middle tier, you need to decide at what level to start and commit transactions; that is, you need to define the transaction layer. It is not a good idea to distribute transaction control and database accesses throughout application code, for a number of reasons, including:

- A coordinated policy for starting and committing transactions should be encapsulated; examples of such policies may include choice of isolation mode and choice of commit mode (e.g., keeping persistent object references alive).
- A coordinated policy for handling database errors should be encapsulated.
- It would make it hard to identify code affected by persistent object model or data model changes.
- A coordinated policy for notification of updates to specific persistent objects or data should be encapsulated.
- A coordinated policy for cleanup of retired persistent objects should be encapsulated.

Instead, there should be a well-defined class of objects that implement a transaction layer. This layer represents the gateway to the database, and implements all policies for accessing that data. It is in this layer that one should coordinate transaction initiation and completion.

Sometimes a component in this layer needs to be able to handle two cases: one being that a transaction is already in progress, and the other that one is not. When this is necessary, most database products provide a method to test if a transaction is in progress for the current thread. Most object database products do not support nested transactions.

This means that complex operations that require several sub-transactions have no built-in protection against being aborted in the middle, after some transactions have been completed but before the overall process has completed. The risk is that data may exist in the database in a logically incomplete state. A good design will explicitly define these intermediate states and transactions will be designed so that they recognize them.

### *Multidatabase Transactions*

If an application needs to access more than one data repository or service to complete a request, it will need a mechanism for coordinating those accesses and monitoring that all accesses complete. There are basically two approaches: a guaranteed delivery mechanism, and a transaction mechanism.

A guaranteed delivery mechanism is a fail-safe system that promises that a message will reach the designated service, even if not right away. An example of such a product is IBM's MQ Series, which provides guaranteed delivery of messages via reliable message queues. There are MQ gateways to a great many applications and services, and so MQ is a powerful way to integrate back-end services into an application. Of course, there is a Java binding for MQ (as for many of IBM's products).

Using MQ, one could, for example, have a Java application which takes an order for a product, makes an entry in a local order database, and then dispatches an MQ message to an order fulfillment center's CICS system. The local application does not have to worry about coordinating a rollback of the local order if the communications link to the CICS system fails because it relies on the MQ system's guaranteed delivery promise that the message will get there and be processed.

Guaranteed delivery messaging systems usually do not provide real-time response. You can safely assume the message will get there—but you do not know when. Therefore, while a messaging approach simplifies system design, it is not practical in an application that must provide end-to-end acknowledgment of service completion in real time.

A different approach is to treat the entire operation as a transaction, with unreliable components. If any operation fails, the entire transaction must be rolled back. To implement this, you may need to rely on transaction services of multiple components. For example, if you need to make insertions into two different databases to complete a unit of work, you can consider these two insertions to constitute a single transaction. Neither database knows about the other transaction, however, and so the application must manage these two transactions, and roll them both back if either fails.

In practice, this is hard to implement, because it requires a two-phase commit process to be implemented by each database. Basically, each database must be told to make a tentative commit, and if all succeeds, they are told to go ahead and make the commit final. Systems that have software components called "transaction managers" are able to participate in such group transactions. Products that support the Enterprise JavaBeans framework take this a step further and greatly simplify the transactional aspect of application design by defining a generic middle-tier architecture and delegating transaction control to a specific component. This is discussed in detail in Chapter 8.

### Cleaning Up Partially Completed Logical Transaction Remnants

It is a misconception that database transaction technology prevents most applications from creating inconsistent results. It certainly helps, but in a high volume system, anything that can happen will, and if an inconsistent result only happens 0.01% of the time, that means that after ten million transactions there will be 1000 inconsistent results in the database. Depending on the nature of the application, this may be ignorable, or it may be absolutely unacceptable.

The reason that errors creep in is usually because complex logical transactions are broken up into multiple separate database transactions, and something goes wrong between one commit and the next. For example, suppose a demographic database has a transaction to set a customer's marital status, and another to set a customer's name. Suppose also that a female customer calls and says, "My boyfriend and I just got married, and my name is no longer Candace Walnoskipanovich (thank goodness!)—it is now Candace Kane." The operator enters and commits a transaction to set Candace's marital status, and then begins to enter another to set her new name, when suddenly the system goes down. There is now a person in the database, who is listed as married, with the last name of Walnoskipanovich. The woman on the phone has already hung up, thinking everything has been taken care of, and the operator is left with no way to correct the error, because in the confusion of the system failure, he has forgotten the caller's very hard-to-remember original last name.

This is a case in which a single logical transaction has been implemented with two independent physical transactions, most likely because the specific logical transaction of a simultaneous name and marital status change was not anticipated. In general, there can be consistency rules in a database that are not thought of at design time, but are discovered afterwards when the system is operational. Until these consistency rules can be added to the system's next release, there needs to be a set of processes for dealing with such inconsistencies, and "reaping remnants" of partially completed logical transactions. In our example, there could be a process for examining all female customers for which marital status was changed, but not the person's name, and producing a report of such instances for inspection and verification.

Inconsistent results can also occur as a result of failure of separate systems that participate in two-phase transactions. Most two-phase transactional systems are advertised as fully reliable, but in fact a series of failures can still result in inconsistencies. Also, to improve throughput, two-phase transactions are often run in a single-phase mode in which the transaction owner does not wait for acknowledgment from all parties before assuming the second phase completed. In general, partially complete results must at some point be reconciled.

### Forward Cache Designs

A forward cache architecture replicates or distributes cached data to clients—possibly within their address space—so that it is accessible where it is needed, perhaps at memory access speed instead of connection speed. This can greatly increase the performance of remote clients that make mostly read accesses to centralized data.

Forward cache systems typically shift the burden of data synchronization to those transactions which perform updates. An update transaction needs to ensure that clients are not reading cached versions of the data that is to be updated before the update can proceed. This can be achieved by requiring the update transaction to obtain a lock which synchronously notifies clients to mark all cached versions of the data as dirty. Clients then know they must refresh the data, and their refresh attempts will block until the update lock is released. This approach is used by the ObjectStore object database.

In multitier applications it may not be practical to distribute the database to all tiers. For example, if the database client is an enterprise JavaBeans container, the end-user clients are far removed and execute in a different address space and probably even a different machine from the database client.

In the case of a multitier system a strategy must be devised for ensuring data integrity across tiers, possibly all the way down to end-user clients. An application-based forward cache can facilitate this while still providing good performance. Forward caches can be implemented using commercial database products which are colocated with clients or with geographically distributed application servers that are located near the end users.

The overhead of performing cache value refreshes in this kind of system can be greatly reduced by coordinating updates so that most of the time they are performed in batches. An approach I have seen used successfully is to employ leases or time-to-live attributes on individual cache entries. For example, consider an application in which clients need to obtain the current prices of items in a catalog. Price data may be stored in a central repository far removed from the client. In fact, it may be in a mainframe and accessible only via a batch extraction process. In this scenario a set of relational databases may redundantly contain the price data and make it available to web clients via a set of application servers. These databases represent a forward cache of the actual price data. If the mainframe price extraction process can be designed to associate a validity period for each price, then the application server clients can know how long a price is good for. If price changes tend to occur at fixed intervals, for example, at midnight each day, the expiration date for large groups of items can be set for the same time, so that application server processes can be designed to obtain new values for those items as a group instead of individually. The update can then be initiated by the application server without the need for any kind of distributed lock, since it is merely

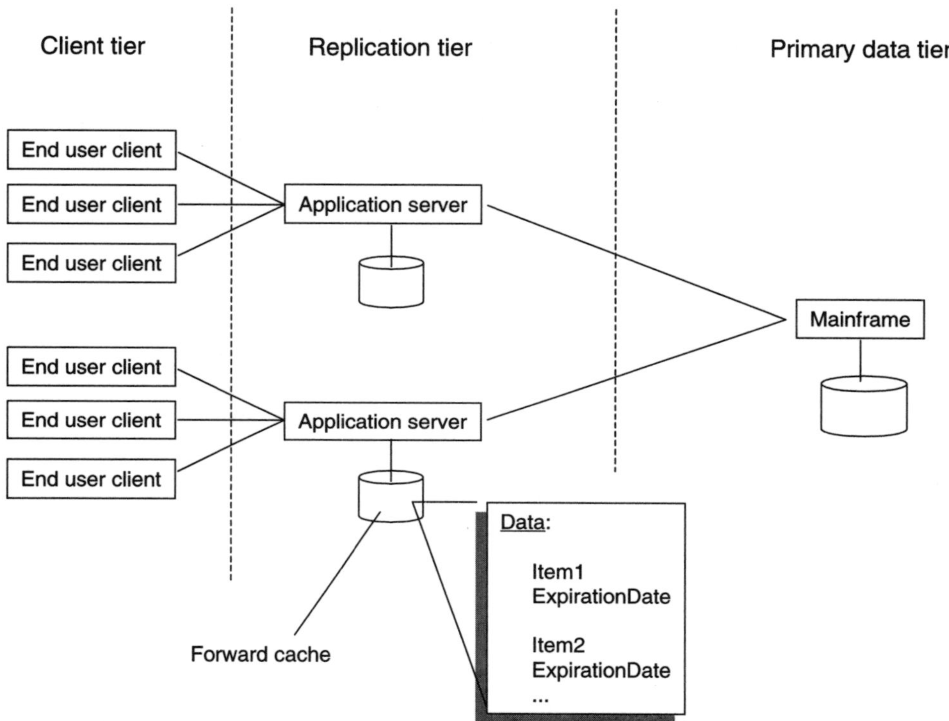


**Figure 6-12** An application-based forward cache design using data with expiration times.

asking for a refresh. A forward cache arrangement with time-to-live application data attributes is shown in Figure 6-12.

Forward cache strategies that employ time-to-live attributes are particularly effective for multitier systems because they allow very effective tiering of the system for scalability and at the same time can deliver in most cases the same performance as if the data resided close to the client.

Using time-to-live attributes does not remove the need to coordinate real-time updates to the central repository. For example, it is possible that a mainframe price might need to be changed ahead of schedule and that all cached copies of that price therefore need to immediately be marked as obsolete before they have expired. In that case a process is needed for notifying the application servers so that they can refresh their copies of the data which is now obsolete. Ideally the process of updating the data in the central price repository is synchronous with regard to the notification of the application servers—that is, the update and the notifications are performed within a single global transaction. In practice this may not always be possible. If it is not, then a procedure will be needed for handling the small number of transactions which complete in the interval when the price is invalid but the application server has not yet been notified.

### *Using Events for Database Client Notification*

In applications in which data is relatively dynamic, client applications must have a means of ensuring that they have data which is up to date. As already discussed, in most business applications, it is not practical to lock the central copy of shared data during "user time," and so the client application has to live with the possibility that data it is working with may be changed by other clients at any time. Provisions must therefore be made within the application to ensure that any client-side cached data is refreshed at appropriate points. This can be achieved by notifying clients when data they are using has changed and allowing the clients to then request a refresh of the data.

An event model is an excellent framework for achieving this. Notification of changes which have been made to a central database view can be propagated to clients with sufficient information for the clients to perform fine-grained refreshes of data they are interested in.

**Event Delivery.** Consideration must be given to which events need to be delivered synchronously—that is, those which must be delivered to all interested clients prior to completion, with failed deliveries resulting in synchronous exception delivery and even possible rollback of the transaction. In a very tightly coupled system, clients might even be required to process event notices before acknowledging. This approach might be necessary in a system in which clients must always exactly reflect the current central model.

Generally, most business client applications do not require synchronous delivery. Notification of updates can be done in a non-synchronous manner (i.e., performed after an update has occurred). A client application receiving notice of an update can then refresh its copy of the affected data. In addition, if event delivery is not synchronous, it is important that clients do not rely on the order of delivery of notification. For example, if a client receives an event indicating that a value in the central database has been set to zero and then receives another event indicating that the value has been incremented, this will have a different effect than if the value is first incremented and then set to zero. If the client assumes the order of delivery is correct, it might choose to optimize accesses by computing the value instead of fetching it. This would lead to incorrect data on the client if events are delivered out of order, which can be expected to occur sometimes with a non-synchronous delivery mechanism.

**Defining the Events.** The operation of an object-oriented system can be usually viewed as a set of logical transactions which result in the construction, promotion, modification, and deletion of composite objects. These changes of state can be signaled by event messages.

The granularity at which database objects can notify remote listeners of these change events is up to the application. In general, fine-grained notification is complex to implement, and must be weighed against the potential number of listeners registered at any one time (which must have open connections or listener linkages of some type for callback). It is possible to put the notification mechanism into the database engine itself, by writing trigger procedures which invoke the event or notification facility.

The four primary categories of events I will introduce in our notification model are:

1. *Database application events*—These are the large-grain events that represent application-level changes of the state of composite objects. These events fall within the broader category of model change events, if the database is viewed as the central model. An example would be the commit of an intermediate or final flight reservation for an airline customer. If the change represents an intermediate state, this implies an optimistic or checkout-based application-level locking model. Within this category, we have these very prevalent subcategories:

    *Obtain (checkout)*: An object's ownership is assigned.

    *Release (checkin)*: An object's ownership is relinquished.

    *Change policy (e.g., from exclusive to nonexclusive)*: Access rights to an object are modified.

    *Construction* (of composite): A new composite object is instantiated.

    *Promotion*: An object is approved in some way, verified, or processed, resulting in its being considered to have transitioned to a new status or level of recognition, or role.

    *Modification*: An object is modified (atomically, of course).

    *Deletion*: An object is deleted from the system, or marked for deletion.

2. *Database physical events*—These are the small-grain events that represent physical insertions and deletions in a database. These are also model-change events. A single physical event does not signify a logically complete (or consistent) change to the database, and any application that reads changes based on physical events has the risk of reading incomplete or tentative data. An example is the addition of an item to an online product order, prior to committing the order. Another example is the entry of the order's bill-to

address. In these two examples, the changes must be made persistent, and so they need to be committed as physical transactions against the database; however, until the order is complete and committed as a unit, most clients would not be interested in these changes. The distinction between physical events and application events becomes more important in applications that are work process in nature, such that users work on changes for a long period before forwarding them to the next stage of processing or approval.

3. *Transaction status events*—These are client-level events that signal changes in the status of transactions initiated by the client. An example would be the successful (or unsuccessful) completion of the commit of changes to the database.
4. *UI events*—These are purely client-level events, and are not represented in the system's data model. Nevertheless, GUI events are often used in the user application to signal user view changes in response to user input. An example of a user event would be a UI component signaling a user action, such as the click of a button.

Database application events, the first category, are those that carry information about model state changes, usable to other transactions, and these are the events that are of most use in synchronizing replicated data between client and server components, and multiple client application views, as I will now discuss.

**Model Synchronization vs. View Synchronization.** Most modern multitier applications provide the user with a windowing interface, freeing the user to engage in multiple simultaneous activities. Within such an end-user application, especially a workflow application which is usually highly concurrent by nature, there are two inherent data synchronization problems that must be addressed:

Inter-view synchronization—UI depictions of an object's data which appear in more than one view at a time must be synchronized.

Inter-model synchronization—If it is possible that there can be more than one local instance of an object representing an actual database persistent object, these multiple local references must be synchronized.

Inter-view synchronization is a UI design problem and is beyond the scope of this book.

The need for inter-model synchronization may arise if two different parts of an application each performs a read on a database object, into a local instance. Depending on the implementation of the underlying persistence mechanism, these references may point to the same cached object, or they may point to different instances, each acting as a distinct proxy for an actual database object. The model synchronization problem can therefore exist within a single application. It

also exists across applications and user sessions, such as when two different users are looking at the same data on their screen. This is the traditional optimistic locking synchronization problem.

Both varieties of inter-model synchronization can be addressed by the same techniques: the data being viewed can be locked (not the best approach); it can be checked out; it can be verified upon commit; or the application can be notified when an externally initiated change occurs. All of these strategies have already been discussed in detail, except for notification, which is being addressed here.

**Achieving Model Synchronization.** Synchronizing one or more client views with a remote data model requires either using a passive strategy such as optimistic locking, or an active strategy such as pessimistic locking or asynchronous change notification. Since the optimistic and pessimistic strategies have already been discussed in an earlier section, I will now look at a technique for implementing active change notification for multiple distributed clients.

Consider Figure 6-13. The component labeled "Model Event Manager" is a component that executes in the database or an application server. Its role is to detect changes to the database and generate notifications for distributed clients, using whatever event or messaging facility has been chosen for the design. The model event manager may be implemented by a set of database triggers, or it may be a set of methods called by Enterprise JavaBeans entity beans. (The latter are discussed in Chapter 8.) The model event manager delegates to the messaging facility the job of maintaining a list of interested clients and delivering the events or messages to those clients.

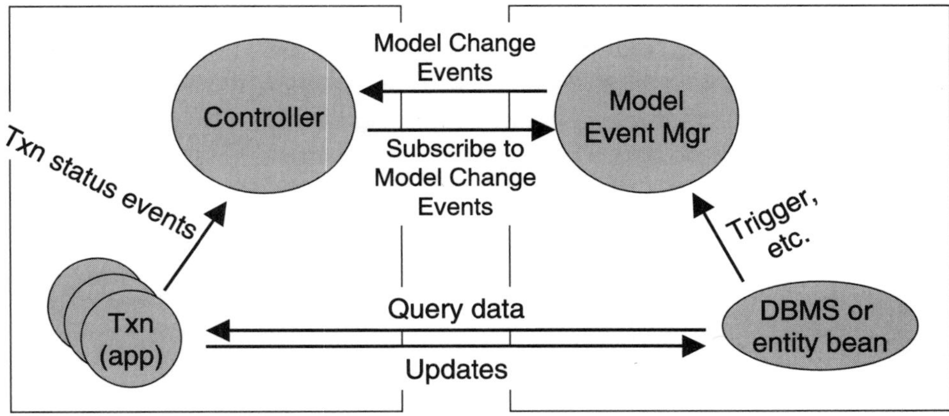


**Figure 6-13** Using events to notify clients of remote data model changes.

The fact that we are assuming that the order of delivery of events is undefined makes it easy to replicate the model event manager, because it alleviates the need for multiple instances of this component to coordinate their operation.

A multitier design could employ filtering across tiers based on the subscriptions of local clients. Many messaging systems provide such filtering. This reduces traffic within tiers, much the way a network bridge filters packets and thereby reduces traffic within network segments.

In order to receive notification, a client must subscribe to the events it is interested in. The client may need to specify additional filtering criteria so that it does not get interrupted by every message on the channel. Ideally it should be interrupted by the messaging system only for events that actually require action—that is, those which affect the client's cached data.

I have chosen to name the client-side component which receives events a "controller." This is because this component needs to control the operation of the client in response to incoming events. It is the job of the controller to determine if the event is actually of interest, and if any of the client's data needs to be refreshed in response to the event. The controller will therefore invoke transactions to retrieve new model data from the remote database.

The link between the controller and the model event manager is a fragile one because the application designer must be diligent to ensure that all database objects or records which need to trigger notificaiton actually have mechanisms which post changes to the model event manager.

Model change events should not convey model information—only that the model has changed, and possibly identify what parts have changed. The model (database) itself should always be consulted for verification. Model change events should be treated as hints only. The controller must also deal gracefully with stale or out-of-order events, and with references to database objects that no longer exist. The model event manager should also deal gracefully with listeners (client adapters) that no longer exist.

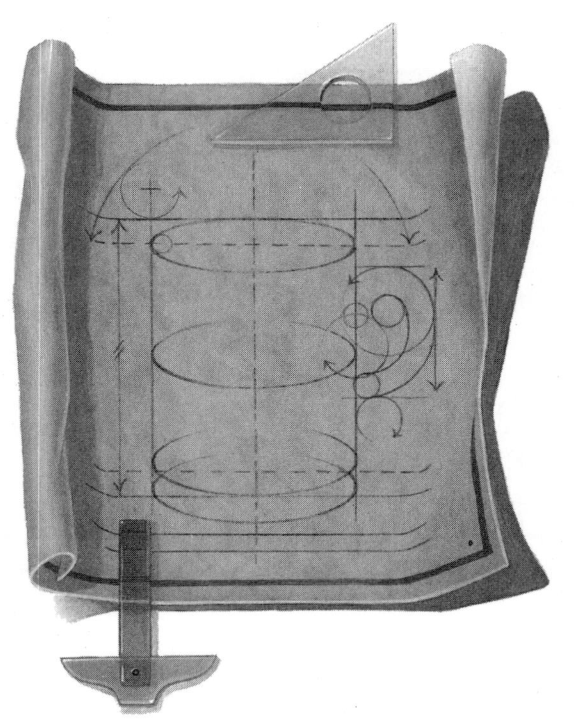

# CHAPTER 7

# Distributed Computing Protocols and APIs

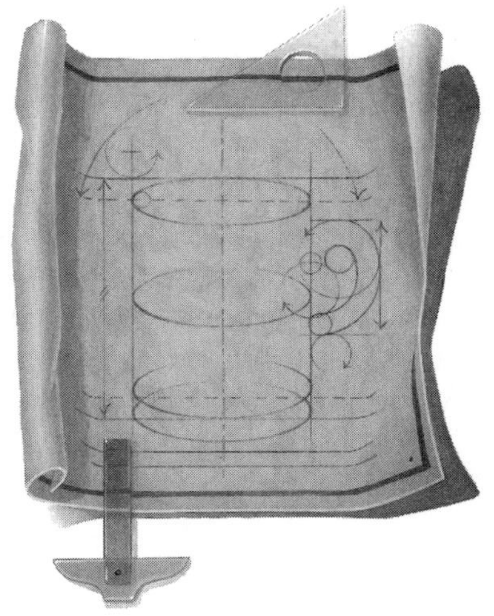

Increasingly, isolated applications within organizations need to be interconnected, providing a uniform set of information sources, processes, and business rules to all business units or branches of an organization, and even between an organization and its customers and partners. The Internet makes this possible, because for the first time there exists a worldwide wide area network with open protocols. The mere availability of this level of connectivity now makes such integration necessary if an organization is to keep abreast of its competition.

Within most organizations, and certainly between organizations, different needs mandate different technology choices, so the task of integrating applications across a wide area network and the Internet almost always involves tying together equipment and software from varied sources. The heterogeneous nature of cross-business unit computing makes a platform-independent language necessary, so that applications of this scope can be developed in a single language and ideally with a single set of open APIs and standards. Java is such a language.

In this chapter I will examine the fundamental Java APIs which make it possible to build distributed applications. The four cornerstones of a distributed application are:

- Data resources
- Naming and lookup of resources and services
- Remote invocation or messaging
- Transaction control

There are standard and open Java APIs to address all of these areas. These include:

JDBC—For access to relational and ODBC data resources. This has been discussed in detail in Chapter 6.

JNDI—Provides a neutral API for accessing directory services and name services, so that resources of most kinds, including database connections and application server objects, can be accessed in a uniform and product-independent way.

RMI—Provides a lightweight and easy-to-use object oriented remote method call service.

CORBA—There are many portable ways to use CORBA with Java; these will be discussed.

XML—Building XML applications with Java is straightforward, and there are many toolkits to enable one to do this.

JMS—Provides an open and neutral API for accessing messaging services such as MQ.

JTA, JTS—Provide standard Java APIs for accessing transaction managers and transaction services provided as part of an application server environment.

It is an enormous challenge to build a distributed system from scratch, even given these building blocks. If the system is to be maintainable, issues which must be addressed include component deployment, the lifecycle of components, management and monitoring, and interfacing to other systems. Many of these issues are addressed by the Enterprise JavaBeans specification, which is discussed in Chapter 8.

The most important class of Java products to evolve to date have been the Enterprise JavaBeans application servers. These products represent the current state of evolution of what historically have been called "transaction managers," products which provide an application infrastructure on a server for building and operating distributed applications. The Enterprise JavaBeans API and product features will be discussed in Chapter 8. To understand these products, it is necessary to understand the underlying APIs which they use, which are listed above. These foundational APIs are the focus of this chapter.

## JNDI

The Java Naming and Directory Interface (JNDI) defines a generic interface for accessing name and directory services. Many Java APIs now rely on or assume the use of JNDI for the function of object and service lookup. For example, JDBC 2 assumes that database drivers will be obtained in this way, and EJB assumes that

JNDI will be used to obtain Enterprise JavaBeans Home interface objects. JNDI can also be used as an interface to directory services such as LDAP, and object name services such as CORBA COS Naming.

### *Retrieving Entries*

Two primary ways to obtain an object using JNDI are to ask for the object by name using the lookup() method, and to search for it based on attributes using a search method. The former is intended primarily for name services and the latter for directory services and other attribute and hierarchical types of name services.

To find an object by name, construct an InitialContext object, and then provide the name of the object you want to find to the lookup method. For example, to look up a persistent CORBA object with the COS Naming JNDI implementation:

```
ORB orb = ORB.init(args, null);

Properties p = new Properties();
p.put("java.naming.factory.initial",
"com.sun.jndi.CosNaming.CNCtxFactory");
p.put("java.naming.corba.orb", orb);

Context context = new InitialContext(p);

Object o =
context.lookup("iiop://myhost:900/MyPersistentCorbaObject");
context.close();

MyCorbaObjectType =
MyCorbaObjectTypeHelper.narrow((org.omg.CORBA.Object)o);
```

In the above, I pass the COS Naming JNDI provider implementation and the ORB to the context constructor as properties. I then perform a lookup, which finds the object, and then I do the obligatory CORBA narrow operation.

Let's look at a JNDI example which uses an LDAP directory service. Here I will reimplement the LDAP search application shown in Chapter 5, but this time using the JNDI interface with an LDAP provider:

```
import java.util.*;
import javax.naming.*;
import javax.naming.directory.*;

public class DemoNaming
{
   public static void main(String[] args) throws NamingException
   {
      Properties p = new Properties();
```

```
// Specify the initial context implementation to use
p.put("java.naming.factory.initial",
   "com.sun.jndi.ldap.LdapCtxFactory");
```

This specifies the JNDI provider implementation to use—in this case Sun's Java LDAP client implementation, which is included with JNDI.

```
// Specify the directory service's host and port number
p.put("java.naming.provider.url", "ldap://myhost:389");
```

Above, I specify the host that contains the LDAP server to which I want to connect. Here I have specified the port explicitly; 389 is in fact the default value for the LDAP service (for LDAP over SSL, it is 636).

At this point you would also provide security credentials if the server requires them. For example, you might set:

```
p.put("java.naming.security.principal", "cliff");
p.put("java.naming.security.credentials", "mypassword");
```

(Note: If your application is an EJB 1.1 Enterprise Bean, security credentials and other JNDI properties are expected to be specified at an administrative level instead of through explicit JNDI properties.)

Now let's establish a search context:

```
DirContext c = new InitialDirContext(p);
```

Here I have used an InitialDirContext instead of an InitialContext. An InitialDirContext is a DirContext, which provides additional functionality appropriate for hierarchical naming systems such as directory servers.

```
// Specify search constraints
SearchControls sc = new SearchControls();
sc.setSearchScope(SearchConstraints.ONELEVEL_SCOPE);
```

In the above code section I have specified that the server should only look immediately within the country and organization context, and not subcontexts. To cause it to look deeper, specify SUBTREE_SCOPE.

```
NamingEnumeration se = c.search
(
   "o=My Company,c=RO",    // searchbase
   "cn=Frank N. Stein",    // filter
   sc                      // constraints
);
```

Above I have specified a search filter, "cn=Frank N. Stein." Search filters are defined in RFC 1558. They can include complex LISP-like expressions, such as "(&(objectClass=Person)(|(sn=Stein)(cn=Frank*)))." The "&" indicates that a match occurs if *all* criteria following it within the same parentheses are met; the "|" means that a match occurs if *any* criteria following it within the same parentheses are met. Continuing with the example, let's now print the search results:

```
        // Print name and atrributes for each entry
        while (se != null && se.hasMoreElements())
        {
            SearchResult sr = (SearchResult)(se.next());
            System.out.println("name=" + sr.getName());

            Attributes as = sr.getAttributes();
            if (as == null) continue;

            for (AttributeEnumeration ae = as.getAll();
                ae.hasMoreElements();)
            {
                Attribute a = ae.next();
                String id = a.getId();
                System.out.println("\t" + id);
                for (Enumeration e = a.getAll(); e.hasMoreElements();)
                {
                    System.out.println("\t\t" + e.nextElement());
                }
            }
        }
    }
}
```

This program was tested also with Netscape's Directory Server product, and it produces the same results as the LDAP API version discussed Chapter 5.

The attributes of an object in a DirContext can be modified with any of the modifyAttributes(...) methods or by rebinding the object, which will replace all the object attribute values.

### *Referrals*

JNDI supports referrals. Referrals are discussed in the context of LDAP in Chapter 5. A referral is a reply from a server containing a redirection. A name or object server sends a referral when it cannot by itself locate an object or entry, but knows where the object or entry can be found. It is then up to the client to try again with the new location.

A JNDI service provider can be configured to automatically follow referrals without involving the end user application. It will do this if the Java environment property `java.naming.referral` is set to "follow." In this case, there is nothing your application needs to do to handle a referral. If this property is set to "ignore," the referral is ignored, and a server response containing a referral will result in an exception.

If the `java.naming.referral` property is set to "throw," a ReferralException is thrown whenever the server returns a referral. The application then handles the exception and decides whether to pursue the referral. In addition, since one referral can lead to another—they can be chained—it is necessary to handle the exception in a loop. For example, this code performs a lookup and handles referrals:

```
Object object = null;  // our result
Context context = new InitialContext(properties);
while (true)  // keep trying until no ReferralException
{
   try
   {
      object = context.lookup("MyObject");
      return object;
   }
   catch (ReferralException e1)
   {
      // The same security credentials will be used,
      // unless you change them here in the properties.
      context = e1.getReferralContext(properties);
      continue;
   }
   catch (NamingException e2)
   {
      System.out.println("Can't find object");
      return null;
   }
}
```

Any directory server that is linked to by referral needs to be trusted to the same degree that the original directory is trusted. At the present time, many JNDI provider implementations do not support strong (certificate-based) authentication. This means that requests and referrals to your directory server from partner organizations or across the Internet should be done with great caution, or using a secure provider implementation that supports encryption and strong authentication.

### *Delegation*

Some JNDI name service providers support delegation, which is the ability of the name server to act as a front end to a different remote server. This evolved because of the Java 1.0 applet security model, which restricted applet remote connections to the applet host. By having a delegating name server on the applet host, which transparently forwards requests to a different remote name server, an applet is able to have name services available from arbitrary name servers, as long as they are permitted by the delegating server.

Name services may also be integrated with server load balancing, since name lookup is the first point at which a server has the opportunity to perform load balancing.

### *Storing Entries*

Storing objects in a repository of some kind requires mapping the object state and definition to the schema of the repository. A Java object can usually be stored in an opaque way, as a serialized "blob," but the disadvantage is that it is then accessible only to Java applications. Depending on the repository, it may be possible to store actual attributes of the object, and be able to retrieve them later either from other applications or from a Java application which knows how to reconstruct the original Java object.

JNDI provides facilities for either approach. In addition, JNDI provides special mappings for certain classes of Java objects, including RMI remote references. In cases where an object must be stored opaquely (as a blob), but the object is not serializable or it is simply not desirable to store it that way, JNDI provides a way to store a proxy for the object, which knows how to later reconstitute or reconnect to the actual object. These are called JNDI Reference objects.

JNDI will therefore store a Java object in one of several ways, depending on characteristics of the object. The basic algorithm it uses to choose is as follows:

```
Object obj = ...object we want to store...
Object newobj = null;
for each classname n listed in java.naming.factory.state,
{
    ObjectStateFactory f = Class.forName(n).newInstance();
    newobj = f.getStateToBind(obj, context, objectName);
    if (newobj != null) break;
}
if (newobj != null) obj = newobj;
if (obj instanceof Referenceable)
{
    obj = ((Referenceable)obj).getReference();
}
```

```
if (obj instanceof Reference)
{
    ...store obj as a Reference...
}

...additional cases - see below...

else if (obj instanceof Serializable)
{
    ...store obj as a serialized value...
}
else if (obj instanceof DirContext)
{
    ...store obj as an attributed directory entry...
}
else ...check for any other classes that getStateToBind() might return...
{
    ...store in whatever manner the provider implementation chooses...
}
```

Some providers may be able to store additional specific forms, such as Java marshalled objects and CORBA object references, and might add these additional cases:

```
else if (obj instanceof org.omg.CORBA.Object)
{
    ...store obj as a CORBA object reference...
}
else if (obj instanceof java.rmi.MarshalledObject)
{
    ...store obj as a javaMarshalledObject...
}
else if (obj instanceof Remote)
{
    ...store obj as a javaNamingReference...
}
```

When this algorithm completes, either the object referenced by the original value of "obj" has been stored in the repository, or a suitable Reference to it has been stored. The choice is implemented by the method getStateToBind() and the predefined preference order shown above. If the object itself is stored, the provider uses an implementation of ObjectStateFactory to determine how to represent the object in the target repository.

It is up to the JNDI service provider implementation to encode this algorithm. Some service provider implemetnations may not adhere to this exactly.

In most cases, you will utilize the provider's built-in techniques for storing objects. You will simply choose a provider appropriate for the kind of directory or repository you are connecting to. However, if you need to take control of how an object is stored, so that other applications can access it non-opaquely, you can implement an ObjectStateFactory to store the object, and possibly an ObjectFactory to read it back in (to Java applications).

### *Implementing References*

If a Java object implements the Referenceable interface, a service provider may store a Reference to an object instead of a serialized or other representation of the object. The Referenceable interface has a single method:

```
public Reference getReference() throws NamingException
```

The service provider calls getReference(), and stores the resulting Reference as a serialized object. (Reference is a serializable concrete class.) If your object implements Referenceable, it returns a suitable Reference object when asked to do so. This means that for objects to be stored this way, they have to know how to construct a Reference object.

To construct a Reference object, the best approach is to use the Reference concrete class, and call one of its constructors or its methods to add the appropriate information to it, including the name and location of an object factory to use to construct a runtime instance of the actual object. I will show an example of this in the next section, using the LDAP provider.

### *Storing (Binding) Java Objects in LDAP Using JNDI*

I discussed storing Java objects in an LDAP directory in Chapter 4. Here I revisit it from the JNDI perspective: storing Java objects in LDAP, but using the JNDI interface and an LDAP provider for JNDI. Storing Java objects in LDAP is much more straightforward this way, because the JNDI LDAP provider has built-in support for the Java-to-LDAP mapping schema described in Chapter 5. If you use an LDAP-specific API, you have to implement the mapping yourself.

Java objects have natural repositories of their own, including the RMI Registry for RMI objects, and ORB naming services for Java CORBA objects. It is convenient for administration purposes to consolidate these disparate directories under one umbrella directory, and LDAP can be used to do this. In this scenario, an LDAP directory does not take the place of the separate application-specific repositories—it augments them. RMI remote references are not supported by the JNDI 1.1 Java LDAP provider, but are in the JNDI 1.2 LDAP provider.

To bind Java objects in LDAP, you must define the LDAP attributes and object classes listed in Chapter 5. To modify attributes of objects, use the DirContext modifyAttributes() method.

If a Java object does not implement Referenceable, the default behavior of the LDAP provider is to map a serializable object to an LDAP entry which has the objectclass attribute values "javaContainer" (it gets the dn attribute from that so it can have a name) and "javaSerializedObject," and through inheritance "javaObject." For example:

```
public class LDAPSer
{
   public static void main(String[] args)
   {
      // Open connnection to LDAP server.
      Properties p = new Properties();
      p.put("java.naming.factory.initial",
         "com.sun.jndi.ldap.LdapCtxFactory");
      p.put("java.naming.provider.url",
         "ldap://<host>/<some-DN>");
      DirContext c = new InitialDirContext(p);

      // Store a serializable object. The LDAP
      // provider will map it to an LDAP entry with
      // the objectclass attributes 'javaSerializedObject',
      // 'javaContainer', and 'javaObject'. This is the
      // default behavior for serializable classes for
      // which there is no installed object factory.
      MySerType mst = new MySerType();
      c.rebind("cn=MyObject", mst, null);
      c.close();
   }

   public static class MySerType implements Serializable
   {
      public int x = 10;
   }
}
```

The result of running this is then a new LDAP entry under the specified distinguished name *<some-DN>*, with the attributes shown in Figure 7-1.

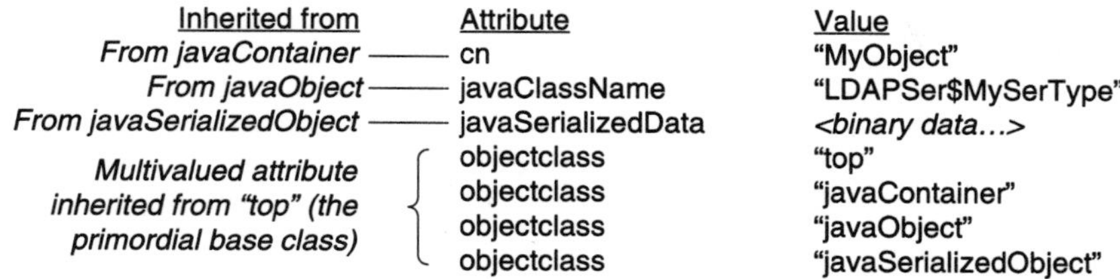


**Figure 7-1** The LDAP entry created by the LDAPSer example.

This newly created LDAP entry will have the distinguished name "cn=MyObject, <*some-DN*>". For example, if <*some-DN*> is "o=My Company, c=RO", the new entry's distinguished name will be "cn=MyObject, o=My Company, c=RO". Note that instead of specifying a starting context in the ldap:// URL, we could have navigated down to the <*some-DN*> context using find() methods.

The new entry is of type {top, javaContainer, javaObject, javaSerializedObject}—that is, it implements all these LDAP classes. For this example to work, *you must have defined these object classes and their attributes in your LDAP schema,* as explained in Chapter 5. The special type "top" is the primordial base class of all object classes. Its only attribute is "objectclass"—hence all object classes have this attribute through implied inheritance from top.

```
public class LDAPRef
{
   public static void main(String[] args)
   {
      ...same as for LDAPSer...
      MyRefType mst = new MyRefType();
      c.rebind("cn=MyObject", mst, null);
      c.close();
   }

   public static class MyRefType implements Referenceable
   {
      public int x;

      public Reference getReference() throws NamingException
      {
         return new Reference
         (
            getClass().getName(),
            "LDAPRef$MyRefTypeObjectFactory",
            factoryCodebase  // JNDI spec incorrectly says this is
               // the URL of the factory class, but actually it
```

```
                // is the URL of the factory class's codebase.
            );
        }
    }

    public static class MyRefTypeObjectFactory
    implements ObjectFactory
    {
        public Object getObjectInstance(Object obj,
            Name name, Context nameCtx, Hashtable environment)
        throws Exception
        {
            // Return an appropriate instance or proxy for MyRefType
            return new MyRefType();  // trivial implementation
        }
    }
}
```

Figure 7-2 shows the LDAP entry created by this program. Note that the LDAP provider has stored the entry as a javaNamingReference instead of a javaSerializedObject.

| Inherited from | Attribute | Value |
|---|---|---|
| *From javaContainer* | cn | "MyRefObject" |
| *From javaObject* | javaClassName | "LDAPRef$MyRefType" |
| *From javaNamingReference* | javaFactory | "LDAPRef$MyRefTypeObjectFactory" |
| *Multivalued attribute inherited from "top" (the primordial base class)* | objectclass | "top" |
| | objectclass | "javaContainer" |
| | objectclass | "javaObject" |
| | objectclass | "javaNamingReference" |

**Figure 7-2** Attributes of the LDAP entry created when storing a MyRefType.

It may be the case that the object being constructed requires credentials or properties of some sort. These can be passed to it by setting these values in the Context used for the bind operation, since the context will pass its environment to the object factory when it calls getObjectInstance(..., Hashtable environment).

What about storing an RMI object reference? A Java remote reference is stored in one of two ways. If the RMI reference uses IIOP, it will be stored using the CORBA LDAP schema. If the RMI reference uses JRMP, it will either be stored using the javaNamingReference schema. In the latter case, usage of the object results in an RMI registry service lookup, and so effectively the object reference is chained to the registry. It is also possible to store an RMI reference directly, in such a way that the registry is not consulted, and the LDAP server acts as the registry.

This is done by first converting the RMI reference to a java.rmi.MarshalledObject, as follows:

```
MarshalledObject mobj = new MarshalledObject(rmiRef);
```

and then storing the marshalled object in LDAP. The LDAP provider will then use the javaMarshalledObject schema, and when the LDAP reference is subsequently accessed through JNDI, the marshalled object will be reconstituted directly, without consulting the registry. For this to work, however, some application needs to always maintain at least one strong reference to the remote object so that it won't be garbage collected.

The advantage of using an LDAP lookup to obtain an RMI reference is that having all your named objects accessed through a central directory allows a system administrator to see them all, and move application-specific services like the RMI registry around without having to go and modify applications. Since the representation of a remote reference in LDAP is non-opaque, an administrator can even modify it manually.

Rather than provide an example of storing RMI objects in LDAP here, I will wait until Chapter 8, where we will look at a much more interesting case: storing EJB references in a central directory using JNDI.

### *JNDI over a Secure Connection*

**LDAP.** Currently certificate-based authentication is not supported by the reference LDAP provider (the latest version at this writing is the version 1.2 early access). However, it does support SSL (as does version 1.02, the current released version). You need to specify the Context.SECURITY_PROTOCOL (java.naming.security.protocol) property, and give it a value of "ssl." For example:

```
env.put(Context.SECURITY_PROTOCOL, "ssl");
```

You can use Sun's SSL socket implementation (the default), in which case you must have those classes installed, or you can specify a conformant implementation. An SSL implementation is conformant if it implements the javax.net.SocketFactory interface. You specify the socket factory class with the java.naming.ldap.factory.socket property:

```
env.put("java.naming.ldap.factory.socket",
"javax.net.ssl.SSLSocketFactory");
```

**CORBA Naming Service.** An application contacts a CORBA Naming service via its installed ORB. Therefore, the ORB implements the socket connection with the remote service. The COSNaming JNDI provider therefore does not specify any connection related properties. These would be set in any properties required by the ORB you choose. You tell JNDI which ORB to use with the java.naming.corba.orb environment property.

**RMI.** Since RMI does not have a built-in security support, there are no security related properties used by the RMI JNDI provider. If you use an secure RMI implementation, the implementation would have its own means of obtaining the required security credentials, and of specifying a socket factory if necessary.

### *Achieving Provider Independence*

Sun has published several provider implementations. In addition, some middleware vendors have developed their own provider implementations for communicating with their proprietary name service. For all providers, proprietary or otherwise, the JNDI API largely shields the application from underlying differences between providers. However, the properties required to initialize a provider are unique to each provider. Therefore, it is a good idea to encapsulate provider environment initialization.

One way to achieve this encapsulation is to create a property adapter, which performs the function of obtaining all connection properties. The property adapter can obtain these properties from a properties file. It can even obtain some properties, such as server-specific credentials, from another repository, such as an LDAP or other authentication server.

For example:

```
public static class MyJNDIPropertyAdapter
{
   public Properties getProperties(String contextName,
      Principal, String password)
   throws MissingResourceException
   {
      // Create a Properties object to return.
      Properties p = new Properties();

      // Obtain the <propertySetName>.properties resource bundle.
      ResourceBundle b =
         ResourceBundle.getBundle(contextName);

      // For each property specified in the resource,
      // read and set its value in our Properties object.
      for (Enumeration e = b.getKeys(); e.hasMoreElements();)
      {
         String key = (String)(e.nextElement());
```

```
            p.put(key, b.getString(key));
        }

        // Get user's credentials for that context.

        ...securely look up connection credentials in a secure server...
        ...this may require logging on to the secure server...

        // Return the constructed properties object.
        return p;
    }
}
```

We can then use this as follows:

```
Properties p = MyJNDIPropertyAdapter.getProperties(
    "MyABCConnection", me, "MyAuthServerPassword");
Context c = new InitialContext(p);
```

A separate property file would then be created for each remote context or root context which needs to be accessed. This allows the encapsulation of JNDI properties for access to remote contexts.

In this example, I have assumed that the remote context being accessed is some kind of service or database. For example, it might be an RMI service, or it might be a JDBC data resource. I have assumed that access to these resources requires separate authentication, and I have included provisions for obtaining the appropriate credentials from a secure directory server. I have also assumed that the calling thread does not have implicit permission to access that directory server, and that credentials for accessing the directory server (i.e., the user ID or Principal and password in this case) are passed in.

In some circumstances a JNDI access may involve a referral. In that case, additional properties may need to be set. The adapter can anticipate this and set those as well, thus fully encapsulating all properties needed for an endpoint access.

### *Using a Directory for Object Management*

Most computing solutions involve multiple products. Applications using Internet technology tend to span organizational units and access multiple data resources and systems, and therefore often span multiple security realms. A system built with multiple servers servicing users from multiple departments can easily become intractable if there is not a centralized strategy for managing user and access control information for the various system components.

Unfortunately it is very difficult at present to seamlessly integrate user and access control management across products. Achieving single-sign-on operation across security realms requires that the realms map user identities and roles. The industry is focusing on LDAP as a standard repository for user and security information, but LDAP still has a way to go in terms of its authentication and replication models to support servers and users across realms. In addition, some of the popular commercial LDAP servers do not expose to network clients needed attributes such as userPassword. Note that to use an LDAP server as a credential repository, other servers must be able to retrieve those credential attributes (in encrypted form usually) across the wire.

An alternative is to use the server platform's native security realm and use the platform as a security server. Many server products now support this. Using the platform's native realm for users and roles requires a commitment to that platform for security management. Another alternative is to use a security server product which provides mappings from the kinds of realms required to a central security repository of some kind. It is also possible to use an LDAP server as a security server and to force application servers to authenticate users to the LDAP server (by performing an LDAP bind).

The problem of where to store access control lists has also not been solved. A logical place for this information is in a repository such as LDAP, but there is no LDAP standard for this type of attribute (in terms of application-defined access control), and an application server or other type of server product which uses an external repository for storing access control information will likely have to cache the information internally to prevent it from degrading the server's performance. Some servers allow externally stored ACL information to be cached internally but do not provide a means for forcing specific entries to be renewed. A superior approach is to use a forward cache design for ACLs. This shifts the performance burden to update operations which occur infrequently for ACLs.

Mapping between realms is commonly a problem even within a system composed of a few heterogeneous components. For example, a web server might provide password and SSL methods for authentication. If servlets are deployed in the web server, these servlets may need to obtain the user's identity and then either propagate this identity to an application server or database, or the servlets can alternatively map the identity to a different identity—perhaps a generic role or account for accessing the backend application server or database. The use of generic roles is usually necessary for resource pools and will continue to be until there exists a standard interface for propagating user identity to data resources.

CORBA products are starting to provide implementations of the CORBA Security 1.2 specification, which provides for the implicit propagation of user identity across CORBA interfaces. Therefore, it is possible that a CORBA-based applica-

tion server will allow user identity to propagate to other supported products, allowing for single-sign-on operation. Some ORB-based application servers allow third-party CORBA security implementations to plug into their infrastructure. The problem then is to map the incoming web user's identity to the CORBA server's realm. This can be done manually by application code in the servlet, but a superior method is to use a web server which can integrate its security framework with the application server you choose. An even more general approach is to use a web server or proxy which can map web credentials to a CORBA Security model so that CORBA-based application servers can access it. Products like the Gradient NetCrusader work this way, allowing web applications to propagate the user's identity to CORBA servers which can utilize Gradient's CORBA Security 1.2 implementation.

Some web security solutions use server-specific APIs such as NSAPI or ISAPI. Since many Java servlet engines run as web server plugins using the same API, it may be difficult to incorporate both the security product and the Java runtime at the same time. One of my engineers came up with the creative solution of writing a security filter gateway which receives all incoming client requests, accesses the security server's client API, and then reposts the request to the same server. This technique allows credentials to be remapped to different credentials depending on the realm or server security domain being accessed. The approach is especially useful if client identity is not determinable from the session or connection but can be determined in some application-specific way, for example, using HTTP POST parameters generated or inserted by a proxy or VPN server. An example of this is the Palm VII network, which permits HTTPS connections between its proxies and other servers on the Internet, but which does not permit HTTPS sessions with the ultimate client—the Palm user. However, the Palm's network makes the user's identity available via a special POST parameter.

## Remote Method Invocation

Remote Method Invocation (RMI) is Java's built-in distributed object protocol. With RMI, you can define objects that export their interface, so that they can be called remotely from other applications in a network. The RMI mechanism handles all the details of packaging method parameters (this is called "marshalling"), sending them across the network to a remote object, unpackaging ("unmarshalling") the parameters at the other end, invoking the correct method with the parameter values, and finally returning the method return result, if any, back to the caller.

Later in this chapter, I will discuss using CORBA from Java. RMI is analogous to CORBA, but it is lighter-weight, and provides a much simpler and standardized model for establishing and managing connections between callers and callees.

All mechanisms of this kind require a facility to handle the packaging of data into a stream. An object-oriented language like Java will require a packaging facility which can package objects. Java's facility for this purpose is the serialization API, which is used by RMI for marshalling and unmarshalling objects. Thus, to understand RMI, we must first look at serialization.

### *Object Serialization*

Java object serialization is a general-purpose mechanism for converting an object's state into an encoded form that is independent of the virtual machine context in which the object was created. An object converted in this way can be saved to a file or sent across a network, and later reconstructed in a different virtual machine, to yield a new object equivalent to the original. The process of serializing an object is often referred to as "freezing" it, and the process of reconstruction is often referred to as "thawing."

For an object to be serializable, it must implement the java.io.Serializable or java.io.Externalizable interface. Objects are written to a java.io.ObjectOutputStream and read from a java.io.ObjectInputStream, using the writeObject() and readObject() methods respectively. First let's discuss the Serializable interface.

There are no methods in the Serializable interface—it is only used as a flag to indicate that the developer of the class intends that users of the class will be able to serialize objects of that type, and can do so without difficulty. Thus, to make an object serializable, simply do this:

```
public class MyClass implements java.io.Serializable
{
    ...
}
```

You can also do this:

```
public interface MySerializableInterface extends
    java.io.Serializable
{
        ...
}

public class MyClass implements MySerializableInterface
{
    ...
}
```

In this case, the class MyClass will be serializable, because it implements an interface that is.

To serialize a Java object, use the ObjectOutputStream.writeObject() method. In this example I start with a ByteArrayOutputStream, but you could use any OutputStream subclass:

```
OutputStream anyOutputStream = new ByteArrayOutputStream();
ObjectOutputStream objectOutputStream = new
ObjectOutputStream(anyOutputStream);
objectOutputStream.writeObject(myObject);
```

To unserialize an object, use the ObjectInputStream.readObject() method:

```
InputStream anyInputStream = new
ByteArrayInputStream(objectOutputStream.toByteArray());
ObjectInputStream objectInputStream = new
ObjectInputStream(anyInputStream);
myObject = (MyObjectType)(objectInputStream.readObject());
```

Note that you have to cast the unserialized object to the type you expect or determine it to be, so that you can then make method calls on it; if it is not of that type, a class cast exception will result.

You can write a sequence of objects to a stream, and in that case, you must read them back in the same order you wrote them. When you write an object, all of its attributes—objects and primitive types—are written automatically, except those that are either unserializable or which have a transient modifier. Static attributes are also not written. Giving an object attribute a transient modifier is like saying, "Don't serialize this, and don't save it in any persistent stores." The serialization process is recursive—all member objects (attributes) are serialized, and all members of the member objects are serialized, and so on, except for the exception cases identified. Object instances are not serialized redundantly, however once an object is added during a serialization operation, it is not added again within the same operation, even if it is referenced by multiple components.

If an object attribute is an object type, and the attribute type is not serializable, the attribute will not be serialized with the referencing object. Instead, when the referencing object is reconstructed, the default constructor for the attribute type will be used to provide a value for the attribute. This is a normal behavior mechanism, and is not considered an error. It is an error, however, if a default constructor needs to be called to initialize a transient attribute or nonserializable class, and no public default constructor exists.

Another caveat is that if a class is serializable, but its superclass is not, none of the attributes of the superclass will be serialized when the object is serialized. This is an important point to remember when extending classes and making them serializable. For this reason, you should consider implementing Serializable in all classes you develop which you intend to be reusable, and which might potentially be serialized or passed using RMI in a future application. RMI can only pass object values that are serializable.

Serialized data is "clear"—anyone can read it by writing a simple program. Therefore, if your program saves or transports serialized objects, you must consider the security ramifications of others intercepting those objects. If there are attributes which should not be serialized for this or another reason (e.g., they may be attributes that have no meaning outside of the originating VM's context, such as a database handle or a socket reference), you can either make the attribute transient, or refrain from making the attribute type serializable, and provide initialization in the type's zero-argument constructor.

Another approach for handling sensitive attributes is to encrypt them. You can accomplish this by overriding the default implementation of the object serialization mechanism. This is not as difficult as it sounds, since you can use default behavior for all but the sensitive attributes. The serialization mechanism automatically looks for a readObject() and writeObject() method in the class of each object that gets serialized, using object reflection. If it finds methods with these signatures, it uses them instead of the default mechanisms. Simply implement a readObject(ObjectInputStream in) and writeObject(ObjectOutputStream out) method for your class, and call in.defaultReadObject() and out.defaultWriteObject() at the beginning of your readObject() and writeObject() method respectively—this will take care of all non-transient attributes for that class. Then, in writeObject(), implement your own behavior for writing and possibly encrypting the sensitive attributes, and in readObject(), implement behavior for performing an inverse operation, perhaps decryption. The readObject() and writeObject() methods only operate on their own class, and not on superclass or subclass attributes.

The Externalizable interface provides a way for a class to completely take control over the way it is serialized, including all of its superclass attributes. The Externalizable interface has two methods: writeExternal() and readExternal(). If the object implements Externalizable (either directly or through a superclass), its writeExternal() method is called whenever the object is serialized. To reconstruct the object, the class's default constructor is called, followed by its readExternal() method. The writeExternal() and readExternal() methods are responsible for all object attribute serialization, including superclass attributes. If the object does not

implement Externalizable but does implement Serializable, the object is written and read using the object stream's default serialization mechanism.

Note that if you write serialized objects to a file, and then make modifications to the corresponding class definitions as part of a system upgrade, the data written previously will be obsolete, and you will probably not be able to read it back in. In general, therefore, serialization should not be used for long-term data storage. I discuss this in Chapter 1 and Chapter 6.

The object reconstruction mechanism automatically loads classes referenced by objects in the stream. It looks for the first non-null class loader on the current thread's stack—normally the class loader of the calling class. Thus, classes are only loaded as needed to represent the objects that get thawed. This is an important feature that is used by RMI, as will be discussed later in this chapter.

Java 2 adds several enhancements to the serialization mechanism, and changes the serialization format. The new deserialization mechanism (implemented in Java 1.1.7 and later) is backward compatible, however, and can deserialize the old format. You can indicate which version to use when serializing with the Java 2 ObjectOutputStream.useProtocolVersion() method. The serialization enhancements are of most interest to tool builders or those who want to implement alternative persistence mechanisms.

#### *How RMI Works*

To use the RMI mechanism, you define a Java interface that constitutes the remote interface you want to export over the network. You then implement that interface with a server object class, and use a special compiler ("rmic") to process that server class to generate what are known as "stub" and "skeleton" classes. These classes serve as the glue that links your remote clients with your server objects.

When your client makes a remote call, it is not actually calling the server object; it is calling a method on a stub class that is deployed with the client code. This stub is a proxy for the server object, and knows how to marshall the input parameters onto an RMI stream and send them to the server using the RMI protocol. At the server end, the skeleton code, through a connection set up by the RMI registry service, receives the stream, unmarshalls its contents, and calls the method identified in the stream. Since the skeleton is actually making the call to your server code, it is the recipient of any return value, and it marshalls this value and sends it back to the client as a stream, where the stub unmarshalls it and creates a new Java object to contain its value. This new object is then returned to the calling routine on the client side. Each method invocation on the server object occurs in its own thread. Your remote methods, therefore, must be thread-safe.

Calls made by your server-side code are local or remote, depending on what they are operating on. If they are operating on the the local server object instance, the calls are local. If they are operating on a remote object passed in as a method parameter from a remote client, or if they are operating on a remote object returned from another remote call, the call to that object will be remote—regardless where the associated object actually resides.

Note that the client does not call "new" for a remote object. It obtains remote objects by using the RMI name registry service to get an initial reference, and all subsequent remote references are obtained as return values in remote calls.

### *Passing or Returning Objects by Reference and by Value*

Java passes and returns all objects by reference—a Java object reference is always a local reference, in the context of the local Java VM. There is no remote referencing built into the Java VM.

When referencing a remote server object, an RMI client is actually referencing a local Java object which serves as a proxy for the server object. RMI will return or pass objects "by reference" or "by value." In this context, we are referring to what is marshalled—a remote reference object, or the contents of the actual object. Do not confuse RMI's remote passing by reference with the Java VM's pass-by-reference semantics. The Java VM always passes objects in and out of methods by reference. With regard to RMI, the difference between passing by value and by reference is what is being referenced—a local proxy for a remote object, or a local copy of the object. Objects passed by value must be serializable so that they can be converted into a stream by the marshalling mechanism, which uses Java serialization.

In a non-remote Java program, when you compare two objects using the "==" operator, you are comparing their identity—that is, you are determining if two references refer to precisely the same instance in memory. In effect, you are comparing their pointer addresses. Since there are no remote semantics built into the Java VM, and Java does not have operator overloading, the "==" operator continues to have this specific meaning even when comparing two references to remote objects. What you end up comparing is the pointer values of the two references, which, for a remote object reference, is actually a reference to the local proxy. Thus, comparing two remote references with the "==" operator determines if the two proxies are identical objects—not if the referenced remote objects are identical, which is probably what you want (in most cases).

Java RMI therefore generates an equals() method for the proxies, and guarantees that this method determines if two remote references refer to the same remote object instance. Thus:

```
remoteObjectA.equals(remoteObjectB)
```

returns true if and only if remoteObjectA, which is actually a local proxy for remote object A, refers to the same remote object (i.e., A) as remoteObjectB—that is, if A and B are the same object. Note that this use of the equals() method carries different semantics than a local equals method, which ordinarily is defined to return true of the contents of two objects are equal. The equals() method for two remote references does not call equals() for the remote object itself to check for the equality of contents of two remote objects—there is no remote call.

In addition, RMI provides a hashcode() method for proxies, so that the value returned by hashcode() for two proxies (stubs) return the same value if the proxies refer to the same remote object.

### *Basic RMI*

To create an RMI application, these are the things you must do:

- Define a remote interface
- Write the server-side implementation of that interface
- Write a server that instantiates and registers that implementation
- Generate stub and skeleton classes, using the RMI compiler (rmic)
- In your client, bind to ("lookup") the remote object
- In your client, make remote calls against the remote object

I will now explain each one with an example.

**Defining the Remote Interface.** Declare a Java interface that contains the methods you want to export as remote methods. When you declare this interface, extend java.rmi.Remote. The Remote interface has no methods, so this is trivial:

```
interface Server extends java.rmi.Remote
{
public String getStuff() throws java.rmi.RemoteException;
}
```

All remote methods must throw java.rmi.RemoteException. You may want to also throw Exception, because you cannot always anticipate what the actual implementation will throw, and if you only declare your remote methods to throw RemoteException, the implementations will not be able to throw anything that does not extend from RemoteException. When a remote method throws an exception, the exception object is marshalled just like any object and sent back to the client.

### *Implementing the Server Object*

The easiest way to implement the actual server object is to extend Unicast-RemoteObject, as follows:

```
public class ServerImpl
extends java.rmi.server.UnicastRemoteObject
implements Server
{
   public ServerImpl() throws java.rmi.RemoteException { super();
}

   public static void main(String[] args) throws Exception
   {
      System.setSecurityManager(new
         java.rmi.RMISecurityManager());
      Server server = new ServerImpl();
      java.rmi.Naming.rebind("MyServer", server);

   }

   public String getStuff() throws java.rmi.RemoteException
   {
      return "hi!";
   }
}
```

In the above example, we create a security manager, because this program will run as an application, so it does not automatically have a security manager unless we create one, and we will be servicing remote clients on the network, which exposes our VM to attack. It is therefore necessary to install a security manager to provide a security sandbox for remote methods to execute in. RMI requires it.

We then create an instance of the server object, and register it with the RMI name registry, so that client programs can perform a lookup to find it and get a remote reference to it. This method call blocks, and so if you want to register more than one object in the same main program you will have to perform the registration in a thread.

The server object must export itself using the exportObject() method. This makes it available to be called remotely. The UnicastRemoteObject constructor does this automatically, as well as other housekeeping things that remote server objects must do, so you will find it convenient to simply extend this class. (If for some reason you must extend another class and so cannot extend UnicastRemoteObject, you can implement the server object functionality yourself by calling the export-Object() method in the constructor for your class, and implementing the hashcode(),

equals(), clone(), readObject(), and writeObject() methods, using the Unicast-RemoteObject implementation as a guide. Usually you will not have to do this, however, since server objects are usually delegators, and do not typically extend from other classes—but this depends on your design.)

Note also that the main method simply exits after the server object registers itself. You might think that this would cause the entire application to terminate, but it does not, because the program is blocked waiting for incoming requests, and this keeps the program alive. Therefore, you do not have to make any special provisions to make the program block, waiting for requests, as this is taken care of. (This is not the case with CORBA applications, as you will see later.)

To generate stub and skeleton classes, run the rmic compiler, as follows:

```
rmic -d . ServerImpl
```

If your server object class is in a package, you would specify the package root after the -d option, and give the fully qualified name for the server class.

**The Client Must Find the Server.** A remote client can use the lookup method to find a server object registered with the naming registry. To look up an object, call the static lookup() method in the RMI Naming class, and specify a URL that identifies the registered name and optionally the host of the object you are trying to find:

```
Server server = (Server)(java.rmi.Naming.lookup(
    "//myhost/MyServer"));
```

If the object is on the same host, you can omit the leading hostname, and just use:

```
Server server = (Server)(java.rmi.Naming.lookup
    ("MyServer"));
```

Now we can make remote calls:

```
String s = server.getStuff();
```

### *Making Callbacks and Local Object Resolution*

In the example above, the remote call getStuff() returns a String. The String class is serializable (it is declared serializable in java.lang.String) so RMI can marshall it and pass it across the network. What the client gets when it makes this call is a copy of the actual string that exists on the server.

If our remote method returns an object whose class implements java.rmi.Remote, the object will be returned by reference—the client will get a proxy (stub) for the actual remote result, and the result object will remain on the server. The proxy can be used to then make calls to the remote object it represents. This is how your remote object methods can return objects that themselves are remote, and so the client does not usually have to call the name registry more than once at the start of a program to get the first reference.

The client can allow the server object to make callbacks to it by passing the server a remote object generated on the client. In this case, the client is sending back a server object, which must itself implement java.rmi.Remote. The main server object (or any other) may use this object sent from the client to make callbacks to the client.

Now suppose a client makes a remote call to the server, and is returned a remote object as a result. The client can pass this same remote object, generated on the server, back to the server, by using it as a parameter in another remote call. What will the server actually get—a remote object, or a reference to its own local object?

RMI does not automatically resolve remote references that are passed back, so the server object's method will receive a stub, even if the actual object represented by the stub exists in the server's VM. Unfortunately, Java 1.1 does not have a mechanism to find the local object. Java 1.2 beta 3 provided a method to find the local object, but the method was removed in beta 4 and the final SDK 1.2.0 release. Hopefully it will return in a future release. Many CORBA implementations perform this local resolution automatically.

***Codebase Issues***

If your server program is going to be accessed remotely by client programs (which is normally the case!), and the stub classes are not resident on the client, the machine hosting the server program will have to have a web server running on it, so that the remote classes can be retrieved by the client as needed. This is true regardless of whether the client program is an applet or not, since RMI uses the HTTP protocol to retrieve classes dynamically. (For testing, you can use a file URL—see below.) Note that analogous to an applet security manager, RMI will restrict downloads to the host to which the RMI connection exists.

The Java 1.1 version of the RMI registry would only encode a class's URL in a returned object stream if the registry itself obtains the class via a URL (i.e., the class is not in the registry process classpath). If the class is in its classpath, it would not encode the URL, and remote client would not know where to download the object's class from. Thus, when the registry was run, you had to make sure that only the JDK classes were in its classpath. In Java 2 this problem seems

to have been fixed, and the registry classpath does not appear to affect the visibility of servant classes to clients, as long as the java.rmi.server.codebase property is set properly when running a server, as I will now describe.

When you run your server program, you must set the codebase property for the program. When the server object registers itself with the registry, the registry will use the codebase property to find classes for that server object. To set the codebase property for a server program, do something like this:

```
java -Djava.rmi.server.codebase=http://myhost/mydir/MyServerClass
```

If you prefer to test your program without a web server, you can use a file URL instead. On Windows NT, use a URL of the form "file:/c:\mydir\"; on UNIX, use "file:/mydir/". (All forward slashes may work in a later Java Windows NT release.)

### *Remote Reflection*

You can remotely perform Java reflection on a remote interface to find out what methods it has, and then call those methods dynamically using the reflection API. This is a rough equivalent to CORBA's Dynamic Invocation Interface, discussed briefly later.

If you have a remote reference to an object, what you really have is a stub for that object. You can get the stub class by calling:

```
currentClass = remoteObject.getClass();
```

From this class, you can traverse the interfaces implemented by the class, and determine which ones implement java.rmi.Remote, again using reflection. For those that do, you can obtain their method signatures using the getMethods() call, which will return a list of Method objects describing each method, including its name and the types of its parameters and return type. This is enough information to allow you to find the corresponding method for the stub class, and then perform an invoke() on the stub object. This invoke results in a remote call, just as if you had called it statically.

### *Automatic Invocation*

Java is an object-oriented language, but most operating systems are not. Operating systems deal in terms of programs, and to create a Java object, you must first start a program. A Java program has a static entry point—main—which is not object-oriented at all. The main() method is just static code, like in any C program. At some point, the main() method may decide to create one or more objects.

RMI is a protocol that acts on objects, so to use it, your program must create some objects, which must implement one or more remote interfaces. In Java 1.1, you first had to start a program manually, to give it a chance to create some objects to export, before you could start making remote calls to those objects. This works fine if you have just one program and a few objects. If you have lots of RMI applications, however, and they create a lot of objects, it is impractical, because if the system needs to be restarted (gee, that never happens!), all these programs need to be restarted as well. Further, if there are lots of remote applications, not all of them may be needed at any one time, and it is inefficient to have all of them running, with all their objects created, just waiting to be invoked. It would be better if the programs could be started automatically when their objects are needed. That way, the system administrator would not have to worry about keeping all these RMI programs running.

CORBA from the beginning has had the concept of automatic object creation and activation, which the OMG refers to as a "persistent" object. Java 2 adds this feature to RMI, and the component that automatically starts object programs (called server programs) is the object activation daemon, "rmid."

When the RMI daemon instantiates a servant object, it needs to establish a Java VM for the servant to run in. This is specified by assigning a servant to an activation group. All activatable servants within an activation group run within the same VM. The activation daemon will start this VM if it is not already running.

To be automatically activatable, an RMI server object must have a constructor of the following form:

```
public <class name>(ActivationID id, MarshalledObject data)
throws java.rmi.RemoteException;
```

The abstract class Activatable provides some default behavior you can use to build activatable objects. You can extend this class, or you can do it yourself. Here is an example that shows how, for both cases:

```
import java.rmi.*;
public interface MyServer extends java.rmi.Remote
{
   public String ping() throws RemoteException;
}

import java.rmi.*;
import java.rmi.server.*;
import java.net.URL;
import java.security.PublicKey;
import java.security.CodeSource;
```

```
import java.rmi.activation.*;
import java.util.*;
public class MyServerImpl implements MyServer
{
   public static void main(String[] args) throws Exception
   {
      String codebase =
         "file:/d:\\servercodedir\\";

      // Install a security manager.
      System.setSecurityManager(new RMISecurityManager());

      // Specify the security policy file to use
      // for this activation group.
      Properties p = new Properties();
      p.put("java.security.policy",
         "d:\\policydir\\java.policy");
```

Above, I first identify the codebase. The codebase is needed to construct an activation descriptor for reactivating the object later—it is used to locate the object's classes. I then install a security manager, which is required for RMI, and specify a policy file to use whenever the server is activated. This is the policy file that will be used whenever the activation daemon starts a new VM to instantiate a servant object, which it must do if a VM of the required activation group is not running.

Next I define an activation group for this server to run in:

```
      // Create the activation group descriptor.
      ActivationGroupDesc ag = new ActivationGroupDesc(p, null);

      // Register the activation group, and obtain
      // an id for it.
      ActivationGroupID agid =
         ActivationGroup.getSystem().registerGroup(ag);

      // Create the activation group.
      ActivationGroup.createGroup(agid, ag, 0);
```

After this, I create a marshalled object, which is used to initialize the server object whenever it is reactivated. This is an optional step, and is useful for server objects that have a customizable or configurable initialization state, such as the name of a database dataset to use. A marshalled object is essentially an object wrapper for a serialized object; the original object can be reconstituted by calling the marshalled object's get() method.

```
      // You can provide an initialization object that
      // encapsulates the object's state.
      // For this to work, "AnyObjectType" must be a serializable
      // class.
      AnyObjectType initObject = new AnyObjectType();

      MarshalledObject mo = new MarshalledObject
         (initObject);
```

Below I construct the activation descriptor, and then register this descriptor with the activation daemon.

```
      ActivationDesc ad = new ActivationDesc(
         agid, "MyServerImpl", codebase, mo);
      MyServer server = (MyServer)Activatable.register(ad);
      Naming.rebind("My Server", server);
}
```

Next I define the constructor that gets called by the activation daemon whenever the object must be reinstantiated. As described earlier, this constructor must have the argument signature (ActivationID, MarshalledObject), and it must export the object to the RMI system, after which it can receive RMI calls.

```
   public MyServerImpl(ActivationID id, MarshalledObject data)
   throws java.rmi.RemoteException
   {
      // If this class extends Activatable:
      super(id, 0);

      // If this class does not extend Activatable:
      this.id = id;
      Activatable.exportObject(this, id, 0);

      // Use the marshalled object data to reconstruct the
      // object's state:
      this.data = (AnyObjectType)(data.get());
   }
   public String ping() throws RemoteException { return "ping"; }

   private AnyObjectType data;
   // If this class does not extend Activatable:
   ActivationID id;   // use this if you want to call
                      // inactive() or unregister()
}
```

To deploy the server, all we have to do is run the main program. We could have put the initialization functionality in a separate class, but that is not necessary. Running the main program will create the activation group, and register the server object. Later, if the server object is invoked but it is not running, it will be instantiated by the activation daemon (as long as the activation daemon is running).

When we run the main program, we should specify the policy file (a URL) which is to be used by the server, thereby using the same set of policies to deploy the object as it uses at runtime. We also need to specify the usual RMI server codebase URL:

```
java -Djava.security.policy=file:/policydir\java.policy
   -Djava.rmi.server.codebase=file:/servercodedir\ MyServerImpl
```

### *How RMI Assigns Server Ports*

Each RMI server process (i.e., program) has a ServerSocket associated with it. This ServerSocket is created when the first servant object bind occurs in the process (not to be confused with a TCP socket bind). This ServerSocket is shared by all RMI servants within the process. The ServerSocket's port is anonymous—it is not specified by your process, and is assigned automatically. The true port number (the port number on which the servant object listens) can be obtained by calling getLocalPort() on the ServerSocket. There is one assigned port per server process, since there is one ServerSocket per server process.

The process also creates a Socket connection to the registry. The Registry.getRegistry() call does not create the Socket; the Socket is only created when servants in the process bind to the registry.

RMI only creates new connections between a client process and server process when it needs to use a connection and none are available (not being used at that moment) between the client and server. Each new connection will require a new client Socket and will result in a new Socket on the server. The new client Socket will have a different local port number than other client sockets on that host, and the new Socket on the server will have the same local port number as other Sockets created by that server process's ServerSocket.

RMI has a legacy built-in connection multiplexing capability which is no longer supported, and therefore should not be relied on. This capability allowed a single connection to support multiple virtual connections. Currently, if all connections are in use, RMI creates a new connection. The multiplexing capability allows a single connection to support multiple virtual connections. This feature was added because Java 1.02 applets cannot create ServerSockets, and therefore cannot act as servers. The multiplexing capability allows an applet client which is connected to a remote server to export a remote object to the server and thereby become a server itself. The server will make callbacks to the client's objects by multiplexing on connections originated from the client. This mechanism still exists in SDK 1.2, but may not in the future. It automatically is used by RMI if an attempt to create a ServerSocket fails.

### *Object Reference Issues*

Within every object reference, RMI by default embeds the IP address of the server which exports the object. It obtains this IP address by calling InetAddress.getLocalHost().getHostAddress(). The problem with this is that IP addresses can change, especially if a DHCP server assigns them dynamically. In practice this is usually not a problem since a DHCP server will try to keep IP addresses constant if it can. Another problem, however, is that if the object is exported across a firewall, the embedded address can expose the host's internal network number. This issue is revisited later when I discuss using RMI across mapped ports.

If you want to override the use of IP addresses in remote references, you can do so by setting the property java.rmi.server.useLocalHostname to true. RMI will then attempt to identify a fully qualified name for the host, using a reverse DNS lookup if necessary. Only if that fails will it then use the machine's IP address.

Unfortunately, InetAddress.getLocalHost().getHostAddress() may not return the IP address you intend. A machine can have more than one IP address if it has multiple network interfaces. The IP address you want in a servant's remote references is the IP address that its intended clients can route to. You can bypass all of this and set the hostname to use by setting the java.rmi.server.hostname property.

If your servant objects are going to be referenced across a mapped port from outside a firewall, you might want to set the above property to a fictitious value, to hide the internal namespace of your network. Making this work is somewhat complex, however. See the discussions later in the subsection "Application Proxy Firewall Port Mapping" on page 490.

If a hostname is used instead of an IP address, the name must be resolved when the reference is used by a client. If the name is not resolvable on the name server being used by the client, then the remote reference will not be usable. This situation is depicted in Figure 7-3.

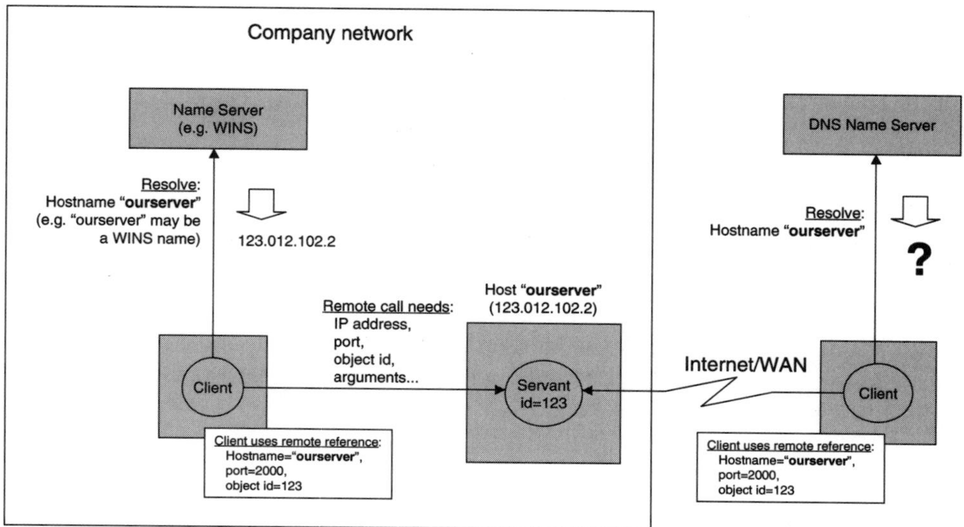


**Figure 7-3** Clients outside a firewall cannot resolve a servant host.

Make sure that the domain name of the server machine is set correctly. An incorrect domain can often go unnoticed because it will not prevent machines from that domain from communicating with each other. If the RMI server's network uses a DHCP server and sets the domain in that way, check that the domain name option is set correctly to the domain that the RMI server belongs to—not the domain that the DHCP server belongs to.

Of course, if the server exports objects from inside a firewall, remote clients will not be able to resolve object reference hostnames nor will they be able to route to object reference IP addresses—so they will not be able to find the servants, unless the clients are designed to access a mapped port on the firewall.

**JDK 1.1.1–1.1.6.** When creating a remote reference, JDK releases 1.1.1 through 1.1.6 do not ensure that the hostname embedded in object references is canonical or standard in any way. For example, these releases do not ensure that it is a DNS name instead of a WINS name, or that it is a complete DNS name: they use whatever the operating system returns as the hostname.

To prevent this problem with these releases, make sure the hostname is resolvable by all clients. If the name is not resolvable on the name server being used by a client, then the remote reference will not be usable.

### Security Permissions that Need to be Enabled

RMI uses network resources. Therefore, when using RMI, you may need to grant these permissions to your application or your system in your server policy file:

```
// Allows your server application to contact the
// host the registry is running on. The registry
// port is 1099 unless you start the registry on
// a different port than its default.
// The <registry-host> may be specified as
// an IP address or a hostname.
permission java.net.SocketPermission
   "<registry-host>:<registry-port>",
   "connect,resolve";

// Allows your server application to receive
// incoming requests on the specified.
// The <servant-host> is normally the machine
// running the server, but you need to specify it,
// since a port is associated with an IP address,
// and the machine may have more than one network
// adapter. It may be specified as an IP address or
// a domain name, but the domain name.
permission java.net.SocketPermission
   "<servant-host>:<servant-port>",
   "connect,accept,resolve";
```

Normally you don't know what port your servant will be listening on, unless you have implemented a technique for controlling the port (discussed in the next section). If you do not know the port, you may need to specify a port range. For example,

```
permission java.net.SocketPermission "<servant-host>:1000-",
   "connect,accept,resolve";
```

allows connections to port 1000 and above.

Client applications will need to specify at least "connect,resolve" SocketPermission for the server host, and possibly "accept" as well if the client exports its own remote objects.

If you create a custom socket factory (discussed in the next section), you will also need to grant this permission:

```
permission java.lang.RuntimePermission "setFactory";
```

Note that you may have three or more security policy files on your system. See Chapter 4 for a discussion of how these are used.

Finally, if you create your own socket factory, and if the registry is not on the same host as the server, the registry host may need appropriate policy settings as well to allow the registry to use your untrusted socket factory code. This is discussed in the next section.

### Controlling Port Numbers and Network Adapter Selection

If you create a socket factory for RMI, you can set the server socket port (the "localport"). This is one way to control this port number, rather than letting it be random. In particular, if you need to configure a firewall to allow an RMI gateway program to listen on a certain port, you would need to set the RMI gateway port number to a specific value, and then "open" that port on the firewall—i.e., allow external connections to that port. (In general there would have to be a strong case for opening a port.)

Java 2 allows you to set a different port for each RMI servant object. If you do not specify a port or socket factory when you call the UnicastRemoteObject constructor, RMI will use a single port for each server program. The firewall will also have to pass requests to the RMI registry, on port 1099—but you can override this value as well and use a different value. The bottom line is that your firewall will have to open at least two ports—which you can set—one port for the registry, and one for your server object.

If your server object does not extend UnicastRemoteObject and it needs to export objects on multiple different ports, you can use the export method added to UnicastRemoteObject in SDK 1.2, which accepts a port number parameter:

```
public static Remote exportObject(Remote obj, int port)
   throws RemoteException
```

The servant class must then also provide RMI-compatible implementations for the equals(), hashCode(), and toString() methods. If your servant extends Activatable instead of UnicastRemoteObject, the Activatable class also has an exportObject() method that takes a port as a parameter. If you are using javax.rmi.PortableRemoteObject (i.e., an IIOP RMI servant), you currently cannot export multiple objects on different ports, because as of this writing PortableRemoteObject does not have an exportObject() method with a port parameter. However, the final release of javax.rmi may.

A client connection has a client-side local port number associated with that connection. This port number is by default assigned by the client's network software, and is anonymous to the client and server. However, it does exist, and has a number—and the firewall will have to allow return packets directed to this port number. This is not a problem in practice, because the firewall sets up its own proxy connection and remembers the client's port number.

If a client exports an object, the client becomes a server, and a ServerSocket is created. In this situation the client (which is now a server also) can control the socket it exports objects on in the same way as described for a server.

Another parameter you might need to control is the network interface used. Some machines have more than one IP address—one for each network card or dialup connection on the machine. If you want your socket connections to use a particular interface, you need to use a socket factory to control it. In the socket factory, the createSocket() method will have to create a socket with the allowed local port number and network interface address. Below I explain how you can provide a socket factory to create custom RMI sockets.

Finally, while connections you make to the RMI registry are transient—they are closed when the call returns—connections you make to remote servers you write are persistent for awhile and timeout. These connections are reestablished automatically as needed, transparent to the application. Therefore you do not need to worry that a large number of inactive RMI clients will tie up lots of communication resources.

### Creating Custom RMI Sockets

The following example shows a socket factory which uses an application-specified port number, but assumes the host it is running on has a single IP address and obtains that:

```
public class MySocketFactory extends RMISocketFactory
{
   private int socketLocalPort;
   private int serverSocketLocalPort;

   public MySocketFactory(int socketLocalPort,
      int serverSocketLocalPort)
   {
      this.socketLocalPort = socketLocalPort;
      this.serverSocketLocalPort = serverSocketLocalPort;
   }

   public Socket createSocket(String host, int port)
   throws IOException
   {
      InetAddress localAddr = null;
      try
      { localAddr = InetAddress.getByName(null); }
```

```
            // null means localhost
        catch (UnknownHostException ex)
        {
            throw new RuntimeException(
            "Can't identify client IP address");
        }

        // Here I am just creating a standard socket for
        // illustraion, but you could create any specialized
        // type of socket.
        return new Socket(host, port, localAddr,
            socketLocalPort);
    }

    public ServerSocket createServerSocket(int port)
    throws IOException
    {
        int p = (port == 0 ? serverPort : port);
        // Here I am creating a standard server socket, but
        // you could create any specialized type of server socket.
        ServerSocket ss = new ServerSocket(port);
        return ss;
    }
}
```

To establish this new socket factory in the RMI runtime, you need to call the setSocketFactory(...) static method. This method requires privilege, so it should be encapsulated in a privileged block, so that the rest of the application does not need to have "setFactory" permission (see Chapter 4):

```
class MyAction implements PrivilegedExceptionAction
{
    private MySocketFactory sf;
    public MyAction(MySocketFactory sf) { this.sf = sf; }
    public Object run() throws java.io.IOException
    {
        // privileged code:
        RMISocketFactory.setSocketFactory(sf);
        return null;
    }
}

MySocketFactory sf = new MySocketFactory(serverPort);
AccessController.doPrivileged(new MyAction(sf));
```

For a client to access a server which provides a socket factory in this way, the client must also install the same socket factory:

```
public class Client
{
   private static MyServer myServer;
   public static void main(String[] args) throws Exception
   {
      int serverPort = Integer.parseInt(args[0]);
      MySocketFactory sf = new MySocketFactory(serverPort);
      RMISocketFactory.setSocketFactory(sf);
      Registry registry =
         LocateRegistry.getRegistry("localhost");
      MyServer myServer =
         (MyServer)(registry.lookup("Server 1"));
      System.out.println(myServer.ping());
   }
}
```

This technique works with both Java 1.1 and Java 2. However, it has the drawbacks that clients must install the required socket factory, and also that an entire application runtime must use the same socket factory. Java 2 provides a way for a server object to specify a socket factory just for itself. That way other RMI servants and clients in the same VM runtime will be able to use the standard RMI socket factory or others they create. This is done by first creating implementations for the Java 2 interfaces RMIServerSocketFactory and RMIClientSocketFactory, and then passing these to the UnicastRemoteObject constructor. Let's look at a simple example. First I will define implementations for RMIClientSocketFactory and RMIServerSocketFactory:

```
public class MyClientSocketFactory implements
RMIClientSocketFactory, Serializable
{
   public Socket createSocket(String host, int port)
   throws IOException
   {
      return new Socket(host, port);
   }
}
public class MyServerSocketFactory implements
RMIServerSocketFactory
{
   private int serverPort;

   public MyServerSocketFactory(int serverPort)
```

```
    {
       this.serverPort = serverPort;
    }

    public ServerSocket createServerSocket(int port)
    throws IOException
    {
       int p = (port == 0 ? serverPort : port);
       ServerSocket ss = new ServerSocket(p);
       return ss;
    }
}
```

Notice that the RMIClientSocketFactory implementation must be serializable, so that the client socket factory can be transported to the client. In the above example, I am again trivially creating standard socket implementations for illustration. In practice, if you were to go to the trouble to create socket factories, you would be creating some kind of specialized socket, such as an SSL socket.

The main difference in the implementation of the server class is that you do not have to statically set an RMI socket factory. Instead you set a client and server socket factory for the individual servant. This is done through the superclass, in the UnicastRemoteObject constructor:

```
public interface MyServer extends Remote
{
    public String ping() throws RemoteException;
}
public class MyServerImpl extends UnicastRemoteObject implements
    MyServer
{
    public MyServerImpl(String name, int serverPort)
    throws Exception
    {
       super(serverPort,
          new MyClientSocketFactory(),
          new MyServerSocketFactory(serverPort));
       LocateRegistry.getRegistry().rebind(name, this);
    }

    public static void main(String[] args) throws Exception
    {
       System.setSecurityManager(new RMISecurityManager());
       new MyServerImpl("My Server", 6000);
    }
```

```
   public String ping() throws RemoteException
   {
      return "ping";
   }
}
```

The client implementation is simpler as well, because the client does not have to also set a socket factory. Instead, the client socket factory is automatically transported to the client as needed:

```
public class Client
{
   public static void main(String[] args) throws Exception
   {
      Registry registry =
         LocateRegistry.getRegistry("localhost");
      MyServer myServer = (MyServer)(registry.lookup(
         "My Server"));
      System.out.println(myServer.ping());
   }
}
```

To set a socket factory, the client and server code will need to have certain permissions, including setFactory and "connect,resolve" SocketPermission. This is true for both the runtime in which you execute your client and server applications, as well as the registry runtime. You can accomplish this for testing by adding these permissions to your jre java.policy file. For final deployment, you should add these permissions for the specific software codesource corresponding to your socket factories.

### *Creating a Registry with Custom Sockets*

The RMI registry can also use a custom socket factory. In Java 1.1, you can only have one socket factory per RMI runtime, so if you use a custom factory for your application, you will need to use the same custom factory for the registry as well. Java 2 is more flexible in that you can use the standard sockets for contacting the registry.

If you choose to use a custom socket factory for the registry as well, you will need to start the registry programmatically, and use the static method:

```
Registry createRegistry(int port, RMIClientSocketFactorycsf,
   RMIServerSocketFactory ssf)
```

To use this registry, however, you need to pass a remote reference to it to a client. Thus, you will need to "bootstrap" the process with a standard registry, or statically install the required socket factory in the client.

### *HTTP Tunnelling*

RMI first attempts to use its native protocol to reach its destination. If this fails, the built-in socket implementation will attempt to use the SOCKS protocol to create an outbound connection to the destination. If the outbound firewall only allows HTTP traffic, these attempts will fail and RMI will try to tunnel using HTTP. This behavior is provided by the default RMI socket implementation. The major disadvantage of this is that it is inefficient, and callbacks are not supported due to the request/response nature of HTTP.

To enable the HTTP tunneling capability (not to be confused with "proxy tunneling"), you will need to set the HTTP proxy properties http.proxyHost, http.proxyPort, and http.nonProxyHosts. These are discussed in Chapter 5.

### *Servants Behind a Firewall*

Accessing services from the outside to the inside, across a firewall, is tricky because firewalls are designed to prevent access from the outside, and most client software provides capabilities for getting out of a firewall but not for getting in. In addition, RMI embeds host names or IP addresses in remote references, and so transporting object references across a firewall results in exposing the internal network address or name space. For this reason, it is usually not a good idea to allow external access to internal RMI servers. Nevertheless, in some scenarios it may be justified.

In most environments access through a firewall from the outside is only allowed by a bastion server, which first front-ends web requests from the Internet. In some cases it may be necessary to allow direct controlled access through the firewall from the outside. One scenario is allowing direct access by trusted and authenticated users such as off-site staff or business partners that may need to access those objects from the outside. Establishing a VPN connection is usually the best approach in this situation. Another scenario is for allowing callbacks, when the objects inside the firewall got there because a client application inside the firewall accessed a server on the outside, and the objects were dynamically created by the client application to provide a callback interface that the server can call. This represents a potential for a Trojan horse, and should be allowed only for trusted applications.

A third scenario for access to an internal server from the outside is when there simply is no static web content required by the application, in which case a front-end web server would serve no purpose. This scenario can occur if all web content is dynamically generated by an application server. If the application server is behind the firewall, it may then be more practical to allow controlled access directly to the application server rather than host a bastion server in a DMZ which would merely provide redirection and nothing more. Internal network addresses are still hidden, because access occurs through the firewall proxy via a mapped port.

Such applications obviously should be carefully restricted in their privileges. Servants inside a firewall cannot easily be reached from the outside because clients cannot see the IP address of their server nor can clients resolve the hostname of the server, and because the firewall restricts traffic to certain ports, the direction of the traffic, and even the type of traffic. Some CORBA products have the ability to automatically proxy objects at a firewall, making use of IIOP's built-in object reference indirection. At this time, RMI does not have this capability. Nevertheless, it is possible to access objects inside a firewall from the outside if special provisions are made. The approach depends on the kind of firewall.

**SOCKS.** If an RMI server object does not know ahead of time what its port will be, it can find out at runtime, and it is the runtime value that is encoded in remote references to the object. However, finding out at runtime is insufficient if the servant is behind a SOCKS firewall, because the firewall needs to be configured to allow port accesses. The SOCKS BIND command enables a server to dynamically register callback ports with a SOCKS firewall, but this SOCKS capability (i.e., BIND) is not implemented yet for Java ServerSockets, which is what is required. Therefore, it is not possible to reach objects inside a SOCKS firewall from outside, unless all port numbers are controlled through a socket factory, and the SOCKS firewall is configured to allow connections to that port.

A more straightforward but potentially risky solution is to implement an object gateway by running a small number of servants on the firewall host, which in turn make calls to servants behind the firewall. More general solutions include using a VPN for access by external partners, or using a generic application gateway (see below).

**Application Proxy Firewall Port Mapping.** RMI cannot utilize natively a mapped port for traversing a firewall. The reason is that object addresses are determined dynamically based on the addresses embedded in object references. To implement port mapping, it would be necessary to either parse RMI messages and rewrite the embedded addresses, or to provide a socket factory which establishes the required proxy connection, similar to the way the Java socket implementation automatically attempts to connect to a SOCKS proxy if appropriate properties are set. Note that a socket factory would have to be provided for the registry as well.

For example, you could define a client socket factory class like this:

```
public class MyClientSocketFactory implements
RMIClientSocketFactory, Serializable
{
   private String firewallHost;
   private int mappedPort = 0;

   public MyClientSocketFactory(String firewallHost,
      int mappedPort)
   {
      this.firewallHost = firewallHost;
      this.mappedPort = mappedPort;
   }

   public Socket createSocket(String host, int port)
   throws IOException
   {
      // Ignore specified host and port; connect to
      // firewall host and mapped port instead.
      return new Socket(firewallHost, mappedPort);
   }
}
```

and a server program like this:

```
public class MyServerImpl extends UnicastRemoteObject implements
   MyServer
{
   static Registry registry;

   public MyServerImpl(String name, String firewallHost,
      int mappedPort, int serverPort) throws Exception
   {
      super(serverPort,
         new MyClientSocketFactory(firewallHost, mappedPort),
         new MyServerSocketFactory(serverPort));
      registry.rebind(name, this);
   }

   public static void main(String[] args) throws Exception
   {
      System.setSecurityManager(new RMISecurityManager());

      // Create servant.
      new MyServerImpl("My Server", <firewall host>,
         <server mapped port>, <server port>);
```

```
   }

   public String ping() throws RemoteException
   {
      return "ping";
   }
}
```

You must also provide a means for external clients to access the registry. You can create a registry instance which uses your client socket factory:

```
public class CreateMyRegistry
{
   public static void main(String[] args) throws Exception
   {
      System.setSecurityManager(new RMISecurityManager());

      // Create a registry.
      registry = LocateRegistry.createRegistry(1099,
         new MyClientSocketFactory(
            <firewallhost>, <registry mapped port>),
         new MyServerSocketFactory(1099));
   }
}
```

A client can then access the RMI server application as long as it uses the client socket factory and provides the appropriate values for the firewall host and the registry mapped port number:

```
public class Client
{
   public static void main(String[] args) throws Exception
   {
      Registry registry =
         LocateRegistry.getRegistry(
            <firewall host>,
            <registry mapped port>,
            new MyClientSocketFactory(<firewall host>,
            <registry mapped port>));
      MyServer myServer = (MyServer)(registry.lookup(
         "My Server"));
      System.out.println(myServer.ping());
   }
}
```

You must still decide how the client will obtain the client socket factory class. The easiest way is to simply deploy that class with the client. If you do not want to do that, you can place the class on a web server and specify that as the java.rmi.server.codebase property when you run the RMI server program. Regardless how you do it, *make sure that the exported objects do not carry with them the internal IP address of your server.* You can check this simply by printing out a remote reference on the client. Again, the embedded addresses can be controlled with the java.rmi.server.codebase property.

Mapping ports, shown in Figure 7-4, is not popular with system administrators because it represents a non-standard configuration, and is also a potential security hole, since the administrator may not know much about the server program running on the destination port, and whether it has vulnerabilities that can represent a threat to the entire network. Nevertheless, it can be the best solution in some cases if routes are carefully controlled. If the only route to the mapped port is from a bastion web server running a servlet engine, then the uncertainties your administrator may have related to these new components may be alleviated since all access is through the web server. An additional firewall can also be placed around the application server, effectively placing it in a DMZ. At some point, however, some non-HTTP protocol is going to have to pass through to access company data resources, unless you replicate your data.

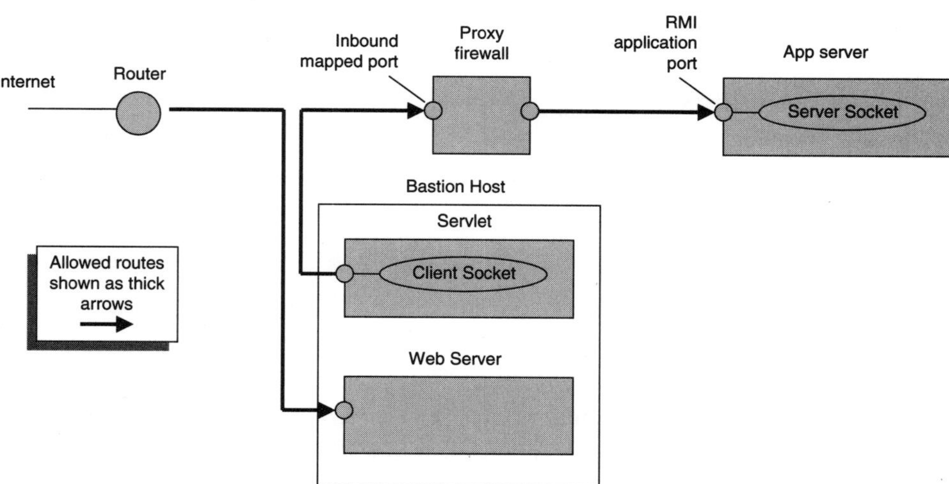


**Figure 7-4** Using RMI socket factories to access mapped ports.

**Application Gateways.** The least problematic way to route RMI requests through a firewall is to write a special gateway application which runs on the firewall machine, receives incoming requests on an "open" port, and generates new equivalent requests to the server behind the firewall. This does not require getting involved with the intricacies of the RMI protocol or object identifiers. Administrators are *most leary of all,* however, of running any non-firewall component on a firewall machine. Exceptions are sometimes made for special firewall proxies, which are designed to pass special protocols which are not supported by the standard firewall and which cannot pass through a mapped port. An example of this is IIOP.

A safer way to deploy a gateway is to run it on an internal machine behind the firewall. In this case, access to the gateway only occurs using a trusted protocol such as HTTP. The gateway receives HTTP requests and either converts them into RMI or other formats or delegates the requested service to an application server. This is depicted in Figure 7-5.

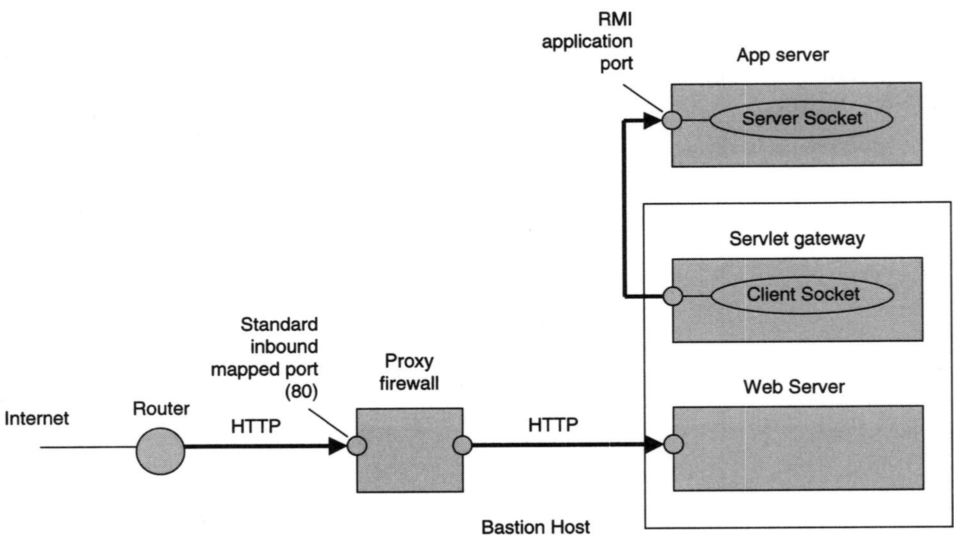


**Figure 7-5** A common gateway configuration for accessing an application server.

A gateway can be written in a generic way to support an application protocol such as RMI, or it can be specific to an application. Writing an application-specific gateway for an RMI server is merely a matter of writing an application with the required services exposed, and delegating those services to an internal server. You can then run an external public registry to allow external applications to look up just those objects which are publicly available. If necessary, it would not be hard to write an authentication layer to access the server, by implementing an appropriate socket factory, or by incorporating authentication into the application.

Generic gateways present a significant security risk, since they allow an arbitrary client to send an arbitrary request to an arbitrary internal destination port using an arbitrary underlying protocol—and in most cases the network administrator does not even know! A gateway should allow for configuration, so that an administrator can specify source and target hosts and ports.

Passing or proxying client requests through the server's firewall is only half the equation. Clients behind a firewall may need a way to be configured to redirect their requests to their own firewall. I have already discussed the proxyHost and proxyPort Java system properties in Chapter 5. In addition, client-side firewalls often do not allow internal clients to connect to external servers on non-standard port numbers (i.e., external port numbers other than 80, 443, etc.).

To service clients behind firewalls that restrict request port numbers, an RMI server may need to be exported on port 80 (or another port that will be allowed by the client's firewall). Alternatively, Sun provides a CGI program with JDK 1.1 which accepts RMI requests wrapped in HTTP and forwards them to the RMI server. The CGI program relies on the fact that RMI client stubs have the ability to automatically wrap their protocol in HTTP when required and route requests to port 80 if all else fails. The client RMI facilities automatically use the proxyHost and proxyPort Java property settings to find the local proxy, and they then reformat HTTP requests to specify the gateway program in the URL. The actual RMI content is then provided as the data in the HTTP stream. Needless to say, this process is quite inefficient and unscalable, so it is most suitable for small, special-purpose applications.

The RMI CGI gateway program executable is called "java-rmi.cgi." Let's look at an example of its use. On the server, run the server program with the -D option specifying the name of the host it is running on, for example,

```
java -Djava.rmi.server.hostname=<this-host> YourServerImplClassName
```

Use the domain name of the host—not its IP address.

The RMI Gateway program is located in the JDK 1.1 bin directory. Install a web server on the server machine if there is not one running there already. Place the java-rmi.cgi program in the web server's cgi-bin directory (you must have a directory called "cgi-bin" immediately under your web root). Set an environment variable for CGI processes (or for your system), called "java.home," to point to where the JRE is installed; this will enable the CGI program to find the Java interpreter.

**The Blocked Registrant Pattern.** If calling a servant through a firewall is not an option, it may be possible in some situations to initiate the call from the other direction and then wait for a reply. This is often practical for implementing callbacks. For example, suppose a client behind a firewall calls a remote RMI server which is outside the firewall. The client itself creates and exports a callback object and passes this as an argument to the remote server. Thus, the client is a server as well. The problem is that the remote server may not be able to use the object passed to it to call back to the client, because the client is behind a firewall. Therefore, instead of passing a callback object reference to the remote server, the client could simply call a special method on the server and wait for a reply; in this case the reply constitutes the callback. This is known as the "blocking registrant" pattern.

To implement this, each client must have a registration thread which calls a registration method in the remote server in a loop. The remote server must provide a special re-entrant registration method, which adds the request to a list and then blocks. Whenever the server wishes to send an event or message to a particular registered client, it interrupts that client's blocked thread. The unblocked thread then calls a method to obtain the event or message and returns it to the caller—which is the client. The client then unblocks as well and receives the returned value. After storing the value and making it available to the client application, the client's registration thread can then can re-register itself in a loop so that it is always waiting for a message. A basic template for this is as follows:

```
public class MyClientImpl implements Runnable
{
   public MyClient() { (new Thread(this)).start(); }
   public void run()   // The registration thread runs this
   {
      while (true)
      {
         Message message =
            myServer.registerForMessage();   // blocks.
         // We have now received a message from the server.
         (new MessageHandlerThread(message)).start();
      }
   }
}
public class MyServerImpl implements MyServer
{
   public Message registerForMessage()
   {
      // Add this thread to list of clients
      clients.addElement(Thread.currentThread());
      try
```

```
        {
            wait();
        }
        catch (InterruptedException ex)
        {
            return messages.getClientThreadsMessage(
                Thread.currentThread());
        }
    }
    public void sendMessageToClient(Thread thread, Message msg)
    {
        messages.insertForClient(thread, msg);
        thread.interrupt();
    }
}
```

For this to work requires that the protocol's (e.g., JRMP or IIOP) service dispatching mechanism creates a new service thread for each incoming request, or at least is able to dynamically grow its service thread pool. This ensures we will not run out of service threads as the number of blocked clients increases. RMI and some IIOP implementations provide this.

This approach is not very scalable unless a tiered architecture is implemented with the actual application server at the top. (See "Multiple EJB Server Tiers" on page 739.) The reason is that a persistent long-term connection is needed for each client, and each client blocks a thread on the server. If there are local messaging servers for each group of clients, and the messaging servers themselves register themselves with the next tier in the same manner, a scalable arrangement can be created. Messaging middleware typically implements this for you, so you do not have to design it.

One difficulty in implementing this is that often HTTP is used by the client to reach the server. If the RMI call is wrapped in HTTP, this approach will require a long-term HTTP connection to the destination host. Depending on the nature of the remote server and whether a gateway through a standard web server is being used, the connection may timeout. The TCP connection may also timeout for other reasons, so your design may need to reconnect when this happens.

### *Implementing Secure RMI*

Adding SSL support to RMI requires installing a socket factory which provides SSL. There are many things to consider in an SSL implementation, including integration with other key management facilities, as well as support for SOCKS and SSL tunneling (also called "proxy tunneling"), which are two alternative ways of passing an SSL session through a firewall. Java sockets have built-in support for SOCKS and HTTP tunneling (not to be confused with proxy tunneling), and you do not want to give these capabilities up if you have a choice. I have already discussed SOCKS and the different forms of tunneling in Chapter 4 and Chapter 5.

Below I will demonstrate how to create a secure RMI server and client using SSL sockets. For this demonstration, I will use the Phaos SSL socket library from Phaos Technologies.

First, define a socket factory class by extending RMISocketFactory. This class has two methods you must implement: createSocket() and createServerSocket(). Note that in this example the CA's certificate is in a file called CACert.der, the server certificate we are using is in a file called MyServerCertificate.der, and the user's (client's) certificate is in a file called MyCertificate.der. Also, the server's private key is in a file called MyServerPrivateKey.der, and the user's private key is in a file called MyPrivateKey.der. In a real application we would obtain all these from a certificate database, or use a user interface to allow the user and/or server administrator to identify them, instead of hard-coding file names as is done here.

I have already shown that you can create an RMI socket factory by implementing the Java 2 interfaces RMIClientSocketFactory and RMIServerSocketFactory, or by extending RMISocketFactory which implements both of these. For this example, I will do the latter for simplicity:

```
import java.rmi.server.*;
import crysec.SSL.*;    // This is the Phaos package
public class SSLRMISocketFactory extends RMISocketFactory
{
```

First we need to implement the createSocket() method for creating client sockets:

```
   public  Socket createSocket(String host, int port) throws
   IOException
   {
      X509 acceptedCACert = new X509(new File("CACert.der"));
      SSLParams params = new SSLParams();
```

If your application requires client authentication, it needs to do something like the following:

```
      // If using client-side authentication:
      SSLCertificate cert = new SSLCertificate();
      cert.certificateList = new Vector();
      // Now load the client certificate and the CA's
      // certificate in DER format.
      // These are the files obtained from the CA.
      // You could replace this with an access to a
      // certificate manager.
```

```
cert.certificateList.addElement(new X509(new
   File("MyCertificate.der")));
cert.certificateList.addElement(acceptedCACert);
cert.privateKey = new RSAPrivateKeyPKCS8(
   "password", new File("MyPrivateKey.der"));
params.setClientCert(cert);
// End client authentication code
```

Now specify what cipher suites the client prefers. The selection of cipher suite is up to the server, but the client has to say what it has.

```
short[] cipherSuites = new short[1];
cipherSuites[0] =
   SSLParams.SSL_RSA_WITH_3DES_EDE_CBC_SHA;
params.setClientCipherSuites(cipherSuites);
SSLSocket s =  new SSLSocket(host, port, params);
```

We have now constructed an SSL client socket. We need to get the server's certificate and validate it. Then I also do some other checks, which you don't have to do, but this is just to illustrate. When these checks are done, return the socket:

```
   SSLCertificate scert = s.getServerCert();
   if (scert == null) throw new IOException("No server
   certificate");
   if (! scert.rootCAvalid())) throw new IOException("CA's
      certificate not valid");

   // Check the CA's distinguished name
   X509 cacert = scert.rootCA();
   if (! cacert.getIssuer().equals
      (acceptedCACert.getIssuer()))
         throw new IOException("Hey - this is not our CA!");

   // Check the CA's public key
   if (! cacert.getPublicKey().equals
      (acceptedCACert.getPublicKey()))
         throw new IOException("Hey - this cert doesn't really
                belong to our CA!");

   // Report that we have accepted the CA
   X509 cacert = scert.rootCA();
  System.out.println("We have accepted a certificate signed by "
      + cacert.getIssuer().toString());

   return s;
}
```

Now we have to implement the createServerSocket() method for creating server sockets. This is very similar, so I will only point out the differences:

```
   public  ServerSocket createServerSocket(int port) throws
      IOException
   {
      SSLParams params = new SSLParams();

      // Get server certificate chain
      SSLCertificate cert = new SSLCertificate();
      cert.certificateList = new Vector();
      // Now load the server certificate and the CA's certificate
      // in DER format.
      // These are the files obtained from the CA.
      // You could replace this with an access to a certificate
      // manager.
      cert.certificateList.addElement(
            new X509(new File("MyServerCertificate.der")));
      cert.certificateList.addElement(new X509(new
         File("CACert.der")));
      cert.privateKey = new RSAPrivateKeyPKCS8(
         "password", new File("MyServerPrivateKey.der"));
      params.setServerCert(cert);

      SSLServerSocket ss =  new SSLServerSocket(port, params);
```

We have now constructed an SSL server socket. If we are requiring client-side authentication, we need to check the client's identity. If the client passes, return the socket:

```
      // If you are using client-side authentication:
      if (ss.getClientCert() == null)
         throw new IOException("No client certificate");
      if (! ss.getClientCert().rootCAvalid()))
         throw new IOException("CA's certificate not valid");
      // End client-side authentication
      return ss;
   }
}
```

We can use the socket factory we have created in our RMI application. All we need to do is create an instance of the factory, and call RMISocketFactory.setSocketFactory():

```
import java.rmi.server.*;
public class MyClientClass
{
```

```
    static
    {
        SSLRMISocketFactory sf = new SSLRMISocketFactory();
        RMISocketFactory.setSocketFactory(sf);
    }

    public static void main(String[] args)
    {
        ...now we can use RMI as we would before...
    }
}

import java.rmi.server.*;
public class MyServerClass
{
    static
    {
        SSLRMISocketFactory sf = new SSLRMISocketFactory();
        RMISocketFactory.setSocketFactory(sf);
    }

    public static void main(String[] args)
    {
        ...now we can use RMI as we would before...
    }
}
```

You also need to create an SSL socket factory for the RMI registry, since your RMI clients will be using SSL sockets, and they will be contacting the registry. Here is an example of an SSL registry implementation:

```
public class SSLRegistryImpl extends RegistryImpl implements
    Registry
{
    public SSLRegistryImpl(int p) throws RemoteException
        { super(p); }

    public static void main(String[] args)
    {
        System.setSecurityManager(new RMISecurityManager());
        RMISocketFactory.setSocketFactory(new
            SSLRMISocketFactory();
        SSLRegistryImpl = new
            SSLRegistryImpl(Integer.parseInt(args[0]));
        synchronized(new Object()) { wait(); }  // block this thread
            forever
    }
}
```

### *RMI Java Properties*

These are the RMI-related Java properties:

**`java.rmi.server.codebase`**—The URL representing a codebase from which to retrieve classes if they are not found in the classpath. This property is set on the server, not the client.

**`java.rmi.server.disableHttp`**—False by default. If true, RMI's HTTP firewall tunneling capability is disabled.

**`java.rmi.server.hostname`**—The hostname or IP address to embed in remote references to all servants exported by this server program. If set, this overrides the built-in mechanism for determining the host IP address or hostname.

**`java.rmi.dgc.leaseValue`**—The time in milliseconds after which an object reference lease expires. When a lease expires, the server decrements its count of clients using the object. If there are no references to an object (including none in the registry), the object will be deleted. Clients holding remote references automatically renew their leases at half the leaveValue interval. The default value for this property is 600000 (ten minutes).

**`java.rmi.server.logCalls`**—If true, enables server call logging. Logging is written to stderr. Default value is false. On Windows, Control-Break will trigger a dump of current thread activity. On Solaris, use Control-\.

**`java.rmi.server.useCodebaseOnly`** —If set to true, when RMI loads classes (if not available via CLASSPATH) they are only loaded using the URL specified by the property java.rmi.server.codebase.

**`java.rmi.server.useLocalHostname`**—If true, then when exporting objects, attempt to determine the server's fully qualified hostname, and only if this fails, use the server's IP address. The java.rmi.server.hostname property overrides this.

**`java.rmi.activation.port`**—The default port to use to contact the activation daemon (rmid). If unspecified, the value 1098 is used, since this is the default port for rmid.

**`java.rmi.activation.activator.class`**—Fully qualified class name of the implementation class for java.rmi.activation.Activator.

**`java.rmi.server.randomIDs`**—If true, a cryptographically secure algorithm is used to generate a random value to use as the object identifier; the identifier is then not guaranteed to be unique, but the probability of a collision is vanishingly small. If this property is false, a different algorithm is used which guarantees uniqueness within the host from which the object is exported.

The properties java.rmi.loader.packagePrefix, java.rmi.registry.packagePrefix, and java.rmi.server.packagePrefix are deprecated.

### *Storing Remote References in LDAP*

A Java remote reference can represent a JRMP object reference or an IIOP object reference, depending on whether the native RMI protocol (JRMP) or IIOP is used. (This is discussed in detail later in this chapter.) Putting use of IIOP aside for the moment and assuming native RMI, the draft IETF standard on the representation of Java objects in LDAP specifies that an RMI reference should be stored in an LDAP database in one of two ways: as a javaNamingReference entry, or as a javaMarshalledObject entry.

The javaNamingReference LDAP object class (introduced in Chapter 5) is the LDAP mapping for a JNDI Reference object. Basically, it provides a chaining facility to allow a JNDI provider layer to look an object up first in LDAP to obtain the object's real location, and then to use that information to automatically go and fetch the real object. One of the attributes of the javaNamingReference object class is javaReferenceAddress, which can provide location information in the form of a URL to obtain the actual object. The javaNamingReference schema class therefore provides a way to create a level of indirection for looking up an RMI object. In this case, the RMI registry is still consulted for the actual object, transparently to a client application.

The second sanctioned way of storing an RMI remote reference in LDAP is to actually store the object reference. Storing an actual remote reference amounts to storing an RMI stub object, which is a serializable type designed to communicate with the server object and act as a proxy for the server. All remote stub objects implement the java.rmi.Remote interface, which in turn implements java.io.Serializable. Therefore, all stubs are serializable.

One disadvantage of a serialized object is that when you read it back in and reconstitute it, you must at that time resolve and obtain its classes. In some circumstances it is desirable to defer that resolution, and have a handy Java container for passing the serialized state around. Java 2 adds the type java.rmi.MarshalledObject for this purpose. One can therefore store a remote reference stub as a javaMarshalledObject entry, and retrieve it and reconstitute it later to access the RMI server represented by the remote reference.

## Java and CORBA

### *CORBA Overview*

CORBA is the acronym for Common Object Request Broker Architecture. CORBA is a standard developed by the Object Management Group, headquartered in Framingham, Massachusetts, a consortium of over 700 companies at the time of this writing. CORBA defines a standard set of protocols and services for building distributed applications using an object model.

CORBA is important because it provides software glue that can be used to tie together different sources of information in an enterprise, regardless of what technologies those components are based on. It is a widely supported and open protocol, and implementations from different sources are interoperable. One therefore has a choice of sources, and can choose a CORBA implementation for a platform based on its advantages for that application without worrying that the choice will have to propagate to other platforms. Of course, this assumes that vendor-specific additions and features are used sparingly.

This makes CORBA solutions extremely flexible, and is a reason why CORBA is the architecture increasingly used by third party middleware. CORBA also defines many useful services, including distributed transactions for cooperating middleware, an event service, a name service, and many, many others.

Java and CORBA are extremely synergistic. Java has given CORBA a tremendous boost, because Java solves the problem of code distribution; CORBA solves the problem of intercommunication between distributed components. This means that combined, they provide an architecture for creating distributed applications that can deploy themselves and run in a cooperative fashion across a network. It is hard to solve one problem without the other; therefore, CORBA and Java are very synergistic.

### ORBs

The central architectural component in a CORBA implementation is the Object Request Broker (ORB). The ORB is the component which manages the communication between a system's CORBA objects and objects on other systems.

Generally, each system has an ORB. This is not a requirement, however. The only requirement is that client stubs be able to bind to an ORB, and that server object adapters be able to bind to an ORB. In practical terms, the ORB is usually within the same computing system; in fact, there may be multiple ORBs within the system. For example, a Java client may have a lightweight ORB, downloaded as part of the applet; this ORB may communicate with the applet host for services, which for a non-applet would be obtained from the execution host.

Netscape bundled the Visigenic VisiBroker 2.5 applet ORB with Navigator 4, and Visigenic's server ORB with some of its server products. Thus, if you want to use a more recent version of that ORB product, you must override the built-in Java properties to point to the desired ORB. This is not hard to do, and Visigenic's documentation addresses this issue.

Most CORBA architectures require at least one ORB per machine. However, as in the case of an applet ORB, it may be a component that does not require installation, and which is simply linked with the program (dynamically in the case of Java, or as a shared library with C++).

### *The Object Adapter*

Conceptually an object adapter (OA) is a plug-replaceable component that implements most of the ORB functionality, and can be selected based on OA-specific features and advantages. For example, a vendor may supply two OAs—one that implements thread pooling for requests, and another that implements a thread-per-connection policy. A server object interacts with an OA, which provides specific deployment, and activation functionality, and the OA in turn interacts with the ORB, which provides generalized ORB-to-ORB connection functionality for the platform.

Two important categories of OA are the Basic Object Adapter (BOA) and the Portable Object Adapter (POA). The BOA has long been a central component in CORBA implementations. The CORBA specifications define the methods and features of the BOA, but the CORBA Java binding does not include it. This is because it was realized that a new kind of object adapter was needed to satisfy web deployment and other requirements, so the Portable Object Adapter (POA) was conceived.

The Java CORBA binding will include POA features when they are finalized. In the meantime, the binding specifies an ORB connect() method for binding an object to the ORB directly without invoking an OA. This is intended for binding transient objects. The POA includes an entire object lifecycle architecture for implementing object persistence and different invocation policies. At the time of this writing, POA implementations are still pending.

### *Stubs and Skeletons*

When you write an application with CORBA, you define a remote interface that defines the interaction between a server object and its clients. This specification is written in a language called Interface Description Language (IDL), and is compiled into a set of software modules that implement that interface. While IDL is language-neutral in the sense that the IDL is the same regardless if the ultimate application is in Java, C, or COBOL, the generated modules are in the implementation language. These modules are called the "stub" and "skeleton."

The stub implements the interface between a client and its ORB, and a skeleton implements the interface between a server object and its ORB and object adapter. The interface serves as the linkage between application code and the application-independent ORB module. These components serve similar functionality to the stub and skeleton components in RMI, except that in the case of RMI, the stub is a component that actually communicates with the remote server, whereas with CORBA, it is ORBs that communicate, and the stub is just an interface layer to the ORB.

### *Repositories*

An implementation repository is the ORB's collection of information about an object type, including how to activate it. There is no public API defined for this repository—it is implementation dependent. It is more of a concept defined by the CORBA specification—the features and policies of object activation are specified, but different implementations provide these features and policies in different ways.

In contrast, an interface repository is a collection of information about the method signatures of objects, so that the objects can be introspected and invoked dynamically at runtime by remote clients. The interface repository provides a public API for doing this remotely. The API for introspecting and invoking CORBA objects dynamically using the interface repository is called the Dynamic Invocation Interface (DII). In contrast, the "normal" way—invoking an object using statically-compiled stubs and skeletons—is called the Static Invocation Interface (SII).

Information about your objects does not automatically get put into the interface repository. To get something into the interface repository, you have to put it there explicitly, using the interface repository API, or a utility.

Many people anticipate that DII is the wave of the future. Perhaps, but my own feeling is that while DII may be useful for integrated tools, it is complex for mainstream business applications to use directly. One advantage is the ability to perform non-blocking calls, since DII has this feature. However, since Java is multithreaded, and it is possible to make multiple requests on a connection or create multiple connections, this advantage is not important in client-side Java applications, because there are other ways to accomplish it that are easily encapsulated, for example, by performing a blocking call in a separate thread. (See the following sidebar "Implementing Nonblocking Calls Using Java.") In addition, some of the leading implementations (e.g., Inprise VisiBroker and IONA Orbix) have had some interoperation incompatibilities in DII, especially with regard to the way they implement the CORBA "pseudo-objects" needed for DII—objects that are built-in.

---

#### Implementing Nonblocking Calls Using Java

It is easy to implement nonblocking method calls using Java threading. Consider the following sequence, which invokes a nonblocking call which encapsulates the operations of starting a thread to run a method.

```
MyRequest r = new MyRequest();
r.start();    // starts a thread, which performs some long
              // operation we don't want to wait for

...continue doing other stuff...
```

```
...later...when we finally need the results of the async
   request,
r.waitTilDone();    // this blocks
...now we continue, knowing the async request has completed...
```

The MyRequest class could extend a base class as follows:

```
public class MyRequest extends Request
{
   public void doStuff() throws Exception
   {
      ...do some stuff that takes a long time...
   }
}

/**
 * Re-usable base class for implementing non-blocking requests
 */
public abstract class Request implements Runnable
{
   private Object o = new Object();    // a semaphore
   private boolean flag = false;

   public void start()
   {
      Thread t = new Thread(this);
      t.start();
   }

   public void waitTilDone() throws InterruptedException
   {
      synchronized (o)
      {
         if (flag) return;
         o.wait();
      }
   }
   public void run()
   {
      synchronized (o)
      {
         // Do stuff that takes a long time...
         try
         {
            doStuff();
         }
         catch (Exception ex)
```

```
            {
               handleException(ex);
            }

            // Signal we're done
            flag = true;
            o.notify();
         }
      }

      public abstract void doStuff() throws Exception;

      public void handleException(Exception ex)
      {
         ex.printStackTrace();
      }
   }
```

### How CORBA Sends Information over the Wire: GIOP and IIOP

To send a remote invocation request from a client to a server object, CORBA uses a stream protocol to encode such requests and the returned results. CORBA allows ORBs to use vendor-specific protocols, but requires that all implementations provide a common protocol defined in the standard, called Internet Inter-ORB Protocol (IIOP).

The actual messages used by IIOP are defined in a CORBA standard called General Inter-ORB Protocol (GLOP). IIOP is merely GIOP, with TCP/IP specified as the transport mechanism. Other transports can be used to communicate with GIOP, and as long as a gateway can bridge two transport protocols, two applications can communicate using GIOP over different transports. In practice, IIOP is almost always the protocol used.

All implementations of IIOP must be compatible (i.e., it must be possible to use a VisiBroker-based client with an Orbix-based server object, perhaps even written in different languages), and vice versa. This is possible if the two ORBs communicate using the same protocol, such as IIOP. Here is a taste of the GIOP specification; you do not actually need to know this to build CORBA applications, but it may help to visualize the basic nature of what is being sent when you make remote calls:

```
module GIOP
{
   enum MsgType
   {
```

```
      Request, Reply, CancelRequest,
      LocateRequest, LocateReply,
      CloseConnection, MessageError
   };

   struct MessageHeader
   {
      char magic [4];
      Version GIOP_version;
      boolean byte_order;
      octet message_type;
      unsigned long message_size;
   };

   struct RequestHeader
   {
      IOP::ServiceContextList service_context;
      unsigned long request_id;
      boolean response_expected;
      sequence <octet> object_key;
      string operation;
      Principal requesting_principal;
   };

   enum ReplyStatusType
   {
      NO_EXCEPTION,
      USER_EXCEPTION,
      SYSTEM_EXCEPTION,
      LOCATION_FORWARD
   };

   struct ReplyHeader
   {
      IOP::ServiceContextList service_context;
      unsigned long request_id;
      ReplyStatusType reply_status;
   };
};
```

A request consists of a message header, request header, and request body. A reply consists of a message header, reply header, and reply body. The request body contains input parameters according to formatting rules defined in the specification. Similarly, the reply body contains parameter and method return values (CORBA allows out parameters).

The specification defines rules for the representation of primitive types (octet, char, etc.) and composite types (struct, arrays, etc.). These rules define the Common Data Representation (CDR). Thus, the entire format of requests and replies is defined, to the byte level.

### *IDL*

Without providing a detailed treatment of IDL grammar rules, let's look at an example, which has the most commonly used features all rolled into one. I will then explain how these features map to Java.

```
module n                  // declare a module
{
   const long c = 3;      // declare a constant
   typedef long T[c];     // declare a new type - an array
                          // of three int's
   enum KindsOfThings { A, B, C };   // an enumeration type
                                     // definition
};

module m
{
   struct s               // declare a struct - analogous to a
                          // C struct
   {
      long i;
      string s;              // an unbounded string with no max size
      string <5> zipcode;    // a string with a max size
      sequence <char, 10> xyz;    // a sequence of 10 char's
   };

   exception SomethingTerrible   // declare a new exception type
   {
      string whatHappened;
   };

   interface b;           // a forward interface declaration

   interface a            // declare an interface - a remote type
   {
      float m(in float x) raises (SomethingTerrible); // a remote
                                                     // method
      oneway void castaway(inout n::T q); // a non-blocking method
      b getB();                      // uses the forward declaration
      any getWhoKnowsWhat();         // returns an "any" type
      readonly attribute n::T a;     // generates a _get_a() method
   };
};
```

An IDL module is a scoping mechanism analogous to a Java package. In fact, the Java binding maps a module to a package. Using modules is optional, just as using packages is optional in Java.

An IDL interface is a declaration of a remote object type. All interface methods are remote methods. An interface is analogous to a Java interface that extends Remote. An IDL interface maps to a Java interface. If the IDL interface has attributes, these map to accessor methods, which are generated to set and get the associated values. A read-only attribute only generates a get accessor. The accessor methods have the form:

```
_get_<attr-name>()
_set_<attr-name>(<attr-type>)
```

For example, the read-only attribute "a" in the above example would generate an accessor with the signature _get_a(long[3]).

A struct is analogous to a C struct. A struct can have no methods—it just contains elements, which may be primitive types, other structs, and interfaces. When a remote call is made that includes a struct type in a parameter or return result, the struct is passed by value—its contents are marshalled and passed in entirety. This is not equivalent to passing objects by value, however, since a struct has no behavior. A struct maps to a Java class that has no methods.

The CORBA Any type is conceptually a typeless object for representing objects that can be of multiple incompatible types, somewhat analogous to void* in C++. The Java binding automatically generates helper classes that have methods to convert objects to and from the Any type.

IDL has "out" and "inout" parameters, but Java effectively has only "in" parameters. Therefore, the mapping defines holder classes for the built-in types, and generates holder classes for the types you define (except those defined with typedefs). You must use these holder types to pass parameters that can be returned as results. Here is an example using the predefined Int holder type:

```
IDL:

interface MyRemoteInterface
{
   void myRemoteMethod(inout long p);
};

Generated Java interface:

public interface MyRemoteInterface
```

```
{
   public void myRemoteMethod(IntHolder p);
}

Java using the remote object type:

...
MyRemoteInterface remoteObject = ...
...
IntHolder ih = new IntHolder(5);
remoteObject.myRemoteMethod(ih);
int returnedValue = ih.value;
...
```

An enumeration type defined in IDL generates a Java class, which contains static instances with names that match the enumeration values. For example:

```
enum MyEnumType { A, B, C };
```

results in a class called "MyEnumType," with static instances MyEnumType.A, MyEnumType.B, and MyEnumType.C. Thus, in your Java code you can do this:

```
MyEnumType met = MyEnumType.A;
if (met == MyEnumType.A) System.out.println("All is well");
```

Note that you should not need to create instances of MyEnumType—in fact, you cannot anyway, because its constructor is private.

IDL has a list of primitive types (see table below), which, as you might expect, includes strings. There are actually two string types: one ("string") that consists of 8-bit characters, and another ("wstring") that can handle Unicode characters.

### *The IDL-to-Java Mapping*

The mapping from CORBA IDL to Java is specified in the CORBA document *Mapping of OMG IDL to Java,* 98-02-61. The mapping specifies a Java binding for CORBA IDL. Thus, you can write CORBA servant implementations and CORBA clients using Java. An IDL-to-Java compiler (e.g., the `idltojava` tool which comes with SDK 1.2 or the more recent `idlj` tool which is part of the RMI-over-IIOP distribution, or any vendor supplied IDL-to-Java compiler) generates the appropriate Java stubs and skeletons, just as IDL-to-C++ compilers generate stubs and skeletons in C++. The binding includes a mapping of IDL data types to Java, as well as a specification of the classes and methods that generated Java stubs and skeletons must have. The latter allows stubs generated by one vendor's compiler to be interchangeable with stubs generated by another vendor's compiler; and

similarly for generated skeletons. Thus, you can take stubs or skeletons generated ahead of time and use them in any CORBA application, regardless whose compiler generated the stubs and skeletons.

The Java binding maps the IDL string type to a Java String object, but if the characters within the Java String are not within the ISO Latin-1 character set, a runtime exception will result during marshalling. Therefore, you should use the wstring type in your IDL if you are writing an application that will process Unicode characters. See Table 7-1.

**Table 7-1** **IDL-to-Java Type Mapping**

| IDL Type | | Java Type |
|---|---|---|
| boolean | ➡ | boolean |
| char, wchar* | ➡ | char |
| octet | ➡ | byte |
| string, wstring* | ➡ | String |
| float | ➡ | float |
| double | ➡ | double |
| long double | ➡ | (not supported) |
| [unsigned]** long | ➡ | int |
| [unsigned]** short | ➡ | short |
| [unsigned]** long long | ➡ | long |
| fixed | ➡ | BigDecimal |

* Use wchar and wstring for Java programs that may contain nonextended-ASCII characters, since the IDL char and string types cannot handle 16-bit characters, but the wchar and wstring types can.

** Unsigned values are not range-checked; if the IDL type is unsigned, you are responsible for making sure that large unsigned values map correctly to the corresponding Java signed type.

An IDL "sequence" is a variable length array, with elements all of a single type, and whose length is available at runtime. The Java binding for IDL maps an IDL sequence to a Java array. If a sequence bound is not specified, it is assumed nevertheless that the sequence represents an object that has fixed bounds, and it is the programmer's responsibility to make sure bounds are not exceeded. IDL also has an array type, whose dimensions are fixed at compile time, and declared like a Java array. An IDL array maps to a Java array.

### *RMI vs. CORBA*

The RMI community often points out that RMI can pass objects by value, whereas CORBA 2 cannot—actually it can, sort of. CORBA passes structs by value, which are analogous to C structs, and have no methods and so are not objects. A struct only has attributes. However, a struct can have an attribute that is a CORBA interface (i.e., an object, on which remote methods can be invoked. So, it is really not so limited).

The principal deficiency that IDL structs have is that an IDL struct is logically a hierarchical structure and therefore cannot reference other structs in a recursive or cyclic manner. This makes it hard to map Java objects because Java objects often contain references to other objects. The recent Objects By Value specification, OMG 98-1-18, adds value semantics to IDL to allow Java-style object graphs to be passed over the wire.

Another advantage of RMI over CORBA is RMI's ability to deploy code as needed. However, even this advantage is not typically realized, since deployment is usually addressed explicitly by other techniques.

The most important advantage of RMI over CORBA in typical organizational applications is its simplicity. RMI is a smaller, simpler mechanism, and does not require learning IDL or the intricacies of the CORBA services. If you have something you want to do quickly and economically, you can whip it up with RMI, and not have to go through the trouble of an ORB vendor selection. Of course, you get what you pay for. Following this route, you are likely to forego performance gains made by commercial ORBs, having a range of service implementations to choose from, as well as object management and monitoring tools.

CORBA does have some built-in advantages as well. For example, the IIOP protocol uses a level of indirection which makes it easier to build firewalls that pass IIOP than RMI's native JRMP. The IIOP protocol also provides header fields which can be used to pass product-specific context information without modifying the basic protocol. This is used commonly for passing transaction context.

In the near future, by using the new class PortableRemoteObject, it will even be possible for RMI applications to directly interoperate with CORBA ones by using the IIOP protocol. Therefore, many of the advantages of using IIOP can be obtained without sacrificing the simplcity of RMI's API.

### *How a Program Finds CORBA Objects*

Normally, remote method calls return object references, which you can use to get additional object references, and so on. However, you need a way to get the first object. You can do this in a variety of ways. Here are four:

- Create the object yourself.
- Use a persistent reference you stored yourself at an earlier time.
- Identify the type of object, and use a service that knows how to create an object of this type.
- Look the object up in a directory service of some kind, such as a name service.

I will now discuss each approach.

**Creating the Object Yourself.** To create a CORBA object that you have defined with IDL, assuming you have run your CORBA toolkit's IDL processor and generated stubs and skeletons, you need to connect to the ORB, and create an instance of the object. Here is an example:

```
// Get an ORB
org.omg.CORBA.ORB orb = org.omg.CORBA.ORB.init();

// Construct the object
MyServer myServer = new MyServerImpl();

// Register the server object with the ORB.
orb.connect(server);    // Resulting object is not persistent -
          // cannot be automatically activated later just from a
          // reference to it
```

The object can now receive remote calls through its ORB. These calls can originate from within the same process. If you want the object to be available to objects in other processes, you will have to use one of the techniques discussed next to publish the object's reference in some way so other processes can find it.

**Using a Persistent Reference.** A persistent reference is a reference to an object that can be transported and used across process boundaries. (This is not to be confused with persistent objects, which will be discussed shortly. Here I am only talking about the object's reference.) For CORBA objects, a commonly used way to create a persistent reference is to convert an object reference to a string, store the string or pass it to another process, and then convert it back to an object reference. For this to work, the corresponding object either must exist, or must be a "persistent" object, as discussed in "CORBA Object Activation" on page 518.

Use the ORB's object_to_string() method to convert the reference to a Java String, and string_to_object(String) to convert the String back to a CORBA object reference. The string representation is standardized so that ORBs from different vendors can interpret each other's stringified references.

**Identify the Object from Its Type.** Some Implementation Repository implementations provide an API to find an object (or an object on any cooperating ORB within a subnet) based on an object's type—in other words the name of its IDL interface. That technique is implementation dependent, and is sometimes used by services that support object replication and create object instances dynamically on demand.

**Finding the Object with a Name Service.** Object references can be stored in a name service or other kind of service that provides a lookup or search capability for persistent objects. Only objects that the ORB recognizes as persistent can be stored in this way. (Making objects persistent is discussed later.) Using a name service is the most important variation of this technique, and now will be discussed in detail.

### *Using a Naming Service*

In using a name service, the first problem is to find the name service itself. There is a slight problem in that the resolve_initial_references() is the method you call to get the name service. However, this method returns a NameContext object—but you cannot create a NameContext until you have a NameContext obtained through the name service—a catch-22! In other words, the CORBA specs do not say how the initial name context is created. One can imagine that a name service might automatically create an anonymous root context, and return this.

It is up to ORB vendors to provide a means of creating and managing root name contexts for a system. For example, VisiBroker allows you to specify a root context name, and the name service creates this root context automatically when you start it. The downside is that you must specify the root context name as a property when running applications that use the name service—a minor inconvenience. The application component which creates the root context is a Java class (ExtendedNamingContextFactory), so you can use it programmatically if desired.

#### Example: Finding a Server Object via a Name Service

To use a CORBA naming service in a program, first we must obtain a local root naming context:

```
org.omg.CORBA.Object ns =
orb.resolve_initial_references("NameService");
org.omg.CosNaming.NamingContext rootContext =
   org.omg.CosNaming.NamingContextHelper.narrow(ns);
```

Next we construct a name service name path for the object we want:

```
org.omg.CosNaming.NameComponent ps =
   new org.omg.CosNaming.NameComponent("MyObject", "");
org.omg.CosNaming.NameComponent path[] = { ps };
```

Finally, we find the object, using the name path, and an automatically generated helper class:

```
// Use the constructed name to locate the object
remoteObject = MyObjectHelper.narrow(rootContext.resolve(path));
```

To use a remote name service, set the org.omg.CORBA.ORBInitialHost property to point to the remote host.

### *Storing IIOP References in LDAP*

Sun Microsystems has also proposed a standard LDAP schema for representing CORBA object references. A CORBA object reference is stored in LDAP by storing its object reference (its IOR) in string form. This is the value you get by ORB calling object_to_string(<your object>). The attribute types and object classes are shown in Figure 7-6 and Figure 7-7.

```
corbaIor
(UTF-8 Directory String)
(single valued)
```

```
corbaRepositoryId
(IA5 String)
```

**Figure 7-6** CORBA LDAP attributes.

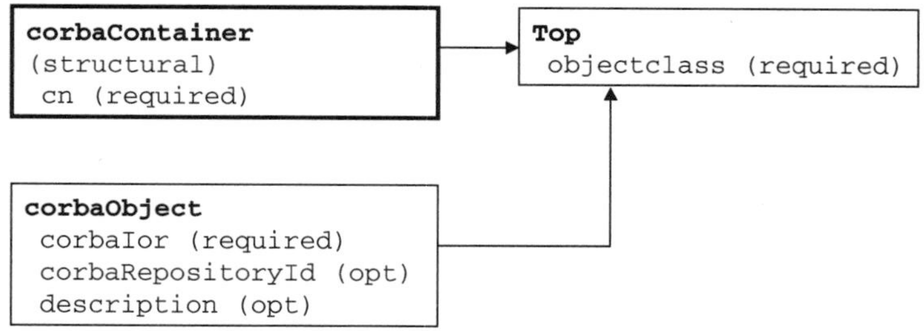


**Figure 7-7** CORBA LDAP object classes.

This mapping is not implemented innately by the LDAP provider that comes with JNDI. However, JNDI state and object factories are provided with the LDAP provider so that an application can install the CORBA mapping. This makes it possible to store RMI-over-IIOP object references in LDAP as well as standard RMI object references.

### *CORBA Object Activation*

CORBA defines four modes in which object instances may be activated (i.e., instantiated and started). Normally, a server program creates a server object. Thus, in these four invocation models, it is assumed that a server process is invoked to create a server object (a server object is often called a "servant"). The process of starting the server process if necessary and instantiating a server object is called "implementation activation." Activating an object may therefore require the ORB's implementation repository to start a server program which knows how to instantiate the required object or objects.

The four activation modes are:

1. Persistent process (server)
2. Shared process (server)
3. Process per connection ("unshared")
4. Process per request ("per-method")

Let's look at an example of each mode.

**Persistent Process (Server).** In this mode, the server program (process) is started manually. A manually-started server program is referred to as a "persistent server." This is not to be confused with a "persistent object," which is a server object which can be automatically re-created, perhaps by automatically restarting the associated server program.

As an example of a persistent server, I will create a simple ping server that is registered with a name service so that it can be found by a client as long as the server is running.

Here is the IDL for the ping service:

```
module pingservice
{
   interface Server
   {
      string ping();
   };
};
```

Here is the server class, which implements the ping service. Notice that it extends the _ServerImplBase abstract class, which is generated by an IDL-to-Java compiler. (In the past, this generation was vendor-specific, but now it must contain a minimum standard set of Java methods.)

```
package pingservice;
public class ServerImpl extends pingservice._ServerImplBase
{
   public String ping()
   {
      return "ping";
   }

   public static void main(String[] args) throws Exception
   {

      // Get an ORB; here we are choosing to explicitly select
      // Visigenic's ORB
      java.util.Properties p = new java.util.Properties();
      p.put("org.omg.CORBA.ORBClass",
         "com.visigenic.vbroker.orb.ORB");
      org.omg.CORBA.ORB orb = org.omg.CORBA.ORB.init(args, p);

      // Construct the ping server object
      Server server = new ServerImpl();

      // Register the server object with the ORB.
      orb.connect(server);

      // Find the naming service's root naming context
      org.omg.CORBA.Object ns =
         orb.resolve_initial_references("NameService");

      // Narrow the reference - all objects must do this
      org.omg.CosNaming.NamingContext nc =
         org.omg.CosNaming.NamingContextHelper.narrow(ns);

      // Now construct a NameService name path for our own ping
      // service object
      org.omg.CosNaming.NameComponent ps =
         new org.omg.CosNaming.NameComponent
         ("PingService", "");
      org.omg.CosNaming.NameComponent path[] = { ps };

      // Register our ping service object, under the newly
           constructed Name Service
      // name path
      nc.rebind(path, server);
```

```
        // Now block forever, so this server process remains
        // persistent
        Object t = new Object();
        synchronized (t)
        {
            t.wait();
        }
    }
}
```

Here is a client that locates and invokes the object:

```
package pingservice;
public class Client
{
    public static void main(String[] args)
    {
      try
      {
         org.omg.CORBA.ORB orb  = org.omg.CORBA.ORB.init();

         // Get the name service
         org.omg.CORBA.Object ns =
            orb.resolve_initial_references("NameService");
         org.omg.CosNaming.NamingContext nc =
            org.omg.CosNaming.NamingContextHelper.
               narrow(ns);
         // Construct a name path to the object we want
         org.omg.CosNaming.NameComponent ps =
            new org.omg.CosNaming.NameComponent
               ("PingService", "");
         org.omg.CosNaming.NameComponent path[] = { ps };

         // Get the ping server object - this should start it
         // if necessary
         Server server = ServerHelper.narrow(nc.resolve(path));
         System.out.println("Bound to server");

         //
         // Now see if we can make calls to our service
         //

         String s = server.ping();
         System.out.println("ping succeeded: " + s);
      }
      catch (Exception ex)
```

```
        {
            ex.printStackTrace();
        }
    }
}
```

**Shared Process (Server).** A shared server is started in response to a request for a persistent object that the server knows how to create. A persistent object is an object which has a name and can be located automatically (and created if necessary) by an ORB in response to an invocation request. The object is located using a locator service, or by using an object reference obtained at an earlier time (which may even have been converted to a string and stored on disk). Once created, the same server object services all requests made to it until it terminates. If a shared server program does not make provisions to stay alive, it will terminate when its invocation is completed. Normally a shared server arranges to stay alive, as will be shown below.

As an example of a shared server, I will modify the above ping server example, and show how you can make it persistent and register it with VisiBroker's implementation repository (which is called the "Object Activation Daemon," or OAD). Having registered it in that way, a client (also shown below) can request the object at any time—as long as the OAD is running—and (transparently) cause the program that knows how to create the object to be automatically started.

```
package pingservice;
public class ServerImpl extends pingservice._ServerImplBase
{
    public String ping()
    {
        return "ping";
    }

    public ServerImpl(String n) { super(n); }

    /**
     * For creating a persistent server object, as a shared server.
     */
    public static void main(String[] args) throws Exception
    {

        // Get an ORB
        java.util.Properties p = new java.util.Properties();
        p.put("org.omg.CORBA.ORBClass",
            "com.visigenic.vbroker.orb.ORB");
        org.omg.CORBA.ORB orb = org.omg.CORBA.ORB.init(args, p);
```

```
        // Get a server object adapter
        org.omg.CORBA.BOA boa = orb.BOA_init();    // For Visigenic

        // Construct the ping server object
        Server server = new ServerImpl("MyServer");
        // With the Visigenic product, a server object becomes
        // persistent if it is given
        // a name when it is conctructed. This also makes "automatic
        // rebinds" possible.

        // Register the server object with the ORB.
        boa.obj_is_ready(server);    // Visigenic's technique for
                // creating persistent objects - this is vendor-
                // specific
        //orb.connect(server);    // Can be used only for
                                  //non-persistent objects

        // Find the naming service's root naming context
        org.omg.CORBA.Object ns =
           orb.resolve_initial_references("NameService");

        // Narrow the reference - all objects must do this
        org.omg.CosNaming.NamingContext nc =
           org.omg.CosNaming.NamingContextHelper.narrow(ns);

        // Now construct a NameService name path for our own
        // ping service object
        org.omg.CosNaming.NameComponent ps =
           new org.omg.CosNaming.NameComponent
           ("PingService", "");
        org.omg.CosNaming.NameComponent path[] = { ps };

        // Register our ping service object, under the newly
        // constructed Name Service name path
        nc.rebind(path, server);

        // Now don't block - just exit
    }
}
```

This program creates the server object as a persistent object, and gives it a name—both in the persistent object store (via the constructor) and in the name service (via the rebind() method). It terminates without blocking, because whenever the server object is needed the object activation daemon will create the object, using the program that follows.

The program performs the same functions as the one above, except that it does not bother to register the object with the name service. I could have consolidated these, but I kept them separate to emphasize that the purpose of these programs is different—one is to create the object, and another is to restore it.

```
package pingservice;
public class SharedServer
{
    /**
     * For restoring persistent server object, as a shared server.
     */
    public static void main(String[] args) throws Exception
    {
        // Get an ORB
        java.util.Properties p = new java.util.Properties();
        p.put("org.omg.CORBA.ORBClass",
        "com.visigenic.vbroker.orb.ORB");
        org.omg.CORBA.ORB orb = org.omg.CORBA.ORB.init(args, p);

        // Get a server object adapter
        org.omg.CORBA.BOA boa = orb.BOA_init();    // For Visigenic

        // Construct the ping server object
        Server server = new ServerImpl("MyServer");
        // With the Visigenic product, a server object becomes
        // persistent if it is given
        // a name when it is conctructed. This also makes "automatic
        // rebinds" possible.

        // Register the server object with the ORB.
        boa.obj_is_ready(server); // Visigenic's technique - this is
        // vendor-specific

        // Now block forever, so this server process remains
        // persistent
        Object t = new Object();
        synchronized (t)
        {
            System.out.println("Waiting...");
            t.wait();
        }
    }
}
```

The client is the same as in the Persistent Process case. Note that the client uses the name service to make reference to an instance that may no longer exist; in that case, the above program will automatically be called by the activation daemon, recreating the object. This program can perform any object state restoration that might be required, although in the example above there is no state to be restored.

Here is the command sequence that you could give to VisiBroker to tell it to register the persistent object so that it knows how to start the process that creates the object when needed. Different CORBA products will have different means of accomplishing this:

```
start oadj -path \MyImplementationRepository
oadutil reg -i pingservice::Server -o MyServer
   -java pingservice.SharedServer -p shared
```

The first line starts the activation daemon, which provides the persistent object activation service. "pingservice::Server" identifies the repository ID —the name by which the implementation repository knows this type of object. "MyServer" identifies the name under which the object was registered as a persistent object. "pingservice.SharedServer" identifies the Java class that contains the main routine to run when starting the server. "shared" specifies that the server be run as a shared server—this affects what the implementation repository does when it receives additional requests for this same object (i.e., whether it will start another process just like this one, start a new process only if the requestor is different, or simply invoke the specified remote method on this object instance).

For the ping service example developed above, which uses the CORBA Name Service, you will also have to start Visigenic's (or any) name service; for example:

```
vbj -DDEBUG -DORBservices=CosNaming -DJDKrenameBug
   com.visigenic.vbroker.services.CosNaming.ExtFactory
   Root MyNameLog.log
```

You must run the ServerImpl program to create the server object, and register it with the name service:

```
java -DORBservices=CosNaming -DSVCnameroot=Root
   pingservice.ServerImpl
```

Now try running the client, even though the server has exited:

```
java -DORBservices=CosNaming
   -DSVCnameroot=Root pingservice.Client
```

The client finds a reference to the server object from the name service, but the object no longer exists, so the activation daemon starts the SharedServer program to re-create it. You should get a message that says, "ping succeeded: ping," indicating the client succeeded.

**Process Per Connection ("Unshared").** In this mode, the server program is also started automatically in response to a request for a persistent object. However, each client connection gets its own server object instance and process. The process dies when the connection is closed. Since the server object serves a single client, and is dedicated to the client for the life of the connection, the server does not ever have to keep a list to correlate clients with state; it maintains state automatically for that client between method invocations.

To demonstrate the process-per-connection mode, I will modify the above program so that the server object contains state, which can be shown to persist between invocations. I will add a variable i, which contains the number of times the ping() method has been called, and each call to ping() will return this value and increment it.

Here is the modified IDL. It merely replaces the ping() return type with an IDL long (an int) instead of a string.

```
module pingservice
{
   interface Server
   {
      long ping();
   };
};
```

Here is the modified server class. Notice that it contains a class variable i, which constitutes state information for the object. If the server is run in process-per-connection mode, this value will be unique for each client, regardless of whether it is declared static or not in Java, since each client gets its own VM.

```
public class ServerImpl extends pingservice._ServerImplBase
{
   private int i = 0;
   public int ping()
   {
      return i++;
   }
```

All we have to do is change the client so that it loops and calls ping() repeatedly, each time printing out the returned value. It should increase because the server stays connected to us, and can maintain state about our connection (i.e., the current value of the server variable i). If the server object is running in a process-per-connection mode, it will behave the same way regardless of how many other clients connect to it, because each clients gets its own instance of the server object.

```
//
// Now see if we can make calls to our service
//

for (;;)
{
   int i = server.ping();
   System.out.println("ping succeeded: " + i);

   // Give it a chance to catch its breath!
   Thread.currentThread().sleep(1000);
}
```

To specify a process-per-connection activation mode for VisiBroker, we can use the oadutil command as in the previous example, but specify an activation mode of "unshared" instead of "shared."

**Process Per Request ("Per-Method").** In the per-request mode, the server program is started automatically in response to each remote method call on an object. The connection is closed, and the process dies at the end of the call. Thus, each request gets its own process. This is somewhat analogous to CGI, in that each CGI request executes in a separate process.

To demonstrate the process-per-request invocation method, we can run the same program as above, but each invocation by the same client will obtain the same value returned by ping()—0. That is because each invocation results in a new process being started to service the request.

To specify a process-per-connection activation mode for VisiBroker, we can use the oadutil command as in the first example, but specify an activation mode of "per-method" instead of "shared."

### *Object Cleanup*

The Java VM takes care of disposing of Java objects when they are not needed. However, this does not relieve you of the need to consider the disposal of non-Java resources. Sometimes you even have to think about Java object disposal, and make sure to set references of unused objects to null so they can be collected (or use Java 2's weak reference facility, which provides a way to define caching references which do not inhibit garbage collection).

CORBA objects are not Java objects. However, from a Java program, you access them using Java objects. This means that you have to make sure you follow CORBA's guidelines for collection of CORBA objects. Also, since a CORBA ORB keeps references to the objects that are exported, it will have a list that references your Java object proxies. If you do not inform CORBA when you are done with its objects, it will never release your Java objects.

If you used the ORB.connect() method to connect to the ORB, instead of an OA adapter bind() or other method, you should use the disconnect() method on the object. If you connected through an OA with activate_object() or a generated helper method, you should call the OA's deactivate_object() method (some implementations use the name deactivate_obj()) to dispose of a server object. This is needed to release ORB resources associated with the object—Java GC will not release these, since they are owned by another object (the BOA or ORB).

When a shared policy is used, you normally want the server program (process) to continue execution after a client connection closes so that other connections can access the server object without having to reinstantiate it. When an unshared policy is used, you want the server process to terminate when the client connection closes. When a per-method policy is used, you want the server process to terminate when the method invocation completes.

In the preceding examples, I use the technique of blocking in a wait() call, to force the server program's main thread to suspend itself so that the process will remain and be ready to service incoming requests. There are no provisions for getting the process to terminate based on the invocation policy. Since the actual implementation of the object persistence mechanism is OA-specific, different products have different ways of providing process termination. The Visigenic BOA provides the method impl_is_ready(), which can be called at the end of the server program. It forces the program to block, and at the same time implements the appropriate process termination, depending on the activation policy that was used. For example, if, instead of:

```
Object t = new Object();
synchronized (t)
{
   System.out.println("Waiting...");
   t.wait();
}
```

we use:

```
boa.impl_is_ready();
```

the server program will terminate appropriately, depending on the policy under which it was activated.

### Connection Models

There is considerable variation in the client and server connection models provided by CORBA products. There are two predominant approaches to client connection management, and two for server connections. For client connections, these are:

> **Multiplexed use of connection on client**—Multiple client threads can make simultaneous requests across a single connection. Requests from multiple threads get forwarded to the server, even if pending requests on other threads have not completed. Thus, each client thread does not need its own connection. Since a single socket connection is used, this also results in less communication resources being used overall.
>
> **Single blocking call per connection**—A connection can process only one request at a time. Requests made by other threads block until the request currently being processed is completed.

For persistent server, shared server, and process-per-connection ("unshared") servers, the predominant approaches are:

> **Thread pool on server**—Each incoming request is assigned a thread from a thread pool. This avoids the overhead of thread creation and destruction, and reduces the number of thread resources that are needed if there are many client connections.
>
> **Thread per connection on server**—Each client connection is assigned a thread that is dedicated to it for the duration of the connection, and this thread is used to process all requests on that connection. This approach is not scalable for lots of client connections.

It is up to the implementation to provide any or all of these models (or alternative models), and currently both Iona and Visigenic provide all of these approaches.

CORBA also provides a facility for defining a Connection context, which allows a shared server to be used for transactional applications. This permits the reestablishment of transaction context from one method call to the next if an unshared activation policy is not being used. This feature is used by the CORBA Transaction Service.

### Object Management

Most CORBA implementations now provide facilities for object management. Ideally you should not have to do any object management. You need to if:

- Objects need to be moved, to balance load

- Objects need to be replicated, and require dynamic assignment to requests and fail-over capabilities
- Objects can get stuck: deadlocked, or hung
- Objects need to be checked (e.g., if they are running or not)
- Objects need to be created manually for replication or for starting
- Objects need to be installed and uninstalled
- Objects need resources assigned to them, and those assignments need to be configured or moved if the objects are moved
- Objects need to be configured (e.g., startup parameters, properties, etc.)
- You need to collect statistics on object utilization

Since most of these conditions exist in a real system, you will probably need object management tools. If a site has many CORBA objects, a common facility for monitoring and configuring them is essential. The facility should conveniently identify which objects are installed, their types (repository IDs) and published names, which are replicatable, each object's activation style, and system resources such as CPU usage, memory, and communication sockets currently used by each.

Some products provide features that include automatic reconnection to an alternate server if a connection is lost due to system failure (failover), and also object replication and automatic selection based on use or a round-robin policy for load balancing. Object migration—the ability to move objects dynamically—is addressed by the CORBA Lifecycle service, and has been implemented by some vendors.

### *Using CORBA with Castanet*

Marimba's Castanet has a sandbox security model, just like an applet, and so it will need a server-side proxy to forward requests to other hosts if it needs services from server objects residing on hosts other than the transmitter host, and to proxy server objects that the channel exports (for callbacks). Unfortunately, a channel is not (necessarily) an applet, and so the ORB.init(Applet) method cannot be used, and even if it could (if the channel were an applet), the applet would not have a proper codebase which the applet ORB could use to locate the host of origin—where the proxy is. For example, the VisiBroker proxy is called "gatekeeper," and the VisiBroker applet ORB attempts to locate the gatekeeper.ior file in the codebase directory.

Different CORBA products will have different approaches to the host access problem. If you are using VisiBroker, there are two solutions:

1. Sign the channel. This eliminates the security sandbox, allowing the channel to contact other hosts. If your CORBA channel does a bind(), run VisiBroker's OSAgent daemon in the same subnet where the channel is deployed, or set the ORBagentAddr property to point to the host where the OSAgent is running, so the gatekeeper will not be necessary (unless you need to penetrate a firewall).
2. Tell the channel program where the gatekeeper is. Note that the gatekeeper provides redirection to the OSAgent for binding (locating), for redirection from the transmitter host, and for firewall penetration using HTTP.

```
public static void main(String[] args)
{
   String myGatekeeperHost = "<your-host's-IP-address>";
   java.util.Properties props = new java.util.Properties();
   props.put( "ORBagentAddr", myGatekeeperHost);
   props.put( "ORBagentPort", "14000" );
   props.put( "ORBdebug", "true" );
   props.put( "GATEKEEPER_ADDR", myGatekeeperHost );
   props.put( "ORBgatekeeperIOR",
      "http://" + myGatekeeperHost + ":15000/gatekeeper.ior");
   org.omg.CORBA.ORB orb = org.omg.CORBA.ORB.init( args, props );
   ...now do a bind(orb, "ServiceName");
```

IONA has a proxy product as well, called Wonderwall. Similar to gatekeeper, it provides IIOP redirection, allowing applets to access CORBA services from other hosts. In addition, it also acts as a firewall which provides IIOP tunneling based on an administator-chosen list of which objects and methods to make visible to the external network.

Note that the Castanet transmitter is available for Solaris, Windows NT, and AIX (there may be others when you read this; check with Marimba), and so if your server objects are on some other architecture, you will either need a proxy such as gatekeeper to forward your ORB requests, or you will need a signed channel that can reach hosts other than the transmitter host.

### *Implementing Secure ORB Connections*

The OMG has defined a security service for CORBA, and in addition has defined an implementation of IIOP, called SECIOP, which uses that service to provide secure connections between CORBA clients and servers. This is a very complex standard, and not all applications can justify the sophistication that SECIOP provides. As an alternative many CORBA vendors have created SSL implementations. Until SECIOP is more widely adopted, it is probably more useful here to look at an SSL CORBA implementation.

The first issue you will have to resolve is whether you need client-side authentication. Generally, intranet applications do not need this unless the server application needs to access a user database of some sort, and needs to perform activities based on who the user is. For example, a call center application might access a sales agent database, and might add transactions that affect the agent's commissions. In such an application, client authentication is probably desirable.

If you need client authentication, you will need to decide where you will keep the client certificates and private keys. Will they be in the form of smart cards, carried by users? Or will they be stored on users' machines with the keys password-encrypted? Let's assume that you have implemented a client certificate database, as demonstrated earlier. You therefore have the capability to retrieve a user's certificate.

It is possible to tunnel IIOP through an HTTPS connection, using an HTTPS connection provided by a browser. This incurs the same kinds of restrictions as tunneling RMI through HTTP or HTTPS. When tunneling with HTTPS, the browser supplies the certificate management and creates and maintains the SSL/HTTP connection. A gateway program is required at the server end to extract the IIOP data from the HTTP stream and forward it to an ORB server. This is a workaround solution if there is no other way to connect through a firewall.

Assuming you are not using browser-based HTTPS tunneling, here is an example of how you might access a Java 2 keystore to obtain a certificate for servicing an SSL CORBA server connection, using VisiBroker's SSL implementation:

```
import org.omg.CORBA.ORBPackage.*;
import com.visigenic.vbroker.ssl.*;
import java.security.*;

public class MyClient
{
   public static void main(String[] args)
   {
      // Specify the Visigenic SSL/IIOP provider
      java.util.Properties p = new java.util.Properties();
      p.put("ORBServices", "com.visigenic.vbroker.ssl");

      // Initialize the ORB
      org.omg.CORBA.ORB orb = org.omg.CORBA.ORB.init(args, p);

      // Get the user's certificate alias
      String alias = ...prompt for alias...

      // Load our client certificate chain
```

```
KeyStore ks = KeyStore.getInstance();
String fname = System.getProperty("user.home")
   + System.getProperty("file.separator") + ".keystore";
InputStream is = new File(fname);
ks.load(InputStream stream, String password);
Certificate[] certChain = ks.getCertificateChain(alias);

// Instantiate a Visigenic "certificate manager"
CertificateManager cm = CertificateManagerHelper.narrow(
   orb.resolve_initial_references
   ("SSLCertificateManager"));

// Provide client certificate chain to the certificate
// manager, which
// will provide it to the server when requested
byte[][] cchain = new byte[certChain.length][];
for (int i = 0; i < cchain.length; i++)
{
   // This is a critical statement: it is how we will
   // pass a certificate, loaded from a Java 2 keystore,
   // to a Visigenic SSL cert manager.
   cchain[i] = certChain[i].getEncoded();
}
cm.setCertificateChain(cchain);

// Get private key password from user
String password = ...prompt...

// Obtain client private key from our database
PrivateKey epk = getPrivateKey(alias, password);

// Provide private key, so that client can answer
// challenges; note that
// it was stored in encrypted form, so the
// CertificateManager will have
// to decrypt it
byte[] encrPK = cm.decodeBase64(epk.getEncoded());
cm.setEncryptedPrivateKey(cncrPK, password);

// Find our server object
OurServer ourServer = OurServerHelper.bind(
   orb, "OurServer");

// Get the "Current" object - this is a proxy for the
// server SSL context
Current c = CurrentHelper.narrow
   (orb.resolve_initial_references("SSLCurrent"));
```

```
      // Verify the server object's certificate
      X509CertificateChain cc =
         current.getPeerCertificateChain(ourServer);
      checkCertChain(cc);

      // Get some other server object, by method call
      SomeOtherServer sos = ourServer.someMethod();

      // Now check that server object's certificate as well
      current.getPeerCertificateChain(sos);
      checkCertChain(cc);

      ...do other stuff...
   }
   static void checkCertChain(X509CertificateChain cc)
   {
      byte[] cbytes = cc.berEncoding();
      Certificate cert = X509Certificate.getInstance(cbytes);
      PublicKey pk = cert.getPublicKey();
      try { cert.verify(pk); }
      catch (java.security.GeneralSecurityException ex)
      { System.out.println("Server certificate not valid!");
         System.exit(0); }
   }
}
```

### Note

To use VisiBroker's IIOP/SSL feature with the Netscape browser, you must add some runtime components to the browser. You must add Visigenic's native SSL library (which includes the RSA BSafe cryptographic algorithms) to your Netscape bin directory, and you must add Visigenic's SSL classes (in a JAR file) to your system's classpath. A similar modification is needed for Internet Explorer.

## RMI-over-IIOP

The native protocol used by RMI to send remote requests and responses over the wire from client to server and back is called Java Remote Method Protocol (JRMP). RMI applications can use an alternative protocol, CORBA IIOP, so that they can be accessed by CORBA clients and can also use some of the additional features of IIOP such as transaction context propagation.

The ability to use the IIOP marshalling protocol from RMI is often referred to as "RMI-over-IIOP." It could more accurately be called "CORBA-pretending-to-be-

RMI." When one uses RMI-over-IIOP one is really doing CORBA, but with a programming model that mimics RMI. For example, when using this protocol, your object references are actually IIOP references instead of RMI references.

The specification that defines RMI-over-IIOP is called the "Java-to-IDL" mapping. As its name reflects, it is a specification of how to map Java objects and data to IDL (I have already discussed the mapping from IDL to Java). Since the IIOP stream protocol is defined for IDL, this accomplishes the objective of mapping Java-to-IIOP. (The Java-to-IDL specification also relies on the IDL extensions defined in the companion Objects By Value specification.)

### *Passing Objects by Value*

RMI allows objects to be passed by value. As discussed earlier in this chapter, CORBA 2 does not. CORBA 2 provides for the definition of IDL structs, which are analogous to C language structs. These struct types cannot contain recursive or cyclic references, nor can they contain methods. A Java object in contrast can have methods and can also contain arbitrary references to other objects, forming an object graph. The CORBA Object By Value specification adds Java-style object types to IDL. This allows Java objects to be passed by value in a CORBA remote call. For example, this IDL defines a CORBA value type:

```
value Score
{
    public long won;
    public long lost;
    public long getNetWinnings();   /* Computes won - lost */
    public Score yesterdaysScore;
}
```

Support for the mapping of methods in IDL value objects is optional. Therefore, you may not be able to narrow a passed value type to its IDL type and portably call its methods. The primary use of value type, therefore, is not to pass objects with behavior, but rather to allow stateful graph structures to be passed. For maximum portability, Java objects which are to be passed by value should not contain any methods.

**Stubs and Skeletons.** A tool which generates RMI-style stubs and skeletons to make remote method calls over the wire using IIOP is required to use the "portability" base types, defined in javax.rmi.CORBA, including the Stub base class for all generated stubs and the Tie interface for all generated tie skeletons. This ensures that you can use stubs and skeletons compiled with RMI compilers from different vendors, and be able to share a single ORB from either vendor.

An IIOP-capable RMI compiler will normally generate the required RMI stubs and skeletons that implement the IIOP behavior for the RMI API. For example, Sun's rmic compiler, if given the -iiop flag, automatically generates Java stubs and tie skeletons directly from the input RMI interface and implementation class. In addition, the compiler can generate IDL. This IDL may then be compiled, using any IDL compiler, into stubs and skeletons in any language (including Java). This allows other applications to communicate with your application regardless of what language they are written in. Thus, you can see that there is a wide variety of choices about the implementation of IIOP servants and clients: servants may be implemented in Java or any language; clients may be in Java or any language. These choices can be summarized as follows:

- An RMI client accessing a remote (Java or otherwise) object using IIOP
- An RMI object exporting itself using IIOP, for access by Java or other kinds of clients
- A Java CORBA client accessing a remote (Java or otherwise) object using IIOP
- A Java CORBA servant exporting itself using IIOP, for access by Java or other kinds of clients

To support these different scenarios, we need to be able to generate these kinds of interface components:

- RMI-over-IIOP Java stubs
- RMI-over-IIOP Java ties
- CORBA Java stubs
- CORBA Java ties or skeletons
- CORBA stubs and ties or skeletons in any other languages with which we are interfacing to

These different scenarios are shown in Figure 7-8, along with the tools that are available to generate them.

The main difference between a Java RMI IIOP stub and a Java CORBA IIOP stub is the API model used. A Java RMI IIOP stub uses the RMI API model, whereas a Java CORBA IIOP stub uses the CORBA API model. Let's look at an example. Assume we have this RMI interface:

```
package pingservice;
import java.rmi.*;

/**
 * Remote interface for our servant, defined as an RMI servant.
```

```
 */
public interface Server extends Remote
{
   String ping() throws RemoteException;
}
```

and this RMI implementation:

```
package pingservice;

import java.rmi.*;
import javax.rmi.*;
import java.util.*;
import javax.naming.*;

/**
 * Servant implementation class, and also main application
 * class (run from command line to instantiate and start a
 * servant). Use -D command line switch to define
 * java.naming.factory.initial
 * to one of the following values:
 * com.sun.jndi.registry.RegistryContextFactory (use
 * for JRMP); or
 * com.sun.jndi.cosnaming.CNCtxFactory (use for IIOP).
 */
public class ServerImpl extends PortableRemoteObject
implements Server
{
      public ServerImpl() throws RemoteException {}

      public String ping()
      {
         return "ping";
      }

      public static void main (String[] args) throws Exception
      {
         if (System.getSecurityManager() == null)
         {
            System.setSecurityManager(new RMISecurityManager());
         }

         Server servant = new ServerImpl();

         InitialContext context = new InitialContext();
         context.rebind("PingService", servant);
      }
}
```

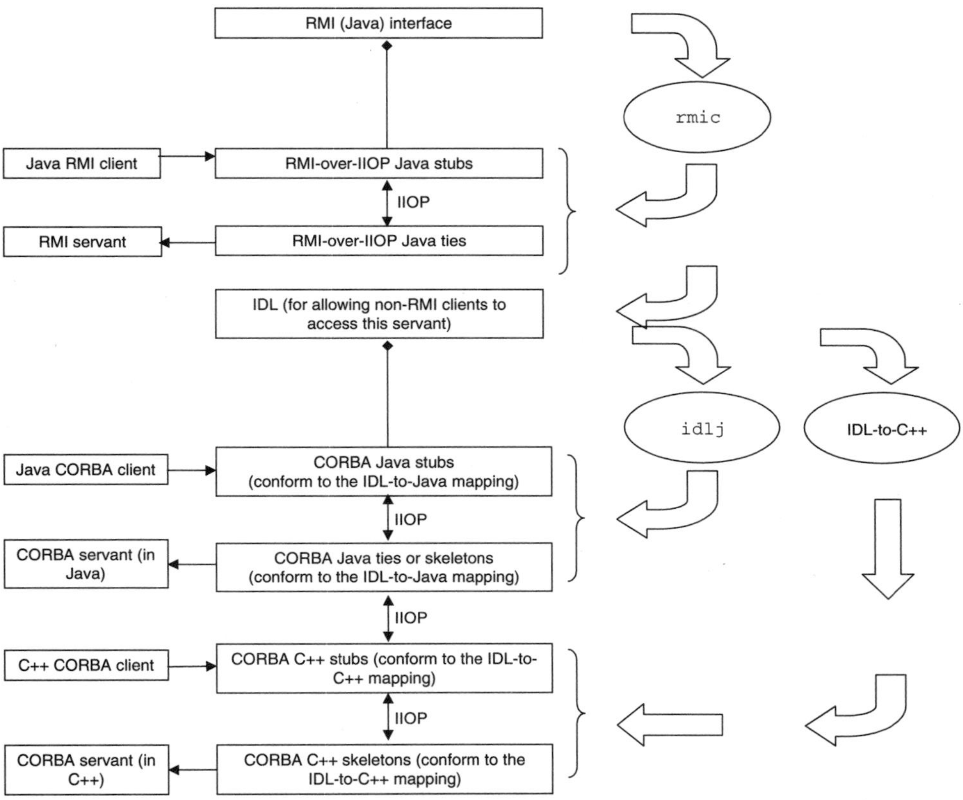

RMI (Java) interface
rmic
Java RMI client
RMI-over-IIOP Java stubs
IIOP
RMI servant
RMI-over-IIOP Java ties
IDL (for allowing non-RMI clients to access this servant)
idlj
IDL-to-C++
Java CORBA client
CORBA Java stubs (conform to the IDL-to-Java mapping)
IIOP
CORBA servant (in Java)
CORBA Java ties or skeletons (conform to the IDL-to-Java mapping)
IIOP
C++ CORBA client
CORBA C++ stubs (conform to the IDL-to-C++ mapping)
IIOP
CORBA servant (in C++)
CORBA C++ skeletons (conform to the IDL-to-C++ mapping)

**Figure 7-8** Different scenarios for generating IIOP stubs and skeletons.

Note that the server object class extends PortableRemoteObject instead of UnicastRemoteObject, as a JRMP RMI servant would do. The PortableRemote-Object gives the server its IIOP behavior.

In order for your programs to work with either RMI or CORBA (purists will says "JRMP or IIOP," but that is not accurate either) you should use the RMI-style interfaces and services. For example, in the ServerImpl class above, I use the JNDI API instead of the CORBA Name Service API. If using a CORBA name service, the name service will be accessed as a JNDI provider—transparent to the server or client code. Using the RMI-style interfaces is extremely important for EJBs, because only then are the beans redeployable across CORBA and non-CORBA application servers.

If you run the RMI compiler `rmic` on our server implementation as follows:

```
rmic -keep -iiop pingservice.ServerImpl
```

it generates this RMI-style IIOP stub:

```
// Stub class generated by rmic, do not edit.

package pingservice;
public final class Server_Stub
     extends javax.rmi.CORBA.Stub
     implements pingservice.Server
{
     // Constructors
     public Server_Stub() {
          super();
     }
     ...
     // Methods from remote interfaces

     // implementation of java.lang.String ping ()
     // throws java.rmi.RemoteException;
     public java.lang.String ping()
          throws java.rmi.RemoteException
     {
          ...
     }
}
```

and it generates the following enhanced RMI-style IIOP tie skeleton. Note that it calls our RMI-style ServerImpl implementation class:

```
// Tie class generated by rmic, do not edit.
// Contents depend on org.omg.CORBA.*.
package pingservice;
public final class ServerImpl_Tie
extends javax.rmi.CORBA.Stub   <---This stub serves also the role
              of the "local stub" which is optional, and allows
              the optimization of process-local calls. It can
              be turned off with the -noLocalStubs rmic option.
implements
      javax.rmi.CORBA.Tie,
      pingservice.Server
{
    pingservice.ServerImpl target = null;
    public void setTarget(java.rmi.Remote target) {
```

```
        This is called automatically to point the tie to
        our servant implementation.
     this.target = (pingservice.ServerImpl) target;
}
...
public org.omg.CORBA.portable.OutputStream _invoke(
  String method, org.omg.CORBA.portable.InputStream _in,
     org.omg.CORBA.portable.ResponseHandler reply)
  throws org.omg.CORBA.SystemException
{
     try {
          org.omg.CORBA_2_3.portable.InputStream in =
             (org.omg.CORBA_2_3.portable.InputStream) _in;
          if (method.equals("ping")) {
               java.lang.String result;
               result = target.ping();
               org.omg.CORBA_2_3.portable.OutputStream out =
                  (org.omg.CORBA_2_3.portable.OutputStream)
                  reply.createReply();
               out.write_Value(result);
               return out;

          } else {
               throw new org.omg.CORBA.BAD_OPERATION();
          }
     } catch (org.omg.CORBA.SystemException ex) {
          throw ex;
     } catch (java.lang.Throwable ex) {
          throw new
                org.omg.CORBA.portable.UnknownException(ex);
     }
}

// Local stub method
public java.lang.String ping()
throws java.rmi.RemoteException {
     java.lang.String result = null;
     try {
          result = target.ping();
     } catch (org.omg.CORBA.SystemException ex) {
          javax.rmi.CORBA.Util.mapSystemException(ex);
     } catch (java.lang.Throwable ex) {
          org.omg.CORBA.portable.UnknownException unknown =
          new org.omg.CORBA.portable.UnknownException(ex);
          javax.rmi.CORBA.Util.mapSystemException(unknown);
     }
     return result;
}
}
```

The generated classes are shown in Figure 7-9.

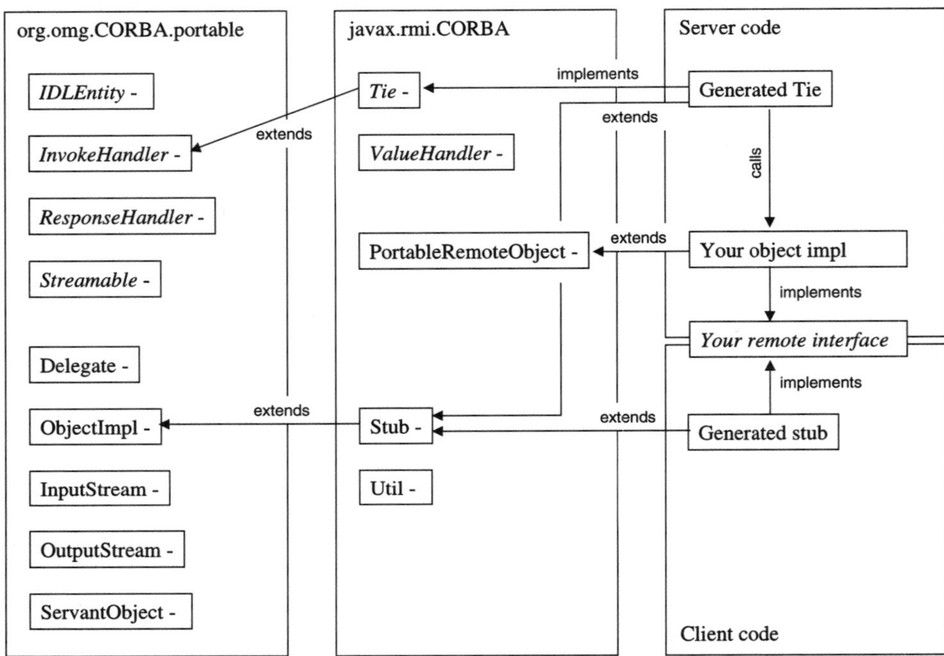


**Figure 7-9** The RMI-over-IIOP generated stub and skeleton classes and their relationship to other CORBA classes.

This RMI server can be accessed by an RMI client in the normal way. However, it is possible to access it using CORBA. This is because our servant is exported with the IIOP protocol. If you run `rmic` to generate IDL, as follows:

```
rmic -idl pingservice.Server
```

it produces this IDL:

```
/**
 * pingservice/Server.idl
 * Generated by rmic -idl. Do not edit
 * Wednesday, February 17, 1999 4:28:20 PM EST
 */
#ifndef __pingservice_Server__
#define __pingservice_Server__
#include "orb.idl"
module pingservice {
```

```
    interface Server {
        ::CORBA::WStringValue ping( );
    };
};
#endif
```

At this point, you now have the option of coding the server in any language, since you have IDL for the RMI interface. We can also, if we wish, implement the server itself as a CORBA server, and use either RMI or CORBA clients. If we run the generated IDL through `idlj`, it produces five (non-POA) CORBA-style client stub classes (each in a separate file) for package pingservice. Here is a portion of the generated stub code:

```
package pingservice;

public interface Server extends ServerOperations,
org.omg.CORBA.Object, org.omg.CORBA.portable.IDLEntity
{
} // interface Server

public interface ServerOperations
{
    String ping ();
} // interface ServerOperations

public class _ServerStub
extends org.omg.CORBA.portable.ObjectImpl
implements pingservice.Server
{
    ...
    public _ServerStub (org.omg.CORBA.portable.Delegate
        delegate)
    {
        super ();
         _set_delegate (delegate);
    }

    public String ping ()
    {
        org.omg.CORBA.portable.InputStream _in = null;
        try {
            org.omg.CORBA.portable.OutputStream _out =
                _request ("ping", true);
            _in = _invoke (_out);
            String __result =
            (String) ((org.omg.CORBA_2_3.portable.InputStream)_in)
```

```
            .read_Value (
            org.omg.CORBA.WStringValueHelper.get_instance ());
         return __result;
      } catch (org.omg.CORBA.portable.ApplicationException _ex)
      {
         _in = _ex.getInputStream ();
         String _id = _ex.getId ();
         throw new org.omg.CORBA.MARSHAL (_id);
      } catch (org.omg.CORBA.portable.RemarshalException _rm) {
         return ping ();
      } finally {
         _releaseReply (_in);
      }
   } // ping
   ...
   public static pingservice.Server narrow (
      org.omg.CORBA.Object obj)
      {
         ...
      }

...
```

and this server tie skeleton class:

```
public class Server_Tie extends org.omg.CORBA.portable.ObjectImpl
implements pingservice.Server
{
      ...
      private static java.util.Hashtable _methods =
         new java.util.Hashtable ();
      static
      {
         _methods.put ("ping", new java.lang.Integer (0));
      }

      public org.omg.CORBA.portable.OutputStream _invoke (
         String method, org.omg.CORBA.portable.InputStream in,
         org.omg.CORBA.portable.ResponseHandler rh)
      {
         org.omg.CORBA.portable.OutputStream out =
            rh.createReply();
         java.lang.Integer __method =
         (java.lang.Integer)_methods.get (method);
      if (__method == null)
         throw new org.omg.CORBA.BAD_OPERATION (0,
         org.omg.CORBA.CompletionStatus.COMPLETED_MAYBE);
```

```
        switch (__method.intValue ())
        {
            case 0:  // pingservice/Server/ping
            {
                String __result = null;
                __result = this.ping ();
                ((org.omg.CORBA_2_3.portable.OutputStream)out)
                .write_Value ((java.io.Serializable)__result,
                org.omg.CORBA.WStringValueHelper.get_instance ());
                break;
            }

            default:
                throw new org.omg.CORBA.BAD_OPERATION (0,
                org.omg.CORBA.CompletionStatus.COMPLETED_MAYBE);
        }

        return out;
    } // _invoke

    public String ping ()
    {
        return _impl.ping();
    } // ping
        ...
} // class Server_Tie
```

We can therefore access our servant using a CORBA client. The client could use a CORBA name service to locate the object, or it could use JNDI with a COS Naming provider (the latter is preferred for Java applications). It is even possible to store CORBA object references in an LDAP server (this is discussed in "CORBA Object Activation" on page 518).

I started this example with an RMI implementation for the server object, but we can choose to implement our servant using a CORBA API instead. This is straightforward since we already have generated an IDL equivalent for our RMI interface. Our CORBA servant can register itself in a CORBA name service, and Java objects can then locate it using JNDI and a COS Naming JNDI provider.

The RMI-to-IIOP mapping shown here is preliminary at this writing, and may change. The exact mappings are not important for the discussion here. I have shown them only so that you can get a feel for the nature of the mappings and their differences.

A goal of the mapping is to have interoperable ("portable") stubs, so that you can use vendor A's stubs and vendor B's stubs at the same time, both sharing a single ORB from vendor A, B, or X; we are not there yet: the standards are not stable yet. (We may also want to use vendor A's skeletons with vendor B's ORB.) This presents a problem for applications that need to access multiple remote ORBs of different kinds. Hopefully a final portability layer will emerge and prove to be interoperable. With the emergence of POA, it is likely to take another year before truly interoperable implementations are widely available.

In the meantime, be cautious if you need to mix CORBA implementations within a single client or server (not a wise thing to do anyway). A workaround for mixed origin clients is to generate all stubs from scratch, using your chosen client ORB's IDL or RMI compiler. These should be able to communicate with any remote implementation. This does not rule out web-based deployment, if all required client code comes from a single source and can therefore be generated with the same set of tools.

On the server side it is likely that a single server program will be built using skeletons generated by a single IDL or RMI compiler, even if it accesses other servants. If those other servants use different ORBs, they are probably in different server processes. Thus, skeleton-level interoperability is less of an issue.

**Transaction Propagation.** The IIOP protocol provides a means to transmit transaction identification information with each request header. A CORBA application will enable this by declaring an object to inherit the TransactionalObject interface. However, if your application is an RMI application—i.e., uses the RMI API—there is no corresponding interface or API for declaring an object to be transactional.

Nevertheless, many deployment environments support transactions. If a thread is associated with a transaction, and needs to use the RMI API to call another object and propagate that transaction context, it is up to the environment to add the required information to the request to achieve that. If IIOP is being used as the marshalling protocol, an EJB server could, for example, add the appropriate transaction information to the IIOP request header, even though the calling object is an RMI object. Transaction propagation will be discussed in detail later in this chapter.

**Programming Differences when Using RMI-over-IIOP.** An application which is coded to the RMI API but uses the IIOP protocol is coded for the most part as a regular RMI application. There are some provisions that need to be made, however, to provide for the special requirements of IIOP. Some of these are:

- *Use JNDI instead of calling the registry directly.* This eliminates dependence on the RMI-specific registry name service. Some organizations may choose to use alternative name services, such as LDAP or a CORBA name service. Thus, for example, your servers should bind object implementations like this:

  ```
  InitialContext context = new InitialContext();
  context.rebind("MyService", myServerImpl);
  ```

  and your clients should obtain object initial references like this:

  ```
  InitialContext context = new InitialContext(p);
  Object myObject = context.lookup("MyService");
  ```

- *Use narrow().* When calling a JNDI method to obtain an initial reference to an object, an RMI application normally casts the returned object to the appropriate application-specific type. CORBA applications have the convention that such "narrowing" be done with a narrow() method. For example:

  ```
  MyServer server = (MyServer)PortableRemoteObject.narrow(
     myObject, MyServer.class);
  ```

  This ensures that any conversion required to implement the narrowing can be done. Unfortunately, this method is specific to PortableRemoteObject, and so you should create your own narrow method which calls PortableRemoteObject.narrow(), so that conversion to JRMP only requires changing your method and does not affect application code. For example, here is a utility adapter for encapsulating RMI narrowing:

  ```
  public class MyRMIAdapter
  {
     public static Object narrow(Object object, Class c)
     {
        return PortableRemoteObject.narrow(object, c);
     }
  }
  ```

  If you import this class, you can then simply use your own narrow method:

  ```
  MyServer server = (MyServer)narrow(
     myObject, MyServer.class);
  ```

- *Encapsulate JNDI property configuration.* As for any JNDI application, you should encapsulate the setting of JNDI properties in an adapter class, so that the property values can be controlled outside the main application and not affect the application code.
- *Unexport all servants when they are destroyed.* Do not rely on RMI's automatic garbage collection of servant objects. An RMI server normally keeps a list of which VMs are currently referencing each servant, and client stubs need to make dirty() and clean() calls to the server periodically to renew object reference leases (this happens transparently, by the underlying RMI mechanism). IIOP does not support this, and so to write code that will work both for JRMP and IIOP, you should explicitly release servant objects in the normal CORBA way by calling the PortableRemoteObject or UnicastRemoteObject method unexportObject(). For example:

```
public void ejbRemove()
{
    ...
    unexportObject(this, true);
}
```

**Invoking Other CORBA Services in an RMI-over-IIOP Application.** Since an RMI-over-IIOP is in a sense really doing CORBA—to the extent that other remote components can tell—you can communicate with those services as with any CORBA application. The critical capability is the ability to exchange object references with CORBA applications. If you export an RMI servant which uses IIOP, then CORBA clients see your servant as just another CORBA servant. A CORBA object reference is called an Interoperable Object Reference (IOR), meaning that it can be exchanged with other ORBs even if they are made by different vendors. The portion of an IIOP object reference which is unique to its ORB is opaque anyway. Therefore, your RMI-over-IIOP application can exchange object references with other CORBA services without concern for interoperability, since the object references are IORs and are interoperable by definition as long as both ORBs implement the recent CORBA pass-by-value extensions.

**Load Balancing and Other Container Services.** It is up to the middleware provider as to how it implements value-added services such as load balancing. Therefore, some products may provide such services for certain protocols but not for others, and you should verify that services you depend on or would like to use are supported with the protocol you choose. Regardless, you should code your application so that it is as independent of the protocol choice as possible.

**Why Use IIOP?** You may be wondering: why go to all this trouble? Why not just use ordinary RMI? Well, there are currently some advantages to using IIOP. For one, it makes your server language-independent, so that it can be accessed from non-Java clients as well. Another advantage, however, is that RMI has no standard way of propagating a transaction context, and so if your Enterprise JavaBeans need to interoperate with other beans deployed on other middleware—of different brands—then IIOP is the way to go. By writing your programs so that they can operate either as RMI or RMI-over-IIOP components, you preserve the most flexibility while sacrificing nothing.

## Messaging

In prior sections I have discussed CORBA and RMI, which are protocols based on a remote invocation model. The protocols operate in real time, in the sense that requests are immediately sent to the destination server, and in most cases responses are generated immediately while the client waits.

Messaging is an alternative model for building distributed systems. The HTTP protocol, discussed in Chapter 5, is a message-oriented protocol of sorts, but is also real time because responses are generated immediately. It is therefore a hybrid. In this section, I am going to discuss message-oriented protocols of the category often referred to as "Message-Oriented Middleware" (MOM). The most important variations of the messaging model are "point-to-point" messaging, in which a message is sent to a specific recipient or set of recipients, and "publish/subscribe," in which a message is sent to all who are interested at any moment.

One important feature of messaging systems is that they tend to be easier to tier. For example, a group of clients can maintain a long-duration connection with a local messaging server, which in turn connects to other messaging servers. Messages which need to travel to distant servers are relayed by intervening servers without requiring a direct connection from the sending client. Similarly, callbacks to clients can be achieved without overburdening a central server with many client connections. Achieving this with a call-based system such as RMI, or CORBA remote method invocation, requires custom programming. A messaging system is therefore well-suited to a system which needs to be highly scalable, and which needs to provide client callbacks to refresh clients.

### *End-to-End QOS*

Quality of service (QOS) refers to the reliability and performance characteristics of a system. These are often the features that distinguish two implementations of a standard. For transactional and messaging systems, quality of service considerations are very similar, and can be grouped as follows:

- Durability—The effect of a committed transaction is persistent, or at least is recoverable. Includes loss of operations performed while connected, and loss of operations performed while not connected.
  - Prevention of repeat operations or duplicates
  - Correctness (garbled messages or data are detected or prevented)
  - Detection and appropriate notification of unresolved problems; no unnecessary notification if problems are handled by the system
- Atomicity—Either all aspects of a transaction complete, or none of it completes. This is very important for ensuring correct results if a system fails, needs to be rolled back and redone, or recovered. Atomicity can apply to:
  - A send or store operation
  - A receipt or retrieve operation
  - An acknowledgment or receipt or storage
  - An end-to-end send or store, receipt or retrieval, and acknowledgment of receipt or retrieval (atomicity of this is not typical for messaging systems, by definition)
- Ordering—Preservation of sequence. Can the application assume that the order of records or messages it obtains from the system represents the order in which they were actually created or sent? Ordering can be relative to:
  - A particular sender or writer. For example, if you receive two messages from a sender, you can be sure that the second message was actually sent subsequent to the first.
  - All senders or writers, and universal time. For example, if A and B both send messages to C, and at the same time send the same messages to D, will C receive all messages in the same sequence that D does? And if A's messages are sent a moment before B's, will both C and D receive A's messages before B's?
- Throughput—How quickly does data pass through the system, in real time?
- Latency, delay—either to send, or to send and receive acknowledgment of receipt; and time to establish a connection.
- Responsiveness to priority.

### *Java Message Service*

The Java Message Service (JMS) API was developed by Sun Microsystems, IBM, Modulus, NEON, OpenHorizon, Oracle, TIBCO, and Vitria to provide a common Java interface to the messaging products offered by those vendors and others. A messaging middleware vendor wishing to provide a Java interface implements a provider layer which plugs into the JMS application layer, thereby making the underlying system specifics transparent to the calling application. Further, because JMS specifies standard protocols for transaction and messaging services, JMS can bridge message services transparently—even those for which there is no JMS provider implementation. JMS is designed for Java 2, and a 1.1-compatible version is not planned.

**Point-to-Point vs. Publish/Subscribe.** JMS supports two models of operation: Point-To-Point (producer / consumer) and Publish / Subscribe (broadcast). In the point-to-point model, applications send and extract messages from named queues. In the publish / subscribe model, applications publish messages to named "topic" channels and listen asynchronously for arriving messages on those topics.

Message producers and consumers are independent—a sender or publisher does not need a receiver or subscriber to be connected to send or publish messages, and a receiver or subscriber can request or wait for messages even if there are no senders or publishers connected.

**Sessions.** A JMS session represents a connection to an underlying messaging service provider. A session provides:

- An interface for creating messages
- An interface for creating message producers (QueueSenders and TopicPublishers) and message consumers (QueueReceivers and TopicSubscribers)

Message delivery from a session to its message listeners is serialized for the session's listeners. Therefore, consumers implemented as listeners can safely share session resources. To implement a producer and consumer within a single client, use separate sessions.

A transactional session maintains a local transaction context for all operations on the session, including its producers and consumers.

**Transactions and Quality of Service.** In JMS, a session may be transactional; that is, queue and publish / subscribe operations can participate in local transactions. Any unacknowledged messages received during the course of the transaction will be redelivered if the transaction is rolled back, or acknowledged automatically if the transaction is commited, and any messages sent will be discarded and not actually sent if the transaction is rolled back, or dispatched if the transaction is committed. A transactional session always has a current transaction in progress—you do not have to explicitly start a transaction.

If the JMS provider layer supports Java Transaction API (JTA) distributed transactions (discussed later in Chapter 8), the JMS system can transparently incorporate its JMS transactions into larger JTA distributed transactions, under the control of XA transaction management. The application code is not specifically affected by this choice, except that if a session is transactional, and the server is using JTS, then the JMS application should refrain from calling commit or rollback on its JMS transaction. Doing so will result in an exception.

Thus, while JMS transactions are like any other simple transaction on a single resource, and define an atomic unit of work for their own resources, a JTA transaction is a composite unit of work that combines several simple transactions across the same resource or multiple resources into one transaction. In contrast, a JMS transaction applies only to the session of which it is a part, and does not extend to other message consumers or producers, even if they make use of the same messages. JTA or underlying XA support is not required by a JMS provider implementation.

JMS defines these message delivery modes:

> PERSISTENT—Guaranteed delivery. Messages will be delivered at least once, and after a receiver acknowledges it, never again to that receiver.
>
> NON_PERSISTENT—Delivery is not guaranteed. The message will be delivered, at most, once.

If a JMS messaging session is transactional, the session automatically acknowledges all messages received upon a commit. Non-transactional sessions may use one of these modes for acknowledgment:

> AUTO_ACKNOWLEDGE—Message receipt is acknowledged automatically by the system when a message is received.
>
> CLIENT_ACKNOWLEDGE—Message receipt is not automatically acknowledged, and applications must explicitly acknowledge them. When a message is acknowledged, all messages received before it are also acknowledged.
>
> DUPS_OK_ACKNOWLEDGE—Messages receipt is automatically acknowledged, but duplicate acknowledgments are permitted.

A session maintains consumed messages until they have been acknowledged by the session, so unacknowledged consumed messages will be redelivered after a rollback. This is the primary purpose of acknowledgment. There is no notification back to the sender of a message when a message is acknowledged; it is merely a

way to notify the messaging system that the message has been received, processed, and will never need to be redelivered.

**Message Filtering.** Both the point-to-point model and the publish/subscribe model support automatic message filtering, in which the underlying messaging system selects incoming messages based on the values of header fields and application-specific message property values. The header fields defined for JMS messages are:

JMSDeliveryMode—Whether delivery is PERSISTENT or NON_PERSISTENT.

JMSPriority—The urgency of the message; 0 is lowest, 9 is highest; a value greater than 4 is considered urgent.

JMSMessageID—A unique ID that identifies a particular message after it has been sent. This field is set by the underlying system when a message is sent, and can subsequently be read by the sender or receiver.

JMSCorrelationID—Optionally used by message senders in an application-specific way to refer to other messages.

JMSType—An application-specific message type. In general, all messages should have this set, since some messaging providers require that each message have a type. However, JMS does not require that any particular types be used.

JMSDestination—The destination to which a message is being sent.

JMSTimestamp—The time a message was sent.

JMSReplyTo—The desired reply destination, specified by the sender.

JMSRedelivered—A flag set by the provider when a message is redelivered due to no acknowledgment of receipt.

JMSExpiration—The GMT time at which the message should be destroyed if it has not been delivered.

Message properties are defined by the application and are set by the sender or publisher by creating a Java Properties object and calling the message's setJMSProperties() method:

```
Properties properties = new Properties();
properties.put("Region", "North America");
message.setJMSProperties(properties);
```

At the receiving end, the JMS system extracts the properties set by the sender, and makes them available for filtering.

Message filters, called "selectors," are expressed using a subset of SQL92, and can make direct references to message header fields or message properties. Filters cannot reference data included in the message body itself. As an example of a selector, suppose the message has a property called "Region," and we are only concerned with urgent messages—those with priorities greater than or equal to 5. We could then filter out all messages that do not meet the criteria specified in our selector expression:

```
String selector = "(Region = 'North America')
   AND (JMSPriority >= 5)";
```

is a selector for selecting only those messages in which the "Region" property is equal to "North America" and the message priority is greater than or equal to 5. When we create a point-to-point queue receiver, we pass in the message selector String. For example, a queue receiver could be created with this selector, using:

```
QueueReceiver receiver = session.createReceiver(queue, selector);
```

To create a filtered topic subscriber, pass in the message selector String in a manner analogous to the queue selector:

```
TopicSubscriber subscriber = session.createSubscriber(topic,
   selector);
```

A more complete example that includes this selector is shown below.

**Message Content Types.** The message content type variants supported by JMS are:

StreamMessage—A stream of data, consisting of supported data types. Data can be retrieved in the sequence written. Retrieval of data can be done using type-specific methods, or using the general object retrieval method readObject().

MapMessage—Named values can be stored and written, using type-specific methods, or using the methods setObject(String name, Object value) and getObject(String name).

TextMessage—For text-based (String) messages, including text consisting of XML.

ObjectMessage—For messages containing a serialized Java object.

BytesMessage—For messages that must have specific byte and numeric formatting to interoperate with an external messaging system. The methods specify the exact format in which data values are written and read.

**An Example.** Let's look at an example of a point-to-point queue which accepts product orders:

```
import javax.jms.*;
import javax.naming.*;

javax.naming.Context nameContext =
   new javax.naming.InitialContext();
Queue orderQueue = (Queue) nameContext.lookup("OrdersQueue");
QueueConnectionFactory factory =
   (QueueConnectionFactory)nameContext.lookup("MyJMSProvider");
```

The above code performs a JNDI lookup of the orders queue and the local JMS provider. The orders queue object encapsulates access to the orders queue as implemented by the message service being used. The factory object encapsulates access to connection creation to the message service. Once we have the factory, we can use it to create a queue connection, from which we can in turn create a queue session:

```
QueueConnection connection = factory.createQueueConnection();
QueueSession session =
   connection.createQueueSession(false,
   Session.AUTO_ACKNOWLEDGE);
```

The boolean parameter in createQueueSession(boolean, int) is a flag indicating whether the session should be transactional or not. If we had wanted this session to be transactional, we would have specified instead in the last line "...create-QueueSession(true, ...)".

From the session, we can create a sender object specific to the queue we are interested in:

```
QueueSender sender = session.createSender(orderQueue);
```

We now have a sender object we can use to send messages to the orders queue. Here I create a map message containing the attributes needed for a customer product order, and then dispatch the message to the queue using the send() method:

```
MapMessage orderMessage = session.createMapMessage();
orderMessage.setString("CustomerName", "Big A. Spender");
orderMessage.setString("ProductName", "L. V. Wallet");
orderMessage.setDouble("Price", (double)(340.00));
sender.send(orderMessage);
```

The point-to-point message sending process is shown in the Figure 7-10.

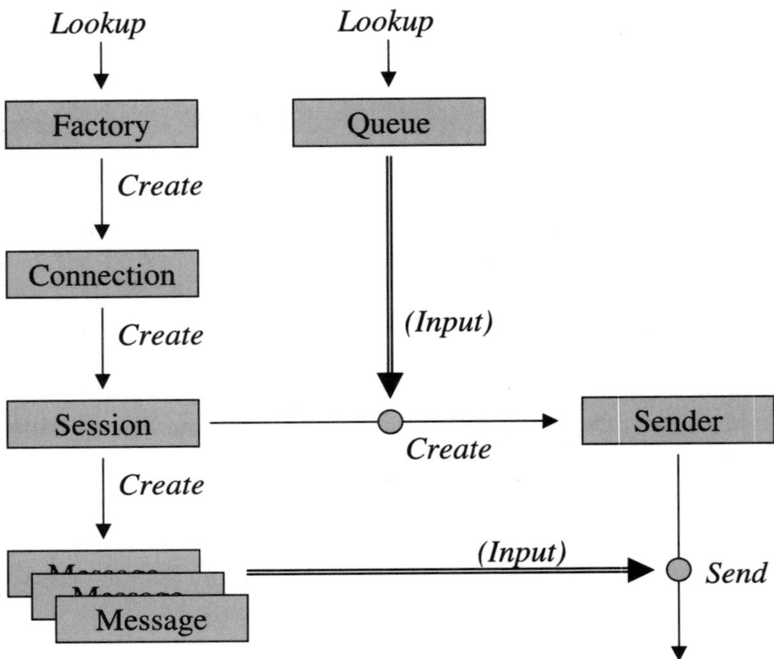


**Figure 7-10** Sending a point-to-point message.

On the receiving end, the receiving application would use the same procedure to connect to the orders queue, and then instead of creating a sender object it would create a receiver, and issue a receive() request whenever it wants another message from the queue. The receive() request blocks until a message arrives:

```
QueueReceiver receiver = session.createReceiver(orderQueue);
Message message = receiver.receive();
```

Thus, the receiving application connects in the same way as the sending application, and the only difference is that the receiver uses a receiver object and calls a receive() method.

The point-to-point message receiving process is shown in Figure 7-11.

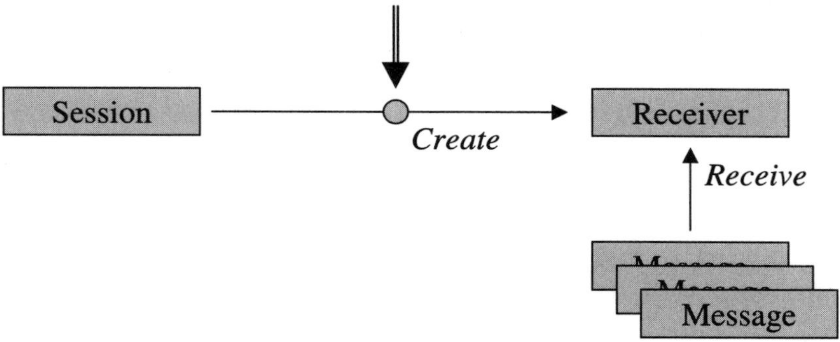


**Figure 7-11** Receiving a point-to-point message.

If the receiving application wants the messaging system to automatically filter messages for it, it can provide a selector expression when it creates the receiver:

```
String selector =
   "(Region = 'North America') AND (JMSPriority >= 5)";
QueueReceiver receiver =
   session.createReceiver(orderQueue, selector);
Message message = receiver.receive();
```

Using the publish and subscribe broadcast model is very similar to using the point-to-point queueing model. The main difference is that instead of using a queue, we use a "topic" to publish and subscribe to:

```
javax.naming.Context nameContext = new
   javax.naming.InitialContext();
Topic orderTopic = (Topic) nameContext.lookup("OrdersTopic");
TopicConnectionFactory factory =
   (TopicConnectionFactory)nameContext.lookup("MyJMSProvider");
TopicConnection connection = factory.createTopicConnection();
TopicSession session =
   connection.createTopicSession(false, Session.AUTO_ACKNOWLEDGE);
```

To publish to this topic, create a publisher object:

```
TopicPublisher publisher =
   session.createPublisher(orderTopic);
```

Now we can use this publisher object to publish messages to the topic, as follows:

```
MapMessage orderMessage = session.createMapMessage();
orderMessage.setString("CustomerName",  "Big A. Spender");
orderMessage.setString("ProductName",  "L. V. Wallet");
orderMessage.setDouble("Price", (double)(340.00));
publisher.publish(orderMessage);
```

Figure 7-12 shows the basic message publishing process.

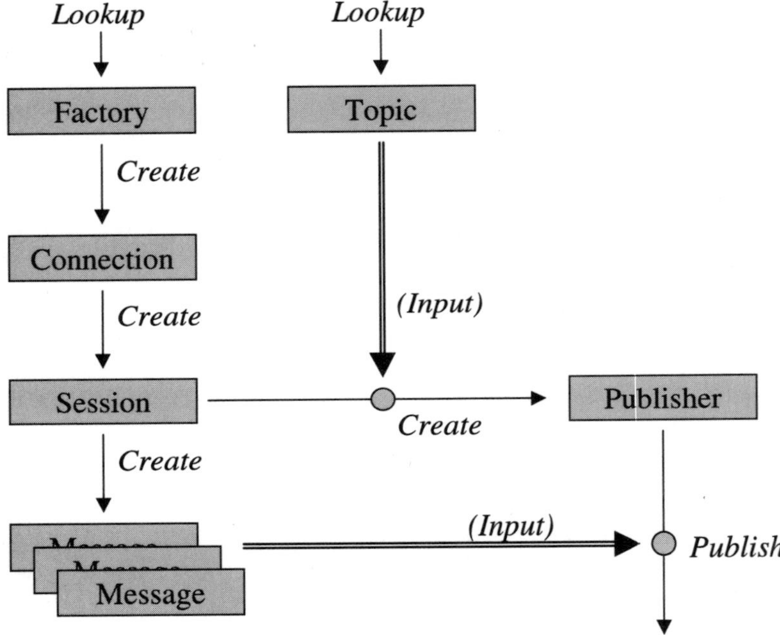


**Figure 7-12** Publishing a broadcast message.

Other applications can subscribe to this topic by creating a subscriber object for the topic:

```
TopicSubscriber subscriber =
   session.createSubscriber(orderTopic);
```

Having subscribed is not sufficient, however. You must define a callback for the JMS system to call when topic messages actually arrive. To do this, you create a message listener—an adapter object which implements the JMS MessageListener interface—and register it with the subscriber object. Whenever a message arrives for the subscribed topic, the listener's onMessage() handler method is called:

```
subscriber.setMessageListener
(
   new MessageListener()
   {
      void onMessage(Message orderMessage)
      {
         try
         {
            // Retrieve data from message
            MapMessage msg = (MapMessage)orderMessage;
            String customerName =
               msg.getString("CustomerName");
            String productName =
               msg.getString("ProductName");
            double price = msg.getDouble("Price");
            // Respond to message with actions...
         }
         catch (JMSException ex) ...
      }
   }
);
```

This is depicted in Figure 7-13.

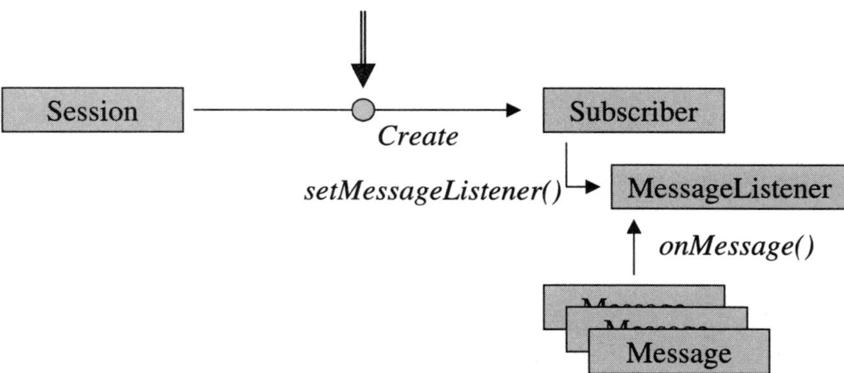


**Figure 7-13** Being notified of a broadcast message arrival.

QueueReceivers can also add message listeners in the same way, for receiving messages asynchronously, instead of calling the receive() method, which blocks. There is also a receiveNoWait() method which does not block, and returns null if there is no message. If you need to control the flow of messages, the connection has methods stop() and start() to temporarily pause and resume incoming message delivery to the associated session's receivers and listeners.

If the application wishes the messaging system to filter topic messages automatically, it can pass a selector expression to the session when it creates the subscriber:

```
String selector =
   "(Region = 'North America') AND (JMSPriority = 5)";
TopicSubscriber subscriber =
   session.createSubscriber(orderTopic, selector);
```

### *CORBA Event Service*

The CORBA Event Service defines a mechanism for the asynchronous dispatching of messages between multiple senders ("suppliers") and multiple interested parties ("consumers"). Unfortunately, the specification does not specify a required quality of service (QOS), so users of the service cannot be sure that if they change vendors, their application will still have the same performance or reliability characteristics. Primary QOS considerations include durability, response time, and the preservation of message order. The service does not require atomicity, and some subscribers may receive messages while others do not. Loss of messages can occur, for example, if an implementation uses queues, and the queue size is reached, causing messages to be discarded—either the oldest or the newest, depending on the implementation. The event service specification leaves it completely up to the vendor to address or not address such QOS issues.

With a minimal QOS implementation, the Event Service is therefore useful mainly as a non-critical notification or advisory system; a design cannot rely on it for correctness, unless acknowledgment and other required QOS features are added by the application. Still, this may be sufficient for many information delivery applications or applications that use notification as a "hint" and do not rely on it for correctness. Also, the Event Service is here today, and Java implementations of it are available from the major CORBA vendors.

The Event Service defines two models: "push" and "pull." They are really the same, in that one is a negative analog of the other. In the push model, a consumer sits and waits for units of work to arrive. In the pull model, it sits and waits for requests for work. In either model, there can be any number of suppliers and consumers. You decide which model you want to use, and then define a supplier and a consumer using interfaces for that model. For example, if you choose a push model, you define a push supplier and a push consumer. If you choose a pull model, you define a pull supplier and a pull consumer.

You can create an event service object in a separate process, or embed its creation in a server program that uses the service. Event channels can be named, but they don't have to be, and if you create a channel in your program, you can use just its reference, instead of having to obtain it by name.

The mechanism for finding event channels is not defined. However, since an event channel is an object, you can register it with the CORBA Name Service, and use that service to look it up from other processes.

Event channels can either be typed or untyped. An untyped event channel dispatches objects of type Any, and your application must convert these objects to the expected application type. You can also define typed event channels, in which the channel type is defined using IDL.

An important issue is how many channels to create. Should you create a separate channel for every kind of event or message in your system, and let clients subscribe to very specific channels? Or should you create a smaller number of generic channels, and effectively broadcast event notification on those channels, and require clients to listen to those for the ones they are interested in? The answer to this depends partly on the implementation of the event service, and how much overhead is involved in creating a channel. In general, you probably do not want to create a separate channel for every kind of event, but you may want to create channels for specific types of important events, to provide notification of application-level events, as described in Chapter 6.

**Example: A Loan Approval Application.** To demonstrate the Event Service, I will create a Loan object, and allow interested parties to register to be notified when the loan is approved. It is assumed that a fallback notification mechanism also exists, possibly less timely but more reliable, perhaps in the form of an approval notification checklist. The event notification is therefore an auxiliary mechanism, used to alert people at the very moment of approval. Here is the code:

```
import org.omg.CosEventComm.*;
import org.omg.CosEventChannelAdmin.*;
import org.omg.CORBA.SystemException;

import com.visigenic.vbroker.orb.*;
import com.visigenic.vbroker.services.CosEvent.*;

public class SingleProcessTest
{
    /**
     * Main program, for demonstrating this. This program creates
     * an instance of a Loan, and
     * an instance of an InterestedParty.
     */
    public static void main(String[] args)
    {
        org.omg.CORBA.ORB orb = org.omg.CORBA.ORB.init();
        org.omg.CORBA.BOA boa = orb.BOA_init();
```

```
        // Create the event channel right here - that way we won't
        // have to give it a name and expect the objects to find it
        EventChannel channel = EventLibrary.create_channel(boa);
        boa.obj_is_ready(channel);

        // Create an instance of a server that generates events
        Loan loan = new Loan(orb, boa, channel);

        // Create an object that will subscribe to the server's
        // events
        InterestedParty interestedParty = new InterestedParty(boa,
           channel);

        // Now approve the loan
        loan.approve(true);
    }
}

public class Loan extends _PushSupplierImplBase
{
    public Loan(org.omg.CORBA.ORB orb, org.omg.CORBA.BOA boa,
     EventChannel channel)
    {
        this.orb = orb;
        this.boa = boa;
        this.channel = channel;
        boa.obj_is_ready(this);

        // Create consumer proxy for the supplier to talk to
        consumerProxy =
           channel.for_suppliers().obtain_push_consumer();
        try { consumerProxy.connect_push_supplier(this); }
        catch ( org.omg.CosEventChannelAdmin.AlreadyConnected ex){}
    }

    public void approve(boolean b)
    {
        try
        {
           org.omg.CORBA.Any message = orb.create_any();
           String s;
           message.insert_string(s = (b ? "Approved" :
              "Disapproved"));
           consumerProxy.push(message);
           System.out.println("Approval message sent: " + s);
        }
        catch(Disconnected e)
```

```
        {
            System.out.println("Disconnected");
        }
        catch(SystemException e)
        {
            e.printStackTrace();
            disconnect_push_supplier();
        }
    }

    public void disconnect_push_supplier()
    {
        try { boa.deactivate_obj(this); }
        catch (org.omg.CORBA.SystemException ex) {}
    }

    private org.omg.CORBA.ORB orb;
    private org.omg.CORBA.BOA boa;
    private EventChannel channel;
    private ProxyPushConsumer consumerProxy;
}
public class InterestedParty extends _PushConsumerImplBase
{
    public InterestedParty(org.omg.CORBA.BOA boa, EventChannel
        channel)
    {
        this.boa = boa;
        this.channel = channel;
        boa.obj_is_ready(this);

        subscribeToChannel(channel);
    }
    public void subscribeToChannel(EventChannel channel)
    {
        // Create a supplier proxy for the subscriber
        ProxyPushSupplier supplierProxy =
            channel.for_consumers().obtain_push_supplier();

        // Connect the subscriber to the channel
        try { supplierProxy.connect_push_consumer(this); }
        catch ( org.omg.CosEventChannelAdmin.AlreadyConnected ex){}
    }

    public void push(org.omg.CORBA.Any data) throws Disconnected
    {
        System.out.println("Loan was: " + data);
    }
```

```
   public void disconnect_push_consumer()
   {
      try { boa.deactivate_obj(this); }
      catch (org.omg.CORBA.SystemException ex) {}
   }

   private EventChannel channel;
   private org.omg.CORBA.BOA boa;
}
```

The issue of persistence is not addressed in this example.

### *CORBA Messaging Service*

The CORBA Messaging Service is a standard under development by the OMG to address MOM requirements in the context of CORBA. The companies actively involved in developing the standard are BEA Systems, Borland (Visigenic), Expersoft, ICL, IONA, IBM, Nortel, Novell, Oracle, PeerLogic, and TIBCO.

The standard is being completed at this writing, and a Java binding does not yet exist. It is not clear exactly how this new CORBA service and JMS will interoperate, but they certainly will. CORBA Messaging is a fairly complex standard. It is likely that, just as RMI provides a Java-friendly interface to IIOP, and JNDI provides, through the CosNaming JNDI provider, a Java-friendly interface to CORBA Naming Service, that, similarly, JMS will provide a Java-friendly interface to the CORBA Messaging Service.

### *Mainframe Transaction Gateways*

Many gateway products have emerged which enable a Java application to communicate directly with mainframe services such as CICS, MQ Series, and so on. For example, Information Builders provides a JavaBean for accessing CICS from their Parlay EJB server. The bean can either access a native CICS gateway and communicate with IBM's native LU6.2 protocol, or it can access a CICS gateway on the mainframe via TCP/IP. Figure 7-14 illustrates the architecture.

IBM is also actively developing Java APIs for accessing most of its mainframe services.

## XML

The Extensible Markup Language (XML) is a World Wide Web Consortium (W3C)-recommended standard (http://w3c.org/TR/REC-xml) for creating information documents. Unlike HTML which contains only words and pictures with some document formatting, an XML document contains syntactic elements which can be used to define information structures.

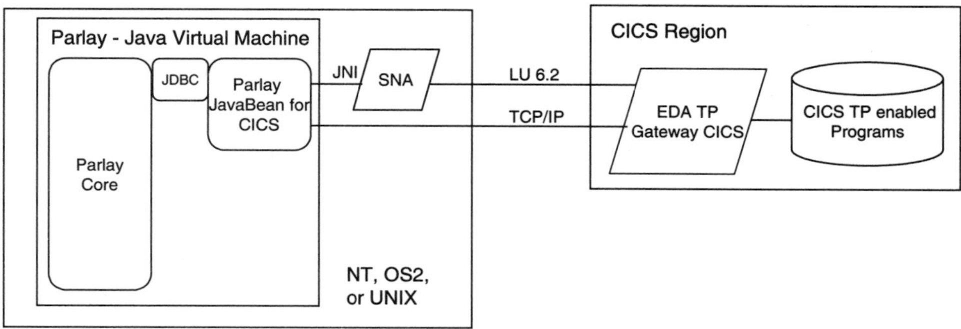


**Figure 7-14** Accessing CICS from an EJB using the Parlay CICS JavaBean Gateway.

XML does this by providing a baseline grammar on which application writers can define new elements and attributes which can be parsed by an XML parser. There is no magic however: even though it is easy to define arbitrary elements and attributes, the semantics of these must be understood by applications which use an XML document. Still, by settling on a basic structure, a generic parser can be used across many applications.

XML can be used to create long-lived documents which can be referenced again and again, or it can be used to create messages for sending from one system to another to convey information and events. XML is likely to find the most use as a messaging or description format for conveying timely structured information between independent systems.

An important difference between distributed systems which use an object oriented interface (such as RMI), and those which use a more data oriented messaging interface such as XML messages, is that the former approach closely links data and semantic behavior whereas the latter completely separates them. Message-oriented systems are appropriate when two communicating systems are loosely coupled in that they have different maintenance cycles and the data to be communicated needs to be defined separately from the invocation and transport mechanisms. Messaging interfaces are only practical for linking distributed systems if the message format and schema is under tight configuration control.

At present, XML is already used in many products and embedded applications. For example, Microsoft Windows uses XML to describe desktop channels and their update characteristics. You can also write your own XML applications and use XML to serve as a message format for linking distributed application components. For example, you might define an XML schema which describes your products and prices, and allow your customers to retrieve up-to-date information as XML and use it in their own ordering process.

The topic of XML is a large and complex one; the purpose of this section is not to teach you all about XML. Instead I will explain how it can be used to send basic messages between two organizations, and show how these messages can be generated and processed using Java.

### *The XML Syntax*

First and foremost, XML is a syntax. Let's look at an example:

```
<?xml version="1.0"?>
<StatusRequest>
   <Cardholder>
      <Cardnumber value="12345 22 3344"/>
      <CardholderName name="Granny Smith"/>
      <ExpirDate month="12" year="02"/>
   </Cardholder>
   <OrderId id="12345abcde"/>
</StatusRequest>
```

The above self-contained XML document defines the tags StatusRequest, Cardholder, Cardnumber, CardholderName, ExpirDate, and OrderId. In addition, it provides values for these tags. Note that some tags end immediately with a "/>" symbol, whereas others have a corresponding </...> tag. The latter have the value consisting of everything that exists between the tag and its corresponding </...> tag. Thus, there are essentially two kinds of tags: those which end immediately and which have attributes, and those which have termination tags and have complex values, possibly consisting of other nested tags.

### *Encoding Semantic Rules*

While the above XML document can stand on its own, it does not specify any rules so that a parsing application can determine if it is defined correctly. For example, it would be nice to be able to specify which tags must be nested within a StatusRequest tag. In the above example, StatusRequest contains a Cardholder and an OrderId, but it might be possible for a StatusRequest to have additional nested tags. Also, it would be desirable to specify the attributes that attributed tags must have, such as the Cardnumber tag. A Document Type Definition (DTD) defines the rules that an XML document must follow. An XML document may identify a DTD which defines the rules to be followed by the document. Here is an example of a DTD for the above XML example:

```
<!ELEMENT StatusRequest (Cardholder, OrderId)>
<!ELEMENT Cardholder (Cardnumber, CardholderName, ExpirDate)>
<!ELEMENT Cardnumber EMPTY>
<!ATTLIST Cardnumber value CDATA #REQUIRED>
<!ELEMENT CardholderName EMPTY>
<!ATTLIST CardholderName name CDATA #REQUIRED>
<!ELEMENT ExpirDate EMPTY>
<!ATTLIST ExpirDate month CDATA #REQUIRED>
<!ATTLIST ExpirDate year CDATA #REQUIRED>
<!ELEMENT OrderId EMPTY>
<!ATTLIST OrderId id CDATA #REQUIRED>
```

The above DTD specifies that the XML document may have a StatusRequest tag, and that the StatusRequest tag must contain a Cardholder tag and an OrderId tag. It defines similar rules for these and other nested tags. It specifies that the Cardnumber tag is self-contained and does not contain any nested tags, and it specifies that this tag contains a required attribute called "value" which is of type "CDATA" (character data). The ExpirDate tag has has two required attributes: "month" and "year," each defined by a separate DTD statement.

You can embed these rules in the XML document itself, but it is far more flexible to keep them in a separate DTD and refer to that DTD in your XML:

```
<?xml version="1.0"?>
<!DOCTYPE StatusRequest SYSTEM "file:/d:/StatusRequest.dtd">
<StatusRequest>
   <Cardholder>
      <Cardnumber value="12345 22 3344"/>
      <CardholderName name="Granny Smith"/>
      <ExpirDate month="12" year="02"/>
   </Cardholder>
   <OrderId id="12345abcde"/>
</StatusRequest>
```

### *Message Transport*

An XML message may be transported by any means, since an XML document is merely a character stream. For example, an XML message can be sent using message-oriented middleware with the Java Message Service API. HTTP can also be used to send XML messages using the POST method. For the purpose of illustration, let's consider a simple case of using HTTP as the message transport.

To send an XML message using HTTP, all you need is the services of a web server at the destination and a servlet or CGI program listening for the message. (You could also use the PUT method.) Open a URLConnection to the destination servlet and send the message in the connection stream. For example:

```
URL url = new URL("http://www.myhost.com/servlet/RequestStatus");
HttpURLConnection uc = (HttpURLConnection)(url.openConnection());
uc.setDoOutput(true);
uc.setDoInput(true);
OutputStream os = uc.getOutputStream();
uc.setRequestMethod("POST");
...write the XML message to the output stream...
```

The destination system may then respond with a message immediately in its HTTP response stream. You might retrieve this as follows:

```
InputStream is = uc.getInputStream();
...read the stream...
```

The overall scenario is shown in Figure 7-15:

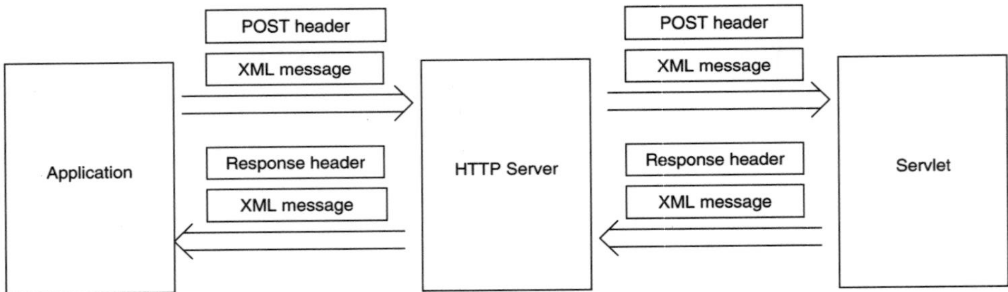


**Figure 7-15** XML message transport using HTTP.

Let's now look at how we might generate an XML message, and then how we might process a message we receive.

### *Message Generation*

There is no reason you cannot construct an XML message from scratch on the fly, or hard-code the required XML constructs in a program to generate a message. It is far more flexible, however, to use a template-based generation technique. There are many ways this can be implemented. One of the more powerful techniques is to use JavaServer Pages, which will be discussed later in this chapter. Regardless how you do it, the basic idea is to predefine a set of XML documents with attributes to be filled in later, and fill those in dynamically when a message is generated using actual data. Each template can have associated with it a DTD so

that its correctness can be verified. At the receiving end, the same DTD would be used to verify the incoming message. Template based XML generation is shown in Figure 7-16.

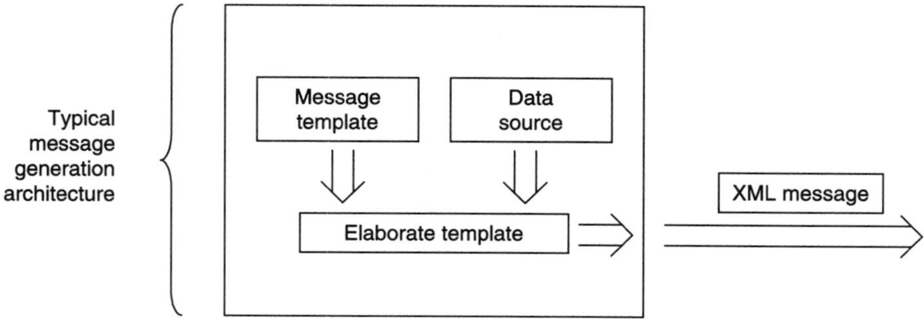


**Figure 7-16** A typical XML message generation scenario.

### *Message Processing*

To process an XML message, you must parse the message first. An effort is underway to standardize the parsing of XML messages. In the meantime, there is a popular standard called SAX developed by David Megginson which is free (http://www.megginson.com/SAX/) and has been widely implemented. It is included with Sun Microsystem's experimental "Project X" distribution.

SAX is a set of Java packages which define an XML parser interface. Many people and companies have written parsers which implement SAX, including Sun, IBM, Oracle, and Microsoft. The Project X distribution includes Java's SAX parser.

There are many ways to write a parser. SAX defines a recognition-based interface, in which the parser calls specific methods for each kind of XML construct as it is recognized. It is up to the application what to do with this information. For example, the application could construct a parse tree. Alternatively, it could maintain a stack of information which is needed later as more and more of the document is recognized. For simple documents, it may be possible to perform the actual desired application processing as constructs are recognized without having to store them.

SAX is modular in that it separates the roles of document parsing (recognition of XML constructs), the handling of those constructs, error handling, locating input, and other functions. To use SAX, your application must provide a module which provides the callbacks that are called when constructs are recognized. This module is called a document handler, and must implement org.xml.sax.DocumentHandler. You register a document handler with a SAX parser by calling the parser's setDocumentHandler() method.

I will not go into all the features of the SAX API, but it is useful to look at an example. Consider the XML grammar we have discussed above. The following program obtains an XML message or document from a file, instantiates a SAX parser, in this case Java's parser, and registers a DocumentHandler class. In practice, the message would more likely come from an HTTP request or some other remote service.

```
import java.io.*;
import org.xml.sax.*;
import org.xml.sax.helpers.ParserFactory;

public class MyDocumentHandler
extends HandlerBase
implements DocumentHandler
{
   private Locator locator;

   private String cardnumber;
   private String cardholderName;
   private String expirMonth;
   private String expirYear;
   private String orderId;

   public static void main(String[] args) throws Exception
   {
      try
      {
         FileInputStream fis =
            new FileInputStream("StatusRequest.xml");

         InputSource is =
         com.sun.xml.parser.Resolver.createInputSource
         (
            "text/xml",    // content type (String)
            fis,           // (InputStream)
            true,          // checkType (boolean)
            "file"         // scheme (String)
         );
         Parser parser = ParserFactory.makeParser
         (
            "com.sun.xml.parser.ValidatingParser"
         );
         parser.setDocumentHandler(new MyDocumentHandler());
         parser.setErrorHandler(new MyErrorHandler());
```

```
      parser.parse(is);
      System.out.println("Success");
   }
   catch (SAXParseException pe)
   {
      System.out.println("Parsing error at line "
         + pe.getLineNumber()
         + " column " + pe.getColumnNumber()
         + ": "
         + pe.getMessage ());
      return;
   }
   catch (SAXException se)
   {
      Exception ne = se.getException();
      if (ne != null) throw ne;
      throw se;
   }
}

static class MyErrorHandler extends HandlerBase
{
   public void fatalError(SAXParseException pe)
   throws SAXException
   {
      throw pe;
   }

   public void error(SAXParseException pe)
   throws SAXException
   {
      throw pe;
   }

   public void warning(SAXParseException pe)
   throws SAXException
   {
      System.out.println("Warning at line "
         + pe.getLineNumber()
         + " column " + pe.getColumnNumber()
         + ": " + pe.getMessage());
   }
}

//
// From DocumentHandler:
//
```

```
public void setDocumentLocator(Locator locator)
{
   this.locator = locator;
}

public void startElement(String name, AttributeList attrs)
throws SAXException
{
   if (name.equals("StatusRequest"))
   {
   }
   else if (name.equals("Cardholder"))
   {
   }
   else if (name.equals("Cardnumber"))
   {
      // Get the attributes.
      cardnumber = attrs.getValue("value");
   }
   else if (name.equals("CardholderName"))
   {
      // Get the attributes.
      cardholderName = attrs.getValue("name");
   }
   else if (name.equals("ExpirDate"))
   {
      // Get the attributes.
      expirMonth = attrs.getValue("month");
      expirYear = attrs.getValue("year");
   }
   else if (name.equals("OrderId"))
   {
      // Get the attributes.
      orderId = attrs.getValue("id");
   }
   else
   {
      throw new SAXParseException(
         "Unexpected element: " + name, locator);
   }
}

public void endDocument() throws SAXException
{
   System.out.println(cardnumber);
   System.out.println(cardholderName);
   System.out.println(expirMonth);
   System.out.println(expirYear);
```

```
        System.out.println(orderId);
    }
}
```

The DocumentHandler class extends a base class for convenience, to provide null implementations for the methods we are not concerned with. It overrides the methods startElement(String name, AttributeList attrs), andDocument(), and some other methods.

The startElement(String name, AttributeList attrs) method is called whenever the parser recognizes a syntactic element such as <StatusRequest> or <Cardholder> or any of the other elements we have defined in our XML. In this way our document handler is notified as each of these constructs is encountered. If the construct has attributes, they are passed in via the attrs argument. Our XML document has attributes defined for the Cardnumber, CardholderName, ExpirDate and OrderId elements.

Once the attributes have all been retrieved, the endDocument() method is called and we can perform some application processing, such as store the recovered data in a database or issue a reply if the message was sent as part of a query. In the simple example here, I merely print the values out.

The overall message processing scenario is shown in Figure 7-17.

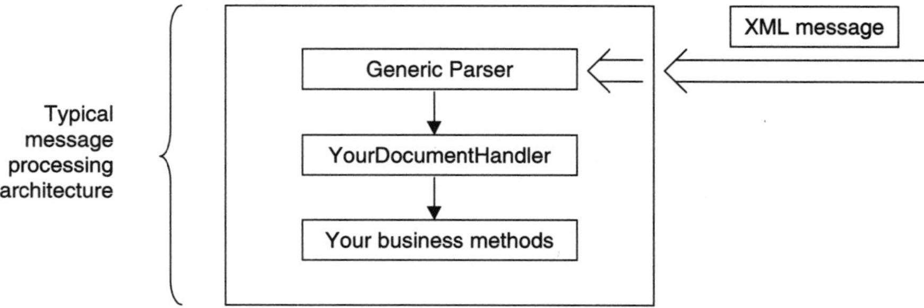


**Figure 7-17** A typical XML message processing scenario.

### *The Document Object Model*

The XML Document Object Model (DOM) defines an object graph structure for representing XML documents. In simple XML applications it may be sufficient to bypass using a DOM representation and to process and generate XML directly. More sophisticated applications can parse XML into a DOM representation and then process the graph structure programmatically. This is a fairly heavyweight approach and should be used only when necessary. Inline processing of parsed data is generally much more efficient that building what amounts to a parse tree.

There are ready-made Java implementations of the XML DOM. Sun Microsystems provides one with their Java XML tools.

### *XML Standards*

You might be wondering if you have to always define your own XML data or if there are existing standards for specific kinds of applications. There are many. A good list can be found at http://www.oasis-open.org/cover/siteIndex.html.

## Distributed Transactions

The increased use of extranets and organization-wide networks has led to attempts to integrate data resources and applications in place within those organizations, to create a larger integrated application framework and improve information flow. Departments can often justify keeping existing processes and data as they are, because they are proven and trusted, and operations depend on them. Therefore, instead of fixing systems that are not broken, wider integration may mean tying together these systems as they are.

Nowadays, most systems are transactional and multiuser. Integrating two transactional systems, however, is not merely a matter of getting data from one system and sending it to another—the integrated process must be transactional for the same reasons that the individual systems are transactional. Transactional operation provides quality of service characteristics that are critical to enterprise level applications, including atomicity, data integrity and isolation during a transaction, and usually recoverability after failure.

Integrating separate transactional systems requires that the separate systems are designed such that they can be integrated. Proprietary systems that support distributed transactions provide their own mechanisms for implementing a cross-system two-phase commit protocol; for such systems to cooperate in multi-system transactions in a nonproprietary way, they must open up their mechanisms for performing transaction control.

Many open transaction protocols exist. Predominantly used is the X/Open XA standard, developed by the X/Open consortium. This protocol is used by many popular transaction managers including such as BEA Systems' Tuxedo. Systems that have components called "transaction managers" which support this protocol can participate in integrated transactions, to tie together separately developed applications.

At the application level, many proprietary systems wrap their native transaction APIs in open standards, most notably the CORBA COS Transactions service

(unofficially known as "OTS"). For example, IBM provides a standards-compliant implementation of OTS over its own Resource Recovery Services.

As discussed earlier, integration of separate applications can be approached using a transactional approach or a messaging approach. Even if a messaging approach is used, often the act of sending or receiving a message is incorporated into a distributed transaction. Thus, the reliable nature of the messaging operations (which may themselves have a local transaction context) cooperates with a reliable distributed transaction mechanism that ties together other components that do not use messaging, to create a more comprehensive end-to-end reliable system. For this to be possible, the messaging system itself (as opposed to the applications using it) must be able to participate in distributed transactions.

## The Java Transaction API (JTA)

### *Overview*

A transaction manager is a component that coordinates the completion of transactions across multiple data resources, possibly of different kinds and from different vendors. Most database products today expose industry standard APIs that transaction managers can use to perform this coordination. A transaction coordinated by a transaction manager, across multiple heterogeneous data resources, is often called a "global transaction." The Java Transaction API (JTA) provides a standard Java interface to transaction management.

When used with a transaction manager, JTA allows the aggregation of separate operations, possibly on different data resources, into a single transaction. This relieves the application of coordinating separate but related changes to multiple data resources, and permits logical transactions to be designed which span multiple heterogeneous data resources.

A primary advantage of EJB application servers is that applications and business objects can be designed to be unaware of where data resources and other business objects are deployed. This makes it possible to separate deployment and infrastructure choices from application architecture, and to allow centralized and consistent management of all applications, rather than each application requiring its own special infrastructure. This can only be accomplished with a location-independent architecture, and EJB with JTA makes this possible.

In most general purpose middle tier programming, one does not need to know about JTA or the underlying transaction services. However, as with any system, it is necessary to have an understanding of it in the event that something goes wrong—otherwise, how can you diagnose the problem? It is also important to understand JTA and its underpinnings to be able to evaluate EJB and other middleware products, since the level of JTA support may not be the same from one product to another, and there may be interoperability issues that involve the lower levels of these APIs. Finally, there might be occasions when you need to manage transactions explicitly within your applications—i.e., write Enterprise JavaBeans deployed as BEAN_MANAGED in their EJB deployment descriptor, or possibly even write "client demarcated" transactions which directly perform their own transaction management on the client.

Following this section, I will also discuss the Java Transaction Service (JTS) in some detail. JTS is the Java binding of the CORBA COS Transactions service (OTS), and since many EJB products are ORB-based and use OTS underneath, it is the API that some ORB-based EJB products provide for writing client-demarcated transactions.

Before I begin discussion of JTA, I must clarify the use of the word "client" in this chapter. Ordinary a client is the component which executes in the end user's process space. However, from the point of view of a transaction manager, the client is the program which originates the transaction. More generally, from the point of view of a server, the client is the program which calls the server, and therefore the client might be a user interface program or it might be another server. In the rest of this chapter, I will intend the word "client" to mean the end user application, but it can usually be generalized to mean the caller, regardless what kind of program the caller is.

### Two-Phase Commit Protocols

A transaction which includes accesses to multiple independent data resources requires a more robust and sophisticated protocol than a simple begin and commit operation to be reliable. The client application still should employ simple begin and commit operations, but underneath there needs to be a handshake between all the data resources involved to ensure that no data resource commits unless all agree to commit. The portion of the overall transaction which is associated with an individual data resource is called a "transaction branch."

A "two-phase" commit protocol accomplishes the coordination of multiple transaction branches by employing a central coordinating entity, called a "transaction manager," and dividing a commit operation into two steps. In the first phase, the transaction manager issues a prepare call to each data resource involved. Each data resource is then required to respond with a vote, indicating its intention to commit or rollback. Once all data resources have responded, the first phase is complete and the second phase begins. If all data resources have responded to the transaction manager with a commit vote, then the transaction manager issues a commit call to each data resource, instructing it to finalize its commit. If, however, any data resource responds with a rollback vote, then the transaction manager issues a rollback call to each data resource. Figure 7-18 shows a successful two-phase commit scenario in which all data resources respond with a commit vote, causing the global transaction to commit.

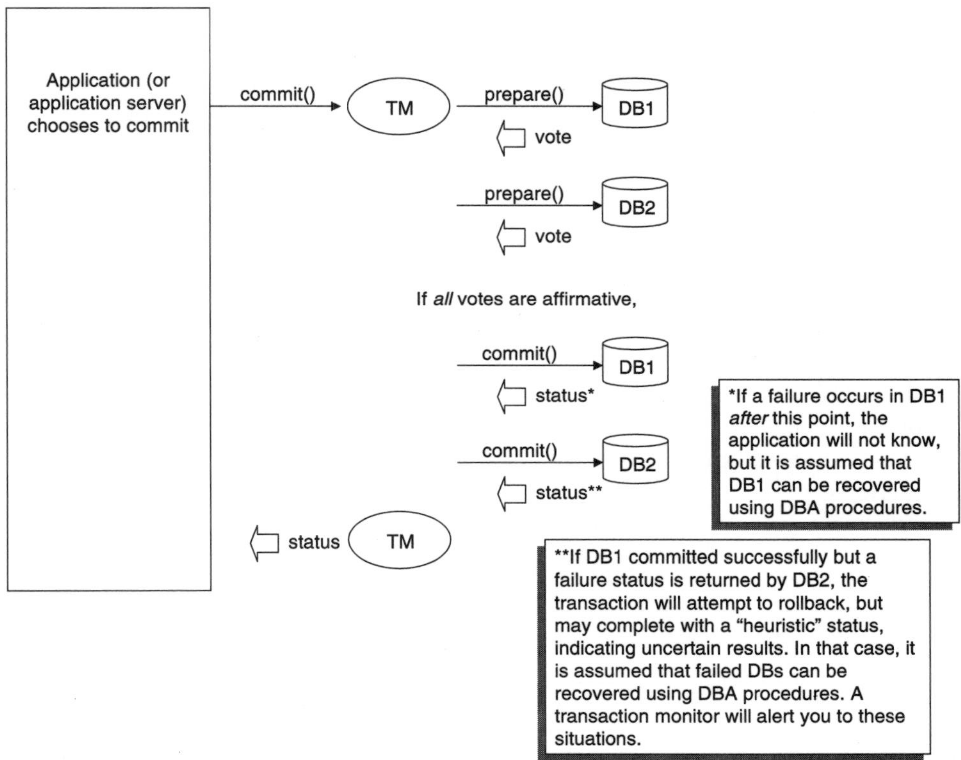


**Figure 7-18** The two-phase commit protocol.

This protocol provides a way to coordinate the commit and rollback of multiple data resources. By itself it does not guarantee reliable operation. The reliability of the system and its global transactions depends on the reliability of the data resources themselves. Most transactional data resources employ logging to provide a way to replay transactions which are lost in the event of a crash. A data resource usually will not respond to a prepare call until it has completed logging its own transaction results. It therefore has a means to recover if it should fail after responding to its prepare call. Since a data resource is inaccessible when it crashes, and it can be assumed that it will not be made accessible again until recovery procedures are run, an administrator can be sure that inconsistency will not result in other data resources as a result of the crash, as long as all lost transactions can be recovered.

The X/Open transaction processing model is shown in Figure 7-19 for comparison. You do not need to know this API for developing Java applications, but it is instructive to see how it relates to the two-phase commit model. The TX begin() operation asks the transaction manager to start a new transaction and associate the current thread with that transaction. In reponse, the transaction manager creates a transaction and then communicates with the data resource using the XA interface to tell it to associate the current thread with the current transaction. It does this with the start() operation. From that point on all operations performed by the client thread on the data resource will be associated by the data resource with the transaction. Note that for this to work the client thread must be the same thread as the thread which calls the start() operation. This implies that these calls are made from a client-side interface within the same address space. To complete a transaction the client invokes the TX commit() operation, which results in an XA prepare() operation and then an XA commit(). The end() operation is only used if the current thread wishes to temporarily leave a transaction so that it can participate in another transaction.

Of course, no system is completely reliable, and it is still necessary to monitor the system and in some cases manually repair failures or abort apparently stuck transactions.

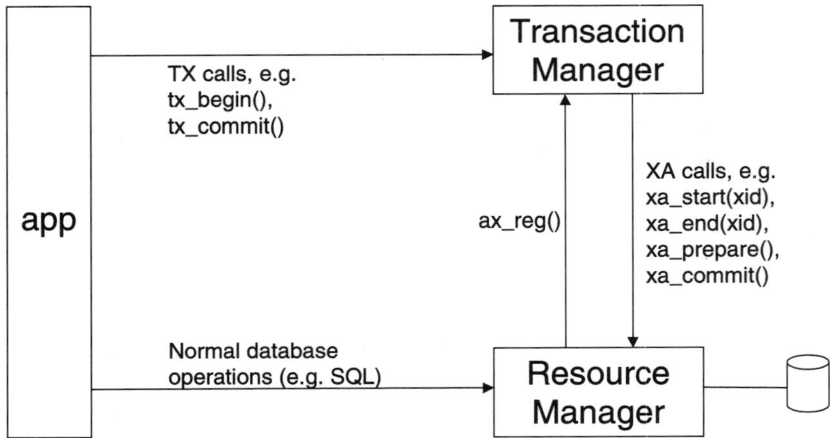


**Figure 7-19** X/Open distributed transaction processing model.

### *Transaction Coupling*

In the context of a single data resource, an ordinary transaction has properties which include atomicity and isolation. These are discussed in Chapter 6 but briefly, atomicity refers to the ability of the data resource to treat operations per-

formed in a transaction as an all-or-nothing proposition: either all operations complete, or none complete. Isolation refers to the ability of the data resource to keep changes private until the transaction commits, so that in-progress work does not affect other users. Atomic operation and isolation are usually achieved by using locks which prevent other transactions from accessing data, and by special buffers for writing changes prior to committing them or for restoring prior contents if a transaction does not complete successfully.

A global transaction has a need for the same kinds of properties. If the branches of a global transaction share the same locks and isolation space, the transaction is said to be "tightly coupled." Otherwise, it is "loosely coupled." Two branches of a tightly coupled transaction can therefore access the same data, and can see each other's pending changes as if they were part of the same transaction branch. OTS and JTS specify that global transactions should be tightly coupled.

Figure 7-20 depicts a tightly coupled global transaction involving a transactional client which makes SQL calls, and which also calls a transactional bean, all within the same global transaction. In this example, both branches of the transaction access the same data resource. It is therefore critical to know whether they will be able to see each other's changes during the transaction.

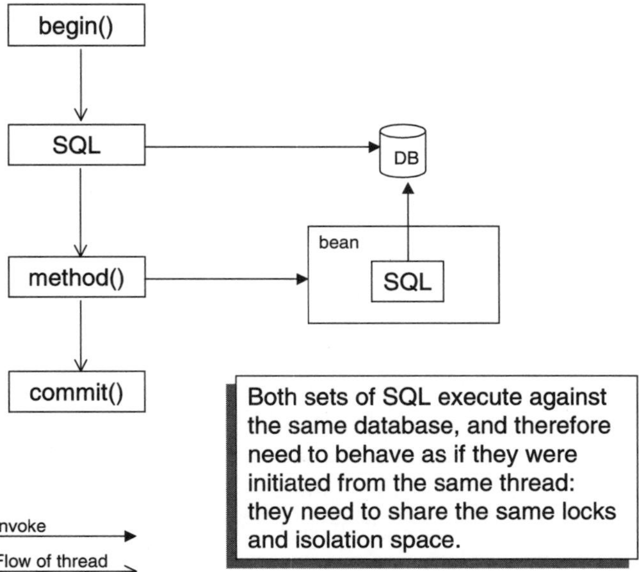


**Figure 7-20** Tightly coupled transaction branches.

The ability to support tightly coupled global transactions is a sophisticated capability. Not all data resource drivers have that ability. In some cases, tightly coupled transactions are supported for some product versions but not others. For example, Oracle supports tightly coupled transactions for Oracle 8, except across separate instances of the Parallel Server product. Since support for tightly coupled transactions is not something one can depend on, this means that it is a good idea to design beans so that the data they use does not overlap.

### Thread Association with Transaction Context

The CORBA Transactions service defines two models for identifying the transaction to associate a method with at runtime: implicit association and explicit association. "Implicit" association assumes that a transaction is associated with a thread, and that at any instant all methods being invoked by a thread belong to no transaction or the same transaction. "Explicit" association assumes no such thread association, and requires a transaction parameter to be passed with all transactional operations, so that the transaction manager knows which transaction to apply the operation against. JTA adopts the implicit model.

The implicit model may seem unusual to some object oriented programmers. However, thread association with runtime properties is not uncommon for other APIs. For example, the Java security framework relies on thread association with class loaders. A security manager can easily determine what code sources are associated with a thread by calling native code which walks up the current thread's call stack and getting the class of each method on the stack. The API that a security manager and privilege manager use to do this is part of the standard Java API. In contrast, the implementation of the association between a thread and a transaction depends on the implementation of the transaction manager interface. Many databases allow only the thread that created a connection to use the connection.

### Mixing of Global and Local Transactions

A "local" transaction is one which is managed by a single data source and which cannot be shared by other data sources or controlled by an external transaction manager. An ordinary JDBC transaction is a local transaction. Some databases allow use of local transactions on XA connections, but some do not. JDBC2 allows it (you can call commit() on a Connection as long as there is no global transaction in progress). DDL statements are usually not supported by XA transactions. They must be done as a local transaction.

### The Platform Layers

JTA operates at several levels. On one level, it provides a means for user applications to explicitly initiate and complete transactions. On a deeper level, it pro-

vides a standard API for middleware to initiate and complete transactions which are not explicitly demarcated. On the deepest level, it provides a standard API framework for building data resource drivers that can participate in global transactions.

JTA is comprised of two packages: javax.transaction and javax.transaction.xa. Package javax.transaction includes five interfaces. Two of these are used by applications:

**UserTransaction**—This is the type that JTA-compliant middleware such as EJB containers must provide to applications that wish to perform their own transaction management. It interposes and forwards application-initiated transaction operations to the container's associated TransactionManager and the thread's current Transaction.

**Status**—This interface merely defines the constant values that are used to indicate a transaction's status, e.g., STATUS_ACTIVE, STATUS_PREPARING, STATUS_COMMITTING, etc.

JTA also defines the following Java interfaces in javax.transaction for application servers to use to interface to a transaction manager implementation. Applications do not normally use these:

**Transaction**—This is the application server's interface to a particular global transaction. Obtained from the TransactionManager by calling getTransaction(), which returns the current transaction associated with the calling thread. This interface is generally not used by applications.

**TransactionManager**—This is the application server's interface to the transaction manager it uses. Applications do not generally use this interface.

**Synchronization**—An application server can register a Synchronization object with a Transaction. Then, the Synchronization object's beforeCompletion() and afterCompletion() methods are called immediately prior to commit and after commit or rollback.

Package javax.transaction.xa includes these interfaces:

**XAResource**—Most APIs that implement JTA (such as JDBC 2 extensions) provide some kind of resource adapter (connection) for communicating with a data resource in a transactional way. This normally includes the ability to manage participation in transactions, as well as data operations on the data resource; e.g., JDBC provides a Connection object type for that purpose. The XAResource is the callback interface that must be provided to the transaction manager by the resource adapter to allow the transaction manager to tell the connection to join, leave, prepare, and commit transaction branches owned by the connection.

**Xid**—A unique identifier that globally identifies a transaction branch. Consists of a globally unique ID for the transaction, and a branch qualifier to identify the branch.

JTA also specifies conceptually the role of a resource adapter, without actually specifying interfaces that such a component must expose to an application. It is up to the domain-specific API, such as JDBC, to specify how a client application obtains a resource adapter. The client then uses the resource adapter to obtain a connection to the actual resource, such as a JDBC Connection. For the purpose of illustration here, I will use the JDBC 2 version of a JTA resource adapter.

The JTA compliant types defined in javax.sql are DataSource, XADataSource, and XAConnection. A user program obtains a DataSource through JNDI. From the user's perspective, it now fills the role that a JDBC Driver used to fill. From the DataSource, one obtains a Connection. The operation of obtaining a Connection triggers many interactions behind the scenes, which we will get into. Also, it is important to realize that the DataSource is implemented *by the middleware*, and is actually an intermediary which interacts with the true driver, which JTA refers to as a "resource factory."

The software layers represented by JTA are shown in Figure 7-21.

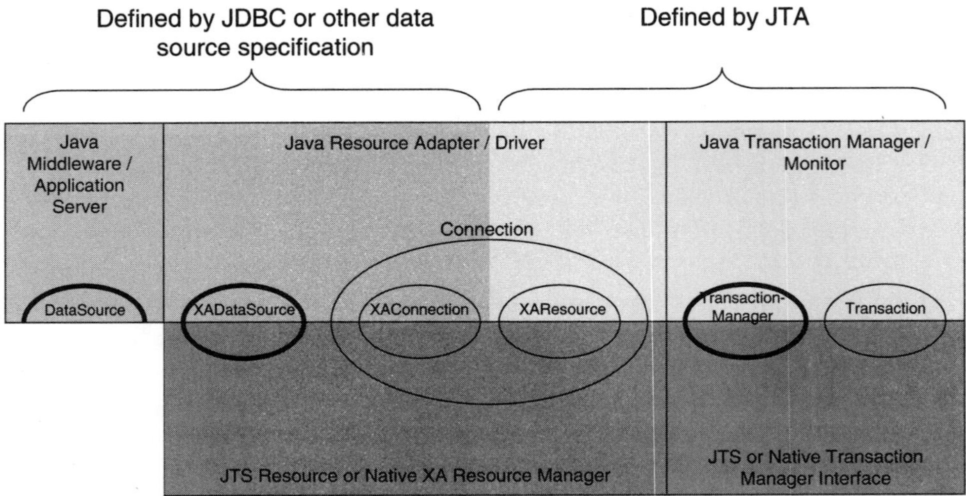


**Figure 7-21** The JTA layers.

The portion on the upper right of the figure, shown in the lightest gray, represents the JTA interfaces, as well as JTA implementation code to adapt to an underlying transaction manager, which may be a native component or have a native interface.

The transaction manager is likely provided by the application server or other execution environment.

Most transaction managers are products which have been around for awhile and are not written in Java. However, to conform to JTA they must now provide a JTA-conformant interface, or the Java middleware must provide one for them. The portion in the figure below the horizontal centerline, in dark gray, represents native or other support for the JTA interfaces. It may consist of a CORBA COS Transactions implementation, or any other adapted transaction manager.

The portion on the upper left, shown in medium gray, represents, for illustration, a JDBC implementation, consisting of a data resource provided by the middleware, as well as code which accesses the driver provided by the database vendor and ultimately provides an application with a connection object. The XADataSource is the JDBC incarnation of the "driver": it serves as the resource factory for creating implementations of the interfaces needed by the application (which needs a Connection) and the transaction manager (which needs an XAResource). The middleware serves the role of coordinating the creation and handoff of these objects, as well as associating them with transactions.

The importance of JTA is this: by having defined these layers, it is now possible to mix and match drivers from compliant vendors, and plug them into the middleware of choice, without sacrificing the ability to work with the middleware's chosen transaction manager.

### *Normal Usage Scenario*

It is expected that most users of JTA will be EJB application servers, and that application developers will not need to access the API most of the time. In fact, JTA itself distinguishes between an application server and a user application, by providing the UserTransaction interface for use by applications, whereas application servers use the Transaction interface directly. Let's see how an application obtains a transaction and then accesses data under that transaction.

Some application domains provide a specific API for obtaining a UserTransaction. For example, Enterprise JavaBeans defines the getUserTransaction() method. Other domains, such as servlets and client environments, do not define a domain-specific way to obtain information. In general, a JTA-enabled container environment is required to provide JNDI-based access to the current UserTransaction. This can be accomplished as follows:

```
Context ic = new InitialContext();
UserTransaction txn = (UserTransaction)ic.lookup(
      "java:comp/UserTransaction");
```

(As of this writing, the use of the JNDI name java:comp/UserTransaction is preliminary, but will likely become standard.)

It is therefore up to the container environment to provide a default JNDI provider which knows how to obtain a Transaction object.

Once the application has an implementation of UserTransaction, it can initiate a transaction by calling begin(). This establishes a global transaction, which the middleware can use to coordinate the operations of any transaction-aware data resources which are accessed by the application.

After the application has accessed all the data resources it needs, it can call commit() on the UserTransaction. The middleware relays this commit to the transaction manager, which propagates it to all the data resources involved. The overall scenario seen by the application is shown in Figure 7-22.

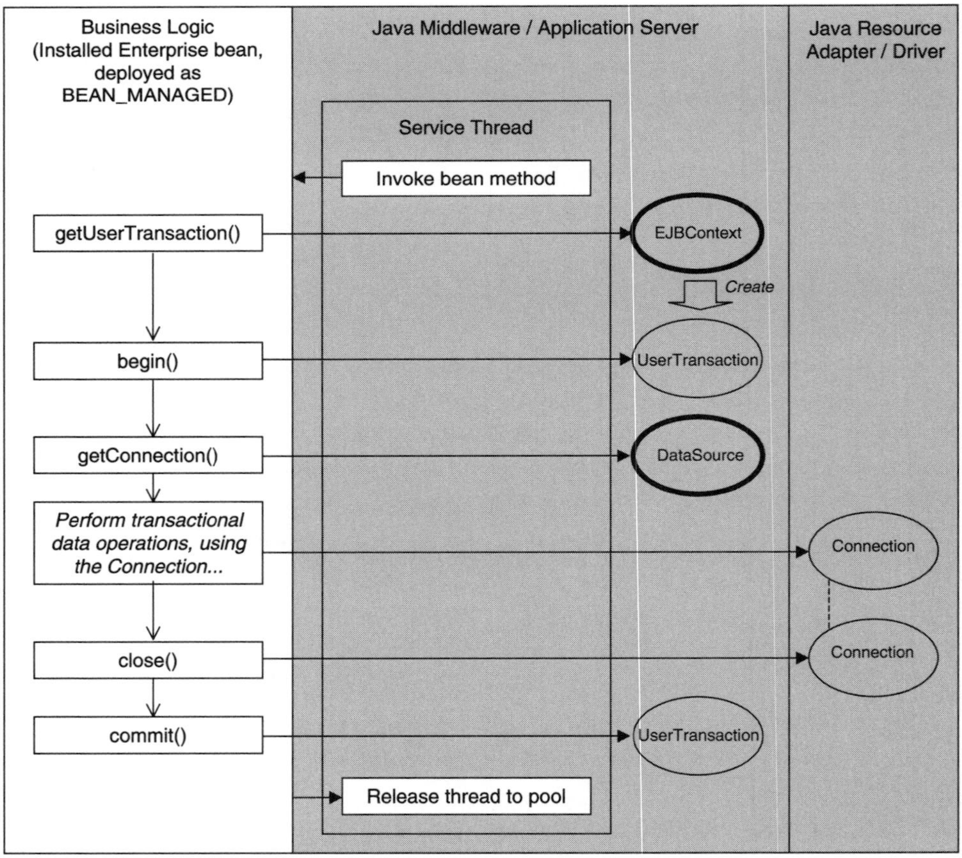

**Figure 7-22** An Enterprise JavaBean obtaining a UseTransaction reference and then beginning and committing a transaction.

### *How It Works*

Figure 7-23 shows the role that a JTA implementation plays behind the scenes when a user begins a transaction. The user application makes a begin() call to the User-Transaction it obtains from its environment or application server. In turn, the User-Transaction implementation delegates the actual begin to the transaction manager, which creates an instance of Transaction and associates it with the calling thread.

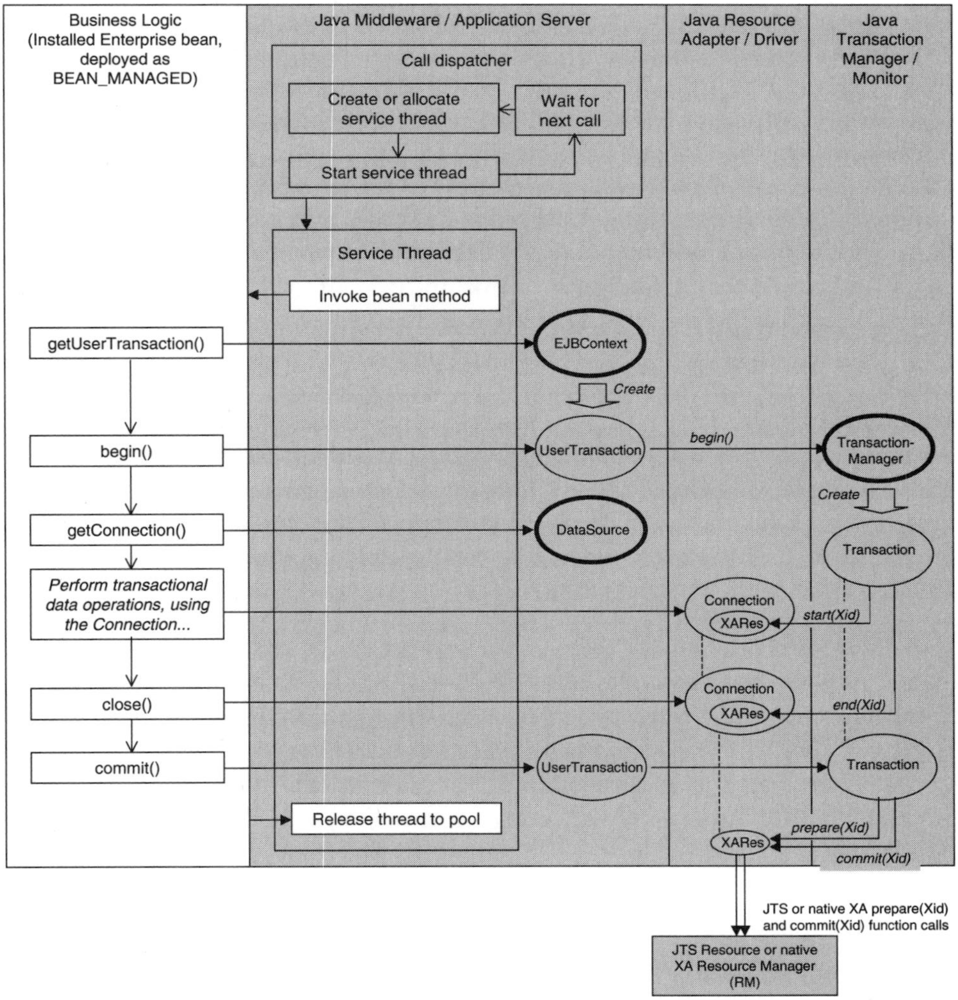

**Figure 7-23** How a transaction manager interfaces to an XAResource to control assignment of resources to transactions.

This association is done internally to the middleware, which is possible because the middleware created the thread that the client application is running in. Note that this scenario is illustrative, and different application servers might implement it differently.

At some point during application processing, the user may obtain connections of various kinds to data resources. For these data resources to participate in global transactions that are managed by the middleware, the data resources must implement the XAResource interface, which provides calls to join and leave transactions, using the start(...) and end(...) methods, respectively. These are callbacks made from the transaction manager to the data resource.

When the user application obtains a data resource connection, it does so through a middleware layer that is specific to the class of data resource being accessed, such as JDBC. The component which provides this connection is referred to as a "resource factory." However the data resource connection is obtained, the middleware layer that provides it obtains an XAResource implementation from the connection and passes that to the Transaction of the current thread. The Transaction is responsible for calling the start(...) method on the XAResource to cause the XA Resource to join the current transaction, and end(...) whenever the middleware needs to cause the data resource to leave the transaction and join another. All the transaction manager has to do is tell the XAResource which transaction to join or leave, and it does this with a unique transaction identifier, the Xid. (See the sidebar "Getting the Xid from JTS/COS Transaction" on page 585.) The XAResource in turn informs the underlying resource manager of the data resource of the join or leave request, causing the underlying connection to be reassigned to the designated transaction.

### *Data Resources*

To obtain a connection to a data resource, you must first obtain a data resource factory. The term "data resource" refers to literally a source and sink for data—a database typically. A "resource factory" is a component which provides a data resource to the application. An example of a resource factory is a DataSource as defined by JDBC2. An example of a data resource is a JDBC Connection.

An application first obtains a data resource factory (for JDBC2, a DataSource) using JNDI. It is therefore up to the middleware vendor to provide for JNDI access for its data resource factories. Once the application obtains a data resource factory in this way, it calls a method to obtain a connection. Again, the exact interface depends on the kind of data resource. For JDBC2 one would call DataSource.getConnection(), and it would return a seemingly plain old java.sql.Connection. Once the application has a connection to the data resource, it can perform data access operations on that connection, e.g., SQL in the case of JDBC2. When the application is done with the connection, it closes it.

### Getting the Xid from JTS/COS Transaction

When the transaction manager invokes the start() and end() methods on an XAResource, it needs to tell the XAResource what transaction to join or leave. Remember that this call is made from a transaction manager thread, most likely independent of any thread associated with the transaction being joined or left. Therefore, these calls need a parameter representing the affected transaction. In the XA world, this is known as the Xid (transaction id). Therefore JTA defines an Xid type for this role.

It is the job of the JTA implementation to create an Xid object representing the transaction. The problem is, how does it do this? The transaction identity ultimately is created by the transaction manager. The JTA layer therefore needs some way of obtaining the identifier used by the transaction manager.

In OTS (and JTS), the counterpart to the JTA Transaction is the Control with its embedded Coordinator and Terminator interfaces. If the transaction manager is accessed by the JTA implementation using an OTS interface, then it can obtain the transaction ID from the Control as follows:

```
Control control =
   <some-TransactionFactory>.create(timeout);
Coordinator coordinator = control.get_coordinator();
PropagationContext pg = coordinator.get_txcontext();
TransIdentity current = pg.current;
otid_t otid = current.otid;
int formatID = otid.formatID;
int len = otid.bequal_length; // (typo in Java
   // mapping: should be "bqual_length", which
   // is short for "branch qualifier length")
byte[] tid = otid.tid;              // includes the branch
   // qualifier and global txn id)
```

From this, it can manufacture an Xid implementation, which must provide these methods:

```
int getFormatId();
byte[] getGlobalTransactionId();
byte[] getBranchQualifier();
```

Little does the application know that behind the scenes, the middleware has given it a connection that is merely a facade for an underlying connection. This connection has two sets of features: data access features, to be used by the application, and transaction control features, to be used by the transaction manager. In the case of JDBC, the driver provides an XAConnection instance to encapsulate the data access features. The driver provides an instance of XAResource to encapsulate all features having to do with transaction management. The middleware registers the XAResource with the transaction manager. In JTA, registration is accomplished with the Transaction method enlistResource(XAResource). This allows the transaction manager to perform its start() and end() calls, as well as its prepare() and commit() or rollback() calls, as a result of events in this or any other transaction branch. This overall scenario is shown in Figure 7-24. Don't get scared —you don't actually have to use this part of the API unless you are writing a data resource manager!

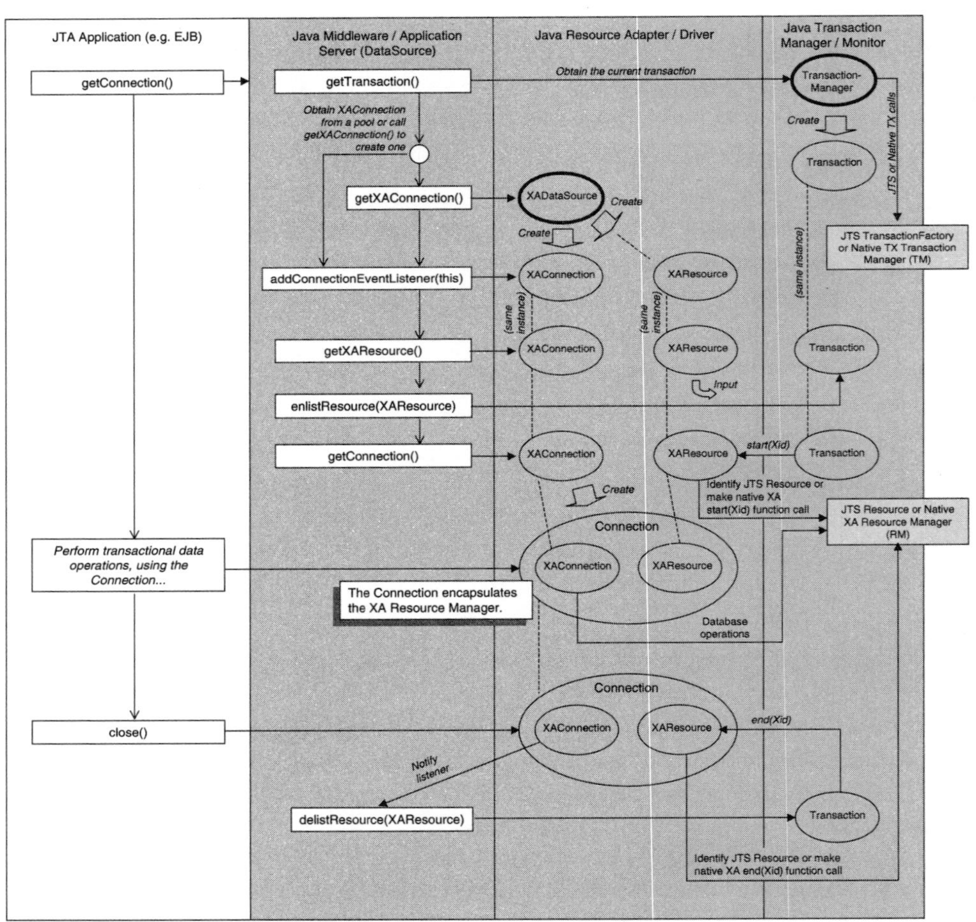


**Figure 7-24** The full details; the two interfaces exposed by a connection: one for data access and the other for transaction management.

**Accessing Multiple Data Resources.** If the transaction accesses multiple data resources, either from the same thread or from different threads (possibly in different Enterprise beans), the middleware automatically identifies the transaction associated with each thread, and makes sure the XAResource is registered with the correct transaction before a data operation is performed on a connection. This assumes that the middleware is involved in the switching between threads. We are not talking about simple Java multithreading here. We are talking about an application environment, such as an EJB server, which has complete control over what object methods are allowed to be executing at any one time. EJB has policies that enforce the required concurrency rules, to prevent multiple clients from accessing a physical bean instance at the same time, and will force a call to block if necessary to satisfy those rules. These policies are discussed in Chapter 8.

Figure 7-25 illustrates two different connections, which may be in the same or in different threads, accessing different data resources. They are part of the same transaction, however, because the middleware has kept track of which transaction each of its clients is associated with.

If you are starting to get the picture that the middleware plays a central role in the operation of JTA, then you have grasped that JTA is not a standalone capability. It is an API that a runtime environment such as a Java middleware platform can implement. A JTA implementation relies on its supporting environment to provide thread association of transactions, and manage what client operations can be invoked at any time, depending on the availability of the data resource connections that it requires.

The environment must also have the ability to remember what resources were involved in a particular transaction, even after the associated connections have been closed by the application. In Figure 7-25, TransactionA issues prepare() and commit() calls to an XAResource, *after* the resource's connection has been closed by the client. Indeed, this XAResource might have several transactions outstanding from different clients, all accessing it via separate connection objects.

Thus, when you close a connection, it frees the underlying resource so it can be used by other transactions. This is true even if your transaction has not yet committed. A commit() executed by the transaction manager against the resource is performed independent of who is currently using the resource, since the commit() explicitly identifies the transaction being committed.

If you fail to close a connection, it may be implicitly closed by the middleware. (It may not actually be closed; it may merely be returned to a resource pool.) If the connection is not closed, the application server may temporarily disassociate the resource from the transaction so that it can be used by other transactions, and reassociate it when the original transaction resumes.

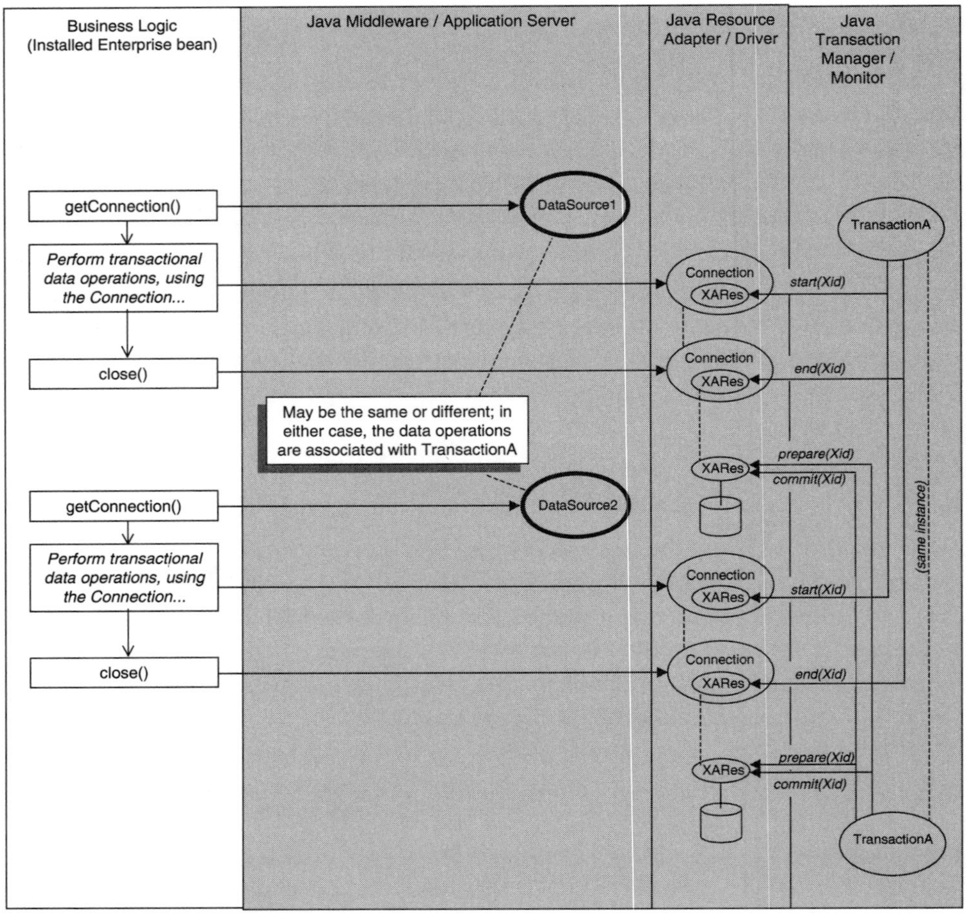

**Figure 7-25** Accessing multiple data resources as part of the same transaction.

### *OO Transactional Data Resources: OTMs*

Object databases can participate in distributed transactions as well. Current transaction specifications such as COS Transactions and the XA specification are not tied to a particular database model and so there is no reason why an object database cannot support either or multiple transaction standards. For example, Object Design (ODI) is developing an EJB container (codenamed "Javlin" at this writing; availability should be announced by the time you read this) for the BEA WebLogic Enterprise server which provides container-managed database operations in the context of global transactions managed by the application server. This is accomplished by a JTS interface which is implemented between the application

server and the object database. ODI also provides an XA interface for their C language product.

### *Propagation of Transaction Context to Another Server*

One of the advantages of JTA is that it allows transaction context to be propagated among cooperating transaction managers. Since EJB transaction association is implicit (a transaction object does not need to be passed with every request, but rather the context is implicit in the operations performed by a thread), this requires that the message protocol automatically includes information about the transaction context. At the present time, RMI does not define a transaction context that is propagated with JRMP messages. IIOP does, however (see Figure 7-26). Therefore, if your application chooses to use IIOP as its message protocol, there is the possibility that transaction context may be propagated between servers when necessary. I say possibility, because while CORBA defines when and how a transaction context is passed, the RMI-over-IIOP mapping does not address the issue, and so it is up to the ORB and middleware vendor whether or not to provide this under the covers for its RMI-over-IIOP implementation. In addition, some vendors have implemented their own version of RMI, which adds the transaction context information. However, while this is a valuable feature, it may present some interoperability issues between servers of different brands. It is not a problem, of course, if all your application servers are from the same vendor.

```
module IOP
{
        ...
        typedef unsigned long ServiceID;
        struct ServiceContext
        {
                ServiceID context_id;
                sequence <octet> context_data;
        };
        typedef sequence <ServiceContext> ServiceContextList;
        const ServiceID TransactionService = 0;
        ...
};
```

*For transactional objects, PropagationContext is sent implicitly in the context_data.*

```
module GIOP
{
        ...
        struct RequestHeader
        {
                IOP::ServiceContextList service_context;
                ...
};
```

**Figure 7-26** Context propagation in IIOP.

Assuming your middleware does have the capability to transmit transaction context implicitly, and that you are making use of it, transaction context is automatically transmitted from caller to callee when you make a remote call. This might be a call from a client to a business object, or a call from one business object to another—possibly in a different server. If multiple servers are involved, the transaction context is then used to establish an inter-transaction manager relationship, and propagate the registration of transactional resources. In this way, when a commit occurs, the transaction manager performing the commit can propagate it to other remotely registered resources. This is transparent to the application. Figure 7-27 depicts this.

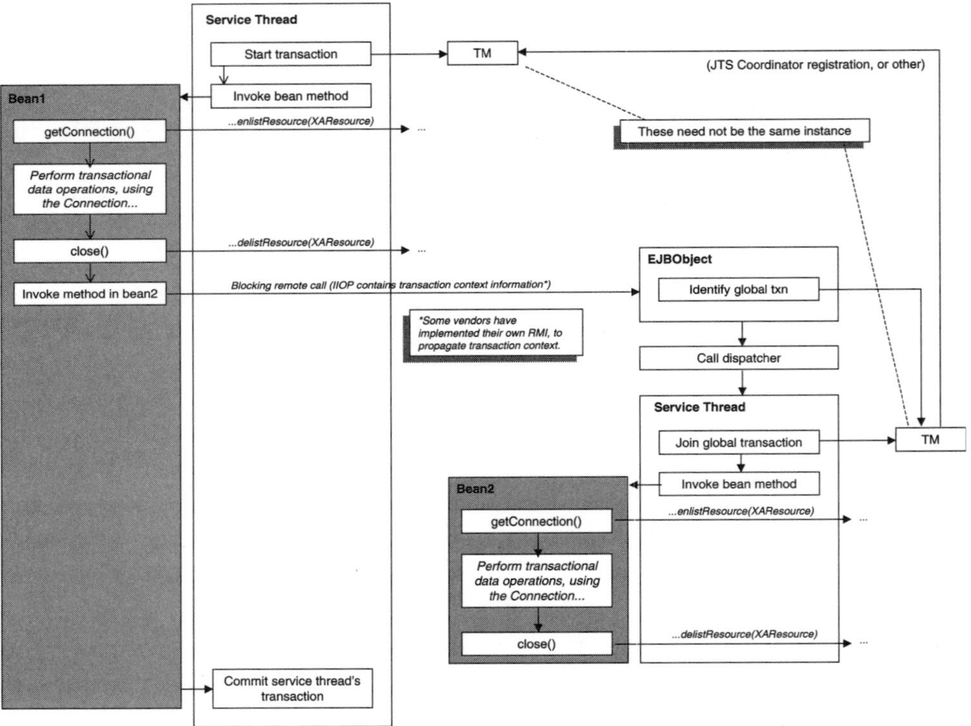


**Figure 7-27** Propagation of transaction context from one server to another.

Unfortunately, while this is nice in theory, at present there is not much support for transaction interoperability between different application server brands. Those application servers which implement CORBA OTS (discussed next) are supposed to have transaction interoperability, because OTS requires it. Interoperability is

achieved through standardization of the context information that is passed between ORBs, which includes a pair of callback objects (a Coordinator and a Terminator) into the originating transaction manager. However, when vendors were surveyed for support of transaction interoperability, responses varied from "not in the near future" to "we don't know"—and senior architects were asked. Apparently it is not on the radar screen of most vendors at present.

Interoperability is an important feature when existing applications start to be interconnected at an enterprise level, so do not overlook it. Tell your application server vendor it is a feature that is important to you.

## JTS and OTS

The Java Transaction Service (JTS) defines a standard Java API for transaction managers to implement. A middleware provider can create a JTA implementation on top of a JTS implementation, and such a JTA implementation is then portable to other JTS-compliant transaction managers. In addition, JTS implementations are interoperable with CORBA COS Transactions implementations, because JTS is essentially the Java binding of COS Transactions.

Understanding JTS is also important because many of the most flexible application servers are ORB-based, for reasons already explained. Those servers typically use OTS for their transaction management implementations, and therefore JTS to implement JTA. The JTS or OTS API may also be exposed to the application programmer, for the purpose of developing client-demarcated transactions.

### *The JTS Packages*

JTS consists of the direct IDL-to-Java mapping of CORBA modules CosTransactions and CosTSPortability, minus one interface (CosTransactions.Current), and with the addition of package javax.jts. This last package contains but one interface: TransactionService.

The most important members of package CosTransactions are these interfaces:

> **TransactionFactory**—Used by an application (e.g., i.e., a client) to begin a transaction. Provides create() and recreate(PropagationContext) (the latter for importing transactions from other ORBs) methods, which return a Control object. A TransactionFactory is the starting point for clients wanting to create a new transaction. In OTS, you get a factory using a CORBA Lifecycle service. In JTS, the method of obtaining a TransactionFactory is undefined and therefore implementation-specific. The TransactionFactory interface is usually not used by client applications, because there is an easier way: the Current interface, which is described next.

**Current**—This is an IDL "pseudo object," which means that it is implemented directly by an ORB and is not a true remote object—you can't call it remotely. It is available only within the ORB process space. The Current interface (not to be confused with org.omg.CORBA.Current, which it extends from) provides a convenience interface, which is an easier programming model than using a TransactionFactory. When you create a transaction using Current, it automatically associates that transaction with the current thread, and remembers that association, so that you can then use Current to perform operations such as begin(), commit(), rollback(), suspend(), resume(). You don't have to identify the transaction—Current identifies it from the thread that is calling it. You can obtain the transaction for the current thread's transaction by calling Current.get_control(), which returns a Control object—which represents the transaction (described next). This is the starting point for server objects to obtain their propagated transaction context. In OTS, a Current is obtained by calling resolve_intial_references ("TransactionCurrent") on the ORB. Unfortunately, Current is omitted from JTS, so its use is outside the scope of JTS.

**Control**—The primary handle used to control and monitor a transaction. Provides get_terminator() and get_coordinator() methods, to get a Terminator and a Coordinator, respectively (these are explained next). Through its delegated Terminator and Coordinator implementations, a Control performs a similar functions to a JTA Transaction.

**Terminator**—This is the interface that a Control exposes to applications for transaction completion. It is used to request a commit or rollback of the transaction. In JTA, the application middleware uses the Transaction interface for this, and so the Transaction, if using JTS underneath, would delegate these operations to a Terminator.

**Coordinator**—This is the interface that a Control exposes to applications for registering resources with the transaction manager, so that it can issue two-phase commit operations on those resources when necessary. In JTA, this role is again performed by the Transaction interface, and so if the JTA implementation uses JTS underneath, it would delegate its resource enlistment to a Coordinator.

**RecoveryCoordinator**—An object which can be stored by resources after they register allows the coordination of recovery later on if a failure should occur.

**Resource**—Analogous to a JTA XAResource and its associated data resource connection. Provides prepare() and commit() to allow the transaction manager to complete a transaction branch. A Resource differs from its JTA counterpart in that a Resource does not provide XAResource's ability to join and leave (start() and end()) transactions. A Resource cannot be shared across multiple transactions—there must be a separate Resource for each transaction on a data resource.

**Synchronization**—This is analogous to JTA Synchronization interface.

**SubtransactionAwareResource**—This is not applicable to JTA-based environments, since JTA does not make use of this.

**TransactionalObject**—CORBA interfaces which extend this type are known to be transactional, causing the ORBs involved to transmit propagation context when necessary and to perform the servant's operations in the context of a transaction. The requirement to implement TransactionalObject only applies, however, to servants coded with the CORBA API, and does not apply to other servants even if they use IIOP. In the latter case, it is up to the ORB implementation to decide how servants are declared to be transactional. If the servants are EJB objects, then the bean deployment descriptor is the declarative means used, and the ORB should propagate transaction context when required.

The propagation of transaction context from a tranactional client to a server uses interfaces defined in package org.omg.CosTSPortability. These interfaces are:

**Sender**—The "sending" ORB uses this transaction manager interface to request a transaction context object (PropagationContext) to embed in a request to be sent to another ORB.

**Receiver**—The "receiving" ORB uses this transaction manager interface to obtain the transaction context (PropagationContext) associated with the incoming remote request.

In addition to these interfaces, JTS adds package javax.jts, which includes the sole interface TransactionService. This interface defines an API for an ORB to obtain the Sender and Receiver objects it needs to initiate and service transactional remote requests.

These interfaces will all be discussed in turn. The JTS, OTS and related packages are shown in Figure 7-28.

An application which uses Control and Terminator objects to begin and end transactions is said to use "direct" transaction context management, because it does not rely on any implicit transaction/thread association provided by the transaction manager interface. An application which uses the Current interface to begin and end transactions is said to use "indirect" transaction context management, because the transaction is implied indirectly by the current thread. For example, several threads, each associated with a different transaction, would share the same Current interface to commit—the Current would determine which transaction was committing based on its internal transaction/thread association. In contrast, when a thread calls commit() on a Terminator, the Terminator does not have to determine which transaction to terminate—it terminates the one it uniquely represents.

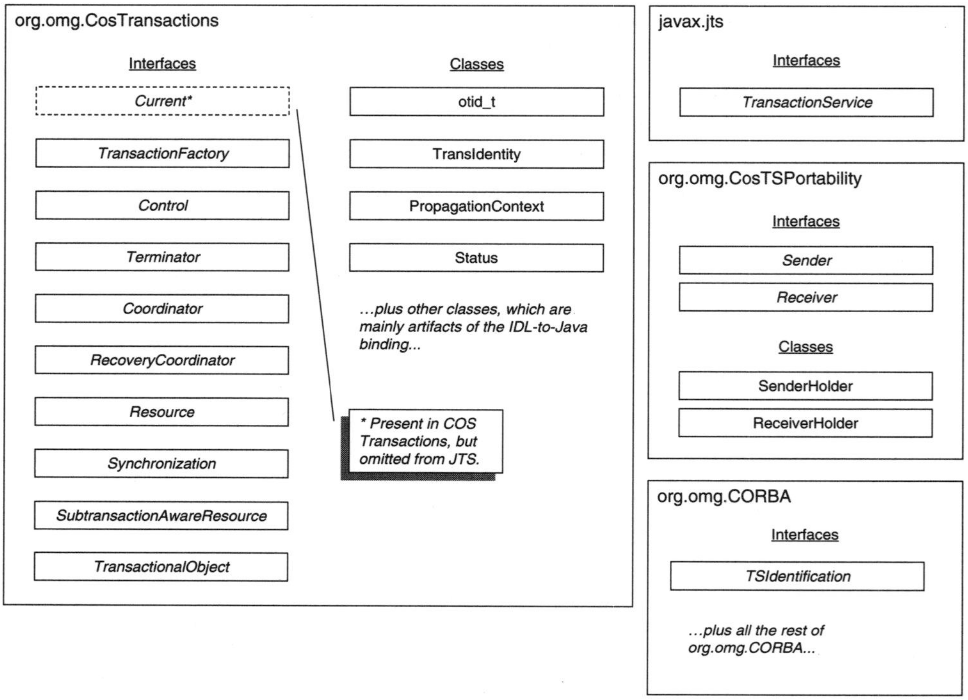

org.omg.CosTransactions

Interfaces: *Current**, *TransactionFactory*, *Control*, *Terminator*, *Coordinator*, *RecoveryCoordinator*, *Resource*, *Synchronization*, *SubtransactionAwareResource*, *TransactionalObject*

Classes: otid_t, TransIdentity, PropagationContext, Status

*...plus other classes, which are mainly artifacts of the IDL-to-Java binding...*

** Present in COS Transactions, but omitted from JTS.*

javax.jts

Interfaces: *TransactionService*

org.omg.CosTSPortability

Interfaces: *Sender*, *Receiver*

Classes: SenderHolder, ReceiverHolder

org.omg.CORBA

Interfaces: *TSIdentification*

*...plus all the rest of org.omg.CORBA...*

**Figure 7-28** The JTS and related packages.

I will first show how direct context management works, to establish the framework for understanding indirect context management. Most likely you will use indirect context management.

### *Direct Context Management*

There is quite a bit of similarity of roles between JTA and JTS interfaces. For example, a JTA application starts out by obtaining a transaction: it either creates a new one, or it obtains the current transaction if one is in progress. A JTS application begins the same way. How it obtains the transaction is not defined by JTS (although it is defined in OTS). However, using some implementation-specific means, it either creates a new transaction, or obtains the current one.

To start a new transaction, the client uses a TransactionFactory to call create(), which creates a new transaction. An alternative offered by most OTS implementations is to obtain a Current, which can then be used to get the Control:

```
org.omg.CosTransactions.Current current =
      (org.omg.CosTransactions.Current)
```

```
        (org.omg.CosTransactions.CurrentHelper.narrow
        (_orb().resolve_initial_references("TransactionCurrent")));

boolean inATransactionAlready =
    (current.get_control() != null);
Control control = null;
if (! inATransactionAlready)
{
        current.begin();
        control = current.getControl();
}
```

I have omitted exception handling for simplicity.

The end result is an instance of Control, from which it can obtain the Coordinator and Terminator interfaces that it needs to register resources and complete the transaction, respectively. This is shown in Figure 7-29.

Once the application has a Coordinator interface, it can register resources. A JTS Resource is highly analogous to a JTA XAResource. The application registers a Resource with the Coordinator for the current transaction, so that the transaction manager can invoke a two-phase commit protocol on the resource at transaction completion. The supplier of the data resource driver can provide the Resource implementation, or the middleware can provide it—in all likelihood the latter. In fact, it is likely that the driver will automatically register its resources with the transaction manager, so that the application does not have to.

#### *Indirect Context Management*

The IDL-to-Java mapping of the CosTransactions.Current interface is:

```
package org.omg.CosTransactions;

public interface Current extends org.omg.CORBA.Current
{
        public void begin() throws SubtransactionsUnavailable;
        public void commit(boolean report_heuristics)
            throws NoTransaction, HeuristicMixed, HeuristicHazard;
        public void rollback() throws NoTransaction;
        public void rollback_only() throws NoTransaction;
        public Status get_status();
        public String get_transaction_name();
        public void set_timeout(int seconds);
        public Control get_control();
        public Control suspend();
        public void resume(Control which) throws InvalidControl;
}
```

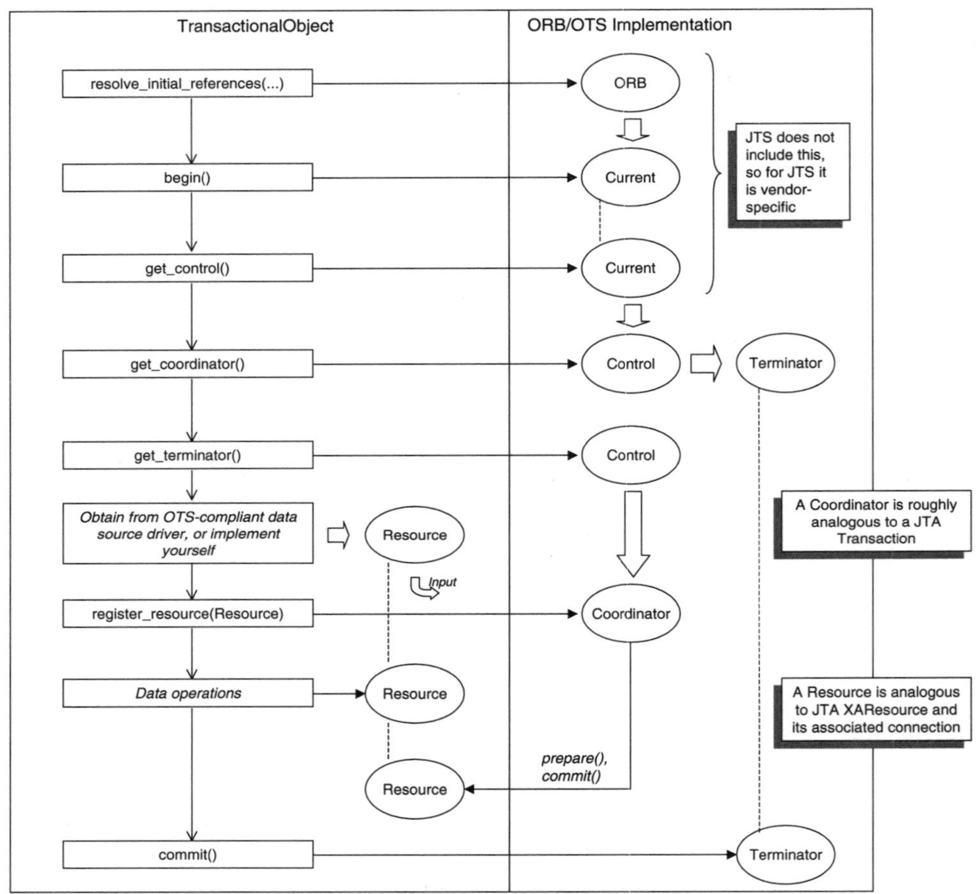


**Figure 7-29** Context management using the Control interface.

To obtain a Current interface, your application calls resolve_initial_references ("TransactionCurrent") on the ORB, and then narrows the object in the standard CORBA way to an org.omg.CosTransactions.Current. You can then use the Current interface to create and complete transactions.

The following client code will attempt to perform the work in a new transaction, or in a subtransaction if a transaction is already in progress and if subtransactions are supported. If subtransactions are not supported, it will perform the work in the existing transaction if there is one in progress, and create a new one otherwise. Subtransactions are not supported by JTA, and so should not be used when the

transactional work involves calls to EJB servers. The example below attempts the transaction three times if a rollback occurs, and then gives up:

```
boolean stillTrying = true;
while (stillTrying)
{
   stillTrying = false;
   try
   {
      org.omg.CosTransactions.Current current =
         (org.omg.CosTransactions.Current)
         (org.omg.CosTransactions.CurrentHelper.narrow(
            _orb().resolve_initial_references(
               "TransactionCurrent")));

      boolean startedNewTransaction = false;
      try
      {
         current.begin();    // Starts a new transaction. Current
               // records the association between that transaction
               // and the current thread.

         startedNewTransaction = true;
      }
      catch (org.omg.CosTransactions.
         SubtransactionsUnavailable ex)
      {
         // Transaction already in progress, and subtransactions
         // are not supported.
      }

         ...perform transactional work...

      if (startedNewTransaction) current.commit();
   }
   catch (org.omg.CORBA.TRANSACTION_ROLLEDBACK ex)
   {
      // try again?
      if ((count++) < 3) stillTrying = true;
      else throw new Exception("Transaction failed");
   }
}
```

These basic operations required for a client demarcated transaction using "indirect" context management are depicted in Figure 7-30.

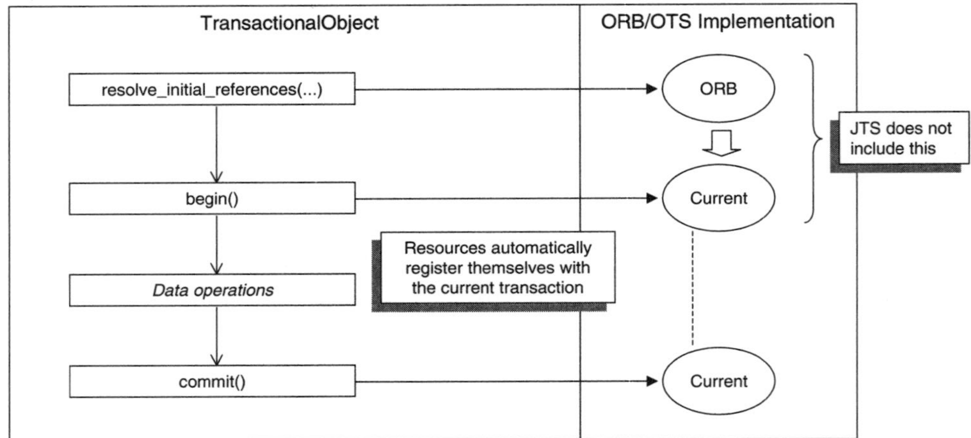


**Figure 7-30** Using OTS to create a client-demarcated transaction.

If your transaction manager implements OTS, this is how you would likely write a client-demarcated transaction. Most products that provide OTS level support and allow you to write client-demarcated transactions provide a Current interface, so you don't have to worry about transaction factories. JTS does not support the Current interface, however, so if you want to be JTS compliant, you need to obtain a Control object from the Current, or, if your OTS implementation provides a TransactionFactory, you would obtain the Control object directly from that. Regardless, you need to obtain a Control. Using the Control instance, you would perform direct context management. The indirect approach hides from you the details of what is going on, whereas the direct approach requires you to code those details.

### *Propagating Transaction Context*

It is the ORB's role to send and receive messages between clients and server objects. It is the transaction manager's role to manage transactions, and maintain a transaction context for each transaction branch. The ORB must include this context in messages that it sends, so that the context can be propagated from one ORB to another, and via the ORB from one transaction manager to another. A JTS transaction manager provides two interfaces for this handoff: the Sender and Receiver interfaces. Basically, a sending ORB obtains the PropagationContext of the current transaction from the transaction manager by calling the transaction manager's Sender.sending_request() method. When a reply to the request is received, the ORB notifies the transaction manager by calling the received_reply() method, and identifies what transaction was replied on by passing back the PropagationContext.

On the other end, so to speak, the receiving ORB obtains the PropagationContext from the message header (from the RequestHeader.service_context—see "How CORBA Sends Information over the Wire: GIOP and IIOP" on page 508), and then must pass this to its transaction manager, to effect the propagation of the transaction. It does this by calling the transaction manager's Receiver.received_request() method, and passing it the PropagationContext sent in the message. When the ORB is ready to reply to the request which came in, it can obtain the PropagationContext suitable for the reply by calling the transaction manager's Receiver.sending_reply() method. These sequences of events are shown in Figure 7-31.

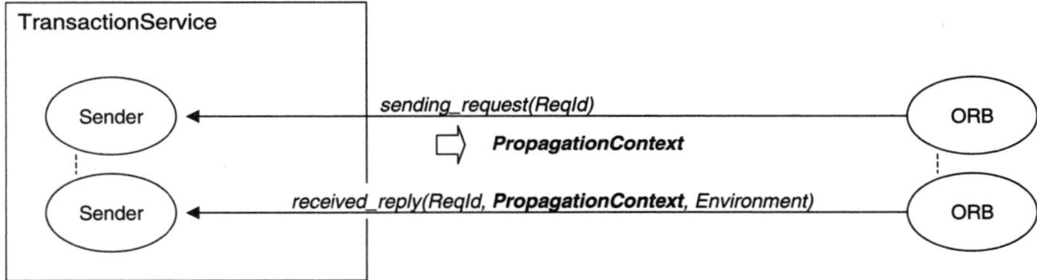


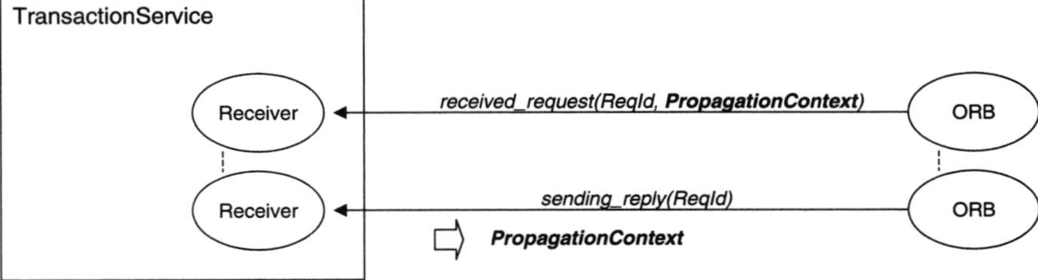


**Figure 7-31** PropagationContext creation and transmission.

One thing I have not mentioned is how the ORB identifies the transaction service instance, which must implement javax.jts.TransactionService. You can probably guess—JNDI! Once the ORB has a handle to the environment's chosen transaction service, it needs to obtain from the transaction service the Sender and Receiver interfaces, for exchanging propagation contexts as described above. It does this by giving the TransactionService a callback: an instance of TSIdentification, on which the TransactionService then calls identify_sender() and identify_receiver() methods, thereby providing the ORB with the Sender and Receiver objects. The ORB is now ready to conduct transactional business. This initialization sequence is shown in Figure 7-32.

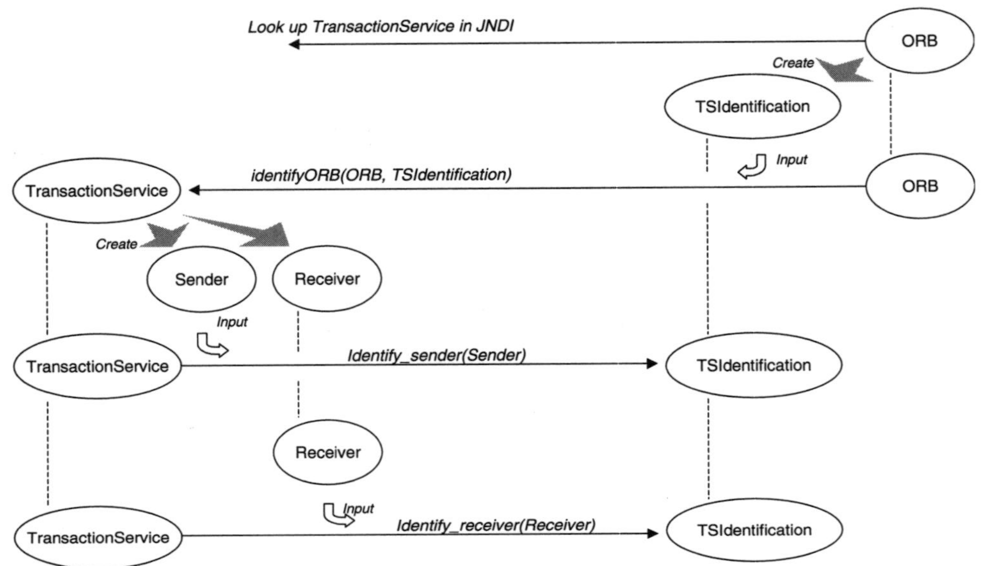


**Figure 7-32** Transaction Service initialization, at server startup.

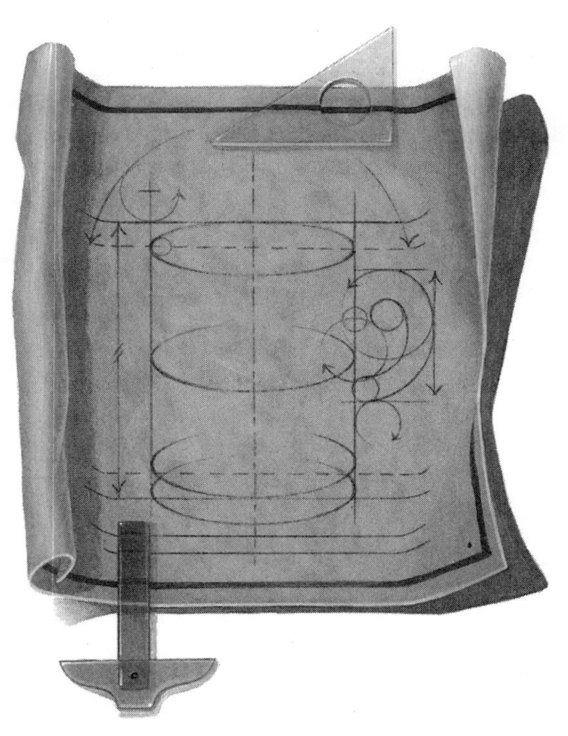

# CHAPTER 8

# Server Frameworks and Architectures

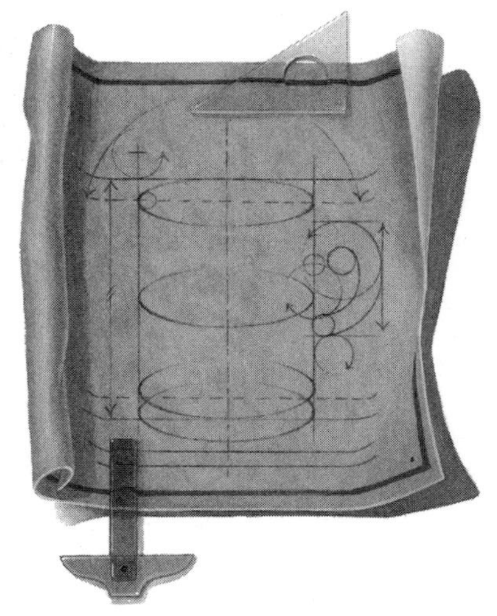

When Java debuted in 1995, its primary deployment platform was web browsers. Netscape's agreement to embed a Java VM in its version 2.0 browser was a public relations coup for Sun, and provided it with a means to make Java ubiquitous very quickly. A consequence, however, was a perception among programmers and the user community that Java was a "client" language, and that its main use was for developing user interfaces.

If you are reading this book you probably know how inaccurate that picture is. One of Java's great benefits is the ability to develop platform-independent business logic and infrastructure. Yet, for the first two years of Java's existence, there was no universally accepted or robust way of deploying Java applications on servers.

This was not due to a lack of support for server protocols. Sun has provided support in the standard Java packages for many Internet communication protocols from early on, and added RMI with Java 1.1. The problem was that there was no accepted standard framework for running Java applications on a server. CORBA provided such a framework, but not all organizations were willing to embrace CORBA just because they were considering Java. Further, Java CORBA implementations had many non-standard features, and suffered from a lack of compatibility.

The Enterprise JavaBeans (EJB) specification finally provided the needed framework for deploying Java server applications. An application server supporting EJB can run Java application components and link them together to allow the creation of distributed server applications. Perhaps the most important result of this for Java acceptance was the fact that EJB-compliant application servers removed the issue of how to "install Java" on a server. Organizations no longer had to evaluate and choose a Java platform and figure out how to set it up if they wanted to build a server application. Instead, they could evaluate EJB products, which are backed by commercial support and documentation. The issue of Java on the server became moot, and selecting a Java server platform became no more controversial than selecting any other infrastructure product.

When this book first appeared, it was the first book to discuss the EJB APIs. At that time, there were only a handful of fledgling products supporting EJB. Since then there has been a remarkable proliferation of Java application servers, nearly all supporting EJB. There are currently around forty such products. This range of choices has given the Java user community a rich set of options, and has greatly accelerated the adoption of Java for enterprise applications. In early 1998, Java server applications were rare, and were executed mainly by more adventurous developers. Today, Java is clearly *the way to go* for developing open protocol distributed applications on TCP networks.

EJB is not the only deployment framework for server side Java. CORBA remains a viable Java server platform, and overlaps EJB in many areas. I will not go further into the CORBA APIs than I already have since there are many good books on that subject. The Java servlet API is another extremely important standard and is supported by many web servers, especially those which come bundled with application servers. The servlet API provides a very convenient and secure framework for creating web server extension programs which can serve dynamically generated HTML, and also can access other network servers such as databases and application servers. Servlets also provide a convenient and comparatively safe gateway for firewalls. Servlets are often used as a web-accessible front end to an EJB back end. The servlet framework includes a facility called JavaServer Pages (JSP), which allows developers to closely couple the specification of generated web content with the business rules for generating that content.

This chapter explains the leading server side frameworks for Java application deployment, including servlets, JavaServer Pages, and EJB. At the end, I will try to pull all this together and discuss value-added features of current commercial frameworks and also show how these products can be used to create entire enterprise information systems.

## Servlets

A servlet is a Java-based web server extension program. It is the Java equivalent of native web server extension technologies, such as Microsoft's ISAPI and ASP and Netscape's NSAPI. The main differences are that:

- The servlet API is a standard Java extension, and therefore portable and platform-neutral.
- Servlets are secure, since they operate within the context of a security manager, similar to applets.
- The servlet API is vastly easier to use than comparable proprietary native APIs.

Server extension APIs have been used mostly in high-performance applications, in which the overhead of a CGI-based solution was unacceptable. The reason is that conventional extension APIs are so difficult to learn and get working reliably that they have been used only when the justification was very strong. Since a native extension API operates within the process context of the web server, a failure of the extension module can bring the server down. Server extensions are extremely hard to test and debug.

On the other hand, CGI has its own very substantial shortcomings. Conventional CGI programs operate as a separate process which must be allocated anew with each request. Thus, there is a great deal of overhead in servicing a CGI request. Furthermore, since the process terminates when the request has completed, it is difficult to implement a service that maintains persistent connections to other services; for example, each request may require the newly started CGI process to open a connection to a database, retrieve data, close the connection, return the data, and then exit. Opening a database connection may require several hundred milliseconds; add this to the CGI process creation time, and it is clear that there is quite a bit which has to occur before the CGI program can return even the smallest amount of data. CGI programs also tend to have a large footprint, and this, combined with the initialization overhead, makes CGI not very scalable.

Server extension APIs, including the Java servlet API and CGI, share the request/response model of HTTP since they operate within the context of an HTTP request. In this model, an incoming request has an input stream associated with it, as well as an environment context and an output stream for results. It is up to the application to perform parsing of the input stream and formatting of the output stream. Most APIs provide methods for retrieving HTTP header and other data from the environment context. The Java servlet standardizes this API, greatly reducing the maintenance problems for which both CGI and server extension programs are notorious. (See Figure 8-1.)

The Java servlet API provides a highly scalable model for adding functionality to web servers. A servlet runs as a thread within the context of the web server's Java virtual machine. Since all exceptions in Java can be trapped by the VM, it would take a bug in the virtual machine itself to crash the web server. It also means that servlets can handle a very large volume of requests, since the footprint of the VM process is shared by all servlets—in fact, even the servlet object instance itself is shared between multiple invocations of the same servlet, and the implication of this is that servlets can provide persistence between invocations for maintaining database and other connections. Servlets therefore have significant advantages over alternatives, in the areas of:

- Stability
- Scalability and performance
- Persistence

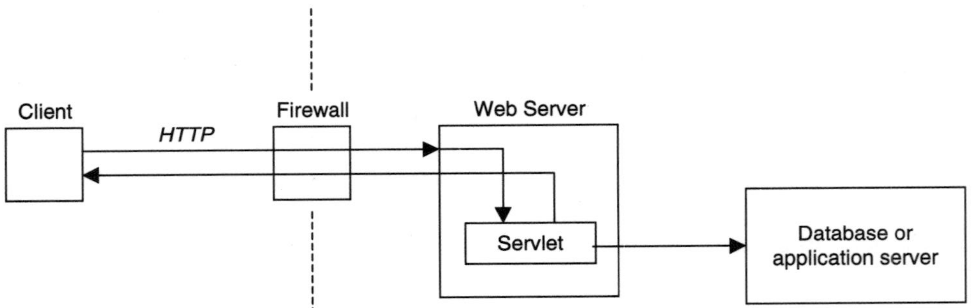


**Figure 8-1** Typical servlet deployment.

### *Security*

Security is no small consideration with any kind of server extension or dynamically invoked program through a web server. CGI is an enormous security hole for administrators, especially ISPs, so much so that many ISPs prohibit CGI programs. Native server extensions are not allowed by ISPs and are only appropriate for internal applications. Servlets change these rules, however, and an administrator could allow servlets to be used with substantial confidence—more so than most CGI programs.

Many ISPs implement a sandbox for CGI processes to run in. UUNet is an example of this: any CGI program invoked by a UUNet web server runs in an "R-box" with a restricted set of resources and privileges. The Java servlet model provides a similar kind of sandbox, but in a standard and portable manner. An administrator familiar with the servlet model as it applies to an Apache web server running on Solaris can directly apply that experience to a servlet running under IIS on Windows NT. The existence of a standard and portable security model is an enormous

advantage for both administrators and developers, who can solve the security problem once for their application instead of once for each platform. Administrators of corporate networks can rest easier, knowing that no servlet can do what it is not specifically configured to do, and further that if one should fail, it will not bring the server down.

### *Servlets as Gateways to Application Servers*

Servlets have become an important adjunct to application servers by providing a web-traversible gateway. Many products extend application server features including security, transaction management, and load balancing to the servlet engine, thereby allowing servlets to become the universal gateway to these services. For example, a servlet can authenticate a user and begin a transaction, and have both the user identity and transaction context propagate to the application server when remote Enterprise JavaBeans calls are made. Load balancing of EJB objects can also be provided by servlet modules used to obtain initial references to EJB objects. Load balancing of the servlets themselves can be provided using standard web load balancing techniques, including DNS-based load balancing. Later in this chapter I will discuss these integration issues more fully. For now, let's look at the servlet APIs up close.

### *Invoking a Servlet*

There are three ways to invoke a servlet.

1. *URL*—The URL of the servlet is specified directly. For example:

   ```
   http://myhost/servlet/mypackage.myservlet?parm1=abc&parm2=def
   ```

   would invoke the servlet *myservlet* in package *mypackage*, in the *servlets* directory on host *myhost*. The exact form of the servlet URL is implementation-specific and depends on the server you are using. A common convention is to use the fictitious "servlet" object base path as shown in the example above, and within that to identify the servlet by its published name or its fully qualified class name. Servlet parameters are specified using the HTTP GET query syntax. They may also be specified as input tags in an HTML form.

2. *HTML-embedded*—The name of the servlet is embedded in an HTML page, similar to the way one embeds an applet in an HTML page. However, in the manner of a server-side include, the <servlet> tag in HTML is processed by the server, and output from the servlet is substituted in its place. For example:

```
<html>
Customer Status...<br>
<servlet name=CustomerStatus code=customer.CustomerStatusImpl>
<param name=firstname value=abe>
<param name=lastname value=lincoln>
</servlet>
<br>
</html>
```

The HTML file must have a .shtml extension. A codebase parameter may be specified as well. However, some servers at present require a servlet deployed in this way to reside in the server's *servlets* directory, even if a codebase parameter is specified.

3. *Chaining*—This is configured by the web server administrator. Chaining allows servlets to be invoked automatically based on the MIME type of a data stream. The technique of chaining can be used to automatically filter or process data of certain types.

### *The Servlet Programming Interface*

You can either extend the abstract class HttpServlet, or implement the Servlet interface directly. You might choose to do the latter if your servlet needs to extend some other class for some reason. The Servlet interface methods are:

**init(ServerConfig)**—This initializes the servlet. The web server instantiates and initializes a servlet the first time it is needed. Once the servlet is initialized, the servlet instance continues to exist until the web server is stopped, or it is explicitly destroyed by an administrator. In the init() method you would normally open database or other server connections required to service requests. In addition, you must save the ServletConfig parameter that is passed in, because the server may ask for it back by calling the getServletConfig() method on the servlet (described next).

**getServletConfig()**—Returns the ServletConfig object reference that the servlet saved in its init(ServletConfig) method.

**getServletInfo()**—Returns author, version, and copyright info.

**service(ServletRequest, ServletResponse)**—This is the method called by the web server whenever an HTTP request invokes the servlet. Each request is serviced in a separate thread, in the virtual machine of the servlet object. The implementation of this method should therefore be thread-safe, since the servlet object instance may be servicing several HTTP requests at the same time, each in a different thread. The HTTP request input stream can be obtained from the ServletRequest argument, and the HTTP output stream from the ServletResponse argument.

**destroy()**—In this method you should release all servlet object resources (close database connections, etc.). This is also your last chance to write or commit persistent data, or make final log entries.

***Example: The Customer Manager Servlet***

I will demonstrate writing a servlet with a complete example, a small application which has two personalities: a servlet personality, and an RMI server personality. The servlet serves the function of letting web-based users query for information on a customer, and the RMI service allows an administrator to obtain more complete information and update the database. The administrator's user interface is shown in Figure 8-2.

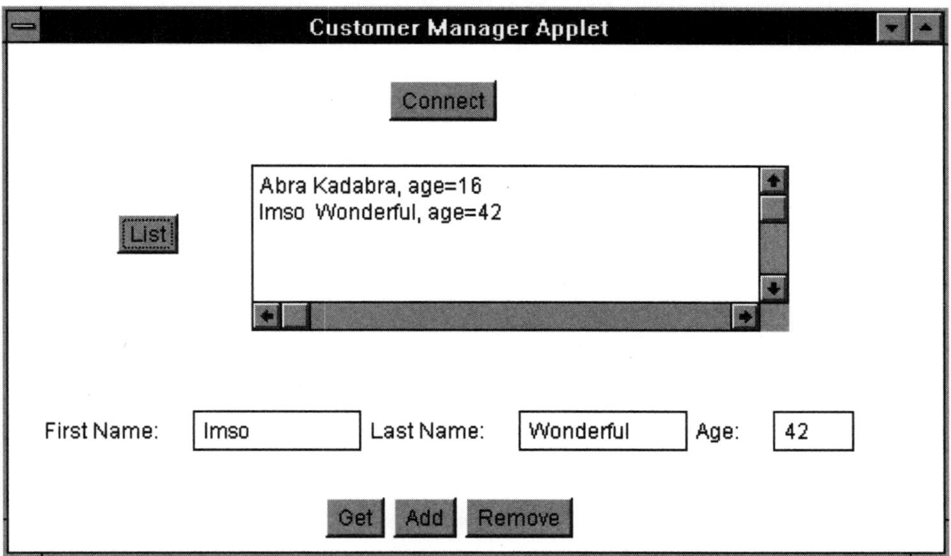


**Figure 8-2** User interface for accessing the Customer Manager servlet's RMI functions.

An administrator would use the above applet to maintain the database of customers. The admin applet accesses the servlet object, which is also an RMI server object, using the RMI protocol. The servlet also provides a servlet interface for nonadministrative web users who want to query the database for information on a customer. In this simple example, the query simply returns the customer's name and age, based on a query string containing the name.

Figure 8-3 shows what happens if you invoke this servlet by entering its URL directly into a browser. The servlet requires two query parameters: *firstname* and *lastname,* and it returns the customer data in a stream to the browser. How it does so will be explained later.

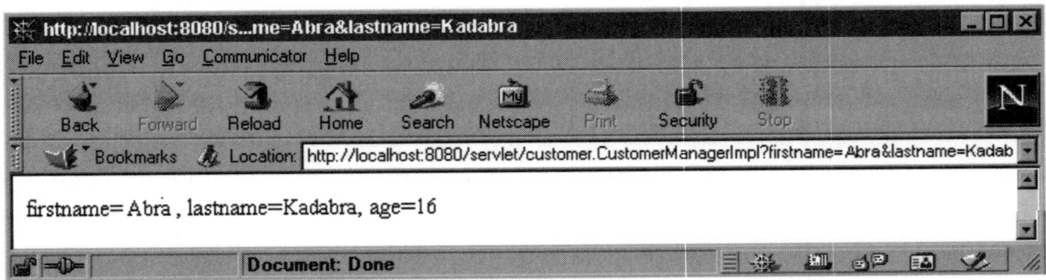


**Figure 8-3** Accessing the servlet using a URL.

Since in this case the servlet is also an RMI server object, it needs a remote interface to export its services. The Java interface for the servlet is shown in the code below.

```
package customer;
import java.rmi.*;

/**
 * Interface for CustomerManager servlet, which has dual-
 * personalities: http and RMI.
 *
 * Allows one to write services that can be accessed from any
 * browser, and across a firewall without tunneling.
 */

public interface CustomerManager extends Remote
{
   public Customer getCustomer(String firstname, String
      lastname) throws RemoteException, Exception;
   public Customer[] getCustomers() throws RemoteException,
      Exception;
   public void addCustomer(String firstname, String lastname,
      int age) throws RemoteException, Exception;
   public void remCustomer(String firstname, String lastname)
      throws RemoteException, Exception;
}
```

Our servlet, as an RMI server object, maintains a persistent database of customer data. For simplicity, I have implemented this database simply as a serialized object file. The Customer class is:

```
package customer;

public class Customer implements java.io.Serializable
{
   private String lastname;
   private String firstname;
   private int age;

   public Customer(String firstname, String lastname, int age)
   {
      this.firstname = firstname;
      this.lastname = lastname;
      this.age = age;
   }

   public String toString() { return "firstname=" + firstname +
      ", lastname=" + lastname + ", age=" + age; }

   public String getFirstname() { return firstname; }

   public String getLastname() { return lastname; }

   public int getAge() { return age; }
}
```

Let's now look at the implementation of the servlet. The init(ServletConfig) method first saves the ServletConfig parameter and then calls the internal method init(), which does the bulk of the initialization, including registering the object as an RMI service, and loading the customer data; in a real application, this would be a database connection. The code for load() and save() is shown at the end of this example.

```
package customer;
import java.io.*;
import javax.servlet.*;

/**
 * Implementation of the CustomerManager.
 */

public class CustomerManagerImpl
   extends java.rmi.server.UnicastRemoteObject
   implements CustomerManager, Servlet
{
   private ServletConfig servletConfig;
   private java.util.Vector customers;
```

```
private boolean bound = false;

public CustomerManagerImpl() throws java.rmi.RemoteException
   { super(); }

//
// Servlet methods...
//

public void init(ServletConfig c) throws ServletException
{
   servletConfig = c;
   init();
}

protected void init() throws ServletException
{
   try
   {
      java.rmi.registry.Registry registry =
         java.rmi.registry.LocateRegistry.getRegistry();
      registry.rebind("CustomerManager", this);
      bound = true;
      System.out.println("Server bound to CustomerManager");
   }
   catch (Exception ex)
   {
      System.out.println("Could not bind:");
      ex.printStackTrace();
   }

   // Load file
   try
   {
      load();
   }
   catch (Exception ex)
   {
      System.out.println("Error reading customer file:");
      ex.printStackTrace();
      throw new ServletException("Terminating due to prior
         error");
   }
}

public ServletConfig getServletConfig()
{
   return servletConfig;
```

```
    }

    public String getServletInfo()
    {
        return "CustomerStatus Servlet";
    }

    public void destroy()
    {
        // Save file
        save();
    }
```

The service() method is the method called by the web server to satisfy servlet invocation requests. In my implementation, I first obtain the two query parameters "firstname" and "lastname." Based on these, I look the customer up in the database and obtain a Customer object for that customer. I then return a stream of data about that customer to the output stream of the current HTTP connection, which can be obtained from the ServletResponse argument:

```
    public void service(ServletRequest request,
        ServletResponse response)
        throws ServletException, IOException
    {
        System.out.println("Service...");

        if (! bound)
        {
            response.getOutputStream().println("Not bound");
            return;
        }

        // Identify customer
        String firstname = request.getParameter("firstname");
        String lastname = request.getParameter("lastname");
        if ((lastname == null) || (firstname == null))
        {
            response.getOutputStream().println(
                "Both last name and first name must be specified");
            return;
        }

        // Retrieve information on the customer
        System.out.println("firstname=" + firstname);
        System.out.println("lastname=" + lastname);
        Customer customer = null;
```

```
        try
        {
           customer = getCustomer(firstname, lastname);
        }
        catch (Exception ex)
        {
           throw new ServletException("Error looking up customer.");
        }

        // Return information on the customer
        if (customer == null)
        {
           response.getOutputStream().println("Customer could not be
              found.");
           return;
        }
        response.getOutputStream().println(customer.toString());
     }
```

The remote services this object exports involve searching for a customer based on a name, getting a list of all customers, adding a customer to the database, and removing a customer. Note that these method implementations are synchronized to protect the customer's object from simultaneous access by multiple servlet request threads; in a real application using a database, this synchronization would probably not be necessary because it would be provided by the synchronization inherent in the database's transaction mechanism.

```
     //
     // CustomerStatus methods...
     // The remote entry point implementations are synchronized,
     // because they may be called my multiple server threads,
     // either as an RMI service, or as a servlet service.
     //


     public synchronized Customer getCustomer(String firstname,
        String lastname) throws java.rmi.RemoteException, Exception
     {
        return findCustomer(firstname, lastname);
     }

     public synchronized Customer[] getCustomers() throws
        java.rmi.RemoteException, Exception
     {
        Customer[] ca = new Customer[customers.size()];
        for (int i = 0; i < customers.size(); i++)
```

```
        {
            Customer c = (Customer)(customers.elementAt(i));
            ca[i] = c;
        }
        return ca;
    }

    public synchronized void addCustomer(String firstname, String
        lastname, int age) throws java.rmi.RemoteException,
        Exception
    {
        Customer c = new Customer(firstname, lastname, age);
        customers.addElement(c);
        save();
    }

    public synchronized void remCustomer(String firstname, String
        lastname) throws java.rmi.RemoteException, Exception
    {
        Customer c = findCustomer(firstname, lastname);
        if (c == null) throw new Exception("Not found");
        customers.removeElement(c);
        save();
    }

    protected Customer findCustomer(String firstname, String
        lastname)
    {
        for (int i = 0; i < customers.size(); i++)
        {
            Customer c = (Customer)(customers.elementAt(i));
            if (c.getFirstname().equals(firstname) &&
                c.getLastname().equals(lastname))
            {
                return c;
            }
        }
        return null;
    }
```

The load() and save() methods are as follows, although again, in a real application, these would perform database accesses.

```
    protected synchronized void load() throws Exception
    {
        // synchronized to protect access to customers object
```

```
        System.out.println("Loading CustomerFile...");
        File file = new File("CustomerFile");
        FileInputStream fis = null;
        try { fis = new FileInputStream(file); } catch
            (FileNotFoundException ex) {}
        if (fis == null)
        {
            customers = new java.util.Vector();
        }
        else
        {
            ObjectInputStream ois = new ObjectInputStream(new
                FileInputStream(file));
            customers = (java.util.Vector)(ois.readObject());
            ois.close();
        }
        System.out.println("...done loading.");
    }

    protected synchronized void save()
    {
        // synchronized to protect access to customers object

        System.out.println("Saving CustomerFile...");
        File file = new File("CustomerFile");
        try
        {
            ObjectOutputStream oos = new ObjectOutputStream(
                new FileOutputStream(file));
            oos.writeObject(customers);
            oos.close();
        }
        catch (IOException ex)
        {
            System.out.println("Error writing customer file:");
            ex.printStackTrace();
        }
        System.out.println("...done saving.");
    }
```

Finally, for testing purposes it helps to have a main method, which is included here for completeness.

```
    public static void main(String[] args) throws Exception
        // for testing only
    {
        System.setSecurityManager(new
```

```
        java.rmi.RMISecurityManager());
        CustomerManagerImpl m = new CustomerManagerImpl();
        m.init();
    }
}
```

The code for the administration applet, which accesses the servlet object via RMI, is not included here because it is not important to understanding servlets. The code is available on this book's web site.

This servlet must be invoked as a servlet prior to being accessed via the administrative tool. The reason is that the init() method is the method which registers the object as an RMI service, and init() is not called until the servlet is invoked for the first time (after a web server restart).

### *Testing and Deployment*

Sun provides a development kit for servlets, called the Java Servlet Development Kit (JSDK), available free from their web site. JSDK 2.0 contains a servlet test bench server called the Servlet Runner. (Release 2.1 adds an improved tool called "Server.") The Servlet Runner is a trivial web server which supports servlets invoked by URL, but not as HTML-embedded servlets. For final testing, you can test your servlets on the Java Web Server, which is Java's full-featured web server written in Java. You can also use the WebLogic Web and application server.

When testing with the servlet runner, you deploy a servlet by specifying it in a servlet.properties file. This servlet.properties file can be identified on the command line when you run the servlet runner. For example, the following line runs the servlet runner with a servlet.properties file located in the c:\dev directory, and the code for the servlet is in the news.jar archive (you can specify a directory instead of an archive), and with c:\test as the document root:

```
start servletrunner -s c:\dev\servlet.properties -d news.jar
   -r c:\test
```

The servlet.properties file lists each servlet (there can be more than one). To list a servlet in the servlet.properties file, include a line of the form:

```
servlet.<servlet name>.code=<servlet class>
```

where <*servlet name*> is the name you want to use for the servlet in servlet URLs, and <*servlet class*> is the fully qualified name of the servlet main class (the class which extends Servlet or HttpServlet). In addition, each servlet which has deployment properties must have an initArgs line which lists all the property values.

These values are retrieved by the servlet at runtime using the getServletConfig().getInitParameter(name) method. You can continue a line onto multiple lines by using the \ character. For example, here is a servlet.properties file for a servlet called "newsgroups" with a main class called "ng.NGServlet." It has two deployment properties, LogfilePath and NsgpDir:

```
servlet.newsgroups.code=ng.NGServlet
servlet.newsgroups.initArgs=\
   LogfilePath=c:\\TEMP\\news\\ng\\ng.log, \
   NsgpDir=c:\\TEMP\\news\\ng
```

A servlet either may be installed locally on a web server, or remotely, in which case the servlet actually resides on another server. Servlets locally installed on a web server should be placed in the *servlets* directory (or, if the servlet is in a package, its package should be in the *servlets* directory), and then identified to the server using its administration tool for security configuration. Servlets installed in this way will have either full or configurable privileges, depending on the server's policy. The Java Web Server, for example, gives full privilege to a locally installed servlet. Remotely installed servlets are considered untrusted by default, and must be in a signed JAR file. An administrator identifies a remote servlet to a server by specifying a URL that ends with the name of the signed JAR file. A remote servlet's privileges are configured by the server's administrator.

Some web servers require a patch to be installed to enable servlet support. Eventually, given the growing importance of Java, most servers will likely include support for Java CGI and Java servlets. In the meantime, installing a patch or plugin is a small price to pay given the tremendous benefits of a standard and robust security model, scalability, maintainability, and single-language development. It must also be contrasted with the comparatively greater difficulty of developing reliable applications using native server extension technologies; for example, it is far easier to create a servlet than to write IIS parse maps and deal with extension control blocks, or NSAPI pblocks and Request data structures.

### *Retrieving GET and POST Data*

It is a little bit unfortunate but not unbearably inconvenient that the API you use to retrieve query parameters supplied with a GET request is different from the API you use to retrieve POST form parameters. Therefore, an HttpServlet must first determine if the data originates from a GET query or a POST. You can determine this using the HttpServletRequest.getMethod() call, which returns a string indicating the HTTP request method (i.e., "GET" or "POST"). Once you know this, you can call the getQueryString() method for a GET request or the getInputStream() method for a POST request, and then call an appropriate parsing method

which is again specific to the request method. For example, this code snippet produces a hashtable containing the request data:

```
public void service(HttpServletRequest req,
   HttpServletResponse res)
throws ServletException, IOException
{
   // Get the input data
   int len = req.getContentLength();
   ServletInputStream sis = null;
   Hashtable data = null;
   String method = req.getMethod();
   if (method.equals("GET"))
   {
      String q = req.getQueryString();
      data = HttpUtils.parseQueryString(q);
   }
   else if (method.equals("POST"))
   {
      sis = req.getInputStream();
      data = HttpUtils.parsePostData(len, sis);
   }
   if (data == null) System.out.println("data is null");
```

**Multipart POST Content.** It is very unfortunate that at the present time, multipart content is not directly supported by the servlet API. If your application needs to supply multipart content to the servlet, you cannot use the parsePostData() method and you must implement your own routines for parsing the raw posted multipart stream.

Multipart content is quite common in many applications. For example, when an HTML form contains an input tag with `type="file"`, the form tag usually specifies `enctype="multipart/form-data"` causing the form data and the attached file to be sent as a multipart stream. This feature permits the use of web pages which allow the user to select a file for upload. The uploaded file is posted as one part of the multipart stream, and the form data itself is posted as the first part.

Writing the code to handle multipart content is not hard, but it would be nice if the standard API handled it.

**Redirection.** A servlet can respond to a web client with a location reply, which will cause a browser to redirect itself to the specified location. This is accomplished with the HttpServletResponse.sendRedirect(String url) method. The argument to this method must be an absolute URL.

### *Class Loader Issues*

Like any Java component environment, a servlet server should generally separate one servlet from another by running it with its own class loader. However, the specification does not require it and many servers (including the Java Web Server 2.0) do *not*. Therefore it is a good idea not to set properties or use non-final static objects or data in a servlet. The Servlet 2.2 specification, which is still in draft form at this writing, states that servlets should be well-behaved with regard to separation from other servlets, although it does not address class loaders specifically and leaves the implementation up to the server provider. Apparently some server vendors felt that defining the behavior in terms of class loaders was too implementation specific, since some vendors may cache classes across VMs and use other means of keeping session data separate. The exact semantics of session separation is therefore a little bit unclear at this time, but it is likely that servers compliant with Servlet 2.2 will provide the separation between servlets that is needed.

### *State Management*

HTTP is a stateless protocol, but defines a mechanism called "cookies" for maintaining state on a client in a way which can be retrieved by a server. There are other techniques which are commonly used, including encoding session state as query parameters in relocation URLs and in URLs that are embedded in content sent back to the client.

The HttpSession type is an abstraction of client session persistence. HttpSession abstracts client state so that the servlet does not have to worry which client session persistence technique is used.

A cookie is just a set of data, defined by a server, which is stored in the user's browser (if the user so permits). Any data can be stored in a cookie, but usually it is minimal and compact, and only enough to correlate the user with previous transactions the user has performed, and possibly containing user preferences as well. For example, a server might store in your browser a cookie containing a unique session ID (which the server creates for you), so that it can keep track of what requests you perform over time. Cookies usually expire, so this state does not persist forever. A cookie may also be set to terminate when the user exists the browser. The user can set whether they want any server to read a cookie, or only the server that set it—otherwise, any web site could examine your cookies to tell what other web sites you had visited recently. Cookies do not impact the HTML content or URLs sent back to the browser, and therefore are preferred for maintaining client state.

To get the current session, use the Servlet getSession(boolean create) method with an argument of true. This will create a session between your servlet and the user's browser, if one does not already exist, and return the new or preexisting session to

you. Most implementations will attempt to use cookies for maintaining session state, and if that fails, use URL encoding. Some servers allow you to specify which technique to use by setting a property or other means.

You can associate data with a session by using the HttpServletRequest.getSession(true) to get the session, and then HttpSession.putValue(String name, Object value) to set a value and the HttpSession.getValue(String name) method to retrieve a session value. Also, to ensure that session state is maintained regardless of the session mechanism used, you should call the getSession() method each time the servlet is invoked; otherwise, session state may be lost if URL encoding is being used.

The actual session data that the session management system stores in a cookie or encodes in URLs is small, and is typically a session ID of some kind. In general, your servlet should be written to assume that URL encoding is the mechanism used for maintaining session state. In fact, when a browser first invokes a servlet, URL encoding may be used to get the session going and then switch to using cookies.

To allow URL encoding to work, you should never manually write URL strings to the output stream for receipt by the browser or for embedding in a web page. Instead, you should pass all written URLs through the encodeURL(String) method to allow the session management system to add any state information it needs. When performing redirects, you should also pass a redirect URL through the encodeRedirectURL(String) method.

**Note**

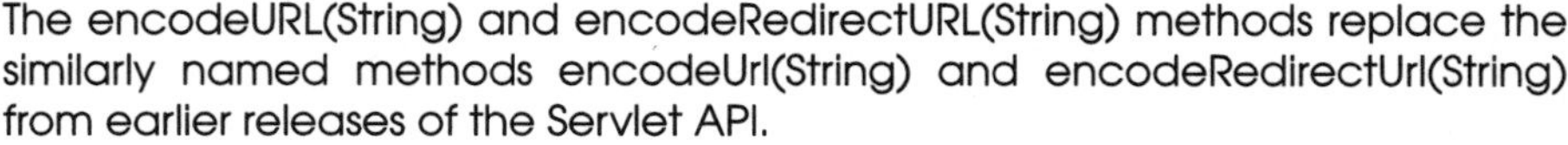

The encodeURL(String) and encodeRedirectURL(String) methods replace the similarly named methods encodeUrl(String) and encodeRedirectUrl(String) from earlier releases of the Servlet API.

Session objects are stored on the server. Therefore, the session state may be local to the VM maintaining the session. If clustering is provided by the web server, the server must either guarantee that a client session will remain with a particular server during the session's lifetime, or the session object must be made available to the other servers in the cluster. Clustering is usually supported by some kind of distributed session state management facility, which may even be persistent, allowing for long-term sessions.

In designing an application's session state, you need to decide if that information needs to be persistent and durable across system restarts, and if it needs to be transactional. It is a good idea to distinguish clearly between session data and persistent application data, since the latter represents true business data and usually needs to be transactional and durable. Any data which needs to be reliably available across server restarts should probably be incorporated into the application data model explicitly rather than treated as session data.

Session data is inherently transient. In fact, a session can go away unpredictably simply by a cookie expiring. Servlet session objects will be reclaimed when the session expires.

### When Session State Is Large

One of the most powerful features of the servlet API is its encapsulation of session state. Most implementations limit the size that the session state can grow to, typically to several kilobytes per user session. This may not be sufficient in all applications. If it is not, you may need to resort to an additional mechanism. For example, you might use session beans, and in that case the servlet state would consist primarily of a key into a hashtable for looking up the session bean reference. If you go down this path, make sure that you cover all conditions which can occur, including the timeout of the session bean, the timeout of the servlet-to-EJB server connection (this will be somewhat rare), servlet timeout, EJB connection loss, and web server restart.

### User-Specific Profiles and Authentication

If you want to provide user-specific profiles for your application, then you need to have users first log in, and then associate their session with their login profile. To do this, you should first check if the user's session is new, and if it is, redirect them to a login page where they log in, and then store in a database an association between their login ID and their current session. For example, this code checks if the session is new, and if so redirects them to a login page:

```
HttpSession session = request.getSession(true);
if (session.isNew())
{
  response.sendRedirect(
      http://www.someserver.com/servlet/login);
}
else
{
   // Session is preexisting; get its ID and apply profile
   // based on that.
}
```

At the login URL, make them provide a user ID and password in a form, which you can retrieve with the parsePostData() method discussed above. Then call getId() on the session, and store the session ID for later use, and redirect the user back to where they just came from.

Note that if your application requires that users log in again after a period of inactivity, you will have to include this in your logic, since isNew() will only return true if there is no session state; if session state is retrieved via a cookie, it will return false. The isNew() method also continues to return false if a session cannot be established for any reason.

Alternatively, you can make use of standard HTTP authentication provided by the web server. If the user is authenticated, you can obtain the user ID by calling HttpServletRequest.getRemoteUser(). You should make the call at the entry point to the web site. If you need to make it at more than one point, you can still use the isNew() method to determine if the user has just connected and therefore if you should obtain the user ID. Here is an example of using web authentication to obtain the user ID:

```
HttpSession session = request.getSession(true);
if (session.isNew())
{
      String user = request.getRemoteUser();
      if (user == null) throw new Exception("Should not happen");
      // Set session state to include the user.
      ...
}
```

The Servlet 2.2 specification (available as a pre-release draft only at this writing, and so this is subject to change) adds the methods getRemoteUserPrincipal() and isRemoteUserInRole(), analogous to methods of the same name defined in the EJB 1.1 specification. While the getRemoteUser() method returns the user ID provided by the user, the getRemoteUserPrincipal() returns the authenticated Principal which the server identified to correspond to the remote user.

Servlet 2.2 compliant servlet engines should unify authentication mechanisms and the getRemoteUserPrincipal() should always return the user authenticated identity (principal) regardless of how the user is authenticated to the servlet server. For example, if basic authentication (password provided to the browser) is used, the getRemoteUserPrincipal() method should return the user's Principal, and if certificate-based authentication is used via a user certificate and private key, the getRemoteUser() method should also return the user's Principal. Pre-2.2 servers may not be able to return the user ID if certificate-based authentication is used; instead a different method must be used to obtain the user identity, as shown below.

You should give some thought to how secure you want the session to be. For example, instead of using a password, you could install the servlet on a secure web server and use SSL, and require users to install a personal digital certificate in their browser. In pre-Servlet 2.2 (and pre-Java 2) servers, a technique supported by some servers for obtaining the user's SSL identity was by getting the attribute "javax.net.ssl.peer_certificates" with the ServletRequest getAttribute() method, which would return an array of javax.security.cert.X509Certificate (with the user's certificate first), and could then get the distinguished name of the certificate owner by calling getSubjectDN(). Here is an example:

```
import javax.security.cert.*;
...
X509Cert certs [] =
   (X509Cert [])
   (request.getAttribute(
      "javax.net.ssl.peer_certificates"));
if (certs == null) throw new Exception(
      "No client certificate; cannot authenticate user");

// Identify user from the certificate.
X509Cert userCert = certs[0];
Principal p = userCert.getSubjectDN();
String dn = p.getName();
...we have now identified the user...
```

As of Servlet 2.2, the standard way to do this is as follows:

```
if (request.isSecure())
{
   java.security.cert.X509Certificate cert =
      request.getAttribute("javax.servlet.request.x509cert");
   if (cert == null) throw new Exception(
      "No client certificate; cannot authenticate user");
   Principal p = cert.getSubjectDN();
   String dn = p.getName();
  ...we have now identified the user...
}
```

Basic web authentication works by having the web client (browser) send an authorization header to the server. If an authorization header is required but was not sent, the server returns an authorization error, and the browser then sends the header (this is called "lazy" authentication). Before doing so, the browser may display a dialog box for the user to enter a user ID and password. The web server is not involved in the creation of this dialog box.

The Servlet 2.2 specification defines a method of authentication called "form-based" authentication which uses an HTML form instead of relying on the authentication dialog and protocol built-in to the web client or on the authentication header. Instead, it uses the HTTP POST method and a special server-based program (servlet) for obtaining the posted authentication parameters and submitting them to the web server's authentication service. An HTML form of the following basic kind must be used to utilize this technique. The form can be customized to depict a look and feel appropriate for the application, but its input parameter names and the action field cannot be changed.

```
<form method="POST" action="j_security_check">
<input type="text" name="J_USERNAME">
<input type="password" name="J_PASSWORD">
</form>
```

Note that the POST action target is the special `j_security_check` servlet program. This program is required to be provided by all servlet engines and it provides the form-based authentication service.

### *Reentrancy*

It is generally a good idea to avoid using multithreading in server business applications, and allow the middleware to manage threading and concurrency. While some middleware component systems such as EJB (discussed later in this chapter) disallow multithreading in server applications, some do not, and it is then necessary for the developer to anticipate the effects of concurrent invocations on objects and code.

Multiple web clients are allowed to access a servlet object concurrently unless the servlet class implements the SingleThreadModel interface. In that case, the servlet is assumed to *not* be reentrant and the servlet can be assured that accesses to it will be serialized (guarded) by the server. To prevent other clients that are trying to access the servlet from blocking, it is then necessary for the server to spawn multiple instances of the servlet, possibly maintaining them in a pool.

In any system which maintains a resource pool, the system must have a policy for determining to what extent the pooled resources are interchangeable. In the case of a servlet pool, the servlet specification requires that servlets be interchangeable. Therefore, you should not leave client-specific state in a servlet object in any way other than via the HttpSession mechanism. Otherwise, instances of the same servlet will not be interchangeable.

### *Multiple UI Frames and Concurrency*

It is common for a servlet to be accessed from a multiframe thin-client page, just as it is common for a heavy-client application to have multiple panels or windows. If each page corresponds to a servlet URL, the servlets will be invoked simultaneously when the UI page is shown.

If the URL of each of two or more frames corresponds to the same servlet, this can represent a special case of general concurrent access to a servlet from a single client session. Servlets are assumed to be reentrant unless the servlet class implements the javax.servlet.SingleThreadModel interface. Therefore, unless the servlet implements SingleThreadModel, both servlet invocations will be performed in separate threads concurrently on the same servlet instance, from the same client session.

This is normally not a problem if the servlet is designed to be reentrant. However, if the servlet accesses an enterprise session bean, there will be a problem because concurrent access to a session bean from the same client session will cause an exception to be thrown by the EJB server (this situation is discussed in "Runtime Concurrency Issues" on page 669). Concurrent access to entity beans is not a problem because access is serialized by the server. The EJB specification *requires* the server to throw a RemoteException if a client tries to access the same session bean from more than one thread.

This presents a problem for client design when the servlet uses session beans. First of all, you must decide how important it is that data shown in separate frames be absolutely in sync. For example, if the frames are populated in series in separate transactions, it is possible that the frames will be inconsistent. If the separate frames do not need to be in sync, then you merely need to ensure that concurrent access to any backend session beans is serialized. This can be achieved by declaring the servlet to be SingleThreadModel, which will serialize access to the servlet itself, thereby accomplishing the required serialized access to the session bean it has created. The potential disadvantage of this approach is that it may reduce performance.

An alternative is to avoid using session beans in servlets and treat the servlet as the "session bean." This is reasonable since the purpose of a session bean is to establish and maintain any required transactional and client state, and the servlet engine may be able to do this (not all servlet engines are transaction enabled). It is important to encapsulate session management logic so that it can be redeployed to a session bean or other framework as required and not to make it architecturally dependent on the servlet framework.

Another alternative which still uses session beans is to explicitly synchronize access to the session bean reference within the servlet. This is permitted since servlets can be multithreaded. However, it is risky and potentially complex. It is a good idea to maintain a single-thread model for server-side components because multithreading can impact the performance and behavior of the server as a whole across clients and can lead to non-repeatable anomalous behavior that is hard to diagnose. Remember that there are conditions which are product specific which can affect behavior, including timeouts, communication problems, and so on.

If separate frames within the client which access the same servlet need to be in sync and always show the same data, the client design itself will have difficulty achieving this because the browser model does not provide a callback mechanism, and it is difficult to affect more than one frame at a time. JavaScript can be used to achieve this, by invoking URLs with target tags that specify other frames. The servlet design is then complicated by the fact that it must be resilient to repeated and unexpected invocations caused by multiple and random clicks by users on the Reload button, the Back and Forward buttons, and other parts of the UI. The servlet engine must be transaction enabled, and all concurrent invocations need to be performed within the same transaction. If session beans are used, these transactions need to propagate to the backend EJB server.

### *Servlet Design*

One of the most challenging aspects of servlets is deciding how to coordinate the functions of obtaining information and presenting it. Servlets operate in a request/response model, and the state which they can maintain between invocations is limited. Therefore it is best to view each invocation as a separate transaction, which is mostly if not completely self-contained, and which is fully responsible for obtaining and displaying its own data. The application therefore cannot be designed to first build a user interface, and then process user interactions with that user interface: the user interface must be rebuilt each time. This makes it difficult to maintain user interface context, such as the current selected item on a screen, and so on.

A servlet generates HTML (typically), and so the user interface is usually based on the HTML or JavaScript document model. There are toolkits which help to generate servlet user interfaces. An example of such a toolkit is WebLogic's htmlKona. This approach is powerful because it allows the servlet to first build an object structure which represents the user interface, and then separately render that object structure when it is done constructing it. Therefore, construction of the user interface elements can be logically decomposed, and need not proceed in the same order as the components are rendered. This makes the task of UI construction similar to the way it would be done for a static UI. The disadvantage of this approach is that HTML has become an enormously complex language, and the mapping between APIs such as htmlKona and HTML's features may not be exact, or may become ridiculously granular. In that case, it may be most practical to mix and match, using the object API for major features but inserting HTML snippets for fine grain control. This creates potential portability problems, but may be the best solution in some cases.

I will not provide details of UI generation here, since UI issues are not the focus of this book. Readers interested in htmlKona can refer to BEA WebLogic's documentation, which is available at http://weblogic.beasys.com.

### Mixing and Matching Servlet Servers and EJB Servers

Most web application servers come bundled with a web server, which includes a servlet engine. Nevertheless it is often possible to mix and match web server, servlet engine, and EJB server from different sources. For example, you should be able to deploy servlets in a Netscape web server which access Enterprise JavaBeans in a WebLogic EJB server. To go a step further, there are many third-party servlet engines for the Netscape web servers. A popular one is JRunner. Thus, it is possible to deploy servlets in a Netscape web server, using a third-party servlet engine, accessing an EJB server of a different brand.

Compatibility between the servlet and the EJB server reduces to the interface between the servlet and the EJB-related services that it accesses. These are usually name services and data resources. If the associated client packages for these services are lightweight, written in Java, and self-contained, it should be possible to deploy them with the client application, and they should be independent of the servlet engine. It should then be possible to deploy them in a servlet regardless of the brand of web server. On the other hand, if the EJB-related services are not lightweight and cannot be separated from the web server, then you are limited to using the EJB server only with its provided web server.

### Deploying Servlets

Prior to Servlet 2.2 there was no standard way to deploy servlets. There was no specification of what could reside in a servlet JAR file, or even if servlets could be deployed as JAR files. There was also no specification stating how servlet codebases were defined, as already mentioned. Nevertheless there have been some de facto standards for deployment and these other aspects of behavior.

**Servlet JavaBeans.** The Java Web Server supports the deployment of a servlet as a JAR file, which may contain the serialized state of the servlet. This is known as a "servlet bean." A servlet bean follows bean conventions and therefore all exposed properties are accessible via getXXX() and setXXX() method. This allows the server to set them at runtime ("hot") in response to configuration changes made

by the administrator. This augments but does not replace the fact that deployment properties set by the administrator are also passed to the servlet via the Servlet-Config object at servlet initialization.

For the Java Web Server, servlet beans are deployed in the servletbeans directory.

**XML-based Deployment.** Sun is making an effort to better define and standardize the way in which Java applications of all kinds are deployed. The Servlet 2.2 draft specification includes an XML definition of a servlet deployment descriptor. The deployment descriptor will be packaged inside of a servlet deployment file, which will be a JAR file, possibly with a .web or .war (WebARchive) extension.

The XML definition is still very preliminary at this point, but here is a taste of what it will likely contain:

```
<web-app>
   <display-name>Sarah's Shiny Servlet</display-name>
   <context-param>
      <param-name>Webmaster</param-name>
      <param-value>webmaster@mycompany.com</param-value>
   </context-param>
   <context-param>
      <param-name>MyEJB</param-name>
      <param-value>ejb/MyEJBv2.3</param-value>
   </context-param>
   <context-param>
      <param-name>SomeDataSource</param-name>
      <param-value>
         jdbc/SomeDataSource2
      </param-value>
   </context-param>
   <session-timeout>30</session-timeout>
   <servlet>
      <servlet-name>My Servlet</servlet-name>
      <servlet-class>com.mycompany.MyServlet</servlet-class>
      <init-param>
         <param-name>myParam</param-name>
         <param-value>123</param-value>
      </init-param>
   </servlet>
   <servlet-mapping>
      <servlet-name>My Servlet</servlet-name>
      <urlpattern>/myservlet/*</urlpattern>
   </servlet-mapping>
   <mime-mapping>
      <extension>xml</extension>
      <mime-type>text/xml</mime-type>
   </mime-mapping>
```

```
   <welcome-files>
      index.jsp, index.html, index.htm
   </welcome-files>
   <security-constraint>
      <web-resource-collection>
         <web-resource-name>My Servlet</web-resource-name>
         <urlpattern>/myservlet/*</urlpattern>
         <http-method>GET</http-method>
         <http-method>POST</http-method>
      </web-resource-collection>
      <userdata-constraint>
         <transport-guarantee>SECURE</transport-guarantee>
      </userdata-constraint>
      <auth-constraint>
         <role-name>webmaster</role-name>
         <role-name>dba</role-name>
         <role-name>corporateuser</role-name>
      </auth-constraint>
   </security-constraint>
   <ejb-ref>
      <ejb-ref-name>MyEJB</ejb-ref-name>
      <ejb-ref-type>Session</ejb-ref-type>
      <ejb-home>com.mycompany.ejb.MyEJBHome</ejb-home>
      <ejb-remote>com.mycompany.ejb.MyEJB</ejb-remote>
   </ejb-ref>
   <resource-ref>
      <res-ref-name>SomeDataSource</res-ref-name>
      <res-type>com.somedrivercompany.SomeDriver</res-type>
   </resource-ref>
</web-app>
```

While this exact syntax may change before you read this (although changes will likely be minimal), there are some basic ideas which will be present. First of all, notice that the syntax allows for a deferred binding between data resource names and their actual JNDI names: in the <resource-ref> section, one identifies a data resource by the name used in the application code's JNDI lookup operation. In this example, that would be the name "SomeDataSource." The deployment descriptor in turn allows the deployer to remap this name to an actual deployed name via a <context-parameter> definition. In this example, the context parameter "SomeDataSource" is mapped to the actual value "jdbc/SomeDataSource2." Thus, JNDI names can be changed at deployment time without changing application code.

A similar procedure is used for mapping EJB names. In this example, the <ejb-ref> section is used to identify an enterprise bean, "MyEJB." A <context-parameter> specification remaps the bean's name to the name "ejb/MyEJBv2.3."

The deployment descriptor also provides a standard way to identify security roles which may access the servlet. It is up to the server environment to map specific users to these roles. Users who authenticate by some means accessible to the web server and belong to those roles will be able to access the servlet.

### *Where to Run a Servlet Server*

An issue that often comes up in application architecture design is where to deploy servlets. In particular, should they be inside the firewall or outside the firewall, and should they be colocated with the application server?

The answer depends on many factors. This is discussed in detail in Chapter 5 and also in the section "Initiating Calls from the Inside" on page 740. However, the short answer is that it depends on how sensitive your data is and how much protection you think you need. It also depends on what protocol the servlet uses to access internal data, whether you trust the protocol, and how much information about the internal network and services the servlet needs to know and store locally to make its requests. The most prudent thing is to keep servlets outside the internal firewall as simple as possible. A common technique is to use a web server inside the DMZ for primarily serving static content, and use a simple servlet gateway or native web server plugin to forward requests which require data to in internal web server, which then makes appropriate data requests to application servers or databases.

You must also consider the fact that the servlets may need to store credentials for accessing those data resources or application servers, and steps should be taken to safeguard the place those credentials reside.

### *JavaServer Pages*

JavaServer Pages (JSP) is an HTML/Java hybrid language for embedding program commands in a web page. These commands are interpreted by the web server prior to returning content to the client. JSP is the modern Java incarnation of what historically were known as "server side includes," which did much the same thing in a more primitive way. While JSP operation can be understood to be interpreted, most implementations will in fact compile portions of a JSP page into one or more runtime objects which can be cached for efficiency.

A draft version of the JSP 1.0 specification has only just been released as of this writing, so it is not yet finalized. In addition, JSP is a huge topic in its own right, and I will not attempt to do anymore here than give you a feel for the nature of JSP and discuss its capabilities. It is an important technology, however, and will find use in web site building as well as in building systems for exchanging data between organizations. You can use JSP today, because Sun's Java Web Server implements it, and as you read this will likely be available for Apache (which has licensed JSP) and other web servers.

Suppose we have a class called mypackage.MyCountryLister which provides a method called getCountries(), which provides a vector list of strings representing countries. It might be something like this:

```
package mypackage;
import java.util.*;
public class MyCountryLister
{
   private Vector countries = new Vector();
   public MyCountryLister()
   {
      countries.addElement("usa");
      countries.addElement("spain");
      countries.addElement("france");
      countries.addElement("singapore");
      countries.addElement("germany");
   }
   public Vector getCountries() { return countries; }
}
```

On the Java Web Server, I deployed the compiled package in the server's `classes` directory (i.e., created the directory "`mypackage`" in the `classes` directory and dropped the class file in it). We could then use this class in a Java Server Page as follows:

```
<html>
<jsp:useBean
   id="myCountryBean" scope="request"
   class="mypackage.MyCountryLister"
/>
<form method="POST" action="/servlet/SelectCountry">
<!--Generate list-->
<select name="COUNTRY">
<%
   for (int i = 0; i < myCountryBean.getCountries().size(); i++)
   {
      String country = (String)
         (myCountryBean.getCountries().elementAt(i));
%>
      <option value="<%=country %>"><%=country %>
<%
   }
%>
</select>
</form>
</html>
```

On the Java Web Server, I dropped this JSP page into the public HTML directory and invoked it. When a browser requests this page, the returned HTML is:

```
<html>
<form method="POST" action="/servlet/SelectCountry">
<select name="COUNTRY">
<option value="usa">usa
<option value="spain">spain
<option value="france">france
<option value="singapore">singapore
<option value="germany">germany
</select>
</form>
</html>
```

This produces an HTML dropdown list containing five countries.

In case you are curious about how this actually works, the web server processed the JSP page by first generating a servlet which contains this section of code (in addition to other boilerplate code) in its service method:

```
out.write("<html>\r\n\r\n");
mypackage.MyCountryLister myCountryBean=
   (mypackage.MyCountryLister)
request.getAttribute("myCountryBean");
boolean _specialmyCountryBean  = false;
if ( myCountryBean == null ) {
   _specialmyCountryBean = true;
   try {
      myCountryBean = (mypackage.MyCountryLister)
         Beans.instantiate(null, "mypackage.MyCountryLister");
   }catch (Exception exc) {
      throw new ServletException (
         " Cannot create bean of class "
         +"mypackage.MyCountryLister");
   }
   request.setAttribute("myCountryBean", myCountryBean);
}
if(_specialmyCountryBean == true) {
}
out.write("\r\n<form method=\"POST\""
   + " action=\"/servlet/SelectCountry\">\r\n"
   + "<!--Generate list-->\r\n<select name=\"COUNTRY\">\r\n");

for (int i = 0; i < myCountryBean.getCountries().size(); i++)
{
   String country =
```

```
            (String)(myCountryBean.getCountries().elementAt(i));
    out.write("\r\n\t\t<option value=\"");

    out.println(country );
    out.write("\">");

    out.println(country );
    out.write("\r\n");
}
out.write("\r\n</select>\r\n</form>\r\n</html>\r\n");
```

As you can see, the generated servlet attempts to instantiate an instance of the MyCountryLister bean. It then writes out sections of the HTML I had encoded in my JSP, and also executes the embedded Java code as part of the servlet's implementation code. Thus, all output to the HTTP response stream is actually generated by the servlet.

There are other ways this could be implemented, and other servers may do it differently. The generated code is presented here so that you can get a feel for the basic model and how it works.

**Serving XML.** An extremely important aspect of JSP is that it is defined as an XML application. Thus a JSP page can be viewed as an XML document with embedded Java code snippets (escaped using XML syntax) which are evaluated at runtime. JSP can therefore be used to create dynamic templates for generating XML messages.

Strictly speaking, JSP is not a pure XML application, as it contains extensions and shortcuts which are not valid XML. However, the specification defines precise XML mappings for all of these extension and shortcut features so that a JSP processor can translate them into equivalent XML. These features are there to make the job of writing JSP easier.

The most important use of JSP's XML compatibility is for writing distributed applications which communicate via XML messages. An XML page with embedded Java can not only generate portions of itself dynamically, but it can access databases, and even communicate with application servers using RMI. When it is done, it produces a completed XML document which can be sent to another system to be interpreted.

Consider the following example of a JSP page which receives and XML message input from an HTTP POST request, parses the message using an XML parser to produce a DOM object tree, extracts an object from the tree, and then generates an XML tag attribute value. The completed result document is then sent back to the client as the HTTP response.

```
<MyData>
<jsp:useBean
   id="myXMLParser"
   class="xml.Parser"
/>
<!--Parse input-->
<%! DOM dom; %>
<%
dom = myXMLParser.parse(input);
%>
<MyTag temperature="<%=dom.abc.def.temperature %>"/>
</MyData>
```

When this JSP page is deployed (or when it is invoked the first time), the server will process the page and generate an equivalent servlet. The portion of the text outside the <% ... %> tags is converted into output statements so that text is sent to the servlet output stream unchanged. The portion inside the <% ... %> tags is treated as Java code and is compiled and incorporated into the servlet. The result is a servlet which generates the surrounding XML text, and in addition, includes the processing statements embedded inside the <% ... %> constructs. Notice that the only embedded Java statement in the example above is a statement which parses the servlet's input stream, assuming it is an incoming XML message; the predefined variable "input" is standard for servlets. When the servlet is run, the embedded Java expressions are evaluated, and the output is a valid XML document which returns to the requestor as a response.

A JSP 1.0 compatible server is not required to handle XML documents. However, JSP 1.1 servers will be required to do so. At that time it will be possible to build XML messaging systems using JSP pages which communicate among themselves via HTTP. The above example is for illustration only, as the details of the servlet XML implementation may change.

## The Enterprise JavaBeans Framework

Note: This discussion reflects the May 7, 1999, public draft of EJB v. 1.1, and the initial public draft of the Enterprise Edition platform specification (c. June 1999).

In the previous chapters we saw some of the tremendous practical difficulties in designing and implementing correct multiuser multitier applications. Intuitively, you should feel that these difficulties should not be necessary; somehow, the tools are not right, or are too complicated. After all, all you want to do in most cases is get data in and out, in such a way that you don't conflict with what someone else is doing. It should be very simple.

Enterprise JavaBeans (EJB) attempts to address these problems by defining a standard architecture for creating multiuser applications based on a three-tier approach. The architecture drastically simplifies the choices the application programmer needs to make, and delegates most of those concerns to an infrastructure layer that is the responsibility of the middleware vendor. The market for middleware is now in a tremendous growth phase, and having a standard architecture that requires interoperability, as the Enterprise JavaBeans framework does, will greatly enhance the value of these products.

### Client, Server, and Data Resource

The EJB model is a three-tier model based on remote method invocation on server objects using RMI. EJB defines an object framework for a set of server object roles and implementations. The model is symmetric, however, in that server objects invoke each other in the same way clients invoke them (i.e., there is no distinction between a local and a remote client). This provides a high degree of object relocatability. (Of course, under the covers, an implementation is free to implement local calls differently, as long as this is transparent to the application.)

Client sessions with server objects are either stateless or stateful. A stateful object retains value between transactions (but not necessarily between client connections). If a connection is stateful, the server object can be either persistent (retains value between client connections) or not persistent. A nonpersistent server object is called a "session" object, and a persistent server object is called an "entity" object. Entity objects are available to all clients, and a server which provides entity objects in effect provides an object database. Session objects, however, are available only to the client for which they were created, and they do not persist after the client connection is terminated.

Even though EJB connections are based on RMI, EJB servers are free to use either RMI's native stream protocol (JRMP), IIOP, or any protocol that can bridge to either of these. This means that EJB objects can interoperate with non-Java clients. Many vendors have also developed EJB-based gateways to their server products, including many mainframe-based applications.

### Transaction Management

Transaction management is a central feature of EJB servers, and all EJB servers either provide transaction management or allow the integrated use of an external transaction manager.

From an API point of view, transactions are manifested as remote calls. You can either take charge of transaction management in your client or server beans, or leave it up to the middleware. The latter is recommended, since that is one of its main advantages. I will assume that unless otherwise specified.

A remote call automatically starts a transaction. The transaction is committed (or aborted if necessary) when the call returns. If the call itself makes other calls, they all automatically use the same transaction by testing whether a transaction is in progress. This can even be the case if the operation spans multiple databases and multiple EJB middleware implementations. A two-phase commit protocol is used if available (i.e., if all middleware involved provides open-protocol transaction management) to implement an atomic transaction from the client's point of view. The EJB server takes care of the implementing of object caching, synchronization, and locking based on the isolation level specified for the underlying data resource. What a wonderful design!

This is significant for portability reasons as well, because transaction control is difficult to implement within application code. JDBC leaves transaction control in the hands of the client; but the transaction and locking facilities available to an application depend on the driver and the database, so users are resorting to using database-dependent SQL and hard-wiring their applications for specific drivers. (JDBC 2 extensions will help to address this problem.) The EJB framework puts the burden back in the lap of the database and middleware vendor to make all these things transparent. EJB server implementors are free to use native APIs to achieve this—the application code does not know or care.

While entity beans represent persistent objects, there is no locking model. For example, you cannot request read locks, intention locks, or write locks. This is because entity beans are not actually data objects—they are components, as will be discussed further below. It is up to the underlying persistence implementation to make use of database locks as required to implement the isolation modes.

Another issue is how an enterprise bean caches non-Java resources, such as connections to other (non-EJB) servers. Entity objects can persist, but they may be disposed of when not in use to reclaim memory. Therefore, if an entity bean must maintain a resource connection such as a database connection, it needs to allow for disposing the resource when the bean is reclaimed, and reobtaining it when the bean is restored. To provide a persistent set of resource connections which are not constantly being closed and opened, most application servers provide a connection pool capability for the databases they support. The EJB 1.1 and related specifications address connection pools explicitly.

An EJB server must support the Java Transaction API (JTA) to the extent that the server must make available a transaction context object (a javax.transaction.UserTransaction) which allows an enterprise bean to begin, commit, and roll back global transactions. A bean would do this if it needed to explicitly manage its transactions, rather than allow the EJB server to automatically begin and commit transactions on behalf of the bean.

**Propagation of Transaction Context.** An interesting situation arises if an organization has more than one application server, and a bean in one application server needs to access a bean in another application server. If the first bean executes in a transaction context, its call to the second bean in the other server needs to execute in the same context. Therefore, the two servers need to be linked, and the first server must be able to transfer the transaction context to the second server.

The ability to transfer or import transaction context is an important feature as an application grows and starts to be used by other departments, and integrated into the infrastructure. Most EJB servers provide this capability, but in different degrees and in different ways. The EJB specification does not require that an EJB server be able to share transaction context with other servers, although it is clear that is a desired and intended feature.

The wonderful thing is that if your application does not need transaction context propagation today, you can always change servers later if you do need it without affecting your application design. At most, you may need to import a different RMI package and change some JNDI properties, but the overall application should not need to change. Taking this a step further, you can design applications without worrying about where components are deployed, because the components can operate within the same transaction even if they are redeployed on different servers. Application components are therefore portable, even if they are transactional. This is depicted in Figure 8-4.

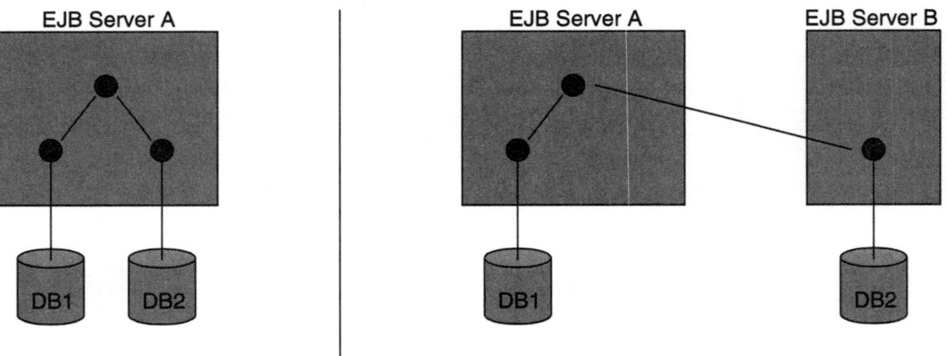


**Figure 8-4** Applications need not change if components are redeployed for improved efficiency.

### *How It Works*

Let's look at the sequence of events that normally occurs, as depicted in Figure 8-5. When a client wants to use a server service, it first establishes a connection by looking up the container object in some directory service via a JNDI interface, and

performing a create(). This creates (or allocates from a pool, if the object is stateless) an instance of the requested enterprise bean. It does not return a reference to this object, however: it creates a server-side proxy, called an "EJB Object" (an unfortunate name, since everything is an object), and returns a reference to that. The proxy object fields calls from the client, and in turn makes identical calls to the Enterprise JavaBean, which in turn makes identical calls to the actual user-written class that implements the business logic. In addition, the proxy object acts as a checkpoint, and performs checks with the container environment regarding security policies.

As you can see, it is the EJB container which actually invokes the Enterprise JavaBeans that you write. The container therefore has the opportunity to perform various actions before it actually makes this invocation, such as identifying your user Principal, what roles your Principal belongs to, and what transaction your call may already be associated with. The container has the job of allocating a thread for the purpose of servicing your request, and then turning the request over to that thread. From that point on, it keeps track of which transaction that thread belongs to. The container also may provide load management services and may provide persistent data resource connection pools. In short, the container provides a protected and managed environment for EJB invocations and performs many of the infrastructure-related housekeeping tasks that you would have to otherwise build into a distributed application.

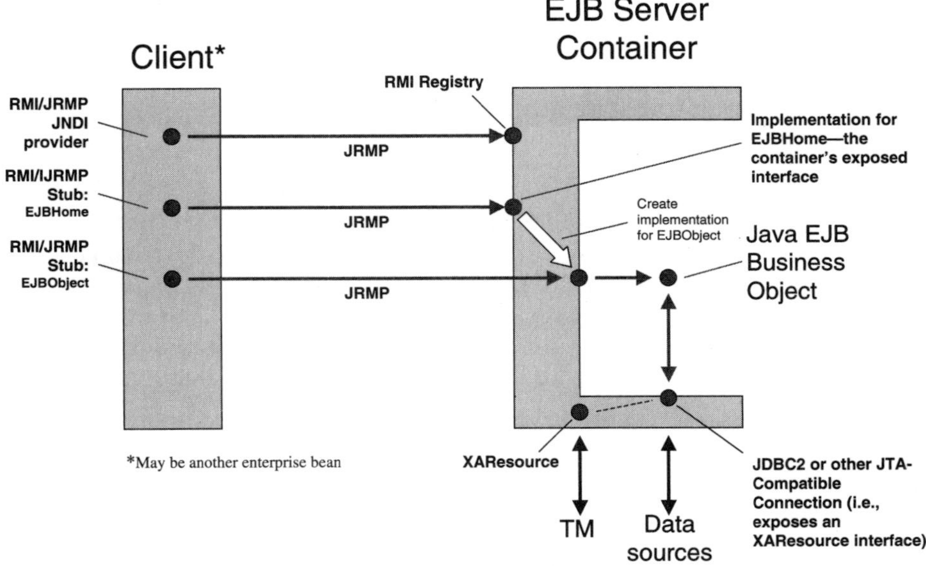


**Figure 8-5** Client and EJB interaction.

### Session Bean vs. Entity Bean

EJB defines two primary kinds of enterprise beans: session beans and entity beans (see Figure 8-6). The difference between a session bean and an entity bean is that an entity bean represents a persistent data item, such as a record in a database. An entity bean instance therefore does not represent a class of items, but represents a particular instance, just as a record is an instance of a row in a relational table. An entity bean instance also has a unique identity, and can be obtained by looking it up using one of its finder methods, just as an indexed row in a relational table can be obtained by performing a query on the value of the index. The lifetime of an entity bean instance is also permanent, and it exists until it is explicitly removed, just as a table row exists until it is deleted.

Entity beans provide an object-oriented view of arbitrary data resources, which may be non-object-oriented in actuality. For example, an entity bean facade may be created to represent a relational data resource so that the application can be coded as if the data resource were object oriented. The EJB server may even provide a tool to generate the entity bean layer for relational or other kinds of data resources that it directly supports.

| | Session Bean | Entity Bean |
|---|---|---|
| Exists until | Server crashes, container is destroyed, or session is terminated | Explicitly removed |
| Access by multiple clients | No | Yes |
| Obtained by | Creating | Creating, using Handle, or finding |
| Can be passivated when in a transaction | No | Yes |

**Figure 8-6** Comparison of session and entity JavaBeans.

Both kinds of beans can be provided to client applications from instance pools in an EJB server. However, the use of instance pooling is a performance feature, and it is largely transparent to clients. In addition, a session bean can be declared to be stateless, allowing the server greater freedom to reuse the bean instance, but whether the server actually makes use of this freedom depends on the server and is transparent to the application.

### Beans Are Components

Entity beans may be small-grain representations of actual persistent data items. Still, an entity bean is a *component*—not a data item. An entity bean instance represents a runtime proxy for an actual data item, typically a complex data item. If your database table has a million rows in it, there are not a million entity beans—there is one entity bean instance for each instance you look up via a findXXX()

method, or obtain a reference to by any means. These instances may be reclaimed at any time to conserve resources, which may cause your application to block briefly the next time it tries to access the instance.

The conceptual difference between components and persistent data objects is an important one. Data objects represent the actual data, and components provide reusable and portable methods of getting to those objects in convenient ways, as well as operations to perform on them. Even if your database is an object database and the objects themselves provide methods, database objects are not inherently portable and self-contained. It is analogous to the difference between a non-enterprise JavaBean and a simple Java program object. An ordinary JavaBean has additional requirements to allow it to be reusable and redeployable, and its getter and setter methods provide a gateway to any real or virtual attributes managed by the bean. Similarly, Enterprise JavaBeans are reusable and redeployable components for accessing data.

#### *Runtime Synchronization*

An extremely important aspect of Enterprise JavaBeans is that runtime access to methods is automatically synchronized by the EJB container so that a programmer does not have to deal with reentrancy issues. This is a departure from the CORBA models which provide shared object access, but require you to write reentrant code and manually keep track of client-specific state.

Bean access synchronization is accomplished without limiting scalability by defining models which support either unshared session-specific state, or shared state which is transactionally managed. These are the session bean and entity bean models respectively. In addition, to support the use of pre-initialized object pools, the model explicitly provides for a special kind of session bean which is declared to not retain state between invocations, thereby allowing it to be pooled after every method call. These bean models will be discussed in greater detail later in this chapter.

#### *Deployment*

EJB 1.0 defined a set of six provider and user roles for enterprise beans. However, the 1.0 specification did not make use of many of these roles, particularly those related to deployment and assembly. The six roles are:

1. Server provider—Integrates and provides the core EJB services required by an EJB container. There is no standard interface between an EJB server and an EJB container (the two are effectively synonymous in current products), and so the server provider is currently the same as the container provider. In the future, there may exist a standard interface between an EJB server and an EJB container, making it possible to obtain containers from third parties

(e.g., containers which provide entity bean access to specialized data resources); then the server provider and container provider may no longer necessarily be the same party.

2. Container provider—Provides an EJB container, which is able to deploy and run enterprise beans with the facilities and APIs required by the EJB specification. The EJB container implements the API seen by an enterprise bean.
3. Bean provider (module developer)—Develops an enterprise bean, in accordance with the EJB specification. The bean is packaged in an EJB JAR file, typically with a tool provided by the EJB server provider. The bean provider specifies deployment information in the EJB deployment descriptor, which is also included in the JAR file. EJB 1.0 used a serialized Java object as a deployment descriptor; EJB 1.1 replaces that with an XML format. The Java 2 Enterprise Edition specification refers to this role with the more generic terms "module developer" and "component developer."
4. Application assembler—Selects a set of enterprise beans to compose a larger application.
5. Application deployer—Installs enterprise beans and enterprise beans applications in an EJB server.
6. System administrator—Configures the runtime resources and security settings needed by the EJB server to support the EJB services, data resources, and containers.

These roles are summarized in Figure 8-7.

The EJB 1.0 specification does not define precise boundaries between roles 1 and 2, or between roles 4, 5, and 6. The 1.1 specification clarifies the roles somewhat and addresses some important issues important to server and container builders.

An enterprise bean is packaged in a JAR file with a deployment descriptor. An EJB 1.0 deployment descriptor is itself a serialized bean, which is an instance of javax.ejb.deployment.DeploymentDescriptor. EJB 1.0 beans had to have a manifest listing each bean's deployment descriptor's serialized file along with the special attribute "Enterprise-Bean: True." For example, this manifest section lists the bean "MyBean":

```
Name: mypackage/MyBeanDeploymentDescriptor.ser
Enterprise-Bean: True
```

**Server Provider**
Builds the application server

**Container Provider**
Builds the container which runs in the application server and exposes EJB services and APIs to the application components

**Component Developer**
May assemble components into an application as well
The result is a highly reusable component, set of components, or applications

**Application Assembler**
Selects and configures components to create an end-use application
The result is an application unit suitable for deployment in a specific kind of environment or a specific environment

**Application Deployer**
Selects and configures applications and components to deploy ("stand up") an end-use application
The result is a fully deployed application users can use

**Application Administrator**
Monitors and administers the application
Makes configuration changes as necessary over time

**Figure 8-7** EJB application lifecycle roles.

The EJB 1.0 deployment descriptor serialized object contains the deployment attributes, which may apply to the entire enterprise bean, or be specific to particular remote methods. The deployment descriptor contains a security descriptor, method descriptors, a transaction attribute, and an object JNDI name.

The security descriptor specifies access rights on a per-user basis. The deployment descriptor may have a set of method descriptors, which specify a security descriptor and transaction attribute on a method-specific basis.

EJB 1.1 deprecates this representation and replaces it with an XML representation, which is discussed below. In addition, EJB 1.1 no longer uses the manifest to identify beans, but instead identifies them from the XML deployment descriptor syntax, which must be stored in the META-INF directory in the JAR file and have the name "ejb-jar.xml."

An EJB server registers an enterprise bean via JNDI, using the object name obtained from the deployment descriptor. This provides object location independence, because other beans can find the object simply by using the JNDI API.

**EJB 1.0 Deployment Descriptors.** EJB 1.0 defines these attributes for bean deployment descriptors:

Name **beanHomeName**—The JNDI Name to use for this bean. (The environment may prefix the name with other path information.)

String **enterpriseBeanClassName**—The full name of the enterprise bean class—i.e., the business class.

String **homeInterfaceClassName**—The full name of the bean's Home interface.

String **remoteInterfaceClassName**—The full name of the bean's remote interface.

boolean **reentrant**—If true, multiple concurrent calls to the same bean instance are permitted. This is necessary for beans that require recursion or which are called back by the beans they call. Use with care, because this capability disables many safeguards, particularly the container's concurrency control mechanisms. This can be set to true only for entity beans.

Properties **environmentProperties**—The customizable properties, with default values, that the administrator may set when the bean is deployed.

**AccessControlEntry**[]

Method **method**—The bean method this access control entry applies to, or null if it applies to the entire bean.

Identity[] **allowedIdentities**—The identities that are permitted to invoke the method (or the bean if method is null).

**ControlDescriptor**[]—Each enterprise bean method may have a control descriptor. It includes the following:

Method **method**—The method the descriptor applies to, or null if the descriptor applies to the entire bean.

int **runAsMode**—One of:

CLIENT_IDENTITY—Use the identity of the client invoking the method.

SYSTEM_IDENTITY—Use a privileged account. The actual account used is determined in a product-specific way.

SPECIFIED_IDENTITY—Use the identity specified in the runAsIdentity property (see below).

Identity **runAsIdentity**—Use this identity, if the runAsMode is set to SPECIFIED_IDENTITY.

int **transactionAttribute**—One of:

TX_BEAN_MANAGED—The *bean* uses JTA to manage transactions itself. It can obtain the current JTA transaction by using EJBContext.getCurrentTransaction().

TX_MANDATORY—If the *client* is not in a transaction when the bean is called, an exception will be thrown.

TX_NOT_SUPPORTED—The bean must not be invoked within a transaction.

TX_REQUIRED—The EJB server starts a transaction for each method invocation (and commits on return), unless one is already in progress for that *client*.

TX_REQUIRES_NEW—The EJB server always creates a new transaction for the call. If the *client* was already in a transaction, that transaction is temporarily disassociated from the caller's thread until the new call (and new transaction) completes.

TX_SUPPORTS—The call executes in the context of the *client's* transaction, if there is one; otherwise it executes without a transaction.

int **isolationLevel**—One of the following. These have the meanings defined in JDBC.

TRANSACTION_READ_COMMITTED

TRANSACTION_READ_UNCOMMITTED

TRANSACTION_REPEATABLE_READ

TRANSACTION_SERIALIZABLE

Session bean descriptors have these additional attributes:

int **sessionTimeout**—A container may destroy a session bean after an inactive period set by this timeout (value is in seconds). A value of zero means a default value should be used.

int **stateManagementType**—One of:

STATEFUL_SESSION—The bean is assumed to retain a modified state after an invocation returns, preventing the bean from being shared with other clients that request a bean of the same kind.

STATELESS_SESSION—The container can assume that the bean does not retain state across invocations, and that the bean may therefore be pooled. It also assumes the bean as a zero-argument create() method.

Entity bean descriptors have these additional attributes:

String **primaryKeyClassName**—The full name of the class that is used to represent the entity bean's primary key value.

Field[] **containerManagedFields**—The specified fields are to be made persistent by the container. The bean makes sure to set the values of these fields during bean initialization, in its ejbCreate() method.

It should be noted that when referring to a session bean deployed as STATEFUL_SESSION, the term "stateless" refers more to the bean's reusability than to whether or not it actually contains state. Session beans are identified as stateless only so that the server can economize on its creation of new session bean instances. If a bean can be returned to a pool of session bean instances, and used for calls by additional clients without those clients being able to detect that the bean has already been used, then the bean is considered to be stateless, even if the bean maintains a resource connection.

**EJB 1.1 Deployment Descriptors.** The EJB 1.1 deployment descriptor uses XML syntax, and its overall structure is shown Figure 8-8. It has three main parts: a header consisting of descriptive information, an "enterprise-beans" section which lists bean definitions, and an "assembly-descriptor" section which adds information related to access control and transaction control.

```
<ejb-jar>
        <description>...text...</description>            optional
        <display-name>...name to be displayed by tools...</display-name>          optional
        <small-icon>...relative pathname of a 16x16 .jpg or .gif...</small-icon>    optional
        <large-icon>...relative pathname of a 32X32 .jpg or .gif...</large-icon>    optional
        <enterprise-beans>
                <session> one or more <session> and/or <entity> definitions
                          ...see below...
                </session>

                <entity>
                          ...see below...
                </entity>
        </enterprise-beans>

        <assembly-descriptor>            optional
                ...see below...
        </assembly-descriptor>
</ejb-jar>
```

**Figure 8-8** EJB 1.1 deployment descriptor structure.

The enterprise-beans section contains <session> and <entity> descriptor entries for describing session and entity beans respectively. A session descriptor entry begins with a descriptive section and then lists the name of the bean, the class name of the home interface, the class name of the remote interface, and the class name of the bean's implementation class. The name of the bean is an informal name, and need only be unique within the JAR file. The session descriptor contains a <session-type> entry, which indicates whether the bean is a stateful session bean. It also contains a <transaction-type> entry which indicates whether its transactions are bean-managed or container-managed.

After that, the session descriptor may contain zero or more of any or all of these kinds of subsections:

<env-entry>—Defines deployment parameters (called "environment properties") which are read by the application. For example, an application might need a parameter specifying the name of an image file resource: this parameter would be specified as an environment entry. Named data resource factories should *not* be listed here; instead they should be identified in <resource-ref> entries.

<ejb-ref>—Enterprise JavaBeans can refer to other beans by looking up their Home interface in a name service. The EJB server may either provide a name service or interpose itself between the bean and an external name service by requiring the use of a specific JNDI provider implementation. In either case, the application does not have to know at coding time the exact class name of other beans: a virtual name can be defined in an ejb-ref, which binds a virtual name to an actual bean home class. An implementation class binding can also be specified, or deferred until final deployment. This allows implementations to be substituted without code changes.

<security-role-ref>—Defines a virtual security role name, which can be bound to a security role defined elsewhere in the JAR file. This indirection allows beans to be coded without knowing actual security role names ahead of time.

<resource-ref>—Binds a JNDI name to a resource adapter or driver class. This is intended for providing naming indirection for accessing resources such as databases. Credentials for accessing the resource are specified in a server-specific manner, perhaps by a tool which allows the administrator to configure the bound resource name. If the <res-auth> subelement has the value "Bean," it is assumed that the bean application code will supply the required resource factory parameters. If instead the <res-auth> value is "Container," then the application server is expected to provide the parameters (by obtaining them from the deployer or administrator).

The layout of a session bean descriptor is shown in Figure 8-9.

```
<session>                             one or more <session> and/or <entity> definitions
        <description>...text...</description>                optional
        <display-name>...see above...</display-name>  optional
        <small-icon>...see above...</small-icon>         optional
        <large-icon>...see above...</large-icon>         optional
        <ejb-name>...arbitrary name, unique within the JAR file...</ejb-name>
        <home>...text...</home>
        <remote>...fully qualified name of the remote interface...</remote>
        <ejb-class>...fully qualified name of the bean class...</ejb-class>
        <session-type>...Stateful or Stateless...</session-type>
        <transaction-type>...Bean or Container...</transaction-type>

        <env-entry>              zero or more of these
                  <description>...text...</description>              optional
                  <env-entry-name>...name...</env-entry-name>
                  <env-entry-type>...data type of this environment
                            entry; one of java.lang.Boolean,
                            java.lang.String, java.lang.Double,
                            java.lang.Integer, java.lang.Float...
                  </env-entry-type>
                  <env-entry-value>...text...</env-entry-value>   optional
        </env-entry>

         The ejb-ref is used to create a binding to another bean:
        <ejb-ref> zero or more of these
                  <description>...text...</description>              optional
                  <ejb-ref-name>...name used to refer to another bean...</ejb-ref-name>
                  <ejb-ref-type>...Entity or Session...</ejb-ref-type>
                  <home>...Fully qualified name of Home interface of referenced bean...</home>
                  <remote>...Fully qualified name of remote interface of referenced bean...</remote>
                  <ejb-link>...Fully qualified name of the referenced bean class...</ejb-link>      optional
        </ejb-ref>

         The security-role-ref is used to create a binding to a security-role:
        <security-role-ref> zero or more of these
                  <description>...text...</description>              optional
                  <role-name>...name...</role-name>
                  <role-link>...text...</role-link>   optional
        </security-role-ref>

         The resource-ref is used to create a binding to a resource:
        <resource-ref>           zero or more of these
                  <description>...text...</description>              optional
                  <res-ref-name>...name...</res-ref-name>
                  <res-type>...fully qualified class/interface type name of the resource...</res-type>
                  <res-auth>...authentication type: either Bean or Container...</res-auth>
        </resource-ref>
</session>
```

**Figure 8-9** Session bean descriptor.

An entity bean descriptor is similar. The differences are that an entity bean descriptor does not have a <session-type> or <transaction-type> entry, but instead must have <persistence-type> and <primkey-class> entry. (All EJB 1.1 entity beans use container-managed transactions.) The <persistence-type> entry specifies if the entity bean uses container managed persistence, and the

<primkey-class> entry identifies the primary key class of the bean. An entity bean descriptor may have zero or more <cmp-field> entries, each of which identifies a container-managed field. If the bean uses container-managed persistence, it may also have a <primkey-field> entry, which specifies the name of the field which is to contain the object's key value. This field must also be listed in the set of <cmp-field> entries. If the key is a compound key (i.e., maps to multiple cmp-fields), a primkey-field is not specified, and the entity bean must have fields which match (in name and type) the fields in the primary key class. The layout of an entity bean descriptor is shown in Figure 8-10.

```
<entity>
        <description>...see above...</description>       optional
        <display-name>... see above...</display-name>  optional
        <small-icon>... see above...</small-icon>        optional
        <large-icon>... see above...</large-icon>        optional
        <ejb-name>...same as for <session>...</ejb-name>
        <home>...same as for <session>...</home>
        <remote>...same as for <session>...</remote>
        <ejb-class>...same as for <session>...</ejb-class>
        <persistence-type>...Bean or Container...</persistence-type>
        <primkey-class>...fully qualified name of primary key class...</primkey-class>
        <reentrant>...True or False...</reentrant>
        <cmp-field>             zero or more of these
                  <description>...text...</description> optional
                  <field-name>...name of a bean container-managed field...</field-name>
        </cmp-field>
        <primkey-field>         optional
                  ...name of primary key field; special rules apply - see discussion...
        </primkey-field>
        <env-entry>             zero or more of these
                  ...same as for <session>...
        </env-entry>
        <ejb-ref>...same as for <session>...</ejb-ref> zero or more of these
        <security-role-ref> zero or more of these
                  ...same as for <session>...
        </security-role-ref
        <resource-ref>
                  ...same as for <session>...
        </resource-ref> zero or more of these
</entity>
```

**Figure 8-10** Entity bean descriptor.

The last part of a deployment descriptor is the <assembly-descriptor> section. This is an optional section which usually is filled in when beans are assembled into an application. It can contain zero of more of any of these sections:

<security-role>—Defines the name of a security role.

<method-permission>—Lists the bean methods which may be accessed by a specified security role. A bean method is identified by specifying its name and type signature. In addition, since a home interface may have methods that have the same name as bean business methods, the qualifier "Home" or "Remote" may be specified to distinguish which interface the method belongs to.

<container-transaction>—Specifies the transaction characteristics of a bean's business methods.

The layout of the <assembly-descriptor> is shown in Figure 8-11.

```
<assembly-descriptor>          optional

    <security-role>          zero or more of these
        <description>...text...</description>              optional
        <role-name>...name defining a security role...</role-name>
    </security-role>

    <method-permission> zero or more of these
        <description>...text...</description>              optional
        <role-name>              one or more of these
                    ...name of role with this permission...
        </role-name>
        <method>    one or more of these
                    <description>...text...</description>              optional
                    <ejb-name>...name...</ejb-name>
                    <method-intf>          optional
                              ... Home or Remote; specifies if this
                              method belongs to the Home or Remote interface...
                    </method-intf>
                    <method-name>...name of a method, or * ...</method-name>
                    <method-param>          zero or more of these
                              ...fully qualified Java type name...
                    </method-param>
        </method>
    </method-permission>

    <container-transaction>              zero or more of these
        <description>...text...</description>              optional
        <method>    one or more of these
                    ...as defined above...
        </method>
        <trans-attribute>
                    ...one of NotSupported, Supports, Required,
                    RequiresNew, Mandatory, or Never...
        </trans-attribute>
    </container-transaction>

</assembly-descriptor>
```

**Figure 8-11** Assembly descriptor.

### *Passivation*

An EJB container can choose to passivate a bean instance to free memory or other resources. Session beans can be passivated at any time as long as they are not in the middle of servicing a request and are not in a transaction. Entity beans can be passivated while they are in a transaction.

Passivation involves serializing the bean's state and writing it to storage. This has nothing to do with an entity bean's persistence mechanism—passivation is a separate mechanism analogous to swapping a bean out without affecting its transaction or state.

Session beans which have fields which are not serializable, such as resource connections, must make those fields serializable before passivation can take place. The bean programmer must do this in the ejbPassivate() method. You don't have to worry that a connection is in use, because the bean container guarantees that only one thread at a time—in this case the passivation thread—can access a session bean. After the EJB container calls ejbPassivate(), it serializes the entire bean and writes its serialized state to storage.

The counterpart to the ejbPassivate() method is the ejbActivate() method. In this method you should restore any connections you closed in ejbPassivate(). The ejbActivate() method is called after the bean's serialized state is restored from storage. After that, the bean is available again to receive remote calls.

Activation can be caused by an attempt by a client to access the bean, and is transparent to the calling application.

Entity beans can be passivated as well. Remember, however, that passivation is separate from an entity bean's persistence mechanism. In fact, for an entity bean, the container will call ejbStore() before it calls ejbPassivate(), to make sure the bean's current state is synchronized with its persistent storage. It does not commit the transaction—ejbStore() merely synchronizes the in-memory object with whatever persistence mechanism is behind the bean. Since most entity bean containers are proxies for an actual persistence mechanism or database, ejbStore() is necessary to perform this synchronization. After the container calls ejbStore(), it then calls ejbPassivate(), which still has the duty to ensure that any non-transient non-container managed fields are serializable.

### *Context*

When an EJB server instantiates an enterprise bean, it passes it a context object (SessionContext for Session beans, and EntityContext for Entity beans), which the bean can use to obtain various services and information. The methods available from the context include:

**getCallerIdentity**()—Returns the java.security.Identity of the client. *Deprecated in EJB 1.1.*

**getCallerPrincipal**()—Returns the java.security.Principal of the client. This method only exists in EJB 1.1.

**isCallerInRole**(Identity identity)—Returns true if the client has the role specified in the server's identity database. *Deprecated in EJB 1.1.*

**isCallerInRole**(String roleName)—Returns true if the client has the role specified. This method only exists in EJB 1.1.

**getUserTransaction**()—Returns the current JTA user transaction. An alternative method of obtaining the UserTransaction is now proposed by the Java 2 EE specification and involves the use JNDI; this is discussed below.

**setRollbackOnly**()—Mark the current transaction for rollback, so that the transaction will not be allowed to commit after this call returns, even if the transaction is distributed and was started by another bean.

**getEnvironment**()—Returns a Properties object that contains the properties for the bean environment seen by the client. This method is deprecated in EJB 1.1; see discussion below.

**getEJBHome**()—Returns a reference to the EJBHome proxy.

The getUserTransaction() method can be used by the bean to obtain a UserTransaction instance representing the current transaction. This assumes that the bean is deployed with a BEAN_MANAGED transaction attribute. The bean can use the UserTransaction object to initiate and complete its own transaction, using begin() and commit() or rollback() calls.

An alternative method of obtaining the UserTransaction is to use JNDI. This is programmatically similar to the way a COS Transactions Transaction object is obtained. You can use JNDI to obtain the UserTransaction as follows:

```
Context ic = new InitialContext();
UserTransaction txn = (UserTransaction)ic.lookup(
      "java:comp/UserTransaction");
```

(As of this writing, the use of the JNDI name "java:comp/UserTransaction" is preliminary, but will likely become standard.)

The getEnvironment() method is deprecated in EJB 1.1. Instead 1.1-compliant beans should obtain environment properties using JNDI from the special runtime initial context "java:comp/env." For example, to obtain the value of an environment property called "MaxTries":

```
import javax.jndi.*;
...
Context ic = new InitialContext();
Context myContext = (Context)(ic.lookup("java:comp/env"));
Integer maxTries = (Integer)(myContext.lookup("MaxTries"));
```

(Note that for this to work, the EJB server must establish the appropriate JNDI properties to point to its JNDI provider implementation, so that the InitialContext() constructor will instantiate that provider.)

The EJB specification recommends that environment properties should be organized in subcontexts under java:comp/env according to their purpose. In particular, resource factories for JDBC (DataSource drivers) should be in the subcontext java:comp/env/jdbc, and JMS connection factories should be in java:comp/env/jms. You can also create your own subcontexts for your application-specific environment properties.

In Chapter 7, I discussed JNDI and explained how context properties are set when creating an initial context. The EJB 1.1 specification recommends that resource connections created within an Enterprise JavaBean should not have to explicitly specify properties. Instead, resource factory properties should be specified administratively at the server level. For example, instead of doing this:

```
Properties p = new Properties();
p.put("some.factory.name.property",
       "com.someone.SomeJNDIFactory");
Context c = new InitialContext(p);
SomeResFac fac = (SomeResFac)(ic.lookup("my.res.factory");
Connection connection = fac.getConnection(
      "somehost", "cliff", "mypassword");
```

one would merely do this:

```
Context c = new InitialContext();
SomeResFac= (SomeResFac)(ic.lookup("my.res.factory"));
Connection connection = fac.getConnection();
```

and the properties for the initial context and connection would be provided by the built-in JNDI provider. There is nothing to stop a bean from using its own JNDI provider for a special purpose, however, or from supplying arguments to a connection factory.

All data resources used by an EJB 1.1 bean which are to be referenced by JNDI look-up should be identified in <resource-ref> entries in the deployment descriptor. This allows the deployment tools to discover the resources that need configuration and present them to the administrator. Resources flagged with the "Bean" res-auth value are assumed to be configured manually in the bean application code.

### Authentication and Security

The getCallerIdentity() method of the EJBContext returns an instance of Identity representing the caller. The method isCallerInRole(Identity) accepts an Identity. The argument represents a role identity—an identity such as "purchaser" or "loan officer" which does not represent an individual, but instead represents a role an individual may have. The EJB server checks its security configuration to see if the caller has the specified role, and if so, returns true; otherwise, it returns false. This is how a bean can programmatically verify that only authorized parties can perform certain functions. In addition, a bean can be deployed with access control entries to control which users or roles are allowed to invoke the bean or a particular method in the bean.

The type java.security.Identity is deprecated in Java 2, and is replaced by java.security.Principal. Therefore EJB 1.1 deprecates use of Identity and the methods getCallerIdentity() and isCallerInRole(Identity), and replaces them with these methods:

```
java.security.Principal getCallerPrincipal()
boolean isCallerInRole(String roleName)
```

The caller identity (Principal) propagates with a call from one bean to the next. Thus, if bean A is called by user Sam, and bean A calls bean B, then if bean B calls getCallerPrincipal() it will receive Sam's identity (Principal) as a result. However, at the present time user identity may not propagate across servers of different brands, since the protocol for this propagation has not yet been standardized. Servers using IIOP will eventually be able to propagate user identity.

**Propagation of Authentication Between Server Components and Drivers.** If your data resources allow you to store user identities and possibly access rights in an external repository, and your app servers can use the same repositories for user and perhaps access control information, then you only need to authenticate the user once. This is known as "single sign-on." Each of your app servers will apply the current user identity (principal) to determine access rights to its beans, and ideally, the app server will also use the same identity for its connection pools. If the current user belongs to the role which is allowed access to the connection pool, the user will be able to access it. The app server will have to present credentials to the data resource when creating the connection pool. If the data resource can use the same repository as the app server uses for its own users, you will only have to administer the users and roles in one place. These scenarios are shown in Figure 8-12.

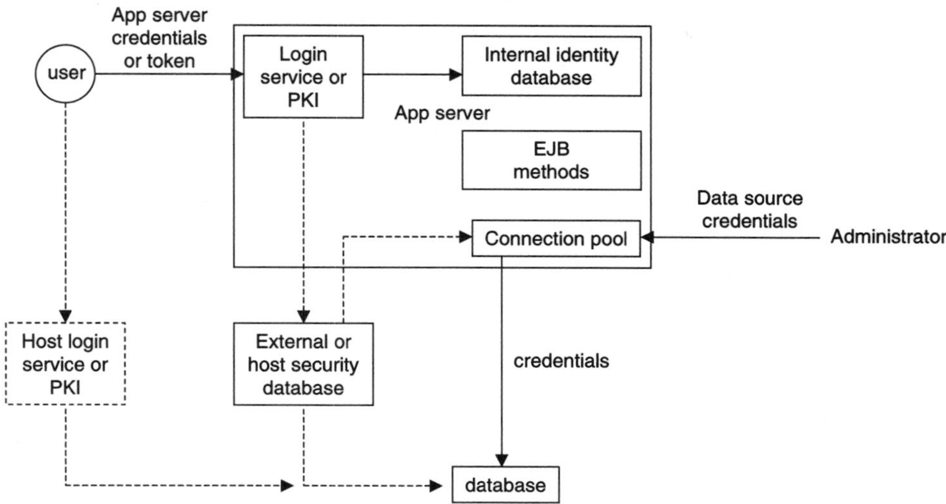


**Figure 8-12** Scenarios for credential entry and sharing.

Even if you are not able to consolidate your user and role administration to this degree, it is still advantageous to use an external repository (perhaps a database, if not a directory server) as your app server's user database, if the app server permits that. Many app servers allow you to choose between a built-in user database, or an external repository such as LDAP or a relational database. This means that user credentials (or a validated certificate for PKI users) will need to be stored in the repository and be retrievable in a secure way by application servers.

Some products also allow connection pools to be created dynamically and to obtain their credential information from an external source such as a database or LDAP server. In all these scenarios, of course, the servers should authenticate each other and may require server certificates for that purpose.

### *Integration with CORBA Security*

The CORBA security model is important for EJB because IIOP has been chosen as the basis for EJB interoperability. The IIOP/SECP model is therefore the model that will be used for EJB, and the stream will have to pass both transaction context and security context in a standard way.

At present there are only a few implementations of CORBA Security, which is an enormously complex standard, and none which extend it into the EJB realm. At this writing it appears that EJB vendors are only now beginning to talk to CORBA Security providers.

Many CORBA Security products are DCE-based, and typically use Kerberos for passing back access rights information to requestors. In some products, SSL sessions can be used, and PKI user identities (typically the user's distinguished name) are mapped to DCE users. The problem for EJB integration will be to map CORBA-Sec users to EJB users, and EJB user roles to CORBA rights and DCE or Kerberos ticket attributes.

The eventual path will be to use LDAP as a security information repository for CORBA security implementations, but LDAP has a long way to go to become scalable, and is presently missing a standard authentication model and features for replication.

### *Adding Application-Specific Authorization*

The EJB model defines a way for a deployer to specify which users or user roles may access a servlet, on a method-specific basis. In many applications, however, this is not sufficient, and authorization must be determined by other factors. In particular, it may be necessary to see if a user belongs to some kind of group which is defined in the application domain but is not defined in the user domain, or access rights might change dynamically depending on the actions of some users. For example, access to a given piece of data might be contingent on one user flagging the data to allow another user to access it.

It almost goes without saying that if the access rules are outside the EJB domain, they must be implemented by the application. This is such a common requirement, however, that it deserves to be addressed. In some cases it is possible to control access to the data using the independent authorization capabilities of the database. Most likely this will not work, because the application server and database represent separate security realms, and also because establishing a database connection for each user is required.

The solution is to write a security manager for your application. You cannot extend the VM's security manager to do this, since that security manager is installed by the EJB server, but you can nevertheless mimic that model and provide a security management class which implements the security policies you need for your application. This is depicted in Figure 8-13.

To make this work, your beans must use the security manager. Every bean method must call the security manager at the beginning of a business method. When doing so, it must pass the authenticated user Principal. This is because, at present, the Java VM does not have a defined interface or capability to associate a user with a thread. (Future VMs will.) The application server most likely has this ability, but if it does, it is not accessible through a standard exposed API.

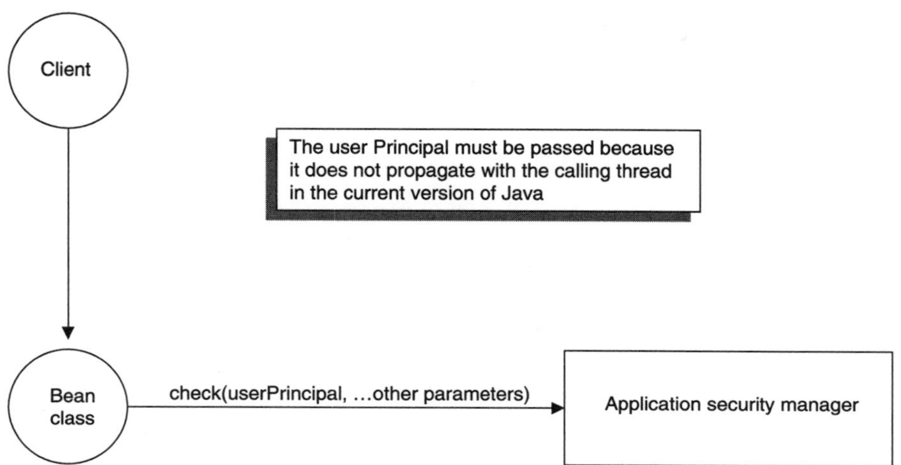


**Figure 8-13** Adding application-specific authorization to your EJBs.

Therefore, you should pass the user's identity with a Principal parameter. Your security manager will then use this and other factors—possibly passed as parameters as well—to determine if the user has the right to perform a designated action. You can follow the Java security manager paradigm and throw an exception if access is denied, or you can simply return a boolean indicating if access is allowed.

One situation which often arises, which was alluded to earlier, is the ability for an application to determine access for one user based on the actions of another—that is, a user who has the authority to approve or delegate an activity authorizes that another user be allowed to perform a specified access or join a certain application-defined role. Those who have used the UNIX "su" command are familiar with the concept of temporarily assuming user roles. In fact, it may be that a user may be given multiple roles or authorizations dynamically and hold several at the same time. This is in essence a workflow authorization model, in which someone needs to be granted access to certain pieces of data at defined points during its lifecycle, in contrast to the relatively static model for access to EJB class methods provided by the EJB security model.

Delegation can be accomplished in many ways, but one way which is straightforward to implement and satisfies most delegation needs is to chain the delegated identities. Therefore, every EJB method requiring authorization would contain an additional parameter consisting of the user's current identity (Principal) chain. A user would then be granted permission to perform an operation based on whether it currently has the required role in the chain. (Most likely additional parameters would be needed by the application security manager to provide context information needed to make its authorization decision, such as which piece of data needs to be granted access to.) Of course, in order to obtain a role and add it to one's chain, an appropriate delegation process must be used and executed by someone with the authorization to run it.

### *What You Write, and What the Tools Generate*

To create an enterprise bean, you have to create three things: a Home interface that defines methods for creating instances of the bean (actually, proxies for the bean); a remote bean interface, which defines the transactions or services that the bean provides; and a class that implements the business logic of these transactions or services. The only implementation code you have to write when doing this is the code that implements the business logic—all the rest is generated by an EJB development tool provided by the middleware vendor.

The middleware tools generate an implemenetation of the Home interface, which maps the create() calls to the bean create methods with corresponding signatures. The middleware tools also generate a bean class and a proxy class. The generated bean class has methods which correspond to methods in the remote interface, and maps these to corresponding methods (which must be present) in the business logic class you have written. The generated proxy has the methods defined in the remote interface, and maps these to the corresponding methods in the bean class. Obviously there must be agreement between all these method signatures. The driving definitions for the method signatures are the home interface and the remote interface you have defined. All this is depicted for a session bean in Figure 8-14.

This is what you need to implement for a session bean:

1. Define the Home interface, with the createXXX(...) methods your application requires. Include create() at a minimum.
2. Define the bean's remote interface, which defines its business methods.
3. Write the implementation—the business class.

In addition to its business methods, your session bean's business class should implement:

> **ejbCreate**(...)—Your bean should initialize all fields in the ejbCreate() method. Some of the initial values will likely come from arguments to the ejbCreate(...) method. If you establish resource connections in the ejbCreate() method, you should close them in the ejbPassivate() method, and reopen them in the ejbActivate() method. If the bean is declared to be stateless, this method must have no arguments.

EJBHome:
void **remove**(Object primKey)
EJBMetaData **getEJBMetaData**()

generated

Home
interf
<remote>* **create**(...)

Home
create(...)

Implementation
class
void **ejbCreate**(...)**

EJB
interf
**methods**

EJB
object
methods

EJB
methods

**methods**

EJBObject:
void **remove**()
EJBHome **getEJBHome**()
Handle **getHandle**()
Object **getPrimaryKey**()
boolean **isIdentical**(EJBObject)

* Return type of a Home create() method must be the bean's remote interface type.

** The ejbCreate() method of a stateless session bean must take zero arguments.

SessionBean:
void **ejbActivate**()
void **ejbPassivate**()
void **ejbRemove**()
void **setSessionContext**(
SessionContext ctx)

optional:

SessionSynchronization:
void **afterBegin**()
void **beforeCompletion**()
void **afterCompletion**(
boolean committed)

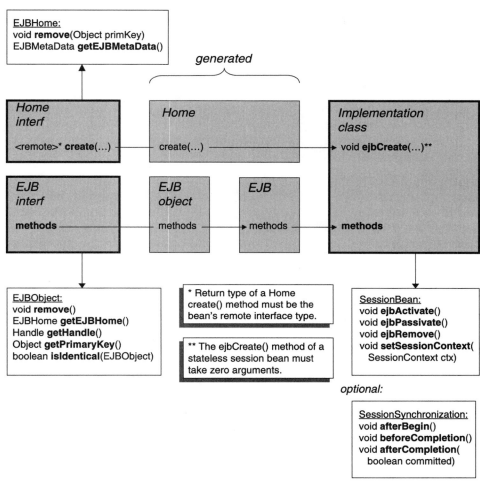

**Figure 8-14** Session Bean interfaces and classes.

**ejbRemove**()—Most likely this will be a no-op for a session bean, but you are required to implement it.

**ejbPassivate**()—This method is called when the bean is not in a transaction, and the container needs to temporarily free the bean's resources—to "swap the bean out." In this method, you must release any resource connections you are holding (such as database connections), and leave the session bean in a *serializable* state. This is necessary so that the container can serialize the bean-write that state to temporary storage. Later, the bean may be "swapped back," and its serialized state restored. After that, the ejbActivate() method will be called, and in that method you can reestablish the bean's resource connections. EJB 1.1 specifies that certain special kinds of references do not need to be Serializable, including remote references to other EJBs, a reference of type SessionContext, and a reference to the container's EJB environment naming context (java:comp/env). Note that *any* EJB attribute marked transient will be ignored during passivation.

**ejbActivate**()—This method is called when a bean is being restored from the passivated state. The bean's serialized state is reconstituted first, and then ejbActivate() is called. In the ejbActivate() method, you have the opportunity to restore any resource connections that you closed in the ejbPassivate() method. Note that some servers may call this before ejbPassivate() is ever called, and in fact may even call it multiple times. Therefore, the implementation of ejbPassivate() should be able to be called repeatedly, and should not assume anything about the prior state of the bean.

**setSessionContext**(SessionContext)—You can elect to save the value passed in. You likely will use it only if the bean manages its own transactions or security roles. Saving this value only makes sense if the session bean is declared to be STATEFUL_SESSION, since stateless beans are never passivated. The variable used to store the session context should not be transient.

If the bean is STATEFUL_SESSION, and its transactions span method calls, you might also need to implement:

**beforeCompletion**()—In this method, make sure any cached state is written to the required data resources. This is your last chance before the middleware invokes commit(), or you may choose instead to call setRollbackOnly() on the EJBContext. Less useful but included here for completeness, you might also implement afterBegin() and afterCompletion(). If your bean performs a complete operation with each call, you may choose to put your database update code right in the business methods instead of in beforeCompletion(). If, however, some of the bean's business methods produce intermediate results, which should only be saved when all the required business methods have been called, you can put the actual database updates in the beforeCompletion() method.

The business methods of your bean have these restrictions:

- Cannot use multithreading or monitors.
- All static fields must be final.
- Unless the bean's deployment defines its transactions as TX_BEAN_MANAGED, it cannot directly access the transaction management services, or perform a commit or rollback.
- Cannot change its java.security.Identity.

Do not provide a constructor for the bean implementation class. The default zero-argument constructor is accessed by the server to instantiate the bean, but the server assumes that all initialization occurs in the ejbCreate() method—*not* in the constructor. This is important because the server may reuse the bean instance for different clients.

If your session bean uses resource connections, such as database connections, you have a choice of opening those connections in the ejbCreate() method and keeping them open for the bean's lifetime (the session), or opening the connections in the business methods that require them and immediately closing them after use. If resource pooling is available for the connection, then there is little overhead in opening and closing a connection, and so opening them as needed is an acceptable option. The right choice depends on how many client sessions you expect to exist at any one time. In general you should only consider keeping connections open if pooling is not available, or if the number of concurrent sessions is expected to be smaller than the pool size.

For an entity bean, the user-written classes and generated code are as depicted in Figure 8-15.

This is what you need to implement for an entity bean:

1. Define the Home interface, with the createXXX(...) and findXXX(...) methods your application requires. Include create() and findByPrimaryKey(...) at a minimum.
2. Define the bean's remote interface, which defines its business methods.
3. Write the implementation—the business class.

In addition to its business methods, your entity bean's business class should implement:

> **ejbCreate**(...)—If your entity bean has no container-managed fields, as specified by its deployment descriptor, then its ejbCreate() method needs to create an instance of the bean in its underlying data resource. Thus, your ejbCreate() method will have database calls if your bean's persistence is not container-managed. If the bean has any container-managed fields, the entire bean is assumed to be container managed. In that case, your bean should initialize all fields in the ejbCreate() method, since the container will then take those initialized values and use them to create the corresponding record in the underlying data resource. Some of the initial values will likely come from arguments to the ejbCreate(...) method. Note that if an entity is created by external means, such as manually entered SQL statements, then an ejbCreate() method will never be called for that instance. The ejbCreate() methods must return the primary key of the entity they create. An attempt to create an entity which already exists must result in a DuplicateKeyException. You may also choose

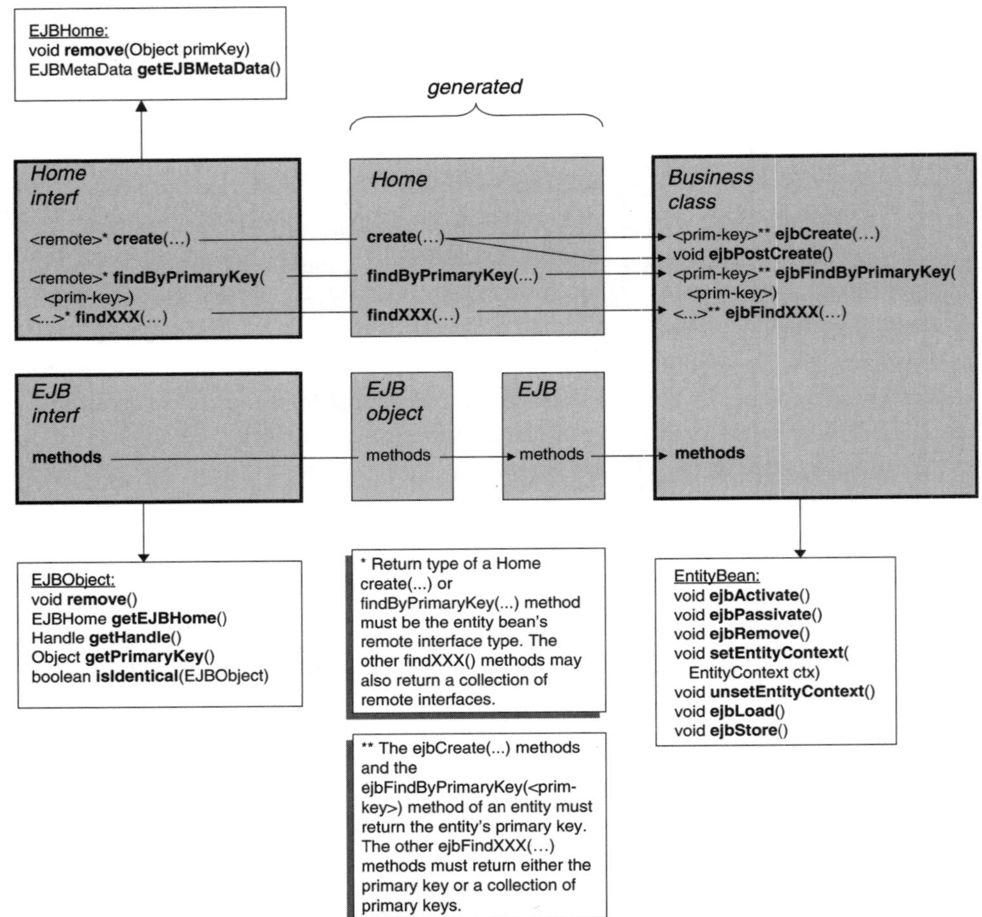


**Figure 8-15** Entity Bean code generation.

to implement an **ejbPostCreate**(...) method. An ejbPostCreate(...) method takes the same arguments as the ejbCreate(...) method with the same signature; it is called after ejbCreate(...) is called. The purpose of the ejbPostCreate(...) methods is that by definition, the entity has been created when they are executed, making the entity's remote reference available.

**ejbRemove**()—This is the method that is called when the bean is destroyed. Its job is to remove all records of the bean from the underlying data resource. If the bean uses container-managed persistence, this method is a no-op; but if it uses bean managed persistence, you must include the appropriate calls to the underlying data resource.

**ejbFindByPrimary**Key(...)—This method must take the primary key as an argument and return the primary key. Thus, it is seemingly a no-op method.

**ejbPassivate()**—The same considerations apply as for a session bean. However, for entity beans, this call may occur in a transaction, but the container then first will call ejbStore() before calling ejbPassivate(). The ejbPassivate() method must free any resources it is holding, and leave all non-transient non-container-managed fields in a serializable state.

**ejbActivate**()—The same considerations apply as for a session bean.

**ejbLoad**()—In a container-managed entity bean, this is called after fields are read in for synchronization. Beans can use this method to uncompress values. If your bean uses bean-managed persistence, you must implement this method and provide the required data resource calls (JDBC or whatever) to load data from the data resource and replicate it in the in-memory bean instance. Note that many EJB server implementations free resources used by an entity without calling ejbPassivate(). Therefore, your ejbLoad() method should not assume that connections established in the ejbCreate() or ejbActivate() methods still exist. In fact, they may even have closed as a result of a database reset.

**ejbStore**()—This method is the inverse of the ejbLoad() method. It is called by the container to replicate the object's in-memory state to the underlying persistent store. If the bean uses container-managed persistence, you do not put any code in this method. If it uses bean-managed persistence, you must implement it and include the required data resource calls to replicate the bean's in-memory state to the underlying data resource. The ejbLoad() and ejbStore() methods do not initiate *global* transaction completion. They merely serve to synchronize object state and database state, since the object typically represents a surrogate for a record or instance of some kind in the database.

**setEntityContext**(EntityContext)—Save the value passed in.

**unsetEntityContext**()—The container calls this when it disposes of a bean instance permanently. This is the last chance to free any resources that were allocation in setEntityContext().

You may also need to implement these:

**ejbFind**<...>()—For beans which use bean-managed persistence, you must implement the find methods you have defined. This will involve searching the underlying data resource to obtain the record, or whatever instance represents the bean instance in that underlying data resource.

### *Comparing EJB References*

Don't use equals() and hashCode() on EJB references. An EJB server is free to pool beans, and you may not have the same actual instance from one call to the next. To compare two EJB references to see if they refer to the same bean (i.e., the same server bean instance, not the same client stub!), use the isIdentical(EJBObject) method on the remote reference.

There are some interesting semantics with the isIdentical() method. The method returns true when used to compare two references to a stateless session bean which have the same Home interface. This is because all stateless beans from the same Home are considered to be equivalent. The same is not true for stateful session beans, and the isIdentical() method will return true for two stateful session bean references only if they are from the same Home and refer to the same session. When isIdentical() is used to compare two entity beans, it will return true only if the two entities are from the same Home and have the same primary key value.

### *What to Deploy with Client Applications*

Clients which access beans do not need the bean server implementation code, as you would expect. What they do need is the bean's remote interface, and all the generated stub classes created by the EJB tools. While it is true that an RMI-based bean will be able to get by with just the Home interface stub, since RMI will download the bean's stub as needed, you should not rely on this because it will not work for IIOP which does not support dynamic downloading of classes. For example, if your bean has a remote interface, a home interface, and an implementation class, an EJB compiler will generate these items:

- Home interface stub
- Bean stub
- Home implementation
- Other classes to implement the interposition layer

Your clients should therefore be deployed with the Home interface, the remote interface, and all the generated stubs.

### *Persistence Mechanism*

The actual data resource access that must be performed by an entity bean implementation is usually one that the EJB server provider specializes in. For example, a product which provides JDBC drivers may also provide a relational mapping layer. The application programmer then creates new entity instances and updates their attributes instead of inserting rows and modifying field values. If the entity implementation code which makes the database calls is included in the bean implementation, accessible to the programmer in the ejbLoad() and ejbStore() methods, this is known as "bean-managed" persistence. If the mapping is transparent and performed automatically by the server, it is known as "container-managed" persistence.

If the entity bean uses container-managed persistence, then the deployment descriptor must state which bean attributes are to be kept persistent. The container then makes sure that these attributes are written to the underlying data resource, according to the bean's deployed transaction rules, immediately prior to whenever a transaction commits. The attributes of a bean which uses container-managed persistence must be declared public in the bean class.

The nice thing about using container-managed persistence is that regardless how the container-managed persistence is implemented, one is not dependent on the mechanism used. It should be possible in most cases to swap one container for another, and use either a relational database or an object database without affecting application code.

**How App Servers Save Entity State.** The way in which a container-managed bean's fields are mapped to a backend store depends, of course, on the kind of storage. EJB servers which provide relational mapping can provide either a very simple mapping which merely maps bean fields to relational table entries, or a sophisticated mapping can be provided which attempts to implement smart references for lazy instantiation to reduce the number of tables that must be accessed. There is great variety in this area. A feature that is especially hard to map is lists or collections, and arrays tend to be hard to map with good performance, since the arrays need to be filled when the bean is instantiated, and this may involve a large number of retrievals. Another problem with mapping beans to relational databases is that the mapping tool needs to make assumptions about the concurrency model used by the database, yet it has no direct control over the database. It is therefore hard to write a generic mapping tool which works with multiple databases without resorting to the most pessimistic policy. Finally, the loose coupling between the relational database and the application server does not provide an opportunity to coordinate caching and load balancing.

Object oriented databases have an easier time providing a mapping from EJB. Essentially each entity attribute becomes an object database persistent object. As such, it must be type-compatible with the types supported by the object oriented database—or the mapping layer must convert it to those types. Object oriented databases also can more effectively map collection types, since they typically supports such types natively.

You might think that an entity persistence layer which maps to an object database might not have to be refreshed, since the entity is stateful and so are the objects it points to. That is not the case however. Object references in most object databases become stale at the end of a transaction. Some databases allow them to remain valid ("hollow"), but in that case, the references are specific to the session or connection, making use of a connection pool impossible. Therefore, an EJB-to-object

database mapping most likely needs to refresh entity attributes just as frequently as a relational mapping would. Still, the task of refreshing is easier since the mapping is more direct.

At this writing, the Gemstone application server is the only widely used product which provides an embedded object database with an EJB container. Others are under development, including a merging of the ODI ObjectStore object database with the WebLogic server. The EJB server and object oriented database combination is a powerful one, and it will be interesting to see how it develops.

**Mapping CORBA References.** In general, the kind of data you plan to map should determine the kind of container you use. Containers are either general purpose or special purpose. General purpose containers will not do a good job of mapping or storing specialized kinds of data. Special purpose containers will do a better job of storing the kind of data they are designed for. It can be expected that a container obtained from an ORB vendor is going to have an efficient and effective means of mapping IIOP object references as well as the CORBA types (including Any, which is Serializable). Other non-ORB containers may resort to generic schemes including Java serialization. Some containers may not be able to automatically map CORBA object references. Eventually, when RMI over IIOP support is required, all EJB containers will be able to store these references.

If you write your own bean-managed persistence mapping, you can, of course, store CORBA object references in stringified form.

**Converting Attribute Types Prior to Storage.** If the bean uses container-managed persistence, the ejbStore() method is called immediately prior to when the container stores the bean's attributes. This provides an opportunity to convert the attributes to storable types before they are actually stored. For example, CORBA references could be converted to stringified form. In that case, the actual references would have to be declared as transient attributes, and the stringified version would be identified in the bean's deployment descriptor as the persistent attributes.

This technique is especially useful when a relational database is used to persistify complex object attributes. If an entity attribute is of a non-built-in type (not an int, a String, etc.), the container tools may not know how to represent it and may store it as a blob, or it may store it in a form which is hard to query using standard relational database query tools. It depends on the sophistication of the container. To avoid this, you can insert code in the ejbStore() method which converts the entity attributes to an attribute-based form, which is more effectively handled by the persistence mechanism and which results in a schema which can be queried with SQL tools. Of course, your ejbLoad() method would have to do the reverse process to convert the attribute-based representation back to an object representation.

You might wonder why you would not simply store the entity's data right from the start in a form which is easily mapped by the container. There are several reasons why this might not be the case. One is that Java applications are object-oriented, and therefore do not naturally result in structures which map to a relational database. In fact, the application might be deployed initially with an object database persistence mechanism. If the application is later migrated to a relational mapped container, it would be nice to have to change as little of the application as possible. The approach outlined here allows changes to be encapsulated within the entity representation.

Another reason why the entity data might be represented with complex objects instead of simple attributes is that the entity might make available a streamable version of itself. The streamable version might implement the business methods, but represent a lightweight version of the object which can be streamed by value to clients so that they can operate on a local instance. The entity bean implementation might incorporate an instance of the steamable class and delegate to it for its behavior. The entity would then only have one attribute: the enclosed streamable object, which is likely to be a complex object. The ejbLoad() method can reveal this object's structure to the container by converting its internal data to entity attributes immediately before storage.

### *Persistified References*

An EJB client can obtain a lightweight storable handle to an EJB object by calling getHandle() or the EJB reference. The Handle can be serialized, and used later. However, it is not portable from one brand of EJB server to another. Since session beans don't have a lifetime beyond the session, it does not make sense to save their handles. Some servers may in fact allow a session bean to continue to exist after a session closes, and the session object may be reobtained by using a persistified handle. The usefulness of this is dubious, however, since it cannot be guaranteed to work.

Saving entity bean handles is of questionable value as well, since all entity beans have a key, and it makes more sense to merely save the key. The handle is therefore of most value for entity container implementations which need to persistify inter-bean references.

### *Embedded References to Other Enterprise JavaBeans*

The Enterprise JavaBeans spec describes entity beans as persistent objects. Most persistent object databases provide a means for objects to reference other objects. What happens if one of your entity beans contains a reference to another entity bean, and you declare that reference field to be persistent, using container-managed persistence? Will the reference be maintained?

The short answer is yes, but let's consider the issues. First of all, if the type of the reference were declared to be a normal Java object reference to the EJB business class, the reference might not be persistifiable because all persistent fields must be of a serializable type. Even if the referenced bean class is serializable, a local reference is not a type of reference you can export to remote clients. What you would need to store is a remote reference. Thus, persistent fields which reference other entity beans should be of the appropriate remote entity bean type, and be set using the normal EJB client APIs. In other words, one entity bean should obtain references to other entity beans the same way that a remote client would, even if both beans are on the same machine. As long as you follow this rule, entity references should be persistifiable.

Many servers implement entity beans as RMI objects. The most common RMI server object base type is UnicastRemoteObject. References to this type are not necessarily usable across a restart of the server. Thus, you cannot reasonably store them on a long term basis. What you can do, however, is obtain the bean's handle using getHandle(), and store that for future use. The handle is guaranteed to be usable across server restarts.

The way in which inter-bean references are implemented for entity beans is therefore up to the application server. You can now see that an EJB server which is backed by a true object database might have a significant advantage for implementing container-managed persistence, since there effectively needs to be no mapping layer, or at most a trivial one: the only requirement is that object references be of a type which is persistifiable by the object database, or a reference to another entity bean. Inter-bean references can be mapped as entity bean handles, if not stored as actual serialized or stringified references. The relational analog is for the EJB server to provide an object-to-relational mapping process for converting inter-bean references into equivalent foreign key lookups. I have already discussed such "blend" products in Chapter 6.

EJB 2 will undoubtedely say more about the persistent reference issue. For one thing, EJB 2 will likely require IIOP, and if a vendor chooses to implement entity beans as persistent CORBA objects, then those object references will be usable across server restarts. However, the vendor might not choose to use persistent objects and still provide IIOP.

The EJB architecture team feels that some vendors may feel reference reuse across server crashes is a quality of service issue, in that if a server is so reliable (or redundant) that it never appears to crash to the user's application, then a reference would not need to be durable in that way. However, the issue of reuse across manual restarts is still open.

A somewhat pathological case is if your entity bean has container-managed fields which are references to session beans. This may seem illogical since session bean

instances are supposed to be private, and storing them in an entity bean effectively shares them with all users of the entity bean. However, as long as the session pointed to by the session references still exists, the stored references should be persistifiable because they will likely be serializable remote object stubs. Despite this, we have observed that some server products throw errors when reconstituting persistified session references in an entity bean.

### *Runtime Concurrency Issues*

In general, the server assumes beans are *not* reentrant. That means that no two concurrent calls will ever share a bean instance (even from the same client), unless the bean is an entity bean and is explicitly declared to be reentrant. Thus, the CORBA "shared server" model—the prevalent one—is not even used by EJB!

An EJB server provides the runtime environment for its business objects. The business object invocation model used is RMI. The server provides the threads that are used to execute incoming remote calls, and so one does not have to implement multithreading as is the case for some ORB products. The server may use the standard RMI invocation that comes as part of Java, or it may provide its own. Regardless, the server component that is actually receiving the call is the EJBObject generated by the middleware tools. This interposed component is then responsible for forwarding the call to the user-written business object. This interposition allows the server to manage how and when the business object actually receives its remote calls.

The assumption of non- reentrancy is a departure from simple RMI semantics, in which incoming calls are automatically routed to the server object, even if it is still in the process of handling an earlier call. Normal RMI assumes that the server object is either reentrant, or that it has taken special steps to serialize or guard its non-reentrant portions. EJB removes this burden from the business object developer by shifting it to the interposed EJB layers.

Therefore, when an Enterprise JavaBean receives a remote call, it can be sure that it is not in the process of handling another call. The EJB server guarantees that all accesses to the bean are serialized (occur one at a time) or that separate instances are used. If the bean is a session bean, concurrent access is prohibited, and the server will throw an exception to the client. If the bean is an entity bean, concurrent accesses belonging to different transactions are serialized, and one call must wait until a prior one completes; or the server is free to create another instance of the entity bean for another transaction in order to provide highter concurrency. Two simultaneous calls to the same logical entity bean instance (i.e., having the same key) from the same transaction will result in an exception.

Note that if a UI allows the user to click again before a session bean method completes, a RemoteException will result. In addition, if two frames of an

HTML page simultaneously access the same servlet using the same session bean, a RemoteException will also result. This scenario has already been discussed in "Multiple UI Frames and Concurrency" on page 626.

A session bean can be declared in its deployment descriptor to be *stateless*—STATELESS_SESSION. This is a declaration by the bean writer that the application does not depend on the state of the bean being saved from one invocation to the next. Given this tip, the EJB server is free to reinitialize the bean with each invocation. This allows the server to place the bean in a pool, and reuse it for other clients. On each invocation of a stateless session bean, the caller requires that the bean is in an initialized state. The caller does not know or care if the bean exists in a pool; as far as it knows, it has a fresh bean, created just for it. The pooling is merely an optimization, to save on Java heap accesses. A stateless bean may have only one create() method in its Home interface, and it may not have any arguments.

You might think that a stateless bean is not good for much, because it cannot retain connections to resources, and reobtaining resource connections with every invocation is too expensive. However, that is not the case. First of all, a stateless bean *can* retain resource connections as long as those connections appear to be stateless across calls to the bean. Second, since resources are typically pooled, reobtaining them is not expensive, and so there is little lost by releasing a resource connection and reobtaining it with every invocation, as long as the resource is a pooled resource. (Still, there may be some overhead in performing the resource lookup, unless this too is cached.)

Another advantage to stateless session beans is that the implementor only has to write the business methods. The implementor does not have to write passivation code to release and later reestablish stateful connections. However, resource connections may still have to be established and released in business methods or in the ejbCreate() and ejbRemove() methods.

Note that if your session bean is not declared stateless, and you neglect to close any connections it uses after you are done with the bean, the connection resources will remain tied up until either you explicitly remove the bean, or the container automatically removes it. It is therefore a good practice to close connections when you are done with them, and to remove your session beans as well.

Entity beans, by definition, maintain state across invocations. Access to a bean's state is protected by the isolation policies of the underlying data resource and the container. The EJB server may use the underlying database to implement concurrency control, or it may impose its own object concurrency control—as long as the effect is consistent with the desired isolation level.

You might think that serializing access to a bean might have severe implications for application concurrency and throughput. The considerations are different for

session beans and entity beans. In the case of a session bean, each client gets its own copy, and so concurrency is not an issue. In the case of an entity bean, an entity bean instance represents a particular element of data, analogous to a row in a table. Serializing access to a single table row does not usually impact performance, unless the row is a singleton of some kind, such as a counter, which all clients must frequently access. The solution to such a singleton not being a bottleneck is to set its isolation level appropriately, or replicate it, and make accesses to it as brief as possible. The entity bean facade, therefore, does not itself impose any special concurrency limiting aspects. It is merely a component object layer on top of a data resource of some kind. In addition, an entity container may create multiple physical instances representing the same logical entity in order to service multiple concurrent transactions.

Not all EJB servers perform this concurrency-improving optimization, however. A peculiar situation arises if a transactional client (a transaction-aware user program or another bean) invokes an entity and then the invocation completes and returns, but the transaction continues for awhile in the client. In that case, the entity which was invoked is still a participant in the transaction, and so it will block against other client calls from other transactions until the first transaction completes—which may be some time later. A more highly optimized container will create additional entity instances for the other transactions so that they do not have to wait.

The difficulty is that to do this, the container has to be aware of the isolation policy of the entity's underlying data. If the entity uses container-managed persistence, the container is intimately familiar with how the data is mapped. If the entity uses bean-managed persistence, it is not, and there is no way to force the entity to "sync" with the container (thereby updating the underlying database of entity state changes) without completing the transaction (you are not supposed to explicitly call ejbStore). Therefore, you should not rely on particular isolation modes when you use entity beans.

#### *Transaction Association*

It is the responsibility of the EJB container to keep track of what transaction is associated with a bean instance. An entity bean can participate in multiple transactions over time, in which case the EJB container can use whatever means it chooses to logically serialize access to the bean's state. One possibility is that the container might rely on the concurrency control mechanisms of the underlying persistent data resource. Alternatively, the container might perform its own concurrency control, and allow only one client to access the bean at a time. In the former case, there are actually multiple transactions associated with the bean. However, for any bean, there is at most one transaction associated with a given remote call, and only one call at a time is possible for a particular physical bean instance.

If the container creates a new transaction to handle the incoming remote call, it must associate that transaction with the thread it dispatches to handle the remote call. If, instead, the incoming call carries a transaction context with it, the container must associate that transaction with the service thread.

Performing this association is not a problem, because the EJB server is responsible for creating all threads that run in it. This is one reason why beans are not allowed to create their own threads, because to do so would be to step outside of the transaction management mechanism.

One possible way an EJB server can create a service thread for an incoming call and then dispatch the call to the bean is shown Figure 8-16. Other designs are possible—this is merely for illustration. In this scenario, a call dispatcher

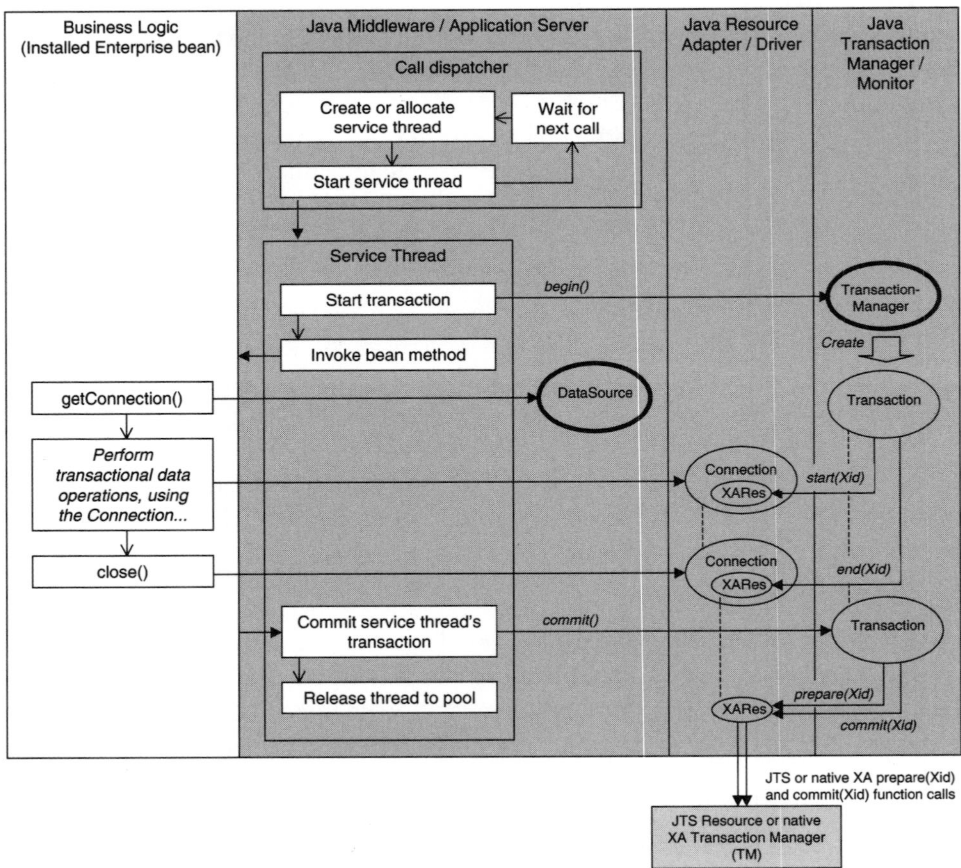


**Figure 8-16** How an EJB server establishes a transaction on behalf of a bean method.

handling incoming calls is responsible for creating an appropriate service thread with transaction context association. This call dispatcher might be part of an ORB, or it might be part of an RMI implementation. An alternative design is to use a standard dispatching mechanism, such as is delivered with Sun's RMI implementation, and create the service transaction association in the EJBObject layer. Regardless, the EJB container is responsible for performing the association, and starting and completing the transaction. Whether this logic is embedded in the service thread itself or is included in a generated layer is up to the implementation.

### Bean Demarcated Transactions

A bean can bypass automatic transaction creation, and initiate and terminate its own transaction. It does so in a way that is integrated with the EJB container, so that callers of the bean, or other beans this bean calls, do not know the bean is managing its own transaction. A bean that creates and manages its own transaction is deployed with the TX_BEAN_MANAGED transaction attribute. Beginning with EJB 1.1, only session beans are allowed to manage their own transactions.

First the bean calls EJBContext.getUserTransaction() to obtain a transaction object. This object is just a handle to the transaction manager—no transaction is in progress at this point. Thus, the bean does not have to locate a suitable transaction manager—it uses the one provided by the EJB server.

Using the transaction object given it by the EJB server, the bean begins a transaction by invoking begin(). From that point on, the bean executes in the context of the new transaction, which is propagated with all requests from that bean to other beans. The transaction remains in effect even if the bean returns from its current remote call without committing or rolling back. When the bean is ready to complete the transaction, it issues either a commit or a rollback on the transaction object. The overall scenario is shown in Figure 8-17. Later I will show an actual example of a bean-demarcated transaction.

### Client Demarcated Transactions (Transactional Clients)

Normally a client is not a participant in a transaction. The transaction executes on the server, on behalf of the client. The transaction begins at the moment the bean method call arrives at the EJB server, and (assuming the bean does not invoke any asynchronous facilities, such as CORBA DII) completes when the method returns. In the process, the bean may call other beans, and propagate the transaction. However, those calls themselves complete in the course of the original method call. Thus, an ordinary client does not actually participate in the transaction directly—it is merely invoking a remote service which performs a transaction on the client's behalf.

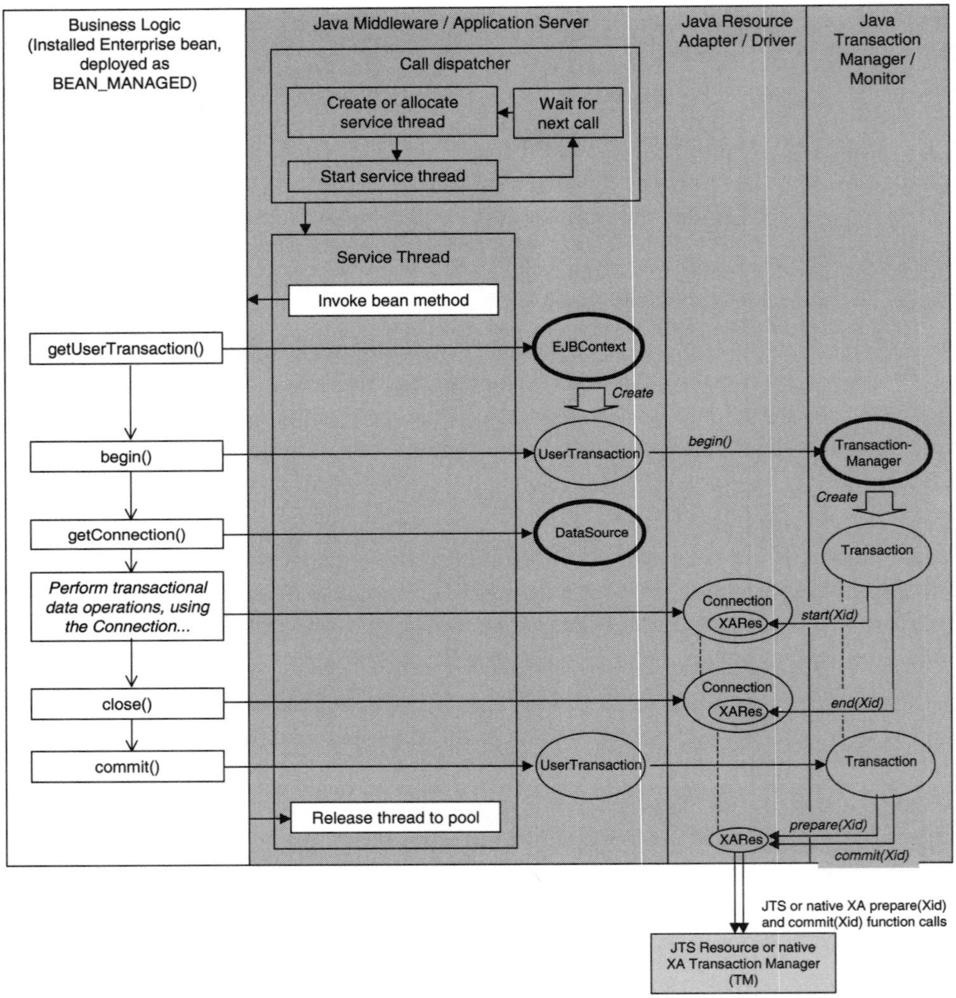

**Figure 8-17** How a TX_BEAN_MANAGED bean method performs its own transaction creation and completion.

This means that if a client thread performs two method calls in succession, each will execute in a separate transaction created just for it. Figure 8-18 depicts this. In fact, even if the client performs the two method calls concurrently in separate client threads, they will still each execute in a separate transaction. A server could, in theory, associate these two transactions, if the server recognizes that they originate from the same client connection. Many server products use a single connec-

tion for all requests from the same client process. However, to combine transactions from separate threads without the client explicitly requesting that would violate the spirit of JTA, which assumes an association between a thread and a transaction: if two separate threads within the same process are to be associated with the same transaction, the client should request that—it should not be automatic.

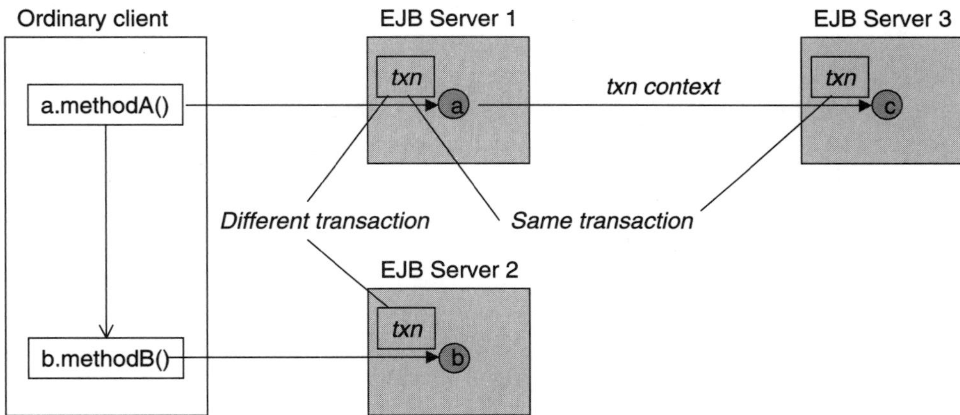


**Figure 8-18** Non-transactional (ordinary) EJB client.

It is possible for the client to directly participate in a transaction by originating the transaction on the client and propagating it to the server. A transaction that is initiated on the client is called a "client demarcated" transaction, and the client is therefore a "transactional client." In that case, the client must obtain a handle to the transaction manager and issue the begin() and commit() calls. An important example of this is a servlet client. Many application servers extend transaction management services to the web servlet server, thereby allowing servlets to initiate transactions which then propagate to the EJB server.

Prior to EJB 1.1, there had been no EJB-defined interface for an EJB *client* executing outside of the EJB container to obtain a transaction object. EJB 1.1 specifies a technique which is not dependent on any EJB interfaces and therefore can be used in other container environment. A transaction-enabled environment can support access to a thread's transaction context by the following method which was discussed earlier in this chapter:

```
Context ic = new InitialContext();
UserTransaction txn = (UserTransaction)ic.lookup(
      "java:comp/UserTransaction");
```

At this time most products do not support this since it is new, but it is likely this will become the standard way of obtaining a UserTransaction context.

An EJB server explicitly makes a transaction object available to a bean (if the bean is deployed to manage its own transactions) via the EJBContext's getUserTransaction() method; however, a client does not have access to this method (unless the client is itself a bean), since the method executes in a bean. Therefore, the API or facility used to obtain a transaction object will depend on the product. Assuming for discussion that the type obtained is either a JTA `UserTransaction` or an OTS `Current` interface, the client would issue the begin() call, then make any required EJB calls. The client's transaction context would propagate to the EJB server, assuming that IIOP (i.e., RMI-over-IIOP) is being used for the EJB calls, and the EJB server has the ability to use a propagated IIOP transaction context. When the client is ready to complete its transaction, it would issue commit() or rollback(), and the transaction manager would coordinate this with any transactional data resources that had been used in that transaction, on this or on any other EJB servers contacted in the process. This scenario is depicted in Figure 8-19.

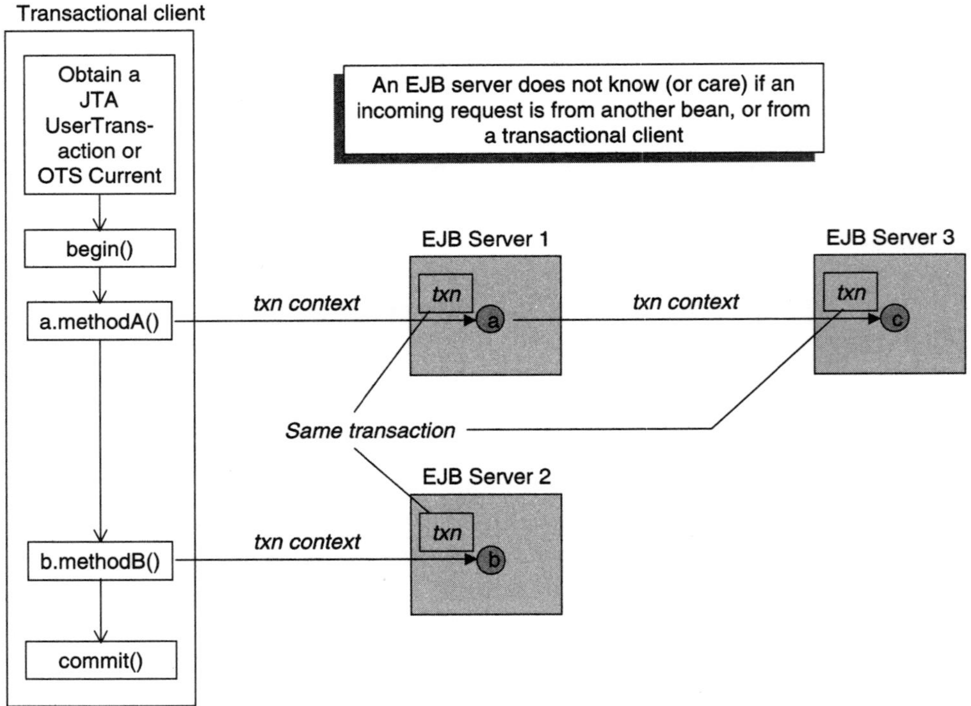


**Figure 8-19** A transactional client.

Therefore, a client which needs to manage its own transaction context and thread association needs to use an additional transaction API, such as CORBA OTS, and the EJB server product the client accesses either will have to provide that facility or be able to interoperate with it. CORBA OTS defines how a client obtains a transaction object that it can use to perform transaction management. Some ORB-based EJB products such as Gemstone/J provide a full OTS capability, and can initiate and propagate client demarcated transactions using RMI-over-IIOP.

The following client code demonstrates a simple but fully elaborated case of checking if a transaction is in progress, and if not, beginning a new one. I have identified all the transaction-related exceptions that can occur. In practice, you will most likely not respond to them all individually.

```
try
{
      org.omg.CosTransactions.Current current =
         (org.omg.CosTransactions.Current)
         (org.omg.CosTransactions.CurrentHelper.narrow
         (_orb().resolve_initial_references(
            "TransactionCurrent")));

      boolean inATransactionAlready =
         (current.get_control() != null);
      if (! inATransactionAlready)
      {
         try
         {
            current.begin();
         }
         catch (SubtransactionsUnavailable su)
         {
            // Should not happen - would only happen if we
            // were already in a transaction, and we have
            // checked that we are not.
         }
      }
```

*...perform EJB calls, using the RMI-over-IIOP API...*

```
      if (! inATransactionAlready)
      {
         try
         {
            current.commit(true); // Use 'true' at great cost,
               // if you need to be sure that all resources
               // have completed their commit when this method
               // returns.
```

```
            }
            catch (NoTransaction nt)
            {
               // Should not happen - would only happen if we
               // were not in a transaction, and we have made
               // sure that we are.
            }
            catch (HeuristicMixed hm)
            {
               // Some resources committed, others did not.
            }
            catch (HeuristicHazard hh)
            {
               // Status unknown - may or may not have committed.
            }
         }
}
// Catch transaction-related CORBA standard exceptions (those
// included implicitly in every method signature).
catch (org.omg.CORBA.NO_PERMISSION np)
{
      // We don't have permission to commit the txn.
}
catch (org.omg.CORBA.TRANSACTION_ROLLEDBACK rb)
{
      // The transaction was rolled back, so a method
      // did not complete.
}
catch (org.omg.CORBA.TRANSACTION_REQUIRED tr)
{
      // A transaction is required, but there is not one
      // associated with the thread calling a method.
}
catch (org.omg.CORBA.INVALID_TRANSACTION it)
{
      // The transaction is invalid.
}
// Catch other CORBA standard exceptions, and all other
// exceptions.
catch (Exception ex)
{
      // Take appropriate action in response to arbitrary failure.
}
```

Note that you have a choice of providing true or false as an argument to the commit() method. A value of true instructs the transaction manager to wait for all transaction branches to complete their commit and individually report back—only then will the commit() method return. Providing an argument of false allows the method

to return after all branches have responded to the prepare phase and the transaction has been logged. A failure could then still occur in one or more branches, but it would most likely be recoverable by recovering the failed server, since the prepare phase ensured tht all servers logged the transaction to recoverable storage.

### *Exceptions*

While your business methods must be declared to throw RemoteException in the interface, your implementations of your business methods do not need to, unless you actually throw a RemoteException. You can of course throw any other kind of exception you choose, and if you do, you must declare it in the throws clause in your interface as well as in the throws clause of the bean method.

In your bean, only declare the exceptions that you actually throw. If you don't throw RemoteException, don't declare it, even if it is declared in the throws clause of your remote interface. This applies to the ejbCreate() and other required methods as well.

Now I will explain the rules defined in EJB 1.0 for what exceptions to throw. You should throw these:

**java.rmi.RemoteException**—In your business methods, when a system-level error occurs, such as a failure to connect to a database. You must declare RemoteException in the throws clause of your remote interface business methods, but need not declare it in the business method implementation unless you actually throw it.

**CreateException**—In your ejbCreateXXX(...) methods, when a failure occurs in that method which causes the entity to not be created. In the special case in which the entity cannot be created because one with the same key already exists, a DuplicateKeyException is thrown. You can choose to declare DuplicateKeyException in your Home interface createXXX() method throws clause, but you don't have to, because DuplicateKeyException is a subclass of CreateException. You *must* declare CreateException in the throws clause of your Home interface createXXX() methods.

**FinderException**—In your ejbFindXXX(...) method, when a failure occurs in that method, and as a result the method cannot complete and therefore the requested object cannot be found. You *must* include this in the Home interface findXXX() method throws clause. (Note that there is an inconsistency in the EJB 1.0 specification, in that in at least two places, it states that this exception must be declared, and in another place it states that it *may* be declared. In practice, EJB servers usually require it.) In the specific case for ejbFindXXX() methods which return a single instance and the requested object cannot be found, but no other failure occurs, then an ObjectNotFoundException should be thrown by the ejbFindXXX() method. You can choose to declare this exception in the Home interface findXXX() method, but you do not have to, since it extends FinderException. Find methods which return a collection return null when a matching object cannot be found.

**RemoveException**—In your ejbRemove() method, when a failure occurs in that method. This is also thrown by the container when a client attempts to remove the object while it is involved in a transaction.

The server will throw these:

**java.rmi.NoSuchObjectException**—When attempt is made to invoke an object that has been removed.

**java.rmi.RemoteException**—When:

An illegal concurrent call or loopback call is attempted.

An attempt to invoke a bean in a different transaction than it is currently in, or in a different isolation level.

**javax.ejb.RemoveException**—When you attempt to remove a bean that cannot be removed, e.g., because a transaction is in progress which involves that bean.

The server will automatically roll back the current transaction if the caller is not a participant in the transaction (e.g., if the caller is not another bean but is a client application operating outside the EJB container).

A bean invoking another bean (or any transactional resource) should specifically catch javax.transaction.TransactionRolledbackException so that it does not do additional work for nothing. In addition, a transactional caller (such as another bean) should check for rollback if any kind of exception occurs, using the getRollbackOnly() method.

EJB 1.1 changes these rules somewhat. For starters, it defines these classes of exceptions:

*Application exceptions*—Includes expected things that can go wrong in the application which represent a user error or logical error, as opposed to a component or system failure of any kind. The business method[1] may choose

---

1. EJB 1.1 considers these to be business methods: ejbCreate(), ejbPostCreate(), ejbRemote(), ejbFindXXX().

Thus, an EJB 1.1 business method *should not throw* RemoteException as an EJB 1.0 business method would. Instead, it throws an application-specific exception a RuntimeException, or an EJBException and allows the server to catch these and either propagate it back to the caller or respond to it and generate a RemoteException.

Note that often the caller is another bean, which possibly initiated the current transaction. This allows the calling bean to decide if it can recover from the condition or if the overall transaction should be terminated. If the caller finds that the bean it calls has thrown an exception type which caused the server to disable the bean, the calling bean should gracefully report this using an application exception rather than throwing some kind of system exception.

to mark the transaction for rollback before throwing an application exception if it determines that the condition is unrecoverable by the caller. Usually it is better to let the caller decide, however, unless the business method has information that cannot be conveyed to the caller. The CreateException, FinderException, and RemoveException are considered to be application exceptions.

*System exceptions*—Anything that is not an application exception. Propagate any RuntimeException or Error; for all others, wrap them in a javax.ejb.EJBException and throw it. The EJB container will roll back the current transaction and disable the bean instance, and throw a RemoteException to the caller. It will also release any resources held by the instance, and most likely generate an error log message to alert the administrator.

If a business method (in particular the ejbLoad() or ejbStore() method) discovers that a requested entity no longer exists in the persistent store, it should throw javax.ejb.NoSuchEntityException. (The ObjectNotFoundException is only thrown by the entity Home interface finder methods. Also, calls to a *session* bean that no longer exists will result in a java.rmi.NoSuchObjectException.)

The non-business methods are not invoked by client calls but instead are invoked by the container to manage the bean. These methods include ejbActivate(), ejbLoad(), ejbPassivate(), ejbStore(), setEntityContext(), setSessionContext(), afterBegin(), beforeCompletion() and afterCompletion(). If any of these methods throws an exception of any kind, the current transaction (if there is one) will be marked for rollback (local transactions will be rolled back immediately), and the bean instance will be disabled and disposed of immediately without cleanup.

### *Some Exception Scenarios for EJB Clients*

Let's look at some scenarios that a client has to consider when it calls business methods on an enterprise bean. Note that a client might be another enterprise bean; it might be a servlet; or it might be a remote heavy client application.

**An Individual Server Instance in the EJB Server Cluster Goes Down, or the Entire Server Goes Down.** The EJB model requires that if a non-AppException propagates out of a bean, the server is required to disable the bean and mark the transaction for rollback. A server failure, however, is not a bean failure, and so this rule does not apply. Clustering makes failover possible, so that if an error occurs outside the bean (e.g., in the server itself or the network) the cluster can hide the condition. If the bean has state that is not managed by the infrastructure, this is difficult to achieve without a special VM. A stateless bean or entity bean with all container-managed fields, however, can theoretically allow failover to be transparent. This is a value-added feature and it outside the scope of the EJB specification. In general, system errors which are not transparent result in a RemoteException, and the client must be prepared to catch this and assume that the session is lost and must therefore create a new session or reobtain the bean instance through a find() or create() method.

**A Bean Fails.** A bean can freeze by going into a loop or by blocking on a resource that does not return or timeout. The server may not detect this. Eventually, the user's session with the bean will timeout, but if the bean is blocked on a resource or in a loop, it appears to be busy and will not timeout. That is why it is important that the server have a monitor facility for seeing how many sessions exist, who is using them, what resources they own, and what activity they are experiencing.

A bean can also experience a runtime or other error. In this case the client will receive a RemoteException. The client does not know if the exception is from a failure which originated from the bean (e.g., the bean threw a RuntimeException and the server therefore disabled it) or communication system failure (the server itself failed causing a loss of connection), and the client therefore does not know if its state has been lost. In general, if a RemoteException is received, it is a good idea to assume the session has been lost and to reobtain the bean from its Home interface. You must also be prepared that the Home interface methods may then throw an exception, in which case you would need to reobtain the Home interface.

**Summary of General Exception Conditions Important for Clients.** The general categories of exceptions thrown to clients from bean methods are summarized as follows:

> **`AppException`**—This represents an exception that the application expects, and so the action that the client should take is application-specific. It does not represent a system failure of any kind. An AppException does not mean the transaction was aborted. Note that if the transaction began when the method was called, the container will attempt to commit the transaction unless the bean marks the transaction for rollback—even if it sends an AppException.
>
> **`RemoteException`**—The session and session state are lost. The client must recreate the session bean or reobtain the entity instance and recall the method. Local transactions (those visible only to the bean) which were started by the container were rolled back by the server.

If client is transactional (e.g., is another bean, or a transaction-aware servlet), it may also receive

> **`TransactionRolledbackException`** (extends `RemoteException`)—Transaction and session (and session state) are lost. The client must recreate the session or reobtain the entity and retry the transaction.

Even if a TransactionRolledbackException does not occur, a transactional client should check for rollback being set if *any* exception occurs, by calling getRollback-

Only() on the SessionContext or EntityContext; or if the client is not a bean (or even if it is), it can instead call getStatus() on the UserTransaction object.

In addition, the bean's Home interface can propagate errors related to connecction loss. In general, every time you access the bean's Home interface object you need to be prepared to receive a RemoteException and respond by reobtaining (looking up) the Home interface.

### *Different Patterns of Enterprise JavaBean Use*

In my examples, I will use the RMI-over-IIOP approach, but I will note where the code is dependent on that API (primarily in client code) so that you can easily modify it if your product does not support RMI-over-IIOP yet. (RMI-over-IIOP is still an early access beta technology at this writing.) The difference is not exposed to EJB code, since the server-side wrapper classes are automatically generated. The fact that your server class may be accessed via a PortableRemoteObject instead of a UnicastRemoteObject is not visible to you, except that the former is more interoperable with other servers in some ways (this is discussed in the section on the Java Transaction API). The main difference to client code is that RMI-over-IIOP clients should use the CORBA-style method `PortableRemoteObject.narrow(Object, Class)` when casting a remotely obtained servant reference. This is shown in the example that follows.

Some application servers also provide their own RMI implementation with value-added features, and in that case, you might need to import their RMI packages instead of the standard java.rmi packages.

**A Stateless Session Bean—ping() Service.** For our first enterprise bean, let's look at the simple case of a session bean which is completely stateless: it has no class variables and therefore is fully reentrant. The example I will use is the EJB incarnation of the ping service example I used when discussing CORBA in the Chapter 7. Here is the enterprise bean's remote interface:

```
package pingservice;
import java.rmi.*;
public interface Server extends EJBObject
{
      public String ping()
         throws RemoteException; <- required
}
```

Here is its Home interface:

```
package pingservice;
import java.rmi.*;
import javax.ejb.*;
```

```
public interface ServerHome extends EJBHome
{
      public Server create()
         throws CreateException, RemoteException; <- both required
                                             for all createXXX() methods.
}
```

Here is the actual bean implementation, containing the business methods, which in this case is the single method `ping()`:

```
package pingservice;
import java.rmi.*;
import javax.rmi.*;
import java.util.*;
import javax.naming.*;

public class ServerImpl
implements SessionBean <- Does not implement your interface!
{
      public ServerImpl() {}

      public String ping() <- but RemoteException not required here, unless
                              your code actually throws it.
      {
         return "ping";
      }

      //
      // Required by EJB design pattern:

      public void ejbCreate() {} <- again, you only declare the exceptions
                                    you actually throw
      public void ejbRemove() {}

      //
      // From SessionBean:

      public void ejbActivate() {}
      public void ejbPassivate() {}
      public void setSessionContext(SessionContext ctx) {}
}
```

That's it! Note that, unlike the CORBA version of this, we only write the servant code—not the server code. In other words, we don't need to provide a main() method, since the EJB framework provides it. A CORBA servant, on the other

hand, requires a main() method to instantiate the servant and export it. The name to use when exporting the servant is provided in the EJB deployment descriptor's beanHomeName attribute. I will call it "pingservice." Also note that even though the bean will be invoked as an RMI servant, we don't have to include any RMI-like declarations in our bean implementation, such as extending PortableRemoteObject or UnicastRemoteObject—all that is done in the EJB linkage code that our EJB server tools will generate. The linkage code in turn invokes our bean. In fact, *your bean implementation does not actually implement your interface!* It only implements SessionBean (or EntityBean for an entity bean). The only RMI dependency in the servant code is that we are required to thrown a RemoteException when something goes wrong, such as a failed database connection. (EJB 1.1 modifies this requirement and defines the situations in which a RemoteException, application exception, and RuntimeException are to be thrown. In addition, since the bean's interface is actually a remote interface, all the arguments and return types of the bean's interface methods must be types which RMI can marshall—i.e., either serializable, or themselves remote references.

These are the steps we must complete to prepare and deploy this bean:

1. Compile the user-written bean and home interfaces, and the bean implementation class, as well as any user-written supporting classes.
2. Create the deployment descriptor and serialize it—your EJB server will have tools for this.
3. Create the manifest file—this will be done automatically by most EJB servers toolkits.
4. Create the JAR file, containing the serialized deployment descriptor, the manifest, and your compiled user-written classes and interfaces.
5. Generate EJB wrapper classes; all EJB products have a tool for this. It is a largely automatic step that requires no intervention (assuming all goes well).
6. Copy the JAR file and generated wrapper classes to a deployment location, and use product-specific tools to deploy and configure them.

These are the EJB 1.0 deployment descriptor attributes, expressed in a Java-like initialization syntax:

```
beanHomeName=pingservice
enterpriseBeanClassName=pingservice.ServerImpl
homeInterfaceClassName=pingservice.ServerHome
remoteInterfaceClassName=pingservice.Server
isReentrant=false
accessControlEntry[]=
{
```

```
        {
            method=ping(),
            Identity[]={everyone}
        },
        {
            method=ejbCreate(),
            Identity[]={everyone}
        },
        {
            method=ejbRemove(),
            Identity[]={everyone}
        }
}
controlDescriptor[]=
{
        {
            method=ping(),
            isolationLevel=TRANSACTION_SERIALIZABLE,
            transactionAttribute=TX_REQUIRED,
            runAsMode=CLIENT_IDENTITY
        }
}
stateManagementType=STATELESS_SESSION
sessionTimeout=0
```

Note that I have declared the ping() method to be TX_REQUIRED, meaning that if the caller does not propagate a transaction context, then the EJB server must start a transaction for the method to execute in. If it does start a transaction, that transaction will complete when the method returns. The bean has also been declared to be STATELESS_SESSION, freeing the server to share the bean with other sessions after each method call completes. We can do this because our bean retains no state after each method call to it completes.

The EJB 1.0 compliant manifest is a text file called Manifest.mf, containing these two lines:

```
Name: DeploymentDescriptor.ser
Enterprise-Bean: True
```

where DeploymentDescriptor.ser is the name of the serialized deployment descriptor file.

The JAR file must contain the deployment descriptor, the manifest file, and all compiled user-written classes and interfaces. To create the JAR file, you can use a line like this:

```
jar cmvf Manifest.mf pingservice.jar DeploymentDescriptor.ser
   pingservice
```

At this point you are ready to use your EJB tools to generate the required EJB wrapper classes, and actually deploy those classes and the bean JAR file you have built. This procedure is tool-specific. Most EJB products provide an interactive user interface to perform these functions.

Here is a client which accesses this service:

```
import weblogic.rmi.RemoteException;
import java.util.Properties;
import javax.naming.InitialContext;
import java.rmi.RMISecurityManager;
import pingservice.*;

public class PingClient
{
      public static void main(String[] args) throws Exception
      {
         //
         // Install a security manager, if there is not one.

         if (System.getSecurityManager() == null)
         {
            // RMI requires a security manager
            System.setSecurityManager(new RMISecurityManager());
         }

         //
         // Identify the name server URL.

         String nameServiceHostUrl = args[0];
         Properties p = new Properties();
         p.put("java.naming.provider.url", nameServiceHostUrl);

         //
         // Look up the ping service, using the name declared in
         // its deployment descriptor.

         InitialContext context = new InitialContext(p);
         Object o = context.lookup("pingservice");
         context.close();

         //
         // We now have the bean's Home interface. For IIOP, we
         // must narrow the returned object's concrete type to the
```

```
// interface type. For JRMP we can skip this step, but
// should leave it in for completeness if our
// implementation allows.

ServerHome serverHome =
   (ServerHome)javax.rmi.PortableRemoteObject.narrow(
      o, ServerHome.class);
// For JRMP, you can simply use this instead:
// ServerHome serverHome = (ServerHome)o;

//
// Create a ping Server.

Server server = serverHome.create();

//
// Invoke the server.

try
{
   System.out.println(server.ping());
   System.out.println("Transaction completed");
}
catch (
   javax.transaction.TransactionRolledbackException rb)
{
   System.out.println("Transaction failed");

   // Depending on how the underlying data resource is
   // configured, you may want to retry, because this
   // might merely represent a contention situation.
   // Some JDBC drivers allow you to configure how
   // the data resource behaves under contention - to
   // wait or to throw an exception.
}
catch (java.rmi.RemoteException re)
{
   System.out.println(
   "Unrecoverable failure - transaction did not
      complete");

   // Note: if this occurs in a transactional client
   // (or in another bean), the transaction may still
   // be in progress, and should be marked for rollback,
   // by calling setRollbackOnly() on the EJBContext.
}
```

Note: you should also catch any exceptions declared in your business method:

```
            //
            // Be a good soldier and remove the object we no
            // longer need.
            // This method is defined in EJBHome, and is provided
            // automatically by the server.

            server.remove();
        }
}
```

A client needs to be able to find the name service that the EJB server used to publish the bean. We called our bean "pingservice" in our deployment descriptor's beanHomeName attribute, so that is the name it is published with. Once this bean is deployed in an EJB server, we can obtain its Home interface by performing a JNDI lookup. JNDI needs to know what kind of name service to use, however—the JNDI provider. The provider is specified by the Java property "java.naming.factory.initial." Thus, as an example, if our EJB server is configured to use, e.g., Sun's implementation of a CORBA Name Service provider, we could set this property on the command line when we run our client, or we could hardcode it in the client code even, if we like. We also need to specify the URL of the name service, so that the provider implementation can find it on the network; this is done by passing to JNDI the host URL as a property argument to the InitialContext() constructor. In the sample client above I pass this URL into the client program as a command-line parameter. Most likely the EJB server will require us to use its own name service provider.

A command line which runs the above client is:

```
java -Djava.naming.factory.initial=
   com.sun.jndi.cosnaming.CNCtxFactory
      PingClient iiop://<name-server-host>:<port>
```

**A Stateful Session Bean—Counting ping() Service.** Let's now look at a similar example, but which maintains state across invocations by the client. I will modify the ping service code to merely contain a single variable "i," which is incremented each time the bean is invoked. Note that this bean must be deployed as STATEFUL_SESSION. This will ensure that the server does not attempt to share our instance with other sessions. Also, a client will only see the state changes of its own session instance, since each client obtains a session instance just for it for the duration of its session with the bean.

```
package pingservice;
import java.rmi.*;
public interface Server extends EJBObject
{
   public int ping() throws RemoteException;
}

package pingservice;
import java.util.*;
import javax.naming.*;

public class ServerImpl
implements SessionBean
{
   private int i;

   public ServerImpl() {}

   public int ping()
   {
       return i++;
   }

   //
   // Required by EJB design pattern:

   public void ejbCreate()
   {
      i = 0;      // Initialize all non-transient fields here
   }
   public void ejbRemove() {}

   //
   // From SessionBean:

   public void ejbActivate() {}
   public void ejbPassivate() {}
   public void setSessionContext(SessionContext ctx) {}
}
```

We must now declare the bean to be a STATEFUL_SESSION bean in its deployment descriptor:

```
stateManagementType=STATEFUL_SESSION
```

The ejbCreate() method must initialize all non-transient class instance variables. In this example the only class instance variable is the variable i, and it is non-transient so that it will be maintained automatically by the container across passivations and reactivations.

We can use the same client program to invoke this bean. Instead of printing "ping," it will now print the value of i, which is incremented each time the method is called. Since the value is not made persistent, it will reset each time the bean is recreated— with each new session at a minimum, or after the bean times out and is reclaimed by the server. Therefore, to test that the bean is really working, we need to place at least two ping() calls in our client program:

```
System.out.println(server.ping());
System.out.println(server.ping());
```

It should print "0" followed by "1."

**A Session Bean with Persistent State.** The fact that we can maintain the value of i in the server-resident bean from one remote call to the next is useful in applications where we need to maintain data on the server during the lifetime of our session, but not beyond the session. In most applications, we want to at least save a final result. Therefore, we need some kind of database connection. Saving the result, however, will make it visible to other sessions.

To make i persistent, we can store its value in a database. Let's assume we have created a relational table to store the value of i, and initialized it with a single record as follows:

```
create table count (i integer);
insert into count values (0);
```

Thus, I have a table called "count," and it contains a single column called "i" with a data type of integer. I have also inserted a single record into the table, containing a value of 0 for the i column. I will not add records to this table; rather, I will use this single record to maintain the current value of i.

Our Server interface would not change as a result of our persistent implementation, but our ServerImpl implementation could change to this:

```
package pingservice;
import java.util.*;
import javax.naming.*;
import java.sql.*;

public class ServerImpl
implements SessionBean, SessionSynchronization
{
```

```
private transient int i;
private transient Connection conn;

public ServerImpl() {}

public int ping() throws java.rmi.RemoteException
{
   //
   // Get the latest value of i from the database.
   // We must do this here because someone else may have
   // updated it since our last transaction.

   Statement stmt = null;
   try
   {
      stmt = conn.createStatement();
      stmt.execute("select * from count");
      ResultSet rs = stmt.getResultSet();
      if (! rs.next())
      {
         // Error - no row found.
         throw new java.rmi.RemoteException(
            "Table Count does not exist");
      }
      i = rs.getInt("i");
      if (rs.next())
      {
         // Error - there is another row; should only be one.
         throw new java.rmi.RemoteException(
         "Multiple Count rows");
      }
   }
   catch (SQLException ex)
   {
      throw new java.rmi.RemoteException(
         "Database is corrupt");
   }
   finally
   {
      try { stmt.close(); } catch (Exception s) {}
   }

   //
   // Increment i and return the new value. Most likely
   // our transaction will commit after this return,
   // causing beforeCompletion() to be called.

   return i++;
```

```
}

public void ejbCreate() throws java.rmi.RemoteException
{
   getConnection();    // Do this here only if you don't
                       // use connection pools.
}

public void ejbRemove() {}

protected void getConnection()
throws java.rmi.RemoteException
{
   // Open connection to database.
   try
   {
      DataSource ds = new DataSource();
      conn = ds.getConnection();
   }
   catch (Exception ex)
   {
      throw new java.rmi.RemoteException(
         "Unable to get connection");
   }
}

//
// From SessionBean:

public void ejbActivate() throws java.rmi.RemoteException
{
   getConnection();
}

public void ejbPassivate() throws java.rmi.RemoteException
{
   // Close connection.
   try
   {
      conn.close();
   }
   catch (Exception ex)
   {
      throw new java.rmi.RemoteException(
         "Unable to close connection");
   }
   finally
   {
      conn = null;
```

```
        }
    }

    public void setSessionContext(SessionContext ctx) {}

    //
    // From SessionSynchronization:

    public void beforeCompletion()
    throws java.rmi.RemoteException
    {
        //
        // Write value of i to database. This method is
        // called whenever a transaction that involved this
        // bean is about to commit.

        Statement stmt = null;
        try
        {
            stmt = conn.createStatement();
            stmt.executeUpdate("update count set i=" + i
                + " where i<" + i);
        }
        catch (SQLException ex)
        {
            throw new java.rmi.RemoteException(
                "Unable to update Count table");
        }
        finally
        {
            try { stmt.close(); } catch (Exception s) {}
        }
    }

    public void afterBegin() {}
    public void afterCompletion(boolean b) {}
}

class DataSource  // Mimic a data resource factory.
{
    private Properties t3props;

    public DataSource() throws Exception
    {
        Class.forName("weblogic.jdbc.jts.Driver").newInstance();
    }

    public Connection getConnection() throws Exception
```

```
    {
        return DriverManager.getConnection(
            "jdbc:weblogic:jts:eng");
    }
}
```

An important difference between this implementation and the previous non-persistent implementation is that this version obtains the value of i from the database each time ping() is called. I have therefore declared i to be transient, and do not bother to initialize it in the ejbCreate() method. The bean can therefore be declared to be STATELESS_SESSION, even though it maintains a database connection, since the connection's transaction is completed with each ping() call, and so the connection is itself stateless across ping() calls. The connection variable is declared transient so that the container will not attempt to serialize it or otherwise store it when the bean is passivated.

Our client program will now display successively increasing values of i, regardless how many times it is run, or the server stopped and restarted. However, other users who invoke this bean will share the same persistent state.

If the server supports connection pools, you would most likely not place the connection establishment code in the ejbCreate() method. The purpose of creating the connection in the ejbCreate() method was so that the connection could be maintained throughout the session without having to reestablish it with each call. This can be very unscalable, however, since each client session will need a connection. A connection pool greatly reduces the connection time seen by a client to obtain a connection, and so with a connection pool there is no difficulty with putting the connection establishment code in the method which actually requires access to the connection, and then immediately closing the connection after it is used.

In most cases you will close connections you are using at the end of the transaction. Note that a stateful session bean may need to keep the connection open across method calls, especially if you have implemented some sort of incremental query method. However, the Java Transaction API does *not* require that a connection associated with a global transaction remain open through the end of the transaction, so if your EJB server is using a transaction manager, you can close your connections as soon as you are done with them, and the transaction should still commit properly.

In this example, I release my database connection in the ejbPassivate() method and reobtain it in the ejbActivate() method. Suppose you have a transaction in progress? For example, you might have a result set open, or you might have an object database session. No fear: a session bean cannot be passivated while it is in a transaction. Thus, if your transactions span multiple method calls you don't have to worry that the bean will be passivated between two calls.

The above example implements the SessionSynchronization interface. I use the beforeCompletion() method to write the value of i to the database. This is not strictly necessary here—I could have written the new value of i in the ping() method itself. It is a good practice, however. The SessionSynchronization methods are called by the container at transaction begin and completion. Since I implement this interface, I also have to provide its other methods, afterBegin() and afterCompletion(), but in this example they are empty.

My implementation uses the ordinary JDBC Driver API, with WebLogic drivers. If your EJB server supports JDBC 2, you should obtain a DataSource implementation. In the code above, I have simulated this, so the change will be minimal. In a real DataSource implementation, you would obtain the DataSource using JNDI.

You might be wondering what the difference is between this implementation and an equivalent entity bean. A session bean is a component which represents a user's session. An entity bean is a component which represents a type of data item. For example, in the above example I do not remove the record when the ejbRemove() method is executed. That would be appropriate for an entity bean, but not a session bean. The session bean does not represent it—it represents *our session*. When you remove it, you are removing the session only—not the data objects that the session happens to access. An entity bean, in contrast, represents data, and when it is removed, that data should be removed as well.

You can use a session bean which implements its own persistence to create a highly scalable service. Since each client connection gets its own session bean instance, the primary resource contention will be for the data resource itself, and not your bean.

**Example of Using an Entity to Represent a Singleton Data Item—Counting ping() Service.** We can choose to implement the above persistent counting ping service as an entity bean. There is an important conceptual difference when doing this, however. By making it an entity bean, we are defining a proxy component class for the data item, and when we create an entity instance, we will hold a proxy instance for the database record which represents the value of i. Thus, all accesses to that value will go through our *single instance* of our entity bean, because that single instance will represent the single record for i in the database. As far as our EJB applications are concerned, our entity bean *is* i. Other non-EJB applications can still access the value of i by going to the database directly if they choose—the entity bean will reload the value of i each time it is accessed, ensuring that it has the latest value, and database locking will automatically enforce concurrency control over the associated database record. An example of use of

this pattern is a logging service which receives events from multiple clients and must synchronously append them to a database or log file. In such an application, the logging service appears as a single entity which exposes a logging interface. (Do not use this approach for benchmarking, however; this is discussed later.)

Such a bean is used differently from the way the former session bean would be used. Instead of merely looking up the service by finding its Home interface and then calling a parameterless create() method, an application now has to ask for a particular instance, using a findXXX() method. The instance returned is a proxy for the particular i value we are interested in (in this simple example we only have one record and one i value, but we could have many). We can make this simpler for applications by defining only a single parameterless find() method, and hard-wiring the instance key into our implementation of find(). However, underneath, it needs to find a particular instance of our entity bean class. If this instance is accessed frequently, it could become a source of contention. However, in the session bean version, the underlying record representing i was a source of contention, so implementing it as an entity bean has not fundamentally changed the contention characteristics.

We need to provide a convenient findXXX() method in our Home interface for applications to obtain the instance of our bean, which happens to be a singleton instance:

```
package pingservice;
import java.rmi.*;
import javax.ejb.*;

public interface ServerHome extends EJBHome
{
   public Server create()
      throws CreateException, RemoteException;
   public Server create(int i)
      throws CreateException, RemoteException;
   public Server find()
      throws FinderException, <- required
         RemoteException; <- required
   public Server findByPrimaryKey(PrimaryKey pk)
      throws FinderException, RemoteException;
}
```

We also have to define a primary key class. For container-managed beans, the primary key cannot be a standard type and must be a class you define. Therefore, even if your bean uses bean-managed persistence and you don't have to define a primary key type, it is a good idea to do so, in case you later choose to change to container-managed persistence: if you define your own primary key type, you won't have to change your Home interface—which is used by all your clients!

```
package pingservice;
public class PrimaryKey implements java.io.Serializable
{
   public int i;
   public PrimaryKey() {}
   public PrimaryKey(int i) { this.i = i; }
}
```

The primary key type must be public and it must be serializable. All its fields must be public and must be a subset of the container-managed fields of the bean. EJB 1.1 relaxes the latter requirement and allows you to use the deployment descriptor to map the key fields to container managed bean fields. The create() methods must return the bean's remote interface type.

Unfortunately the primary key type must be a concrete class—it cannot be an interface. (EJB 1.1 allows it to be an Object as well.) This means that it is not possible to defer the specification of the concrete type of a primary key to the bean's implementation; it must be selected when the EJB interfaces are designed. Your primary key type should also provide correct implementations of clone(), equals(), and hashcode(), as most EJB servers use these methods on the primary key.

You must always implement the ejbCreate() methods of the bean class. For a container-managed bean, however, your ejbCreate() methods actually would not do any creating. Instead, it needs to merely initialize its fields, and the container will then use those initialization values to create a database record or object instances. The return type of an entity bean's ejbCreate() methods must be the entity's primary key type. (For a session bean, the return type must be void.)

If your bean is container-managed, you do not have to implement the findXXX() methods that you define in your Home interface. The EJB server tools will generate those methods. Different EJB products will have different ways of allowing you to define precisely what the find methods do. Some products may allow you to specify the findXXX() method parameters and an expression for the method to evaluate, such as an SQL expression. Others may support a set of searching rules that the tools can use to generate an equivalent findXXX() method. It depends on the kind of data resource that is being used by the container to provide the persistence. I am assuming for my example here that the EJB development tools allow me to define the required behavior of my find() method, such that it will find the singleton record in the database that I have created to contain the value of i.

Your EJB tools will also provide you with a means of associating your container-managed bean fields with items (e.g., columns or persistent object classes) in the underlying database.

A finder method can either return a single instance, or a collection. EJB 1.0 requires that if a finder method returns a single instance, the return type must be the remote interface. If it returns a collection, the return type must be an Enumeration. Again, for container-managed beans these methods are generated by the EJB tools, and your tool documentation will tell you how to define these interfaces. EJB 1.1 allows additional types to be returned by the finder methods, including Java 2 Collection types. In either case, the elements of the returned Enumeration or Collection must be entity bean references, and must implement the bean's remote interface.

Find methods which return an enumeration or collection return null when a matching object cannot be found. Find methods which return a single instance throw ObjectNotFoundException when the specified object cannot be found.

The findXXX() methods are not static methods: they are called on an instance. Nevertheless, do not assume that a findXXX() method is called on a properly initialized instance of the bean. The server may use a pooled instance in which the instance fields have undetermined values. Therefore a findXXX() method should not read instance data unless it is reading values that it set itself.

Let's first see what a container-managed implementation would look like. Our interface still does not change, but here is an implementation which relies on the EJB container to persistify the value of i:

```
package pingservice;
import java.util.*;
import javax.naming.*;

public class ServerImpl implements EntityBean
{
   private int i;

   public int ping()
   {
      return i++;
   }

   public PrimaryKey ejbCreate()
   throws java.rmi.RemoteException
   {
      return ejbCreate(0);       // Default: start with 0.
   }
```

```
   public PrimaryKey ejbCreate(int i)
   throws java.rmi.RemoteException
   {
      this.i = i;    // Here we merely initialize the fields, since
                     // the bean is container-managed, and it will
                     // create the underlying database records.

      return new PrimaryKey(i);    // For entity beans, the
                     // create methods must return the primary key.
   }

   public void setEntityContext(EntityContext ec) {}
   public void unsetEntityContext() {}
   public void ejbRemove() {}
   public void ejbActivate() {}
   public void ejbPassivate() {}
   public void ejbLoad() {}
   public void ejbStore() {}
}
```

In the deployment descriptor, we must declare a container-managed field called "i":

```
containerManagedFields[]={i}
```

The EJB container will now ensure that the value of i is replicated to and from the database as necessary, and use whatever locks are necessary to ensure the serialization level specified in the bean's isolationLevel deployment descriptor.

We need to configure our deployment descriptor so that we have permission to call our findXXX() methods. Thus, in our deployment descriptor, we need to add these access control entries:

```
{
   method=ejbFind(),
   Identity[]={everyone}
},
{
   method=ejbFindByPrimaryKey(pingservice.PrimaryKey),
   Identity[]={everyone}
}
```

Our client applications now need to identify the instance they want. If we use our existing client, which calls create(), it will create an new entity each time. Instead, we need to modify the client to perform a find operation:

```
Server server = serverHome.find();
```

Alternatively:

```
Server server = serverHome.findByPrimaryKey(
   new PrimaryKey(val));
```

would find the entity as long as its i column has a value of val.

The ability to find the value assumes that the value exists. We can use the table we created in the previous session bean example. After all, remember that an entity is often just a proxy for an actual database value. The database value is the real entity—our entity class is merely acting on its behalf.

Also, our existing client performs a remove() at the end. We don't want to do that now, because our bean now represents a data item, and is not just a servant. Therefore, we need to remove our remove() call. Entity beans have an additional API for being removed: you can call remove(Object) and supply the primary key as the parameter.

In this application, it is possible we may want to restrict clients from creating more instances of the entity. To accomplish that, do not define any create() methods in the Home interface, and in the bean class only implement the primary ejbCreate() method, which takes no arguments. Clients then will not be able to call a create() method, and the only way to create an entity then will be through manually inserting a record in the database, as we did in this case. You can also control access to the createXXX() and remove() methods by using access control settings in the deployment descriptor.

**Using Bean-Managed Persistence—Still Assuming a Singleton Entity.** We can choose to implement our own persistence instead of turning it over to the container. In that case, applications use the bean the same way: the only difference is internal to our bean.

To implement our own entity persistence, we must add behavior to the ejbCreate() methods to make them actually create persistent database records or objects instead of merely initializing fields. Similarly, we will need to implement ejbRemove() so that it deletes the associated data from the database. To retrieve existing data from the database, we need to implement the ejbLoad() method, and we must implement ejbStore() to write data back to the database. We must also implement ejbFindXXX() methods corresponding to our Home interface findXXX() methods.

If we implement our own bean-managed persistence, we must make sure we release and restore needed connections in the ejbPassivate() and ejbActivate()

methods respectively, if we are not using a connection pool and need to hold our connections long-term. Note that an entity bean can be passivated even if it is currently involved in a transaction. That is why EJB 1.1 does not allow entity beans to manage their own global transactions.

If your bean uses bean-managed persistence, there is nothing to stop it from participating in local transactions on non-JTA connections. Passivation will not happen asynchronously in the midst of a bean method call—it will only occur if no other method is currently in progress on the instance. If a transaction is still in progress on the instance, it can still be passivated, and it must release all database connections. If they are JTA connections the transaction will not be lost, but if they are local transactions, the local transactions may be lost. Therefore, if you use bean-managed persistence and use local transactions, make sure all your local transactions complete in each method call.

Here is an example of how we could modify our ping server entity to provide its own persistence:

```
package pingservice;
import java.util.*;
import javax.naming.*;

public class ServerImpl implements EntityBean
{
   public int i;
   private transient Connection conn;

   public int ping()
   {
      return i++;
   }

   public PrimaryKey ejbCreate()
   throws java.rmi.RemoteException, CreateException
   {
      return ejbCreate(0);        // Default: start with 0.
   }

   public PrimaryKey ejbCreate(int i)
   throws java.rmi.RemoteException, CreateException
   {
      this.i = i;

      getConnection();    // There is no problem opening the
                  // connection here as long as there are only
                  // a few entities. If there are many entities,
```

```
            // it would be better to open the connection
            // in the ejbLoad() method, and then immediately
            // close it as soon as we are done with it.

    //
    // Create a new instance of i. Do not allow duplicates,
    // since i is the primary key.

    Statement stmt = null;
    try
    {
        stmt = conn.createStatement();
        stmt.execute("select * from Count where i=" + i);
        ResultSet rs = stmt.getResultSet();
        if (rs.next())
        {
            throw new DuplicateKeyException();
        }

        stmt.close();
        stmt = conn.createStatement();
        stmt.executeUpdate("insert into Count values (" + i
            + ")");
    }
    catch (SQLException ex)
    {
        throw new CreateException(ex.getMessage());
    }
    finally
    {
        try { stmt.close(); } catch (Exception s) {}
    }

    return new PrimaryKey(i);    // For entity beans, the
            // create methods must return the primary key.
}

public void setEntityContext(EntityContext ec) {}
public void unsetEntityContext() {}

public void ejbRemove()
throws RemoveException, java.rmi.RemoteException
{
    //
    // Delete i from the database.

    Statement stmt = null;
    try
```

```
    {
        if ((conn == null) || conn.isClosed()) getConnection();
        stmt = conn.createStatement();
        stmt.executeUpdate("delete from Count where i=" + i);
    }
    catch (SQLException ex)
    {
        throw new RemoveException(ex.getMessage());
    }
    finally
    {
        try { stmt.close(); } catch (Exception s) {}
    }
}

public PrimaryKey ejbFind()
throws FinderException, java.rmi.RemoteException
{
    //
    // It is important to realize that finder methods
    // are NOT NECESSARILY called from an active bean - they
    // may be called using an inactive instance. Therefore,
    // finder methods should not assume that any class
    // variables have been initialized.

    Statement stmt = null;
    try
    {
        if ((conn == null) || conn.isClosed()) getConnection();
        stmt = conn.createStatement();
        stmt.execute("select * from Count");
        ResultSet rs = stmt.getResultSet();
        if (rs.next())
        {
            // Check for multiple rows.
            // Note that if we allowed multiple rows, this
            // method would have to return an Enumeration
            // of primary keys.

            if (rs.next())
            {
                // A duplicate - we don't allow that.
                throw new java.rmi.RemoteException(
                    "Unexpected duplicate");
            }

            return new PrimaryKey(i);
        }
```

```
            else
            {
                throw new ObjectNotFoundException();
            }
        }
        catch (SQLException ex)
        {
            throw new FinderException(ex.getMessage());
        }
        finally
        {
            try { stmt.close(); } catch (Exception s) {}
        }
    }

    public PrimaryKey ejbFindByPrimaryKey(PrimaryKey pk)
    throws FinderException, java.rmi.RemoteException
    {
        Statement stmt = null;
        try
        {
            if ((conn == null) || conn.isClosed()) getConnection();
            stmt = conn.createStatement();
            stmt.execute("select * from Count where i=" + pk.i);
            ResultSet rs = stmt.getResultSet();
            if (rs.next())
            {
                // Check for duplicates. The schema can prevent
                // it, but we will also check for it here for
                // completeness.

                if (rs.next())
                {
                    // A duplicate - we don't allow that.
                    throw new java.rmi.RemoteException(
                        "Unexpected duplicate");
                }

                return new PrimaryKey(pk.i);
            }
            else
            {
                throw new ObjectNotFoundException();
            }
        }
        catch (SQLException ex)
        {
            throw new FinderException(ex.getMessage());
```

```
    }
    finally
    {
        try { stmt.close(); } catch (Exception s) {}
    }
}

public void ejbPassivate() throws java.rmi.RemoteException
{
    // Close connection. Only do this if it is opened in
    // ejbCreate().
    try
    {
        if ((conn != null) && (! conn.isClosed())) conn.close();
    }
    catch (Exception ex)
    {
        throw new java.rmi.RemoteException(
            "Unable to close connection");
    }
    finally
    {
        conn = null;
    }
}

public void ejbActivate() throws java.rmi.RemoteException
{
    // Some EJB servers call this method even if
    // ejbPassivate() has not been called, and it may
    // be called multiple times.

    getConnection();    // Only do this here if it is closed
                        // in ejbPassivate().
}

public void ejbLoad() throws java.rmi.RemoteException
{
    Statement stmt = null;
    try
    {
        if ((conn == null) || conn.isClosed()) getConnection();
            // The above is necessary because the server might
            // lose or close the database connection, without
            // passivating the instance.

        stmt = conn.createStatement();
        stmt.execute("select * from count");
```

```
      ResultSet rs = stmt.getResultSet();
      if (! rs.next())
      {
         // Error - no row found.
         throw new java.rmi.RemoteException(
            "Table Count does not exist");
      }
      i = rs.getInt("i");
      if (rs.next())
      {
         // Error - there is another row; should only be one.
         throw new java.rmi.RemoteException(
            "Multiple Count rows");
      }
   }
   catch (SQLException ex)
   {
      throw new java.rmi.RemoteException(
         "Database is corrupt");
   }
   finally
   {
      try { stmt.close(); } catch (Exception s) {}
   }
}

public void ejbStore() throws java.rmi.RemoteException
{
   // Write value of i to database.
   Statement stmt = null;
   try
   {
      stmt = conn.createStatement();
      stmt.executeUpdate("update count set i=" + i
         + " where i<" + i);
   }
   catch (SQLException ex)
   {
      throw new java.rmi.RemoteException(
         "Unable to update Count table");
   }
   finally
   {
      try { stmt.close(); } catch (Exception s) {}
   }
}

protected void getConnection()
```

```
    throws java.rmi.RemoteException
    {
        // Open connection to database.
        try
        {
            DataSource ds = new DataSource();
            conn = ds.getConnection();
        }
        catch (Exception ex)
        {
            throw new java.rmi.RemoteException(
                "Unable to get connection");
        }
    }

    public void ejbPostCreate() {}
     public void ejbPostCreate(int status) {}
}
```

The DataSource is the same as in the persistent state session bean example.

In this case, the deployment descriptor does not declare any container-managed fields, nor do we instruct the EJB tools to generate any findXXX() methods for us—we have written the find methods ourselves. This is necessary because the EJB tools do not know how we are going to choose to implement persistence, so they cannot possibly generate our find methods. In the case of container-managed persistence, the tools can generate the find methods, because the tools are generating the persistence implementation as well.

**Entity with Bean-Managed Persistence—Assuming Many Entities.** I have assumed in our ping() examples thus far that our application has a singleton persistent data instance (the value i) which we first accessed with a session bean and then with an entity bean. If there are multiple data items represented by an entity class—possibly thousands or millions, e.g., if they represent rows in a database and there are many rows, then the entity class represents a component which knows how to provide access to those data items, and the entity's Home interface is a component which knows how to manufacture entities on demand for the purpose of accessing data items. Calling remove() on an entity removes the actual data item from the persistent store. That is not the same as destroying the entity class instance, which the server may do if it is not being used. The entity is not the data—it is a means of accessing the data. Thus, if you have a million rows in the database, there will not be a million entities—there will be some number representing how many rows are being accessed by all the clients at that instant.

What if you need to retrieve large result sets? Does that mean that the server will create a number of entities equal to the number of rows in the result set? In general, the answer is yes. For example, if you have a findXXX() method which returns a collection, the collection will contain entity references. On the other hand, the server is free to give you a "smart" collection which instantiates the actual entity references (stubs) in a lazy manner. If that is the case, then the act of scrolling through the collection is what will actually cause stubs to be instantiated. The server is not even required to create an entity instance until the instance is accessed from a client (a stub), and so the only entities that might be instantiated would be those on which you actually make remote calls. This all depends on the implementation, however, and so you can see there can be a large difference in behavior from one product to another in terms of how large result sets are handled.

You cannot control this aspect of the Home interface methods. However, in general, it is advisable in business methods when returning multiple results to the client to return lightweight references instead of actual entity references—i.e., return primary key values. This relieves the server from having to support a potentially large and dynamic collection of remote references for every query.

**Bean-Managed Transaction.** Session beans are allowed to manage their own transactions. (EJB 1.0 allowed entity beans to do so as well, but you should not use that feature because it is disallowed in EJB 1.1.) Since session beans are often used to implement a transactional session layer from non-transactional clients, it is not unexpected that sometimes the session layer might want to explicitly control the transactions it initiates. Once initiated, a bean transaction may span multiple calls to the bean until the transaction completes, even if the client is non-transactional. This is because the EJB server associates the session with the transaction, and does not lose that association across remote calls. This multi-call transaction retention is only possible for stateful session beans.

A common use of session-managed transactions is logging. For example, the session might want to log each attempt to perform an operation, even if the operation fails. Therefore, a session method might need to initially operate outside the transaction which will be used to access the application data so that it can first perform a logging transaction. The logging transaction might make an entry in a list of attempted order entries. This list might consist of a file or some other database. Once the entry is made, it might attempt the actual order entry by beginning a transaction and then proceeding to do work.

Let's look at an example of a stateful session bean which begins its own transaction, and then allows operations on that transaction in other method calls.

```
public void m1()
{
    ...do some stuff that needs to occur before the transaction starts...
    t = ejbContext.getUserTransaction();
    t.begin();
}

public void m2()
{
    con = ds.getConnection();
    ...do stuff with connection...
    con.close();
}

public void m3()
{
    t.commit();
}
```

Now if we call m1, and then call m2 several times and finally call m3, all operations on the data resource (and any other data resources we access in that session between the transaction begin and the commit) will occur in the same transaction. Since the session is associated with the session bean, the transaction therefore encompasses all operations on that session bean, as well as all operations performed by that session bean between the begin and the commit.

Transactional resources (those using global transactions, not local transactions) can be closed and reopened—they will still occur in the same transaction, even across bean invocations, as long as the transaction has not yet been completed.

**Incorporating Mainframe and Legacy Transactions.** If you have existing transactions which have been built in a non-Java transactional environment, one approach to incorporating those transactions is to build a CORBA bridge to them. However, if that environment is not a CORBA environment, it may be easier to bridge to that environment using the transaction manager that environment is designed around. For example, the BEA Tuxedo product is a widely used non-Java transactional application server for accessing Tandem and other mainframe and high-availability systems. If the environment is a Tuxedo environment, it is likely there are Tuxedo transactions which can be accessed remotely.

The BEA WebLogic server currently supports Tuxedo distributed transactions through the use of the WebLogic Jolt data resource drivers. These are actually Tuxedo drivers, and Tuxedo is used to define transactions against specific data resources. All operations performed within the context of the transaction,

whether they are against the same data resource or not, occur as global Tuxedo transactions and are committed or rolled back as a unit.

For example, assume we have defined a pair of Tuxedo transactions called PING and PONG. The PING transaction executes against an Oracle server, and is implemented by a query which returns a single column value. The PONG transaction executes against a DB2 server and also returns a single column value. To use these two transactions, you must use them within the same Tuxedo session. An example of this is shown below:

```
public class PingPongServerImpl implements SessionBean
{
   private SessionContext context;
   private transient SessionPool joltSession;
   public String pingpong() throws Exception
   {
      bea.jolt.pool.Transaction transaction =
         joltSession.startTransaction(sessionTimeout);
      Result pingResult = joltSession.call(
         "PING", new DataSet(), transaction);
      String ping = (String)pingResult.getValue(
         "PING", null);
      Result pongResult = joltSession.call(
         "PONG", new DataSet(), transaction);
      String pong = (String)pingResult.getValue(
         "PONG", null);
      transaction.commit();
      return ping + pong;
   }
   public void ejbActivate()
   {
      javax.naming.Context c =
         new javax.naminjg.InitialContext(
            context.getEnvironment());
      String joltPoolName =
         poolAcontext.getEnvironment().get("joltPoolName");
      SessionPoolManager sPoolManager =
         (SessionPoolManager)
            c.lookup(SessionPoolManager.POOLMANAGER_NAME);
      joltSession = (SessionPool)
         sPoolManager.getSessionPool(joltPoolName);
      if (joltSession == null) throw new Exception(
         "Error intializing Jolt session pool");
   }
...
```

As you can see, it is actually Tuxedo that is coordinating the transaction to its own data resources.

However, the transaction used by the Tuxedo server is the same global transaction used by the EJB application server, and so any transactional data resources accessed by EJB server as part of that transaction will be included in the same global commit or rollback. Notice also that the Tuxedo Jolt connections are available through a pool so that there is little overhead with connecting and releasing connections at will within the application.

**Multiprocessing from a Single Bean Using Non-Blocking Calls.** The EJB model prohibits the explicit use of multithreading by applications. The reason is because service threads are created and managed by the server to enforce access control to beans. If a bean created a separate thread, that thread might remain running when the main service thread was returned to a thread pool and another client tried to access the bean, violating the EJB concurrency control model.

Normally this means that an application only can perform a single operation at a time. However, there is no reason why you cannot use a server-based multiprocessing facility which is integrated with the server and therefore cooperates with the EJB server's multithreading. For example, if the server is an ORB-based server which provides an interface repository, then you can use the DII interface to perform non-blocking "deferred-synchronous" CORBA method calls, continue other processing tasks, and then rendevous with the DII call. If the EJB server provides global transaction management, the DII call will propagate your bean's transaction context in the IIOP request header, thereby allowing your CORBA calls to participate in the EJB transaction. The scenario is shown in Figure 8-20.

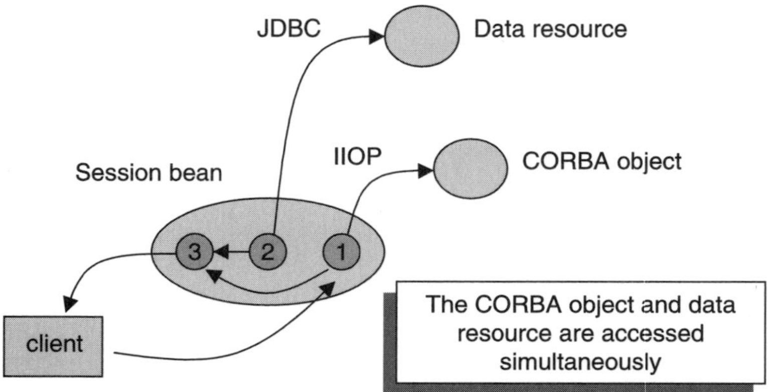


**Figure 8-20** Using CORBA's DII facility to implement multiprocessing from within an Enterprise JavaBean.

Let's look at an example of doing this. Suppose your bean is a session bean and needs to access two separate remote services: a database and a CORBA service (which might provide access to a database). Suppose the CORBA service is represented by the following IDL:

```
interface SomeService
{
   long getTotal();
}
```

Suppose the database you need to access is accessible via a connection pool called "SomeDatabase," and that you want to total a column called "SALES" from a set of rows of a table called "ATLANTA" in the database, and add that to the total you receive from SomeService. This might be your bean's remote interface:

```
public interface GetAllData extends EJBObject
{
   public int getGrandTotal() throws java.rmi.RemoteException;
}
```

Your bean business method implementation might look like this:

```
public int getGrandTotal()
{
   // Initiate non-blocking DII call to SomeService.
   SomeService someService = ...look up and narrow SomeService...
   org.omg.CORBA.Request request =
      someService._request("getTotal");
   request.set_return_type(
      orb.get_primitive_tc(
         org.omg.CORBA.TCKind.tk_long));
   request.send_deferred();// does not block

   // Perform access to database while the DII request
   // is being processed...
   java.sql.Statement statement = connection.createStatement();
   java.sql.ResultSet rs = statement.executeQuery(
      "SELECT sum(SALES) from ATLANTA");
   int totalA = rs.getInt(1);

   // Rendevous with the DII call.
   request.get_response();// blocks
   int totalB =
      request.result().value().extract_long();
```

```
    // Return both results in an AllData instance.
    return totalA + totalB;
}
```

You have now achieved what the EJB spec seems to preclude: doing two things at once, both initiated from the same client thread! Assuming the IIOP protocol, DII interface, and global transaction management are all supported by your EJB server and all data resources accessed, it will work, and without disturbing the EJB container or infrastructure.

It should be pointed out that doing this will not necessarily increase application throughput. It may even reduce throughput. The impact depends on the degree to which the remote resources are being utilized, as well as the EJB system load. It is likely it will decrease latency for a particular client, however, unless all clients use the technique.

**Using SessionSynchronization to Achieve Change Notification via Callbacks.** A common requirement for multiuser applications is to notify one user when another user has changed something. I address this at length elsewhere in this book, in terms of callback models and messaging models for both synchronous and non-synchronous change notification.

The optional SessionSynchronization interface of a session bean can be used to implement callback notification. For example, if your session bean implements SessionSynchronization, it must provide these methods:

```
void afterBegin()
void beforeCompletion()
void afterCompletion()
```

Your afterCompletion() method might have this implementation:

```
public void afterCompletion()
{
    // Use a JMS connection to notify all interested
    // parties that
    MapMessage msg = session.createMapMessage();
    msg.setString("EventName",  "ValueChanged");
    publisher.publish(msg);
}
```

This will notify all subscribers via a JMS provider that the specified event has occurred. Those subscribers then can access the appropriate bean or data object to obtain any new values they require. You can also provide the data in the event

message itself as long as clients understand that it might change again by the time they get the message.

There may be also be cases in which you want a bean to listen for JMS or other message events. In a future JMS release, the JMS API will be able to directly activate Enterprise JavaBeans. In the meantime, the best approach is to write a JMS listener application which waits for messages and then invokes the required bean methods in response.

**The Session Layer as a Transaction Encapsulation Layer.** If your client application is primarily a data access application, you might be tempted to conclude that you do not need any session beans and that all your accesses can go directly to the required entity beans. This works fine, as long as you only need to access one entity at a time. If your client is transactional, such as a transaction-capable servlet or other transactional client, you will be also be ok: you will be able to access multiple entity beans within the same transaction. If you need to access multiple entities within a single transaction and your client is non-transactional, however, you will need a server-side session within which to perform your transaction—you will need a session bean. Your session bean then exists for the purpose of starting and completing your transactions.

A server-side transaction layer made up of session beans can be very useful and powerful. For example, you can implement an optimistic locking policy in that layer, or a checkout policy, relieving clients from having to deal with the details of object timestamp or value comparison or object reservations. You can completely hide this functionality in your session layer. I have already outlined the techniques of these locking policies in an earlier chapter and so I will not repeat that here. However, there are still some issues that need to be dealt with, most prominent of which is the durability of the session.

Another reason to consider using session beans for maintaining client session state is that if session state is maintained in the servlet layer, only HTTP clients will be able to access it. If all your clients are thin clients this is not a concern, but if the application provides both heavy- and thin-client user interfaces, session portability across client types may be required.

**Durable Sessions.** Sessions are volatile in that if a server is shut down, all sessions are lost and are most probably not restored—session restoration is not required by the EJB model.

If you are using your sessions to implement a long-term session state which should not be lost in the event of server shutdown or failure, you should store that state in a durable resource such as a database. This can be done in many ways. Some application server products provide a distributed state management

facility for storing session data without tying the user to a particular session instance, which is nevertheless durable and survives across server restarts. A more standards-based approach, however, is to use either an entity bean for storing long-term session state, or to store the state directly in a database. I have already presented a technique for storing session state data from a session bean. If you use an entity bean, you can represent session state with a database table or object database collection which uses your session user ID as a primary or non-primary key, and then define a findXXX() method for retrieving the instance which represents your session. To protect the privacy of your session data, you will probably want to encode user principal-based access control in the entity bean as discussed previously in the section "Adding Application-Specific Authorization" on page 656.

Using an entity bean is a good solution for long-term logical transactions and work-process applications. Session state is automatically recoverable, and is not tied to a particular workstation, allowing for mobility of the user.

### *Tradeoffs Between Heavy EJB Clients and Thin EJB Clients*

The decision of whether to employ heavy clients or to use "thin" web clients (i.e., browsers and HTML / JavaScript) is an important decision which has a large effect on application usability. Thin clients benefit from quick startup and zero installation, but suffer from poor responsiveness and an inferior user interface compared with an executable heavy client and a total inability to receive callbacks.

There are some other tradeoffs besides the user interface. A heavy EJB client must obtain and most likely maintain a connection with an EJB server rather than with an HTTP server. This has potential negative ramifications for scalability. On the other hand, a heavy client has the ability to maintain all session state within the client itself, relieving the server from maintaining any session state; this has positive ramifications for scalability.

While EJB server products vary greatly, generally speaking, EJB servers have limits in the tens of thousands in terms of how many client connections they can concurrently support. Web servers on the other hand can easily support many more than this because of their inherently stateless connection model. Once again there is no reason why EJB server connections cannot be implemented in a similarly scalable way, but at present the focus is more on persistent connections which have less scalability than the weakly persistent or intermittent connections provided by web servers. The relative scalability of the different client models is discussed later in "Scaling Multitier Java Applications" on page 749.

### *EJB (User) Session and Persistent Database Session Association*

As EJB products mature, object databases will become increasingly important as implementations of container managed persistence. The standard object database model is the ODMG model. (At this writing there is an effort underway to recast this model in a more Java-centric way, under a new but very similar standard called "JDO.") The ODMG model prescribes that object database object references become stale at the end of a transaction, and so each transaction must reestablish full context within the database from scratch. Many object database products, however, extend this model and provide a means for object references to remain valid across transactions. The set of object references are associated with a particular client database session. A session is usually associated with a runtime thread.

This session is distinct from a session the user may have with the EJB server. If the user's session bean accesses a database session, either directly or indirectly via an entity bean, the user's thread must leave the session when the EJB call returns, because the thread belongs to the EJB server and will be returned to a thread pool. The problem is to reconnect to the same database session when the client makes the next EJB call. In addition, if the bean managing the session is an entity bean, the bean must ensure that no other client session accesses the database session until after the user which effectively belongs to a particular user. In other words, the session is reserved for the user which started it.

To recap, this issue only exists if one is attempting to persist EJB sessions across EJB calls. Transactions are not a problem, because the EJB container knows how to manage transactions across calls. Database sessions which persist across transactions are another matter, however, and are not considered by the EJB model. To draw a relational database analogy, it is as if one had a result set which endured after a transaction completed, and which was scrollable and lasted until explicitly closed by the client. The session association problem is depicted in Figure 8-21.

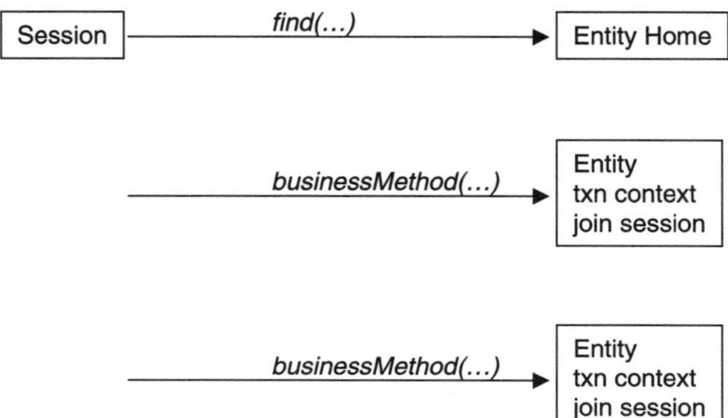


**Figure 8-21** Client session and object database session association.

There are two choices. One is to avoid this situation and refresh all object references anew with each transaction. The other is to build database session management into your beans as an optimization. This makes the implementation reliant on a non-standard feature, but it is hidden in the persistence implementation. In fact, it may be a feature of a container-managed persistence product.

### *The Double Interface Pattern to Provide Strong Typing of Your Implementation and Entity Interface*

A surprising feature of the EJB specification is that a bean's implementation does not have to implement the bean's interface. The implementation must implement either SessionBean or EntityBean, and the remote interface must extend EJBObject; but that is all. The deployment tools enforce the required mapping between a bean's interface and its implementation methods, but it would be nice if the compiler could catch mismatch errors as well between the interface and the implementation.

Another difficulty related to this occurs when you have a requirement for several bean implementations which all must inherit default behavior from a base class. The problem is that if the base class is a bean, it will have to implement SessionBean or EntityBean, and therefore have to implement all the many methods of one of those interfaces.

A solution is to define a business method interface separately from the bean's remote interface. The bean remote interface can extend the business interface, and the bean implementation base class can implement the interface as well. Bean concrete implementations can extend the base class, which implements the business interface. The concrete implementations can also implement SessionBean or EntityBean, which is required for them to be beans.

The result is that you have an interface type which truly represents your pure business method requirements apart from the fact that it is manifest as a remote bean. In designing the interface, make sure that the business methods throw an exception type which meets the requirements of bean remote methods, but that is all you need to do to make this work. A sample scenario depicting this for a session bean is shown in Figure 8-22.

### *Writing a Utility Layer to Handle Complex Data Relationships*

If you have an entity-relationship schema for your application, it is normal to use container-managed persistence and make each persistent object type an entity bean. Applications which need to operate very efficiently may need to be hand-coded, however. In that case, you would likely use bean-managed persistence.

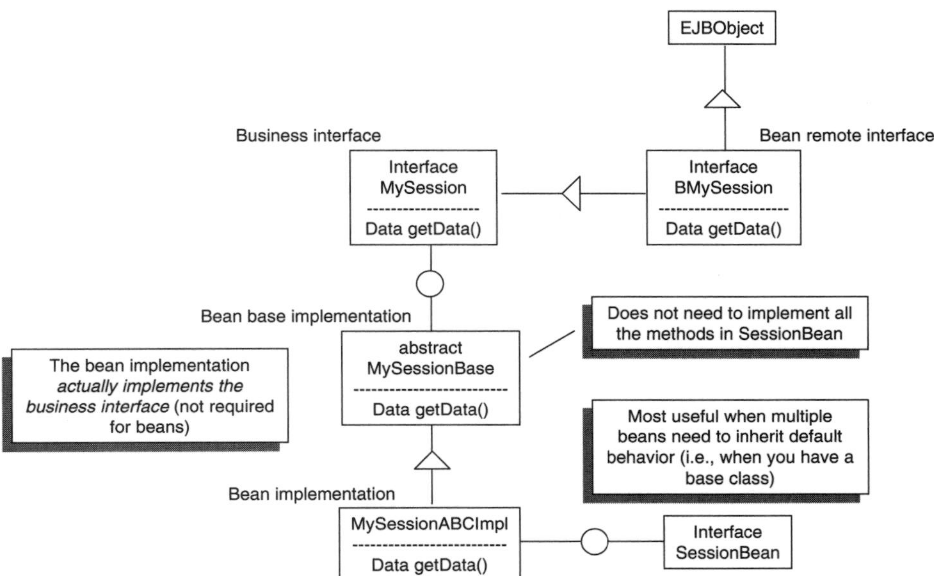


**Figure 8-22** The double-interface pattern for EJBs.

Using bean-managed persistence allows you to be more creative with regard to the implementation of your persistence layer, and there is no reason why you must make each object type an entity bean. In fact, a good strategy is to first develop a persistence utility layer, which operates directly on the underlying persistence mechanism, such as a relational database, and encode the primitive transactions that your application will need. On top of that, you can provide entity beans if desired for those objects which serve as entry points to the data. Purists may balk at this, but it results in a high performance design without sacrificing flexibility. This is true as long as isolation and concurrency control is provided by the underlying database, which is the case if you are using a relational database.

For example, suppose your object model defines an Account object and a Person object, with a many-to-one relationship between them. These objects are shown at the top of Figure 8-23. As shown in the figure, this type of object schema can easily be mapped to equivalent relational tables, consisting of an Account table, a Person table, and a relationship table to capture the many-to-one relationship between Account and Person.

To capture this kind of schema with EJB container managed persistence, the EJB server has to provide a mechanism for persistifying the relationship between Account and Person. One approach is to use an object-to-relational mapping compiler, to generate an equivalent relational schema and the code to access it.

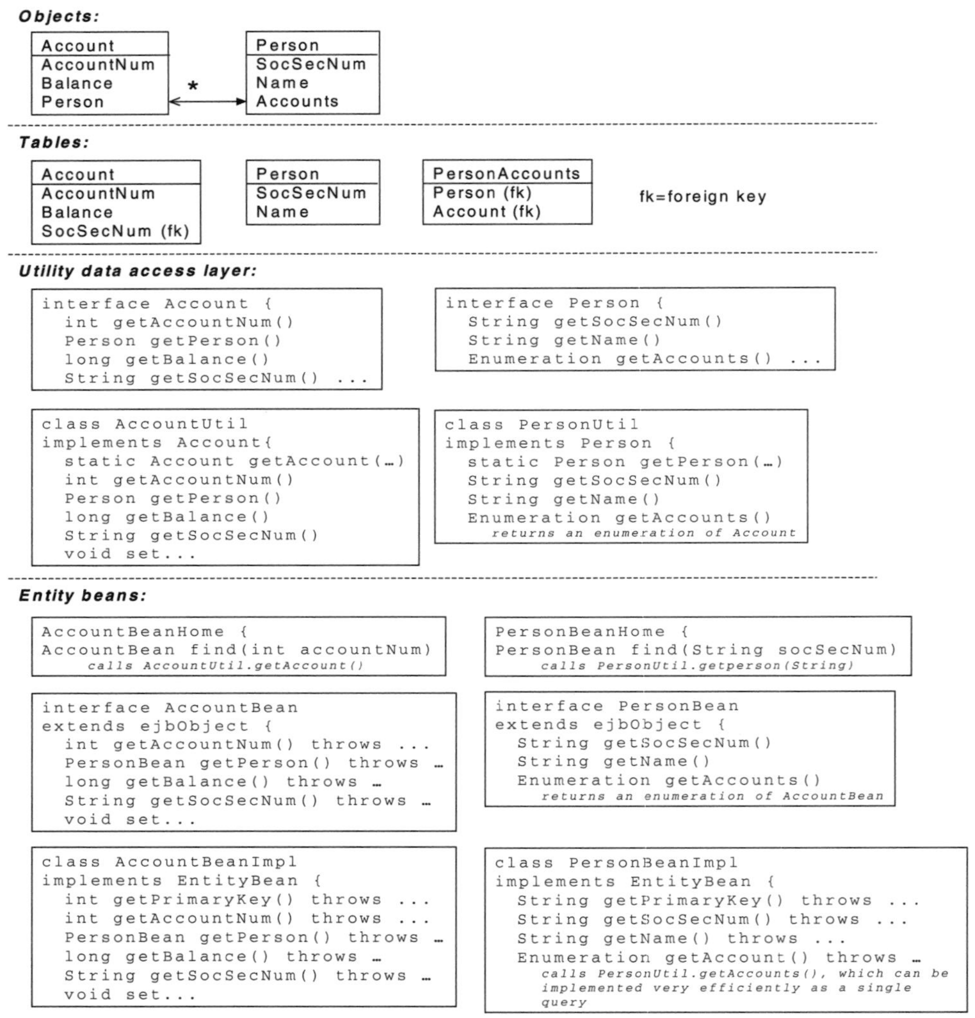


**Figure 8-23** A utility layer for mapping objects to tables, and ultimately to entity beans.

An alternative is to code the mapping by hand. If you plan to do this, you can make your job easier by first coding a transactional persistence layer based on your object schema. After that is working, and you have determined that it meets the needs of all of your application's transactions, you can write an entity bean layer on top of it. The entity bean layer provides keyed access to the data objects, and allows them to be accessed remotely in the context of the EJB server. This

approach separates the task of database access from EJB deployment, which allows programmers to concentrate on one aspect of the problem at a time. It also makes it possible to encode the persistence operations much more efficiently.

For example, the object model consisting of Persons and Accounts, shown in Figure 8-23, can be mapped to a relational schema. The application processing requirements can then be analyzed, and an object-oriented data access and utility layer can be designed which provides transactional access to the underlying relational tables and also provides convenience methods for performing commonly required operations, such as joins, in an efficient manner. This access layer is unaware of whether clients will be local or remote, and its purpose is to provide efficient and transactional access to the data, anticipating the needs of client applications. For transactional isolation, it relies on the underlying database. In the example, the classes AccountUtil and PersonUtil provide the utility methods. For example, PersonUtil provides the static method getPerson(...), which retrieves a person record from the database based on parameters specified. PersonUtil also provides the method getAccounts(...), which efficiently implements the one-to-many relationship between Person and Account. Other methods might perform complex joins to return result sets or collections. All this is done directly against the database without any interposition from an EJB infrastructure.

Once a utility access layer has been implemented which provides the fundamental search and retrieval operations that clients will need, EJB entity beans can be built on top of this layer. The entity bean designers do not have to worry about concurrency control because that has been addressed in the utility access layer. The EJB designers only have to build an efficient remote access layer (i.e., an entity bean layer) on top of the utility layer. Complex session-oriented processing needs for clients can then be built using session beans which access the entity beans as transactional persistent objects.

The advantage of this approach is that it leads to an efficient persistence implementation, instead of leaving it up to a persistence mapping tool. Also, since the database is used for concurrency control, non-EJB clients can safely access the same data using other protocols.

### *Session Beans for Encapsulating Application Processes*

If your bean client is transactional, for example, a transaction-aware servlet engine, you may be able to maintain all session state in the client closer to where it is needed without burdening the EJB server with session state. However, there is a tradeoff in doing this in that it means that every entity bean access will result in a remote call from the EJB client to the EJB server. These calls may be more efficient if they occur locally within the EJB server.

The solution is to clearly separate what constitutes session state and what constitutes well-defined operations which primarily access backend data resources and which can be encapsulated in session beans. For example, suppose your application session must make calls to two separate entity beans in order to obtain separate results, which it then integrates in some way (e.g., totals) and displays for the client. Rather than perform separate client calls to each entity, it may be more efficient to create a session bean which performs the integrating (e.g., totaling) operation and have the clients call this instead, resulting in a single call instead of multiple client calls.

In fact, such business methods are reusable and should be first encapsulated in reusable classes which then are wrapped in session beans. That allows these reusable classes to be redeployed in other frameworks if the need arises. If bean-managed persistence is being used for the entity beans, it may even be possible to write the session methods separate from the EJB model and then wrap all the required session and entity accesses in beans, as discussed in the previous section.

### *Session Beans as Entity Factories*

It is often the case that a session must access unanticipated kinds of entities. The session might be passed an argument which specifies the name of the Home interface to look up. Once the desired Home interface is found, the session can call a findXXX() method on the Home interface.

The problem is that to make that call, the session must operate on the exact type of the Home interface—not a base type. This is because Home interface methods must return the exact type of the entity they represent, and therefore their methods cannot be extended. Therefore, a session cannot have a statement of the form:

```
EntityHomeBaseType eh =
   (EntityHomeBaseType)context.lookup("MyConcreteEntityHome");
EntityBaseType e = eh.create();
```

because the return type of the create() method of the Home interface of each entity type will be different from each other, making it impossible to override the method in derived Home classes.

A solution is to use reflection to interrogate the stub for a create() method and invoke it. Consider a set of entity types, all which have Home interfaces with a create() method that takes an argument of type `ArgsBaseType`. As long as there is a create(ArgsBaseType) in each Home interface we can use reflection to invoke the create(ArgsBaseType) method on the Home interface stub:

```
Class c = eh.getClass();
Method m = c.getMethod("create", new Class[] {
```

```
   Class.forName("ArgsBaseType") });
bio = (BIO)(m.invoke(ioh, new Object[] { roleArgs }));
```

Note that the create() method of each concrete type must have *exactly* the same argument signature. In the above example I use an argument of type ArgsBaseType, which can be subclassed, but still each create() method must be declared to take an argument of type ArgsBaseType—not a subclass of it. If a subclass is desired, each concrete create() method can cast internally the argument type to a subclass:

```
public void create(ArgsBaseType args)
{
   MyExtendedArgsType a = (MyExtendedArgsType)args;
   ...use a instead of args...
}
```

The same considerations apply to the findXXX() methods.

### *Don't Invoke Methods on "This"*

The keyword "this" is dynamically bound to the runtime type of the object which owns the enclosing method, even if the object is a subtype of the class in which the method is defined. When an EJB method is invoked, the actual object may be a subclass, of the bean implementation class. Therefore "this" will refer to that subclass if there is one. In any case, it will never be a remote stub.

If a bean implementation passes "this" as an argument to another bean, the object passed will be either the bean implementation class type or a subclassed type. Further, the passed object will not implement the bean's EJB remote interface, which extends the EJBObject interface. It will therefore be missing important methods which are used by the server's interposition layer.

In general, unless they are declared to be reentrant, beans are not allowed to invoke themselves through another bean. Passing "this" provides an avenue to shortcut this against the rules, since if the receiver of "this" invokes a method on the passed reference, which is the actual implementation and not a stub, there is no opportunity for the server to interpose itself. The server will end up trying to marshall the bean implementation. (Passing "this" in a remote call to another bean would only work under special circumstances anyway; in most cases it would generate an error.) Bean implementations should therefore not pass "this" as an argument when invoking other beans.

If your bean implementation needs to pass itself to another bean, obtain the current bean's SessionConext or EntityContext and call the context's getEJBObject() method on the context. This returns an EJBObject implementation which can be passed to other beans.

### *Passing Entities by Value*

In Chapter 6, I provide an example of a remote application which has the ability to provide remote object interfaces or alternatively provide the remote objects by value. The value representations are lightweight streamable versions of the server-based objects—they are not even derived from the same base type. These lightweight objects were viewed as messages and were therefore logically immutable. After all, clients should not think that they can modify the streamed objects, or they might also think that those modifications would propagate to the server—which they would not.

It is often useful to provide to clients a lightweight streamable version of an entity. This allows the client to peruse the entity locally instead of making a remote call for every accessor. The streamed version should have all serializable attributes, ideally defined to be public and final. The streamable version may implement the business interface of the entity if the double-interface pattern is used, but in that case, any setter methods or methods which change the state of the entity instead should throw an application exception.

The streamable message objects should be small and represent a logically composite value, and not carry information that is peripheral to the entity's purpose. Primary keys should be sent for all embedded references to other entities rather than sending along those entities as well.

The associated entity might have a getValue() method which would return the streamed value, or thrown an application level exception if a streamable version of the entity is not available or possible. The example shown in the next section will illustrate this, along with many other concepts that I have been discussing. (This example is based on research I did in collaboration with the CORBA and EJB design staff at the National Security Agency, and I would like to thank them for their valuable object analysis and insight.)

### *A More Comprehensive Example*

This example will illustrate several concepts:

- The double-interface pattern
- A factory pattern for obtaining multiple arbitrary entities from a transactional session
- Providing a getValue() method for entities
- Using the ejbLoad() method to convert the persistent representation into an object representation

The goal of this example is to serve as a general template for a very common usage of enterprise beans: when a transactional user session must access one or

more entities within the same transaction, possibly of different kinds, and most or all entities derive from a common base class which provides generic behavior—including the EntityBean default behavior. This example may seem complex, but it represents the general case well and illustrates many of the issues we have discussed.

Let's consider a trivial application which needs to provide stockbrokers with access to information about stocks. The basic business interface, called Stock, might be defined as follows:

```
public interface Stock
{
   String getSymbol() throws RemoteException;
   void setSymbol(String sym) throws RemoteException;
}
```

I have added the throws clauses because as we have seen, they will be necessary to be able to implement an EJB interface which provides these methods.

We might also want to define some remote behavior that only the remote interface would possess. Rather than define the EJB interface just yet, let's define a separate interface which contains the remote behavior:

```
public interface RStock extends Stock
{
   public SStock getValue() throws NotSerializableException;
}
```

The method I have chosen to add is a method which returns a streamable version of the entity. This is the method a client will call to obtain the entity by value—with the proviso that any changes made to the value copy only affect the local copy. The getValue() method returns an SStock which I will define as follows:

```
public interface SStock extends Stock, java.io.Serializable {}
```

This defines a streamable version of the Stock interface, and it has the same methods as the business interface. The implementation actually returned will possibly restrict the use of some of the methods. Consider this base class implementation of SStock:

```
public abstract class SStockBase implements SStock
{
   private String symbol;
```

```
   public SStockImpl(String sym) { this.symbol = sym; }

   public String getSymbol() throws RemoteException
   {
      return symbol;
   }

   public void setSymbol(String sym) throws RemoteException
   {
      throw new Exception("Method not available");
   }
}
```

As you can see, if a client attempts to use the setSymbol() method on the streamed copy, they will get an exception advising them that they are trying to change a local copy.

Let's now define the EJB interface for the entity:

```
public interface BStock extends RStock, EJBObject {}
```

The EJB interface is therefore merely an aggregator which combines the RStock interface with the EJBObject interface. This is the interface seen by remote clients of the bean we are going to define. I chose to define the remote interface in RStock, instead of adding it directly to the EJB interface, because now I will be able to make the entity implementation class implement RStock instead of the EJB interface. I will obtain compile-time type checking on all my business methods, without having to implement the remote interface, which would require me to define additional methods that are intended for the server's interposition layer and should not be in the implementation class.

Before defining the bean implementation class, I might want to define a base class which multiple implementation classes can inherit to obtain standard EJB behavior and possibly other behavior that I might want to provide as a default. Here is such a base class:

```
public abstract class StockEntityBase implements RStock,
EntityBean
{
   // ----------------------------------------------------
   // Private instance state.

   private EntityContext entityContext;
   private String symbol;
```

```
// -----------------------------------------------------
// Persistent fields. These must be public if
// container-managed persistence is used.

public Key key;    // The primary key for all stock entities.

// -----------------------------------------------------
// Methods from RStock:
//

public Object getValue() throws
   java.io.NotSerializableException
{
   throw new java.io.NotSerializableException();
}

// -----------------------------------------------------
// Methods from Stock:
//

public String getSymbol() { return symbol; }
public void setSymbol(String sym) { symbol = sym; }

// -----------------------------------------------------
// EntityBean methods:
//

/**
 * An ejbCreate() method is called to initialize the entity.
 * If container-managed persistence is used, an ejbCreate()
 * method merely sets initial values for fields, and the
 * container persistence mechanism will write those values
 * to storage. For bean-managed persistence, an ejbCreate()
 * method must also write to persistent storage, most likely
 * creating a new record or persistent object in the process.
 */
public OID ejbCreate(String sym) throws
   java.rmi.RemoteException
{
   init(sym);
   return key;
}

/**
 * For bean-managed persistence, this method must
 * actually remove the entity representation from storage.
 * For container-managed persistence, this is usually a no-op.
 */
```

```
   public void ejbRemove() {}

   public void setEntityContext(EntityContext ec)
      { entityContext = ec; }
   public void unsetEntityContext() { entityContext = null; }
   public void ejbActivate() {}
   public void ejbPassivate() {}

   /**
    * For container-managed persistence, this is called after
    * fields are reloaded. For bean-managed persistence, this
    * method must actually read fields from storage.
    */
   public void ejbLoad() {}

   /**
    * For container-managed persistence, this is called before
    * fields are stored. For bean-managed persistence, this
    * method must actually write fields to storage.
    */
   public void ejbStore() {}

   public void ejbPostCreate() {}
   public void ejbPostCreate(int status) {}

   // ---------------------------------------------------
   // Protected methods.
   //

   protected void init(String sym)
   {
      key = new Key(sym);
   }
}
```

Now that this base class is defined, we can not only reuse it, but we do not have to clutter our business logic implementation class with all this behavior, which is largely boilerplate.

We have discussed all the EJB methods already; the topic of most interest here is the class structure, so I will not go into the above methods.

All the interfaces and classes discussed so far logically comprise a set of public resources for accessing stocks. I will assign them to a package called "stock," the structure of which is shown in Figure 8-24. For simplicity, I have omitted a Home interface.

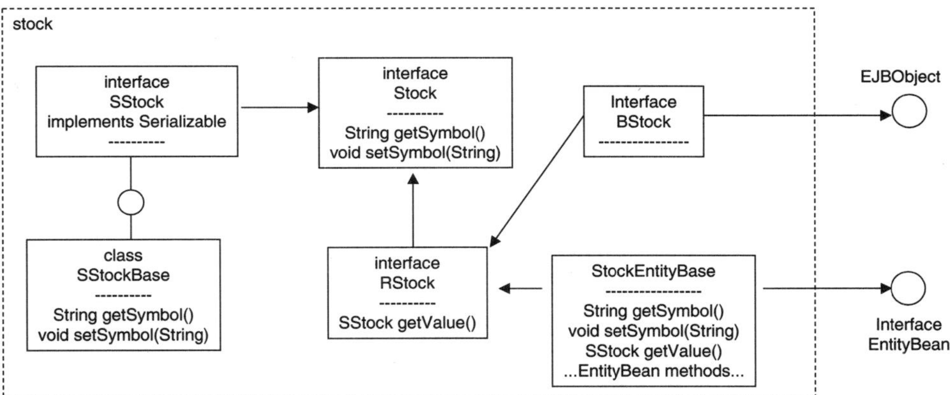


**Figure 8-24** The `stock` package.

We can now specialize this set of tools, say for New York Stock Exchange stocks, by creating a package called "nyse," which draws on the stock interfaces and classes and extends or implements them. I will define in package nyse an interface called NYSEStock which extends the basic business interface of the stock package—Stock—and adds methods which might apply to NYSE stocks. Remember this is an artificial example for the purpose of examining EJB class structure—do not bother to compare it too closely with real world stock exchanges!

The NYSEStock interface is as follows:

```
public interface NYSEStock extends Stock
{
   public int getPrice() throws RemoteException;
   public void setPrice() throws RemoteException;
}
```

I have specialized the Stock interface by adding two additional methods. The function of the methods is not important for our purposes; what is important is that the NYSE specialization of Stock has additional methods.

Once again I will follow our pattern and define a streamable version of this, which I will call SNYSEStock. This interface extends the streamable SStock interface defined earlier as well as the NYSEStock interface. Thank goodness for double inheritance of interfaces!

```
public interface SNYSEStock extends SStock, NYSEStock {}
```

I will also define a concrete implementation of this interface, which will extend the SStockBase base class defined earlier:

```
public class SNYSEStockImpl extends SStockBase implements
SNYSEStock
{
   private int price;

   public SNYSEStockImpl(String sym, int price)
   {
      super(sym);
      this.price = price;
   }

   public int getPrice() throws RemoteException { return price; }

   public void setPrice(int p) throws RemoteException
   {
      throw new Exception("Method not available");
   }
}
```

This is the actual concrete type a client will get if they call the getValue() method on a Stock EJB entity interface. It is a lightweight version of a Stock, and permits a client to peruse the object without making remote call after remote call. Of course, it does not have the remote behavior of the remote version, and clients must use the streamable version accordingly. Notice that as for the getSymbol() method of the base class, it does not allow a client to modify it by changing the price, as a reminder that this is merely a copy of the actual object.

The corresponding EJB interface for a NYSEStock is as follows:

```
public interface BNYSEStock extends BStock, NYSEStock {}
```

Once again, this is merely an aggregator. I did not bother to define a separate remote interface because I do not desire to add any remote behavior in the NYSE specialization.

We are now ready to define the actual concrete EJB class representing a NYSE-Stock. I will call that class NYSEStockEntity:

```
public class NYSEStockEntity extends StockEntityBase implements
   NYSEStock
{
   private transient NYSEStock stock;
   public int price;    // Must be public so container can
                        // persistify it.
```

```
    public String symbol;    // "

    public int getPrice()
    {
       return stock.getPrice();
    }

    public void setPrice()
    {
       stock.setPrice();
    }

    public void ejbLoad()
    {
       //
       // Convert persistent representation into an object
       // representation. In this case I use a separate
       // object to illustrate how a composite pattern
       // can be used with relational persistence.

       stock = new NYSEStockImpl(symbol, price);
    }

    public void ejbStore()
    {
       //
       // Synchronize values before persistification.

       symbol = stock.getSymbol();
       price = stock.getPrice();
    }
}
```

Notice that this implementation of the entity uses an internal instance of NYSE-StockImpl to provide its behavior. We have not yet discussed this class. I am assuming that it implements important business behavior for NYSEStock objects. The entity class could use and extend this behavior to provide the required remote and persistent semantics. I could define the business behavior directly in the `NYSEStockEntity` EJB implementation class, but I wanted to illustrate an important point: I have delegated the entity's behavior to the embedded NYSE-Stock instance according to a composite pattern. This might be convenient for constructing a streamable representation of the entity. More importantly, I can encapsulate the construction of this internal NYSEStock instance, which allows me to more easily use a different representation for storing the object's state to a non-object oriented data resource.

To clarify this, in the above example I use the ejbStore() method to read the contents of the embedded NYSEStock instance into non-transient attributtes. The reference to the NYSEStock instance is itself transient, so a container persistence mechanism will ignore it. The attributes price and symbol are public and non-transient, so they will automatically be stored by the container when necessary. The ejbStore() method and ejbLoad() methods provide for the synchronization of the storable attributes with the internal NYSEStock instance. If we were to allow the NYSEStock instance to be stored directly by a non-object oriented (e.g., relational) persistence mechanism, there is no telling how it might get mapped. We might like the way it gets mapped, but we might not—it will depend on the container. The technique used here provides an escape to use when you have an ill-suited container.

The actual implementation of NYSEStockImpl is not important. It could be identical to the SNYSEStockImpl class, except that it would not throw an exception when its setter methods are used.

The nyse package is shown in Figure 8-25. Again, the Home interface is omitted for simplicity.

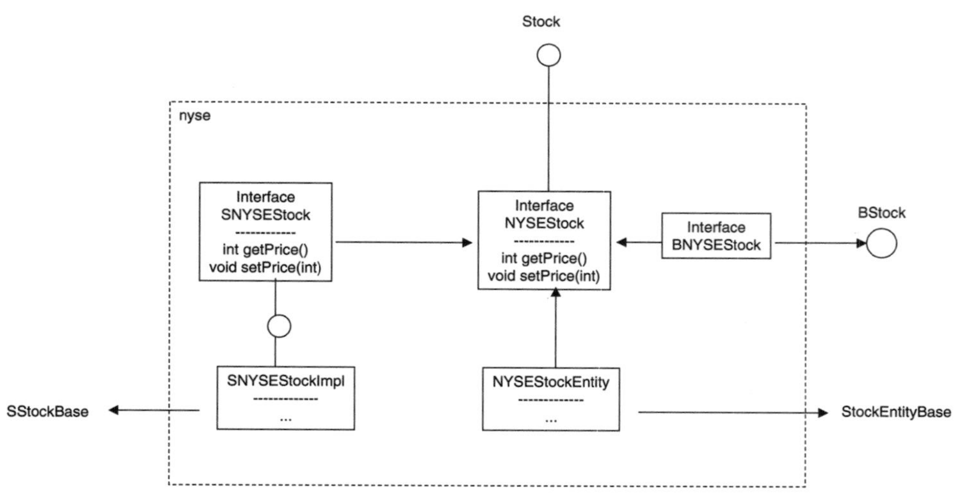


**Figure 8-25** The `nyse` package.

We should now consider how a client would use this entity. Non-transactional clients might need to access more than one entity at a time within a single transaction, and so we clearly need a stateful session interface to provide a transaction context that can span multiple method calls. In addition, a client might want to

access stock entities of other specialized types in addition to the NYSEStock type. The session therefore cannot be hard-wired for NYSEStock entities or the NYSE-Stock Home interface.

Let's now look at the Home interface for a NYSEStock. The create() and find() methods appearing in the Home interface must have the return type of the entity's EJB interface—the return type cannot be a base type. Therefore, one cannot overload Home interface methods. The NYSEStock Home interface might look like this:

```
public interface NYSEHome
{
   public BNYSEStock create(String sym)
      throws CreateException, RemoteException;
   public BNYSEStock findByPrimaryKey(Key key)
      throws RemoteException, FinderException;
}
```

A session bean which provides access to our entity type might have this interface:

```
public interface Facade
{
   public BStock getStock(String exchange, String sym)
   throws RemoteException;
}
```

As you can see, I am allowing for the possibility that there might be different kinds of stocks in addition to NYSE stocks by requiring the session client to specify an exchange, such as "NYSE," "ASE" (for the American Stock Exchange), and so on. The session bean interface for this might be:

```
public interface BFacade extends Facade, EJBObject {}
```

Clients can create a BFacade session which provides them with transactional context and session state management. The session would manage the user's session state information and provide services such as optimistic data access policies, and possibly user interface management. The session can access entity beans as components which provide access to persistent data resources and other kinds of multiuser state. The session can access other session objects for business rules, which should be encapsulated according to discrete and well-defined functions. In most cases, sessions accessed indirectly in this way by other sessions will be stateless, and the only sessions with state would likely be sessions designed for end-use access, although this is not a hard and fast rule.

A session bean which wants to access an entity's Home interface does so by looking it up using a JNDI context. Once the remote reference to the Home interface is obtained, it can call a create() or findXXX() method to obtain a reference to the desired entity. When looking up the Home interface, the session bean will have to specify the exact published name of the Home interface for the entity class. In other words, we cannot use a generic Home interface to serve for us several different kinds of entities—e.g., NYSE entities, ASE entities, and so on, based on a create() or findXXX() argument. We need to look up the Home interface that is specific to the entity type we want. Once obtained, the Home interface cannot have an overridden findXXX() method which we can call using a base Home interface type—we have to invoke the appropriate findXXX() method on exactly the Home type that applies to the entity. This means that either the session object must have a separate call for every kind of entity it might access, or alternatively it can use Java reflection to construct a call, with the assumption that all entities will adhere to a certain pattern for its findXXX() methods.

Here is an implementation of our EJB session interface:

```
public class FacadeSession implements Facade, SessionBean
{
   // ---------------------------------------------------
   // Private instance state.
   //

   private SessionContext sessionContext;

   // ---------------------------------------------------
   // Methods from Facade:
   //

   public BStock getStock(String exchange, String sym)
   throws FacadeException
   {
      //
      // Look up the Home interface for the specified exchange.

      StockHome shome = lookUpStockHome(exchange);

      //
      // Retrieve the object from the repository.

      BStock bstock = null;
      Class c = shome.getClass();
      Method m = null;
      try
```

```
   {
      m = c.getMethod("findByPrimaryKey", new Class[] {
         Class.forName("stock.Key") });
      bstock = (BStock)(m.invoke(shome, new Object[] { sym }));
   }
   catch (Exception exf)
   {
      exf.printStackTrace();
      throw new FacadeException(exf);
   }
   return bstock;
}

// ----------------------------------------------------
// SessionBean methods:
//

public void ejbPassivate() {}

public void ejbActivate() {}

public void ejbCreate() {}
{
   // Initialize all non-transient fields here.
}

public void ejbRemove() {}

public void setSessionContext(SessionContext ctx) {
   sessionContext = ctx; }

public void beforeCompletion() {}

// ----------------------------------------------------
// Protected methods.
//

protected StockHome lookUpStockHome(String exchange) throws
   FacadeException
{
   Context ic = null;
   String jndiName =
      /* "ejb/" + */   // for 1.1
      getHomeName(exchange);
   StockHome shome = null;
   try
   {
      ic = new InitialContext();
```

```
            shome = (StockHome)ic.lookup(jndiName);
        }
        catch (NamingException ex)
        {
            throw new FacadeException("Unable to look up "
                + jndiName, ex);
        }

        return shome;
    }

    protected String getHomeName(Class role)
    {
        return exchange + "Home";
    }
}
```

Notice the use of Java reflection against the Home interface stub to invoke a findByPrimaryKey() method against a Home type which is not statically known to the application. Note also that the caller—a session bean in this case—needs to have foreknowledge of the name and type signatures used by the findXXX() methods it intends to use.

The session package, which I have called "facade" for lack of a better word, is as shown in Figure 8-26. (I did not want to call the package "session" since I would then be inclined to call the bean class "SessionSession," which would be confusing.) Once again, the Home interface is omitted for simplicity.

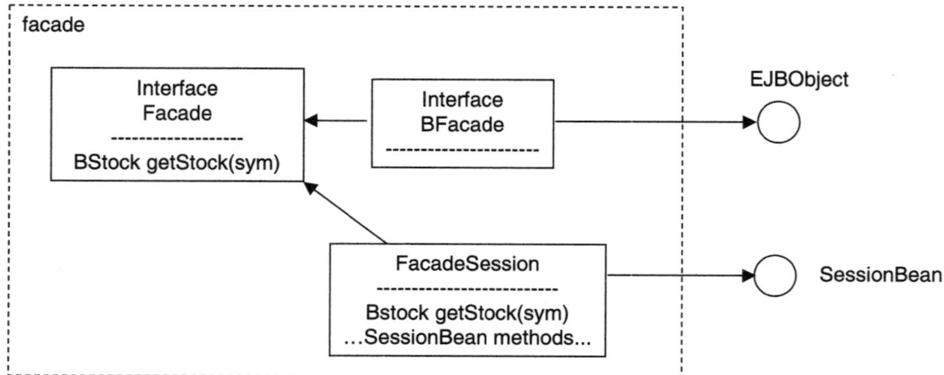


**Figure 8-26** The facade package.

This is quite a lot of code to implement for an infrastructure that is supposed to make the programmer's job "automatic." It makes one stop and question for a moment what value the EJB infrastructure provides. The value, of course, is distributed transaction management, session state management, concurrency control, deployment facilities, and many other things. Reliable multiuser multidata resource distributed applications are impossible without these things.

### *Running CORBA from Inside an EJB; Accessing Beans from CORBA Servants*

You should not export a CORBA servant in a bean, because that will create a non-EJB thread and will violate the EJB single-thread model. However, your bean can be a CORBA client and you can use IIOP to communicate with external ORBs. If your EJB server is a CORBA-based EJB server, it will also be able to export beans with both an EJB interface and a CORBA (IDL) interface by providing IDL for the Home and bean interfaces, making the Home interface available from a CORBA name service, and exposing the home's interface and bean's interface in an interface repository.

Some CORBA-based EJB servers provide a facility for pooling CORBA connections to non-EJB CORBA objects. In this case the connection is treated the same as an external pooled resource. Present implementations are stateful and typically do not participate in EJB load management. Such connections are usually dedicated to a particular CORBA object instance once established, although there is no reason they cannot have their own load management service.

### *Storing EJB References in an LDAP Server*

It is possible to store EJB references in an LDAP server. EJB references—including the Home interface reference—are merely RMI or IIOP references. Since both of those kinds of references can be stored in an LDAP repository, you can store an EJB reference in an LDAP repository. Here is an example of doing just that:

```
// Identify the RMI registry and LDAP context URLs.
String nameServiceHostUrl = rmi://registryhost
String ldapContextUrl = ldap://ldaphost/o=myorg

// Set the RMI provider.
Properties p = new Properties();
p.put("java.naming.factory.initial",
   "weblogic.jndi.TengahInitialContextFactory");
p.put("java.naming.provider.url", nameServiceHostUrl);

// Obtain the context.
InitialContext context = new InitialContext(p);
```

```
// Look up the bean.
Object o = context.lookup("pingservice");
context.close();

// Narrow the returned object's concrete type to
// the interface type. )If we were using IIOP, we
// would use PortableRemmoteObject.narrow().)
ServerHome serverHome = (ServerHome)o;

// Set the LDAP JNDI provider.
p = new Properties();
p.put("java.naming.factory.initial",
   "com.sun.jndi.ldap.LdapCtxFactory");
p.put("java.naming.provider.url", ldapContextUrl);

// Obtain the context.
InitialDirContext context_ldap = new InitialDirContext(p);

// Bind the bean Home reference.
context_ldap.rebind("cn=pingservice_ldap",
   serverHome, null);
```

The last statement above is critical. The behavior of the LDAP provider will depend on the types that serverHome implements. If it implements java.rmi.Remote, the appropriate Java LDAP schema classes will be used to map the Home reference as an RMI reference. (Note that EJBHome extends java.rmi.Remote.) If our serverHome object uses IIOP instead of JRMP, then it will implement org.omg.CORBA.Object, and the corresponding CORBA LDAP schema classes will be used to map the Home reference. (The CORBA LDAP mapping is discussed in Chapter 7.)

Otherwise, if the Home reference implements java.io.Serializable, it will be stored as a serialized byte stream, using the LDAP javaSerializedObject schema. If the Home object uses a proprietary RMI mechanism and does not implement java.rmi.Remote, but does implement Serializable, then the Home reference will be stored opaquely as a serialized object.

Now let's attempt to look up and use the LDAP entry we just created:

```
// Look up the bean Home using the LDAP entry we
// just created.
Object b = context_ldap.lookup("cn=pingservice_ldap");

// Narrow the return value to the Home type.
ServerHome serverHome_ldap = (ServerHome)b;
```

```
// Create an instance of the bean.
Server server_ldap = serverHome_ldap.create();

// Invoke the bean.
try { System.out.println(server_ldap.ping()); }
catch (java.rmi.RemoteException re) {
   System.out.println(
   "Unrecoverable failure - transaction did not complete");
}
```

Typically an EJB server will come with its own JNDI provider for registering and looking up enterprise beans. This does not present a problem in itself for portability, since the provider dependence is easily encapsulated. In addition, the name service provider may represent a significant value-added feature and set of capabilities, including load balancing. On the other hand, the EJB server's name service may be LDAP based, since many server products now come with an integrated LDAP server or allow you to use your own.

One glitch you may encounter is that if you use other JNDI providers in your application, for example, an LDAP provider, they must all use the same version (or at least compatible versions) of JNDI, because these providers are all accessed from the same program. Since JNDI has evolved somewhat between the 1.1 and 1.2 releases, and server products are not always completely up to date with revisions of extension packages (such as package javax.naming), you should check which version of JNDI your app server JNDI providers use before planning to mix providers from other sources.

There is also the problem of security. The LDAP service will almost certainly require authentication to access it. Your EJB server will either have to be able to exchange credentials automatically, or you will have to provide them programmatically when creating the JNDI context. This is discussed in detail in Chapter 7.

### *Multiple EJB Server Tiers*

The basic model defined for RMI, CORBA, and EJB is based on a three-tier arrangement in which a client invokes a remote method on a server tier which then accesses a data tier. As the number of clients grows, the number of connections between clients and the single server increases and at some point becomes too burdensome for the server.

Of course many variations on this are possible, including interposing a web tier between the clients and the server. This allows the web tier to pool server connections, and since web connections are transient and easily scaled, the burden on the server is relieved. A solution is still needed for the general problem, however, of tiering application servers. Intranets in particular need a way to scale their internal services without resorting to building web interfaces when web interfaces are not needed.

Message-oriented systems have long ago solved this problem by allowing messaging servers to broker messages for each other, and route them only as needed to reach a final destination. This allows clients to maintain persistent connections with their local messaging server, permitting notification callback messages. The same can be achieved with remote invocation protocols, such as CORBA and RMI, if it is designed into the application. What is needed is a messaging tier, which can be implemented with the remote invocation protocol or with a messaging protocol. A messaging tier has these characteristics:

- Allows a callback architecture, without the overhead
- Solves the problem of synchronizing clients
- First server tier acts as a switch into the messaging tier

Clients create EJB sessions with a local server. The local server provides beans that act as proxy services to its clients and behave as if they were the actual service provider. When a service arrives, the proxy beans determine where the service can be obtained and forward the request, either to a next level tier or to the actual service provider.

This arrangement is scalable because each tier only needs to maintain a connection to each of its own clients and also a small pool of connections to its parent in the message tier.

Client callbacks are practical if the required number of permanent client connections is handled in a scalable way, either through tiering or because the number of clients is within the range of what the primary server tier can handle. When implementing callbacks, be careful that you do not introduce additional connection protocols unless absolutely necessary. It is common for Java programmers to assume that they can just export a standard Java RMI server object in their client and then create an RMI connection back to the client from a server object. If you do this from a server which uses a protocol other than the standard Java RMI implementation (or perhaps not even RMI), you will have an additional socket connection just for the callback in addition to whatever server connection your client normally has. Make sure that the protocol package you use for any callback objects is the same as what the server uses, unless you feel you have no choice but to use a different protocol.

### *Initiating Calls from the Inside*

Many Internet applications employ a design which receives web requests from the Internet through an outer firewall and in which servlets or other web-based programs in the "DMZ" (the area between the outer firewall and the inner fire-

wall) then make data requests through an internal firewall to internal protected EJB servers or data resources.

Even if you trust the protocol which passes through your inner firewall and you are confident that your routers can effectively filter against packet level attacks, the mere fact that a connection originates from the outside and passes into your protected network introduces the risk of penetration by very sophisticated attacks. It is considered far safer if all TCP connections orignate from *inside* your network and none originate from outside.

This is problematic for most protocols such as RMI, HTTP, and so on, because with these protocols the requestor originates the TCP connection. However, as we saw in "The Blocked Registrant Pattern" on page 496, it is possible to service externally originated requests by using an internally originated communication connection. To implement this you could employ a bastion application server in the DMZ which receives a blocked registration request from an application server inside the protected network.

A more common way of dealing with this problem is to employ a message-based interface, in which requestors insert their requests into a request queue and a servicer behind the inner firewall removes requests and services them by returning responses into a response queue. This is secure as long as the queue implementation employs connections which originate from the inside.

An alternative is to replicate your data and place the replicated copies in the DMZ region outside the inner firewall. This safeguards the actual data sources, since the replication process always moves from the inside to the outside. See the section "Forward Cache Designs" on page 439 in Chapter 6 for a pattern of how to build an effective replication system.

If you have high confidence in your firewall or your data resources are all considered non-critical or replaceable, you may not need to go to this extreme to protect your data. However, if you have systems which are critical to your business which need to be accessed in real time by external clients, you should consider a design which does not require externally originated connections to pass into your protected network.

## Java 2 Enterprise Edition

The Java 2 Enterprise Edition specification defines a Java platform with features aimed at enterprise level computing environments. It builds on the Standard Edition specification mostly in the areas of security, deployment, and interoperability.

The specification defines a packaging model for applications which consist of multiple modules. A module consists of an independently developed and packaged unit, typically comprised of a JAR file. A module is self-contained and reus-

able, but usually is not executable by itself, although it may be. An application assembler obtains modules required for an application, assembles and packages them, and configures the package to reflect the way the modules refer to each other and possibly to external resources. The application configuration information is encoded in an application level deployment descriptor that augments the individual module deployment descriptors.

The individual deployment descriptors may be copied and customized as well to add attributes which refer to other modules and to resources. The modules and all the deployment descriptors are packaged into an application unit consisting of a JAR file with the extension ".ear." (One would hope that tool builders do not use the obvious graphical metaphor when building application assembly toolbars.) An example of an application package is shown in Figure 8-27.

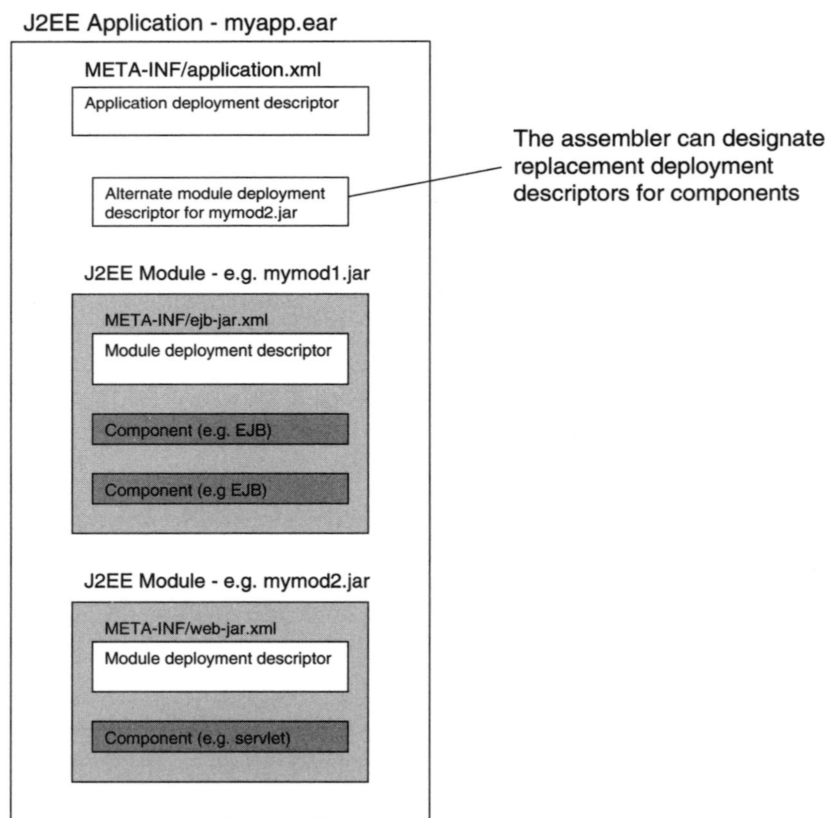


**Figure 8-27** A J2EE application assembly and deployment unit.

The actual component (module) deployment descriptors are not modified typically, since they are signed and their original form should be preserved. Instead, they are copied and the copies modifed for deployment.

Here is an example of a J2EE application deployment descriptor:

```
<application>
   <icon>
      <small-icon>
         MotherIcon16.gif
      </small-icon>
      <large-icon>
         MotherIcon32.gif
      </large-icon>
   </icon>
   <display-name>
      Mother Of All Applications
   </display-name>
   <description>
      Assembly consisting of two modules:
      Sarah's new Shiny EJB and Harry's
      trusty servlet.
   </description>
   <module>
      <ejb>
         shiny/shiny.jar
      </ejb>
      <alt-dd> <!--Application-customized depl. desc.-->
         shinyejb/shiny.xml
      </alt-dd>
   </module>
   <module>
      <web>
         <web-url>
            <!--The archive file containing
            the servlet and JSP module.-->
            harry/harry.web
         </web-url>
         <context-root>
           <!--Content deployed with the
           servlet is below this location.-->
           harry/stuff
         </context-root>
      </web>
      <alt-dd> <!--Application-customized depl. desc.-->
         harrys_servlet/harry.xml
      </alt-dd>
   </module>
```

```
   <security-role>
      <role-name>
         administrator
      </role-name>
   </security-role>
   <security-role>
      <role-name>
         corporateuser
      </role-name>
   </security-role>
</application>
```

This application assembly consists of two modules: an enterprise bean shipped as "shiny.jar" and a servlet shipped as "harry.jar." The two modules are added to the application assembly JAR ("EAR") file, which must have a .ear extension, and which must include the assembled application's XML deployment descriptor, such as the one shown above.

Notice that the <alt-dd> tags identify module-specific deployment descriptors which override the deployment descriptors embedded in the modules. These overriding deployment descriptors are based on the original ones, but incorporate changes that reflect assembly-specific information. The configuration of an assembly deployment descriptor will be UI-driven for most J2EE environments.

## Electronic Commerce Server Applications

Electronic commerce is an increasingly important aspect of Internet applications. Most companies planning enterprise applications now include Internet commerce portals as part of their systems, to allow customers not only to obtain information but also to place orders and manage their own accounts.

A full treatment of electronic commerce is beyond the scope of this book. However, it is an especially important category of applications, and we need to see how it relates to the concepts discussed so far.

Electronic commerce across the Internet was pioneered by Netscape when it released the SSL protocol. At that time, any server which provided SSL was known as a "commerce server." Now most web servers provide SSL, so the definition of commerce server is somewhat narrower. An electronic commerce server typically provides three kinds of functionality that distinguish it from application servers and web servers in general. These are:

- Communication is secure in order to protect the customer's sensitive financial and account information, such as credit card number and customer number.

- There are facilities and features to enable the easy construction of commerce-related functions, such as online catalogs and shopping baskets.
- There are payment gateways to financial service networks which are authorized by banks to transfer funds and debit credit card and other accounts.

Enterprise product data and price databases often reside on high-reliability mainframe systems. The same is often true of order-processing and fulfillment systems. Therefore, it is common for commerce servers to act as gateways to these systems. Commerce servers, therefore, often need features that facilitate building such gateways, such as mainframe gateways for services such as CICS, MQ, and Tandem. These gateways as well as commerce service interfaces are often accessed by native APIs, and so the application server must provide a means to incorporate native gateways into the application server's services. This can be accomplished by writing CORBA objects which are accessed by servlets or enterprise beans. Eventually it is expected that JMS wrappers and EJB entity containers will be widely available as well for mainframe transactional services.

At present most such mainframe gateways exist in the form of JavaBeans components which can be dropped into an application to provide access to CICS and other systems. These are available from companies that specialize in such gateways, such as Information Builders.

It is also common that access to certain mainframe data such as product data is available only in a batch mode. If this kind of data is relatively non-volatile, then changes to it can be transferred on a daily basis, possibly using a forward caching strategy as discussed in Chapter 6.

### *The Electronic Commerce Process*

The main aspects of a typical electronic commerce application are:

**Goods presentation**—An online catalog which allows the user to peruse the items that are available for purchase and to view information about the items, such as price.

**Shopping basket**—A facility for the user to select items. The item selections are retained in some manner throughout the session.

**Invoice presentation**—At the user's command, computes the total cost and applicable shipping fees and taxes and displays these along with a manifest of the items being purchased.

**Payment options presentation**—Allows the user to choose between the payment methods or instruments that are supported by the merchant.

**Payment authorization**—Contacts a payment authorization service network to obtain authorization of the amount to be charged.

**Fulfillment**—The actual shipment or transport of goods. Most systems notify the customer when fulfillment occurs, so that the customer can watch for the arrival of the package.

**Settlement**—Charges previously authorized are actually applied against the customer's account. In some systems, settlement occurs at the time of fulfillment; in other systems, settlement occurs at the time of authorization.

A common implementation pattern for electronic commerce applications is shown in Figure 8-28.

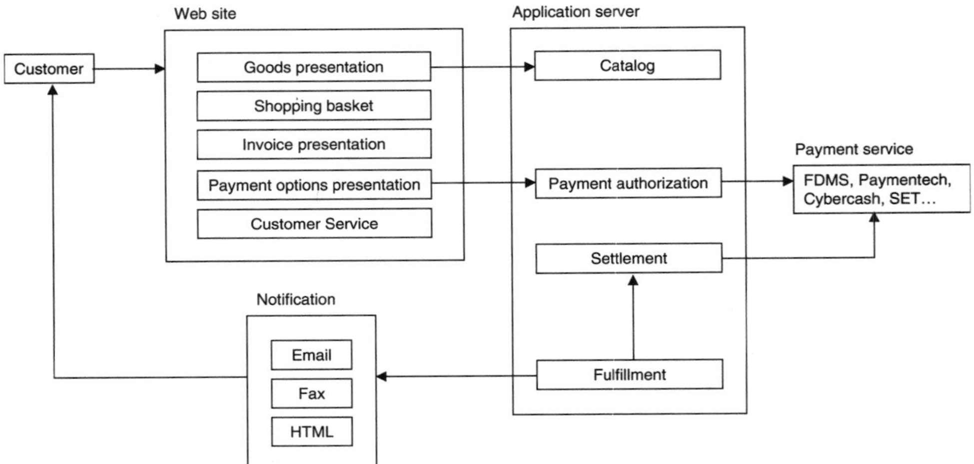


**Figure 8-28** Typical electronic commerce processes.

### *Handling Payment*

Authorization of payment occurs through private networks run by financial organizations. Two widely used networks are First Data Merchant Services (www.firstdata.com) and Paymentech Network Services (First USA Financial Services; www.paymentech.com). Newer systems which operate across the Internet include SET and Cybercash.

Cybercash is probably the easiest system for a merchant to set up because it is accessed using HTTP. All you need to do is obtain a Cybercash account and then incorporate standard HTTP POST requests in your application. The POSTs are sent to Cybercash's web servers, where authorization and fulfillment occurs, depending on the request. The only twist is that you need to encrypt the messages you send using Cybercash's DES3 library and decrypt the responses (SSL is not currently used, mainly for historical reasons, and may be used in the future).

Using Cybercash's library is quite easy, however. The JNI-compliant interface can be loaded and accessed from Java using the following Java native interface:

```
package com.cybercash.cychmck;
public class MessageBlock {

    static {
        System.loadLibrary("cychmck");
    }
    public native String Decrypt(String input,
        String merchantKey, String merchantKeyId);

    public native String Encrypt(String input,
        String merchantKey, String merchantKeyId);
}
```

Cybercash maintains a fleet of web servers which handle all the interaction with proprietary payment-authorization networks, and merchant commerce servers only have to interface to these web servers using the HTTP protocol. Here is an example of posting a credit card purchase authorization request and receiving the response. Note that a request containing payment information is formed, encrypted, and then POSTed to Cybercash's web server:

```
String request = "order-id=" +
URLEncoder.encode(generateOrderID());
request += "&amount=" + URLEncoder.encode("usd 49.95");
request += "&card-number=" +
URLEncoder.encode("4111111111111111");
request += "&card-exp=" + URLEncoder.encode("1/00");
request += "&card-name=" + URLEncoder.encode("Joe Somebody");
request += "&card-address=" + URLEncoder.encode("123 Main St.");
request += "&card-city=" + URLEncoder.encode("San Francisco");
request += "&card-state=" + URLEncoder.encode("CA");
request += "&card-zip=" + URLEncoder.encode("91111");
request += "&card-country=" + URLEncoder.encode("USA");
request += "&version=" + URLEncoder.encode("MCK-3.2.0.2");

// encrypt the request

MessageBlock mb = new MessageBlock();
request = mb.Encrypt(request,
    "gmRJp8rbzzcRdI5g8eLRScFeeQSWew5FsBzq6bxJDSJIiWhq7f",
    "test-mck");

// add http headers to the request
```

```
String outMsg;
outMsg = "POST http://cr.cybercash.com"
    + "/cgi-bin/cr21api.cgi/mauthcapture/test-mck "
    + "HTTP/1/1\r\n";
outMsg += "User-Agent: MCK-3.2.0.2\r\n";
outMsg += "Content-type: "
    + "application/x-www-form-urlencoded\r\n";
outMsg += "Content-length: "
    + Integer.toString(request.length()) + "\r\n";
outMsg += "\r\n";
outMsg += request;

// send the request

Socket sock = new Socket(InetAddress.getByName(
    "cr.cybercash.com"), 80);
OutputStream out = sock.getOutputStream();
for (int ix= 0; ix < outMsg.length(); ix++)
{
    out.write((byte)outMsg.charAt(ix));
}
out.flush();

// receive the response

String response = "";
DataInputStream dataInput =
    new DataInputStream(sock.getInputStream());
boolean readingHeaders = true;
for(;;)
{
    String line = dataInput.readLine();
    if (line == null) break;

    if (readingHeaders)
    {
        if (line.length() == 0)
            readingHeaders = false;
    }
    else
    {
        response += line;
    }
}
dataInput.close();
sock.close();

// decrypt the response
```

```
response = mb.Decrypt(response,
    "gmRJp8rbzzcRdI5g8eLRScFeeQSWew5FsBzq6bxJDSJIiWhq7f",
    "test-mck");
```

The long string provided to the Encrypt and Decrypt methods is an example of a merchant key. This is obtained from Cybercash when a merchant account is set up.

## Scaling Multitier Java Applications

### *Understanding the Overhead of Each Tier*

When a request arrives at a server, it must go through a dispatching mechanism which obtains a service thread in which to process the request, performs housekeeping such as associating session state with the request, and finally passes control to the service thread. There is usually a limited number of service threads available from a pool. Thread pools are usually growable but have an upper limit so that the pool cannot grow past a certain point. Most application servers are designed to support under 100 concurrent service threads, although this can vary depending on the server design and the operating system. Operating systems also usually have a limit on the number of threads they can manage, and this can be configured within a certain range. A typical limit is 400.

Request dispatching in its most basic form, therefore, typically requires two management threads: one to insert incoming requests into a request queue, and another to remove them from the queue and assign each request to a service thread from a thread pool. The queue decouples the incoming request rate from the service dispatching rate so that the system can gracefully handle more requests than it has threads to process for short periods of time. This design is depicted in Figure 8-29.

In addition to the dispatching overhead of a connection, there is the overhead of marshalling request and reply data, and the delay incurred by session state assignment and lookup of the application- or protocol-specific service method to invoke. When one adds all this up, it can be significant, and that is the price one pays for using general-purpose remote service protocols and service platforms. With a three-tier system this overhead and its associated latency are usually tolerable, but if one chains together additional tiers, response can quickly degrade. For example, consider a five-tier system which includes a remote client, a set of servlets running in a web server, session beans running in an EJB server which communicate with entity beans on the same server, and a backend database accessed via the entity beans. The actual layers of this system are shown in Figure 8-30.

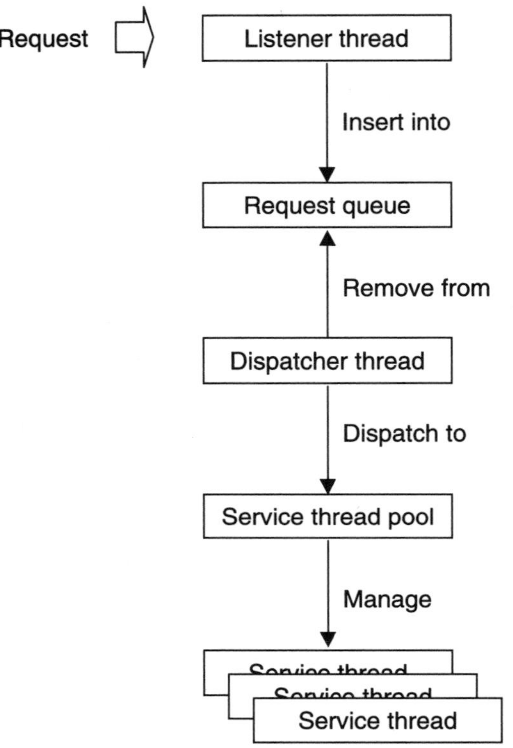


**Figure 8-29** Request queueing and thread dispatching in an application server.

This system has somewhere between seven and ten queues, or more, depending on the implementation, not counting communication system queues, and each incoming request must go through several kinds of marshalling or data transformation before the result is obtained. After that, the result must return through the same route. It is unlikely a system with this many layers can achieve subsecond response with general-purpose components unless queries are very small or sophisticated result caching is used in the web or EJB tiers.

Of course, subsecond response is not always the goal. This system may be very scalable. If clients perceive two-second response 90% of the time, that may be sufficient. Depending on the clustering and scalability features of the components, the system may be highly scalable and be able to handle very large volumes.

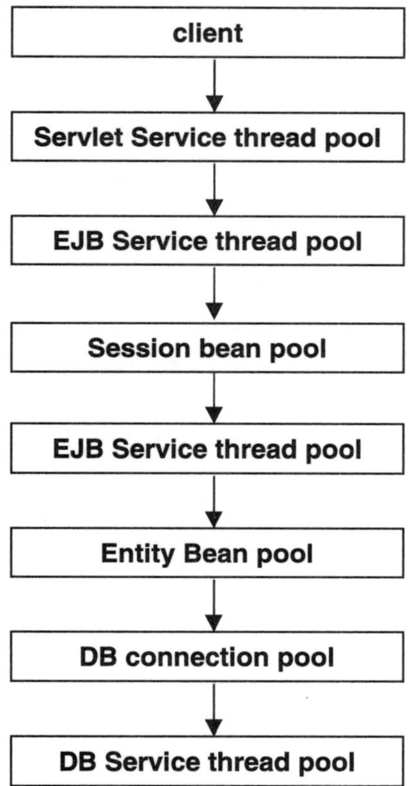


**Figure 8-30** The many pools involved in servicing a request in a five-tier EJB application.

Consider an alternative design which does not need to handle large volume but which must have very quick response. This might consist of a remote client which makes HTTP requests to servlets in a web server which directly accesses the back-end database using pooled native drivers. Such a system can easily be designed to provide subsecond response. The performance objectives of the system, therefore, strongly dictate its fundamental design, and this must be considered from the outset.

### *Scalability of Servlet Sessions vs. EJB Sessions*

If you employ only a web front end, you may not need session beans. The servlet layer can provide session state management, and possibly transaction management and security context management. Non-web clients need session beans for session state management. To make your application code independent of whether it is deployed in servlets or session beans, encapsulate all accesses to session state object classes which can be substituted with servlet or session bean versions. Make your business logic independent of how it is deployed.

Servlets generally scale better when it comes to maintaining client sessions. In terms of servlets, there is usually a limit on the size of state that each client can maintain, for example, 4K. For 20,000 sessions, this would be 80Mb of cached client session state, which is still manageable on a single machine. With a large number of sessions, the server's mechanism for dispatching and managing requests and its application-processing throughput will likely be stressed more than its ability to contain the required session state. In addition, there does not need to be a separate servlet instance for each client session. The EJB model, on the other hand, requires a separate session bean for each session. In practice, these session instances may be shared using pooling and passivation techniques, reducing the number of active objects. If all clients tend to be active, however, the pool will need to be very large.

If the servlets are accessing stateful session beans, this somewhat defeats the scalability of the servlet model because there are in effect two different and possibly redundant session models. One should try not to mix two session state models in the same application unless it represents a small or intermittent portion of the usage profile.

Session beans are also not needed if you have heavy clients. A heavy client (e.g., a client-side persistent Java application) can maintain its own state much more efficiently than a server-resident object. The disadvantage is that the client's state is then only accessible from one workstation and it may be harder to provide recovery of or backup for the session state.

### Lookups and Reconnects

Servlets handle incoming requests from web clients. A request is made in the same way each time, by resolving a URL to the target network and routing the request to a suitable server containing the desired servlet. There is no application-specific client programming involved. Accessing an EJB, in contrast, involves first obtaining a remote reference to a factory object—the EJB Home—followed by obtaining a reference to the actual desired bean. Only then can a method on the bean be invoked.

The steps of looking up the Home interface and then obtaining the bean reference can be performed as needed or once at the beginning of the program. There is usually considerable overhead associated with performing a Home interface lookup, and somewhat less overhead in obtaining a bean reference. You should therefore optimize the frequency with which you obtain these. Most of the overhead is usually incurred the first time you do something which requires a server connection.

In general, you should obtain a bean's Home interface no sooner than you are sure you will need it, but only once during the lifetime of a server connection. In other words, if you have a heavy client, it makes sense to obtain the Home interfaces you need only once, but be prepared to reobtain them if a connection is lost—i.e., if you receive a RemoteException.

On the other hand, if your configuration uses load balancing and if the load balancing is triggered by the Home interface lookup, you should consider reobtaining the Home interface at somewhat regular intervals to allow the load-balancing algorithms to function.

Session bean references can be reused for multiple transactions, so, in general, one creates a session bean once during a session—typically when the client application starts or first accesses the server. If a client only accesses the server intermittently, it is usually acceptable to hold a session reference but to provide for reobtaining a session if it times out on the server (in that case, you will likely lose your session state). There are generally four kinds of session loss: connection timeout, session timeout (set by the timeout attribute in a session bean's deployment descriptor), explicit disposing of the session or closing of the connection by the client, and loss of connection due to a network error or server restart. RMI will restablish a connection as needed if it times out, but some customized RMI implementations require the client to catch the timeout exception and reestablish the connection if it is needed.

Stateless session beans do not really represent a session. Therefore, there is usually little overhead involved with maintaining the session bean reference—it is just a remote reference. The server connection will likely remain open even if the session bean is explicitly removed by the client, so there is usually no advantage to doing so. This behavior depends on the server product. Note that it depends on the connection protocol between the client and server. Many servers use RMI, but many do not; some use optimized versions of RMI that manage connections differently from standard RMI.

If the client (which may be another bean) accesses an entity bean, there generally will be few resources maintained for the client in between entity transactions, since entity beans to not maintain client-specific session state. The only overhead is the connection itself. Again, if the server maintains connections across bean creation and deletions, there may be little to be gained by disposing of the entity reference. Removing an entity bean removes the shared data object from the server, so this is not appropriate as a means of economizing resource usage. It generally makes sense to maintain entity references as long as you think you might need them, but, as with session beans, always be prepared to reobtain the reference (and probably the Home interface as well) in the event of a connection failure.

A common configuration is for a servlet to access one or more EJBs. In this scenario, the servlets should attempt to reuse their EJB connections either by using bean connection pools or by maintaining an EJB reference across servlet invocations. In this case, the primary load balancing occurs at the front end where the servlets are accessed. Load balancing of the EJBs can be done as well, but care needs to be taken that connections are not being recreated excessively, which can severely damage response time. Examine the load-balancing system closely to see when connections are reestablished. In one experiment we did, the introduction of EJB load balancing improved server utilization but increased user response time by a factor of ten! In that case, the load-balancing technology made the assumption (incorrect in this case) that session bean creations would be infrequent and that bean references would be maintained over long periods.

### *Some Session Profile Scenarios*

Let's consider three patterns for multitier applications which represent a challenge for scalability:

- Lots of heavy clients.
- Lots of thin clients, with short sessions.
- Lots of thin clients, with long sessions.

**Lots of Heavy Clients.** This is the easiest case and represents the traditional client/server problem. Clients maintain their own state, lending the system to a stateless middle tier. This arrangement also allows for client callbacks to notify clients to refresh when data has changed. This can be done in a scalable way by tiering services and using messaging middleware.

A stateful client relieves a considerable burden from the server. The disadvantages are that clients must be deployed and maintained and the design does not support mobility, for example, doctors roaming in a hospital.

**Lots of Thin Clients, with Short or Inactive Sessions.** This scenario consists of HTML or JavaScript clients accessing servlets in a web server. The servlet layer establishes and maintains session state. If the servlet container provides transaction support, servlets can initiate transactional operations which propagate to compatible data resources and enterprise beans. The user's identity context can also be established in the servlet layer and ideally can be propagated to other resources it accesses. As I have explained, this often requires accessing credential stores, although ideally the user's identity will propagate automatically.

A critical parameter is the size of each user's session state. If the session state is large, you can write it to storage programmatically or you can use stateful session beans. A third alternative is to store session data with an entity bean. The size of

the session state can be reduced by redesigning the application to divide it up into a larger number of separate transactions, each representing a different processing step. This might eliminate the need for session beans, which represent another stateful layer on top of the servlet sessions.

If session beans are necessary, the design can still be scalable. Since this scenario supposes that sessions are short or relatively inactive, the number of active session beans can be kept low. Thus, a thousand sessions may only require 100 or fewer active session bean instances at any one time, most of the time. This is what would be expected in an application which has been divided into short transactions which use optimistic concurrency techniques and only access data resources when absolutely necessary.

In general, if latency is a concern, move the access to data resources forward, possibly into the servlets, and reduce the size of the session state by redesigning the application.

**Lots of Thin Clients, with Very Active Long Sessions.** The picture changes considerably for thin client designs if sessions are long in duration. This is the hardest case because the server cannot effectively share or pool session objects. A system with ten thousand clients each maintaining a very active session may potentially need to maintain as many active client state records or objects in its cache. This is what one might see, for example, in a call center.

An application server with a very efficient distributed cache is needed to service the clients effectively in this case. Alternatively, one can programmatically store session data in a database or some other shared or clusterable repository, possibly accessible via entity beans. The system will operate most efficiently if stateful session requests are routed back to the same server so that the session cache or database cache is usually where it is needed. The most scalable configuration may be to rely primarily on the web front end—i.e., the servlets—to maintain session state and use an EJB engine as needed for aggregating or intermittently accessing backend data resources and as a platform for sending messages to other parts of the system, such as an administrative system.

### *Configuration and Server Resources*

The performance and responsiveness of a server are typically affected by many factors. These may include:

> **Memory**—It is now common for servers to have a Gb or more of RAM per processor. Many application servers have minimum requirements of over 100 Mb just to run the application server and its administrative tools. It is necessary to determine the baseline memory requirements and the incremental memory requirements per client in order to project requirements as usage increases.

**Processors**—Adding processors is a cost-effective way to increase throughput, especially on machines which can handle large amounts of IO and therefore which will not become IO bound. For this reason, most servers now have multiple processors, typically from 2 to 64. Some high-end systems (e.g., Silicon Graphics servers) can have hundreds of processors, but these are used mostly in tightly coupled database or computational applications. Web applications are more commonly scaled by adding server machines to a cluster.

**TCP connections (ulimit)** —Many operating systems are configured by default to support some maximum of file descriptors, typically around 1000. A Java socket object may require two system file descriptors. For high usage applications, this limit may need to be increased so that it covers a range that is sufficiently beyond the average expected number of clients. Otherwise, clients will not be able to connect.

**Threads**—Application servers typically pool threads. The number of threads a server can efficiently support is commonly in a range significantly under a hundred. Most products do not run well if the number of threads is larger than this.

**Connection resources or caches**—In addition to the raw socket connection used by a client, the application server may experience a certain incremental memory footprint of its own for each connection.

**Timeouts**—Some protocols, for example, RMI, reconnect as needed. Others don't. Your application should tune the use of timeouts. TCP will also timeout an inactive connection after some interval, typically two minutes.

**Application-level multiplexing**—Depending on the server design, reponse to client requests may be relatively insensitive to the number of clients, or it may increase linearly or in some other relationship.

**Session pool size**—Session beans are normally pooled objects. The size of the pool is usually not a large factor in terms of resource usage. An application with lots of clients will scale better if beans are stateless, or if state can be maintained on the client. If there are 20,000 clients, it may be impractical to maintain 20,000 active stateful session beans on the server. In general, the pool needs to grow to the number of currently active beans, such that beans do not "thrash." This varies greatly with the kind of application. If stateful session beans are used and clients are active, the pool may need to be very large to prevent thrashing. You may need to gather statistics on how much thrashing is occurring. This can be done by instrumenting the bean's activate() and passivate() methods.

### *Running Web and Application Servers (and Other Servers Too) on the Same Machine*

Some architectures (e.g., UNIX) handle multiple processes better than others and can ensure that no one process swamps a machine. The decision of whether multi-

ple servers can effectively be run on a single machine therefore depends partly on the hardware platforms chosen. In any case, each machine should have enough resources so that process-specific resources are rarely swapped or paged. Note that, generally speaking, if a server is doing fewer things, there are likely to be higher hit rates on all system caches.

Generally, the clustering mechanisms used for web and bean requests are different and, therefore, do not impact each other appreciably, so there is usually no conflict or risk in using the same physical or logical cluster for these different classes of server. The cluster may provide a distributed state mechanism which is shared across web and bean systems, but such a service is usually itself scalable and replicatable.

### *Running Multiple Application Server Instances on a Server*

Most systems which have multiple processors can apply them as needed across processes. That is, each time a thread is scheduled, it is assigned to a (potentially different) processor. (This is not true on all architectures, however.) Therefore, on most architectures, having fewer processes does not imply having idle processors, and having more processes does not imply making the processors busier. If processors are relatively idle, it is likely that the communication resources are a bottleneck. Since this rarely happens on multiprocessor systems (which typically have very high bandwidth IO and communication systems), idle processors usually mean the system is not taxed, or that there is some other bottleneck, such as a database or other service. External services may be more highly utilized by using more connections to them and ensuring the system has the required bandwidth. Software-based resources such as transaction queues can also be bottlenecks and keep multiprocessors from being fully utilized.

Running multiple software instances on a single server does not generally increase throughput unless instances have dedicated resources of some kind which are bottlenecks, or unless the server program itself has internal non-reentrant activities which are bottlenecks. For example, if you have two boxes, each with two processors, it may be advantageous to run two instances on each if it turns out that the server software has significant internal bottlenecks that multiple processors cannot resolve but which multiple instances can resolve because each instance will then have its own copy of the resource. Several commercial application servers on the market are known to have such bottlenecks and can therefore sometimes benefit from running multiple instances on a multiprocessor system.

To determine if this helps your situation, you will have to try it empirically since it depends on so many factors. You should measure the shape of the latency and throughput curves with one instance and with two. If two instances improve processor utilization, the second latency curve will be signficantly flatter than the first over a wide range until other resources saturate; and the second throughput curve should be significantly steeper than the first until hardware bottlenecks begin to have an effect.

### *Bean Lookup and Identification; Load Balancing and Clustering*

To obtain a bean, you must locate its Home interface and then either look it up if it is an entity bean and already exists, or create it using a create...() method provided by the bean's Home interface. The Home interface is therefore the portal to obtaining an instance of the bean.

Most EJB products provide some kind of object load balancing. This is often implemented through the name service, since that is the first point at which a remote object is accessed. When a client needs to access an enterprise bean object, it must first obtain the bean's Home interface. It does this using the JNDI interface, but behind the scenes the JNDI provider code supplied by the application server implements whatever protocol is needed to access the application server's load-balancing mechanism. The final result is that a stub is delivered to the client code, and the stub, which implements the server's communication protocol, may contain additional load-balancing-related code.

Web servers can provide load balancing as well, usually in the form of a server plugin or proxy which knows how to manage client state on top of HTTP. There are also techniques which are application protocol-independent, including DNS-based load balancing and network (IP-based) load balancing. While these latter techniqes are usually the concern of the network administrator, it is important to understand these approaches so that you know what the options are for the design of a replicated server configuration and what their pros and cons are. In order to lay a foundation for discussing clustering services, which are server-based techniques usually embedded in the application server technology, I will first explain the common DNS and network-based techniques.

### *DNS-Based Load Balancing vs. Network-Based Load Balancing*

Enhancements have been made to DNS implementations in recent years to allow them to be used for load balancing. This relies on the ability of DNS to store and supply more than one address mapping for a name. Client socket libraries try each in sequence until a connection is established.

The problem with DNS-based load balancing is that it is not real time. DNS load balancing is not responsive to load variations on the destination systems because it uses a random or round-robin policy rather than obtaining current information about load to make its name resolution decisions. It is also not responsive to the removal of a server from a network either, as it requires the connection attempt to timeout before it will try another and is dependent on the time-to-live of client-

side cached DNS entries to refresh entries (unless client DNS systems receive real-time update notifications from the server's DNS system, but this is not a scalable approach). DNS-based load balancing is therefore considered an inferior technique compared to alternatives.

Network-based load balancing typically consists of mapping a DNS entry to a single virtual IP address, and then using a load-balancing router to map the virtual external IP address (and port) to a real internal IP address (and port) dynamically, based on some policy which can be round robin or can employ a (usually proprietary) load-information protocol. (The internal IP addresses are not visible to the outside because the router rewrites them in all packets that leave the system.)

The problem with network-based load balancing is that it often cannot work well with stateful protocols, especially if clients are behind their own firewall. Stateful application protocols either require successive client requests to return to the same server as the one on which the session began or they work best if this is so. Since client firewalls hide the client's network identity, a smart load-balancing router must attempt to use application protocol information to identify clients. Some protocols do not provide sufficient information. The HTTP protocol does not assign client IDs, and so a smart load balancer does not know how to reroute to the same server. An exception is SSL: in that case, clients have non-opaque IDs, and some load-balancing routers can use that to make routing decisions.

### Clustering

Protocol-specific load balancing is usually implemented by software which either uses open features of the application protocol to make routing decisions or adds features to the protocol to facilitate load balancing. This is also called "clustering" because it is usually implemented as a backend service tightly coupled with the server and its protocols, providing a "cluster" of servers which behave as if they were one larger server. Clustering involves a replicated proxy service on the server side which knows how to move, access, or connect to the client's session cache or to special clients (e.g., load balancing name service lookup stubs or object stubs). There are also forms of clustering that are OS-supported and not application specific. OS-supported clustering usually operates by the OS allocating processes to nodes within a high-speed backend network and employing a shared disk array so that all nodes see the same file system.

Web clustering can be achieved most easily if the clustering service is integrated with the web server's state management facility. For example, the web server's servlet engine maintains stateful sessions for clients by returning cookies to clients or by using URL-rewriting. If the load balancer is aware of how the state is encoded, it can read the state and use it to route successive requests to the appro-

priate server, even across connection timeouts. This type of clustering is often provided in the form of a web server plugin.

In the case of a non-HTTP server such as an EJB server, clustering can be implemented in the object factory stub or in the object stub, as described earlier. This is usually done by providing cluster-aware stubs for either or both the Home interface and EJB servant objects.

Any clustering technology must address two fundamental issues: assignment of client requests to servers and ultimately servants; and if client sessions are stateful, assignment or reassignment of client state to requests. These issues are depicted in Figure 8-31.

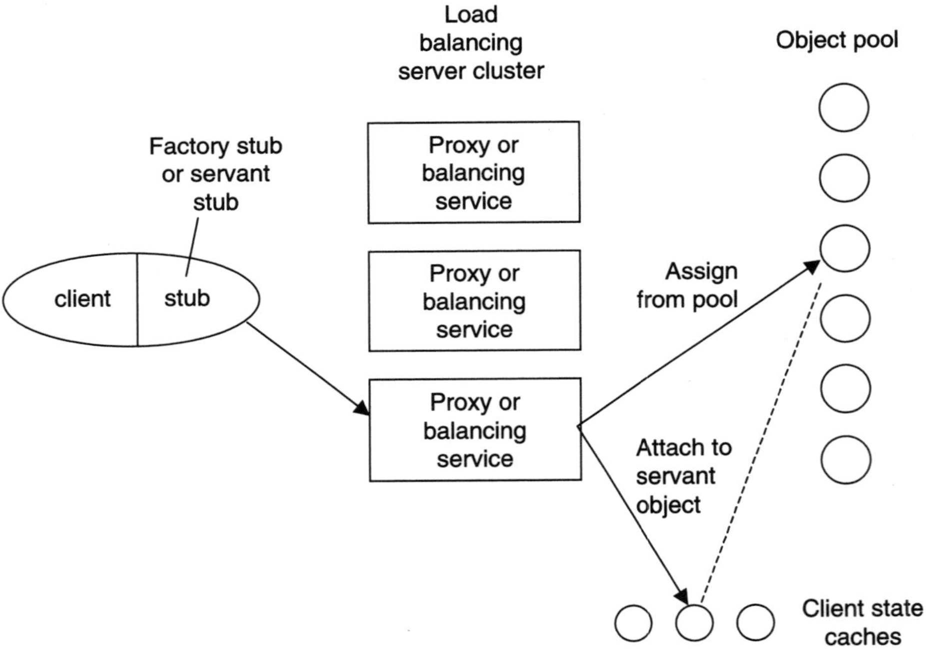


**Figure 8-31** The two-pronged problem of assigning requests to servers and reattaching to session state.

There are a great many variables in terms of how the overall system can be configured. The most important of these are:

**Servant connections**—Connections from client to the server selected by the load-balancing algorithm can be through a direct socket connection to the target server or can be proxied by a server dedicated to the client. The

advantage of making a direct connection is that the servers do not have to spend time processing pass-through traffic. Direct connections require the constant breaking and establishment of server connections, however, whereas if the same server connection is reused by a client for all traffic, the session establishment overhead is lower. In any case, load-balancing client stubs must be prepared to contact backup or alternate servers in case the one they are connected to fails.

**Distribution of state**—Stateful sessions can be supported by rerouting a client back to the same server. This ensures that the client's session state is present. However, if the server fails, there needs to be a failover mechanism to make the client's state available on an alternate server. Thus, regardless of whether stateful clients can migrate from server to server during normal operation, there needs to be a state migration mechanism if transparent failover is supported. Client state can be distributed; it can be centrally located, as in a database; or it can be moved as needed. If the state is distributed, it can be in the form of a distributed cache or it can be a replicated cache maintained on a primary or secondary pair of servers or replicated to all servers.

**Duration of assignment and attachment**—Servers can be assigned to clients anew with each request. They can be assigned for the duration of a transaction, for the lifetime of a session (i.e., for the lifetime of the validity of the session's object reference), or for the duration of the client's server connection. The more dynamic the assignment, the more effectively the system can balance its load. However, a highly dynamic model incurs greater overhead and complexity, impacts the way connections are managed, and increases the frequency with which they need to be created.

**Where decisions are made**—Load-balancing decisions can be made by the client, through the stubs used by the client to access the server; or the decisions can be made by a central (but redundant) load-balancing service. Client-based decisions can be made using load information or using a random policy. The load-balancing service can periodically broadcast load information to clients or clients can query for load information when needed. Server-based decisions can be made directly in response to client service or lookup requests.

### *Load-Balancing Algorithms*

Network-based solutions are often implemented in combination with a server-load management system which provides information directly to the load-balancing components (e.g., routers). This is a very effective solution when network-based techniques can be used.

The algorithms used to make dispatching decisions in clustered systems may depend on the kind of service or object being dispatched to. In particular, different policies might be used for stateless services than for stateful services. For example, a statistical or parametric algorithm might be used to select stateless session beans, whereas a deterministic algorithm (such as a hash on the bean's address, name, or ID) might be used to select stateful session beans and entity beans, thereby assuring that a session remains with the bean for the lifetime of the session. A more sophisticated policy would migrate an object's state cache as needed in order to balance load. If the application server uses an object database to implement container persistence, it has the opportunity to integrate the object database cache with the application server cluster cache and thereby migrate or distribute stateful beans as part of load management.

### *Visibility of Failures to Clients*

Ideally, the cluster (usually through code in the client stub) will try another server if an operation fails due to a communication failure, that is, if the server goes down. It can do this, however, only if it can distinguish between failures which had side effects and those which did not. For example, if the stub determines that the failure resulted in a transaction rollback and the bean is declared to be stateless, the stub knows it can safely and automatically retry the transaction without throwing an exception to the client. In that case, it should in the end only throw an exception if all available servers have been tried and all failed, or if an application exception or rollback exception occurs.

### *Accessing Non-Clustered Resources; Pinning an Object to a Server*

Sometimes it is desirable to have an object type execute on a specific server while other object types are clustered. You might want to do this if the object needs to access a service which is only accessible from one server but not the others. In a clustered environment not all resources are necessarily clustered. For example, IIOP connections or database connections may not participate in the app server's EJB clustering. In that case, the resources are server-specific, and therefore the resources (pool names) may need to be defined identically in each server so that they can be found by the beans. If the resources are only available from a single server, this will not work, and you must ensure that the bean class which accesses the resource always executes on the server that has access to that resource. You can usually accomplish this by configuring the cluster appropriately, for instance, by omitting it from the list of clustered bean classes or not tagging it as clusterable when the bean is configured in the server's administration interface.

### *Benchmarking a Configuration*

Benchmarking a system's components and configuration is important for predicting the behavior of the system under load. You never know how a system will behave until you measure it live; however, it is wise to have measurements

behind you which predict with some confidence what performance you will see. It is often difficult to accurately simulate a system before turning live users loose on it, so benchmarking it is critical to obtain an understanding of its behavior and how it scales. Benchmarking is also valuable for proof of concept studies.

The primary goal of benchmarking should not be to obtain final results for a planned configuration, since you cannot truly do that until the system is in operation, but to obtain an understanding of the relationships between the different configuration parameters and how steeply the behavior changes as parameters and load change as well as where the inflection points are.

The immediate objective of benchmarking should be to obtain statistics over a range of configuration parameters. Ideally, a benchmark effort is divided into two or more sessions, so that the results of the first session can be examined and plotted and used to design additional tests for successive sessions. Sometimes seemingly innocuous system parameters like the timeout period of clients can have an unanticipated large effect on results, and a second round of testing may be needed to determine which system parameters are truly the most important ones to focus on.

Before engaging in a full-scale benchmarking session, it is a good idea to conduct the tests on a smaller scale first and get an understanding of the system that way, and then verify that understanding at the upper range of interest in full-scale testing.

One of the most difficult problems in performing a benchmark is how to simulate the required number of clients. If server performance is being measuered, it is important that clients are not overburdened and that the load on the clients does not skew the results. Also, many server products utilize a single server connection for all client sessions within the client's VM. This means that to simulate multiple clients from a machine, you need to use separate VMs. A VM's minimum footprint on AIX is about 6 Mb. If each client test machine has 3 Gb, this means that each machine has sufficient memory for upward of 500 clients, and that 20 machines would be needed at a minimum to simulate 10,000 clients. In actuality, this number of clients on a single machine will overwhelm the machine, in terms of its threading resources and processing capabilities as well as its network communication bandwidth. Client machines may also need to be high IO bandwidth machines in order to handle logging requirements as well, depending on the amount of data being collected. A quick calculation should be done of the amount of data being written to see if the machine can handle it without adding substantially to its load.

Care should be taken that logging does not skew results. Do not use a shared singleton instance on a server for logging, since this can result in contention for the log. Have each system keep its own log; tally and correlate all logs afterward.

Pay attention to important but often hidden, system characteristics such as the behavior of protocol connections, timeouts, and so on.

You will need to understand how the system works. The first step of planning a benchmark is to develop a model of how the system works. The model may be parameterized, and in that case your tests should be designed to measure the parameters. This is usually done by plotting numbers on a curve and measuring the slope over both normal and high-load regions. This gives you the incremental performance degradation with each unit of change in load or change to a configuration parameter. Be sure to include backend services which will affect final system performance, such as clustering or load-balancing services.

### *Building a Scalable Architecture*

A scalable design often requires replication of services, for performance as well as for reliability. It is important that there be no single point of failure in the system if high availability is required. This includes network components as well as servers. Routers and firewalls may need to be replicated to provide redundancy and increase throughput. A highly redundant configuration is shown in Figure 8-32.

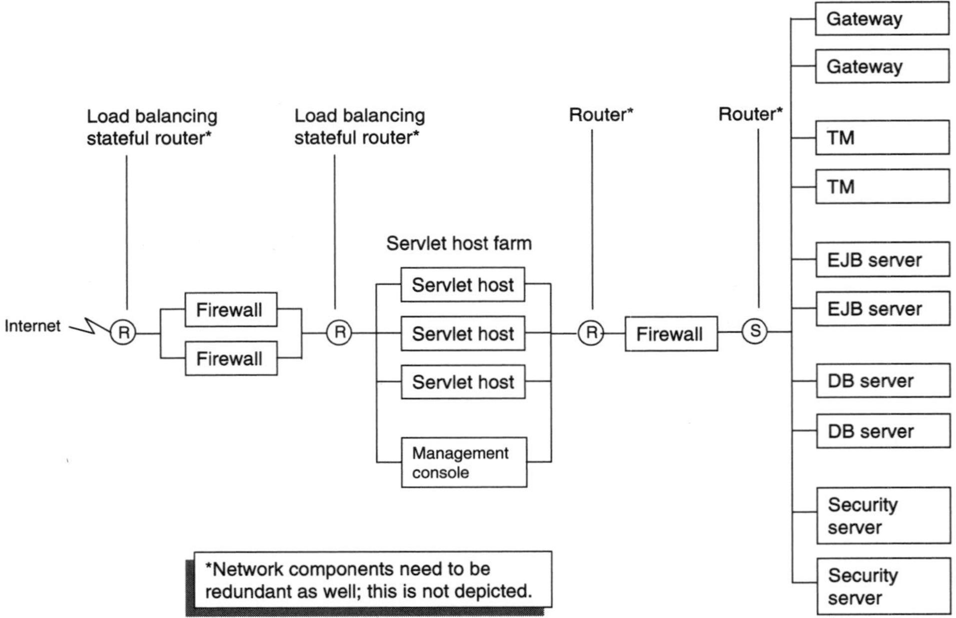


**Figure 8-32** Achieving scalability and high availability through replication.

In this design, the web servers are located behind the Internet firewall because there is assumed to be extensive use of servlets requiring configuration files and credentials for accessing data sources. The web servers therefore need to be well protected. A separate management server is included in the design to focus on the need to consolidate the management of all the different components and to allow servers to be added and removed from clusters without affecting the management server. Presumably, all of the management services can be operated from other hosts in an emergency, in case the dedicated management server fails.

This configuration assumes a web-based application implemented with servlets. The servlets are the primary stateful objects, and they need to run efficiently and responsively. The servlet engines available in the marketplace should be benchmarked and evaluated for features to select the one that meets the architectural requirements of the application. EJB load balancing is most likely not critical in this configuration because most functionality and load balancing are likely to be at the servlet side.

The EJB servers are included to provide a platform for handling events which must propagate to other components. For example, database triggers may need to call EJB methods and possibly send JMS messages, or CORBA services may need to call enterprise beans to provide notification of some kind, for instance in response to the completion of an asynchronous operation or in reponse to the receipt of a message.

The EJB servers also provide convenient access to backend resources such as databases. The EJB servers most likely provide transaction management services, but the design also allows for the possibility that some resources (such as CORBA objects) may need non-EJB transaction management. Therefore, it is assumed that a transaction manager is chosen which is decoupled from the EJB server and which exposes an interface such as OTS. That way a single set of redundant TMs can be used for all resources. Note that most Java mainframe gateway components are presently implemented as Java beans—not EJB beans. These beans usually interface directly to mainframe databases or transaction managers.

In designing the system configuration it is important to identify any content and services that will be accessed from outside the network. Constantly bouncing across networks can have a drastic effect on performance, since server keep-alive features are prevented from operating.

The primary database used by the application needs to provide its own form of redundancy while appearing logically as a single resource. This will simplify application design and still provide the necessary redundancy of all services. Most scalable database products provide redundancy through failover and mirroring options.

The largest wildcard in the configuration is how security is handled. Each product provides its own security service. A global security service is needed to manage the many different classes of users across products and components, including administrative users. Administrative users will likely have PKI based credentials due to the importance of securing administrative access to the system, while web users will likely have passwords. It would be desirable to administer the firewalls, all servers, and even the network using a single redundant security database. At present, it is possible but extremely difficult to achieve this, depending on the choice of products. Still, it is of great utility to have at least a central set of redundant credential repositories which can be administered in a secure manner.

# Index

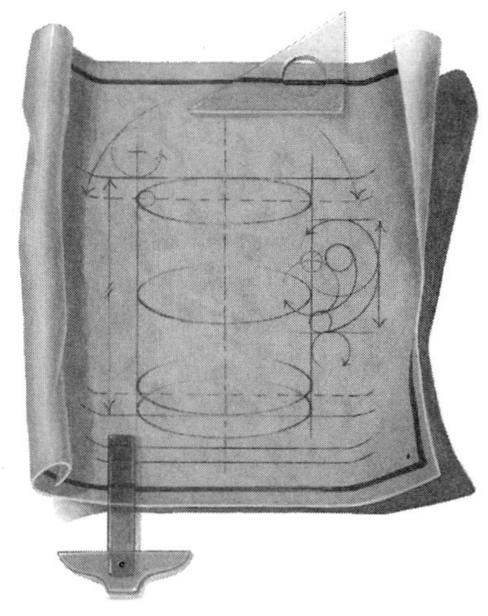

## Numerics



## A

## B



## C

## D

## E

## F

## J

## P

## Q



## R

## S

## T

## U



## V



## W



## X

785